A Chanticleer Press Edition

GRASSLANDS

By Lauren Brown

Birds
John Bull, Field Associate, The American Museum of Natural History; John Farrand, Jr., Editor, *American Birds,* National Audubon Society; and Miklos D. F. Udvardy, Professor of Biological Sciences, California State University, Sacramento

Butterflies
Robert Michael Pyle, Consulting Lepidopterist, International Union for Conservation of Nature and Natural Resources

Insects and Spiders
Lorus Milne and Margery Milne, Lecturers, University of New Hampshire

Mammals
John O. Whitaker, Jr., Professor of Life Sciences, Indiana State University

Mushrooms
Peter Katsaros, Mycologist

Reptiles and Amphibians
John L. Behler, Curator of Herpetology, New York Zoological Society; and F. Wayne King, Director, Florida State Museum

Trees
Elbert L. Little, Jr., former Chief Dendrologist, U.S. Forest Service

Wildflowers
William A. Niering, Professor of Botany, Connecticut College, New London; Nancy C. Olmstead, former Research Associate, Connecticut Arboretum; and Richard Spellenberg, Professor of Biology, New Mexico State University

Alfred A. Knopf, New York

This is a Borzoi Book
Published by Alfred A. Knopf, Inc.

Published in the United States by Alfred A. Knopf, Inc.,
New York, and simultaneously in Canada by Random House of
Canada Limited, Toronto. Distributed by Random House, Inc.
New York.

Prepared and produced by
Chanticleer Press, Inc., New York.

Printed and bound by Dai Nippon, Tokyo, Japan.
Typeset in Garamond by Dix Type Inc., Syracuse, New York.

First Published March 1985
Second Printing, September 1989

Library of Congress Cataloging in Publication Data
Brown, Lauren, 1947–
The Audubon Society nature guides. Grasslands.
Includes index.
1. Grassland ecology–United States–Handbooks, manuals,
etc. 2. Grasslands–United States–Handbooks, manuals, etc.
3. Grassland fauna–United States–Identification. 4. Plants–
Identification.
I. National Audubon Society. II. Title III. Title: Grassland
QH104.B76 1985   574.5'2643'0973   84-48675
ISBN 0-394-73121-2 (pbk.)

Cover photograph: A White-tailed Deer, its tail flipped up as
a sign of alarm, speeds across the Nebraska sandhills.

CONTENTS

Part I

Grasslands
How to Use This Guide 8
Introduction 19
Tallgrass Prairie 30
Mixed Prairie 45
Shortgrass Prairie 54
Desert Grasslands 64
Intermountain Grasslands 73
California Grasslands 84
Eastern Grasslands 93
How to Use the Color Plates 116

Part II

Color Plates
Grasslands 1–30
Mammals 31–90
Grasses and Shrubs 91–114
Wildflowers 115–294
Butterflies and Moths 295–348
Insects and Spiders 349–396
Trees 397–486
Birds 487–552
Mushrooms 553–564
Amphibians and Reptiles 565–618

Part III

Species Descriptions
Mammals 322
Grasses 354
Wildflowers 366
Butterflies and Moths 445
Insects and Spiders 475
Trees 496
Birds 529
Mushrooms 554
Reptiles and Amphibians 559

Part IV

Appendices
Glossary 582
Bibliography 589
Credits 590
Index 595

ACKNOWLEDGMENTS

Many people throughout the country have kindly provided information on local grasslands. Although they are too numerous to mention by name, I particularly want to thank staff members at the field offices of The Nature Conservancy, as well as those of the associated Heritage Programs. From the Atlantic to the Pacific, these professionals have been most cordial and helpful, and have given me valuable information on grassland habitats. The staff of Yale University Kline Science Library also deserves special mention for helping me track down obscure bits of information.

I am grateful to Durward L. Allen for reviewing the manuscript and for his helpful comments, and also to Nate Gibbons for his review. Special thanks go to Erin O'Hare for her intelligent and enthusiastic contributions, and to Paul Stamler for technical advice and instruction. I thank John Herzan for his unending patience.

The staff of Chanticleer Press has gained my unbounded admiration, especially Mary Beth Brewer. I also appreciate the hard work of Susan Costello, Ann Whitman, Marian Appellof, Constance Mersel, David Allen, and Jane Opper, among others.

Lauren Brown

THE AUTHOR

Lauren Brown
Author of *Weeds in Winter* and *Grasses: An Identification Guide*,
Lauren Brown studied botany at Swarthmore College and at
the Yale School of Forestry and Environmental Studies. She is
curator of the Connecticut Audubon Society Birdcraft Museum
and lives in Branford, Connecticut, where she is active in local
conservation organizations.

HOW TO USE THIS GUIDE

This guide is designed for use both at home and in the field. Its clear arrangement in four parts—habitat essays, color plates, species descriptions, and appendices—puts information at your fingertips that would otherwise only be accessible through a small library of field guides.

The habitat essays enable you to discover the many kinds of grasslands, the relationships among the plants and animals found there, and highlights not to be missed. The color plates feature grassland scenes and over 600 photographs of different plant and animal species. The species descriptions cover the most important information about a plant or animal, including a description, the range, specific habitat, and comments. Finally, the appendices include a bibliography, a glossary, and a comprehensive index.

Using This Guide at Home

Before planning an outing, you will want to know what you can expect to see.

1. Begin by leafing through the color plates for a preview of grasslands.
2. Read the habitat section. For quick reference, at the end of each chapter you will find a list of some of the most common plants and animals found in that habitat.
3. Look at the color plates of some of the animals and plants so that you will be able to recognize them later in the field. The table called How to Use the Color Plates provides a visual table of contents to the color section, explains the arrangement of the plates, and tells the caption information provided. The habitats where you are likely to encounter the species are listed in blue type so that you can easily refer to the correct habitat chapter. The page number for the full species description is also included in the caption.
4. Turn to the species descriptions to learn more about the plants and animals that interest you. A range map or drawing appears in the margin for birds, mammals, reptiles, and amphibians, and for many of the trees and wildflowers. Poisonous reptiles are indicated by the danger symbol ⊗ next to the species name.
5. Consult the appendices for definitions of technical terms and suggestions for further reading.

Using This Guide in the Field

When you are out in the field, you will want to find information quickly and easily.

1. Turn to the color plates to locate the plant or animal you have seen. At a glance the captions will help you narrow down the possibilities. First, verify the habitat by checking the blue type information to the left of the color plate. Next, look for important field marks, which are also indicated in blue type— for example, how and where a mushroom grows, an insect's food, or a caterpillar's host plants. To find out whether a bird, mammal, reptile, or amphibian is in your area, check the range map next to the color plate.
2. Now turn to the species description to confirm your identification and to learn more about the species.

First frontispiece: A Bison grazing on June Grass at Yellowstone National Park, Wyoming.

Second frontispiece: A Pronghorn races across the prairie at Wind Cave National Park, South Dakota.

Third frontispiece: Black-tailed Prairie Dogs watch for intruders near their burrows in the shortgrass prairies of Wind Cave National Park, South Dakota.

Fourth frontispiece: Tiger Swallowtails take nectar in a Vermont meadow.

Fifth frontispiece: A hawkweed meadow blazes with summer color in Kalamazoo, Michigan.

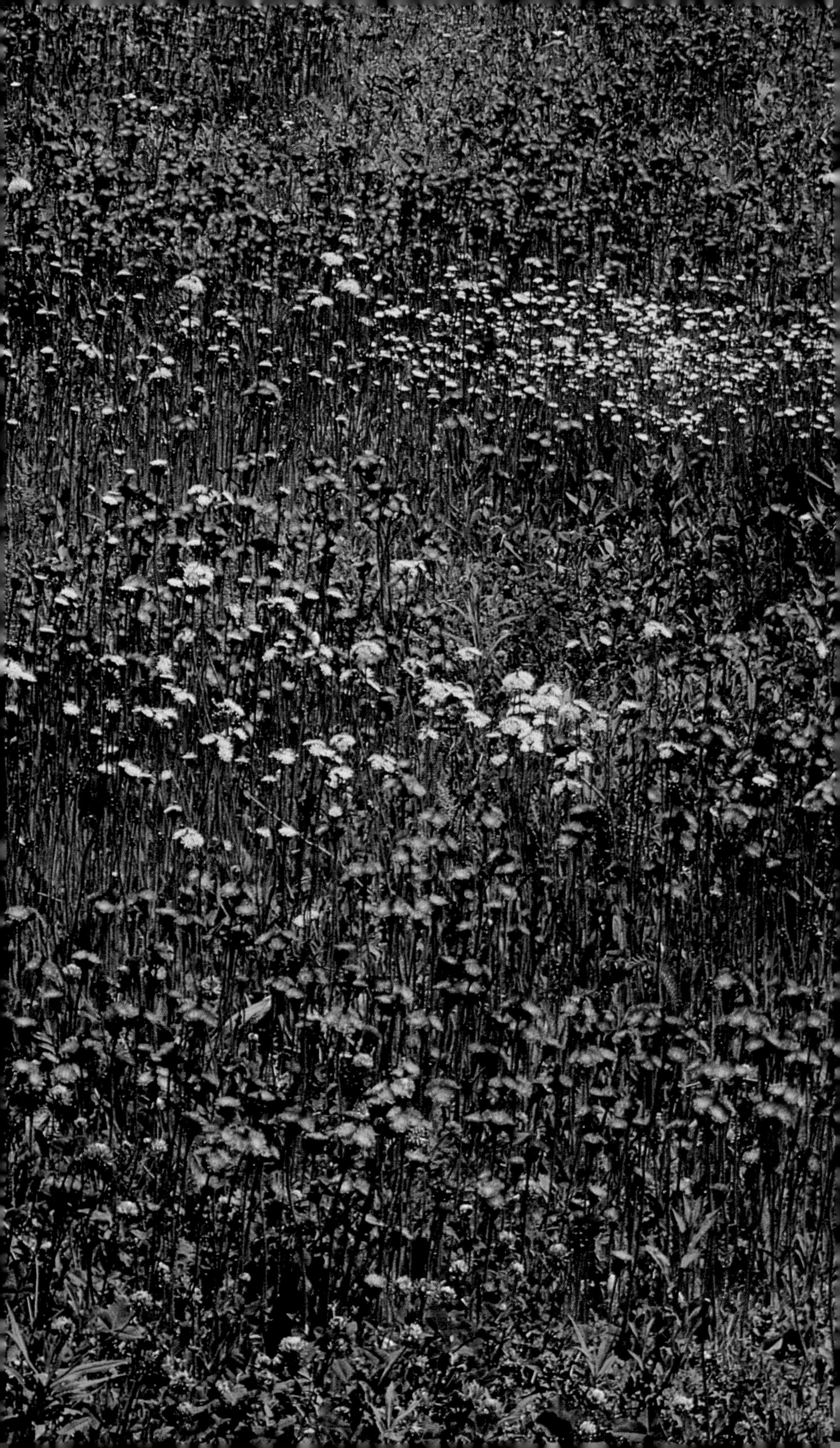

PART I GRASSLANDS

PREFACE

There is today an enthusiastic ground swell of interest in grasslands. Traditionally, nature lovers and outdoorspeople have turned to the mountains and the seashores for relaxation and enjoyment. Until recently, a city dweller would hardly consider taking a vacation in the Midwestern prairies, and like our forebears on the Oregon Trail, most of us have hurried to get across our grasslands—from one coast to the other—as quickly as possible.

This lack of interest in grasslands has been reflected in the national parks and monuments that have been created which are mainly those that include unusual landscapes. Thus, as this book goes to press—and we hope that it will soon be inaccurate—there is not one national park dedicated exclusively to the preservation of grassland.

Why preserve grasslands? Because they are one of the most extensive, productive ecosystems in the United States. Why have they not been preserved? Because they were too productive, and were quickly transformed to croplands; and because, in their vastness, they were considered the quintessence of monotony and were taken for granted.

While most publications on grasslands focus on one group of animals—such as wildflowers or birds—or on one geographical area—most often the tallgrass prairie, this book, covers all types of wildlife that we are most likely to notice in a grassland, and it discusses grasslands throughout the country. If you are standing in the middle of a prairie preserve, surrounded by stiff spikes of purple flowers, and a medium-sized bird with a yellow breast trills overhead while a large moth with pink markings on its wings hovers like a hummingbird in front of one of the flowers, you do not need to have carried three separate field guides with you. You can use this book to find that a White-lined Sphinx was taking nectar from a Prairie Blazing Star, in the territory of a male Western Meadowlark.

Unfortunately, few of us are able to walk down the road to an undisturbed native grassland. One must search to find good examples of the landscape that so overwhelmed the pioneers. Once you do find these places, however, they are there for you to enjoy throughout the year. For a twentieth-century Sunday afternoon walker, the prairie is a relatively benign environment, and you do not need to take any extraordinary precautions beyond what good common sense and a little experience will tell you. Take decent walking shoes, maybe a hat to keep off the sun, and whatever equipment you might want for studying natural history.

The enjoyment of natural history can be a solitary activity, and it has attracted some famous loners. However, especially if you are just starting, you can help yourself learn, and have more fun, by getting together with others who have similar interests. If this does not appeal to you, by all means stay on your own and discover and enjoy. For this is what it is all about, whether alone or with others, on a camping trip or on a Sunday afternoon walk: personal exploration and discovery.

INTRODUCTION

Some seventy or eighty million years ago, grasses began to evolve. Shortly thereafter, animals that lived off these grasses emerged and in turn modified the environment chiefly by grazing as to encourage the continued growth of grasses. Fire doubtless swept these early grasslands, and the plants and animals developed adaptations that enabled them to survive—and even thrive—under these conditions. This combination of grasses, grassland animals, and fire was so successful that grasslands now cover one quarter of the earth's surface.

Unlike most other flowering plants, grasses commonly grow in vast concentrations, most often in a semiarid climate. While humid climates support forests and dry ones support deserts, the grasslands require a moisture level somewhere in between. Moreover grasslands have a distinctive character. Unlike deserts, the vegetation forms a relatively solid cover over the ground, and unlike forests, the space is open and the views are endless.

Grasslands support more than just grasses. Within them one may find many kinds of wild flowers, desert plants, and even occasional trees. They also provide food and habitat for birds, mammals, reptiles, insects, amphibians, and countless microscopic soil organisms.

The colors in a grassland are both brilliant and subtle. Open space seems to stretch out indefinitely; indeed it can inspire an observer to feel, if only for a moment, that there are no bounds or limits on one's existence.

In spite of the limitations imposed by climate, grasslands present tremendous diversity as they change throughout the seasons and over the years. Moreover, grasslands in different locations vary considerably from one another. All of the continents except Antarctica contain some type of grassland. In Asia they are called steppes; in South America, pampas; and in South Africa, the veld. In the United States, the greatest stretch of grassland supports the prairie, a plant community that occupies the relatively flat land stretching west from the Appalachians. The prairie blends into the grassland type known as the plains, which then extends to the Rockies. Other grasslands exist in the Southwest, the Far West, and the East. Although these grasslands differ in some ways, they are all dominated by grasses.

The existence of the American grasslands is marked by irony. After millennia of evolution, they were transformed within half a century by the European settlers. The rich soils and unbroken spaces lured hungry settlers and were quickly exploited for human use. The existing plants and animals gave way to new species that were either cultivated by human beings or were able to adapt to the conditions created by human beings. As a result, the natural, or "true," grasslands in the United States have all but vanished.

They have not vanished completely, though. In a few places, one can still explore grasslands that retain their original beauty, looking as they did before our ancestors altered most of them. From suburban New York to coastal California, bits and pieces have survived, thanks either to chance or to the efforts of conservationists. Ranging in size from less than an acre to 8000 acres, these places offer an opportunity to see grassland plants and animals, and—even in preserves of a few acres—to get a feeling for the landscape that once covered a large part of the country.

Characteristics of Grasslands

All grasslands in the United States—except the eastern systems—have certain characteristics in common. They generally exist on flat or rolling terrain, and, although underlain by a variety of rock types, all occur on similar soils —those that are rich in organic matter, slightly alkaline, and very fertile.

American grasslands exist in areas where the annual precipitation averages between ten and thirty-nine inches. However, quantity alone does not tell the whole story. The time of year when the precipitation falls is also important. In most grasslands, precipitation is concentrated in peak periods; thus stretches of drought occur annually. Moreover, there are great fluctuations from year to year. Evaporation must be considered as well. In warmer, drier places, more of the yearly precipitation is lost to evaporation. From north to south, evaporation rates increase; thus, in southern areas, more rainfall is necessary to support the same vegetation that grows with less rainfall in the north. Shortgrasses, for example, may grow in Montana with fourteen inches of rainfall, while in Colorado they need seventeen, and in Texas they require twenty-one. Climatologists refer to this variable amount of necessary precipitation as "effective" or "equivalent" rainfall.

Because there are few obstacles to air movement, wind is an important factor in the climate of grasslands. Especially in the midcontinental grasslands, the wind seems to blow constantly. As it blows, the wind evaporates water, thereby exacerbating the already arid conditions. Wind also contributes to the spread of fire.

Whether caused by lightning or set by human beings, fires spread quickly through grasslands—partly because the dense cover of dead stalks provides plentiful fuel and partly because high winds push the fire along, and there are few rivers in prairie country to stop it. Some grasslands seem to vacillate between being grasslands and being forests. The agent that tips the balance in these cases is fire. Most trees are killed or weakened by fire, but grasses have adapted to survive it and may even grow better after a conflagration. Fire removes litter (dead plant material), which would otherwise shade the soil and keep it from warming up in the early spring. Furthermore it releases the nutrients that are locked up in the litter. The grasses thus begin to grow earlier in the season, and they reach greater heights.

Types of Grasslands

Even a novice who cannot name a single plant can see differences between, for example, a grassland in Missouri and

Grasslands

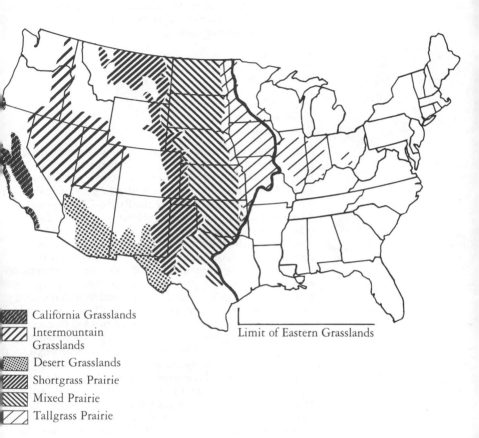

California Grasslands
Intermountain Grasslands
Desert Grasslands
Shortgrass Prairie
Mixed Prairie
Tallgrass Prairie

Limit of Eastern Grasslands

one in Arizona. The vegetation differs in size, color, and general aspect from area to area. Although boundaries between communities or types (areas defined by their dominant plant species) are rarely precise, important differences between them do exist across the country. This book recognizes and describes the following communities:

Tallgrass prairie
Mixed prairie
Shortgrass prairie
Desert grasslands
Intermountain grasslands
California grasslands
Eastern grasslands

Missing from this list are two other natural, self-sustaining grassland communities found in the United States: the mountain meadow, which is found in western mountains above the tree line; and the tidal wetlands, which line the Atlantic coast and grace parts of the Pacific. These systems, which still support undisturbed vegetation, are described in other volumes of this series.

The largest unbroken grassland formation is a huge area covered by tallgrass, mixed, and shortgrass prairies that stretches from the Appalachians to the Rockies. The names of these three grassland types are descriptive: The tallgrass prairie, which requires a moister environment than the other two, supports grasses that are over five feet high; the mixed prairie supports grasses ranging between two and four feet; and the shortgrass prairie, which requires the least moisture, supports grasses that are less than two feet tall. Although these height classifications are somewhat arbitrary, they roughly correspond to the natural heights of the species that characterize each community. These communities succeed each other along a gradient of decreasing moisture from east to west. They are not separated by distinct linear boundaries, but instead grade into each other in broad transitional zones that shift over time, depending on the weather. In a dry spell lasting several years, shortgrass species will expand their range to include areas occupied by mixed prairie, and species of midgrasses will expand into the domain of the tallgrasses. During wet years, the process is reversed. This phenomenon was dramatically illustrated during and after the great drought of 1933–39. Large areas of prairie were transformed by the dry conditions; when precipitation resumed, the previous communities reappeared.

These three prairie types are not absolutely restricted to separate geographic zones. In an area labeled mixed prairie on the map, a tallgrass community may grow in low, wet spots, and a shortgrass community may cover the dry, rocky outcrops. In such instances, soil moisture is the controlling factor—rather than yearly precipitation and evaporation. In spite of the intermingling and hopscotching of the three prairie types, they are still distinct enough to be mapped as three separate zones.

The other grassland communities are separated as much by geography as by vegetation. Although the desert grasslands support vegetation that is similar to that found in the shortgrass prairie, they are found at higher elevations, on the edges of the southwestern deserts. Sagebrush grasslands (discussed in the chapter entitled "Intermountain Grasslands") are found in the flat, intermountain basins of the Basin and Range province; the Palouse prairie (also in "Intermountain Grasslands"), though botanically similar to the sagebrush grassland, is found on the volcanic soils of the Columbia Plateau. The California grasslands are found in the Central Valley and the foothills of the California section of the Coast Range. The eastern grasslands are in a separate class, as the soils and the climate in the region where they occur foster the growth of trees rather than grasses. With time, and without human intervention, they become forests. Thus they are temporary features on the landscape, and indeed are sometimes technically designated "temporary or successional grasslands," for they are still grasslands, even though not in the true ecological sense.

Grassland Plants

The grass family is considered to be the third largest family of flowering plants in the world. This family has two scientific names—Gramineae and Poaceae—either of which can be used. Grasses are found from pole to pole and contain more species that are distributed worldwide than any other family of plants.

As a group, grasses are easy to recognize. However, their lack of brightly colored flowers may make them seem dull as well as difficult to distinguish from each other. Thus many naturalists find grasses confusing and ignore them. This prejudice is unfortunate, given their large numbers and their importance in the evolution and survival of mankind. Many of the most important crop plants are grasses: wheat, rice, corn, oats, sorghum, millet, barley, rye, and sugarcane. Almost all of our food comes—either directly or indirectly—from grasses. Meat-producing animals may, for example, eat corn, a grass, or they may graze on the open range, eating grass leaves, which human beings are incapable of digesting.

Grasses are herbaceous: They do not form woody tissue nor do they increase in girth, as trees do. Therefore, with a few exceptions, such as bamboo, sugarcane, and Reed, grasses are relatively small—shorter than a person. Members of the grass family have narrow leaves with parallel veins. The stems are hollow except at the node, the point where the leaf joins the stem. Grass flowers are small and inconspicuous, and are arranged either in tight, vertical clusters called spikes or in many-branched clusters called panicles. Grasses are distinguished from two similar families, the sedges and the rushes, by their hollow, round stems, by the way the flowers are arranged on the stem, and by the detailed structure of their flowers.

Grasses have features that enable them to minimize the dilemma experienced by all plants: On one hand, leaf surfaces must be exposed to the sun in order for photosynthesis to take place, but at the same time, it is desirable to have less leaf exposure, since water is lost through these surfaces. Although the narrow leaves of grasses, arranged more or less vertically along the stem, present less surface area, they are also arranged for maximum photosynthetic efficiency.

Several other characteristics of the grasses represent adaptations to the grassland environment. First, a large proportion of their biomass (living matter, expressed in weight or volume) exists underground in their root systems. In a seventy-day-old seedling of Big Bluestem, a widespread prairie grass, the above-ground growth is barely visible, but the extensively branched root is almost two feet long. Fully grown grass plants have enormous, fibrous root systems, sometimes reaching a depth that is twice the height of the above-ground shoots. A comparison by ecologists of a prairie and an oak forest in Minnesota revealed that the percentage of total plant biomass existing underground was greater in the prairie. During the growing season, about half of the biomass in the prairie was underground, while in the oak forest, the underground biomass represented less than ten percent.

The extensive root system presents several advantages. In areas of sparse and irregular precipitation, it makes sense for the seedling to establish contact with the deeper, moister layers of soil as soon as possible. Another advantage of the large root system is the defense it provides against grazing (or mowing, a mechanical form of grazing) and fire. Plant tissue, even that within the root system, represents the end product of the process of photosynthesis and thus contains stored energy, which can be drawn upon to produce new tissue. When a significant portion of the above-ground tissue of a prairie plant is removed or destroyed, enough energy is stored in the root system to make new growth possible.

Perennial grasses' defense against grazing is a sophisticated process which involves the leaves' unusual growth system. In most plants, the actively growing and dividing cells are located at the tips of the leaves. Thus a tree seedling with only two small leaves would die if it were clipped close to the ground, because it would lose its power to produce new tissue. In grasses, however, the growing center is at the base of the leaf, where it joins the stem, and the tip of the leaf is the oldest tissue. Therefore, if the tip of the leaf is cut, it can renew growth from its base. In addition, young shoots are hidden inside older shoots in a series of wraparound tubes. If the top of the shoot is bitten off, the protected young shoots can take over.

Many grass plants produce shoots called tillers, which are offshoots of the seedling or of other, already-established tillers. This accounts for the tufted growth form of many grasses, including some of those that grow in lawns. These side shoots sometimes travel, either above ground (as stolons) or below ground (as rhizomes), before sending out leaves. The grasses with runners that travel only a short distance form dense sod, which not only keeps them from being pulled out of the ground when they are clipped, but also prevents the establishment of competing plants. Other grasses do not form sod, but grow in discrete bunches with space between the plants. And some grasses can do either, depending upon environmental conditions. Generally, dry conditions lead to the dominance of bunchgrasses, and wet ones, to the formation of sod.

All herbaceous plants grow as annuals, biennials, or perennials. Annuals have a one-year life cycle, which means they germinate, set seed, and die in one growing season. They last through the winter, or the dry season, as seeds. A biennial has a two-year life cycle; it survives its single winter as a root and a tuft of basal leaves. In the second year, it sends up a flowering shoot, sets seed, and dies. A perennial can live for a period lasting from a few years to decades and, like the biennials, survives the winter in the form of its root system and a few basal leaves.

Most native prairie grasses and broad-leaved plants are long-lived perennials, but when the vegetation is stripped and the soil is laid bare from either overgrazing or trampling, annuals often appear. Although the perennials might seem to have superior adaptations to prairie conditions, the annuals turn out to be equally adapted in their own way.

Despite shallow root systems—which are theoretically unsuited to a dry climate—annuals are able to survive because of their telescoped life cycle. They germinate as soon as it rains, grow quickly, and set seed while there is still adequate moisture. It does not matter if the soil dries out and the plant dies; its work is done: The soil is filled with seeds for the following year. If the annual is a species that is not strictly tied to day length as a signal for flowering and germination, it can even produce several generations during one year.

Thus annuals represent an important part of the grassland flora. They are not capable of invading a well-established prairie sod, but any grassland contains disturbed areas, where annuals may become established. The dominant plant species of natural grasslands, however, are perennial grasses.

Long before anyone knew much about plant physiology, ranchers noticed that some grasses grew the most in spring and fall, while others were inactive until the heat of the summer. They called these, respectively, cool-season and warm-season grasses. In the 1960s, researchers discovered that this phenomenon was not mere coincidence, but was the result of different biochemical processes—different forms of photosynthesis—which cause some plants to do better in warm, dry conditions and others to thrive in a cool, moist environment. With warm- and cool-season plants interspersed in a grassland, nothing is wasted; the two combine to make efficient use of seasonal trends.

The plants that share grasslands with the grasses—the forbs— also share some of the grasses' adaptations, and have others of their own. These herbs have broad leaves relative to the grasses and thus present a larger surface, which means higher levels of evaporation. Even so, they are not as broad as the leaves of most plants in the humid, eastern forests. Many of the forbs' leaves are stiff and leathery or covered with bristly hairs—common defenses of desert plants against both drought and grazing. Unlike desert plants, few grassland plants have thorns.

The perennial forbs match the grasses in root adaptations as well. Although few have the fibrous root systems that the grasses do, most have deep taproots with several branches. The roots of some prairie forbs delve as deep as twenty feet. In times of severe drought, certain species outlive the surrounding grasses. With their slightly different root systems, grasses and forbs are able to exploit different resources in the grassland system.

Grassland Animals

When most people think of grasslands, a few dominant species come to mind: Bison (also called Buffalo), which almost became extinct; Pronghorn (also known as "American Antelope," although it is not really an antelope), which is the fastest animal in the Western Hemisphere; Coyote; jack rabbits; and a host of rodents, including prairie dogs. However, these and other grassland animals have undergone significant changes in population levels and ranges as a result of nineteenth-century human settlement.

Most of the grassland species—particularly large mammals—are wide-ranging in distribution and can adapt to a great variety of climates and food supplies. Some of the smaller mammals are more restricted in their ranges, but closely related species occupy parallel niches elsewhere.

Grassland animals share characteristics and habitats that are different from those of their forest counterparts and which help them to survive in the grassland environment. Accordingly, one of the first things one is likely to notice about grassland fauna is a preponderance of burrowing animals. Prairie dogs, ground squirrels, and pocket gophers are the most obvious ones, but many snakes and even a bird—the Burrowing Owl—also spend time in these rodents' burrows. There are also burrowing predators: weasels, ferrets, the Swift Fox, and the Badger.

The burrowing habitat is widespread for several reasons. Above ground, the prairie provides few hiding places. Furthermore, the prairie can be a place of extreme variation in climate—ranging from hot, humid summers to bitterly cold winters—but a constant environment exists underground. Finally, a burrow serves as an excellent hideaway during a fire. Prairie fires burn fast, but they rarely even burn the soil surface, let alone reach underground. Since most burrowing animals do not roam far from their burrows, they can quickly duck inside during a fire and wait it out.

Running is another adaptive ability of grassland animals. It makes sense; if there is no place to hide from a predator, it

helps to be able to run. The Swift Fox, which has been
clocked at twenty-five miles per hour, the Coyote, clocked at
forty miles per hour, and the Pronghorn, at seventy miles per
hour, are a few of the animals that have refined the running
habit. Many birds, though capable of flying, instead rely on
running to escape; these include the quails, the grouse, and
the Road Runner, to name a few. To the ostriches, emus, and
rheas—grassland inhabitants of other continents—running is
so important that they have lost the ability to fly.

The grassland environment has influenced the social behavior
of its inhabitants. The numbers of animals witnessed in one
location have been staggering: In presettlement days, millions
of Buffalo could be seen in one herd; millions of prairie dogs,
in one town; and 20,000 jack rabbits, the victims of angry
farmers, could be rounded up in one day. Comparisons of
woodland and grassland animals show a much greater degree
of sociability in the grasslands. In the grasslands, prairie dogs,
for instance, live in large, highly organized social units. Their
eastern woodland counterpart, the Woodchuck, rarely
interacts with its fellows; their western mountain counterpart,
the Yellow-bellied Marmot, is only slightly social. Among
birds, flocking species form a much higher percentage of the
total number of species than in woodlands.

The social habit may be a response to lack of cover (witness
the prairie dogs with their effective alarm system), but it is a
response to other factors as well. Birds, which rely heavily on
sound for communication, are hampered in open grassland,
where sound is swallowed up, absorbed by the ground, and
lost in the wind. Flocking could be a solution to this problem.
Other solutions have evolved: various members of the Grouse
family hold their courtship rituals, which include strange
sounds, at dawn or dusk, when the air is still and the sound
travels farther. Other grasslands birds, lacking perching posts,
deliver their territory and courtship songs in flight. Out of
necessity most grassland birds nest on the ground.

The raptors, or birds of prey, are more conspicuous in the
grasslands than elsewhere. The open spaces favor animals with
good vision, and an abundance of small mammals provides a
good food supply for hawks and eagles.

Insects are legion. The most notorious among them are the
grasshoppers, of which hundreds of species occur in the North
American grasslands. Amphibians, most of which are
dependent upon water for mating, are common only around
ponds, but the grasslands are a good habitat for many
drought-tolerant snakes. The snakes hunt small rodents and
insects—as well as birds and birds' eggs, most of which are
conveniently found in ground-level nests.

There is also an "invisible prairie," which consists of countless
numbers of microscopic organisms that live in the soil and on
the ground, where they feed on dead plants and animal
matter. These organisms actually do most of the work of the
prairie. This is because, in spite of the overwhelming numbers
of herbivores, it appears that they consume only a small
proportion of the green matter available to them. Even the

insects, which collectively eat prodigious amounts, waste most of their food; a grasshopper will clip a leaf, chew a bit, and then let the rest of it fall to the ground. Bacteria and fungi consume much of this "wasted" plant material, either above-ground as litter, or after it has begun to rot underground. According to some recent estimates, the total weight of soil microorganisms in a given area of grassland is about equal to the total weight of the vegetation.

There is evidence that herbivory—the act of animals eating plants—both stimulates greater production of roots in relation to shoots and, in general, encourages increased plant growth. This happens through the release of the enzyme thiamine in the animals' saliva. Thus the herbivores appear to have adapted in ways that will ensure continued production of their food supply; however, at the same time, they tend to drive the plants underground, where their most likely consumers will be bacteria, fungi, and nematodes—or the "invisible prairie."

When the native grassland animals met up with the nineteenth-century settlers, the encounter was not a happy one. Habitat alteration caused a number of them to suffer severe population decreases, although others were able to adapt to the human-induced changes, and some even increased. However, most of the animals were considered pests and thus became the victims of deliberate extermination programs. These efforts met with varied success. Both the Bison and the prairie dogs were nearly eliminated, while the jack rabbits somehow managed to increase in number. The Bison, the lifeblood of the Indians, was, for a time, a target for destruction; in fact it was government policy to destroy the Bison and thereby the Indians as well. The prairie dogs were targeted because they were seen as agricultural pests. As for the jack rabbits, which ate crops, the early settlers organized drives in which they herded tens of thousands of the animals into enclosed areas and clubbed them to death. In California, ground squirrels were cited in a gubernatorial proclamation, which offered prizes to the schoolchildren who killed the most animals. Coyote control continues to this day, at a cost of millions of dollars. However, the Coyote has held its own and is presently increasing its range into areas that it never used to occupy.

Uses of Grasslands for Agriculture and Grazing

We cannot eat grass leaves directly. We can and do eat grass seeds, which are the grains—corn, wheat, and so on—that are so important to our diet. In some American grasslands, human beings have removed the native grasses and planted other species: corn on the tallgrass prairie, and wheat on the mixed prairie. Other grasslands are too dry for crop production, but they are still useful to human beings. On rangeland, the grass is eaten by animals that can digest it—principally cows—and is thus converted into food that we can eat: beef and dairy products. Sheep can graze land that is even poorer than that which is acceptable to cattle; they provide us with mutton and wool. In the East, where there is very little open range, grass is cut and dried to make hay, which is fed to livestock in the winter. Hay is also harvested in the western grasslands.

Of course an infinite number of cattle cannot feed on a finite amount of land. When too many animals are placed on a range, it becomes overgrazed and no longer produces valuable forage. Overgrazed rangeland may recover over time, but not all sites have this capability. Vast areas of the western range have been overgrazed; some have been permanently degraded.

Although much altered now, grasslands have had and continue to play an important role in the shaping of this country's landscape, history, and economy. Where the native grass cover has been removed, the land is valuable for agriculture, and where the original grasses remain, it is valuable for grazing. The settlement of the grasslands—and the early settlers' eventual triumph over the hardships they encountered—represents one of the most impressive chapters of the nation's history, even if the flip side of this event—the taking of the grasslands from the original inhabitants—can hardly be so acclaimed.

In spite of all the changes, grasslands can still be seen today. We can still watch the native grasses wave in the wind, with Compass Plants and prairie dock towering over them in the late summer. We can still witness prairie fires (even if they are deliberately set by scientists), and afterwards see the grass grow back lush and green. We can view meadowlarks and prairie chickens as well as Pronghorns and prairie dogs. We can also notice how plants have adapted to their environment and understand how animals have affected the growth of plants. And we can see differences—differences between various types of grasslands, resulting from the forces of climate and geology across the country. A detailed description of various types of grasslands—their differences and similarities as well as what one might find in them and why—follows.

TALLGRASS PRAIRIE

In its original state, the tallgrass prairie—also known as the true prairie—was probably the most dramatic of all American grasslands. Early settlers wrote of grass reaching as high as a horse's back and said that grazing cattle could only be found by standing up in the saddle and looking for movement in the grass. In some places, the grass grew as high as twelve feet.

Early Settlers' Impressions of the True Prairie

While there were patches of mid-size grasses, for the most part, the grass was uniform in height and seemingly endless in extent. In its overall size and sameness, it suggested a vast body of water. This comparison was made over and over again by early writers. In *Sketches of Iowa and Wisconsin,* a booklet by John Plumbe, Jr. published in the 1840s, a Judge Hall wrote:

These plains, although preserving a general level in respect to the whole country, are yet in themselves not flat, but exhibit a gracefully waving surface, swelling and sinking with an easy slope, and full, rounded outline. . . . It is said that surface which . . . is called rolling, and which has been said to resemble the long, heavy swell of the ocean, when its waves are subsiding to rest after the agitation of a storm. . . . the whole of the surface of these beautiful plains is clad throughout the season of verdure with every imaginable variety of color, from "grave to gay." It is impossible to conceive a more infinite diversity, or a richer profusion to hues . . .

One woman wrote: "When I saw a settler's child tripping out of home bounds, I had a feeling that it would never get back again. It looked like putting out to Lake Michigan in a canoe."

The grasses were not this imposing all year round. In the fall, the stalks died, and over the course of the winter, they were beaten to the ground by wind and snow. The new stalks did not again reach full height until mid-July, following heavy June rains. In the meantime, the spring forbs and cool-season grasses had their day in the sun, and the prairie progressed through a series of color changes and flowerings. The ecologist J. E. Weaver described the spring wild flowers as "the gems of nature, manifold in variety, radiant in beauty, endless in recurrence." The flowering began with more than forty low-growing spring plants—pasque flowers, Bird-foot Violet, strawberries, ground plums—and progressed to tall, rough wild flowers—Prairie Dock, Compass Plant, coneflowers, Blackeyed Susan, Blazing Star, as well as dozens of others.

The tallgrasses flowered in late summer. These species turned a multitude of subtle yet rich colors encompassing all shades of bronze, copper, crimson, yellow, and gold, and were quite beautiful to behold.

Although some observers found the tallgrass prairie to be insufferably monotonous, and perhaps a little frightening in

its broad silence, most travelers told of a landscape marked by diversity and splendor.

Range

The designation "true prairie" is ironic, because the tallgrass prairie has a tenuous hold on being a prairie at all. The past tense is often used in describing the tallgrass prairie, as this vegetation type no longer exists except in small, isolated patches. This is because the rich soil on which it occurred was too attractive to settlers to be left for Big Bluestem and Indian Grass, native tallgrass prairie plants. By the turn of the century, most of the tallgrasses had been plowed under, and the land had been replanted in corn—the tallgrass prairie was largely gone. It remained in small areas such as railroad rights-of-way and old cemeteries, and also in a few large areas, such as the Flint Hills of eastern Kansas.

The tallgrass prairie has historically occurred in the Midwest, in parts of Iowa and Minnesota, and on the eastern edges of Kansas, Nebraska, South Dakota, and North Dakota—from which it extends northward into Canada. But although its range is known, its exact boundaries are hard to define.

The eastern boundary is particularly problematic, for a large area consisting of much of Iowa, Missouri, Illinois, parts of Indiana, and little pieces of Ohio is not quite prairie, is not forest, nor is it a hybrid. This area is called the Prairie Peninsula. The word "peninsula" is fitting, for on a map the area looks like a tongue of prairie surrounded on three sides by forest. When the peninsula is viewed up close, however, the situation is more complicated; indeed some have said that it should be called "the Prairie Archipelago," for it consists of islands of prairie surrounded by forest. (See "The Prairie Peninsula," at the end of this chapter, for further discussion of this area.)

The western boundary of the tallgrass prairie is somewhat simpler, though it is not delineated by an obvious geographical feature, such as a mountain range or a river. Rather, it is a broad transition zone that runs from north to south through the eastern part of the Dakotas and Nebraska, central Kansas, and into central Oklahoma. Outliers of the tallgrass prairie occur in the interior of Texas and along the Gulf Coast in Texas and Louisiana.

The transition zone between tallgrass and mixed prairies basically reflects a decrease in precipitation, an increase in evaporation, and therefore a decrease in soil moisture. One of the reasons that both the eastern and western boundaries are not exact is that the tallgrass prairie becomes dominant during wet years and thins out when conditions are drier. During the great drought of 1933–39, scientists documented an eastward retraction of one hundred to 150 miles on the prairie's western border. Conversely, when rainfall resumed, they witnessed a westward expansion.

Notwithstanding the above, those who define the boundary with a fixed line are not terribly inaccurate, for, in spite of its fluctuations, the border between the two grassland provinces never veers far from an uncompromisingly straight line: the ninety-eighth meridian of longitude. According to the historian Walter P. Webb, the ninety-eighth meridian is an absolute boundary between two completely different environments and ways of life.

Despite these "border disputes," a farmer is not likely to have much difficulty in defining this habitat, as the tallgrass prairie is also known as the corn belt. Farther west, corn can be grown successfully only on irrigated land.

Physical Features

The present configuration of the midcontinental prairie can be explained by three factors:

1. The craton. A craton is a relatively immobile portion of the earth's crust. The western and eastern parts of this country are in a state of ongoing geological upheaval—the recent eruption of Mt. St. Helens and the frequent earthquakes in both the East and the West are examples—while the part of the continent between the Rockies and the Appalachians has been stable since the beginning of Cambrian time, or about 500 million years ago. The underlying rocks in this middle area are among the oldest known, having been formed about 600 million years ago during the Precambrian Era. They are strong and can resist tectonic deformations in the earth's crust. This circumstance explains why the Midwest is basically flat. These ancient, Precambrian rocks are overlain by various layers of rock that were deposited during the Mesozoic Era as shallow seas advanced and retreated. These younger, sedimentary rocks include limestones and sandstones, and their nature and location sometimes determine local soil characteristics. The Precambrian Shield protrudes above the sedimentary strata in some places, including the Sioux uplift in South Dakota, the Ozark uplift in Missouri, the Arbuckle and Wichita mountains in Oklahoma, the Llano uplift in Texas, the Black Hills in South Dakota, and the Front Range in the Rockies.

2. The Rocky Mountains. The Rocky Mountains began uplifting at the end of the Mesozoic Era, roughly 65 million years ago. Even as they rose, wind and water incessantly and inexorably eroded them. Over the eons, the detritus that eroded from the Rockies spread across the Midwest. This explains why the land rises imperceptibly from near sea level at the base of the western edge of the Appalachians to over a mile high at the eastern foot of the Rockies.

3. The glaciers. While the craton and the Rocky Mountains are responsible for the landscape as a whole, the glaciers are responsible for its smaller features—the variations that would affect a settler's decisions on such matters as where to build a house, where to plant, and where to locate a road. During the Pleistocene Epoch, the ice cap spread south and covered much of the continent; in some places, ice sheets were a mile thick. There were four periods of very cold weather. In chronological order, the four glacial periods were the Nebraskan, the Kansan, the Illinoian, and the Wisconsin. Glaciers did not cover the entire country, but in the places they did cover, they

reorganized the landscape. They scraped away rocks and deposited them elsewhere, dumped huge piles of gravel and debris that became hills, and deposited gravel in sheets that formed plains. Stranded blocks of ice created depressions that are now potholes, ponds, and lakes.

Between and after the glacial periods came times of extreme dryness, during which loose material was blown around by westerly winds. When such material has a fine texture, it is called loess, from the German word for "loose." Extensive deposits of loess formed a rich soil along the Mississippi and Missouri rivers, and the loess was sometimes shaped by the wind into distinctive bluffs along the riverbanks. More heavily textured, sandy material was also on occasion picked up by the wind and deposited in large dunes. The Nebraska Sandhills, which occupy most of the north-central part of Nebraska, constitute the largest of such areas.

The formation of soil is a slow process that is brought about by the action of weather and vegetation on rock. The character of the soil is initially determined by the climate and the bedrock, but as plants become established, vegetation also plays a part. Because of variations in bedrock geology and changes caused by glaciation, the soils in the tallgrass prairie vary in color, texture, and chemical properties. Yet they have all been similarly modified by the growth of grasses over the centuries.

As grasses die and rot, they provide the beginnings of a deep surface layer, which eventually becomes dark in color and rich in organic matter. When the surface soil dries, it does not harden but instead remains soft; thus such soils are called mollisols, a term derived from the Latin *mollis* for soft. Especially where underlain by limestone, the mollisols are alkaline or neutral. Thus, since bacteria are inhibited by acidic conditions, these soils provide a good environment for their growth and, consequently, one that encourages the decomposition by the bacteria of plant material and the liberating of the nutrients therein.

An important feature of the tallgrass prairie is that the subsoil remains moist year-round. Furthermore, precipitation is sufficient to leach various substances from the soil into the groundwater; thus they do not accumulate in the soil. All of these characteristics make for a soil that is favorable for the growth of crops.

Climate

Precipitation in the tallgrass prairie ranges from approximately twenty-five to about thirty-nine inches per year, with somewhat less falling on its western edges. Over half of this arrives during the growing season. In Lincoln, Nebraska, for example, records of precipitation over a fifty-year span show an annual average of twenty-eight inches, with eighty percent falling as rain during the growing season. On average, fourteen inches, or fifty percent, fell during May, June, and July. A second, smaller peak period occurred in September. Summers can be hot and humid, with the heat alleviated only by constant winds. Winters vary from mild in the south to severe in the northern prairie habitats.

A seemingly characteristic feature of many grassland climates —the tallgrass prairie included—is an extreme variability in yearly precipitation, and drought is a frequent occurrence. The following excerpt from Weaver's work suggests what it felt like to be on the tallgrass prairie, the prairie community with the most moisture, during the drought of 1933–39:

> The most trying period began about June 20. The half-cured little bluestem on hillsides and xeric slopes crunched like snow when one tread upon it. Even the accompanying big bluestem was half dried. Then followed a period of most intensive drought. A terrific heat wave swept over the prairie. It continued until the last week in July. During this time the scorching sun seared the prairie as if by fire, and life in all but the most deeply rooted species retreated underground.

Vegetation

A stand of tallgrass prairie looks wonderfully diverse— especially in the spring, when it hosts a striking variety of wild flowers and many different kinds of grasses. However, if one were to count the stems in a square meter, or to cut them down, sort them by species, and weigh them, it would become evident that most of the biomass is produced by a few species—all of which are grasses. Such dominance of large areas by a few species is a characteristic of most grasslands.

Warm-Season Grasses

One of the dominant species in the tallgrass prairie is Big Bluestem. This species is not blue, but it is big. The flower stalks, which jut high above the leafy bases, may grow to a height of twelve feet, though a height of four to nine feet is more common. Big Bluestem is also known as Turkey Claw because of the fingerlike arrangement of its flower stalks. It is a somewhat gangly-looking plant, but as it matures in the late summer, it becomes quite handsome, displaying a variety of colors ranging from steely gray to wine red. Big Bluestem is an excellent forage grass that is readily eaten by livestock. In the tallgrass prairie, it prefers moist, but not wet, soil. It is often found in broad valleys and on lower slopes, where it may constitute eighty percent of a stand. Land on which Big Bluestem grows is also good for corn.

Indian Grass, which occupies the same habitat as Big Bluestem, is characterized by tall, lustrous, golden-brown flower stalks. The sight of these stalks waving in the wind is a sign of late summer. In the northern parts of the tallgrass prairie, Indian Grass is not as plentiful as Big Bluestem, but in southern areas, it can take over ninety percent of a stand. It is somewhat more opportunistic and drought-tolerant than Big Bluestem, and can invade bare soil. It, too, provides excellent forage.

Unlike Big Bluestem, Prairie Cordgrass dominates land that is too wet for corn. Prairie Cordgrass, whose relatives grow chiefly in salt marshes, is one of the tallest, densest prairie grasses, growing up to twelve feet high in thick, luxuriant stands. Another name for this species is Ripgut, a reference to the small barbs that line the edges of its leaves and make working in a Prairie Cordgrass stand a miserable experience. The barbs do not seem to bother cattle, however, and Prairie Cordgrass provides good forage. Early accounts of tall, impenetrable stands of grass were probably referring to Prairie Cordgrass.

Slightly uphill from Prairie Cordgrass, Switchgrass appears. It does not grow as tall or as dense, but it is also a good forage plant. This plant's delicate flower clusters contain hard, bony seeds. It it slightly less shade-tolerant than the other dominant prairie grasses. In the eastern states, Switchgrass grows in dry soil on the upper edges of salt marshes.

On upland sites, one finds Little Bluestem, which, like its larger namesake, is not blue, except when the young leaves emerge in the spring. It is little only in relation to Big Bluestem, as it grows to an average height of three feet. Unlike the species described above, it often grows as a bunchgrass rather than a sod grass, depending on soil moisture. In the fall, it turns a rich gold.

Cool-Season Grasses

These are all warm-season grasses, but there are cool-season grasses as well, which grow and flower in the spring before being shaded out by the taller, warm-season species. Needlegrass, Junegrass, and Prairie Dropseed—all cool-season species—are each named for a particular characteristic: Needlegrass for the long bristles attached to its seed husks; Junegrass for the time of year that it flowers; and Prairie Dropseed for its large tear-shaped seeds. These grasses contribute a fresh, green aspect to the prairie in the spring.

Forbs

In spite of the overwhelming dominance of grasses—in terms of both space and weight—it is the diversified forbs that catch one's eye. They usually grow among the grasses, occurring only rarely in solid stands. Most of them are about the same height as or shorter than the grasses, but some of them, such as Rosinweed and Compassplant, tower above. The dominant groups are the legumes—plants with pealike flowers and seeds in a pod—and the composites, which are daisylike flowers. The composites, most of which appear in the late summer, include various sunflowers, goldenrods, Blazing Star, coneflowers, asters, and members of the genus *Silphium*. The forbs' brilliant colors add delight to the prairie landscape.

Trees

Although descriptions of the tallgrass prairie dwell on the endless sea of grasses, trees do grow in this habitat—chiefly along the riverbanks, but also in the midst of the grasses. The riverbank trees include cottonwoods, American Elm, Green Ash, Box Elder, and various hackberries, but the most widespread upland prairie tree is the Bur Oak.

The Bur Oak is a magnificent tree with a broad, spreading crown and thick, dark green leaves. Its name comes from the distinctive, bristly caps on its large acorns, which are dispersed by Fox Squirrels. In adapting to prairie conditions, a Bur Oak seedling puts down a four-foot-long taproot in its first year; thus, like the grasses, it can draw on deep reservoirs of soil moisture in dry years. The leathery coating on its leaves cuts down on water loss, and the thick, corky bark resists fire.

The tallgrass prairie resembles a forest in several ways. Like a miniature tree, a full-grown grass plant spreads its leaves well beyond the area covered by its base and casts deep shade on the ground. Only one to three percent of the sunlight reaching the top of the grasses penetrates to the bottom. As in a forest, though, the lower grass leaves are oriented so that they can receive sunlight even in this dense tangle. Moreover, the relationship between the vegetation and the seasons in the prairie is somewhat analogous to that occurring in the forest: In both, the low-growing plants crowd their entire life cycle —from the emergence of the first leaves to the development of flowers and fruits—into the spring, before they are enveloped by shade. In addition, both a forest and a mature grass stand can resist invasion by other species. An individual grass plant may live ten to twenty years, during which time it develops a dense, fibrous root system, so that invading species do not stand a chance.

If the dominant grasses are grazed or cut too frequently, the sunlight reaching the ground will promote the establishment and spread of other native perennial species, which are called increasers. The replaced dominants—those that cannot withstand heavy grazing—are called decreasers. Once cattle can no longer rely on the decreasers, they turn to the increasers, even though the latter usually provide forage that is less nutritious. As the increasers are cropped or trampled, more sunlight reaches the ground, and in time, bare spots may appear. At this point, the area is ripe for an influx of invaders, which are usually annual species that are adapted to bare soil. In the past, areas such as Buffalo wallows provided suitable places for invaders to catch hold.

These opportunistic annuals bide their time, producing abundant seed crops every year as they wait for a chance to spread. They usually produce inferior forage, both in quantity and quality, and many possess sharply pointed seeds that irritate grazing animals. These species will fill up a cleared field once it is taken out of cultivation. If grazing is stopped, or if the cleared land is left alone long enough, this process can reverse itself, although slowly. The long-lived native perennial species will come back, usually within twenty years.

Wildfires

The grasses and forbs that dominate and define the tallgrass prairie would not be dominant if it were not for fire. Early travelers wrote with great awe about the spectacular fires that burned the prairies. One observer wrote that settlers without wood used bundles of dried Prairie Cordgrass for fuel, and that enough could be tied together in an hour to warm a house for a day. Imagine, then, the fires that could rage through miles of dried Prairie Cordgrass. Alfred Brunson, a Methodist circuit rider traveling through Illinois in 1835, wrote:

The last 12 miles we travelled after sundown and by fire light over the Prairie, it being on fire. This was the grandest scene I ever saw. . . . We had a view at one time from one to 5 miles of fire in a streak, burning from 2 to 6 feet high. In high grass it sometimes burns 30 feet high, if driven by fierce winds. By the light of this fire we could read fine print for ½ a mile or more. . . . Till I saw this, I could never understand one part of the scripture. The cloud which overspread the camp of Israel and kept off the rays of the sun by day, was a *pillar of fire by night*. It was literally so with the smoke which rose from these fires.

Following settlement, wildfires became less and less frequent. There were several reasons for this: Land was converted to agriculture; towns and cities were constructed; and thus there was less fuel, and less unbroken grassland for fires to burn through. In addition, the settlers attempted to control and prevent fires. Trees started to invade the remaining segments of the prairie that did not burn. They eventually shaded out the grasses, and the forest replaced the prairie.

If a tallgrass prairie is regularly subjected to fire—as they apparently were for a long time—it will remain a tallgrass prairie. Fearsome as these fires might have looked, they did not last long or burn very thoroughly. Experiments recreating prairie fire conditions have shown that even some of the dead grass is not burned, the fire moves so quickly. Although the soil surface may heat up to as high as 400° F for a few minutes, temperatures below ground rarely change. Thus, for such a dramatic event, the results are often far short of catastrophic. The basal shoots of the green plants are usually unaffected, and the roots are not in the slightest bit damaged.

In fact, overall grass growth is better after a fire. There are several possible reasons: The nutrients previously locked up in the dead plant material are released by fire (although some of them wash away with the next rain); the soil warms up sooner in the spring, since it is not covered with dead grass; and new shoots get more light.

The fate of the animals in the path of a fire is mixed. Burrowing animals can take shelter in their insulated, underground homes, and many other species can run or fly away from a blaze. However, the fate of certain other animals is not so positive. In 1891 John H. Schaffner, a Kansas farmer, wrote, somewhat grimly: "Insects and rabbits and birds fled but often too late to escape death; and as we walked over the still warm ashes, we found many snakes and small quadrupeds that had been burned. By the aid of the bright flames we could see hundreds of burned bird's nests, some with the little birds still writhing in the agonies of death."

The larvae of butterflies and other insects, which are relatively immobile, may be killed in large numbers. And prairie travelers sometimes wrote of seeing singed and blind Buffalo bellowing in pain after a fire.

Researchers, though, find surprisingly few dead animals after a fire in relation to the populations that inhabited the burned areas before the fire. Evidently, grassland species have evolved in ways that enable them to survive frequent fires.

Prairie Animals

The animal populations of the tallgrass prairie provide a reminder of this habitat's underlying similarities to the eastern forests and at the same time call into question the appropriateness of calling this habitat the true prairie. For most of the animals that we think of as quintessentially prairie inhabitants—prairie dogs, the Pronghorn, and the Black-tailed Jackrabbit—are not found at all on the tallgrass prairie. In fact only a few species occur exclusively in the tallgrass prairie. Among the few mammals that are restricted to the tallgrass prairie are the Plains Pocket Gopher (misnamed, like some other prairie animals; the plains are farther west) and Franklin's Ground Squirrel. Both have close relatives in other American grasslands; these other species are also restricted to their particular habitats. The habits of the related species are generally similar, so the following discussions of these two tallgrass prairie species will apply somewhat to their relatives elsewhere.

The Latin name for pocket gopher, *Geomys,* means "earth mouse." Fittingly enough, Plains Pocket Gophers rarely come above ground except when they are young or during mating season. They dig vast, labyrinthine burrows, in which they eat, raise their young, and die. The burrows can be as much as one hundred feet long and may have side chambers for food storage and excrement; each animal lives alone in its own burrow.

Because soil is such a good insulator, these pocket gophers are not adapted to heat; they can die within an hour if exposed to a hot summer sun. Their principal food consists of the roots of plants—especially grasses—which they cut with their large front teeth. Their lips close behind their teeth, so that they do not get dirt in their mouths; if necessary, they use their teeth for digging.

Because they so rarely surface, Pocket Gophers suffer less mortality from predators than do other grassland rodents. One such predator is the Badger, a creature adapted to catch burrowing animals. With its short front legs ending in recurved claws, its flattened body, and its shovel-like hind claws, this predator can dig as well as any rodent.

Badgers live in dens and dig different ones for various uses, which include daytime resting, food storage, giving birth, and raising their young. When hunting Pocket Gophers, a Badger digs several short, vertical holes along the length of a Gopher's extensive burrow. It descends one, then moves a short distance in each direction along the tunnel, enlarging the passageway

as it goes and using its sense of smell to locate its prey. If the
Badger does not find the Gopher right away, it resurfaces and
uses a different vertical passage. Thus it avoids having to
burrow great distances.

Franklin's Ground Squirrel, although also a burrower, feeds on
the surface. While some rodents, such as prairie dogs, require
a shortgrass environment so that they can see their enemies,
Franklin's Ground Squirrel prefers tallgrasses, which help
conceal the entrance to its burrow. Like most of its sibling
species, its populations fluctuate without damage to the
overall population, and it can adapt quickly to a change in
conditions. In the tallgrass prairie, it was considered a pest
when the land was first broken—its numbers tended to
increase—but the populations generally declined within a few
years, and people recognized that the creature was beneficial,
as it eats voles and grasshoppers. Although usually secretive
and elusive, Franklin's Ground Squirrel makes its presence
known at mating time by its mating call—a high-pitched
whistle—which gives it another name: "Whistling Ground
Squirrel."

The tallgrass prairie's affinities to both prairie and forest, and
the considerable intermingling of these two habitats within
tallgrass areas—especially in Illinois, Ohio, Wisconsin, and
Michigan—have resulted in a great diversity of animal life
within its boundaries. Ecologists have been aware for a long
time of "the edge effect"—the fact that the boundary between
two habitats, such as woodland and grassland, supports many
more species than either habitat does by itself. This is because
more than one habitat is available to meet the animals'
requirements.

The Fox Squirrel, for instance, basically an arboreal species,
seems to do well in country where woodlands abut grasslands.
Its original habitat was probably the riverbank forests of the
prairie, where it nested and did much of its feeding, and from
which it apparently also ventured out into open spaces. As
agricultural acreage increased in the East, thereby causing a
greater intermingling of habitats, the Fox Squirrel thrived and
expanded its range.

Another classic edge species is the White-tailed Deer, which
abounds in the tallgrass prairie. Moreover, the Elk, one of the
most impressive American hoofed animals, favored the
tallgrass prairie as well.

The Prairie Peninsula

Little of the Prairie Peninsula remains now, for most of it is
either under cultivation or buried beneath housing
developments, but historically it has occurred in the eastern
portion of the tallgrass prairie. During its heyday, it contained
a bewildering variety of habitats. In parts of the peninsula,
islands of prairie ranging between one and twenty miles in
diameter were surrounded by forest; in other sections, islands
of forest were surrounded by prairie; and in yet other places,
islands of savanna—grassland with scattered trees—were
surrounded by forests. These forests were dry and were made

up mainly of oaks and hickories; they were thus substantially different from many of the forested areas immediately to the east, which were dominated by beech and maples. The transition between the forest and prairie communities was abrupt. This is not usually the way of nature; different but adjacent plant communities generally grade into each other in such a way that boundaries are indefinable.

In the early twentieth century, the presence of these prairie islands puzzled American ecologists, who believed that climate was the primary influence determining the vegetation of a particular area. Annual precipitation in the Prairie Peninsula was sufficient to support the growth of trees; why, then, was a healthy tallgrass prairie present instead? Edgar Transeau of Ohio State University, the biologist who coined the term "Prairie Peninsula," performed detailed analyses of weather records and concluded that the climate of the tallgrass prairie was subtly different from that of the surrounding areas. Among other things, it had lower relative humidity in the summertime and greater irregularity of precipitation. However, his findings have not solved the dilemma of the prairie islands' existence to the satisfaction of everyone.

Scientists have examined the properties of the local soils—particularly soil moisture—in search of an explanation for the variations within this area, but have not been successful. The Prairie Peninsula exhibited little correlation between vegetation and soil type, except that the soils under the prairie were soils that had developed under grassland and those under the forested areas were forest soils—which only indicates that both plant communities had been where they were for a long time. The existence of the prairie islands violated known patterns of plant distribution. Generally trees require more water than grasses and thus grow in wet soils, while grasses occur on the drier sites. In the Prairie Peninsula, however, patches of forest were found both in moist soils, such as those on the eastern sides of lakes, and on rocky bluffs and steep slopes, where the soil was dry. The grasses likewise grew in either wet or dry soils.

It has been suggested that the location of forests on the eastern edges of lakes and on steep bluffs was at least partially related to fire. According to this theory, fires generally came from the west with the prevailing winds, and lakes served as natural firebreaks. On bluffs and steep slopes, the grasses did not grow densely enough to provide fuel. Thus forests were able to establish themselves.

Once the pattern of forests and grasslands had been somewhat established, fire helped to maintain the status quo. Fires tend to occur in grasslands more than in forests; the grassland environment is conducive to fire, while the forest environment discourages the spread of fire, as trees both help the air to retain moisture and block the wind. Not only does the forest discourage fire—to which the prairie grasses are adapted—but in addition, prairie grasses do not grow well in the shade, and thus do not favor spots under the forest canopy. Therefore it seems that once established, each plant community created conditions that favored its perpetuation.

But the question remains: How did the prairie islands and the dry oak-hickory forests become established in the first place? Ironically enough, scientists have looked for the answer in bogs. Although the bog habitat is not at all like the prairie, it provides an acidic environment in which little decay takes place. Pollen drifting down from the plants can be preserved over tens of thousands of years; these remnants can help to identify the species that previously inhabited the areas. As sediments accumulate in a lake bottom and pollen lands on the sediment, a long-term record of vegetation builds up, forming a bog. One can extrapolate the climate from the dominant vegetation of a period.

The pollen record in the Prairie Peninsula provides good evidence that there were two periods of warm, dry weather following successive periods of glaciation. During these periods, prairie plants from the Southwest and forest plants from the Southeast could have invaded the Prairie Peninsula. Thus the grassland islands, or relicts, may be holdovers from yet another climatic period that have been maintained since then by fire and grazing.

None of the theories explaining the origins of the Prairie Peninsula are fully accepted, and they have become harder to test as the large grazing animals have disappeared, fires have been controlled, and the prairie islands have been altered or destroyed. Further complicating the matter is the fact that the boundaries of the islands seeem to have always been unstable: In a series of dry years, one could see small oak trees die and grasses take over; in a sequence of wet years, oak seedlings could become established in the grasslands, and the forest would expand a bit.

The Future of the Tallgrass Prairie

Many preserves, including the Flint Hills and other, smaller areas, are scattered throughout the Midwest. The Flint Hills are underlain at a shallow depth by rocky soil; thus the area was never considered worth plowing and so has remained basically unchanged. The Nature Conservancy now owns 8000 acres of the Flint Hills, which it maintains as a presettlement prairie.

The tallgrass prairie is also being deliberately restored and recreated along highway rights-of-way, on institutional grounds, and even in residental settings. There is an encouraging trend toward prairie landscaping, as homeowners are finding that the prairie community, the best suited to the climate, requires minimum maintenance.

Thus, although the tallgrass prairie will probably never again be seen in its original vastness, it will persist.

TALLGRASS PRAIRIE: PLANTS AND ANIMALS

Mammals
Badger 51
Coyote 37, 38
Deer Mouse 62
Eastern Chipmunk 90
Eastern Cottontail 48
Eastern Mole 77
Eastern Spotted Skunk 50
Fox Squirrel 80
Franklin's Ground
Squirrel 84
House Mouse 61
Least Shrew 76
Least Weasel 54
Long-tailed Weasel 53
Meadow Jumping
Mouse 67
Meadow Vole 56
Plains Pocket Gopher 78
Plains Pocket Mouse 75
Prairie Vole 59
Red Fox 41, 42, 44, 45
Striped Skunk 49
Thirteen-lined Ground
Squirrel 89
Western Harvest Mouse 63
White-tailed Deer 33
White-tailed Jack
Rabbit 47
Woodchuck 79

Grasses and Shrubs
Big Bluestem 101
Foxtail Barley 107
Indian Grass 94
Little Bluestem 97
Needlegrass 99
Prairie Cordgrass 105
Switch Grass 95

Wildflowers
Bird Foot Violet 286
Black-eyed Susan 176
Bladder Campion 140
Blue Salvia 271
Blue Vervain 274
Boneset 150
Butterfly Weed 228
Calico Aster 135
Camphorweed 168
Carolina Anemone 139
Common Barberry 209
Common Milkweed 241
Common Strawberry 126

Common Sunflower 175
Compass Plant 171
Crazyweed 267
Death Camas 144
Dense Blazing Star 262
Evening Primrose 205
Fall Goldenrod 214
Flowering Spurge 146
Giant Sunflower 173
Great Lobelia 276
Hairy Golden Aster 170
Hoary Cresss 147
Horse Nettle 123
Illinois Tick Trefoil 153
Indian Blanket 226
Indian Paintbrush 225
Ivy-leaved Morning
Glory 283
Jerusalem Artichoke 172
Lance-leaved Goldenrod 213
Leadplant 275
Locoweed 265
Marijuana 117
Maximilian's Sunflower 177
Mouse-ear Chickweed 138
New England Aster 246
New York Ironweed 247
Panicled Aster 134
Pasqueflower 281
Plains Larkspur 156
Pointed Blue-eyed
Grass 289
Prairie Acacia 159
Prairie Blazing Star 261
Prairie False Indigo 154
Prairie Larkspur 155
Prairie Mimosa 158
Prairie Rose 238
Prairie Smoke 249
Purple Prairie Clover 253
Queen-of-the-prairie 258
Ragged Fringed Orchid 120
Rattlesnake Master 116
Rough Blazing Star 259
Rough-fruited
Cinquefoil 186
Rough-stemmed
Goldenrod 215
Showy Evening
Primrose 235
Shrubby Cinquefoil 191
Silverleaf Scurf Pea 272
Smooth Aster 293
Spotted Joe-pye Weed 248

Spreading Dogbane 234
Stiff Goldenrod 208
Sweet Goldenrod 216
Tall Goldenrod 214
Tall Ironweed 294
White Prairie Clover 142
White Snakeroot 148
White Sweet Clover 151
Wild Blue Phlox 290
Wild Lupine 269
Woolly Locoweed 268
Yellow Thistle 162

Butterflies and Moths
Acmon Blue 322, 323
Acraea Moth 303
American Painted Lady 337
Artichoke Plume Moth 315
Beard-grass Skipper 317
Buckeye 345
Cabbage White 307
Checkered White 309
Common Checkered
Skipper 311
Common Sulphur 296
Eastern Black
Swallowtail 331
Eastern Tailed Blue 328
Gray Hairstreak 319
Greenish Blue 327
Meadow Fritillary 344
Milkweed Tiger Moth 306
Monarch 335
Orange-bordered Blue 324
Orange Sulphur 295
Painted Lady 338
Pearly Crescentspot 340
Pipevine Swallowtail 320
Prairie Ringlet 297
Red-spotted Purple 321,
330
Regal Fritillary 336
Silvery Blue 326
Sleepy Orange 298
Sod Webworm Moth 305
Viceroy 334
Woolly Bear Caterpillar
Moth 301
Yellow Woolly Bear
Moth 304

Insects and Spiders
American Hover Fly 365
Digger Bees 373

Digger Wasp 369
Early Tachinid Fly 372
Golden Northern Bumble
Bee 374
Goldenrod Spider 342, 396
Green Midges 359
Honey Bee 375
House Mosquito 362
Jumping Lynx Spider 394
Large Bee Flies 370, 371
Malaria-carrying
Mosquitoes 360
Metaphid Jumping
Spider 393
Nebraska Conehead 355
Nine-spotted Ladybug
Beetle 380
Orb Weavers 395
Paper Wasps 368
Pennsylvania Firefly 383
Pyralis Firefly 384
Red-blue Checkered
Beetle 381
Robber Flies 361
Rose, Pea, and Potato
Aphids 391
Spur-throated
Grasshoppers 352
Three-lined Potato
Beetle 388
Toxomerus Hover Flies 366
Tumblebugs 379
Two-striped
Grasshopper 354
Yellow-faced Bees 363

Trees
American Plum 418, 455
Apple 422, 452
Bigtooth Aspen 433
Biltmore Hawthorn 434,
454
Black Cherry 419, 458
Black Locust 444, 453, 484
Blackjack Oak 437
Bur Oak 439
Common Chokecherry 421,
457, 472
Common Persimmon 412,
468, 470
Common Prickly-ash 450
Eastern Cottonwood 432
Eastern Redcedar 400
European Buckthorn 426

Fanleaf Hawthorn 435
Glossy Buckthorn 409, 47⊕
Mexican Plum 423
Oneflower Hawthorn 427
Osage Orange 411, 459,
469
Paper Birch 429
Post Oak 441
Prairie Crab Apple 424
Quaking Aspen 430
Russian Olive 467
Shining Sumac 449, 464
Smooth Sumac 448, 465
Siberian Elm 416

Birds
American Goldfinch 552
American Kestrel 496
Barn Owl 512
Barn Swallow 522
Bobolink 544
Bobwhite 503
Brewer's Blackbird 549,
550
Clay Colored Sparrow 531
Cliff Swallow 521
Common Nighthawk 515
Dickcissel 529
Eastern Bluebird 524
Eastern Kingbird 518
Eastern Meadowlark 547
Field Sparrow 532
Grasshopper Sparrow 537
Gray Partridge 497
Greater Prairie Chicken 50⊕
Horned Lark 520
Killdeer 506
Lark Sparrow 534
Loggerhead Shrike 528
Long-billed Curlew 508
Mourning Dove 509
Northern Harrier 489
Northern Shrike 527
Red-tailed Hawk 491, 492
Red-winged Blackbird 545
546
Ring-necked Pheasant 498
Sharp-tailed Grouse 502
Short-eared Owl 514
Tree Sparrow 530
Turkey Vulture 488
Upland Sandpiper 507
Vesper Sparrow 533
Western Meadowlark 548

MIXED PRAIRIE

On its western edge, the tallgrass prairie grades into a broad north-south belt dominated by grasses of medium height— those that are approximately two to four feet tall. This area is primarily known as the mixed prairie, although it is also sometimes called the midgrass prairie, the mixed-grass prairie, the bluestem bunchgrass prairie, or the Great Plains. Some feel that the mixed prairie should not exist as a separate province, arguing that it merely represents a transition zone between the tallgrass and shortgrass prairies. If the mixed prairie is a transition zone, however, it is an extremely broad one: It is wider than either of the two zones it is supposed to bridge. Furthermore, the mixed prairie has a distinct look of its own, and possesses certain discrete characteristics that set it apart.

"The Great American Desert"

In addition, the distinction between the tallgrass-prairie and mixed-prairie habitats has been an important one in the history of American settlement. In some scholars' minds, the mixed prairie marks the true transition between forest, where trees grow, and plains, where they do not. To settlers this distinction was a crucial one. Trees were necessary for fuel, buildings, and fences, and their absence represented a very real impediment. The distinction was also important in a somewhat less tangible way, as the psychological reaction to treeless landscapes had a profound effect. For a long time, some people believed that land on which trees did not grow would not support crops. Americans had grown up surrounded by trees. Even though in the East—and in Europe—the trees had to be cleared before agriculture was possible, an environment that was devoid of trees was perceived as alien and inhospitable. Because of this belief, settlement of the prairies was postponed for many years. Unwilling to live in a treeless landscape, thousands of people died while attempting to cross the most fertile land in North America to get to Oregon, an area where trees were abundant.

In 1820 Maj. Stephen H. Long was sent by the U.S. Congress on an exploring expedition along the Platte River to the Rocky Mountains. In his report, he labeled this area "The Great American Desert." It was, he said, "wholly unfit for cultivation, and of course uninhabitable by a people depending upon agriculture for their subsistence. Although tracts of fertile land considerably extensive are occasionally to be met with, yet the scarcity of wood and water, almost uniformly prevalent, will prove an insuperable obstacle in the way of settling the country. . . . The whole of this region seems peculiarly adapted as a range for buffaloes, wild goats, and other wild game; incalculable multitudes of which find ample pasturage and subsistence upon it."

Although many educated, influential explorers and decision-makers soon realized that Long's statements represented a misconception, the idea of a "Great American Desert" stuck in the popular imagination, and for decades afterward, geography books carried that label. Despite the inaccuracy of Long's

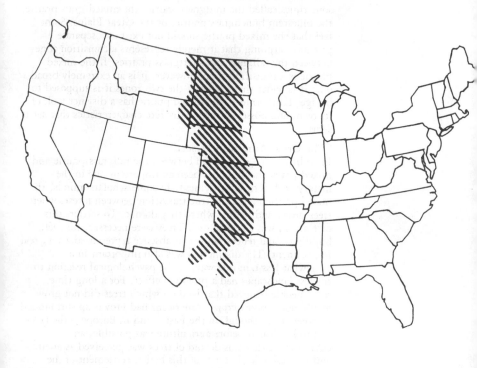

pronouncement, a degree of wisdom was contained in it, for the presence of trees in an area was correctly equated with a certain minimum yearly precipitation. Nonetheless, although such an amount of precipitation is needed to support a forest, it is not required—as most settlers then believed—to support the growth of crops.

In the nineteenth century, much debate centered around the question of why there were so few trees in the American prairies; differing theories abounded. Horace Greeley, the noted journalist, proposed that the trees had been pushed over by strong winds. His idea may seem laughable now, but it too contains a germ of truth, as the wind is an important factor in the life of the prairie.

Today the mixed prairie still contains large areas of land that support native midgrasses, as well as quite a bit that has been given over to farming. During the early settlement days, wheat, hay, and other dry land crops—sunflowers, sugar beets, and flax—were grown. In recent years, the technique of pivot irrigation has also made possible the growth of corn. From the air, pivot-irrigated fields look like great circles of green in an otherwise brown or golden landscape.

Range and Physical Features

The mixed prairie occupies most of the Dakotas, much of Nebraska and Kansas, the central part of Oklahoma, and parts of north-central Texas. Like the tallgrass prairie, its boundaries may shift according to cycles of weather. Any map of its area is merely an approximation of the mixed prairie range.

In broad terms, the mixed prairie is not significantly different, in a geological sense, from the tallgrass prairie: It is underlain by the same stable bedrock and is covered by a similar variety of sedimentary rocks—sandstones, limestones, and shales. In the northern areas, the soil has resulted from the same combination of glacial action and subsequent vegetation; the most noticeable differences in vegetation are caused by the presence of low, wet areas or sandy soil. The Nebraska Sandhills, mentioned in the tallgrass prairie discussion, are in the mixed prairie area. In the Dakotas, the glacial retreat left a myriad of depressions that subsequently filled with water; these became the prairie potholes. These watery spots are famous for the huge number of birds that visit them, particularly during periods of migration.

The soils are similar to those of the tallgrass prairie, but are not as rich. Because there is less precipitation, there is also less organic matter in the soil, which can be more brownish in hue than black. The smaller amount of precipitation also causes salts to accumulate in a hard layer three to six feet below the surface. Farther west, this lime layer is closer to the surface. Its existence is one of the distinguishing features of the mixed and shortgrass prairies.

Precipitation ranges between fourteen and twenty-three inches per year, and average wind velocities and evaporation rates are higher than on the tallgrass prairie; thus aridity is higher. As in the tallgrass prairie, most of the precipitation falls in the summer and is subject to great yearly fluctuations.

The great drought of the 1930s affected the mixed prairie ever more severely than it did the tallgrass prairie; parts of the region became known as the Dust Bowl. Topsoil, made barren by excessive wheat cultivation and overgrazing, blew eastward in huge, suffocating clouds that blackened midday skies. The drought, which occurred during the Depression, contributed to economic disaster and aroused national concern. The loss of topsoil and the general collapse of the local economy are still cited as a result of intemperate and shortsighted land use.

Little Bluestem and Other Typical Grasses

If the mixed prairie could be characterized by a single plant species, it would be Little Bluestem. This grass is also common on the dry uplands of the tallgrass prairie, but in the mixed prairie it is the usual dominant, covering great areas. Big Bluestem is also present in the mixed prairie, but it occupies the areas that, farther east, are inhabited by Prairie Cordgrass—namely, the moister areas along river terraces. Little Bluestem is no more blue than Big Bluestem, but it is smaller: It reaches a height of about two or three feet. The two species do not look similar, as Little Bluestem does not have the fingerlike flower arrangement that Big Bluestem does. Indeed many botanists feel that it should be considered a separate genus and have thus named it *Schizachyrium scoparius.* Its fuzzy flowers are borne on wiry stalks, which run the length of the stem and jut out from the axils of the many curly leaves.

Little Bluestem, a warm-season grass, is not the only dominant species; cool-season grasses such as Junegrass and the needlegrasses *Stipa comata* and *Stipa spartea* are dominant associates.

In the northern part of the mixed prairie, Western Wheatgrass, a cool-season sod former, also dominates, sometimes to the extent that it temporarily eliminates Little Bluestem. This happens in years that start with good rainfall but then dry up. Western Wheatgrass gets a head start in the spring and, by spreading vigorously via rhizomes, overruns areas dominated by Little Bluestem. As the soil becomes drier, Western Wheatgrass becomes semidormant, but it persists, and Little Bluestem cannot catch up. Given moist weather, Little Bluestem eventually reestablishes its position of dominance.

By the time the grasses are full-grown in the summer, the tallgrass prairie is virtually a uniform stand, with few, if any, species of different heights. The mixed prairie, on the other hand, is more open and thus more layered. Buffalo Grass and Grama Grass, the two dominant species of the shortgrass prairie, commonly grow in the midst of Little Bluestem. In addition, forbs dot the mixed prairie, and dense stands of shrubs appear on sheltered hillsides. Some of these shrubs, such as Shining Sumac, form brilliant masses of color in the fall. Trees occur here too, primarily along the riverbanks,

where the usual riparian species—cottonwoods, elms, Green
Ash, willows, and Hackberry—hold sway.

The Role of Fire

Fire is an important factor in the mixed prairie, but it is not
always a beneficial agent. Because ranchers are interested in
promoting optimum growth of grass, and managers of natural
preserves are interested in keeping out invading shrubs, a
considerable amount of research has been done on prairie
burning. Although burning is generally good for the prairie,
the effect of burning varies considerably with such factors as
the weather, the time of year, the intensity of the fire, and the
interval between burnings. Some species respond well to
burning, while others do not. Individually, Little Bluestem is
well adapted to fire, but if a stand is burned during a dry year
or on a generally dry site, productivity can decrease, perhaps
because there is no litter layer left to prevent a loss of soil
moisture. In a wet year, however, burning will increase
productivity on the mixed prairie as it does for the tallgrasses.

The Story of the Bison

The mixed prairie is an important faunal boundary. It
constitutes the eastern edges of the ranges of many grassland
animals, including prairie dogs, Pronghorn, Swift Fox, Black-
tailed Jack Rabbit, and Desert Cottontail. Here we begin to
find sizable concentrations of the animal that most aptly
symbolizes the midwestern grasslands: the Bison. Bison were
once found as far east as the Appalachians, but these stragglers
from the Plains populations quickly disappeared after the
arrival of the white settlers. They were also found in the
tallgrass prairie, but again not in huge numbers. The true
Bison habitat occurs west of the tallgrass prairie, in the mixed
prairie.

Accounts of the enormous numbers of Bison abound: The
naturalist W.T. Hornaday, author of the 1887 report of the
U.S. National Museum on "The Extermination of the
American Bison," wrote: "Of all the quadrupeds that have
lived upon the earth, probably no other species has ever
marshaled such innumerable hosts as those of the American
bison. It would have been as easy to count or to estimate the
number of leaves in a forest as to calculate the number of
buffaloes living at any given time during the history of the
species prior to 1870."

A regional governor wrote in 1853: "About five miles from
camp, we ascended to the top of a high hill, and for a great
distance ahead every square mile seemed to have a herd of
buffalo upon it. Their number was variously estimated by
members of the party, some as high as half a million. I do not
think it any exaggeration to set it at 200,000. I had heard of
the myriads of these animals inhabiting these plains, but I
could not realize the truth of these accounts until to-day,
when they surpass everything which I could have imagined
from the accounts I had received."

And yet another traveller wrote: "Not even a buffalo was now
to be seen to relieve the dull monotony of the scene; although

at some seasons (and particularly in the fall) these prairies are literally strewed with herds of this animal. Then, 'thousands of tens of thousands' might at times be seen from this eminence."

These observations are not inconsistent, as the Bison did indeed move around the prairie; they had to in order to support such large numbers in such concentrated herds. The dense masses of Bison that people wrote about probably occurred during seasonal movements or wanderings; it was usually evident that these immense herds were made up of many smaller ones. Even in smaller groups, the Bison had a significant impact and could leave an area virtually bare as a result of the animals' grazing, trampling, and their habit of creating wallows, or bare areas where the Bison liked to roll in the dust (it is thought that the thick coating of dust on their fur discouraged mites and insects). Hornaday wrote that the Bison "at times so completely consumed the herbage of the plains that detachments of the United States Army found it difficult to find sufficient food for their mules and horses." These areas, once devastated, would then go through the same phases of recovery that an overgrazed prairie does now. Various animals would take advantage of each phase. The prairie dogs used the area while the Bison were grazing, for the herds' activities kept down the grasses and increased visibility. Later, Pronghorns ate the shrubs that became established in the grazed areas.

The Bison played an important role in our history (as did we in its survival), because it formed the base of subsistence for the Indians. Ironically, the Plains Indians did not exploit the Bison much before the eighteenth century. Indeed, until long after the horse was introduced into the area in 1541 by the Spaniards, the Plains Indians were chiefly farmers. Limited in mobility, they were also limited in the use they could make of the Plains resources. By the early 1700s, the Indians were making more use of the horse; thus Bison hunting became easier, and they could follow the herds in their nomadic movements. In a relatively short time, their way of life changed as they became completely dependent on the Bison; it provided everything: food, shelter, and clothing.

For several centuries, the Indians and the Bison evolved a complex set of adaptations and dependencies, aided by a crucial agent—fire. The Indians depended on the Bison, the Bison depended on grass, and grass could not maintain itself without fire. The Indians would set fires—either to drive the Bison to a place where they could easily be killed, or to attract them with the fresh growth of short, green grass. Once begun, this cycle tended to perpetuate itself.

All of this was disrupted by the white man. His cattle cropped the grass more closely, so that there was less fuel for fire. Fires threatened his settlements, so he tried to control them. He cleared large areas of land for agriculture, and these spaces served as firebreaks. He subdued the Indians and confined them to reservations. And he systematically exterminated the Bison.

Of course no methodical count was made of the number of
Bison on the prairie when the settlers arrived, nor is there any
way of knowing whether the sizable herds that were reported
were typical or represented periods of high population.
However, by piecing together historical accounts, computing
how much land was available to support a given number of
Bison, and guessing how many calves were lost to predation,
historians have estimated the number of Bison on the prairie
before 1870 to be between thirty million and seventy million.
Within thirty years, this figure had shrunk to less than 1,000.
Were it not for the efforts of conservationists, the species
could have become extinct. Present populations, which exist
primarily in national parks and nature preserves, number
about 65,000.

Why was this highly successful animal, which roamed the
Plains with virtually no competition and relatively little
predation, so quickly eliminated, while others that were
equally persecuted, such as the jack rabbit, only increased
their numbers? The Bison's size is certainly one reason—Bison
cannot easily hide and it is difficult for a marksman to miss a
target that is seven feet high and weighs a ton. Their herding
behavior also made them easy to find, and their lack of speed
did not help them. And once the onslaught started, their low
reproductive rate made it impossible for the populations to
keep up with the losses.

Just as the Bison played an important role in our history, it
presumably also played an important role in the ecology of the
Plains. However, the full effect of the Bison on its
environment is not well understood, because the animal no
longer makes its home there, and its former habitat has been
seriously fragmented and diminished.

It is tempting to consider domestic cattle the ecological
grassland equivalent of the Bison, since they basically occupy
the same niche, but there are important differences between
the two animals. Cattle are more selective in their feeding,
and less efficient; thus they must eat more forage to produce
the same amount of flesh. The Bison were free to roam, while
cattle are fenced in. And Bison were a more essential part of
the system. Their dung returned nutrients to the prairie earth,
and when they died, their carcasses either were eaten by local
animals or decayed and returned to the earth.

It is difficult to imagine the central grasslands as they were
when the Bison was the dominant herbivore. One thing is
clear: In spite of all the glowing accounts of endless seas of
green grass, there must have been times when the prairie was
bare and ravaged. It presumably recovered after such periods,
as it does now after cultivation or heavy grazing.

The story of the Bison emphasizes that the prairie has been a
constantly changing ecosystem. Plant and animal communities
changed—sometimes gradually, sometimes suddenly—with
changes in weather, topography, and soils, or in response to
events such as fires and Bison migrations. Although a broad
swath across the middle of the country was called prairie,
endless variation occurred within this region.

MIXED PRAIRIE: PLANTS AND ANIMALS

Mammals
Badger 51
Black-tailed Jack Rabbit 46
Black-tailed Prairie Dog 87
Coyote 37, 38
Deer Mouse 62
Eastern Cottontail 48
Eastern Mole 77
Fox Squirrel 80
Franklin's Ground
Squirrel 84
Fulvous Harvest Mouse 64
House Mouse 61
Least Weasel 54
Least Shrew 76
Long-tailed Weasel 53
Meadow Vole 56
Mule Deer 35
Northern Pygmy Mouse 74
Ord's Kangaroo Rat 72
Plains Pocket Gopher 78
Plains Pocket Mouse 75
Prairie Vole 59
Red Fox 41, 42, 44, 45
Richardson's Ground
Squirrel 83
Striped Skunk 49
Swift Fox 40
Thirteen Lined Ground
Squirrel 89
Western Harvest Mouse 63
White-tailed Deer 33
White-tailed Jack
Rabbit 47

Grasses and Shrubs
Big Bluestem 101
Blue Grama 108
Buffalo Grass 103
Foxtail Barley 107
Indian Grass 94
Kentucky Bluegrass 91
Little Bluestem 97
Needle-and-thread 110
Needlegrass 99
Prairie Cordgrass 105
Switch Grass 95

Wildflowers
Bird-foot Violet 286
Black-eyed Susan 176
Bladder Campion 140
Blue Salvia 271
Blue Vervain 274

Boneset 150
Butterfly Weed 228
Camphorweed 168
Carolina Anemone 139
Common Milkweed 241
Common Mullein 219
Common Strawberry 126
Common Sunflower 175
Compass Plant 171
Crazyweed 267
Death Camas 144
Evening Primrose 205
Fall Goldenrod 214
Flowering Spurge 146
Giant Sunflower 173
Gumweed 182
Hairy Golden Aster 170
Hoary Cress 147
Horse Nettle 123
Illinois Tick Trefoil 153
Indian Blanket 226
Indian Paintbrush 225
Ivy-leaved Morning
Glory 283
Jerusalem Artichoke 172
Leadplant 275
Locoweed 265
Many-spined Opuntia 161
Marijuana 117
Maximilian's Sunflower 177
Mouse-ear Chickweed 138
Pale Agoseris 163
Panicled Aster 134
Pasqueflower 281
Plains Larkspur 156
Pointed Blue-eyed
Grass 289
Prairie Acacia 159
Prairie Blazing Star 261
Prairie False Indigo 154
Prairie Gentian 282
Prairie Mimosa 158
Prairie Rose 238
Prairie Smoke 249
Purple Prairie Clover 253
Rough Blazing Star 259
Sego Lily 122
Shrubby Cinquefoil 191
Silverleaf Scurf Pea 272
Spotted Joe-pye Weed 248
Spreading Dogbane 234
Stiff Goldenrod 208
Sweet Goldenrod 216
Tall Goldenrod 214

Teasel 252
Wild Blue Flax 287
Woolly Locoweed 268

Insects and Spiders
American Hover Fly 365
Brown Daddy-long-legs 388
Digger Bees 373
Digger Wasp 369
Early Tachinid Fly 372
Field Cricket 350
Golden Northern Bumble
Bee 374
Goldenrod Spider 392, 396
Green Lacewings 358
Green Midges 359
Honey Bee 375
House Mosquito 362
Jumping Lynx Spider 394
Large Bee Flies 370, 371
Malaria-carrying
Mosquitoes 360
Metaphid Jumping
Spider 393
Mormon Cricket 351
Nine-spotted Ladybug
Beetle 380
Orb Weavers 395
Paper Wasps 368
Pennsylvania Firefly 383
Pyralis Firefly 384
Red-blue Checkered
Beetle 381
Robber Flies 361
Rose, Pea, and Potato
Aphids 390
Three-lined Potato
Beetle 388
Toxomerus Hover Flies 366
Tumblebugs 379
Two-stripped
Grasshopper 354
Yellow-faced Bees 363

Trees
American Plum 418, 455
Apple 422, 452
Biltmore Hawthorn 434, 454
Black Cherry 419, 458
Black Locust 444, 453, 484
Blackjack Oak 437
Bur Oak 439
Common Chokecherry 421,
457, 472

Common Persimmon 412,
468, 470
Common Prickly-ash 450
Eastern Cottonwood 432
Eastern Redcedar 400
European Buckthorn 426
Glossy Buckthorn 409, 474
Mexican Plum 423
Oneflower Hawthorn 427
Osage Orange 411, 459,
469
Post Oak 441
Prairie Crab Apple 424
Quaking Aspen 430
Russian Olive 467
Shining Sumac 449, 464
Siberian Elm 416
Smooth Sumac 448, 465

Birds
American Goldfinch 552
American Kestrel 496
Barn Owl 512
Barn Swallow 522
Black-billed Magpie 523
Bobolink 544
Bobwhite 503
Brewer's Blackbird 549,
550
Burrowing Owl 513
Chestnut-collared
Longspur 542
Clay-colored Sparrow 531
Cliff Swallow 521
Common Nighthawk 515
Dickcissel 529
Eastern Bluebird 524
Eastern Kingbird 518
Eastern Meadowlark 547
Ferruginous Hawk 493
Field Sparrow 532
Grasshopper Sparrow 537
Gray Partridge 497
Greater Prairie Chicken 500
Horned Lark 520
Killdeer 506
Lark Bunting 535
Lark Sparrow 534
Loggerhead Shrike 528
Long-billed Curlew 508
Mourning Dove 509
Northern Harrier 489
Northern Shrike 527
Red-tailed Hawk 491, 492

Red-winged Blackbird 545,
546
Ring-necked Pheasant 498
Sandhill Crane 505
Sharp-tailed Grouse 502
Short-eared Owl 514
Smith's Longspur 541
Swainson's Hawk 490
Tree Sparrow 530
Turkey Vulture 488
Upland Sandpiper 507
Vesper Sparrow 533
Water Pipit 526
Western Kingbird 517
Western Meadow Lark 548

Mushrooms
Common Psathyrella 555
Fairy Ring Mushroom 554
Fried Chicken
Mushroom 559
Hemispheric Agrocybe 556
Japanese Umbrella Inky 553
Meadow Mushroom 560
Purple-gilled Laccaria 561
Shaggy Mane 562
Smooth Lepiota 558
Tumbling Puffball 563
White Waxy Cap 557

Reptiles and Amphibians
Coachwhip 614
Common Garter Snake 592
Corn Snake 603
Eastern Fence Lizard 589
Fox Snake 608
Great Plains Skink 582
Great Plains Toad 570
Lesser Earless Lizard 585
Many-lined Skink 577
Milk Snake 611
Plains Black-Headed
Snake 615
Plains Spadefoot 567
Prairie Kingsnake 607
Prairie Skink 579
Racer 618
Red-spotted Toad 568
Slender Glass Lizard 581
Western Box Turtle 574
Western Hognose
Snake 604
Western Rattlesnake 605
Woodhouse's Toad 569

SHORTGRASS PRAIRIE

The shortgrass prairie, also known as the Great Plains and the High Plains, is the most arid of the midcontinental grasslands. While its eastern edge is vaguely defined by a rather indefinite transition zone between it and the mixed prairie, its boundary to the west is abruptly marked by the Rocky Mountains.

Spaces in the shortgrass prairie seem even vaster than they do in the mixed prairie. Here, distance that one traverses between settlements is greater, and it is possible to travel farther and longer without seeing a house, a building, or a human being.

Description

As is typical with prairie communities, the shortgrass prairie has been defined in various ways. The nineteenth-century ecologist J.E. Weaver denied it even existed, declaring that it was nothing but an overgrazed mixed prairie. He contended that if grazing were stopped, the midgrasses would come back as proof, he described many locations where he saw midgrasses and shortgrasses growing together, a common association in the mixed prairie region.

The range ecologist H.L. Shantz, however, wrote in 1923 that the shortgrass prairie was distinct. He separated it from the mixed prairie on the basis of their different soil characteristics. Others find the distinctions between the two communities to be less rigid, but agree that the shortgrass prairie is distinguishable as an area where the plants use all available moisture before the end of the growing season. By late summer, the subsoil is usually dry—a phenomenon that does not generally occur in the tallgrass and mixed prairies, where the available moisture lasts longer.

As a result of western movies, the general image of the High Plains is one of parched, yellow hillsides. For a short time every year, however, the Plains are actually green. During the summer, the grasses dry out and enter a dormant phase. But this stage may be only temporary: If autumn rainfall is adequate, they will resume growth and sometimes even flower again. Because moisture, rather than temperature, is the crucial factor governing the growth of plants in the region, the distinctions between cool- and warm-season grasses do not seem to be so important here. Both types of grasses maintain similar schedules, growing and becoming dormant at about the same time of year.

In terms of height and structure, the appearance of the shortgrass prairie varies considerably. Sometimes the grass forms a dense, gray-green turf, and sometimes it has a rather rugged, uneven appearance because of the mixture of midgrasses and shortgrasses. In drought years, stands of these plants may be patchy, with spots of bare soil occurring between the grasses.

Range

The shortgrass prairie is bounded on the west by the Rocky Mountains, although it is also found in the mountains at lower elevations. To the east, it follows an irregular boundary line

that angles slightly from the northwest to the southeast. There
are different theories about what causes the boundary to fall
where it does—among them, the suggestion that perhaps it
follows the line of effective rainfall. The shortgrass prairie
occupies much of Montana, eastern Wyoming, eastern
Colorado, western Kansas, the Oklahoma panhandle, northern
Texas, and eastern New Mexico.

Physical Features

The most significant feature of the shortgrass prairie is the
small amount of precipitation it receives. In some places, the
annual average is as low as ten inches. Although most of the
precipitation comes during the growing season—May through
July—the moisture is soon used up, and the plants go into a
state of dormancy during the summer, when the weather
becomes less congenial to growth.

Other weather phenomena also combine with the low
precipitation to make life difficult for plants. One important
element is the wind, which here reaches higher velocities than
anywhere else on the plains; another is hailstorms—an average
of four per year. The latter may be particularly destructive
during the growing season.

Geologically, the shortgrass prairie is part of the same
formations that the tallgrass and mixed prairies belong to. But
the soils in the shortgrass region are more varied. Large areas
contain grassland mollisols like those found farther east, but
these are lighter in color and poorer in organic matter. In
other areas within the shortgrass prairie, the soils may be
shallow, rocky, or sandy.

Throughout the midcontinental prairie, calcium is constantly
leached out of the surface layers of the soil to form a hard layer
underneath. From east to west, as precipitation decreases, this
layer is located in an increasingly shallow position; in some
places, it lies only six inches from the surface. It was this layer
that Shantz used to define the shortgrass area, whose boundary
with the mixed prairie he determined to be the point where
the lime layer comes within two feet of the surface of
the soil.

Dominant Grasses

In the dominant plants of the shortgrass prairie, the
adaptations to dryness are more varied and more pronounced
than are those in the dominant species of the tallgrass and
mixed prairies. As elsewhere, the species are constantly
battling for dominance within a community. Each species has
its own habits and features that enable it to do better in some
circumstances and cause it to do more poorly in others.
Because of the constant fluctuations in weather and animal
populations, the vegetation is perpetually changing.

Fire is not as important in the maintenance of the shortgrass
habitat as it is in the mixed and tallgrass prairies. Since the
grasses are shorter and sparser, there is simply less fuel to carry
a fire. Grazing, however—on the part of many different kinds
of animals—plays a very important role in maintaining the
shortgrasses.

Trees do invade sometimes; then fires help to keep them down. The Bison is an unwitting conspirator in this destructive process, as it scratches its head and rubs its horns on the young Ponderosa Pines that invade from higher elevations. This rough scratching may either kill or uproot a tree, or significantly weaken it—to the extent that this normally fire-resistant species will succumb to the next conflagration.

Blue Grama and Buffalo Grass

The dominant grasses are Blue Grama and Buffalo Grass, two nutritious forage plants. Blue Grama is easily recognizable by its delicate, arched flower stalks with flowers lined up along one side, and its wiry, often curled tufts of blue-green basal leaves. Although the flower stalks may grow to a length of between six and twenty inches, the tufted leaves rarely exceed three to five inches.

Buffalo Grass, a shorter plant, is immediately identifiable because of its habit—unusual among the grasses—of spreading by stolons, or above-ground stems. The stolons take root as they spread, putting out new tufts of green grass. They can grow an inch or two a day and may extend as much as two-and-a-half feet. Thus Buffalo Grass can colonize a bare site easily. This plant's name is apt. Not only did the Bison apparently like it, but its stoloniferous habit enabled the grass to recolonize a wallow or an area otherwise laid bare by the Bison.

Buffalo Grass is further unusual among the grasses because its male and female flowers are located on separate plants. The male flower stalks resemble Blue Grama stalks, but they tend to grow in clumps and are not as graceful. The female flowers are enclosed in short bulblike structures, which often lie near the ground. The seeds are enclosed in spiny husks, which can easily travel in the Bison's fur—thus it appears that the Bison reseeded its range as it went along!

Like all prairie grasses, the shortgrasses have long, fibrous roots, but the root system of a shortgrass forms a much larger proportion of the plant than do those of the midgrasses and tallgrasses. A grass that is only a few inches high might have a four-foot root system. This represents an adaptation not only to drought, but also to grazing, which the shortgrasses are able to withstand remarkably well.

Midgrasses

In spite of the name "shortgrass prairie," midgrasses occur here—among them, Junegrass, Western Wheatgrass (both of which are also found to the east), Red Three-awn, and Needle-and-thread. Red Three-awn is a distinctive-looking, silver-gray grass with reddish flower clusters. Its common name derives from three long bristles that are attached to the seed coating; its scientific name means "long-bristled bristle." Needle-and-thread also gets its common name from its bristle, which emerges from the top of the seed coating in such a way that it looks like a threaded needle.

These two species are but a few of the many bristle-seeded

grasses found in dry, western country. The frequency of bristles suggests that the bristles have an adaptive function. They may serve the same function as thorns do on certain desert plants—to protect the plants from granivores. (It is not known what protects the nonbristly species; grasses are not known to have poisons or repulsive flavors that discourage herbivores.) Moreover, it has been suggested that the bristles serve as dispersal mechanisms, as they get caught on animals' fur. This theory has never been scientifically demonstrated, but to anyone who has ever walked through a field of brome grass and afterwards examined his or her socks, it appears quite reasonable.

The bristles also seem to have a role in germination. Many of these awns are hygroscopic—that is, they absorb water. In the process of absorption, they twist and untwist. The twisting moves the seed across the soil surface until it reaches a good site for germination—perhaps a slight depression or a crack in the soil surface, where water can accumulate. This characteristic is an important one—especially in a dry climate, where subtle differences between spots of ground only centimeters apart may affect the likelihood of seed germination.

The bristles sometimes push the seed so that it goes into the ground with its bottom end down. Hairs often point upward from this end, making it difficult for the seed to move back up again. The seeds germinate better in this position since the emerging shoot is not able to push the seed back up out of the ground. Burial seems to be important for other reasons as well The seed is better protected against granivores, and the new roots are less likely to dry out.

Forbs, Shrubs, and Cacti

Forbs are not as plentiful on the shortgrass prairie as on the mixed and tallgrass prairies. Those that are present have even deeper roots than the grasses and are thus quite drought-resistant. Many of the eastern prairie forbs—such as Blazing Star, prairie clovers, and goldenrods—grow here, but they grow smaller and less abundantly than they do to the east. Some of the more typical shortgrass prairie forbs are Red False Mallow, Purple Loco, Western Wallflower, and Curlycup Gumweed, to name just a few. Many of these are unpalatable—even poisonous—to cattle and thus increase on overgrazed ranges.

Shrubs also exist on the shortgrass prairie. One of the most prevalent is Fringed Sage, a species that is related to Big Sagebrush. Like all species of sagebrush, of which there are several in the West, Fringed Sage is recognizable as a sagebrush by its silvery-gray leaves. It increases during conditions of overgrazing, at which time it provides a good food source for browsers such as Mule Deer and Pronghorn. The shrubs and forbs of the shortgrass prairie exhibit some of the same adaptations to dryness that are seen in desert plants: light colors and protective coatings. Many have gray-green, silvery-green, or blue-gray leaves, which are often fuzzy. This similar coloration is probably not a coincidence, as the light color reflects the sun's rays and thus reduces water loss from the leaf surfaces. The coating of hairs serves to reduce evapotranspiration from the leaves. Another adaptation to dryness is succulence. On the shortgrass prairie, cacti—succulents normally associated with the desert —are common. The most common cacti are the prickly pears. When conditions are favorable, these plants have a remarkable number of strategies for spreading—both by seed and vegetative reproduction. In spite of the spines, many animals, including the Coyote and jack rabbits, eat the sweet, succulent cactus fruits. They then excrete the seeds, unharmed, far from the parent plant. The seeds are also spread by rodents, which bury them in caches and later fail to collect them. Vegetative reproduction in prickly pears is extremely effective. After cattle or other animals have broken the pads loose and kicked them around, the pads take root and grow almost anywhere. The plants also produce secondary shoots along the length of their horizontal roots, in much the same way that Buffalo Grass produces shoots along its above-ground stolons.

Cacti do well under dry conditions. They store water in their pads, which are actually stems, and they have wide-spreading, shallow roots. The roots can absorb water even from a light rainfall; this gives the cacti a competitive advantage over deeply rooted plants. Under moist conditions, however, cacti do not do well. They are attacked by root rot fungus, and the insects that eat cacti require moist weather.

During the drought of the 1930s, cacti spread prolifically over the shortgrass prairie, sometimes becoming so thickly distributed that large animals could not lie down between the plants. When rainfall resumed, the cacti were attacked by their insect enemies; they lost their competitive advantage against the deeply rooted grasses, as they could not draw on deep water reserves. Their numbers dropped dramatically.

Domain of Prairie Dogs

"True" grassland animals are found on the shortgrass prairie. Most of them are more at home here than in other grasslands. They cannot survive among tallgrasses—not so much because of their food habits, for they are largely generalists, but because of their defense and escape mechanisms. Prairie dogs and the Pronghorn rely on their ability to see a predator from long distances, or to detect a hawk or an eagle by its shadow. Once faced with a predator, the Pronghorn, the jack rabbits, and the Swift Fox depend upon speed for their escape. These animals require open country, as it enables them to make use of their defensive traits.

A good complement of shortgrass fauna can be witnessed in a prairie dog town. To a range manager, a dog town is a sorry sight. Since the dogs do not venture far from their burrows to feed, the grass in many places has been clipped short or is gone altogether. These areas look weedy.

To many plains animals, a dog town is an ideal habitat. The

Burrowing Owl, the only species of owl that does not nest in trees, hatches and raises its young in prairie dog towns, often in prairie dog burrows. These birds do not hesitate to eat young prairie dogs, and prairie dogs do not hesitate to eat owl eggs; nonetheless, both species survive. Several ground-nesting birds are found in prairie dog towns: among them, the Horned Lark, the Killdeer, and the Mountain Plover.

The Prairie Rattlesnake—and sometimes even the Diamond-backed Rattlesnake—frequents dog towns, and often appropriates the burrows for the winter. These snakes also eat young prairie dogs, but—except in a few cases—do not seem to have a serious effect on the towns' populations.

Harvester ants, which have burrowing habits similar to those of the prairie dogs, are attracted to these bare areas; they create their hills on prairie dog mounds. The ant colonies, which may contain up to 10,000 ants, are equally attractive to prairie dogs, which sometimes start burrows in anthills.

Last but certainly not least, Bison can be found in the dog towns. They seem to prefer these sites for feeding and wallowing. Prairie dogs, in turn, often establish new towns where Buffalo have been. Both species are attracted by the shortgrass habitat created and maintained by the other. Sometimes, in their wallowing, the Bison destroy a few dog burrows, but the dogs rebuild them.

Decades ago, prairie dogs were legion. In 1901 Vernon Bailey of the Bureau of Biological Survey, an agency that preceded the U.S. Fish and Wildlife Service, described a prairie dog town in Texas that covered 25,000 square miles and contained 400 million prairie dogs. Whether or not this particular example is true cannot be conclusively determined, but it is known that prairie dogs and their towns were once far more extensive than they are now.

After the Bison disappeared, the adaptable prairie dog followed the cattle and started building towns in cattle pastures. This did not please ranchers, who were concerned that the prairie dogs were competing with their cattle for food. Since large populations of prairie dogs were concentrated in one place, and their burrows could be sealed off and gassed, the prairie dogs were easy prey for settlers. Their numbers declined drastically as a result, and today they persist in only a few places.

Although most of the prairie dog's associates and predators have adapted to its decline, finding new food sources and habitats (the Killdeer and the Horned Lark may now be found on golf courses), a couple of species apparently declined with the prairie dog: the Mountain Plover and the Black-footed Ferret. The Black-footed Ferret, which was probably never common, is now the rarest mammal in North America.

Changes in the Shortgrass Prairie

The shortgrass prairie was never considered attractive for agriculture in the way that the tallgrass and mixed prairies were. Therefore little of it was plowed under and planted in wheat or other crops. But it was not left untouched.

In the mid-nineteenth century, the western cattle industry started growing, spurred by the opening of the West and the growth of the eastern cities, which provided a market. The fortunes of the industry rose and fell more than once—until the 1880s, when several factors combined to make a boom. The railroads were reaching farther than they ever had, providing an easy way to get the cattle to market; the Indians had been subjugated; and, most important, easterners and Europeans with extra money were looking for investments. The winter of 1881–82 was mild, and the cattle grew fat. This fueled speculators' hopes, and thus the year 1882 saw a wild frenzy of rising prices for cattle, along with a heavy level of stocking in response to the increased investment—a level that could not last long.

The cattle boom of 1881–82 ended in disaster: Drought arrived in 1883, cattle died by the hundreds of thousands, and prices crashed. And the shortgrass prairie was devastated. The shortgrasses probably could have come back—indeed in many places they did—if overgrazing had not continued on a large scale throughout the next century. Countless acres of range have been overgrazed and perhaps permanently destroyed. Still the shortgrass prairie is less altered than the other two prairie systems. Most of it still supports uncultivated vegetation. The native perennial grasses persist and, in some cases, even dominate. The shortgrass prairie continues to survive even if it is no longer the domain of the Bison and the prairie dog.

Mammals
Badger 51
Black-tailed Jack Rabbit 46
Black-tailed Prairie Dog 87
Coyote 37, 38
Elk 32
Fox Squirel 80
Fulvous Harvest Mouse 64
Grasshopper Mouse 70
House Mouse 61
Long-tailed Weasel 153
Mule Deer 35
Northern Pygmy Mouse 74
Ord's Kangaroo Rat 72
Plains Pocket Gopher 78
Plains Pocket Mouse 75
Prairie Vole 59
Red Fox, 41, 42, 44, 45
Richardson's Ground
Squirrel 83
Sagebrush Vole 58
Spotted Ground Squirrel 88
Striped Skunk 49
Swift Fox 40
Thirteen-lined Ground
Squirrel 89
Western Harvest Mouse 63
Western Jumping Mouse 66
White-tailed Deer 33
White-tailed Jack
Rabbit 47

Grasses and Shrubs
Blue Grama 108
Buffalo Grass 103
Indian Grass 94
Needle-and-thread 110

Wildflowers
Arrowleaf Balsam Root 174
Blackfoot Daisy 130
Broom Snakeweed 203
Buffalo Gourd 196
Camphorweed 168
Common Sunflower 175
Cowpen Daisy 179
Crazyweed 267
Death Camas 144
Desert Plume 217
Feather Peabush 231
Field Milkvetch 230
Green Pitaya 119
Gumweed 182
Hairy Golden Aster 170

Hooker's Evening
Primrose 190
Hoary Cress 147
Indian Blanket 226
Indian Paintbrush 225
Little Golden Zinnia 185
Locoweed 265
Many-Spined Opuntia 161
Mule's Ear 169
Pale Agoseris 163
Pasqueflower 281
Plains Larkspur 156
Plains Wallflower 210
Prairie Gentian 282
Prairie Mimosa 158
Prairie Smoke 249
Prairie Star 137
Purple Groundcherry 285
Purple Prairie Clover 253
Rocky Mountain Bee
Plant 260
Sego Lily 122
Shrubby Cinquefoil 191
Silverleaf Scurf Pea 272
Snakeweed 211
Spreading Fleabane 133
Tahoka Daisy 292
Texas Bluebonnet 270
Vase Flower 232, 233
Velvety Nerisyrenia 125
Western Pink Vervain 243
White Prairie Clover 142
Wild Blue Flax 287
Woolly Locoweed 268
Yellow Bee Plant 204
Yellow Bell 198

Butterflies and Moths
Acmon Blue 322, 323
Acraea Moth 303
Alfalfa Looper 310
American Painted Lady 337
Artichoke Plume Moth 315
Beard-grass Skipper 317
Buckeye 345
Cabbage White 307
Checkered White 309
Common Blue 329
Common Checkered
Skipper 311
Common Sulphur 296
Eastern Black
Swallowtail 331
Eastern Tailed Blue 328

nereal Duskywing 316
ray Hairstreak 319
reat Gray Copper 318
reenish Blue 327
leadow Fritillary 344
lilkweed Tiger Moth 306
lonarch 335
range-bordered Blue 324
range Sulphur 295
ainted Lady 338
early Crescentspot 340
ipevine Swallowtail 320
rairie Ringlet 297
ed-spotted Purple 321, 30
lvery Blue 326
leepy Orange 298
od Webworm Moth 305
iceroy 334
Vestern Tailed Blue 325
Voolly Bear Caterpillar
loth 301
ellow Woolly Bear
loth 304

nsects and Spiders
merican Hover Fly 365
rown Daddy-long-legs 388
igger Bees 373
igger Wasp 369
arly Tachinid Fly 372
olden Northern Bumble
ee 374
oldenrod Spider 392, 396
reen Lacewings 358
reen Midges 359
reen Valley
rasshopper 353
loney Bee 375
louse Mosquito 362
umping Lynx Spider 394
lalaria-carrying
losquitoes 360
letaphid Jumping
pider 393
lormon Cricket 351
line-spotted Ladybug
eetle 380
rb Weavers 395
aper Wasps 368
ennsylvania Firefly 383
yralis Firefly 384
ed-blue Checkered
eetle 381

Robber Flies 361
Rose, Pea, and Potato
Aphids 390
Three-lined Potato
Beetle 388
Toxomerus Hover Flies 366
Tumblebugs 379
Yellow-faced Bees 363

Trees
Common Chokecherry 421,
457
Eastern Cottonwood 432
Honey Mesquite 445, 461,
485
Osage Orange 411, 459,
469
Quaking Aspen 430
Russian Olive 467
Siberian Elm 416
Smooth Sumac 448, 465

Birds
American Goldfinch 552
American Kestrel 496
Barn Owl 512
Barn Swallow 522
Black-billed Magpie 523
Bobolink 544
Brewer's Blackbird 549,
550
Burrowing Owl 513
Cassin's Kingbird 516
Chestnut-collared
Longspur 542
Cliff Swallow 521
Common Nighthawk 515
Eastern Bluebird 524
Eastern Kingbird 518
Ferruginous Hawk 493
Field Sparrow 532
Golden Eagle 494
Grasshopper Sparrow 537
Gray Partridge 497
Horned Lark 520
Killdeer 506
Lark Bunting 535
Lark Sparrow 534
Lesser Prairie Chicken 501
Loggerhead Shrike 528
Long-billed Curlew 508
McCown's Longspur 539
Mourning Dove 509
Northern Harrier 489

Northern Shrike 527
Red-tailed Hawk 491, 492
Red-winged Blackbird 545,
546
Ring-necked Pheasant 498
Roadrunner 511
Sage Grouse 499
Sandhill Crane 505
Scissor-tailed Flycatcher 519
Short-eared Owl 514
Smith's Longspur 541
Snow Bunting 543
Swainson's Hawk 490
Tree Sparrow 530
Turkey Vulture 488
Upland Sandpiper 507
Vesper Sparrow 533
Water Pipit 526
Western Kingbird 517
Western Meadowlark 548

Mushrooms
Common Psathyrella 555
Fairy Ring Mushroom 554
Fried Chicken
Mushroom 559
Hemispheric Agrocybe 556
Japanese Umbrella Inky 553
Meadow Mushroom 560
Purple-gilled Laccaria 561
Shaggy Mane 562
Smooth Lepiota 558
Tumbling Puffball 563
White Waxy Cap 557

Reptiles and Amphibians
Coachwhip 614
Common Garter Snake 592
Corn Snake 603
Eastern Fence Lizard 589
Great Plains Skink 582
Great Plains Toad 570
Lesser Earless Lizard 585
Many-lined Skink 577
Milk Snake 611
Plains Black-headed
Snake 615
Plains Spadefoot 567
Red-spotted Toad 568
Western Box Turtle 574
Western Hognose
Snake 604
Western Rattlesnake 605

DESERT GRASSLANDS

When many people think of the Southwest, they visualize forests of tall Saguaro cactus, Roadrunners, and rattlesnakes. It comes as a surprise to some people when they discover that grasslands exist in the Southwest that are similar to those found in the Great Plains.

Description and Range

The desert grassland habitat, also known as the desert plains grassland, is found principally in southeastern Arizona, southwestern New Mexico, parts of Texas, and northern Mexico, at elevations just above those where the true desert communities occur—generally between 4000 and 8000 feet. The grasslands usually occur on gentle slopes—sometimes as unbroken stretches, sometimes interspersed with various shrubs and cacti.

There are some who think that these grasslands are merely an unstable transitional zone between the desert and the forest, that they do not exist as a distinct ecosystem. However, unlike some of the other grasslands, which have been irrevocably altered or have disappeared, these exist today. A traveler in the Southwest will encounter these desert grasslands again and again, and there is good evidence that they covered an even greater area in earlier times. Desert grasslands have been and remain an important ecological and economic resource for the southwestern states.

Physical Features

Geologically, this part of the country is still considered part of the Basin and Range province, which is an area of isolated mountain ranges separated by broad, flat basins. This basin and range topography causes air pollution problems in southwestern cities. Inversions take place, in which the cold air sinks and is then trapped—along with pollutants from the cities—by the warm air that has moved in above to replace it.

The mountain ranges are made up chiefly of granite, an igneous rock, and metamorphic gneisses and schists. Over the millennia, frequent lava flows have produced outcrops of basalt —where spectacular displays of spring wild flowers can be found—and towering, fantastically patterned cliffs of rhyolite, a fine-grained volcanic rock. The basins, many of which are underlain by sedimentary rocks, are filled with unconsolidated gravel, sand, and clay that gradually eroded off the mountains.

The landscape is a dramatic one. A traveler may climb up tortuous, isolated mountain roads, passing through changing biotic zones, and suddenly emerge to overlook a new basin. Such an ascent constantly reveals unexpected and spectacular panoramas.

As in the intermountain habitat, the vegetation varies according to its location—the particular side of a slope—and elevation. Within a given area, the desert grassland appears, vanishes, and reappears, forming a landscape mosaic with the actual desert and the pinyon, juniper, and oak woodlands.

The soils of the desert grassland differ from the soils of most other grasslands in the country, because they have developed where rainfall is insufficient to leach salts and chemicals out of the soil. These salts accumulate in the subsoil and form a hard layer. In the Southwest, this hard layer is called by its Spanish name, caliche. It occurs at various depths. Unlike the black or brown prairie soils, the desert soils are light-colored at the surface and are low in organic matter.

The desert grassland is the most arid of all the grasslands in the country, with an annual rainfall of eleven to seventeen inches. Although this is more precipitation than the intermountain grasslands receive, the sun here shines more frequently and intensely; Yuma, Arizona, for example, which is not far from the area here described, has more hours of sunshine per year than any other place in the United States. Thus evaporation is higher, and less moisture is available for plants. The shortage of atmospheric moisture also means that the ground heats up faster during the day and cools more rapidly at night; this rapid heating and cooling causes strong winds, which draw additional moisture out of the plants and from the soil.

Rain falls in both winter and summer—slowly and gently in the winter, quickly and violently in the summer. Summer storms are often localized, but the rapid, intense runoff can start a flash flood that may spread to a rainless area. People are killed every year by these floods. Most of the rain falls in the summer, and thus the grasses grow most during this season, in spite of the fact that the winters are relatively mild. April, May, and June are completely dry.

Warm-Season Bunchgrasses and Other Plants

The dry climate of the desert grassland dictates a dominance of short, warm-season bunchgrasses. Among the most prevalent members of the grassland flora are the various species of the genus *Bouteloua,* or grama grasses (the word "grama" derives from the Spanish word—and ultimately from the Latin term —for grass). There is a species of *Bouteloua* to fit almost every niche in this grassland. Blue Grama, Sprucetop Grama, and Slender Grama are excellent perennial forage grasses, because they can withstand continued grazing. Hairy Grama and Black Grama are good forage, but weaken if heavily grazed during their summer growing period. The annual *Boutelouas,* Six Weeks Needlegrass and Six Weeks Grass, behave like the annuals elsewhere. They rapidly colonize bare soils, grow profusely for a short while, and then dry out. These types are generally a sign of an exhausted range. They are low in nutritional value and are distasteful to cattle, which pull up the roots along with the grass and get dirt in their mouths. Many of the *Bouteloua* species are also found in the Great Plains; but at the low elevations and in the heavier soils of the Southwest, one also finds a grass that is restricted to the region: Tobosa. Tobosa is slightly larger than Blue Grama—it grows to a height of two feet—and is generally coarser. Compared with Blue Grama, it is not as good as forage, nor is it as tough. Tobosa flats have proven to be highly susceptible to invasion by shrubs.

An interesting feature of the southwestern desert is the dominance of succulents, semisucculents, and shrubs. Succulents are such plants as the cacti, which depend for survival primarily on their ability to store water in their stems. The semisucculents—yucca is an example—have no stems to speak of, but are characterized by large tufts of fleshy basal leaves and by long flower stalks extending well beyond the leaves. Their survival depends more on their ability to reduce water loss from their leaves than on a capacity to store water. The succulents and semisucculents punctuate the desert grassland. The pads of prickly pear cacti point in all directions, and the Agaves (century plants) litter the hillsides with the carcasses of their spent flower stalks. Yuccas, which the Indians used for food and fiber, are scattered about.

The desert shrubs have evolved various mechanisms for drought survival. During the dry season, Creosote Bush, which grows successfully in the hottest, driest deserts of the continent, sheds not only its resinous, strong-smelling leaves, but also its twigs and even its branches. After a rain, it produces a quick flush of new growth. Ocotillo, which is often used as a hedge, employs the same strategy; it can completely cover itself with a new set of green leaves within forty-eight hours. Species of mesquite, a genus of thorny shrubs or trees in the pea family, seem to be adapted by virtue of their deep roots. These roots ordinarily grow sixty to seventy feet deep, but they have been discovered in mine shafts at depths of up to 175 feet.

The shrubs are invaders. Snakeweed, Burroweed, and Jimmyweed are but a few of those that have accompanied mesquite and Creosote Bush on an unrelenting encroachment, one probably initiated by human beings.

Changes in the Desert Grassland

Like other grasslands in the country, the desert grassland went through radical, large-scale alterations under the influence of nineteenth-century settlement. Early settlers wrote about broad, grassy marshes along sluggish streambeds, which teemed with Wild Turkeys. Upland grasslands apparently extended to lower elevations then than they do today; in general, much larger areas seem to have been cloaked in grassland than at present.

The cattle boom hit the Southwest just as it hit the Northwest and the Great Plains. In Arizona, for example, there were 5000 cattle in 1870; by 1890 the number was 1,095,000. By the early years of this century, seventy-five percent of these cattle had died of starvation. In the intervening years, they had stripped away the grasses and trampled the soil; this led to increased runoff, which led in turn to a phenomenon called trenching, in which the once-sluggish streams carved deep gullies. Trenching caused a lowering of the water table, a condition that favored mesquite because of its deep roots. A mesquite stand transpires more water than does a stand of grass that is similar in size; thus the water table was further affected, and the regrowth of the grasses became even less likely.

In drier places, the erosion that followed overgrazing led to dune formation, a condition to which mesquite is also adapted, as it can survive burial by sand and then grow through a dune. An established mesquite plant can trap drifting sand and thus cause the formation of still more dunes. Originally, mesquite had been restricted to the floodplains, but during the mesquite invasion that followed the cattle boom, it spread to higher elevations. Some scientists believe that this spread was caused by cattle ingesting the seeds, which germinate better after passing through a cow's digestive tract. Thus the cow was perhaps responsible for the proliferation of mesquite in another, more direct, way: It may have been the prime dispersal agent that brought the plant up out of the floodplains.

Mesquite was not the only shrub to increase. Areas of former grassland now support Creosote Bush as far as the eye can see, and many of the Tobosa flats are now choked with Lotebush, Allthorn, Ocotillo, and Mormon Tea, to name but a few of the invading species.

Mainly for economic reasons—namely, to increase rangeland —many landowners are trying to restore grassland. Fire has proved an effective tool, especially in Tobosa stands. Like most native perennial grasses, Tobosa responds well to fire in years with adequate rainfall—to the subsequent warmer soil temperatures and to the release of nutrients in the spring. As a result of the fire, cacti are parched and weakened to the point that they are easily devoured by insects. Mesquite bushes are either killed or weakened and are thus subject to attack by insects. Borers carve interior tunnels in the branches so that when a second fire comes along, the bushes are so well aerated that the flames can sweep through and kill them. Although grassland restoration efforts are bringing the landscape closer to its presettlement state, they are having some adverse affects on animal populations.

Animal Life

The present situation is one of a highly diversified fauna. Among the mammals, we again find several familiar grassland species: Pronghorn, Mule Deer, White-tailed Deer, Coyote, Badger, and Black-tailed Jackrabbit. Two desert grassland mammals—the Collared Peccary and the Bighorn Sheep—are seen in few other places. The Collared Peccary is one of the few animals that regularly eats prickly pear cacti—spines and all—and is the only native pig in North America. Peccary populations are threatened by the efforts of ranchers to restore true grassland, not only because they need the cover provided by shrubs, but also because there is greater competition in true grassland areas for the protein-rich, green forbs that grow in the summer.

The Bighorn Sheep ranges throughout the western mountain ranges, but its populations have been so reduced by hunting, range competition, and diseases from domestic sheep that it is now only found in a few, isolated wildlife refuges. One of these is in southwestern New Mexico, where this species has recently been reintroduced. The Bighorn Sheep is not strictly a grassland animal—steep slopes and rocky cliffs are a more critical feature of its habitat—but it does spend time foraging in grasslands at upper elevations.

Here—even more than in other grasslands—rodents abound. In the true desert, half of all the mammalian species are rodents. The desert grassland rodents include cotton rats, woodrats, ground squirrels, pocket gophers, and the ubiquitous Deer Mouse. We also find Kangaroo rats, a group more or less restricted to the Southwest and California. Three species—Ord's, Bannertail, and Merriam's—are found in the desert grassland. The name "kangaroo rat" reflects the fact that this animal has strong hind feet and a long tail, which enable it to jump like a kangaroo instead of running on all fours as other rodents do.

A visitor to the Southwest is struck by the abundance of lizards. It is no coincidence that these animals thrive in the desert and the desert grassland, because, since they are cold-blooded, they benefit from the desert heat. In fact, they are among the few animals that can tolerate the heat. Thus they provide food for the daytime predators, such as hawks and the Roadrunner. They are also able to take advantage of the food source represented by the diurnal insects.

The Southwest is a good place for birdwatching. The openness of the landscape makes the birds easy to see, and the year-round warmth supports many species not found elsewhere in the country. And of course there is always the possibility that one might see species that have wandered northward from Mexico.

With the changes in land use over the past century, bird life changed too. Ornithologists noted the decline and disappearance of grass-dependent species such as Masked Bobwhite, Botteri's Sparrow, and Mearn's Quail. Populations of Scaled Quail, which is recognized by a cottony tuft on its head, seem to have declined and then recovered. The Horned Lark, which loves shortgrass also seems to have flourished with the increase in grazing.

On the unbroken grasslands, one can still find many of the Plains birds: Lark Bunting, Grasshopper Sparrow, Mountain Plover, Prairie Chicken, meadowlarks, Long-billed Curlew, and Burrowing Owl. But in the scrub areas, a large variety of birds take advantage of the structural diversity and the increased opportunities for cover. Where cacti are part of the shrub layer, some of the more typical desert species—such as Cactus Wren and Verdin, both of which make their nests in cacti—can be seen. Lucy's Warbler and many others nest in mesquite.

Ground birds are also common: the Gambel and Scaled Quails scurry along the ground in large flocks; and the Roadrunner, a bird that has come to symbolize the Southwest, perhaps epitomizes the generalization that grassland animals are runners. The Roadrunner, skilled at survival in this habitat, can run up to fifteen miles per hour, and, though the running habit is thought to have evolved as a response to wide-open spaces, the Roadrunner combines speed with agility and easily darts in and out among bushes and grasses.

Adaptions of Desert Grassland Animals

Diurnal desert animals face great problems of temperature regulation. The Roadrunner seems to meet this challenge by changing its temperature throughout the day. In the dark or the shade, it can lower its body temperature; when it moves into the sunlight, it can raise it again by holding its plumage erect to expose dark patches of skin on its back. Some of the diurnal mammals, such as the Antelope Ground Squirrel—a more strictly desert species—adapt by first accumulating heat for a while and then discharging it during a rest in the shade. Kangaroo rats are also known for their many adaptations to dry conditions: They never drink water, but instead synthesize it metabolically; their kidneys are very powerful, and thus their urine is highly concentrated and does not carry away a lot of water; and their feces are hard and dry.

To avoid the desert heat, almost all desert grassland rodents are nocturnal and nest in underground burrows. To evade predators, they come out for about an hour at night, stuff food into their cheek pouches, and return to their burrows to eat it. Ecologists have often wondered how so many species with similar food preferences and similar habitats are able to coexist in the same place. It turns out that what looks like one place to us is really a myriad of microhabitats to the eyes of the rodents. Kangaroo rats tend to forage in areas that are slightly more open than do nearby pocket mice or harvest mice, probably because their jumping habit better enables them to escape from predators.

The desert grassland does not support hordes of animals. Bison apparently did not occur in vast numbers here. But this habitat does support diversity. It also provides a living textbook of remarkable adaptations to a climatic extreme.

DESERT GRASSLANDS: PLANTS AND ANIMALS

Mammals
Badger 51
Black-tailed Jack Rabbit 46
Black-tailed Prairie Dog 87
Collared Peccary 36
Coyote 37, 38
Deer Mouse 62
Fulvous Harvest Mouse 64
House Mouse 61
Kit Fox 39
Long-tailed Weasel 53
Mule Deer 35
Northern Grasshopper Mouse 70
Northern Pygmy Mouse 74
Ord's Kangaroo Rat 72
Plains Pocket Mouse 75
Spotted Ground Squirrel 88
Striped Skunk 49
Western Harvest Mouse 63
White-tailed Deer 33
White-tailed Prairie Dog 86

Grasses and Shrubs
Common Sagebrush 113
Creosote Bush 114
Tobosa Grass 109

Wildflowers
Arrowleaf Balsam Root 174
Blackfoot Daisy 130
Broom Snakeweed 203
California Poppy 223
Centaury 242
Chickweed 136
Common Owl's Clover 264
Common Sunflower 175
Cowpen Daisy 179
Cream Cup 189
Death Camas 144
Devil's Claw 118
Elegant Camas 124
Feather Peabush 231
Fiddleneck 160
Field Milkvetch 230
Goldfields 178
Green Pitaya 119
Gumweed 182
Hoary Cress 147
Hooker's Evening Primrose 190
Little Golden Zinnia 185
Many-spined Opuntia 161
Pale Agoseris 163

Plains Larkspur 156
Prairie Gentian 282
Prairie Smoke 249
Purple Groundcherry 285
Rabbit Brush 212
Rain Lily 195
Red Clover 229
Rocky Mountain Bee Plant 260
Sheep Sorrel 221
Shrubby Cinquefoil 191
Snakehead 180
Snakeweed 211
Spreading Fleabane 133
Tahoka Daisy 292
Threadleaf Grounsel 167
Twinleaf 188
Vase Flower 232, 233
Velvety Nerisyrenia 125
Western Pink Verrain 243
White Clover 157
White Prairie Clover 142
Yellow Bee Plant 204

Butterflies
Acraea Moth 303
Alfalfa Looper 310
American Painted Lady 337
Artichoke Plume Moth 315
Cabbage White 307
Common Checkered Skipper 311
Common Sulphur 296
Eastern Black Swallowtail 331
Gray Hairstreak 319
Greenish Blue 327
Monarch 335
Mylitta Crescentspot 341
Orange-bordered Blue 324
Orange Sulphur 295
Painted Lady 338
Pearly Crescentspot 340
Pipevine Swallowtail 320
Silvery Blue 326
Sleepy Orange 298
Small Checkered Skipper 313
Sod Webworm Moth 305
Variegated Fritillary 342
Western Tailed Blue 325
West Coast Lady 339
Woolly Bear Caterpillar Moth 301

Yellow Woolly Bear
Moth 304

Insects and Spiders
American Hover Fly 365
Digger Bees 373
Digger Wasp 369
Early Tachinid Fly 372
Golden Northern Bumble
Bee 374
Goldenrod Spider 392, 396
Green Lacewings 358
Green Midges 359
Green Valley
Grasshopper 353
Honey Bee 375
House Mosquito 362
Jumping Lynx Spider 394
Large Bee Flies 370, 371
Malaria-carrying
Mosquitoes 360
Metaphid Jumping
Spider 393
Mormon Cricket 351
Orb Weavers 395
Paper Wasps 368
Rose, Pea, and Potato
Aphids 390
Rough Harvest Ant 376
Three-lined Potato
Beetle 388
Toxomerus Hover Flies 366
Tumblebugs 379
Yellow-faced Bees 363

Trees
Alligator Juniper 399, 477
Common Juniper 401, 475
Eastern Cottonwood 432
Gregg Catclaw 443, 462
Honey Mesquite 445, 461,
485
Huisache 446, 463
Oneseed Juniper 399
Siberian Elm 416
Smooth Sumac 448, 465
Soaptree Yucca 408
Utah Juniper 398, 476

Birds
American Kestrel 496
Barn Swallow 522
Caracara 495
Cassin's Kingbird 516

Cliff Swallow 521
Common Nighthawk 515
Ferruginous Hawk 493
Golden Eagle 494
Grasshopper Sparrow 537
Horned Lark 520
Killdeer 506
Lark Bunting 535
Loggerhead Shrike 528
Mourning Dove 509
Red-tailed Hawk 491, 492
Red-winged Blackbird 545,
546
Roadrunner 511
Scaled Quail 504
Scissor-tailed Flycatcher 519
Swainson's Hawk 490
Turkey Vulture 488

Mushrooms
Common Psathyrella 555
Fairy Ring Mushroom 554
Fried Chicken
Mushroom 559
Hemispheric Agrocybe 556
Japanese Umbrella Inky 553
Meadow Mushroom 560
Shaggy Mane 562
Smooth Lepiota 558
Tumbling Puffball 563

Reptiles and Amphibians
Coachwhip 614
Corn Snake 603
Eastern Fence Lizard 589
Great Plains Skink 582
Great Plains Toad 570
Lesser Earless Toad 585
Many-lined Skink 577
Plains Black-headed
Snake 615
Plains Spadefoot 567
Racer 618
Red-spotted Toad 568
Western Box Turtle 574
Western Hognose
Snake 604
Western Rattlesnake 605
Western Spadefoot 566
Woodhouse's Toad 569

INTERMOUNTAIN GRASSLANDS

Although much of the intermountain West is often referred to as grassland, the dominant feature throughout most of it is sagebrush, which is not a grass. In fact, such grasslands are also known as sagebrush grasslands, sagebrush scrub, and shrub steppes. In earlier times, however, sagebrush was probably not as abundant in this area as it is today. The exact nature of the former vegetation is unknown, but historically this intermountain region has provided sufficient forage value to sustain grazing animals such as cattle; thus it has been considered a grassland.

Land of the Sagebrush

Sagebrush, a small, gray-green shrub in the daisy family (Asteraceae or Compositae), grows throughout vast areas in the western states. There are several species of sage, but the most common one—especially in this region—is Big Sagebrush. The strong turpentinelike smell of sagebrush leaves —which is evident after a rainstorm or even when one walks through a stand of bushes—is characteristic of the arid, open West.

A sagebrush landscape can at first seem overwhelmingly monotonous; from a distance, sage seems to be the only living thing for miles around. Up closer, though, one can find good stands of widely spaced bunchgrasses growing among the sage, along with a variety of forbs.

Sagebrush grasslands cover millions of acres and constitute the most extensive community in the intermountain region. A good deal of the sagebrush grasslands are now owned by the federal government, which uses some of the land for military purposes, leaving other portions as rangeland.

The Palouse Prairie

Also within the intermountain area, a specialized grassland known as the Palouse prairie occupies the southeastern corner of the state of Washington. The name Palouse comes from the French word *pelouse,* which means "lawn." The Palouse prairie probably never looked like a lawn, but the early French explorers very likely had no words to express what they were seeing and thus did the best they could in giving a name to the area.

Because of the differences between the geological history of the Palouse prairie and that of the intermountain grasslands, the soils of the former are more fertile and have historically supported purer stands of grass with fewer shrubs. Like the tallgrass prairie, the fertility of the Palouse led to its demise: Within half a century, almost all of it was converted to agriculture—primarily the cultivation of wheat and peas. The transformation was so rapid that little is now known about the original Palouse prairie, but since the remaining wild vegetation is not very different from that of the intermountain area, the two are discussed together.

Range

The intermountain grasslands occur in the large area known as the intermountain, or basin and range, province. Both names

are descriptive, for the area is flanked by the Rockies to the east and the Sierra Nevada and Cascade ranges to the west, and—with the exception of the Columbia Plateau in southeastern Washington—is characterized by a large number of small, discrete mountain ranges, which are separated by flat basins. The region also includes the Great Basin, a vast area without drainage to the sea. The intermountain west encompasses Utah and Nevada, as well as parts of eastern California, the section of Arizona that lies north of the Colorado River, and small parts of southern Idaho, southeastern Wyoming, eastern Oregon, and southeastern Washington.

Physical Features

A U.S. Army geologist during the nineteenth century described the intermountain area as "an army of caterpillars crawling northward out of Mexico." This observation reflects the fact that all except one of the mountain ranges—and thus the basins as well—run in a north-south direction, some extending for 150 miles. Certain basins are as wide as 250 miles. The basins are between 3000 and 6000 feet above sea level, while the crests of the mountains range from 7000 to 12,000 feet. Most of the few rivers in the area drain into the Great Salt Lake, but a few ranges are drained internally.

The present landscape seems to have been shaped primarily during the relatively recent Pliocene Epoch—about five million years ago. Before this time, the Sierra Nevada Mountains were lower than they are now. Waters from the intermountain region apparently drained into the Pacific, and the area was covered with coniferous forests. Even earlier, in the Tertiary Period, swampland vegetation occupied this region. During the Pliocene, however, two simultaneous processes occurred that determined the area's present climate and configuration. First, extensive block faulting—a process whereby adjacent surfaces of rock are displaced relative to each other—took place. Simply stated, the parts of the rocks that were dislodged in an upward direction became mountains, while the parts that were pushed downward became basins. At the same time, the Sierra Nevada Mountains were uplifted; as they rose, they cast over the region a longer rain shadow—the lee area of a mountain where there is less rain.

Erosion wore the mountains to their present shapes and continues to mold them. The mountains are cut by steep, V-shaped canyons; runoff feeds into these canyons from smaller V-shaped canyons. From the air, such gullies and channels look like giant, dark fern leaves painted on the mountainside. The sediment washed down from the canyons fills the valleys and creates flat basin floors. Most of the sediment is fine-grained, the product of invisible weathering, but flash floods still occur in the spring after a winter of heavy snowfall and may carry anything from sand to boulders. Landslides are common on the faces of the mountains.

The resulting soils are rocky, thin, and low in organic matter. However, because of their high mineral content, they can be

made productive through irrigation. It is said that the
Mormons could tell from the size of the sagebrush whether
land was worth irrigating for agriculture; if the sagebrush was
waist-high, it was; if it was only knee-high, it was not. Only
about one percent of this area is farmed.

At the northern edge of this region, the Columbia Plateau—
where Palouse prairie occurs—has quite a different geological
history from the basin and range area. The plateau is the result
of a series of lava flows that began during the late Oligocene
and early Miocene Epochs—or about twenty-six million years
ago, before the uplifting of the western mountains. The lava
flowed out of deep fissures and sometimes traveled as far as
200 miles, gradually filling in the valleys and covering the
hills of the existing landscape. Between successive flows, lakes
and rivers formed. The lava flows continued for a long time,
each successive flow hardening into tough basalt. In some
places, the basalt is now 1000 feet thick.

Later, during the Pliocene Epoch, the Cascades began
uplifting, as the Sierra Nevadas had to the south, and cast a
rain shadow over the Columbia Plateau. As the climate
became drier, the trees died out, and the forest was replaced
by grasses and shrubs from the east and the south. Meanwhile
the basalt was continually weathering and forming soil. The
vegetation, however, was not well enough developed to
stabilize the soil, so loose soil was blown about into giant
dunes, some as high as 150 feet. These high, rolling hills are
now the dominant feature of Palouse topography.

The Columbia Plateau was later affected by glaciation. In
eastern Washington, the last glacier left great piles of sand
and gravel at its toe, and the glacial meltwater formed huge,
powerful rivers that scraped away all the soil in their path.
The rivers cut deep canyons, named coulees by the French
explorers. This scouring process did not reach the Palouse
prairie area, though; this is one reason that the area has proved
so fertile for agriculture. Although the land to the west of the
Palouse is underlain by the same rich basalt, it supports dry
sagebrush scrub. The locals call it "the scablands" because of
its frequent rock outcrops and poor soil. Most of the rich,
wind-blown soil was long ago washed away from here into
the sea.

Climate

If you were to walk in a straight line from east to west across
the Great Basin, the constant changes in elevation would not
only make you tired, but would also make it necessary for you
to frequently add or subtract articles of clothing. The climate
changes constantly with altitude. The mountains catch most of
the little available moisture, so as elevation increases, more
precipitation falls; the temperatures drop as well. The climate
on a mountain's northern slope is different from that on the
southern slope: The southern slope receives more sunlight and
is thus warmer and drier. In addition—as one might expect—
the climate changes gradually with latitude.

Generally, the climate in the intermountain west is extremely arid; precipitation averages ten to fifteen inches per year. This is not much different from the yearly average in the shortgrass prairie, but there is a significant difference in yearly distribution. Here most of the precipitation occurs during fall and winter, and very little rain falls during the growing season. In the Great Basin area, much of the winter moisture is lost to sublimation, which is direct transfer of water from a solid to a vapor. The little rain that falls during the growing season comes from sporadic, unpredictable thundershowers. Thus plants start the season with a reservoir of ground water, but it is quickly used up.

The growing season is short, extending from late spring to early fall, and summer frosts may occur at night. During the day summer temperatures often exceed 100° F. In short, this climate is not hospitable to the growth of most plants. One of the reasons that agriculture is successful in the Palouse prairie —in spite of this harsh climate—is that the fine-textured soils are able to hold water longer. Also, winters on the Columbia Plateau tend to be foggier and cloudier, so that less moisture is lost to sublimation.

Vegetation

The climatic changes due to altitude and latitude cause variations in plant life. As a result, the vegetation of the intermountain region forms a kind of crazy quilt, which is difficult to map except in minute detail. Fortunately the differences in climate are repeated often and regularly enough that the vegetation forms distinct zones, each zone surviving under a certain combination of temperature and rainfall.

The sagebrush grassland does not survive in the hottest and driest parts of the region—the southerly basins. In the southern part of the region, it is found only on the lower slopes of the mountains, while in the northern parts, it also occupies the vast basins.

The overall shortage of moisture dictates the dominance of widely spaced bunchgrasses. The soil moisture directly beneath one plant is simply not sufficient to support it; each must spread its roots horizontally, precluding the growth of other plants. The lack of summer rainfall dictates the dominance of cool-season species, which are inactive during the summer.

The dominant grass that grows with sagebrush is Bluebunch Wheatgrass. This species is aptly named, for the plant is blue-green, it grows in clumps, and it is distantly related to wheat. There are, of course, other shrubs and grasses, and annual and perennial forbs also occur here, though not in abundant displays. Lupines, larkspurs, phloxes, and violets brighten up the landscape here and there, and the large basal leaves of Mule's Ears and Arrow-leaved Balsamroot are present throughout the year, sending up bright yellow, sunflowerlike blossoms from May to July. The Sego Lily, which is the state flower of Utah and a food source that tided the Mormons through times of scarcity, is also found in the sagebrush grassland.

Animal Life

The summer drought has also had important consequences for the animal life of the region. Most of the animals found in the shortgrass and mixed prairies are here, but animals that need a year-round supply of green grass have not been able to survive. The large, plant-eating animals that do occur here are Mule Deer, Elk, and Pronghorn, all of which eat shrubs as well as grasses. Also missing is the Black-tailed Prairie Dog, but its niche is filled by a close relative, the White-tailed Prairie Dog. The two have similar diets and serve the same ecological function by dramatically altering large areas of the landscape with their feeding and burrowing. Although White-tails do not interact with each other in an organized manner to the extent that Black-tails do, they do live in colonies, which—like those of the Black-tail—seem to provide an attractive habitat and even housing for a host of other animals ranging from crickets to Coyotes. One study found almost forty different species—just among the vertebrates—that were spending time in some way or another in a White-tailed Prairie Dog town.

The typical prairie birds—Dickcissel, longspurs, and Lark Bunting—are less common here, but the opportunistic Horned Lark and the ever-present Western Meadowlark are often found. The sagebrush grassland supports a small diversity of birds, with the raptors and the runners being most common. One of the most abundant birds is—appropriately —the Sage Grouse. Like its smaller, eastern relatives, the Prairie Chicken and the Sharp-tailed Grouse, this normally nondescript bird becomes quite spectacular during its annual mating display.

Small rodents abound. Although their diversity in any one spot might be low, diversity over the whole intermountain area is high, especially among the ground squirrels, which are thought to have started their process of speciation in this area. Of the twenty-two species of ground squirrels in the United States, nineteen are found within 500 miles of the shores of the Great Salt Lake, most of them within similar habitats and small ranges. In spite of the rich speciation among small rodents in this area, one of the most common rodents is the Deer Mouse, an animal that is common from Maine to California.

Pocket gophers are here too. They are different species from those in the tallgrass prairie, but these also spend most of their lives underground and continually turn the soil. Perhaps because they are insulated from temperature extremes, they do not hibernate or aestivate. Pocket gophers also provide housing for many associates—one researcher counted twenty-two species of animals using pocket gopher burrows, including many reptiles and amphibians.

The small rodents are food for the usual grassland predators— Coyote, skunks, Badger, and weasels, as well as the hunting birds. The intermountain area is also home to a group of carnivores now barely found in the midcontinental grasslands: wild cats, including Mountain Lion, Bobcat, and Lynx.

Among large herbivores, the Mule Deer and the Pronghorn reign supreme. They vary their diets according to the availability of food and exploit the wide-open spaces in their seasonal migrations and wanderings.

The wild horse, an animal particular to this area, has caused unusual problems. Ironically, horses were once native to this continent, but they mysteriously disappeared in North America after the glaciers retreated, near the end of the Pleistocene and were not seen again until the arrival of the Spaniards. They then started forming wild herds as they either escaped or were abandoned. The descendants of the Spaniards' horses were undoubtedly joined over the next four centuries by horses that drifted away from various explorers, traders, and miners, and by those that were abandoned during the great drought of the 1930s. The wild horses were considered free game for the pet-food market—until protective legislation was passed in 1971. Then populations expanded so much that the horses were considered a threat to ranching efforts. A compromise between protectionists and ranchers is reflected in the current policy, whereby a certain number of horses are rounded up every year and sold as pets.

The critical feature of the Intermountain fauna is the absence of a large, demanding herbivore like the Bison. Just as the characteristics of the vegetation affected those of the animal population, the characteristics of the animal populations, in turn, had important consequences for the vegetation.

Changes in the Intermountain Grasslands

Visitors to the sagebrush grassland today will not see much grass, at least not much Bluebunch Wheatgrass. They will see a great deal of sagebrush, however—probably more than was present a hundred years ago—and, in the early spring, a silvery-green carpet formed by an alien grass called Downy Brome, or Cheatgrass. A hundred years ago, brome was not here; now it practically coats the intermountain west.

According to ecologists, this invasion is one of the more remarkable plant invasions that has taken place in this country —and one that has affected millions of acres of land. Like most plant invasions, it was made possible by changes in environmental conditions, the cultivation of wheat in the Palouse area, and the cattle boom of the 1880s.

Downy Brome evolved on the steppes of Asia, in roughly the same part of the world that wheat originated. It has a life cycle and requirements that are similar to those of wheat. An annual, it germinates quickly in response to soil moisture. Most of the seeds germinate in the spring, set seed by early summer (when the soil moisture is just about depleted), and die. Some plants, however, germinate with the fall rains, survive the winter as seedlings, and then flower and set seed the following spring.

Downy Brome has been a weed in wheat fields for centuries, which explains the origin of its other name, Cheatgrass. Farmers used to plant wheat and then be astounded when Downy Brome came up the next year. (In fact, up until the nineteenth century, it was commonly believed that one plant could be transformed into another; this belief was fostered by weed invasions such as this.) In all probability, a shipment of wheat seed that had been poorly sorted included a few Downy Brome seeds—enough to start an invasion in the fresh, bare soil.

Ironically, when the Washington Territory was first being settled—and its potential was viewed with skepticism—the territorial governor, Isaac Stevens, performed a detailed scientific evaluation of the region, in which he compared the Palouse to the steppes of Asia, an area with a similar climate, where agriculture had been successful for centuries. Little did he realize the further implications of the climatic similarity. The climate of the Columbia Plateau suited Downy Brome perfectly, and overnight it became—and it continues to be— major competitor of wheat.

The similarity between the two areas had further implications The steppes of Asia were grazed year-round by wild horses and camels; thus Downy Brome had evolved to withstand grazing. The native Bluebunch Wheatgrass and other perennial bunchgrasses did not withstand the heavy grazing that took place during the cattle boom. As they weakened and died, Downy Brome quickly took over. It has retained its dominance for the last hundred years.

Unlike the prairie grasslands, which seem to come back after disturbance, the sagebrush grassland does not seem able to recover quickly from a Downy Brome invasion, even in places where grazing has been reduced and Bluebunch Wheatgrass seeds have been planted. Because Downy Brome is an annual and thus does not take a firm hold in the soil, this lack of recovery is surprising.

Some think that Downy Brome obtains an advantage through its root system, which consists of longer—although weaker— roots. Since Bluebunch Wheatgrass is a perennial, it "wastes" a lot of energy in the first year by building a tough, almost woody, root that will survive many years. Deep, vertical growth takes place in subsequent years. Downy Brome, an annual, does not need this tough root, so—unlike Wheatgrass —its energy goes into vertical, downward growth. This is important in an arid climate, for every centimeter of downward growth brings the plant into contact with more water. Since the soil dries out from the top down, the Brome seedlings have the advantage of a few more days of water, a few more days in which the plant can flower and set seed.

There is a tendency to denounce all alien invaders as undesirable and to see these invasions as punishment for our greed. Downy Brome, at least from a cattle rancher's point of view, is not absolutely bad. Many alien invaders are less nutritious for livestock than the plants they replace, but in a year of good rainfall, Downy Brome can produce decent early forage. Its drawbacks are that its yearly growth is entirely dependent on rain, and its production can vary by 1000 percent from one year to the next. (Perennial grasses also vary in production, but not to such a wide degree as annuals.) In addition, the sharply barbed seeds of Downy Brome can pierce the eyes and mouths of livestock and wildlife that are out on the range after the plant has gone to seed.

Subsequent to the Downy Brome invasion, the sagebrush grassland has experienced other changes in vegetation. With the demise of the native bunchgrasses, the amount of land covered by sagebrush and other shrubs has increased—to the detriment of the rancher. The scrub environment, however, with its diversity of food sources and cover, is a much better habitat for wildlife. Mule Deer, Pronghorn, Sage Grouse, and many other species of animals benefit from the presence of shrubs. The larger animals depend upon them for food; the smaller ones, for cover.

As in the desert grassland, however, extensive range restoration efforts are underway, and an estimated five to six million acres of sagebrush have been burned, sprayed, and planted in grass. While this practice is perhaps bringing the landscape closer to its presettlement aspect, the result is also less diversity of wildlife as well as a cause for dispute between the hunter and the rancher. In addition, it makes us realize how vulnerable the landscape is; it is perhaps unsettling to see how easily we can control it.

Although to some the sagebrush grassland can be a place of extreme desolation, there is power in its monotony and inhospitality and in the fact that plants and animals have and can survive in this overwhelmingly vast area. Despite this harshness the sagebrush grassland has succumbed to human interference perhaps more irreversibly than any of the other grassland ecosystems in the country. In this respect, it will be interesting to track its development. Is Downy Brome here to stay? Have a few decades of human activity produced an irreversible change in the flora? Perhaps the original vegetation will reassert itself, but if this happens, it will do so only slowly because of the harsh climate. Only time will tell.

INTERMOUNTAIN GRASSLANDS:
PLANTS AND ANIMALS

Mammals
Badger 51
Black-tailed Jack Rabbit 46
Colombia Ground
Squirrel 81
Coyote 37, 38
Deer Mouse 62
Elk 32
Great Basin Pocket
Mouse 69
House Mouse 61
Kit Fox 39
Long-tailed Weasel 53
Meadow Vole 56
Mule Deer 35
Northern Grasshopper
Mouse 70
Ord's Kangaroo Rat 72
Red Fox 41, 42, 44, 45
Richardson's Ground
Squirrel 83
Sagebrush Vole 58
Striped Skunk 49
Uinta Ground Squirrel 82
Western Harvest Mouse 63
Western Jumping Mouse 66
White-tailed Jack Rabbit 47
White-tailed Prairie Dog 86

Grasses and Shrubs
Bluebench Wheatgrass 112
Common Sagebrush 113
Idaho Fescue 100

Wildflowers
Arrowleaf Balsam Root 174
Broom Snakeweed 203
Centaury 242
Common Sunflower 175
Crazyweed 267
Cream Cup 189
Death Camas 144
Desert Plume 217
Elegant Camas 124
Fiddleneck 160
Field Milkvetch 230
Flatpod 115
Hoary Cress 147
Locoweed 265
Many-spined Opuntia 161
Mule's Ear 169
Pale Agoseris 163
Plains Wallflower 210
Prairie Smoke 249

Prairie Star 137
Rabbit Brush 212
Sego Lily 122
Showy Thistle 251
Shrubby Cinquefoil 191
Snakehead 180
Snakeweed 211
Spreading Dogbane 234
Sweet Fennel 207
Threadleaf Phacelia 236
Threadleaf Groundsel 167
Vase Flower 232, 233
White Prairie Clover 142
Wild Blue Flax 287
Yellow Bee Plant 204
Yellow Bell 198

Butterflies and Moths
Acmon Blue 322, 323
Acraea Moth 303
Alfalfa Looper 310
American Painted Lady 337
Artichoke Plume Moth 315
Cabbage White 307
Common Blue 329
Common Checkered
Skipper 311
Common Sulphur 296
Funereal Duskywing 316
Gray Hairstreak 319
Great Gray Copper 318
Monarch 335
Mylitta Crescentspot 341
Orange-bordered Blue 324
Orange Sulphur 295
Ornate Tiger Moth 302
Painted Lady 338
Pearly Crescentspot 340
Pipevine Swallowtail 320
Prairie Ringlet 297
Silvery Blue 326
Small Checkered
Skipper 313
Sod Webworm Moth 305
Viceroy 334
West Coast Lady 339
Western Tailed Blue 325
Woolly Bear Caterpillar
Moth 301
Yellow Woolly Bear
Moth 304

Insects and Spiders
American Hover Fly 365

Brown Daddy-long-legs 388
Digger Bees 373
Digger Wasp 369
Early Tachinid Fly 372
Field Cricket 350
Golden Northern Bumble
Bee 374
Goldenrod Spider 392, 396
Green Lacewings 358
Green Midges 359
Honey Bee 375
House Mosquito 362
Jumping Lynx Spider 394
Large Bee Flies 370, 371
Malaria-carrying
Mosquitoes 360
Metaphid Jumping
Spider 393
Mormon Cricket 351
Nine-spotted Ladybug
Beetle 380
Orb Weavers 395
Paper Wasps 368
Rose, Pea, and Potato
Aphids 390
Three-lined Potato
Beetle 388
Toxomerus Hover Flies 366
Tumblebugs 379
Yellow-faced Bees 363

Trees
Common Juniper 399
Curlleaf Cercocarpus 414,
486
Eastern Cottonwood 432
Quaking Aspen 430
Russian Olive 467
Siberian Elm 416
Singleleaf Pinyon 480
Smooth Sumac 448, 465
Utah Juniper 398, 476

Birds
American Goldfinch 552
American Kestrel 496
Barn Owl 512
Barn Swallow 522
Black-billed Magpie 523
Bobolink 544
Brewer's Blackbird 549,
550
Cliff Swallow 521
Common Nighthawk 515

Eastern Kingbird 518
Ferruginous Hawk 493
Golden Eagle 494
Grasshopper Sparrow 537
Horned Lark 520
Killdeer 506
Loggerhead Shrike 528
Long-billed Curlew 508
Mountain Bluebird 525
Mourning Dove 509
Northern Harrier 489
Northern Shrike 527
Red-tailed Hawk 491, 492
Red-winged Blackbird 545,
546
Ring-necked Pheasant 498
Sage Grouse 499
Sandhill Crane 505
Short-eared Owl 514
Swainson's Hawk 490
Tree Sparrow 530
Turkey Vulture 488
Vesper Sparrow 533
Water Pipit 526
Western Kingbird 517

Mushrooms
Common Psathyrella 555
Fairy Ring Mushroom 554
Fried Chicken
Mushroom 559
Hemispheric Agrocybe 556
Japanese Umbrella Inky 553
Meadow Mushroom 560
Shaggy Mane 562
Smooth Lepiota 558
Tumbling Puffball 563
White Waxy Cap 557

Reptiles and Amphibians
Common Garter Snake 592
Racer 618
Western Rattlesnake 605

CALIFORNIA GRASSLANDS

Description of the California grasslands is best left to the naturalist John Muir:

So on the first of April, 1868, I set out afoot for Yosemite [from Oakland]. It was the bloom time of the year over the lowlands and coast ranges; the landscapes of the Santa Clara Valley were fairly drenched with sunshine, all the air was quivering with the songs of meadowlarks, and the hills were so covered with flowers that they seemed to be painted. Slow indeed was my progress through these glorious gardens, the first of the California flora I had seen. Cattle and cultivation were making few scars as yet, and I wandered enchanted in long wavering curves, knowing by my pocket map that Yosemite Valley lay to the east and that I should surely find it.

Looking eastward from the summit of Pacjeco Pass one shining morning, {I found before me} a landscape . . . that after my wanderings still appears as the most beautiful I have ever beheld. At my feet lay the Great Central Valley of California, level and flowery, like a lake of pure sunshine, forty or fifty miles wide, five hundred miles long, one rich furred garden of yellow compositae. And from the eastern boundary of this vast golden flowerbed rose the mighty Sierra, miles in height, and so gloriously colored and so radiant, it seemed not clothed with light, but wholly composed of it, like the wall of some celestial city.

Appearance and Range

Originally, grasslands covered one fourth of the state of California. However, like other American grassland systems, they have been either obliterated or radically altered. The California grasslands, also known as the Pacific Prairie, fall into two separate communities, which are similar in some ways but also quite distinct: the coastal grassland and the valley grassland. The coastal grassland covers middle-elevation hillsides from San Francisco to southern Oregon. It is not continuous, but alternately appears and vanishes, depending on elevation and aspect. It sometimes appears miles inland as a bald in the middle of the forest; in places it cascades directly to the sea. Although the present-day species found in coastal grasslands are not the same as those found in past times, the coastal system is, nonetheless, grassland. Modern-day Californians can say there is prairie of sorts in at least part of their state.

The valley grassland occurs in the large Central Valley of California—principally on the flatlands, but it sometimes rises into the foothills surrounding the valley. Occasionally it can be found on the south-facing slopes of the southern coastal mountain ranges.

The combination of soil and climate in the valley has proved irresistible to farmers, so much of this original grassland community has disappeared. Where citrus groves or cotton fields have not taken over the land, however, grasslands may persist, but the dominant species are completely different from those found 150 years ago by settlers.

In spite of all these changes, botanists and wild flower lovers are still attracted to the Central Valley by the dazzling display of annual spring wild flowers and low, wet areas known as vernal pools or, informally, hog wallows. These depressions, which are sometimes half of a mile wide, fill with water during the spring and dry out during the summer. A limited number of species have evolved so that they can tolerate these unusual conditions; some of these are quite rare. For example, a vernal-pool grass grows nowhere else in the world. Like many other unusual habitats, vernal pools are disappearing; they are being drained, filled, or cultivated.

Physical Features

The geology of coastal California is complex. The Coast Ranges are a product of tectonics—specifically, of the collision of the Pacific continental plates with the North American continent. Successive periods of land immersions and emersions, as well as deformations resulting from a variety of causes, have created what geologist Philip King has called "a melange of tectonically disordered blocks and slices." The geological composition and soil basis are thus quite varied, as all three rock types exist in close proximity. The area is still one of great geological instability: It is subject to frequent floods, mudslides, and earthquakes.

The bedrock contains large areas of granite, as well as sedimentary shales, sandstones, and conglomerates intruded by igneous rocks. The character of the vegetation is not so markedly influenced by the nature of the underlying bedrock, as it is in the Palouse in Washington and Idaho, except in a few places where the igneous rocks have been metamorphosed into a greenish rock called serpentine. The high concentrations of magnesium in serpentine make plant growth difficult, and, as is the case with the vernal pools, these serpentine outcrops support a very specialized flora. The outcrops attract botanists' attention not only because of their unusual and restricted flora, but also because they are one of the few places where native grasses persist. The Central Valley is geologically simpler than the Coast Range. It was once covered by a vast inland sea, which has since evaporated.

Annual precipitation in the two habitats varies from six to twenty-nine inches, with the coastal area generally receiving more. As in the intermountain area, precipitation is concentrated in the fall, winter, and spring months; very little rain falls during the summer. This pattern helps to form a Mediterranean climate, or one characterized by mild, rainy winters and hot, dry summers. The vegetation becomes green with the first rainfalls in late October or early November and remains green but does not grow during the winter. Spring arrives in late February. By late April to early May, the grasslands have dried to a golden color; they stay that way until fall, at which time the "green-to-gold cycle" begins again. Ironically, the source of the gold color is primarily alien grasses; the original vegetation probably changed from green to a less striking brown.

In the valley, summer temperatures can be punishing, often reaching over 100° F; on the coast, the summer heat is mitigated by the sea breezes and frequent fogs rolling in off of the Pacific. Aside from the rich soil, one of the attractions of the area for farmers is the long growing season. Although heavy frosts occur, they last but a short time, so crops can be grown virtually year-round.

Animal and Plant Life

John Muir's description of the uniform blanket of daisies notwithstanding, the Central Valley once possessed a great variety of habitats, which contained a diversity of species. The north-facing slopes at the edge of the valley supported shrub communities, and the rivers that drained the valley were lined with riparian forests and broad marshes.

Such variety created excellent wildlife habitats. Pronghorn, feeding on grass and shrubs, roamed the valley in large numbers, and Tule Elk, a subspecies of the Elk, migrated seasonally from the valleys to the hills. Large populations of jack rabbits were food for Coyotes, while the Badger probably concentrated on the burrowers: pocket gophers, ground squirrels, and pocket mice. Mule Deer and Black-tailed Deer frequented the forest borders along the foothills. The valley even contained Grizzly Bears, now totally gone from California and declared an endangered species. Along with the Meadowlark, John Muir probably also saw or heard the Horned Lark, Brewer's Blackbird, and the Desert Sparrow Hawk—perhaps even the California Condor, which is also now endangered. One bird he could not have seen elsewhere is the Yellow-billed Magpie.

The picture is different now. The balance has shifted considerably in favor of small, herbivorous mammals. Predator populations have declined because of control programs and loss of habitat, while large stretches of farmland and cattle ranges are a veritable banquet table for ground squirrels and numerous species of mice.

The government has tried to eliminate these rodents. In 1918, citing $30 billion in crop damage, the governor of California proclaimed Ground Squirrel Week and offered prizes to the schoolchildren that killed the most ground squirrels. His efforts had little effect, however. Today the rodents reign supreme in the California grassland; these small animals continue to exert considerable influence over its productivity and composition.

Although we have a good picture of the animals that used to inhabit the Central Valley, no one is certain about the plant life that used to grow in the valley grassland. Based on the small amount of information that is available, it is thought that the dominant grass was Purple Needlegrass, a bunchgrass found only in California. Purple Needlegrass is indeed purplish, and in the summer, the dried stalks must have lent a distinctive color to the valley grasslands. Of what was growing on the coastal grassland before the settlers arrived, we are equally uncertain, but the best candidates for dominant species are California Oatsgrass, Idaho Fescue, and Red Fescue, all perennial bunchgrasses.

The climate also favored an abundance of annuals that could complete their life cycles during the brief wet period before the onset of summer drought. Since the survival of an annual species depends upon the success of next year's seedlings, most annuals produce a large number of seeds and hence—in proportion to their size—many flowers. The relative composition of species varied from year to year, depending upon the weather, but apparently in March, April, and May brilliant color displays were produced by various species of wildflowers, including Indian paintbrushes, Owl's Clover, Brodiaeas, lupines, gilias, and nemophilas. After the dry summer, Yellow-flowered Tarweed burst into bloom, in masses sometimes extending for miles.

In 1851 a surveyor noted that the valleys and foothills in the Mt. Diablo area west of San Francisco were covered with Wild Oats, an introduced species that afforded "excellent pasturage to the extensive droves of cattle and horses that were scattered abroad over this magnificent range and also the herds of elk, antelope, and deer that abound here." The "extensive droves" of cattle and horses became more extensive in time. In 1918 the well-known ecologist Frederic Clements commented on "the obliteration of many hundreds of miles of nearly continuous associations of *Stipa pulchra* and the establishment of *Avena fatua* [Wild Oats] as the great dominant throughout." The arrival and proliferation of the cattle and horses constituted one of the principal reasons for the disappearance of the California grasslands.

Like the bunchgrasses of the Palouse and the intermountain area, the native California grasses did not evolve under a system of heavy grazing. Large herbivores were present—Elk, Pronghorn, and deer—but their diets were not limited to grasses. And, most important, because of the natural attrition due to disease and predation, their numbers probably were never as great as those of the domestic herds. However, when heavy grazing began, the native bunchgrasses were destroyed, and conditions became ripe for the influx of a host of annuals that were alien, or introduced from abroad. Most of these annuals came from the Mediterranean, some perhaps brought in accidentally by the Spanish explorers centuries before. Today almost 400 alien species grow in the California grasslands.

If many of the original grasslands "disappeared" in the sense that their species composition changed naturally, many more of those in the Central Valley truly disappeared: They were obliterated in the face of agricultural pressures. Lettuce, tomatoes, walnuts, almonds, and avocadoes are but a few of the crops being produced on these former grasslands. The coastal grasslands, however, often occurred on steep slopes, were not as attractive for intensive cultivation, and were thus left mainly for grazing. But now they too are facing the threat of obliteration as suburban and vacation housing developments creep inexorably over the hills.

In spite of certain purists' revulsions to the California grasslands' current, altered character, these areas hold a fascination for ecologists because they are never the same from year to year. There are wars and fluctuations between the plant species—just as on the midcontinental prairie—but they happen more quickly and noticeably, since the entire plant population dies at the end of each growing season.

Two of the factors that seem to control both total and relative abundance of species are weather and rodent populations. A study of such factors can tell us a lot about ecosystems in general.

The amount of precipitation in winter and early spring can make a tremendous difference in total growth and may favor some species over others. A wet year will bring forth a staggering profusion of showy annual wild flowers, while in a dry year, the seeds simply might not germinate or, if they do, the seedlings might not survive.

The rodents' effect is related to their habit of clipping green vegetation, as well as their consumption of seeds. High populations of rodents can significantly reduce the cover of green grass. The resulting increased light and warmth reaching the soil—along with the decreased litter layer—can affect the next year's germination. When the grasses go to seed, some of the rodents seem to have strong preferences, which in turn influence plant concentrations. For instance, in one area where Wild Oats made up only four percent of the plant cover, seventy-five percent of their seeds were eaten by Voles. In laboratory experiments, when the Voles were given a choice of several seeds, they made a beeline for the Wild Oats, showing that, for whatever reasons, they clearly preferred it. Maybe their preference for Wild Oat seed explains why this species formed such a small percentage of this particular stand.

Many rodents, especially Voles, experience fluctuations in population—in a cycle marked by a buildup of the local population to a high level, and a subsequent crash. The reasons for this cycle are a continuing puzzle for biologists. The most dramatic representation of this phenomenon is the much-exaggerated "migration" of lemmings in Scandinavia. But it occurs in California as well. The rodent populations' ups and downs in turn affect the vegetation that they feed upon.

Future of California Grasslands

Will the annuals' domination of these grasslands persist indefinitely? Have they taken over the native perennial grassland for the forseeable future—or is there hope for a recovery of the native grassland? A rangeland that is no longer grazed may be dominated by annuals for as long as twenty-five years. However, the answer to the last question seems to be a guarded "yes."

The evidence comes from surprising quarters. First, a story that illustrates the capability of grasslands: the invasion and subsequent repression of Klamath Weed.

Known to most of us as St. Johnswort (although it is but one

member of the St. Johnswort family), Klamath Weed is a
small and innocuous herbaceous wildflower. It was apparently
brought to this country in 1696 by the Rosicrucians, a
mystical religious sect that settled in the Philadelphia area.
The species spread, but was never more than a roadside flower
until it arrived in California grasslands at the turn of the
century. There its population exploded. The reasons for this
explosion may never be fully understood, but one clearly is the
fact that it is poisonous to cattle—so they avoided it. By 1940
this economically destructive plant covered over 200,000 acres
in northern California.

Although range managers initially despaired of finding a way
to control the plant, the story has a happy ending. The
solution that was found represents one of the first successful
cases of biological control in the country. The Klamath Weed
Beetle, which eats only St. Johnswort, was introduced into the
region in 1946. It flourished and brought the plant
populations under control. In some areas, Klamath Weed
disappeared completely within two years.

The rangelands were carefully observed both before and after
the release of the beetle. In some pastures, Klamath Weed had
made up fully half of the vegetation, so its demise left
extensive bare ground for colonizing species. Scientists had a
grand opportunity to witness the process of succession. The
first plants to arrive were annual forbs; these were followed by
annual grasses. These grass species were in turn replaced by
native perennial grasses—notably California Oatsgrass—
within ten years.

The second piece of evidence came from a military reservation
that was off limits to the public and therefore unobserved for
several decades. Controlled burning had been taking place
there on thousands of acres since 1942, in order to reduce the
amount of dry matter that could catch fire from test
explosives. The land is covered with fine stands of perennial
bunchgrasses.

Burning is now being practiced elsewhere on an experimental
basis, and the results are dramatic. The reasons are not well
understood, but fields completely dominated by annuals begin
showing perennial growth within three years. Even species
that were not visible before the burning have begun
to appear.

However, in 1938 the eminent ecologists J.E. Weaver and
Frederic Clements wrote, in their textbook *Plant Ecology*, "The
native bunch-grass prairie of California has been . . . largely
destroyed by overgrazing and fire." In 1968 an ecologist,
maintaining that the annual grasses were here to stay, wrote
that twenty-nine years of protection from grazing and fire
produced grasslands in Monterey County which were still
dominated by [annual aliens]. Perhaps because of the truly
serious damage caused by wildfires in this part of the country,
fire was, until recently, thought of as only a destructive force.
If experimental burning continues and keeps causing a
regrowth of perennial grasses, perhaps our understanding of
this grassland ecosystem will be improved.

CALIFORNIA GRASSLANDS: PLANTS AND ANIMALS

Mammals
Badger 51
Black-tailed Jack Rabbit 46
California Vole 57
Deer Mouse 62
Eastern Mole 77
Elk 32
Heermann's Kangaroo
Rat 73
House Mouse 61
Long-tailed Weasel 53
Meadow Vole 56
Mule Deer 35
San Joaquin Pocket
Mouse 68
Striped Skunk 49
Western Harvest Mouse 63

Grasses and Shrubs
Idaho Fescue 100
Purple Needlegrass 111
Sweet Vernal Grass 96
Velvet Grass 92

Wildflowers
Baby Blue Eyes 284
Buffalo Gourd 196
California Poppy 223
Centaury 242
Common Madia 181
Common Owl's Clover 264
Common St. Johnswort 202
Common Sunflower 175
Cowpen Daisy 179
Cream Cup 189
Desert Plume 217
Devil's Claw 118
Douglas' Iris 279
Douglas' Meadow
Foam 128
Elegant Brodiaea 280
False Baby Stars 239
Farewell to Spring 240
Fiddleneck 160
Field Milkvetch 230
Flatpod 115
Goldfields 178
Hooker's Evening
Primrose 190
Miniature Lupine 273
Pale Agoseris 163
Prairie Star 137
Rabbit Brush 212
Red Clover 229

Rocky Mountain Bee
Plant 260
Rosin Weed 184
Showy Thistle 251
Shrubby Cinquefoil 191
Snakehead 180
Spreading Dogbane 234
Sweet Fennel 207
Teasel 252
Threadleaf Phacelia 236
Tough-leaved Iris 278
Vinegar Weed 277
Wild Blue Flax 287
Yellow Bee Plant 204
Yellow Bell 198
Yellow Mariposa Tulip 194

Butterflies and Moths
Acmon Blue 322, 323
Acraea Moth 303
Alfalfa Looper 310
American Painted Lady 337
Artichoke Plume Moth 315
Buckeye 345
Cabbage White 307
Common Blue 329
Common Checkered
Skipper 311
Common Sulphur 296
Eastern Tailed Blue 328
Funereal Duskywing 316
Gray Hairstreak 319
Great Gray Copper 318
Monarch 335
Mylitta Crescentspot 341
Orange Sulphur 295
Ornate Tiger Moth 302
Painted Lady 338
Pearly Crescentspot 340
Pipevine Swallowtail 320
Silvery Blue 326
Small Checkered
Skipper 313
Sod Webworm Moth 305
Variegated Fritillary 342
West Coast Lady 339
Western Tailed Blue 325
Woolly Bear Caterpillar
Moth 301
Yellow Woolly Bear
Moth 304

Insects and Spiders
American Hover Fly 365

Brown Daddy-long-legs 388
Digger Bees 373
Digger Wasp 369
Early Tachinid Fly 372
Field Cricket 350
Golden Northern Bumble
Bee 374
Goldenrod Spider 393
Green Lacewings 358
Green Midges 359
Honey Bee 375
House Mosquito 362
Jumping Lynx Spider 394
Large Bee Flies 370, 371
Malaria-carrying
Mosquitoes 360
Metaphid Jumping
Spider 393
Nine-spotted Ladybug
Beetle 380
Orb Weavers 345
Paper Wasps 368
Rose, Pea, and Potato
Aphids 390
Three-lined Potato
Beetle 388
Toxomerus Hover Flies 366
Tumblebugs 379
Yellow-faced Bees 363

Trees
California Black Oak 438
Canyon Live Oak 420, 482
Coast Live Oak 425
Curlleaf Cercocarpus 414,
486
Smooth Sumac 448, 465
Valley Oak 440, 483

Birds
American Goldfinch 552
American Kestrel 496
Barn Owl 512
Barn Swallow 522
Bobolink 544
Brewer's Blackbird 549,
550
Cassin's Kingbird 516
Cliff Swallow 521
Common Nighthawk 515
Eastern Kingbird 518
Golden Eagle 494
Grasshopper Sparrow 537
Horned Lark 520

Killdeer 506
Lark Sparrow 534
Loggerhead Shrike 528
Mountain Bluebird 525
Mourning Dove 509
Red-tailed Hawk 491, 492
Red-winged Blackbird 545,
546
Roadrunner 511
Turkey Vulture 488
Vesper Sparrow 533

Mushrooms
Common Psathyrella 555
Fairy Ring Mushroom 554
Fried Chicken
Mushroom 559
Hemispheric Agrocybe 556
Japanese Umbrella Inky 553
Meadow Mushroom 560
Shaggy Mane 562
Smooth Lepiota 558
Tumbling Puffball 563
White Waxy Cap 557

Reptiles and Amphibians
Coachwhip 614
Common Garter Snake 592
Racer 618
Western Rattlesnake 605
Western Spadefoot 566

EASTERN GRASSLANDS

Eastern grasslands, which are sometimes referred to as successional grasslands, form a unique category. They are not, for the most part, "natural" grasslands; rather, to survive they must be maintained by human intervention. Left to their own devices, eastern grasslands revert to their original, forested state.

Origins of Eastern Grasslands

When the colonists arrived on the eastern seaboard, they found themselves surrounded by forest. Writers such as James Fenimore Cooper and Nathaniel Hawthorne have given the impression that these forests were dark, sinister, and impenetrable, but this is somewhat erroneous. Instead, the forests at this time were generally more open than those we are accustomed to, because the Indians had been burning the understory—both to make for easier traveling and perhaps to improve the habitat for their game, especially deer. There were also clearings where the Indians grew crops, as well as natural grasslands along the riverbanks and the shoreline. Nevertheless, the dominant vegetation of the region was forest.

The settlers set themselves to the arduous task of clearing the land for agriculture. This process reached its peak in the first half of the nineteenth century. It is difficult to imagine how different the landscape must have been then. The state of Connecticut, for instance, was seventy-five percent cleared, according to estimates; today seventy-five percent of the land supports forest.

The opening of the Erie Canal, the building of the railroads, and the settlement of the tallgrass prairie to the west had a profound effect on the eastern landscape. At the same time, the continuing waves of immigration to the United States, an increasing emphasis on industrialization, and the consequent growth of cities significantly enlarged the market for farm produce. Once the fertility of the midwestern soils was realized, and the Erie Canal and the new railways provided transport to the markets of the East, eastern farmers began to abandon their rocky fields. Thus began a trend of declining farm acreage in the East, which continues to this day.

Types of Grasslands and Range

Three types of grasslands now exist in the East: agricultural grasslands, old fields, and relict communities. Agricultural grasslands are areas that have been planted in grass and are preserved by mowing or grazing. A grassland that is cut periodically for hay is called a meadow; if it is grazed continually, it is a pasture. The second type, an old field, succeeds an agricultural field when grazing or cutting ceases; different species of grass take over. Ultimately, if undisturbed, an old field becomes a forest. Relict grasslands are mysterious outliers of the prairie—rare, isolated, natural grassland communities whose origin, survival, and dynamics still constitute a puzzle.

The various types differ somewhat in appearance. Meadows may remain green through most of the summer if cut; they consist of grasses that are one to two feet high. Pastures are short-cropped, a rich green, and frequently support a population of robust weeds. Old fields and relict grasslands are filled with coarse, yellow grasses and a wide assortment of shrubs and forbs.

For purposes of this discussion, "eastern" encompasses the area ranging from the Atlantic Coast westward about as far as the tallgrass prairie, including the Prairie Peninsula area. Southern Florida, whose tropical influences cause it to support different vegetation from the rest of the East Coast, is excluded.

Physical Features

Since the eastern grasslands—excluding relict communities—are a product of human activity rather than of underlying natural forces, a detailed description of the varied and complex geology of the eastern part of the United States is not really relevant to this discussion. What is important is the eastern grassland soils, which are quite different from those that exist in other grassland areas. The eastern soils are podzols, which form beneath vegetation on the forest floor, where organic matter accumulates. As this matter decays, organic acids are formed. These acids leach minerals from the upper layers of the soil; the soil, in consequence, turns an ashy-gray color. (The word podzol derives from the Russian words for "under" (*pod*) and "ash" (*zola*).) Podzols are infertile—both as a result of their acidity and because they lack important minerals.

True podzols are formed under cold, wet conditions; thus, in the East, these extremely poor soils are found only in northern New England and New York. Although the process of podzolization can also take place in warmer climates, the amount of leaching and acidity lessens from north to south. Thus the soils south of central New York are relatively fertile. The soil in New England is infamous for its rockiness, which is a result of its geologic history—one marked by extensive glacial activity. Glaciation left extensive deposits of glacial till, which is a mixture of sand, rocks, and gravel. In spite of the relative fertility of the New England soils, the presence of rocks tends to reduce the land's value for agriculture. New Englanders joke that the soil grows rocks; indeed the alternate freezing and thawing of the soil during the winter does cause rocks to move upward through the soil profile, and a whole new "crop" to appear every spring.

Throughout the East, areas of sand are interspersed among the dominant podzols. These sand plains are either the remains of wind-blown deposits from postglacial lake beds or the result of centuries of outwash from the uplands. No matter what its origin is, sandy soil drains faster than other types and thus produces a drier environment for plant growth. Relict grasslands are often found in sand plains.

The climate in the East is characterized by ample rainfall: between thirty-five and fifty-five inches annually, with most areas receiving an average of forty-five inches. Generally a peak period of precipitation occurs in the springtime, but with the occasional exception of late summer, the region does not generally experience prolonged periods of drought. Drought years may occur, but they are not as overtly devastating to the eastern grasslands as they can be in the prairie region.

Typical Plants in Meadows and Pastures

Meadows and pastures in an eastern landscape have such a natural appearance and evoke such nostalgic connotations that it may be difficult to accept the fact that they are completely artificial ecosystems, no more natural than a planted bed of perennial flowers. In fact that is basically what they are; the only difference is that they are cut and harvested every year. In order to create a meadow or a pasture, the land must be cleared of forest and the grasses planted—and if the land is to continue to support grassland, it will have to be reseeded several times during the owner's lifetime. Between seedings, a meadow or pasture must periodically be fertilized and spread with lime to compensate for the acid nature of the podzolic soils.

The grasses in agriculture grasslands are not native ones; they are species that were brought from northern Europe, where the climate is similar. Like cultivated crops or garden flowers, they have been the object of extensive experimentation on the part of plant breeders. New varieties, which have particular traits to suit particular situations, are constantly being introduced.

One of the most common forage grasses is Timothy, which is easily recognized by its long, cylindrical flower stalk. This is one meadow grass that might be indigenous, but its origins, although recent, cannot be confirmed. According to one account, it was native to the New World and was first found growing in New Hampshire. A man by the name of Timothy Hanson introduced it to commerce and gave it his name. It was then apparently sent almost immediately to Europe, where it was widely used. Subsequently it was sent back to America; thus it has often been attributed to Europe. Other sources say that it has grown in Europe since the Stone Age, but was only discovered and put to use in America. When horses were the principal means of transportation, this forage plant was an especially important cash crop.

Other grasses in an eastern meadow include Kentucky Bluegrass, which is also the most common lawn grass in the East (it does not come from Kentucky); Tall Fescue; Orchard Grass; Smooth Brome, which is planted for hay on the northern Great Plains as well; and Redtop. Most of these are also used by highway departments for roadside planting; thus, since they spread easily, they may be seen almost anywhere in the East.

Few flowers appear in a meadow early in the spring, but from late spring through fall, many wild flowers—both alien and native—grow interspersed with the grasses. These include hawkweeds, milkweeds, Oxeye Daisy, lupines, vetches, and goldenrods.

On an intensively used meadow, the grasses are usually planted along with a legume, either a clover or Alfalfa. This

practice has been in effect for centuries (the first documented
case occurred in 1613). The legumes enrich the soil by fixing
atmospheric nitrogen into a form that plants can use; they also
provide a high-protein forage when they are cut and dried.
The grasses in a pasture are similar to those in a meadow, but
the wildflower component in a pasture is likely to be different,
since most wild flowers get cropped. Especially on a worn-out
or overrun pasture, the non-grass plants are most likely to be
thorny shrubs, which the cows leave alone. Among these are
various barberries, hawthorns, and junipers, and a relentless
invader, the Multiflora Rose. The Multiflora Rose was brought
into this country by the U.S. Soil Conservation Service to
control erosion. Its white, cascading flowers are lovely, and its
tasty fruits provide food to many birds, but it has become a
curse to farmers because of its aggressive and tenacious growth
habits.
When eastern meadows and pastures are deserted, they begin
to undergo the process of succession, which is the changing of
species composition and dominance over time. Such
abandoned, or old, fields may initially be dominated by any of
a number of species—often clone-forming wild flowers such as
milkweeds or goldenrods, which spread by rhizomes and form
persistent patches. In the next stage, old fields are generally
characterized by grasses of the genus *Andropogon,* which also
cover much of the midwestern prairie.
An old field can also evolve from abandoned cropland—that
is, on bare soil. On such sites, "weeds"—annual grasses and
annual or perennial forbs—usually dominate for several years
before the perennial grasses become established. The more
common of these "weeds" are Horseweed, pigweeds,
ragweeds, Camphorweed, Witch Grass, crabgrasses, and
Yellow Aster, to name but a few. For various reasons, in spite
of abundant seed production, these plants do not last a long
time; eventually the perennial grasses become established.
The sight of these coarse, yellow grasses is a familiar one to
many. In the Northeast, Little Bluestem, the dominant grass
of the mixed prairie, is prominent; in the Southeast, the most
common species is Broom Sedge, an *Andropogon* that is
inaccurately named, as it is not a sedge. Superficially the two
species look quite similar, but the flowers are slightly
different, and Broom Sedge is leafier and a paler yellow.
Especially in wet areas or on the coastal plains, a variety of
Broom Sedge (considered by some to be a separate species
called *Andropogon glomeratus*) may grow masses of leafy tufts at
the top of the stem; thus this subspecies is easily recognized.
Unlike the other *Andropogons,* Broom Sedge has a short, weak
root system and does not provide good forage. It generally
grows in poor soils. Little Bluestem, on the other hand, occurs
on good rangeland and provides good forage. Even so, either it
was not prevalent enough, seed was too difficult to collect, or
the colonists were simply too set in their ways to try it, for
they complained about the native grasses and imported seeds
of their own English grasses almost immediately upon
arriving. As late as 1859, when the tallgrass prairie was

actively being settled and the value of the native grasses was becoming known, the author of *American Weeds and Useful Plants,* a widely used farming manual, wrote of Little Bluestem: "This, and the other native species, are remarkably worthless grasses and apt to abound in poor old neglected fields. Where they prevail, no further evidence is required to demonstrate the unprofitable condition of the land, or the miserable management of the occupant."

The grasses are inevitably replaced by trees. The invading tree species also vary, but there is nonetheless a predictable zonation of old field invaders from north to south. In northern Maine, the invader is White Spruce; in northern New England, it is White Pine; in southern New England and the Middle Atlantic states, Redcedar; in Virginia and the higher elevations of the Carolinas, Virginia Pine; and in the rest of the Carolinas and Georgia, Loblolly Pine. Other invaders include Gray Birch, Black Cherry, and Sweetgum, and many additional species will invade if a seed source happens to be nearby.

The length of time necessary for a tree invasion to take place varies. In the Southeast, where succession takes place faster than in the North, pines begin appearing within three to five years after a grass stand takes root. However, if a seed source does not exist nearby, a Broom Sedge community can last indefinitely. In the North, trees also appear within a few years, but decades will pass before a full cover is established. As the conifers grow, the grasses die because of shade and root competition, and the conifer stand is eventually established. Within one hundred years or so, it is the conifers' turn to succumb—except in the far North—for the conifers cannot germinate in deep shade. Hardwoods can, however, and species of oaks, maples, and beeches grow slowly underneath the conifers, awaiting their chance. When the conifers die or are cut, the hardwoods take over. Once a hardwood forest is established, it tends to maintain itself unless struck by catastrophic disturbances, such as fire, a wind storm, or insect infestation.

Relict Grasslands

Scattered here and there in small areas around the East, isolated grassland formations seem to have resisted this pattern. Insignificant though these might be in terms of size, they are interesting to botanists because they harbor rare species, and to ecologists as violations of the rule; the fact that these grasslands occur where they should not invites a closer look at the causes of plant distribution. As thoroughly examined as they are, these grasslands are sometimes the subject of controversy out of proportion to their size; indeed ecologists cannot even agree whether they are grasslands, shrublands, or something else. For lack of a better term, these areas are here referred to as relict grasslands, the word "relict" alluding to the theory that these grasslands are a hangover from the warm, dry period following the retreat of the glaciers.

Some of the relict grasslands occur on serpentine barrens. They are scattered throughout the valley and ridge province of southeastern Pennsylvania and northern Maryland, where they are found on outcrops of serpentine, a rock that is high in magnesium. These barrens are generally never farmed and have a savannalike vegetation—open glades of Redcedar interspersed with grasses and various herbaceous plants. There seem to be many causes for the unusual flora of these barrens, all of them probably intertwined: thin soil, subsequent lack of water, high concentrations of magnesium, and low concentrations of calcium.

Similar to these are the shale barrens occurring from south-central Pennsylvania to southwestern Virginia and adjacent West Virginia, and the limestone barrens of western Maryland, Virginia, and Tennessee. These support not only stands of old field species such as Little Bluestem and Broom Sedge, but also prairie grasses such as Side-oats Grama, a plant that is almost never found in the East. The grasslands occurring on these sites seem to be fairly easily explained again by the thin, dry soil, as well as by the usually southern exposure of the slopes on which they occur; however, some barrens in Tennessee and Pennsylvania are found on wet soils with a shallow hardpan layer, which limits the depth to which roots can penetrate.

Some relict grasslands are found on sandy soil; these are even more of a mystery. The islands Martha's Vineyard and Nantucket in Massachusetts harbor some of them, as does the central part of Florida. The Massachusetts grasslands are dominated by *Andropogon* and False Wild Indigo; the Florida prairies, by Wiregrass, a species known for its adaptation to fire. Wiregrass comes back well after a fire, and even apparently contains flammable chemicals, which make it an especially good fuel.

The sandy soil would seem enough of an explanation for these grasslands, were it not for the fact that, throughout the eastern states, vast acreages of sandy soils that are similar to those upon which these grasslands occur are covered with pine or oak forests. Cape Cod, Long Island, the New Jersey Pine Barrens, and the sand plains of the Southeast are good examples. Fire is often pointed to as a factor responsible for the persistence of the sandy relict grasslands, but the pine or oak sand plain forests are equally well adapted to—and in fact dependent upon—fire, so repeated fires are not a satisfactory explanation.

West-central Pennsylvania has some even more mysterious grasslands, which some observers claim are nothing but old corn fields, but others consider to be extreme eastern outliers of the Prairie Peninsula. One person suggested that these are former passenger pigeon roosts, which were rendered infertile by the droppings of thousands of birds. Some low, grassy summits, or balds, in the Great Smoky Mountains are dominated by Mountain Oat Grass. Well below the tree line, these balds have so far stumped ecologists, who have suggested without conclusiveness every possible cause for the lack of trees: wind, fire, ice injury, grazing, postglacial climate, and Indian land-use practices.

Another grassland that defies explanation is the Hempstead Plain on Long Island in New York. Originally fifty square miles in extent but now reduced by dense suburban development to twenty acres, the Hempstead Plain is underlain by soil that is slightly more fertile and organically rich than that in the surrounding areas, which is basically sand. It now supports mainly Broom Sedge, but before disturbance and development, it contained over one hundred species of flowers, trees, and shrubs, including huge populations of Birdfoot Violet, a prairie species that gave the Plains "a celestial hue" as late as 1949.

Wildlife in Meadows, Pastures and Fields

Since extensive grasslands are a relatively recent feature on the eastern landscape, many of the "true" grassland animals found on the prairie do not occur in the eastern grasslands. Nor are their adaptations evident in the animals that live here. However, many animals—at all trophic levels—have adapted to take advantage of the variety provided by the ever-changing meadows and old fields.

An important factor in eastern grasslands is the edge effect, which is the improvement in habitat brought about by the juxtaposition of two ecosystems, such as a field and a forest. Many studies have scientifically documented this observation, which hunters and birdwatchers have already made. The edge between a forest and a field will contain not only more individuals, but also more species, than either the forest or the field by themselves.

This is because a number of animals find things they need from both habitats. Birds can find seeds or insects to eat in the field, and nesting sites in the forest. Skunks and foxes venture out into the fields to hunt mice and Meadow Voles or to feast on the late-summer crops of blackberries that take over a late-stage field, then return to the forest for shelter and to grub under dead logs for insects. Cottontail rabbits eat grass in the open fields all night, when they are less visible to predators, and then retire to the woods, where they remain concealed during the day. The White-tailed Deer enjoys green grass, fresh goldenrod shoots, and sometimes garden produce during the summer; in winter, when these plants are covered by snow, it resorts to the twigs and evergreen leaves of the nearby woody species for nourishment.

Similarly, an old field just going over to shrubs and small trees provides a better habitat for many animals than an unbroken stand of grass, largely for the same reasons. A study that compared Field Sparrow populations in a field over a twenty-year span found a large increase over the period in the number of birds inhabiting the field, correlating with a proportionate increase in the number of Redcedar trees. The birds born in Redcedar nests were far more likely to fledge successfully than those born in ground nests, doubtless because their location provided protection from predators. Over the years, when

rabbit hunting has been popular and landowners have sought
to improve the habitat for cottontails, one of the most
frequent recommendations has been to plant thorny shrubs.
The creator of the fictional character Br'er Rabbit knew what
he was talking about when he had Br'er Rabbit conniving to
get himself thrown into the brier patch, a sure place of safety
for him. An old field that is just beginning to go over to trees
and shrubs provides not only protected sites, but is also likely
to have blackberries, cherries, Russian olives, and other fruits
that are attractive to wildlife. A meadow or an old field by
itself might not be a very prolific habitat; however, a field
next to a forest (which is usually the case) or a field in the
middle stages of succession (as every field inevitably is) can be
a prolific habitat.

The clearing of the eastern forests created new habitats, and
many animals that we now take for granted throughout the
Northeast extended their original ranges to take advantage of
these new habitats. The Red Fox, considered to be a hybrid of
the native fox and introduced species, expanded south from
Canada and its centers of introduction, while the White-tailed
Deer apparently moved north with the clearing of the land.
The Thirteen-lined Ground Squirrel spread eastward from the
shortgrass prairie to Ohio, where it is at home in old fields,
golf courses, and cemeteries. Even the Coyote, a denizen of the
open plains, moved east, where it is most successful in areas
supporting a mixture of woods and old fields.

Many prairie birds moved east as the land was cleared—
among them, the Horned Lark, the Brown-headed Cowbird,
the Cliff Swallow, the Dickcissel, and the Loggerhead Shrike.
Other grassland birds, such as the Eastern Meadowlark, the
Savannah Sparrow, the Upland Sandpiper, and the
Grasshopper Sparrow, probably nested originally in grassy
sand dunes or on salt marshes and then expanded their habitat
into these new fields. Now that open grasslands in the East are
decreasing in total area as they are either developed or replaced
by forest, many of these birds are becoming less common.
Others, however, have adapted to even newer grassland
habitats: The Miami, Florida, airport, for example, supports a
population of Burrowing Owls thousands of miles from any
other members of the species, and small, grass-strip airports
are visited by experienced birdwatchers looking for
Grasshopper Sparrows, Upland Sandpipers, Lapland
Longspurs, pipits, and Snow Buntings, all birds
of the prairie.

Among the mammals, only a few true grassland species—the
Prairie Deer Mouse, the Meadow Vole, and the Eastern Mole
—are found in the eastern grasslands. The food sources
available to these three grassland burrowers have been nicely
divided: The diet of the Deer Mouse consists mainly of seeds
and nuts, as well as insects; the Meadow Vole eats green plant
material; and the Eastern Mole eats primarily earthworms. The
denser the grass cover, the more likely one is to find mice and
voles, which build underground nests and then create little
runways in the grass.

Another grassland burrower is the Woodchuck, which is actually a kind of squirrel and is related to the prairie dog. Its name comes from an Indian word and does not refer to its habitat. The Woodchuck has a diet similar to that of the prairie dog—principally green leaves. It is not a social animal; but as is the case with the prairie dogs' burrows, the Woodchuck's burrows are freely used by others, including skunks, snakes, rabbits, Raccoons, Virginia Opossums, foxes, and mice. Although, like the prairie burrowers, Woodchucks are considered a terrible nuisance by farmers, they do improve the soil with their constant tilling activity.

Insects are legion in the eastern grasslands. In the early part of this century, a writer who studied pastures and meadows in upstate New York counted 6843 insects on a one-hundred-square-foot plot over the course of one summer. He then calculated that two species of leafhoppers alone consumed more plant material per season than did the cows, which were presumably grazing the pasture to capacity. This finding is consistent with measurements taken on the western range, where it is estimated that grasshoppers eat as much grass as do cattle. In the eastern meadows as well as on the prairies, it appears that the large animals—birds included—barely make a dent in the supply of green plants available for consumption. The honor of being the most active consumers goes to the insects and the soil microorganisms.

The eastern grasslands support an assortment of wildflowers and are thus good places to find butterflies, which also need warmth and sunlight. Snakes inhabit this habitat too—most often the Common Garter Snake, but also the Northern Brown, Milk, King, and Rat snakes.

Future of Eastern Grasslands

Eastern grasslands constitute an ever-changing, diverse habitat. Even though few of them are natural, their temporary existence has had wide-ranging effects on animal distribution, and has changed the face of the landscape. As these pastures and meadows disappear to the bulldozer and the forest, there is growing concern about their future and an interest in preserving them—not only as inherent natural features, but also simply because they are satisfying to look at. They can be maintained—an old field by burning, a meadow by mowing, and a pasture by grazing—but clearly only if the intent is there. As less and less land is farmed in the eastern states, this job becomes more difficult. One can only hope that the combined efforts of conservationists, governments, and landowners will reverse this tide.

EASTERN GRASSLANDS: PLANTS AND ANIMALS

Mammals
Deer Mouse 62
Eastern Chipmunk 90
Eastern Cottontail 48
Eastern Harvest Mouse 65
Eastern Spotted Skunk 50
Fox Squirrel 80
Hispid Cotton Rat 60
House Mouse 61
Least Shrew 76
Least Weasel 54
Meadow Jumping Mouse 67
Oldfield Mouse 71
Red Fox 41, 42, 44, 45
Southern Bog Lemming 55
Striped Skunk 49
White-tailed Deer 33
Woodchuck 79

Grasses and Shrubs
Big Bluestem 101
Blue Grama 108
Broomsedge 98
Foxtail Barley 107
Indian Grass 94
Kentucky Bluegrass 91
Little Bluestem 97
Orchard Grass 104
Redtop 93
Reed Canary Grass 102
Sweet Vernal Grass 96
Switch Grass 95
Timothy 106
Velvet Grass 92

Wildflowers
Bindweed 121
Birdsfoot Trefoil 199
Black-eyed Susan 176
Bladder Campion 140
Blue Salvia 271
Blue Vervain 274
Bluets 288
Boneset 150
Butterfly Weed 228
Calico Aster 135
Camphorweed 168
Canada Lily 224
Common Barberry 209
Common Mullein 219
Common St. Johnswort 202
Common Strawberry 126
Common Sunflower 175
Common Tansy 183

Common Winter Cress 206
Cow Vetch 266
Deptford Pink 244
Elecampane 166
English Daisy 131
English Plantain 143
Evening Lychnis 141
Evening Primrose 205
Fall Goldenrod 214
Great Lobelia 276
Hoary Cress 147
Horse Nettle 123
Indian Blanket 226
Indian Paintbrush 225
Ivy-leaved Morning
Glory 283
Jerusalem Artichoke 172
Lance-leaved Goldenrod 213
Marijauana 117
Meadowsweet 149
Moth Mullein 192
Mouse-ear Chickweed 138
Multiflora Rose 127
New England Aster 246
New York Ironweed 247
Nodding Thistle 255
Orange Hawkweek 227
Oxeye Daisy 132
Paniceled Aster 134
Pointed Blue-eyed
Grass 289
Queen Anne's Lace 145
Queen-of-the-Prairie 258
Ragged Fringed Orchid 120
Ragged Robin 245
Red Clover 229
Rough-fruited
Cinquefoil 186
Rough-stemmed
Goldenrod 215
Sheep Sorrel 221
Showy Evening
Primrose 235
Shrubby Cinquefoil 191
Smooth Aster 293
Spotted Joe-pye Weed 248
Spreading Dogbane 234
Steeplebush 263
Sweet Fennel 207
Sweet Goldenrod 216
Tall Goldenrod 214
Tall Ironweed 294
Teasel 252
White Clover 157

White Snakeroot 148
White Sweet Clover 151
Wild Bergamot 257
Wild Blue Phlox 290
Wild Lupine 269
Wild Madder 152
Yarrow 129
Yellow Hawkweed 164
Yellow Rattlebox 200
Yellow Sweet Clover 218

Butterflies and Moths
Acraea Moth 303
American Painted Lady 337
Artichoke Plume Moth 315
Beard-grass Skipper 317
Buckeye 345
Cabbage White 307
Common Checkered
Skipper 311
Common Sulphur 296
Eastern Black
Swallowtail 331
Eastern Tailed Blue 328
Gray Hairstreak 319
Greenish Blue 327
Indian Skipper 300
Little Metalmark 343
Meadow Fritillary 344
Milkweed Tiger Moth 306
Monarch 335
Orange-bordered Blue 324
Orange Sulphur 295
Painted Lady 338
Pearly Crescentspot 340
Pipevine Swallowtail 320
Prairie Ringlet 297
Red-spotted Purple 321,
330
Regal Fritillary 336
Silvery Blue 326
Sod Webworm Moth 305
Variegated Fritillary 342
Viceroy 334
Woolly Bear Caterpillar
Moth 301
Yellow Woolly Bear
Moth 304

Insects and Spiders
American Hover Fly 365
Brown Daddy-long-legs 388
Chinese Mantid 357
Digger Bees 373

Digger Wasp 369
Early Tachinid Fly 372
Eastern Wood Ticks 378
European Earwig 377
Field Cricket 350
Giant Hornet 367
Golden Northern Bumble
Bee 374
Goldenrod Spider 392, 396
Green June Beetle 387
Green Lacewings 358
Green Midges 359
Honey Bee 375
House Mosquito 362
Japanese Beetle 386
Jumping Lynx Spider 394
Large Bee Flies 370, 371
Locust Treehopper 349
Malaria-carrying
Mosquitoes 360
Meadow Spittlebug 389
Metaphid Jumping
Spider 393
Nebraska Conehead 355
Nine-spotted Ladybug
Beetle 380
Orb Weavers 395
Paper Wasps 368
Pennsylvania Firefly 383
Praying Mantis 356
Pyralis Firefly 384
Red-blue Checkered
Beetle 381
Robber Flies 361
Rose, Pea, and Potato
Aphids 390
Spur-throated
Grasshopper 352
Striped Blister Beetle 385
Tarnished Plant Bug 382
Three-lined Potato
Beetle 388
Toxomerus Hover Flies 366
Tumblebugs 379
Two-striped
Grasshopper 354
Yellow-faced Bees 363

Trees
American Plum 418, 455
Apple 422, 452
Balsam Poplar 431
Bigtooth Aspen 433
Biltmore Hawthorn 434, 454

Black Cherry 419, 458
Black Locust 444, 453, 484
Blackjack Oak 437
Common Chokecherry 421,
457, 472
Common Juniper 401, 475
Common Persimmon 412,
468, 470
Common Prickly-ash 450
Eastern Cottonwood 432
Eastern Redcedar 400
Eastern White Pine 405,
478
European Buckthorn 426
Fanleaf Hawthorn 435
Glossy Buckthorn 409, 474
Gray Birch 428
Loblolly Pine 404
Longleaf Pine 406
Mexican Plum 423
Oneflower Hawthorn 427
Paper Birch 429
Pin Cherry 417, 456, 473
Post Oak 441
Prairie Crab Apple 424,
451
Russian Olive 467
Sassafras 442, 466
Shining Sumac 449, 464
Shortleaf Pine 403, 479
Slash Pine 407
Smooth Sumac 448, 465
Southern Catalpa 410
Southern Crab Apple 415
Staghorn Sumac 447, 471
Sweetgum 436, 481
Virginia Pine 402

Birds
American Goldfinch 552
American Kestrel 496
Barn Owl 512
Barn Swallow 522
Bobolink 544
Bobwhite 503
Cattle Egret 487
Cliff Swallow 521
Common Nighthawk 515
Eastern Bluebird 524
Eastern Kingbird 518
Eastern Meadowlark 547
Field Sparrow 532
Grasshopper Sparrow 537
Ground Dove 510

Henslow's Sparrow 538
Horned Lark 520
Killdeer 506
Loggerhead Shrike 528
Mourning Dove 509
Northern Harrier 489
Red-tailed Hawk 491
Red-winged Blackbird 545,
546
Ring-necked Pheasant 498
Tree Sparrow 530
Turkey Vulture 488
Upland Sandpiper 507
Vesper Sparrow 533
Western Meadowlark 548

Mushrooms
Common Psathyrella 555
Fairy Ring Mushroom 554
Fried Chicken
Mushroom 559
Giant Puffball 564
Hemispheric Agrocybe 556
Japanese Umbrella Inky 553
Meadow Mushroom 560
Purple-gilled Laccaria 561
Shaggy Mane 562
Smooth Lepiota 558
Tumbling Puffball 563
White Waxy Cap 557

Reptiles and Amphibians
Coachwhip 614
Common Garter Snake 592
Corn Snake 603
Eastern Fence Lizard 589
Eastern Hognose Snake 606
Fox Snake 608
Milk Snake 611
Prairie Kingsnake 607
Prairie Skink 579
Racer 618
Slender Glass Lizard 581
Western Box Turtle 574
Woodhouse's Toad 569

1 Mixed grasses and thistle Manhattan, Kansas

Mixed Prairie

2 Switch Grass Ellsberry, Missouri

Tallgrass Prairie

3 Sandhill Bluestem Grass Fort Robinson State Park, Nebraska

Mixed Prairie

Mixed grasses and forbs in early spring   Flint Hills, Kansas

Tallgrass Prairie

Blazing Stars in mixed grasses   Belmont Prairie Preserve, Downers Grove, Illinois

Tallgrass Prairie

Aster with grasses   Near Chicago, Illinois

Tallgrass Prairie

7 Split rock in mixed blowing grass   Western North Dakota

Mixed Prairie

8 Wheatgrass   Roosevelt National Park, Medora, North Dakota

Mixed Prairie

9 Sand Reedgrass   Big Foot Pass area, Badlands National Park, South Dakota

Mixed Prairie

0 Little Bluestem and other grasses   Valentine National Wildlife Refuge, Nebraska

Mixed Prairie

1 Mixed forbs   Northeast of Fort Collins, Colorado

Shortgrass Prairie

2 Sunflower in Western Wheatgrass   Custer Battlefield National Monument, Montana

Shortgrass Prairie

13 Sagebrush association

Sangre de Cristo Mountains, northeastern New Mexico

Desert Grasslands

14 Mesquite grassland association

Near Santa Rita Mountains, southeastern Arizona

Desert Grasslands

15 Broom Snakeweed

Plains of Saint Augustine, southern New Mexico

Desert Grasslands

16 Sagebrush association

Hoyt Mountains, Oregon

Intermountain Grasslands

17 Foxtail Barley

Near Leadore, Idaho

Intermountain Grasslands

18 Mixed grasses

Oneida County, Idaho

Intermountain Grasslands

19 Hillside with annual grasses   Catalina Island, California

California Grasslands

20 Baby Blue Eyes   San Luis Obispo County, California

California Grasslands

21 Lupines and Tidy Tips in coastal meadow   San Francisco area, California

California Grasslands

2 Chicory meadow   Kent Pond area, near Killington, Vermont

Eastern Grasslands

3 Smooth Aster and Goldenrod meadow   Stony Creek, Connecticut

Eastern Grasslands

4 Hawkweed meadow   Gould City, Michigan's Upper Peninsula

Eastern Grasslands

25 Old field

Licking County, Ohio

Eastern Grasslands

26 Old field with Horseweed

New Hanover County, eastern North Carolina

Eastern Grasslands

27 Old field with Broom Sedge

Pender County, southeastern North Carolina

Eastern Grasslands

28 Dry prairie

Upper Kissimmee Prairie, Florida

Eastern Grasslands

29 Wet prairie

Kissimmee Prairie, Florida, north of Lake Okeechobee

Eastern Grasslands

30 Prairie grasses and flowers

Near Gainesville, Florida

Eastern Grasslands

HOW TO USE THE COLOR PLATES

The color plates on the following pages include nine major groups of animals and plants: mammals, grasses and shrubs, wildflowers, butterflies and moths, insects and spiders, trees, birds, mushrooms, and amphibians and reptiles.

Table of Contents
For easy reference, a table of contents precedes the color plates. The table is divided into two sections. On the left, we list each major group of animals or plants. On the right, the major groups are usually subdivided into smaller groups, and each small group is illustrated by a symbol. For example, the large group of trees is divided into small groups based on characteristics such as leaf shape, flower color, or fruit type. Similarly, the large group of amphibians and reptiles is divided into small groups made up of distinctive animals such as salamanders, turtles, or snakes.

Captions for the Color Plates
The black bar above each color plate contains the following information: the plate number, the common and scientific names of the animal or plant, its dimensions, and the page number of the full species description. To the left of each color plate, the habitats where you are likely to encounter the species are always indicated in blue type. Additionally, you will find either a fact helpful in field identification, such as the food that an insect eats (also in blue type), or a range map or drawing.

The chart on the facing page lists the dimensions given and the blue-type information, map, or drawing provided for each major group of animals or plants.

CAPTION INFORMATION

Dimensions	Blue Type/Art
Mammals Length of adult	Range map
Grasses and Shrubs Plant height	Specific habitat
Wildflowers Plant height and flower length or width	Drawing of plant or flower
Butterflies and Moths Wingspan of fully spread adult	Caterpillar's host plants
Insects and Spiders Length of adult, excluding antennae and appendages	Major food
Trees Leaf, leaflet, or needle length; flower width, length, or diameter; fruit length or diameter	Winter tree silhouette
Birds Length, usually of adult male, from tip of bill to tail	Range map showing breeding, winter, and/or permanent range
Mushrooms Approximate size of mature mushroom: height or width of stalked mushroom; width of round or unusually shaped mushroom	Specific habitat
Amphibians and Reptiles Maximum length of adult	Range map

Mammals

Deer and Other Hoofed Mammals
31–36

Coyote and Foxes
37–45

Rabbits
46–48

Skunks and Badger
49–51

Weasels
52–54

Mouselike Mammals
55–78

Squirrels and Their Relatives
79–90

Grasses and Shrubs

Grasses and Shrubs
91–114

Wildflowers

Green
115–120

White
121–159

Wildflowers (*continued*)

Yellow
160–219

Red or Orange
220–228

Pink
229–268

Blue or Purple
269–294

Butterflies and Moths

Green or Yellow
295–296

Orange
297–301

Boldly Patterned
302, 308–309, 320–321, 330–348

White
303–304, 306–309, 322–329

Blue or Gray
305, 312, 318–319, 322–329

Brown
310–311, 313–317

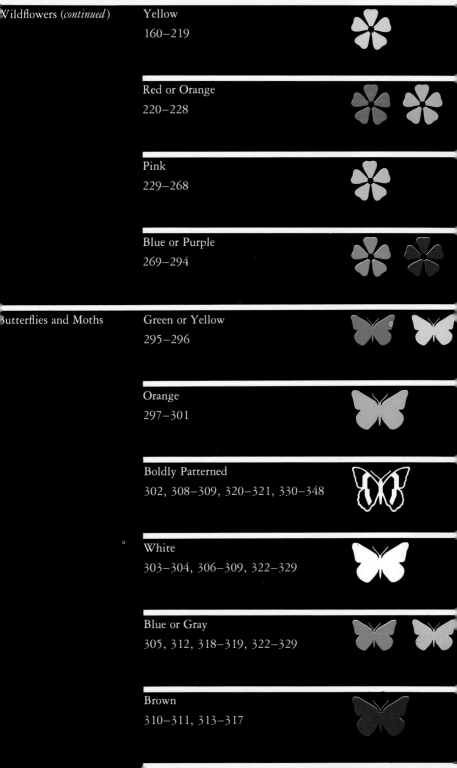

Insects and Spiders

Hopper, Crickets, and Grasshoppers
349–355

Mantids and Lacewing
356–358

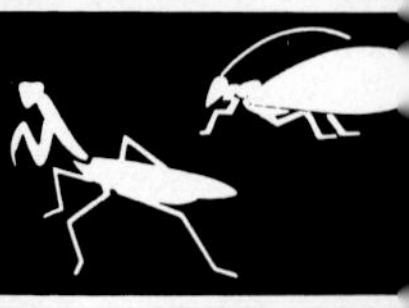

Flies
359–362, 365–366, 370–372

Beelike and Wasplike Insects
363–375

Ant and Earwig
376–377

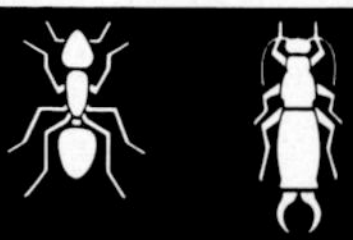

Tick
378

Beetlelike Insects
379–388

Spittle Bug and Aphid
389–390

Daddy-long-legs and Spiders
391–396

Trees

Needle-leaf and Scale-leaf Conifers
397–407

Yucca

408

Simple Leaves

409–442

Compound Leaves

443–450

Pink Flowers

451–452

White or Cream Flowers

453–459

Yellow or Green Flowers

460–468

Fleshy Fruit

469–470

Berrylike Fruit

471–477

Cones

478–480

Ball-like Fruit

481

Trees (*continued*)	Acorns 482–483	
	Pods 484–485	
	Tufted Fruit 486	
Birds	Egret 487	
	Hawklike Birds 488–496	
	Pheasants, Grouse, and Quails 497–504	
	Crane 505	
	Killdeer, Sandpiper, and Curlew 506–508	
	Doves 509–510	
	Roadrunner 511	

Birds (*continued*)

Owls
512–514

Nighthawk
515

Perching Birds
516–552

Mushrooms

Stalked Mushrooms
553–562

Puffballs
563–564

Amphibians and Reptiles

Frogs and Toads
565–573

Turtles
574–576

Lizards
577–582, 584–591

Salamander
583

Snakes
592–618

31 Bison
Bison bison
p. 323
Length: 10–12½′ males; 7–8′ females

Shortgrass and Mixed
prairies

32 Elk
Cervus elaphus
p. 323
Length: 6¾–9¾′

Shortgrass Prairie;
Intermountain and
California grasslands

33 White-tailed Deer
Odocoileus virginianus
p. 324
Length: 4½–6¾′

Tallgrass, Mixed and
Shortgrass prairies; Desert
and Eastern grasslands

34 Pronghorn　　　*Antilocapra americana*　Length: 49¼–57⅛″
　　　　　　　　　　　　p. 325

Mixed and Shortgrass
prairies; Intermountain
Grasslands

35 Mule Deer　　　*Odocoileus hemionus*　Length: 3¾–6½′
　　　　　　　　　　　　p. 326

Mixed and Shortgrass
prairies; Intermountain,
Desert, and California
grasslands

36 Collared Peccary　*Dicotyles tajacu*　Length: 34¼–40″
　　　　　　　　　　　　p. 327

Desert Grasslands

37 Coyote
Canis latrans
p. 327
Length: 41⅜–52"

Tallgrass, Mixed and
Shortgrass prairies;
Intermountain and Desert
grasslands

38 Coyote
Canis latrans
p. 327
Length: 41⅜–52"

Tallgrass, Mixed and
Shortgrass prairies;
Intermountain and Desert
grasslands

39 Kit Fox
Vulpes macrotis
p. 328
Length: 23–31"

Intermountain and Desert
grasslands

Swift Fox

Vulpes velox
p. 329

Length: 23⅜–31½″

Mixed and Shortgrass prairies

41 Red Fox

Vulpes vulpes
p. 329

Length: 35⅜–40⅜″

Tallgrass, Mixed and Shortgrass prairies; Intermountain and Eastern grasslands

42 Red Fox

Vulpes vulpes
p. 329

Length: 35⅜–40⅜″

Tallgrass, Mixed and Shortgrass prairies; Intermountain and Eastern grasslands

43 Gray Fox

*Urocyon
cinereoargenteus*
p. 330

Length: 31½–44¼″

Tallgrass and Mixed
prairies; Desert and Eastern
Grasslands

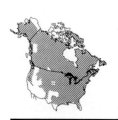

44 Red Fox

Vulpes vulpes
p. 329

Length: 35⅜–40⅜″
Cross phase

Tallgrass, Mixed and
Shortgrass prairies;
Intermountain and Eastern
grasslands

45 Red Fox

Vulpes vulpes
p. 329

Length: 35⅜–40⅜″
Silver phase

Tallgrass, Mixed and
Shortgrass prairies;
Intermountain and Eastern
grasslands

6 Black-tailed Jack Rabbit

Lepus californicus
p. 331

Length: 18¼–24¾"

Mixed and Shortgrass prairies; Intermountain, Desert, and California Grasslands

7 White-tailed Jack Rabbit

Lepus townsendii
p. 332

Length: 22¼–25¾"

Tallgrass, Mixed and Shortgrass prairies; Intermountain Grasslands

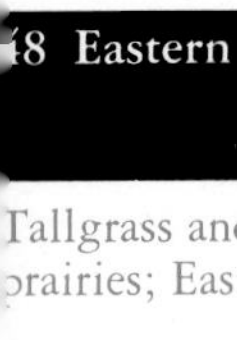

8 Eastern Cottontail

Sylvilagus floridanus
p. 332

Length: 14¾–18¼"

Tallgrass and Mixed prairies; Eastern Grasslands

| 49 Striped Skunk | *Mephitis mephitis*
p. 333 | Length: 20½–31½" |

All North American
prairies and grasslands

| 50 Eastern Spotted
Skunk | *Spilogale putorius*
p. 334 | Length: 13½–22¼" |

Tallgrass Prairie and
Eastern Grasslands

| 51 Badger | *Taxidea taxus*
p. 334 | Length: 20½–34¼" |

Tallgrass, Mixed and
Shortgrass prairies;
Intermountain, Desert and
California grasslands

2 Ermine

Mustela erminea
p. 335

Length: 7½–13½"

allgrass and Mixed
rairies

3 Long-tailed Weasel

Mustela frenata
p. 335

Length: 11–21¾"

allgrass, Mixed and
hortgrass prairies;
ntermountain, Desert and
California grasslands

4 Least Weasel

Mustela nivalis
p. 336

Length: 6¾–8⅛"

Tallgrass and Mixed
rairies; Eastern Grasslands

55 Southern Bog Lemming

Synaptomys cooperi
p. 337

Length: 4⅜–6⅛"

Eastern Grasslands

56 Meadow Vole

Microtus pennsylvanicus
p. 337

Length: 5½–7¾"

Tallgrass and Mixed prairies; Intermountain and Eastern grasslands

57 California Vole

Microtus californicus
p. 338

Length: 6¼–8⅜"

California Grasslands

8 Sagebrush Vole *Lagurus curtatus* Length: 4¼–5⅝"
p. 338

Shortgrass Prairie and Intermountain Grasslands

9 Prairie Vole *Microtus ochrogaster* Length: 5⅛–6¾"
p. 338

Tallgrass, Mixed and Shortgrass prairies

10 Hispid Cotton Rat *Sigmodon hispidus* Length: 8¼–14⅜"
p. 339

Eastern Grasslands

61 House Mouse

Mus musculus
p. 339

Length: 5⅛–7¾"

All North American
prairies and grasslands

62 Deer Mouse

Peromyscus maniculatus
p. 340

Length: 4¾–8¼"

Tallgrass and Mixed
prairies; Intermountain,
Desert, California, and
Eastern grasslands

63 Western Harvest Mouse

*Reithrodontomys
megalotis*
p. 340

Length: 4½–6¾"

Tallgrass, Mixed and
Shortgrass prairies;
Intermountain, California
and Desert grasslands

64 Fulvous Harvest Mouse

Reithrodontomys fulvescens
p. 340

Length: 5¼–7⅞"

Mixed and Shortgrass prairies; Desert Grasslands

65 Eastern Harvest Mouse

Reithrodontomys humulis
p. 341

Length: 4¼–5⅞"

Eastern Grasslands

66 Western Jumping Mouse

Zapus princeps
p. 341

Length: 8½–10¼"

Shortgrass Prairie and Intermountain Grasslands

67 Meadow Jumping Mouse *Zapus hudsonius* p. 342 Length: 7¼–10″

Tallgrass Prairie and
Eastern Grasslands

68 San Joaquin Pocket Mouse *Perognathus inornatus* p. 342 Length: 5–6⅜″

California Grasslands

69 Great Basin Pocket Mouse *Perognathus parvus* p. 342 Length: 5¾–7¾″

Intermountain Grasslands

Shortgrass Prairie; Intermountain and Desert grasslands

1 Oldfield Mouse   *Peromyscus polionotus*   Length: 4¾–6"
p. 343

Eastern Grasslands

72 Ord's Kangaroo Rat   *Dipodomys ordii*   Length: 8⅛–11⅛"
p. 344

Mixed and Shortgrass prairies; Intermountain and Desert grasslands

73 Heermann's Kangaroo Rat   *Dipodomys heermanni*   Length: 9¾–13⅜"
p. 345

California Grasslands

74 Northern Pygmy Mouse   *Baiomys taylori*   Length: 3⅜–4⅞"
p. 345

Mixed and Shortgrass prairies; Desert Grasslands

75 Plains Pocket Mouse   *Perognathus flavescens*   Length: 4⅜–5⅛"
p. 345

Tallgrass, Mixed and Shortgrass prairies; Desert Grasslands

76 Least Shrew *Cryptotis parva* Length: 2¾–3½"
p. 346

Tallgrass and Mixed
prairies; Eastern Grasslands

77 Eastern Mole *Scalopus aquaticus* Length: 3¼–8¾"
p. 346

Tallgrass and Mixed
prairies; Eastern Grasslands

78 Plains Pocket Gopher *Geomys bursarius* Length: 7⅜–14⅛"
p. 347

Tallgrass, Mixed and
Shortgrass prairies

79 Woodchuck

Marmota monax
p. 347

Length: 16½–32¼"

Tallgrass Prairie and
Eastern Grasslands

80 Fox Squirrel

Sciurus niger
p. 348

Length: 17⅞–27½"

Tallgrass, Mixed and
Shortgrass prairies; Eastern
Grasslands

81 Columbian Ground Squirrel

Spermophilus columbianus
p. 348

Length: 12⅞–16⅛"

Intermountain Grasslands

82 Uinta Ground Squirrel

Spermophilus armatus
p. 349

Length: 11–11⅞"

Intermountain Grasslands

83 Richardson's Ground Squirrel

Spermophilus richardsonii
p. 349

Length: 9¾–14"

Mixed and Shortgrass prairies; Intermountain Grasslands

84 Franklin's Ground Squirrel

Spermophilus franklinii
p. 350

Length: 15–15⅝"

Tallgrass and Mixed prairies

85 Belding's Ground Squirrel

Spermophilus beldingi
p. 350

Length: 10–11¾"

Intermountain Grasslands

86 White-tailed Prairie Dog

Cynomys leucurus
p. 351

Length: 13⅜–14⅜"

Intermountain and Desert grasslands

87 Black-tailed Prairie Dog

Cynomys ludovicianus
p. 351

Length: 14–16¼"

Mixed and Shortgrass prairies; Desert Grasslands

8 Spotted Ground Squirrel

Shortgrass Prairie and Desert Grasslands

Spermophilus spilosoma
p. 352

Length: 7¼–10"

9 Thirteen-lined Ground Squirrel

Tallgrass, Mixed and Shortgrass prairies

Spermophilus tridecemlineatus
p. 352

Length: 6¾–11¾"

0 Eastern Chipmunk

Tallgrass Prairie and Eastern Grasslands

Tamias striatus
p. 353

Length: 8½–11¾"

91 Kentucky Bluegrass

Poa pratensis
p. 355

Height: 1–3′

Tallgrass, Mixed, and
Shortgrass prairies;
Intermountain, California,
Desert, and Eastern
grasslands

Habitat
Moist or dry soil,
meadows, and fields

92 Velvet Grass

Holcus lanatus
p. 355

Height: 12–25″

California and Eastern
grasslands

Habitat
Fields, meadows,
roadsides, moist places

93 Redtop

Agrostis alba
p. 355

Height: 8–30″

Tallgrass, Mixed, and
Shortgrass prairies;
California and Eastern
grasslands

Habitat
Fields, roadsides, and low
places

04 Indian Grass

Sorghastrum nutans
p. 356

Height: 3–8'

Tallgrass and Mixed
prairies

Habitat
Prairies and dry fields

05 Switch Grass

Panicum virgatum
p. 356

Height: 3–6'

Tallgrass and Mixed
prairies; Eastern Grasslands

Habitat
Moist prairies, open
ground, roadsides, and
upper edges of salt marshes

06 Sweet Vernal Grass

*Anthoxanthum
odoratum*
p. 357

Height: 12–28"

California and Eastern
grasslands

Habitat
Fields, roadsides, and
waste places

97 Little Bluestem
Andropogon scoparius
p. 357
Height: 1½–4½'

Tallgrass, Mixed, and
Shortgrass prairies; Eastern
Grasslands

Habitat
Old fields, prairies, open
woods, and roadsides

98 Broomsedge
Andropogon virginicus
p. 358
Height: 20–40"

Eastern Grasslands

Habitat
Fields, roadsides, dry soils,
open woods

99 Needlegrass
Stipa spartea
p. 358
Height: 1¾–7'

Tallgrass and Mixed
prairies

Habitat
Prairies and sandy soil

00 Idaho Fescue *Festuca idahoensis* p. 359 Height: 11–40"

Intermountain and California grasslands

Habitat
Rocky slopes, open woods, sagebrush plains, and mountain meadows

01 Big Bluestem *Andropogon gerardi* p. 359 Height: 3½–7'

Tallgrass and Mixed Prairies; Eastern Grasslands

Habitat
Prairies, fields, roadsides, dry woods, and rocky shorelines

02 Reed Canary Grass *Phalaris arundinacea* p. 359 Height: 2–7'

Eastern Grasslands

Habitat
Low wet places, riverbanks, and marshes

103 Buffalo Grass

Buchloe dactyloides
p. 360

Height: 4–12"

Mixed and Shortgrass
prairies

Habitat
Dry plains

104 Orchard Grass

Dactylis glomerata
p. 360

Height: 1⅓–5'

Eastern Grasslands

Habitat
Meadows, roadsides, and
waste places

105 Prairie Cordgrass

Spartina pectinata
p. 361

Height: 1½–7'

Tallgrass and Mixed
prairies

Habitat
Wet prairies, shores,
roadsides, and salt marsh
edges

06 Timothy

Phleum pratense
p. 361

Height: 1½–3′

Tallgrass and Mixed
Prairies; Eastern Grasslands

Habitat
Fields, roadsides, and
clearings

07 Foxtail Barley

Hordeum jubatum
p. 362

Height: 1–2′

Tallgrass and Mixed
Prairies; Eastern Grasslands

Habitat
Waste places, roadsides,
meadows, and bare soil

08 Blue Grama

Bouteloua gracilis
p. 362

Height: 6–20″

Mixed and Shortgrass
Prairies

Habitat
Dry plains

109 Tobosa Grass

Hilaria mutica
p. 363

Height: 1–2′

Desert Grasslands

Habitat
Plains, low hills, and
valleys

110 Needle-and-Thread

Stipa comata
p. 363

Height: 1–2′

Mixed and Shortgrass
prairies

Habitat
Prairies, plains, and dry
hills

111 Purple Needlegrass

Stipa pulchra
p. 363

Height: 2–3½′

California Grasslands

Habitat
Native grasslands,
serpentine barrens, and
open places

12 Bluebunch Wheatgrass

Agropyron spicatum
p. 364

Height: 1⅔–3⅓′

Intermountain Grasslands

Habitat
Dry slopes, plains, and open woods

13 Common Sagebrush

Artemisia tridentata
p. 364

Height: 2–7′

Intermountain and Desert Grasslands

Habitat
High plains, dry mountain slopes, and dry woods

114 Creosote Bush

Larrea tridentata
p. 365

Height: to 7′

Desert Grasslands

Habitat
Low plains, sandy flats, and dry slopes

115 Flatpod
Idahoa scapigera
p. 367
Plant height: 1–5"
Flower length: about ⅛"

Intermountain and
California grasslands

116 Rattlesnake Master
Eryngium yuccifolium
p. 367
Plant height: 2–6'
Flower width: ¾"

Tallgrass Prairie

117 Marijuana
Cannabis sativa
p. 367
Plant height: 3–10'
Flower width: to ⅛"

Tallgrass and Mixed
prairies; Eastern Grasslands

18 Devil's Claw

Proboscidea altheaefolia
p. 368

Creeper
Flower length: 1–1½"

Desert and California
Grasslands

19 Green Pitaya

Echinocereus viridiflorus
p. 368

Plant height: 1–10"
Flower width: ¾–1"

Shortgrass Prairie and
Desert Grasslands

**120 Ragged Fringed
Orchid**

Habenaria lacera
p. 369

Plant height: 1–2'
Flower length: ½"

Tallgrass Prairie and
Eastern Grasslands

121 Bindweed

Convolvulus arvensis
p. 369

Plant height: 1–3′
Flower width: about 1″

Eastern Grasslands

122 Sego Lily

Calochortus nuttallii
p. 369

Plant height: 6–18″
Flower width: 1–2″

Mixed and Shortgrass
prairies; Intermountain
Grasslands

123 Horse Nettle

Solanum carolinense
p. 370

Plant height: 1–3′
Flower width: ¾–1¼″

Tallgrass, Mixed, and
Shortgrass prairies; Eastern
Grasslands

24 Elegant Camas   *Zigadenus elegans*   Plant height: 6–28"
p. 370   Flower width: about ¾"

ntermountain and Desert
grasslands

25 Velvety Nerisyrenia   *Nerisyrenia camporum*   Plant height: 8–24"
p. 371   Flower width: about ¾"

hortgrass Prairie and
Desert Grasslands

**126 Common
Strawberry**   *Fragaria virginiana*   Creeper
p. 371   Flower width: ¾"

Tallgrass and Mixed
prairies; Eastern Grasslands

| 127 Multiflora Rose | *Rosa multiflora*
p. 372 | Plant height: 6–16"
Flower width: ³⁄₄–1½" |

Eastern Grasslands

| 128 Douglas' Meadow Foam | *Limnanthes douglasii*
p. 372 | Plant height: 4–16"
Flower width: about ³⁄₄" |

California Grasslands

| 129 Yarrow | *Achillea millefolium*
p. 373 | Plant height: 1–3'
Flower width: about ¼" |

Eastern Grasslands

130 Blackfoot Daisy

Melampodium leucanthum
p. 373

Plant height: 6–20"
Flower width: about 1"

Shortgrass Prairie and Desert Grasslands

131 English Daisy

Bellis perennis
p. 373

Plant height: 2–8"
Flower width: about 1"

California and Eastern grasslands

132 Oxeye Daisy

Chrysanthemum leucanthemum
p. 374

Plant height: 1–3'
Flower width: 1–2"

Eastern Grasslands

133 Spreading Fleabane

Erigeron divergens
p. 374

Plant height: 4–28"
Flower width: about 1"

Shortgrass Prairie; Desert
and California grasslands

134 Panicled Aster

Aster simplex
p. 375

Plant height: 2–5'
Flower width: ³⁄₁–1"

Tallgrass and Mixed
prairies; Eastern Grasslands

135 Calico Aster

Aster lateriflorus
p. 375

Plant height: 1–5'
Flower width: less than ½"

Tallgrass Prairie and
Eastern Grasslands

| 136 Chickweed | *Stellaria media* p. 376 | Plant height: 3–8″ Flower width: ¼″ |

All North American grasslands

| 137 Prairie Star | *Lithophragma parviflorum* p. 376 | Plant height: to 20″ Flower width: ½–1″ |

Shortgrass Prairie; Intermountain and California grasslands

| 138 Mouse-ear Chickweed | *Cerastium vulgatum* p. 377 | Plant height: 6–12″ Flower width: ¼″ |

Tallgrass and Mixed prairies; Eastern Grasslands

139 Carolina Anemone   *Anemone caroliniana*   Plant height: 4–10″
    p. 377   Flower width: about 1½″

Tallgrass and Mixed
prairies

140 Bladder Campion   *Silene cucubalus*   Plant height: 8–30″
    p. 377   Flower width: 1″

Tallgrass and Mixed
prairies; Eastern Grasslands

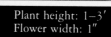

141 Evening Lychnis   *Lychnis alba*   Plant height: 1–3′
    p. 378   Flower width: 1″

Eastern Grasslands

42 White Prairie Clover
Petalostemon candidum
p. 378

Plant height: 1–2'
Flower length: less than ¼"

Tallgrass, Mixed, and
Shortgrass prairies;
Intermountain and Desert
grasslands

43 English Plantain
Plantago lanceolata
p. 379

Plant height: 6–20"
Flower length: about ⅛"

Eastern Grasslands

44 Death Camas
Zigadenus nuttallii
p. 379

Plant height: 1–2½'
Flower width: about ½"

Tallgrass, Mixed, and
Shortgrass prairies;
Intermountain and Desert
grasslands

| 145 Queen Anne's Lace | *Daucus carota*
p. 380 | Plant height: 1–3'
Flower width: 3–7" |

Eastern Grasslands

| 146 Flowering Spurge | *Euphorbia corollata*
p. 380 | Plant height: 10–36"
Flower width: ⅜" |

Tallgrass and Mixed
prairies

| 147 Hoary Cress | *Cardaria draba*
p. 380 | Plant height: 8–20"
Flower length: about ⅛" |

All North American
grasslands

| 48 White Snakeroot | *Eupatorium rugosum*
p. 381 | Plant height: 1–3′
Flower length: about ⅕″ |

Tallgrass Prairie and
Eastern Grasslands

| 49 Meadowsweet | *Spiraea latifolia*
p. 381 | Plant height: 2–5′
Flower width: about ¼″ |

Eastern Grasslands

| 50 Boneset | *Eupatorium perfoliatum*
p. 382 | Plant height: 2–4′
Flower length: to ¼″ |

Tallgrass and Mixed
Prairies; Eastern Grasslands

151 White Sweet Clover *Melilotus alba* p. 382

Plant height: 3–8'
Flower length: ¼"

Tallgrass, Mixed, and
Shortgrass prairies;
California and Eastern
grasslands

152 Wild Madder *Galium mollugo* p. 383

Plant height: 1–3'
Flower width: about ⅙"

Eastern Grasslands

153 Illinois Tick Trefoil *Desmodium illinoense* p. 383

Plant height: 2–5'
Flower length: to ½"

Tallgrass, Mixed, and
Shortgrass prairies

54 Prairie False Indigo *Baptisia leucantha* Plant height: 2–5′
p. 383 Flower length: to 1″

Tallgrass and Mixed
prairies

55 Prairie Larkspur *Delphinium virescens* Plant height: 1–3′
p. 384 Flower length: about 1″

Tallgrass, Mixed, and
Shortgrass prairies

156 Prairie Larkspur *Delphinium virescens* Plant height: 1–3′
p. 384 Flower length: about 1″

Tallgrass, Mixed, and
Shortgrass prairies; Desert
Grasslands

| **157 White Clover** | *Trifolium repens* | Creeper |
| | *p. 384* | Flower length: ¼–½″ |

Eastern Grasslands

| **158 Prairie Mimosa** | *Desmanthus illinoensis* | Plant height: 2–4′ |
| | *p. 385* | Flower width: cluster about ½″ |

Tallgrass, Mixed, and
Shortgrass prairies

| **159 Prairie Acacia** | *Acacia angustissima* | Plant height: 1–5′ |
| | *p. 385* | Flower width: minute; clusters ¾″ |

Tallgrass and Mixed
prairies

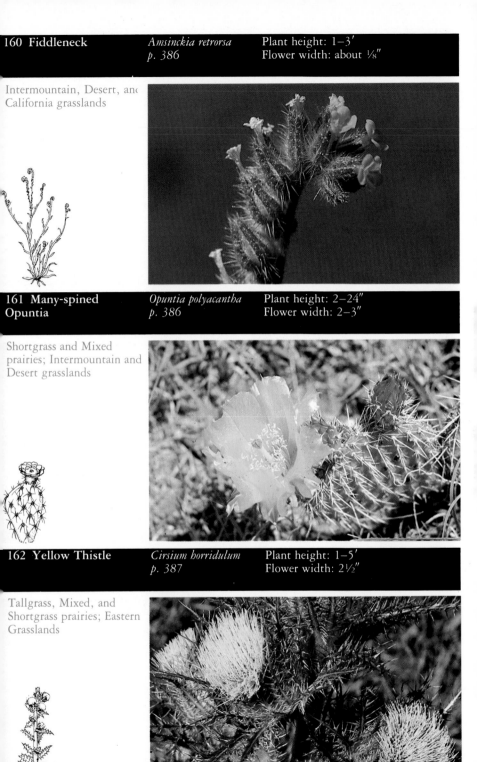

160 Fiddleneck

Amsinckia retrorsa
p. 386

Plant height: 1–3′
Flower width: about ⅛″

Intermountain, Desert, and
California grasslands

**161 Many-spined
Opuntia**

Opuntia polyacantha
p. 386

Plant height: 2–24″
Flower width: 2–3″

Shortgrass and Mixed
prairies; Intermountain and
Desert grasslands

162 Yellow Thistle

Cirsium horridulum
p. 387

Plant height: 1–5′
Flower width: 2½″

Tallgrass, Mixed, and
Shortgrass prairies; Eastern
Grasslands

| 163 Pale Agoseris | *Agoseris glauca*
p. 387 | Plant height: 4–28"
Flower width: ½–1¼" |

Mixed and Shortgrass
prairies; Intermountain,
Desert, and California
grasslands

| 164 Yellow Hawkweed | *Hieracium pratense*
p. 388 | Plant height: 1–3'
Flower width: ½" |

Eastern Grasslands

| 165 Yellow Goatsbeard | *Tragopogon dubius*
p. 388 | Plant height: 1–3'
Flower width: 1–2½" |

All North American
grasslands except Desert
Grasslands

66 Elecampane *Inula helenium* Plant height: 2–6′
　　　　　　　　　 p. 389 Flower width: 2–4″

Eastern Grasslands

167 Threadleaf *Senecio douglasii* Plant height: 1–3′
Groundsel *p. 389* Flower width: 1¼″

Intermountain and Desert
grasslands

168 Camphorweed *Heterotheca* Plant height: 1–3′
　　　　　　　　　　 subaxillaris Flower width: ½–¾″
　　　　　　　　　　 p. 389

Eastern Grasslands

| 169 Mule's Ears | *Wyethia amplexicaulis* p. 390 | Plant height: 12–32″ Flower width: 3–5″ |

Shortgrass Prairie and
Intermountain Grasslands

| 170 Hairy Golden Aster | *Chrysopsis camporum* p. 390 | Plant height: 1–2′ Flower width: 1″ or more |

Tallgrass, Mixed and
Shortgrass prairies

| 171 Compass Plant | *Silphium laciniatum* p. 391 | Plant height: 3–12′ Flower width: to 3″ |

Tallgrass and Mixed
prairies

| **172 Jerusalem Artichoke** | *Helianthus tuberosus*
 p. 391 | Plant height: 5–10′
 Flower width: to 3″ |

Tallgrass and Mixed
prairies; Eastern Grasslands

| **173 Giant Sunflower** | *Helianthus giganteus*
 p. 392 | Plant height: 3–12′
 Flower width: 1½–3″ |

Tallgrass and Mixed
prairies

| **174 Arrowleaf Balsam Root** | *Balsamorhiza sagittata*
 p. 392 | Plant height: 8–32″
 Flower width: 4–5″ |

Shortgrass Prairie;
Intermountain and Desert
grasslands

| 175 Common Sunflower | *Helianthus annuus* p. 392 | Plant height: 3–10′ Flower width: 3–6″ |

All North American
grasslands

| 176 Black-eyed Susan | *Rudbeckia hirta* p. 393 | Plant height: 1–3′ Flower width: 2–3″ |

Tallgrass and Mixed
prairies; Eastern Grasslands

| 177 Maximilian's Sunflower | *Helianthus maximiliani* p. 393 | Plant height: 3–10′ Flower width: 2–3″ |

177 Maximilian's
Sunflower

78 Goldfields

Lasthenia chrysostoma
p. 394

Plant height: 4–10″
Flower width: ¾–1″

Desert and California grasslands

79 Cowpen Daisy

Verbesina encelioides
p. 394

Plant height: 4–60″
Flower width: 1½–2″

Shortgrass Prairie; Desert and California grasslands

180 Snakehead

Malacothrix coulteri
p. 395

Plant height: 4–20″
Flower width: 1–1½″

Intermountain, Desert, and California grasslands

181 Common Madia	*Madia elegans* p. 395	Plant height: 1–4' Flower width: 1¼–2"

California Grasslands

182 Gumweed	*Grindelia squarrosa* p. 396	Plant height: 6–36" Flower width: about 1"

Mixed and Shortgrass prairies; Desert Grasslands

183 Common Tansy	*Tanacetum vulgare* p. 396	Plant height: 2–3' Flower width: ½"

Eastern Grasslands

California Grasslands

Shortgrass Prairie and
Desert Grasslands

**86 Rough-fruited
Cinquefoil** *Potentilla recta* Plant height: 1–2′
p. 397 Flower width: ¾″

186 Rough-fruited
Cinquefoil

187 Douglas' Meadow Foam

Limnanthes douglasii
p. 372

Plant height: 4–16"
Flower width: about ¾"

California Grasslands

188 Twinleaf

Cassia bauhinioides
p. 398

Plant height: 4–16"
Flower width: ½"

Desert Grasslands

189 Cream Cup

Platystemon californicus
p. 398

Plant height: 4–12"
Flower width: ½–1"

Intermountain, Desert, and California grasslands

90 Hooker's Evening Primrose

Oenothera hookeri
p. 399

Plant height: 2–3′
Flower width: 2–3″

Shortgrass Prairie; Desert and California grasslands

191 Shrubby Cinquefoil

Potentilla fruticosa
p. 399

Plant height: 6–36″
Flower width: about 1″

All North American grasslands

192 Moth Mullein

Verbascum blattaria
p. 400

Plant height: 2–4′
Flower width: 1″

Eastern Grasslands

| 193 Common Buttercup | *Ranunculus acris* p. 400 | Plant height: 2–3′ Flower width: 1″ |

Eastern Grasslands

| 194 Yellow Mariposa Tulip | *Calochortus luteus* p. 400 | Plant height: 8–24″ Flower width: 1–1½″ |

California Grasslands

| 195 Rain Lily | *Zephyranthes longifolia* p. 401 | Plant height: to 9″ Flower length: ¾–1″ |

Desert Grasslands

96 Buffalo Gourd

Cucurbita foetidissima
p. 401

Creeper
Flower width: 2–3"

Shortgrass Prairie and
California Grasslands

97 Devil's Claw

Proboscidea altheaefolia
p. 368

Creeper
Flower length: 1–1½"

Desert and California
Grasslands

98 Yellow Bell

Fritillaria pudica
p. 402

Plant height: 4–12"
Flower length: ½–1"

Shortgrass Prairie;
Intermountain and
California grasslands

199 Birdsfoot Trefoil	*Lotus corniculatus* *p. 402*	Plant height: 6–24" Flower length: ½"

Eastern Grasslands

200 Yellow Rattlebox	*Rhinanthus crista-galli* *p. 403*	Plant height: 4–32" Flower length: ½"

Eastern Grasslands

201 Butter-and-eggs	*Linaria vulgaris* *p. 403*	Plant height: 1–3' Flower length: about 1"

Eastern Grasslands

**02 Common
t. Johnswort**

Hypericum perforatum
p. 403

Plant height: 1–2½′
Flower width: ¾–1″

California and Eastern
grasslands

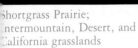

03 Broom Snakeweed

Gutierrezia sarothrae
p. 404

Plant height: 6–20″
Flower width: ¼″

Shortgrass Prairie;
Intermountain and Desert
grasslands

204 Yellow Bee Plant

Cleome lutea
p. 404

Plant height: 1½–5′
Flower length: about ¼″

Shortgrass Prairie;
Intermountain, Desert, and
California grasslands

205 Evening Primrose

Oenothera biennis
p. 405

Plant height: 2–5′
Flower width: 1–2″

Eastern Grasslands

206 Common Winter Cress

Barbarea vulgaris
p. 405

Plant height: 1–2′
Flower width: ⅓″

Eastern Grasslands

207 Sweet Fennel

Foeniculum vulgare
p. 406

Plant height: 3–7′
Flower width: 2–7″

Intermountain, California, and Eastern grasslands

208 Stiff Goldenrod
Solidago rigida
p. 406
Plant height: 1–5'
Flower length: about ⅓"

Tallgrass and Mixed
prairies

209 Common Barberry
Berberis vulgaris
p. 407
Plant height: 3–10'
Flower width: about ¼"

Eastern Grasslands

210 Plains Wallflower
Erysimum asperum
p. 407
Plant height: 6–14"
Flower width: ½–1"

Shortgrass Prairie and
Intermountain Grasslands

| 211 Broom Snakeweed | *Gutierrezia sarothrae* p. 404 | Plant height: 6–20″ Flower width: ¼″ |

Shortgrass Prairie; Intermountain and Desert grasslands

| 212 Rabbit Brush | *Chrysothamnus nauseosus* p. 407 | Plant height: up to 7′ Flower height: ¼–½″ |

Intermountain, Desert, and California grasslands

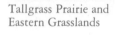

| 213 Lance-leaved Goldenrod | *Solidago graminifolia* p. 408 | Plant height: 2–4′ Flower length: about ⅓″ |

Tallgrass Prairie and Eastern Grasslands

14 Tall Goldenrod
Solidago altissima
p. 408
Plant height: 2–7′
Flower length: about ⅛″

Tallgrass and Mixed prairies; Eastern Grasslands

215 Rough-stemmed Goldenrod
Solidago rugosa
p. 409
Plant height: 1–6′
Flower length: about ⅛″

Tallgrass Prairie and Eastern Grasslands

216 Sweet Goldenrod
Solidago odora
p. 409
Plant height: 2–3′
Flower length: about ⅙″

Tallgrass and Mixed prairies; Eastern Grasslands

217 Desert Plume

Stanleya pinnata
p. 410

Plant height: 1½–5'
Flower length: ⅜–⅝"

Shortgrass Prairie;
Intermountain and
California grasslands

218 Yellow Sweet Clover

Melilotus officinalis
p. 410

Plant height: 2–5'
Flower length: ¼"

Eastern Grasslands

219 Common Mullein

Verbascum thapsus
p. 410

Plant height: 2–6'
Flower width: ¾–1"

Eastern Grasslands

220 Curly Dock

Rumex crispus
p. 411

Plant height: 2–4'
Flower length: about 1/6"

All North American
grasslands

221 Sheep Sorrel

Rumex acetosella
p. 411

Plant height: 6–12"
Flower length: about 1/12"

All North American
grasslands

222 Winged Dock

Rumex venosus
p. 412

Plant height: 6–20"
Flower length: 1/2–1 1/2"

Shortgrass Prairie;
Intermountain and
California grasslands

| 223 California Poppy | *Eschscholtzia californica* p. 412 | Plant height: 8–24″ Flower width: 1–2″ |

Desert and California grasslands

| 224 Canada Lily | *Lilium canadense* p. 413 | Plant height: 2–5′ Flower width: 2–3″ |

Eastern Grasslands

| 225 Indian Paintbrush | *Castilleja coccinea* p. 413 | Plant height: 1–2′ Flower length: about 1″ |

Tallgrass, Mixed, and Shortgrass prairies; Eastern Grasslands

226 Indian Blanket

Gaillardia pulchella
p. 414

Plant height: 8–16"
Flower width: 1–3"

Tallgrass, Mixed, and
Shortgrass prairies; Eastern
Grasslands

227 Orange Hawkweed

Hieracium
aurantiacum
p. 414

Plant height: 1–2'
Flower width: ¾"

Tallgrass Prairie and
Eastern Grasslands

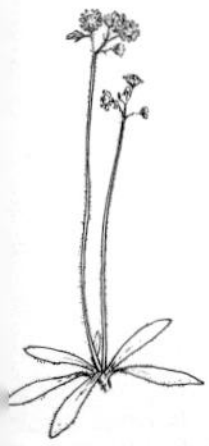

228 Butterfly Weed

Asclepias tuberosa
p. 415

Plant height: 1–2½'
Flower width: ⅜"

Tallgrass and Mixed
prairies; Eastern Grasslands

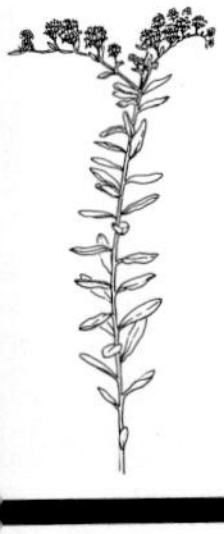

229 Red Clover

Trifolium pratense
p. 415

Plant height: 6–24″
Flower length: ½″

Eastern Grasslands

230 Field Milkvetch

Astragalus agrestis
p. 415

Plant height: 2–12″
Flower width: about ¾″

Shortgrass Prairie;
Intermountain, Desert, and
California grasslands

231 Feather Peabush

Dalea formosa
p. 416

Plant height: 1–3′
Flower width: about ½″

Shortgrass Prairie and
Desert Grasslands

| 232 **Vase Flower** | *Clematis hirsutissima* p. 416 | Plant height: 8–24″ Flower length: about 1″ |

Shortgrass Prairie;
Intermountain and Desert
Grasslands

| 233 **Vase Flower** | *Clematis hirsutissima* p. 416 | Plant height: 8–24″ Flower length: about 1″ |

Shortgrass Prairie;
Intermountain and Desert
Grasslands

| 234 **Spreading Dogbane** | *Apocynum androsaemifolium* p. 417 | Plant height: 1–4′ Flower width: ⅓″ |

All North American
grasslands except Desert
Grasslands

235 Showy Evening Primrose

Oenothera speciosa
p. 417

Plant height: 8–24"
Flower width: 3"

Tallgrass Prairie and
Eastern Grasslands

236 Threadleaf Phacelia

Phacelia linearis
p. 418

Plant height: 4–20"
Flower width: ⅜–¾"

Intermountain and
California grasslands

237 Corn Cockle

Agrostemma githago
p. 418

Plant height: 1–3'
Flower width: 2"

Eastern Grasslands

38 Prairie Rose *Rosa suffulta* Plant height: 2′
p. 419 Flower width: about 2″

Tallgrass and Mixed
Prairies

39 False Baby Stars *Linanthus androsaceus* Plant height: 2–12″
p. 419 Flower width: ½–¾″

California Grasslands

40 Farewell to Spring *Clarkia amoena* Plant height: 6–36″
p. 419 Flower width: ¾–1½″

California Grasslands

| 241 Common Milkweed | *Asclepias syriaca* p. 420 | Plant height: 2–6' Flower width: ½" |

Tallgrass and Mixed
prairies; Eastern Grasslands

| 242 Centaury | *Centaurium calycosum* p. 420 | Plant height: 5–24" Flower width: ⅜–½" |

Intermountain, Desert, and
California grasslands

| 243 Western Pink Vervain | *Verbena ambrosifolia* p. 421 | Plant height: 8–16" Flower width: ¼–½" |

Shortgrass Prairie and
Desert Grasslands

Eastern Grasslands

Eastern Grasslands

Tallgrass Prairie and
Eastern Grasslands

247 New York Ironweed

Vernonia noveboracensis
p. 423

Plant height: 3–6'
Flower width: about 1/3"

Tallgrass Prairie and
Eastern Grasslands

248 Spotted Joe-Pye Weed

Eupatorium maculatum
p. 423

Plant height: 2–6'
Flower width: 1/3"

Tallgrass and Mixed
prairies; Eastern Grasslands

249 Prairie Smoke

Geum triflorum
p. 423

Plant height: 6–16"
Flower length: to 3/4"

Tallgrass, Mixed, and
Shortgrass prairies;
Intermountain and Desert
grasslands

250 Coyote Thistle

Eryngium leavenworthii
p. 424

Plant height: 20–40"
Flower length: 1½"

Mixed and Shortgrass
Prairies

251 Showy Thistle

Cirsium pastoris
p. 424

Plant height: 2–4'
Flower length: 1½–2½"

Intermountain and
California grasslands

252 Teasel

Dipsacus sylvestris
p. 425

Plant height: 2–6'
Flower length: less than ½"

Eastern Grasslands

253 Purple Prairie Clover

Petalostemum purpureum
p. 425

Plant height: 1–3'
Flower length: about ⅙"

Tallgrass, Mixed, and Shortgrass prairies

254 Bull Thistle

Cirsium vulgare
p. 426

Plant height: 2–6'
Flower width: 1½–2"

Eastern Grasslands

255 Nodding Thistle

Carduus nutans
p. 426

Plant height: 2–9'
Flower width: 1½–2½"

Tallgrass, Mixed, and Shortgrass prairies; Eastern Grasslands

256 Canada Thistle *Cirsium arvense* Plant height: 1–5'
p. 427 Flower width: 1"

Eastern Grasslands

257 Wild Bergamot *Monarda fistulosa* Plant height: 2–4'
p. 427 Flower length: 1"

Eastern Grasslands

258 Queen-of-the-Prairie *Filipendula rubra* Plant height: 3–6'
p. 428 Flower width: ⅓–½"

Tallgrass Prairie and
Eastern Grasslands

| 259 Rough Blazing Star | *Liatris aspera*
p. 428 | Plant height: 16–48″
Flower width: about ¾″ |

Tallgrass and Mixed
prairies

| 260 Rocky Mountain
Bee Plant | *Cleome serrulata*
p. 428 | Plant height: ½–5′
Flower length: ½″ |

Shortgrass Prairie; Desert
and California grasslands

| 261 Prairie Blazing Star | *Liatris pycnostachya*
p. 429 | Plant height: 2–5′
Flower width: about ½″ |

Tallgrass and Mixed
prairies

262 Dense Blazing Star *Liatris spicata* Plant height: 1–6'
p. 429 Flower width: ¼"

Tallgrass Prairie

263 Steeplebush *Spiraea tomentosa* Plant height: 2–4'
p. 430 Flower width: less than ¼"

Eastern Grasslands

264 Common Owl's *Orthocarpus* Plant height: 4–16"
Clover *purpuracens* Flower length: 1–1¼"
p. 430

Desert and California
grasslands

265 Locoweed

Oxytropis splendens
p. 431

Plant height: 4–12"
Flower length: about ¾"

Tallgrass, Mixed, and
Shortgrass prairies;
Intermountain Grasslands

266 Cow Vetch

Vicia cracca
p. 431

Vine
Flower length: ½"

Eastern Grasslands

267 Crazyweed

Oxytropis lambertii
p. 432

Plant height: 8–12"
Flower length: about ¾"

Tallgrass, Mixed, and
Shortgrass prairies;
Intermountain Grasslands

68 Woolly Locoweed   *Astragalus mollissimus*   Plant height: 8–18″
                           p. 432   Flower length: 1″

Tallgrass, Mixed, and
Shortgrass prairies

269 Wild Lupine   *Lupinus perennis*   Plant height: 8–24″
                        p. 433   Flower length: up to ⅔″

Tallgrass Prairie and
Eastern Grasslands

270 Texas Bluebonnet   *Lupinus subcarnosus*   Plant height: 12–15″
                             p. 433   Flower length: ½″

Shortgrass Prairie

271 Blue Salvia	*Salvia azurea* *p. 434*	Plant height: 2–5' Flower length: ⅔–1"

Tallgrass and Mixed
prairies; Eastern Grasslands

272 Silverleaf Scurf Pea	*Psoralea argophylla* *p. 434*	Plant height: 1–2' Flower length: ⅓"

Tallgrass, Mixed, and
Shortgrass prairies

273 Miniature Lupine	*Lupinus bicolor* *p. 434*	Plant height: 4–16" Flower length: about ⅜"

California Grasslands

74 Blue Vervain

Verbena hastata
p. 435

Plant height: 2–6'
Flower width: ⅛"

Tallgrass and Mixed
Prairies; Eastern Grasslands

275 Leadplant

Amorpha canescens
p. 435

Plant height: 1–3'
Flower length: about ⅙"

Tallgrass and Mixed
Prairies

276 Great Lobelia

Lobelia siphilitica
p. 436

Plant height: 1–4'
Flower length: about 1"

Tallgrass Prairie and
Eastern Grasslands

| 277 Vinegar Weed | *Trichostema lanceolatum* p. 436 | Plant height: 2–5′ Flower length: about ½″ |

California Grasslands

| 278 Tough-leaved Iris | *Iris tenax* p. 437 | Plant height: to 16″ Flower width: 3–4″ |

California Grasslands

| 279 Douglas' Iris | *Iris douglasiana* p. 437 | Plant height: 6–32″ Flower width: 3–4″ |

California Grasslands

280 Elegant Brodiaea

Brodiaea elegans
p. 438

Plant height: 4–16"
Flower length: 1–1½"

California Grasslands

281 Pasqueflower

Anemone patens
p. 438

Plant height: 6–16"
Flower width: about 2½"

Tallgrass, Mixed, and
Shortgrass prairies

282 Prairie Gentian

Eustoma grandiflorum
p. 439

Plant height: 10–28"
Flower length: 1¼–1½"

Mixed and Shortgrass
prairies; Desert Grasslands

| 283 Ivy-leaved Morning Glory | *Ipomoea hederacea* p. 439 | Vine Flower width: about 1½" |

Tallgrass and Mixed prairies; Eastern Grasslands

| 284 Baby Blue Eyes | *Nemophila menziesii* p. 439 | Plant height: 4–12" Flower width: ½–1½" |

California Grasslands

| 285 Purple Groundcherry | *Physalis lobata* p. 440 | Creeper Flower width: about ¾" |

Shortgrass Prairie and Desert Grasslands

286 Bird-foot Violet

Viola pedata
p. 440

Plant height: 4–10"
Flower width: often 1½"

Tallgrass and Mixed
prairies; Eastern Grasslands

287 Wild Blue Flax

Linum perenne
p. 441

Plant height: 6–32"
Flower width: ¾–1½"

Mixed and Shortgrass
prairies; Intermountain and
California grasslands

288 Bluets

Houstonia caerulea
p. 441

Plant height: 3–6"
Flower width: about ½"

Eastern Grasslands

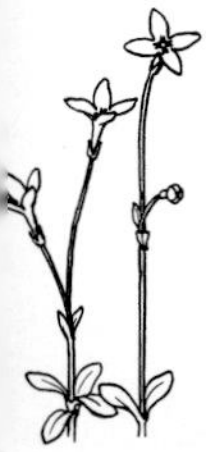

| 289 Pointed Blue-eyed Grass | *Sisyrinchium angustifolium* p. 442 | Plant height: 4–20″ Flower width: ½″ |

Tallgrass and Mixed prairies; Eastern Grasslands

| 290 Wild Blue Phlox | *Phlox divaricata* p. 442 | Plant height: 10–20″ Flower width: ¾–1½″ |

Tallgrass Prairie and Eastern Grasslands

| 291 Chicory | *Cichorium intybus* p. 443 | Plant height: 1–4′ Flower width: to 1½″ |

Eastern Grasslands

92 Tahoka Daisy

Machaeranthera tanacetifolia
p. 443

Plant height: 4–16"
Flower width: 1¼–2½"

Shortgrass Prairie and
Desert Grasslands

93 Smooth Aster

Aster laevis
p. 443

Plant height: 2–4'
Flower width: to 1"

Tallgrass Prairie and
Eastern Grasslands

94 Tall Ironweed

Vernonia altissima
p. 444

Plant height: 3–7'
Flower width: about ¼"

Tallgrass Prairie and
Eastern Grasslands

All North American
grasslands

Host Plants
A variety of herbaceous
legumes including alfalfa
(*Medicago sativa*) and white
clover (*Trifolium repens*)

All North American
grasslands

Host Plants
Various legumes, especially
clovers (*Trifolium*)

Tallgrass, Mixed, and
Shortgrass prairies;
Intermountain and Eastern
grasslands

Host Plants
Various grasses (Poaceae)

Tallgrass, Mixed, and
Shortgrass prairies; Desert
Grasslands

Host Plants
include senna (*Cassia*),
clovers (*Trifolium*), and
other legumes

Eastern Grasslands

Host Plants
Timothy (*Phleum pratense*)

Eastern Grasslands

Host Plants
Prairie grass (*Panicum*),
fescue (*Festuca*), and
crabgrass (*Digitaria*)

301 Woolly Bear Caterpillar Moth

Isia isabella
p. 449

Wingspan: 1⅝–2″

All North American grasslands

Host Plants
Low herbaceous plants of many kinds, mostly wild

302 Ornate Tiger Moth

Apantesis ornata
p. 449

Wingspan: 1⅛–1⅝″

Intermountain and California grasslands

Host Plants
A variety of herbaceous plants

303 Acraea Moth

Estigmene acraea
p. 450

Wingspan: 1⅞–2″

All North American grasslands

Host Plants
Herbaceous plants, including cord grasses (*Spartina*) in salt marshes

304 Yellow Woolly Bear Moth

Diacrisia virginica
p. 450

Wingspan: 1½–2"

All North American grasslands

Host Plants
A variety of herbaceous plants

305 Sod Webworm Moth

Crambus spp.
p. 450

Wingspan: ½–1½"

All North American grasslands

Host Plants
Stems, crowns, and roots of grasses (Poaceae)

306 Milkweed Tiger Moth

Euchaetias egle
p. 451

Wingspan: 1–1¾"

Tallgrass, Mixed, and Shortgrass prairies; Eastern Grasslands

Host Plants
Milkweed foliage (*Asclepias*)

307 Cabbage White

Artogeia rapae
p. 451

Wingspan: 1¼–1⅞"

All North American
grasslands

Host Plants
Many crucifers
(Brassicaceae), as well as
nasturtiums
(Tropaeolaceae) and other
plants

308 Becker's White

Pontia beckerii
p. 452

Wingspan: 1⅜–1⅞"

Shortgrass Prairie;
Intermountain and
California grasslands

Host Plants
Include bladderpod
(*Isomeris arborea*), golden
prince's plume (*Stanleya
pinnata*), black mustard
(*Brassica nigra*), and
probably other crucifers
(Brassicaceae)

309 Checkered White

Pontia protodice
p. 452

Wingspan: 1¼–1¾"

Tallgrass, Mixed, and
Shortgrass prairies

Host Plants
Include many crucifers
(Brassicaceae) and some
capers, such as bee plant
(*Cleome*)

Autographa californica   Wingspan: 1⅛–1⅝"
p. 453

Mixed and Shortgrass
Prairies; Intermountain,
Desert, and California
Grasslands

Host Plants
Alfalfa (*Medicago sativa*),
cereals, vegetables, garden
flowers, ornamental shrubs,
and orchard trees

11 Common Checkered Skipper   *Pyrgus communis*   Wingspan: ¾–1¼"
p. 453

All North American
grasslands

Host Plants
Available mallows
(Malvaceae)

312 Yucca Giant Skipper   *Megathymus yuccae*   Wingspan: 2–2⅞"
p. 454

Tallgrass, Mixed, and
Shortgrass prairies;
Intermountain and Eastern
grasslands

Host Plants
All U.S. yuccas except
Whipple's yucca (*Yucca whipplei*)

313 Small Checkered Skipper

Pyrgus scriptura
p. 454

Wingspan: ⅝–1"

Mixed Prairie;
Intermountain, Desert, and
California grasslands

Host Plants
Alkali mallow (*Sida hederacea*), globemallow (*Sphaeralcea coccinea*), and probably other mallows

314 Dakota Skipper

Hesperia decotae
p. 455

Wingspan: 1–1⅜"

Tallgrass and Mixed prairies

Host Plants
Include grama grass (*Bouteloua*), beard grass (*Andropogon*), Three-awn (*Aristida*), and other grasses (Poaceae)

315 Artichoke Plume Moth

Platyptilia carduidactyla
p. 455

Wingspan: ¾–1⅛"

All North American grasslands

Host Plants
Tender foliage and buds of artichoke (*Cynara scolymus*) and thistles (*Carduus; Cirsium*)

316 Funereal Duskywing

Erynnis funeralis
p. 456

Wingspan: 1⅛–1¾"

Shortgrass Prairie;
Intermountain and
California grasslands

Host Plants
Woody and herbaceous
legumes (Fabaceae)

317 Beard-grass Skipper

Atrytone arogos
p. 456

Wingspan: ⅞–1¼"

Tallgrass, Mixed, and
Shortgrass prairies; Eastern
Grasslands

Host Plants
Beard grass (*Andropogon
gerardi*); perhaps panic
grass (*Panicum*) in Georgia

318 Great Gray Copper

Gaeides xanthoides
p. 457

Wingspan: 1¼–1¾"

Shortgrass Prairie;
Intermountain and
California grasslands

Host Plants
Several docks (*Rumex
hymenosepalus,
R. conglomeratus, R. crispus,
R. obtusifolia*)

319 Gray Hairstreak

Strymon melinus
p. 457

Wingspan: 1–1¼″

All North American grasslands

Host Plants
Include corn (*Zea mays*), oak (*Quercus*), cotton (*Gossypium*), strawberry (*Fragaria*), and mint (*Lamiacea*), legumes (Fabaceae) and mallows (Malvaceae) preferred

320 Pipevine Swallowtail

Battus philenor
p. 458

Wingspan: 2¾–3⅜″

All North American grasslands

Host Plants
Chiefly pipevines, Dutchman's pipevine (*Aristolochia macrophylla*) or Virginia Snakeroot (*A. serpentaria*) in East, and 2 other species (*A. californica* and *A. longiflora*) in West

321 Red-spotted Purple

Basilarchia astyanax
p. 458

Wingspan: 3–3⅜″

Tallgrass, Mixed, and Shortgrass prairies; Eastern Grasslands

Host Plants
Include willows (*Salix*), poplars and aspens (*Populus*), cherries (*Prunus*), hawthorns (*Crataegus*), apples (*Malus*), and hornbeams (Carpinus)

22 Acmon Blue

Icaricia acmon
p. 459

Wingspan: ¾–1″

Tallgrass, Mixed, and Shortgrass prairies; Intermountain and California grasslands

Host Plants
Wild buckwheat (*Eriogonum*), locoweed (*Astragalus*), bird's-foot trefoil and deer weed (*Lotus*), lupine (*Lupinus*), other legumes, and knotweed (*Polygonum aviculare*)

323 Acmon Blue

Icaricia acmon
p. 459

Wingspan: ¾–1″

Tallgrass, Mixed, and Shortgrass prairies; Intermountain and California grasslands

Host Plants
Wild buckwheat (*Eriogonum*), locoweed (*Astragalus*), bird's-foot trefoil and deer weed (*Lotus*), lupine (*Lupinus*), other legumes, and knotweed (*Polygonum aviculare*)

324 Orange-bordered Blue

Lycaeides melissa
p. 460

Wingspan: ⅞–1¼″

Tallgrass, Mixed, and Shortgrass prairies; Intermountain, Desert, and Eastern grasslands

Host Plants
Vary geographically and altitudinally, and include lupine (*Lupinus*), alfalfa (*Medicago sativa*), crazyweed (*Oxytropis*), and wild licorice (*Glycyrrhiza*); lupine preferred eastward

325 Western Tailed Blue

Everes amyntula
p. 460

Wingspan: ⅞–1⅛″

Mixed and Shortgrass prairies; Intermountain, Desert, and California grasslands

Host Plants
Locoweed (*Astragalus*), peas (*Lathyrus*), and vetch (*Vicia*)

326 Silvery Blue

Glaucopsyche lygdamus
p. 461

Wingspan: 1–1¼″

All North American grasslands

Host Plants
Legume family (Fabaceae): deer weed (*Lotus scoparius*), lupine (*Lupinus*), wild pea (*Lathyrus*), vetch (*Vicia*), locoweed (*Astragalus*), and others

327 Greenish Blue

Plebejus saepiolus
p. 462

Wingspan: ⅞–1¼″

Tallgrass, Mixed, and Shortgrass prairies; Desert and Eastern grasslands

Host Plants
Clover flowers (*Trifolium monanthum, T. longipes, T. wormskioldii*), and probably others

28 Eastern Tailed Blue
Everes comyntas
p. 462
Wingspan: ³⁄₄–1″

Tallgrass, Mixed, and Shortgrass prairies; California and Eastern Grasslands

Host Plants
Many legumes, especially clover (*Trifolium*), slender bush clover (*Lespedeza*), beans (*Phaseolus*), tick trefoil (*Desmodium*), wild pea (*Lathyrus*), and others

29 Common Blue
Icaricia icarioides
p. 463
Wingspan: 1–1³⁄₈″

Mixed and Shortgrass prairies; Intermountain and California grasslands

Host Plants
Over 40 species or forms of *Lupinus* recorded

30 Red-spotted Purple
Basilarchia astyanax
p. 458
Wingspan: 3–3³⁄₈″

Tallgrass, Mixed, and Shortgrass prairies; Eastern Grasslands

Host Plants
Include willows (*Salix*), poplars and aspens (*Populus*), cherries (*Prunus*), hawthorns (*Crataegus*), apples (*Malus*), and hornbeams (*Carpinus*)

331 Eastern Black Swallowtail

Papilio polyxenes
p. 464

Wingspan: 2⅝–3½"

Tallgrass, Mixed, and Shortgrass prairies; Desert and Eastern grasslands

Host Plants
Members of the carrot family, including Queen Anne's Lace (*Daucus carota*), and some members of the citrus family (Rutaceae), including rue (*Ruta graveolens*) and Texas turpentine broom (*Thamnosoma texana*)

332 Tiger Swallowtail

Pterourus glaucus
p. 464

Wingspan: 3⅛–5½"

All North American grasslands

Host Plants
Mostly broadleaf trees and shrubs; favorites include willows and cottonwoods (Salicaceae), birches (Betulaceae), ashes (*Fraxinus*), many cherries (*Prunus*), and tulip-poplars (*Liriodendron tulipifera*)

333 Dark Zebra Swallowtail

Eurytides philolaus
p. 465

Wingspan: 2½–3½"

Shortgrass Prairie

Host Plants
Arctic sagebrush (*Artemisia arctica*) in Alaska

334 Viceroy

Basilarchia archippus
p. 465

Wingspan: 2⅝–3"

Tallgrass, Mixed, and Shortgrass prairies; Intermountain and Eastern grasslands

Host Plants
Willows (*Salix*) preferred, but also poplars and aspens (*Populus*), apples (*Malus*), and cherries and plums (*Prunus*)

335 Monarch

Danaus plexippus
p. 466

Wingspan: 3½–4"

All North American grasslands

Host Plants
Milkweeds (*Asclepias*) and dogbane (*Apocynum*)

336 Regal Fritillary

Speyeria idalia
p. 467

Wingspan: 2⅜–3⅜"

Tallgrass and Mixed prairies; Eastern Grasslands

Host Plants
Violets (*Viola*)

337 American Painted Lady

Vanessa virginiensis
p. 467

Wingspan: 1¾–2⅛″

All North American grasslands

Host Plants
Species of everlastings (*Gnaphalium, Antennaria, Anaphalis*) or other composites (Asteraceae)

338 Painted Lady

Vanessa cardui
p. 468

Wingspan: 2–2¼″

All North American grasslands

Host Plants
Thistle (*Cirsium*), but also a variety of other composites (Asteraceae) and mallows (Malvaceae)

339 West Coast Lady

Vanessa annabella
p. 469

Wingspan: 1¾–2″

Intermountain, Desert, and California grasslands

Host Plants
Mallows (Malvaceae), including cheeseweed (*Malva parviflora*), sidalceas (*Sidalcea*), hollyhocks (*Althaea*), and globemallows (*Sphaeralcea*); occasionally nettles (*Urtica*)

All North American
grasslands

Host Plants
Asters (*Aster*)

Intermountain, Desert, and
California grasslands

Host Plants
Thistles (*Cirsium*), mild
thistle (*Silybum marianum*),
and plumeless thistle
(*Carduus pycnocephalus*)

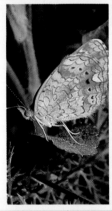

Desert, California, and
Eastern grasslands

Host Plants
include violets and pansies
(*Viola*), flax (*Linum*),
passionflower (*Passiflora*),
stonecrop (*Sedum
lanceolatum*), moonseed
(*Menispermum*), and
plantain (*Plantago*)

343 Little Metalmark

Calephelis virginiensis
p. 471

Wingspan: ⅝–¾″

Eastern Grasslands

Host Plants
Yellow thistle (*Cirsium horridulum*) in Texas

344 Meadow Fritillary

Clossiana bellona
p. 471

Wingspan: 1¼–1⅞″

Tallgrass, Mixed, and Shortgrass prairies; Eastern Grasslands

Host Plants
Violets (*Viola*)

345 Buckeye

Junonia coenia
p. 472

Wingspan: 2–2½″

Tallgrass, Mixed, and Shortgrass prairies; California and Eastern grasslands

Host Plants
Include plantain (Plantaginaceae), figwort (Schrophulariaceae), stonecrop (Crassulaceae), and vervain (Verbenaceae) families

346 Eyed Brown

Satyrodes eurydice
p. 473

Wingspan: 1⅝–2″

Tallgrass and Mixed prairies; Eastern Grasslands

Host Plants
Sedges (*Carex*)

347 Riding's Satyr

Neominois ridingsii
p. 473

Wingspan: 1½–1⅞″

Shortgrass prairie and Intermountain Grasslands

Host Plants
Probably grasses (Poaceae)

348 Large Wood Nymph

Cercyonis pegala
p. 474

Wingspan: 2–2⅞″

All North American grasslands

Host Plants
Various grasses (Poaceae)

349 Locust Treehopper

Thelia bimaculata
p. 476

Length: ⅜–½"

Eastern Grasslands

Food
Plant juices of locust and other leguminous trees and shrubs (Fabaceae)

350 Field Cricket

Gryllus pennsylvanicus
p. 476

Length: ⅜–1"

All North American grasslands

Food
Plant materials outdoors including seeds and seedlings of wild and crop plants, small fruits, and when available, dying and dead insects

351 Mormon Cricket

Anabrus simplex
p. 476

Length: 1–2⅜"

Mixed and Shortgrass prairies; Desert and Intermountain grasslands

Food
Lupine (*Lupinus*), sagebrush (*Artemisia*), and many plants including grains and vegetables

352 Spur-throated Grasshopper   *Melanoplus ponderosus*   Length: 1–1⅜″
p. 477

Tallgrass Prairie and
Eastern Grasslands

Food
Native grasses (Poaceae)

353 Green Valley Grasshopper   *Schistocerca shoshone*   Length: 1½–2¾″
p. 477

Shortgrass Prairie and
Desert Grasslands

Food
Grasses (Poaceae)

354 Two-striped Grasshopper   *Mermiria bivittata*   Length: 1⅛–2⅛″
p. 478

Tallgrass and Mixed
prairies; Eastern Grasslands

Food
Grasses (Poaceae)

355 Nebraska Cone-head *Neoconocephalus* Length: 1⅛–1¼" (males);
nebrascensis 1⅛–1⅜" (females)
p. 478

Tallgrass Prairie and
Eastern Grasslands

Food
Flowers and foliage of trees

356 Praying Mantis *Mantis religiosa* Length: 2–2½"
p. 478

Eastern Grasslands

Food
Diurnal insects including
caterpillars, flies (Diptera),
butterflies and some moths
(Lepidoptera), and bees
(Apoidea)

357 Chinese Mantid *Tenodera aridifolia* Length: 2½–3⅜"
p. 479

Eastern Grasslands

Food
Large caterpillars,
butterflies, flies, bees,
wasps, and day-flying
moths

Chrysopa spp.
p. 479

Length: ³⁄₈–⁵⁄₈″

All North American
grasslands

Food
Small insects, especially
aphids (Aphididae,
Eriosomatidae) and nymphs
of scale insects and their
kin (Margarodidae,
Diaspididae)

Tanytarsus spp.
p. 480

Length: ¹⁄₄–³⁄₈″

All North American
grasslands

Food
Wet organic matter,
mostly in silt at bottom of
quiet ponds, streams, or
marshes

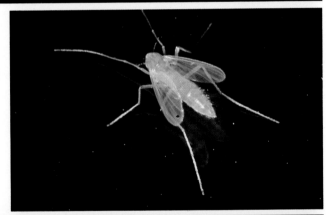

Anopheles spp.
p. 480

Length: ¹⁄₈″

All North American
grasslands

Food
Males: plant juices;
females: blood of warm-
blooded animals and
humans; larvae:
microscopic algae

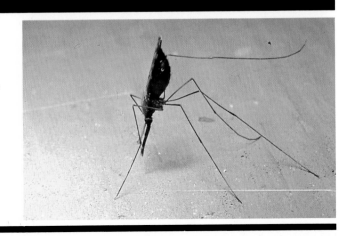

361 Robber Flies
Tolmerus spp.
p. 481
Length: ⅜–¾″

Tallgrass, Mixed, and Shortgrass prairies; Eastern Grasslands

Food
Body juices from many flying insects; insect larvae, especially of beetles (Coleoptera)

362 House Mosquito
Culex pipiens
p. 481
Length: ⅛–¼″

All North American grasslands

Food
Males: plant juices; females: blood from birds and mammals, including humans; larvae: microscopic algae

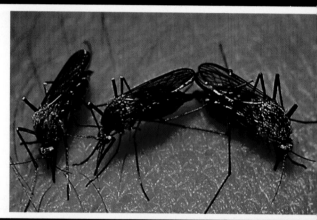

363 Yellow-faced Bees
Hylaeus spp.
p. 481
Length: ¼″

All North American grasslands

Food
Nectar and pollen

364 Yellow Jackets

Vespula spp.
p. 482

Length: ½–⅝″

All North American grasslands

Food
Nectar and insects

365 American Hover Fly

Metasyrphus americanus
p. 482

Length: ⅜″

All North American grasslands

Food
Nectar; aphids (Aphididae, Eriosomatidae), larvae of scale insects (Margarodidae, Diaspididae)

366 Toxomerus Hover Flies

Toxomerus spp.
p. 483

Length: ¼–½″

All North American grasslands

Food
Nectar; aphids (Aphididae, Eriosomatidae)

367 Giant Hornet
Vespa crabro germana
p. 483
Length: ¾–1⅛"

Eastern Grasslands

Food
Nectar and insects

368 Paper Wasps
Polistes spp.
p. 483
Length: ½–1"

All North American
grasslands

Food
Nectar; juices from crushed
and rotting fruits; insects

369 Digger Wasp
Scolia dubia
p. 484
Length: ½–¾"

All North American
grasslands

Food
Juices and larvae of Green
June Beetles (*Cotinus nitida*)

All North American
grasslands

Food
Nectar; larva parasitizes
nests of solitary bees
(Apoidea)

All North American
grasslands

Food
Nectar; larva parasitizes
nests of solitary bees
(Apoidea)

All North American
grasslands

Food
Nectar; larva an internal
parasite of moth or
butterfly (Lepidoptera)
caterpillar

373 Digger Bees

Anthophora spp.
p. 485

Length: ⅝"

All North American
grasslands

Food
Nectar and pollen

374 Golden Northern Bumble Bee

Bombus fervidus
p. 485

Length: ⅜–⅝" (male drones); ½–¾"
(workers); ¾–⅞" (queen)

All North American
grasslands

Food
Nectar and honey

375 Honey Bee

Apis mellifera
p. 486

Length: ⅝" (male drones); ¾" (queen);
⅜–⅝" (sterile female workers)

All North American
grasslands

Food
Nectar, honey, and royal
jelly

Desert Grasslands

Food
Seeds and grains

Eastern Grasslands

Food
Vegetables, orchard fruits,
garden flowers, garbage;
mites (Tetranychidae,
Hydrachnellae,
Trombidiidae); insect
larvae and pupae

Eastern Grasslands

Food
Larger animals and blood
of mammals, especially
deer (Cervidae); rodents
(Rodentia)

379 Tumblebugs

Canthon spp.
p. 488

Length: ⅜–¾″

All North American
grasslands

Food
Dung

380 Nine-spotted Ladybug Beetle

Coccinella novemnotata
p. 488

Length: ¼″

All North American
grasslands except Desert
Grasslands

Food
Aphids (Aphididae,
Eriosomatidae), small soft
insects, mites
(Tetranychidae,
Hydrachnellae,
Trombidiidae)

381 Red-blue Checkered Beetle

Trichodes nutalli
p. 489

Length: ⅜″

Tallgrass, Mixed, and
Shortgrass prairies; Eastern
Grasslands

Food
Thrips (Thripidae,
Aeolothripidae), other
small insects, pollen; larvae
of wasps and bees
(Hymenoptera)

382 Tarnished Plant Bug

Lygus lineolaris
p. 489

Length: ¼"

Eastern Grasslands

Food
Plant juices from foliage, soft stems, and fruits including strawberries (*Fragaria*), wild mustard (Brassicaceae), goldenrod (*Solidago*), aster (Asteraceae), and on vegetable, fruit, and alfalfa (*Medicago sativa*) crops

383 Pennsylvania Firefly

Photuris pennsylvanicus
p. 490

Length: ⅜–⅝"

Tallgrass, Mixed, and Shortgrass prairies; Eastern Grasslands

Food
Soft-bodied insects, snails and slugs (Gastropoda), mites (Tetranychidae, Hydrachnellae, Trombidiidae); also their own species

384 Pyralis Firefly

Photinus pyralis
p. 490

Length: ⅜–½"

Tallgrass, Mixed, and Shortgrass prairies; Eastern Grasslands

Food
Insect larvae; slugs and snails (Gastropoda)

385 Striped Blister Beetle

Epicauta vittata
p. 490

Length: ½–⅝″

Eastern Grasslands

Food
Crops and weeds;
grasshopper (Acrididae)
eggs deposited in soil

386 Japanese Beetle

Popilla japonica
p. 491

Length: ⅜–½″

Eastern Grasslands

Food
Leaf tissues and ripening
fruit of more than 200
plants including vines,
flowers, shrubs, and trees;
larva eats roots, especially
those of grasses (Poaceae),
vegetables, and nursery
plants

387 Green June Beetle

Cotinus nitida
p. 491

Length: ¾–⅞″

Eastern Grasslands

Food
Pollen from open flowers
including hollyhock
(*Sidalcea, Sphaeralcea*);
ripening fruit, especially
peaches (*Prunus persica*);
foliage and fruit of many
trees and shrubs; larva eats
roots of grasses (Poaceae),
alfalfa (*Medicago sativa*),
vegetables, tobacco
(*Nicotiana*), ornamental
plants, and many others

388 Three-lined Potato Beetle

Lema trilineata
p. 492

Length: ¼"

All North American grasslands

Food
Members of the nightshade family (Solanaceae) including potatoes (*Solanum tuberosum*)

389 Meadow Spittlebug

Philaenus spumarius
p. 492

Length: ⅜"

Eastern Grasslands

Food
Juice of many different plants

390 Rose, Pea, and Potato Aphids

Macrosiphum spp.
p. 492

Length: ⅛"

All North American grasslands

Food
Juices of various host plants; preference varies according to species

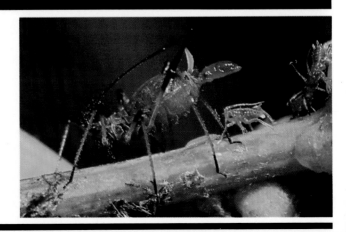

391 Brown Daddy-long-legs

Phalangium opilio
p. 493

Length: ⅛–¼″

All North American grasslands

Food
Small insects and decaying organic matter

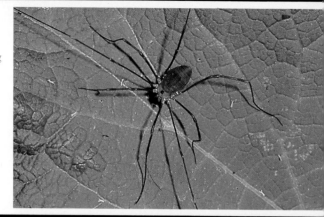

392 Goldenrod Spider

Misumena vatia
p. 493

Length: ⅛″ (males); ¼–⅜″ (females)

All North American grasslands

Food
Flower-visiting insects

393 Metaphid Jumping Spiders

Metaphidippus spp.
p. 494

Length: ⅛–¼″ (males); ⅛–¼″ (females)

All North American grasslands

Food
Small insects

394 Jumping Lynx Spiders

Oxyopes spp.
p. 494

Length: ⅛–¼″ (males); ⅛–⅜″ (females)

All North American grasslands

Food
Small insects

395 Orb Weavers

Araneus spp.
p. 495

Length: ¼″ (males); ⅜–¾″ (females)

All North American grasslands

Food
Insects

396 Goldenrod Spider

Misumena vatia
p. 493

Length: ⅛″ (males); ½–⅜″ (females)

All North American grasslands

Food
Flower-visiting insects

397 Alligator Juniper

Juniperus deppeana
p. 497

Leaf length: 1/16–1/8"; scalelike

Desert Grasslands

398 Utah Juniper

Juniperus osteosperma
p. 497

Leaf length: 1/16"; scalelike

Intermountain and Desert grasslands

399 Oneseed Juniper

Juniperus monosperma
p. 498

Leaf length: 1/16"; scalelike

Desert Grasslands

400 Eastern Redcedar   *Juniperus virginiana*   Leaf length: ⅟₁₆″; scalelike
                              p. 498

Tallgrass and Mixed
prairies; Eastern Grasslands

401 Common Juniper   *Juniperus communis*   Leaf length: ⅜–½″
                            p. 499

Intermountain, Desert, and
Eastern grasslands

402 Virginia Pine   *Pinus virginiana*   Needle length: 1½–3″
                           p. 499

Eastern Grasslands

403 Shortleaf Pine
Pinus echinata
p. 500
Needle length: 2¾–4½"

Eastern Grasslands

404 Loblolly Pine
Pinus taeda
p. 500
Needle length: 5–9"

Eastern Grasslands

405 Eastern White Pine
Pinus strobus
p. 500
Needle length: 2½–5"

Eastern Grasslands

06 Longleaf Pine *Pinus palustris* Needle length: 10–15″
p. 501

astern Grasslands

07 Slash Pine *Pinus elliottii* Needle length: 7–10″
p. 501

astern Grasslands

408 Soaptree Yucca *Yucca elata* Leaf length: 1–2½′
p. 502

Desert Grasslands

409 Glossy Buckthorn   *Rhamnus frangula*   Leaf length: 1½–2¾"
p. 503

Tallgrass and Mixed
prairies; Eastern Grasslands

410 Southern Catalpa   *Catalpa bignonioides*   Leaf length: 5–10"
p. 503

Eastern Grasslands

411 Osage-orange   *Maclura pomifera*   Leaf length: 2½–5"
p. 504

Tallgrass, Mixed, and
Shortgrass prairies; Eastern
Grasslands

12 Common Persimmon

Diospyros virginiana
p. 504

Leaf length: 2½–6"

Tallgrass and Mixed Prairies; Eastern Grasslands

13 Pussy Willow

Salix discolor
p. 505

Leaf length: 1½–4¼"

Tallgrass Prairie and Eastern Grasslands

14 Curlleaf Cercocarpus

Cercocarpus ledifolius
p. 506

Leaf length: ½–1¼"

Intermountain and California grasslands

415 Southern Crab Apple

Malus angustifolia
p. 506

Leaf length: 1–2¾"

Eastern Grasslands

416 Siberian Elm

Ulmus pumila
p. 507

Leaf length: ¾–2"

Tallgrass, Mixed, and Shortgrass prairies; Intermountain and Desert grasslands

417 Pin Cherry

Prunus pensylvanica
p. 507

Leaf length: 2½–4½"

Eastern Grasslands

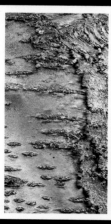

18 American Plum   *Prunus americana*   Leaf length: 2½–4"
p. 508

Tallgrass and Mixed
Prairies; Eastern Grasslands

19 Black Cherry   *Prunus serotina*   Leaf length: 2–5"
p. 508

Tallgrass and Mixed
Prairies; Eastern Grasslands

20 Canyon Live Oak   *Quercus chrysolepis*   Leaf length: 1–3"
p. 509

California Grasslands

421 Common Chokecherry

Prunus virginiana
p. 509

Leaf length: 1½–3¼"

Tallgrass, Mixed, and
Shortgrass prairies; Eastern
Grasslands

422 Apple

Malus sylvestris
p. 510

Leaf length: 2–3½"

Tallgrass and Mixed
prairies; Eastern Grasslands

423 Mexican Plum

Prunus mexicana
p. 511

Leaf length: 2–4½"

Tallgrass and Mixed
prairies; Eastern Grasslands

Tallgrass and Mixed
Prairies; Eastern Grasslands

California Grasslands

Tallgrass and Mixed
Prairies; Eastern Grasslands

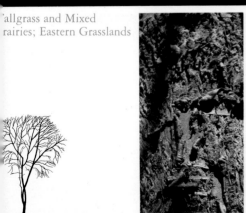

427 Oneflower Hawthorn   *Crataegus uniflora*   Leaf length: ¾–1½"
                                     p. 513

Tallgrass and Mixed
prairies; Eastern Grasslands

428 Gray Birch   *Betula populifolia*   Leaf length: 2–3"
                             p. 513

Eastern Grasslands

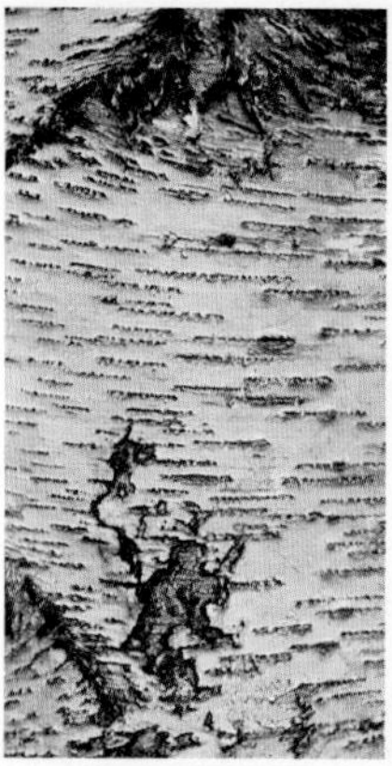

429 Paper Birch   *Betula papyrifera*   Leaf length: 2–4"
                              p. 514

Tallgrass Prairie and
Eastern Grasslands

430 Quaking Aspen   *Populus tremuloides*   Leaf length: 1¼–3"
                          p. 515

Tallgrass, Mixed, and
Shortgrass prairies;
Intermountain Grasslands

431 Balsam Poplar   *Populus balsamifera*   Leaf length: 3–5"
                          p. 515

Eastern Grasslands

432 Eastern Cottonwood   *Populus deltoides*   Leaf length: 3–7"
                               p. 516

Tallgrass, Mixed, and
Shortgrass prairies;
Intermountain, Desert, and
Eastern grasslands

433 Bigtooth Aspen
Populus grandidentata Leaf length: 2½–4″
p. 517

Tallgrass Prairie and
Eastern Grasslands

434 Biltmore Hawthorn
Crataegus intricata Leaf length: 1–2½″
p. 517

Tallgrass and Mixed
prairies; Eastern Grasslands

435 Fanleaf Hawthorn
Crataegus flabellata Leaf length: 1½–3″
p. 518

Tallgrass Prairie and
Eastern Grasslands

436 Sweetgum

Liquidambar styraciflua
p. 518

Leaf length: 3–6"

Eastern Grasslands

437 Blackjack Oak

Quercus marilandica
p. 519

Leaf length: 2½–5"

Tallgrass and Mixed prairies; Eastern Grasslands

438 California Black Oak

Quercus kelloggii
p. 520

Leaf length: 3–8"

California Grasslands

439 Bur Oak *Quercus macrocarpa* Leaf length: 4–10"
p. 520

Tallgrass and Mixed
prairies

440 Valley Oak *Quercus lobata* Leaf length: 2–4"
p. 521

California Grasslands

441 Post Oak *Quercus stellata* Leaf length: 3¼–6"
p. 521

Tallgrass and Mixed
prairies; Eastern Grasslands

442 Sassafras *Sassafras albidum* Leaf length: 3–5"
p. 522

Eastern Grasslands

443 Gregg Catclaw *Acacia greggii* Leaflet length: ⅛–¼"
p. 522

Desert Grasslands

444 Black Locust *Robinia pseudoacacia* Leaflet length: 1–1¾"
p. 523

Tallgrass and Mixed
prairies; Eastern Grasslands

445 Honey Mesquite   *Prosopis glandulosa*   Leaflet length: ⅜–1¼″
p. 524

Shortgrass Prairie and
Desert Grasslands

446 Huisache   *Acacia farnesiana*   Leaflet length: ⅛–¼″
p. 524

Desert Grasslands

447 Staghorn Sumac   *Rhus typhina*   Leaflet length: 2–4″
p. 525

Eastern Grasslands

448 Smooth Sumac *Rhus glabra* Leaflet length: 2–4"
p. 526

All North American
grasslands

449 Shining Sumac *Rhus copallina* Leaflet length: 1–3¼"
p. 526

Tallgrass and Mixed
prairies; Eastern Grasslands

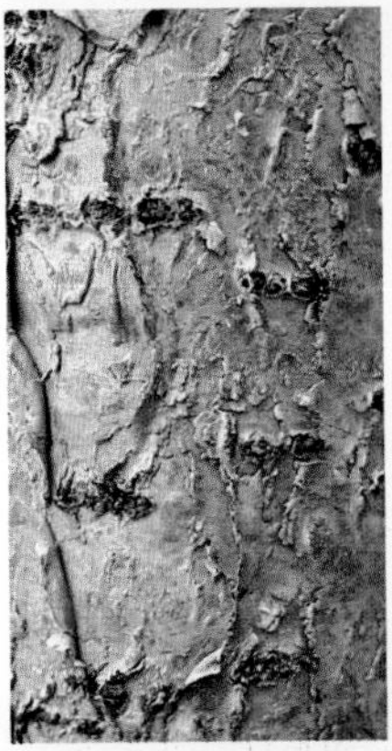

**450 Common Prickly-
ash** *Zanthoxylum
americanum* Leaflet length: 1–2"
p. 527

Tallgrass and Mixed
prairies; Eastern Grasslands

451 Prairie Crab Apple
Malus ioensis
p. 511

Flower width: 1½–2"

Tallgrass and Mixed
prairies; Eastern Grasslands

452 Apple
Malus sylvestris
p. 510

Flower width: 1¼"

Tallgrass and Mixed
prairies; Eastern Grasslands

453 Black Locust
Robinia pseudoacacia
p. 523

Flower length: ¾"

Tallgrass and Mixed
prairies; Eastern Grasslands

54 Biltmore Hawthorn
Crataegus intricata
p. 517

Flower width: ⅝″

Tallgrass and Mixed
Prairies; Eastern Grasslands

455 American Plum
Prunus americana
p. 508

Flower width: ¾–1″

Tallgrass and Mixed
Prairies; Eastern Grasslands

456 Pin Cherry
Prunus pensylvanica
p. 507

Flower width: ½″

Eastern Grasslands

| 457 Common Chokecherry | *Prunus virginiana* p. 509 | Flower width: ½" |

Tallgrass, Mixed, and Shortgrass prairies; Eastern Grasslands

| 458 Black Cherry | *Prunus serotina* p. 508 | Flower width: ⅜" |

Tallgrass and Mixed prairies; Eastern Grasslands

| 459 Osage-orange | *Maclura pomifera* p. 504 | Flower diameter: clusters less than 1" |

Mixed and Shortgrass prairies

460 Pussy Willow *Salix discolor* Flower length: 1–2½"
p. 505

Tallgrass Prairie and
Eastern Grasslands

461 Honey Mesquite *Prosopis glandulosa* Flower length: ¼"
p. 524

Shortgrass Prairie and
Desert Grasslands

462 Gregg Catclaw *Acacia greggii* Flower length: ¼"
p. 522

Desert Grasslands

463 Huisache   *Acacia farnesiana*   Flower length: ³⁄₁₆″
                     p. 524

Desert Grasslands

464 Shining Sumac   *Rhus copallina*   Flower width: ⅛″
                         p. 526

Tallgrass and Mixed
prairies; Eastern Grasslands

465 Smooth Sumac   *Rhus glabra*   Flower width: less than ⅛″
                        p. 526

All North American
grasslands

66 Sassafras *Sassafras albidum* Flower length: ⅜″
p. 522

Eastern Grasslands

67 Russian-olive *Elaeagnus angustifolia* Flower length: ⅜″
p. 527

Tallgrass, Mixed, and
Shortgrass prairies;
Intermountain and Eastern
Grasslands

468 Common *Diospyros virginiana* Flower length: ⅜″ (male); ⅝″ (female)
Persimmon p. 504

Tallgrass and Mixed
Prairies; Eastern Grasslands

469 Osage-orange   *Maclura pomifera*   Fruit diameter: 3½–5″
p. 504

Mixed and Shortgrass
prairies

**470 Common
Persimmon**   *Diospyros virginiana*   Fruit diameter: ¾–1½″
p. 504

Tallgrass and Mixed
prairies; Eastern Grasslands

471 Staghorn Sumac   *Rhus typhina*   Fruit diameter: ³⁄₁₆″
p. 525

Eastern Grasslands

472 Common Chokecherry *Prunus virginiana* Fruit diameter: ¼–⅜"
p. 509

Tallgrass, Mixed, and Shortgrass prairies; Eastern Grasslands

473 Pin Cherry *Prunus pensylvanica* Fruit diameter: ¼"
p. 507

Eastern Grasslands

474 Glossy Buckthorn *Rhamnus frangula* Fruit diameter: ⁵⁄₁₆"
p. 503

Tallgrass and Mixed prairies; Eastern Grasslands

475 Common Juniper   *Juniperus communis*   Cone diameter: ¼–⅜″
p. 499

Tallgrass, Mixed, and
Shortgrass prairies; Eastern
Grasslands

476 Utah Juniper   *Juniperus osteosperma*   Cone diameter: ¼–⅝″
p. 497

Intermountain and Desert
grasslands

477 Alligator Juniper   *Juniperus deppeana*   Cone diameter: ½″
p. 497

Desert Grasslands

78 Eastern White Pine *Pinus strobus* Cone length: 4–8″
p. 500

Eastern Grasslands

79 Shortleaf Pine *Pinus echinata* Cone length: 1½–2½″
p. 500

Eastern Grasslands

480 Singleleaf Pinyon *Pinus monophylla* Cone length: 2–3″
p. 528

Intermountain Grasslands

481 Sweetgum
Liquidambar styraciflua
p. 518

Fruit diameter: 1–1¼"

Eastern Grasslands

482 Canyon Live Oak
Quercus chrysolepis
p. 509

Acorn length: ¾–2"

California Grasslands

483 Valley Oak
Quercus lobata
p. 521

Acorn length: 1¼–2¼"

California Grasslands

84 Black Locust

Robinia pseudoacacia
p. 523

Fruit length: 2–4"

Tallgrass and Mixed
Prairies; Eastern Grasslands

85 Honey Mesquite

Prosopis glandulosa
p. 524

Fruit length: 3½–8"

Shortgrass Prairie and
Desert Grasslands

486 Curlleaf Cercocarpus

Cercocarpus ledifolius
p. 506

Fruit length: ¼"

Intermountain and
California grasslands

487 Cattle Egret
Bubulcus ibis
p. 530
Length: 20"

Eastern Grasslands

488 Turkey Vulture
Cathartes aura
p. 530
Length: 26–32"

All North American
grasslands

489 Northern Harrier
Circus cyaneus
p. 530
Length: 16–24"

Tallgrass, Mixed, and
Shortgrass prairies;
Intermountain and Eastern
grasslands

Mixed and Shortgrass Prairies; Intermountain and Desert grasslands

All North American grasslands

All North American grasslands

493 Ferruginous Hawk *Buteo regalis* Length: 22½–25″
p. 532

Mixed and Shortgrass
prairies; Intermountain and
Desert grasslands

494 Golden Eagle *Aquila chrysaetos* Length: 30–41″
p. 532

Shortgrass Prairie;
Intermountain, Desert, and
California grasslands

495 Crested Caracara *Polyborus plancus* Length: 20–22″
p. 532

Desert Grassland

496 American Kestrel

Falco sparverius
p. 533

Length: 9–12"

All North American
grasslands

497 Gray Partridge

Perdix perdix
p. 533

Length: 12–14"

Tallgrass, Mixed, and
Shortgrass prairies

498 Ring-necked
Pheasant

Phasianus colchicus
p. 533

Length: 30–36"

Tallgrass, Mixed, and
Shortgrass prairies;
Intermountain and Eastern
grasslands

499 Sage Grouse

*Centrocercus
urophasianus*
p. 534

Length: 26–30″ (males);
22–23″ (females)

Shortgrass Prairie and
Intermountain Grasslands

500 Greater Prairie-Chicken ○

Tympanuchus cupido
p. 534

Length: 16–18″

Tallgrass and Mixed
prairies

501 Lesser Prairie-Chicken

*Tympanuchus
pallidicinctus*
p. 535

Length: 16″

Shortgrass Prairie

502 Sharp-tailed Grouse
Tympanuchus phasianellus
p. 535

Length: 16–18″

Tallgrass and Mixed Prairies

503 Northern Bobwhite
Colinus virginianus
p. 535

Length: 8–11″

Tallgrass and Mixed Prairies; Eastern Grasslands

504 Scaled Quail
Callipepla squamata
p. 536

Length: 10–12″

Desert Grasslands

505 Sandhill Crane
Grus canadensis
p. 536
Length: 34–48"

Mixed and Shortgrass
prairies; Intermountain
Grasslands

506 Killdeer
Charadrius vociferus
p. 537
Length: 9–11"

Tallgrass, Mixed, and
Shortgrass prairies;
Intermountain, Desert,
California, and Eastern
grasslands

507 Upland Sandpiper
Bartramia longicauda
p. 537
Length: 12"

Tallgrass, Mixed, and
Shortgrass prairies; Eastern
Grasslands

Tallgrass, Mixed and
Shortgrass prairies;
Intermountain Grasslands

All North American
grasslands

Eastern Grasslands

511 Greater Roadrunner

Geococcyx californianus Length: 24"
p. 538

Shortgrass Prairie; Desert
and California grasslands

512 Common Barn-Owl

Tyto alba Length: 18"
p. 539

Tallgrass, Mixed, and
Shortgrass prairies;
Intermountain, California,
and Eastern grasslands

513 Burrowing Owl

Athene cunicularia Length: 9"
p. 539

Mixed and Shortgrass
prairies

514 Short-eared Owl

Asio flammeus
p. 539

Length: 16"

Tallgrass, Mixed, and
Shortgrass prairies;
Intermountain Grasslands

515 Common Nighthawk

Chordeiles minor
p. 540

Length: 10"

Tallgrass, Mixed, and
Shortgrass prairies;
Intermountain, Desert,
California, and Eastern
grasslands

516 Cassin's Kingbird

Tyrannus vociferans
p. 540

Length: 8–9"

Shortgrass Prairie; Desert
and California grasslands

517 Western Kingbird

Tyrannus verticalis
p. 541

Length: 9"

Mixed and Shortgrass
prairies; Intermountain
Grasslands

518 Eastern Kingbird

Tyrannus tyrannus
p. 541

Length: 8½"

All North American
grasslands except Desert
Grasslands

519 Scissor-tailed Flycatcher

Tyrannus forficatus
p. 541

Length: 14"

Shortgrass Prairie and
Desert Grasslands

520 Horned Lark   *Eremophila alpestris*   Length: 7–8″
p. 542

All North American
grasslands

521 Cliff Swallow   *Hirundo pyrrhonota*   Length: 5–6″
p. 542

All North American
grasslands

522 Barn Swallow   *Hirundo rustica*   Length: 5¾–7¾″
p. 542

All North American
grasslands

523 Black-billed Magpie *Pica pica* p. 543 Length: 17½–22″

Mixed and Shortgrass prairies; Intermountain Grasslands

524 Eastern Bluebird *Sialia sialis* p. 543 Length: 7″

Tallgrass, Mixed, and Shortgrass prairies; Eastern Grasslands

525 Mountain Bluebird *Sialia currucoides* p. 543 Length: 7″

Intermountain and California grasslands

526 Water Pipit   *Anthus spinoletta*   Length: 6–7″
                            p. 544

Mixed and Shortgrass
prairies; Intermountain
Grasslands

527 Northern Shrike   *Lanius excubitor*   Length: 9–10½″
                            p. 544

Tallgrass, Mixed, and
Shortgrass prairies;
Intermountain Grasslands

528 Loggerhead Shrike *Lanius ludovicianus*   Length: 8–10″
                            p. 545

All North American
grasslands

529 Dickcissel

Spiza americana
p. 545

Length: 6"

Tallgrass and Mixed
prairies

530 American Tree Sparrow

Spizella arborea
p. 545

Length: 5½–6½"

Tallgrass, Mixed, and
Shortgrass prairies;
Intermountain and Eastern
grasslands

531 Clay-colored Sparrow

Spizella pallida
p. 546

Length: 5–5½"

Tallgrass and Mixed
prairies

532 Field Sparrow   *Spizella pusilla*   Length: 5¼"
p. 546

Tallgrass, Mixed, and Shortgrass prairies; Eastern Grasslands

533 Vesper Sparrow   *Pooecetes gramineus*   Length: 5–6½"
p. 547

Tallgrass, Mixed, and Shortgrass prairies; Intermountain, California, and Eastern grasslands

534 Lark Sparrow   *Chondestes grammacus*   Length: 5½–6½"
p. 547

Tallgrass, Mixed, and Shortgrass prairies; California Grasslands

535 Lark Bunting
Calamospiza melanocorys
p. 547

Length: 6–7½"

Mixed and Shortgrass prairies; Desert Grasslands

536 Savannah Sparrow
Passerculus sandwichensis
p. 548

Length: 4½–6"

Tallgrass, Mixed, and Shortgrass prairies; Intermountain and Eastern grasslands

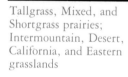

537 Grasshopper Sparrow
Ammodramus savannarum
p. 548

Length: 4½–5"

Tallgrass, Mixed, and Shortgrass prairies; Intermountain, Desert, California, and Eastern grasslands

Eastern Grasslands

Shortgrass Prairie

All North American
grasslands except California
Grasslands

541 Smith's Longspur   *Calcarius pictus*   Length: 5¾–6½"
p. 550   Female

Mixed and Shortgrass
prairies

**542 Chestnut-collared
Longspur**   *Calcarius ornatus*   Length: 5½–6½"
p. 550

Mixed and Shortgrass
prairies

543 Snow Bunting   *Plectrophenax nivalis*   Length: 6–7¼"
p. 550

Shortgrass Prairie

Tallgrass, Mixed, and
Shortgrass prairies;
Intermountain, California,
and Eastern grasslands

All North American
grasslands

All North American
grasslands

547 Eastern Meadowlark *Sturnella magna*   Length: 9–11″
p. 552

Tallgrass and Mixed
prairies; Eastern Grasslands

548 Western Meadowlark   *Sturnella neglecta*   Length: 8½–11″
p. 552

Tallgrass, Mixed, and
Shortgrass prairies; Eastern
Grasslands

549 Brewer's Blackbird   *Euphagus cyanocephalus*   Length: 8–10″
p. 552   Female

Tallgrass, Mixed, and
Shortgrass prairies;
Intermountain, and
California grasslands

550 Brewer's Blackbird

Euphagus cyanocephalus
p. 552

Length: 8–10"

Tallgrass, Mixed, and Shortgrass prairies; Intermountain and California grasslands

551 Bronzed Cowbird

Molothrus aeneus
p. 553

Length: 6½–8¾"

Shortgrass Prairie

552 American Goldfinch

Carduelis tristis
p. 553

Length: 4½–5"

Tallgrass, Mixed, and Shortgrass prairies; Intermountain, California, and Eastern grasslands

553 Japanese Umbrella Inky

Coprinus plicatilis
p. 555

Cap width: ⅜–1″

All North American grasslands except Desert

Habitat
Grassy areas

554 Fairy Ring Mushroom

Marasmius oreades
p. 555

Cap width: ⅜–1⅝″

All North American grasslands except Desert

Habitat
Grassy areas

555 Common Psathyrella

Psathyrella candolleana
p. 555

Cap width: 1–4″

All North American grasslands except Desert

Habitat
Grassy areas, and on or near hardwood stumps

56 Hemispheric Agrocybe

Agrocybe pediades
p. 556

Cap width: ⅜–1″

All North American grasslands except Desert

Habitat
Grassy areas and wood mulch

557 White Waxy Cap

Hygrophorus eburneus
p. 556

Cap width: 1–4″

All North American grasslands except Desert

Habitat
Grassy areas; also coniferous, beech, or mixed forest

558 Smooth Lepiota

Lepiota naucina
p. 556

Cap width: 2–4″

All North American grasslands except Desert

Habitat
Grassy areas

559 Fried-chicken Mushroom

Lyophyllum decastes
p. 556

Cap width: 1–5"

All North American grasslands except Desert

Habitat
Grassy areas

560 Meadow Mushroom

Agaricus campestris
p. 557

Cap width: 1–4"

All North American grasslands except Desert

Habitat
Grassy areas

561 Purple-gilled Laccaria

Laccaria ochropurpurea
p. 557

Cap width: 2–8"

Tallgrass, Mixed, and Shortgrass prairies; Eastern Grasslands

Habitat
Open oak woods and grassy areas

All North American
grasslands except Desert

Habitat
Grassy areas, wood chips,
and hardpacked soil

All North American
grasslands except Desert

Habitat
Pastures and open woods

Eastern Grasslands

Habitat
Pastures and open woods

Tallgrass, Mixed, and
Shortgrass prairies

Desert and California
grasslands

Mixed and Shortgrass
prairies; Desert Grasslands

68 Red-spotted Toad

Bufo punctatus
p. 561

Length: 1½–3″

Mixed and Shortgrass
prairies; Desert Grasslands

69 Woodhouse's Toad

Bufo woodhousei
p. 561

Length: 2½–5″

Tallgrass and Mixed
prairies; Desert and Eastern
grasslands

70 Great Plains Toad

Bufo cognatus
p. 561

Length: 2–4½″

Tallgrass, Mixed, and
Shortgrass prairies; Desert
Grasslands

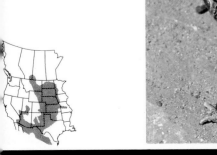

571 Striped Chorus Frog *Pseudacris triseriata* Length: ³⁄₄–1½″
p. 562

Tallgrass, Mixed, and
Shortgrass prairies; Eastern
Grasslands

572 Plains Leopard Frog *Rana blairi* Length: 2–4⅛″
p. 562

Tallgrass and Mixed
prairies

573 Green Toad *Bufo debilis* Length: 1¼–2⅛″
p. 563

Mixed and Shortgrass
prairies; Desert Grasslands

74 Western Box Turtle   *Terrapene ornata*   Length: 4–5¾"
p. 563

Tallgrass, Mixed, and
Shortgrass prairies; Desert
Grasslands

75 Painted Turtle   *Chrysemys picta*   Length: 4–9⅞"
p. 563

Tallgrass, Mixed, and
Shortgrass prairies; Eastern
Grasslands

576 Snapping Turtle   *Chelydra serpentina*   Length: 8–18½"
p. 564

Tallgrass and Mixed
Prairies; Eastern Grasslands

577 Many-lined Skink   *Eumeces multivirgatus*   Length: 5–7⅝"
p. 564

Mixed and Shortgrass
prairies; Desert Grasslands

578 Western Skink   *Eumeces skiltonianus*   Length: 6½–9⁵⁄₁₆"
p. 564

Intermountain and
California grasslands

579 Prairie Skink   *Eumeces septentrionalis*   Length: 5–8⅛"
p. 565

Tallgrass and Mixed
prairies

580 Racerunner — *Cnemidophorus sexlineatus* p. 565 — Length: 6–10½"

Tallgrass and Mixed prairies; Eastern Grasslands

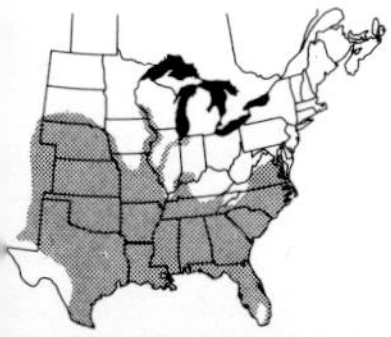

581 Slender Glass Lizard — *Ophisaurus attenuatus* p. 565 — Length: 22–42"

Tallgrass and Mixed prairies; Eastern Grasslands

582 Great Plains Skink — *Eumeces obsoletus* p. 566 — Length: 6½–13¾"

Mixed and Shortgrass prairies; Desert Grasslands

583 Tiger Salamander   *Ambystoma tigrinum*   Length: 6–13⅜"
                                       p. 566

Tallgrass, Mixed, and
Shortgrass prairies;
Intermountain and Desert
grasslands

**584 Bluntnose Leopard
Lizard**   *Gambelia silus*   Length: 8–9½"
                              p. 566

California Grasslands

585 Lesser Earless Lizard   *Holbrookia maculata*   Length: 4–5⅛"
                                p. 567

Mixed and Shortgrass
prairies; Desert Grasslands

586 Texas Horned Lizard
Phrynosoma cornutum
p. 567
Length: 2½–7⅛"

Shortgrass Prairie and
Desert Grasslands

587 Spot-tailed Earless Lizard
Holbrookia lacerata
p. 567
Length: 4½–6"

Shortgrass Prairie

588 Western Whiptail
Cnemidophorus tigris
p. 568
Length: 8–12"

Intermountain, Desert, and
California grasslands

589 Eastern Fence Lizard

Sceloporus undulatus
p. 568

Length: 3½–7½"

Tallgrass, Mixed, and Shortgrass prairies; Desert and Eastern grasslands

590 Side-blotched Lizard

Uta stansburiana
p. 568

Length: 4–6⅜"

Intermountain and Desert grasslands

591 Collared Lizard

Crotaphytus collaris
p. 569

Length: 8–14"

Mixed and Shortgrass prairies; Desert Grasslands

**92 Common Garter
nake** *Thamnophis sirtalis*   Length: 18–51⅝"
p. 569

allgrass, Mixed, and
hortgrass prairies;
ntermountain, California,
nd Eastern grasslands

93 Plains Garter Snake   *Thamnophis radix*   Length: 20–40"
p. 570

Tallgrass, Mixed, and
Shortgrass prairies

**594 Checkered Garter
Snake**   *Thamnophis marcianus*   Length: 18–42½"
p. 570

Desert Grasslands

| 595 Western Ribbon Snake | *Thamnophis proximus* *p. 570* | Length: 19–48½" |

Tallgrass and Mixed prairies

| 596 Lined Snake | *Tropidoclonion lineatum* *p. 571* | Length: 7½–21" |

Mixed and Shortgrass prairies

| 597 Western Terrestrial Garter Snake | *Thamnophis elegans* *p. 571* | Length: 18–42" |

Intermountain Grasslands

598 Pine-Gopher Snake

Pituophis melanoleucus
p. 571

Length: 48–100"

Mixed and Shortgrass prairies; Intermountain, Desert, and California grasslands

599 Western Diamondback Rattlesnake

Crotalus atrox
p. 572

Length: 34–83⅞" ⊗

Shortgrass Prairie and Desert Grasslands

600 Massasauga

Sistrurus catenatus
p. 572

Length: 18–39½" ⊗

Tallgrass, Mixed, and Shortgrass prairies; Desert and Eastern grasslands

601 Glossy Snake
Arizona elegans
p. 573
Length: 26–70"

Shortgrass Prairie and
Desert Grasslands

602 Northern Water Snake
Nerodia sipedon
p. 573
Length: 22–53"

Tallgrass and Mixed
prairies; Eastern Grasslands

603 Corn Snake
Elaphe guttata
p. 573
Length: 24–72"

Tallgrass, Mixed, and
Shortgrass prairies; Desert
and Eastern grasslands

604 Western Hognose Snake
Heterodon nasicus
p. 574
Length: 16–35¼"

Mixed and Shortgrass Prairies; Desert Grasslands

605 Western Rattlesnake
Crotalus viridis
p. 574
Length: 16–64"

Mixed and Shortgrass Prairies; Intermountain, California, and Desert Grasslands

606 Eastern Hognose Snake
Heterodon platyrhinos
p. 575
Length: 20–45½"

Tallgrass Prairie and Eastern Grasslands

607 Prairie Kingsnake
Lampropeltis calligaster Length: 30–52⅛"
p. 575

Tallgrass and Mixed
prairies; Eastern Grasslands

608 Fox Snake
Elaphe vulpina Length: 34–70½"
p. 576

Tallgrass and Mixed
prairies; Eastern Grasslands

609 Longnosed Snake
Rhinocheilus lecontei Length: 22–41"
p. 576

Intermountain and Desert
grasslands

10 Ground Snake   *Sonora semiannulata*   Length: 8–19"
p. 577

Shortgrass Prairie and
Desert Grasslands

11 Milk Snake   *Lampropeltis*   Length: 14–78¼"
triangulum
p. 577

Tallgrass, Mixed, and
Shortgrass prairies; Eastern
Grasslands

512 Ringneck Snake   *Diadophis punctatus*   Length: 10–30"
p. 578

All North American
grasslands except California
Grasslands

613 Rat Snake
Elaphe obsoleta
p. 578
Length: 34–101"

Tallgrass and Mixed
prairies; Eastern Grasslands

614 Coachwhip
Masticophis flagellum
p. 579
Length: 36–102"

Tallgrass, Mixed, and
Shortgrass prairies; Desert,
California, and Eastern
grasslands

615 Plains Blackhead Snake
Tantilla nigriceps
p. 579
Length: 7–14¾"

Mixed and Shortgrass
prairies; Desert Grasslands

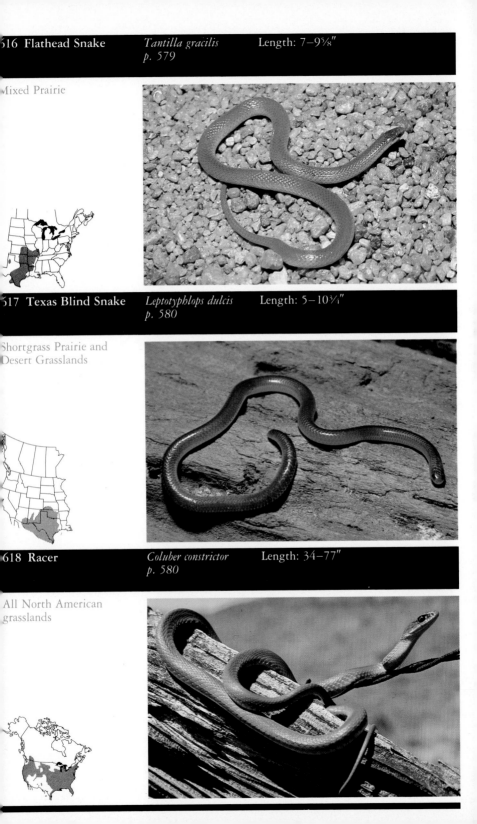

516 Flathead Snake   *Tantilla gracilis*   Length: 7–9⅝"
p. 579

Mixed Prairie

517 Texas Blind Snake   *Leptotyphlops dulcis*   Length: 5–10¾"
p. 580

Shortgrass Prairie and
Desert Grasslands

618 Racer   *Coluber constrictor*   Length: 34–77"
p. 580

All North American
grasslands

MAMMALS

The North American grasslands provide a variety of habitats for many different kinds of mammals, large and small. Bison, once very numerous, are still at home in some regions, while foxes, deer, rabbits, and a large assortment of smaller animals can be found throughout the prairies and plains. Some mammals, such as the Prairie Dogs, live in complex burrow systems; others, such as the Elk, range widely in search of food. This section describes these and other common mammals of the grasslands.

Bison
Bison bison
31

Males: 10–12½' (304–380 cm) long. Females: 7–8' (210–240 cm) long. Largest terrestrial animal in North America. Dark brown, with shaggy mane and beard. Long tail with tuft at tip. Broad, massive head; humped shoulders; short legs clothed with shaggy hair; large hooves. In both sexes, short black horns curving out, then up, and in at pointed tips. Horn spread to 3' (90 cm).

Sign
In wooded habitat, trees ringed with pale "horn rubs" or "head rubs" where bark is worn away; trampled ground underneath such trees or around rubbed boulders.
Wallows: Especially in plains habitat, are dusty saucerlike depressions, 8–10' wide, 1' deep, where Bison have rolled and rubbed repeatedly, dust-bathing to relieve itching and rid coats of insects. Bulls may urinate in dry wallows and then cake themselves with mud as protection against insect pests.
Tracks: Similar to those of domestic cow but rounder and somewhat larger, about 5' wide for a mature bull. On hard ground, cleft between facing crescent lobes may not show, and tracks may then resemble horses' hoofprints.

Breeding
After a gestation period of 270–285 days, a single calf is born in May; occasionally there are twins. The reddish newborn stands to nurse in 30 minutes, walks within hours, and in 1 or 2 days joins the herd with its mother.

Habitat
Varied: primarily plains, prairies, river valleys, sometimes forests.

Range
Free-ranging Bison occur only at Wood Buffalo National Park, Northwest Territories, Canada, and in Yellowstone National Park, Wyoming.

Comments
Commonly known as the Buffalo, Bison are most active in early morning and late afternoon but sometimes also on moonlit nights. In the midday heat, they rest, chewing their cuds, or dust-bathing. Usually 4–20 Bison herd together, with sexes separate except during breeding season; occasionally herds gather into bands of several thousand. They will stampede if frightened, galloping at speeds up to 32 mph. By 1900 fewer than 1000 Bison remained, and a crusade of rescue and restoration was begun. Today more than 30,000 Bison roam national parks, national Bison ranges, Canadian Buffalo parks, and privately owned rangelands.

Elk
Cervus elaphus
32

6¾–9¾' (203.2–297.2 cm) long. Large deer, with slender legs, thick neck. Brown or tan above; darker underparts. Rump patch and tail yellowish brown. Males have dark brown mane on throat and large, many-tined antlers: 6 tines on each side when mature, with main beam up to 5' (150 cm) long.

Females lack antlers, are approximately 25 percent smaller than males.

Sign
During the rut, thrashed saplings and large shrubs; "rubs" on saplings and small trees made as the animals polish their antlers.
Wallows: Depressions dug in ground by hooves and antlers, where copious urine and feces give a strong, musky odor.
Tracks: Cloven hearts, much larger and rounder than those of White-tailed or Mule deer; 4–4½" long. When walking, hindprints slightly ahead of and partly overlapping foreprints; stride 30–60". When running and bounding, foreprints and hindprints are separate and stride up to 14'. In snow or mud, dewclaws often print behind lobed main prints.

Breeding
After a gestation of about 255–275 days, a cow leaves the herd to give birth usually to 1 calf, sometimes 2.

Habitat
Variable: chiefly high, open mountain pastures in summer; lower wooded slopes, often dense woods, in winter.

Range
Vancouver Island, much of central and W. Washington, W. Oregon to NW. California; central Manitoba to south-central Colorado; central Saskatchewan to S. Manitoba; isolated populations in California, Nevada, Utah, Arizona, New Mexico, Oklahoma, South Dakota, Minnesota, and Michigan; very small numbers in several eastern states, notably Pennsylvania and Virginia. Great numbers in Colorado, Wyoming, Montana, and Washington.

Comments
Although Elk now seem to be mainly inhabitants of mountainous, remote areas, there is evidence that they were once among the major herbivores in some of the American grasslands. The Elk is primarily nocturnal but especially active at dusk and dawn. Unlike the much smaller White-tailed Deer, which is often heard crashing through the brush, the Elk moves through the forest rapidly and almost silently. Bulls can run up to 35 mph, and both bulls and cows are strong swimmers. Also called Wapiti, Elk feed on many kinds of plants but are primarily grazers; east of the Continental Divide, they feed more heavily on woody vegetation.

White-tailed Deer
Odocoileus virginianus
33

4½–6¾' (134–206 cm) long. Tan or reddish brown above in summer; grayish brown in winter. Belly, throat, nose band, eye ring, and inside of ears white. Tail brown, edged with white above, often with dark stripe down center, white below. Black spots on sides of chin. Bucks' antlers with main beam forward and several unbranched tines behind; a small brow tine. Antler spread to 3' (90 cm). Does normally lack antlers. Fawns spotted.

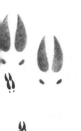

Sign
Bed: Shallow, oval, body-size depression in leaves or snow. "Buck rubs": Polished scars or oblong sections where bark removed from bushes, saplings, or small trees, usually close to ground; made when a buck lowers its head and rubs antlers against a tree to mark territory; trees chosen to fit antlers (for example, a rub on a tree 4–5″ in diameter indicates the rub was made by a very large buck).

Raggedly browsed vegetation: Lacking upper incisors, deer rip away vegetation instead of snipping it neatly like rabbits.

Tracks: Like narrow split hearts, pointed end forward, about 2–3″ long; dewclaws may print twin dots behind main prints in snow or soft mud. In shallow snow (1″ deep), buck may drag its feet, leaving drag marks ahead of prints; in deeper snow, both bucks and does drag feet. Straddle 5–6″ wide. Stride, when walking, 1′; when running, 6′ or more, and hindprints sometimes register ahead of foreprints; when leaping, 20′.

Breeding
Gestation is 7 months; a once-bred doe usually produces 1 fawn but later has 2 or possibly 3 if food is abundant.

Habitat
Farmlands, brushy areas, and woods.

Range
Southern half of southern tier of Canadian provinces; most of United States except most of California, Nevada, Utah, N. Arizona, SW. Colorado, and NW. New Mexico.

Comments
If alarmed, the Whitetail raises, or "flags," its tail, exhibiting a large, bright flash of white; this "hightailing" communicates danger to other deer or helps a fawn follow its mother in flight. Once nearly exterminated in much of the Northeast and Midwest, Whitetails are now more abundant than ever, owing in part to hunting restrictions.

Pronghorn
Antilocapra americana
34

49¼–57⅛″ (125–145 cm) long. Medium-size; long-legged; deerlike. Upper body and outside of legs pale tan or reddish tan; sides, chest, belly, inner legs, and rump patch white. 2 broad white blazes across tan throat. Cheeks and lower jaw usually white. Buck has broad, black band from eyes down snout to black nose and black neck patch. Horns black: bucks' 12–20″ (30–50 cm) long when full grown, lyre-shaped, curving back and slightly inward near conical tips, each with 1 broad, short prong jutting forward and slightly upward usually about halfway from base; does' seldom more than 3–4″ (7.5–10 cm) long, often without prongs. Short erectile mane.

Sign
Tracks: Shaped like split hearts about 3″ long; hindprints slightly shorter than foreprints. Tracking usually relatively unimportant for field observer, since Pronghorn inhabits open terrain and can often be seen at a great distance.

Breeding
Breeds in fall. After delayed implantation of 1 month and gestation of 7 months, the young are born in May or June, with unspotted coats and weighing 2½–13 lb. A doe's first breeding usually produces 1 fawn; subsequent breedings bring twins, rarely triplets.

Habitat
Grasslands; grassland-brushlands; bunch grass-sagebrush areas.

Range
S. Saskatchewan south to California, Arizona, New Mexico, and W. Texas; also in northern Mexico.

Comments
The fastest animal in the Western Hemisphere and among the fastest in the world, the Pronghorn, making 20' bounds, has been clocked at 70 mph for 3–4 minutes at a time. Speeds of 45 mph are not unusual, and 30 mph is an easy cruising speed, which it can maintain for about 15 miles. It runs with its mouth open, not from exhaustion but to gasp extra oxygen. Active night and day, it alternates snatches of sleep with watchful feeding.

Mule Deer (includes Black-tailed Deer)
Odocoileus hemionus
35

3¾–6½' (116–199 cm) long. Stocky body with sturdy legs. In summer, reddish brown or yellowish brown above; in winter, grayish above. Throat patch, rump patch, inside of ears, inside of legs white; lower parts cream to tan. Large ears. Bucks' antlers branch equally, each a separate beam forking into 2 tines. Antler spread to 4' (120 cm). 2 major subspecies: Mule Deer with tail white above, tipped with black; Black-tailed Deer, with tail blackish or brown above. Males larger than females.

Sign
Browse marks, buck rubs, scrapes, beds, and droppings similar to those of White-tailed Deer.
Tracks: Foreprints and hindprints 3¼" long (males), 2⅜" long (females); walking stride 22–24". Distinctive bounding gait ("stotting"), with all 4 feet coming down together, forefeet printing ahead of hind feet.

Breeding
After a gestation of 6–7 months, a single fawn is produced by a once-bred doe, while the older does usually have twins. Newborns weigh about 8 lb.

Habitat
Mixed habitats, forest edges, prairies, mountains and foothills.

Range
S. Yukon and Mackenzie south through western United States to Wisconsin and W. Texas; also northern Mexico.

Comments
These deer have large ears that move independently and almost constantly and account for the common name.

Primarily active in mornings, evenings, and on moonlit nights, deer may also be active at midday in winter. Summer forage is chiefly herbaceous plants but also blackberry, huckleberry, salal, and thimbleberry; winter browse includes twigs of Douglas-fir, cedar, yew, aspen, willow, dogwood, serviceberry, juniper, and sage. Acorns and apples are also eaten.

ollared Peccary
icotyles tajacu
6

34¼–40″ (87–102 cm) long. Piglike. Grizzled grayish or blackish above and below, with yellowish tinge on cheeks and whitish to yellowish irregular collar from shoulder to shoulder. Heavy, bristly hair from head to back can be erected into a mane. Inconspicuous tail; piglike snout; tusks (canines) nearly straight. 4 toes on forefeet, 3 on hind feet; all feet with 2 hooves. Young brownish with a black stripe down back.

Sign
Rooted-up ground; chewed cactus, especially prickly pear, and other low vegetation. Sometimes a light skunky odor.
Tracks: Cloven hooves are rounded oblongs, generally about 1–1½″ long, with hindprint slightly smaller than foreprint. Stride, short, usually 6–10″ between pairs of overlapping foreprints and hindprints. Similar to pig's but smaller.

Breeding
Breeding may occur at any time of the year, as food is abundant the year round in their mild habitat, but most births occur in summer. After a 4-month gestation, 2–6 young, usually twins, are born with yellowish or reddish hair.

Habitat
Brushy deserts, rocky canyons, and wastelands.

Range
SE. Arizona, extreme SE. and SW. New Mexico, central and S. Texas; also northern Mexico.

Comments
Active mainly in the early morning and late afternoon, the Peccary, or Javelina, often beds down in a hole rooted in the earth or takes shelter in a cave during the midday heat. Peccaries travel in herds of 6–30, grunting softly while feeding. As they move about, a musk gland on their back exudes a mild skunky scent, which probably serves as a bonding mechanism, helping to keep members of the group together. The musk gland also serves as an alarm signal: when a Peccary is agitated, the hairs on its back become erect, uncovering the gland, which then involuntarily discharges scent.

oyote
anis latrans
7, 38

41⅜–52″ (105–132 cm) long. Grizzled gray or reddish gray with buff underparts; long, rusty or yellowish legs with dark vertical line on lower foreleg; bushy tail with black tip. Nose pad to 1″ (25 mm) wide. Ears prominent.

Sign

Dens: Favored sites are riverbanks, well-drained slopes, sides of canyons or gulches. Den mouths usually 1–2' wide, often marked by mound or fan of earth and radiating tracks.
Tracks: Similar to dog's, but in a nearly straight line; 4 toes, all with claws; foreprint about 2½" long, slightly narrower; hindprint slightly smaller; stride 13" when walking, 24" when trotting, 30" or more when running, often with much wider gaps signifying leaps. Tracks and scat most often seen where runways intersect or on a hillock or open spot, vantage points where Coyotes linger to watch for prey.

Breeding

Mates February–April; may pair for several years or life, especially when populations are low; 1–19 young born April–May; in a crevice or underground burrow.

Habitat

In the West, open plains; in the East, brushy areas.

Range

E. Alaska, northern and western Canada, all of western United States east to at least New England, N. New York, New Jersey, Ohio, Tennessee, and Louisiana. Additional isolated records of Coyotes all over the East.

Comments

The best runner among the canids, the Coyote can leap 14' and cruises normally at 25–30 mph and up to 40 mph for short distances; tagged Coyotes have been known to travel great distances, up to 400 miles. The Coyote runs with its tail down, unlike wolves, which run with tail horizontal. A strong swimmer, it does not hesitate to enter water after prey. Calls include barks and yelps followed by a prolonged howl.

Kit Fox
Vulpes macrotis
39

23–31" (60–80 cm) long. Buffy gray above with buff along sides and underside of tail. Tail tip black. Large ears. Soles of feet with long fur.

Sign

Den: Often an old kangaroo rat mound. Opening 8" wide. Usually surrounded by small mound of earth.
Tracks: Small, less than 1½" long; prints may not show pads or claws because of heavy hair on the feet.

Breeding

Pairs form in fall, October–November. Monogamous for breeding season, but may switch mates in other years. Breeding occurs in winter, December–February; young are born in spring, March–April. 4–5 pups per litter.

Habitat

Deserts, grasslands, and montane areas with trees.

Range

SE. Oregon; SW. Idaho, and Utah; south into Mexico; east to central and SE. New Mexico, W. Texas.

Comments
This mostly nocturnal fox excavates its own den or enlarges burrows of ground squirrels and kangaroo rats. Food includes rodents, ground-dwelling birds, lizards, insects, and even scorpions. These beautiful foxes are alert and elusive. They can be quite irascible when trapped or cornered. Some consider the Kit Fox to be a subspecies of the Swift Fox.

Swift Fox
Vulpes velox
40

23⅝–31½″ (60–80 cm) long. Buff yellowish above, whitish below. Tail with black tip and often a black spot at upper base. Feet light-colored; ears large, triangular; dark spots below eye.

Sign
Den: In ground with 3–4 entrances 8″ wide; usually with mound of earth; sometimes scattered with small bones or scraps of prey.
Tracks: Similar to Gray Fox's but smaller, usually less than 1½″ long; all prints show 4 toes and claws.

Breeding
Mates January–February, usually for life; 3–5 young born March–April in chamber 3′ below ground.

Habitat
Shortgrass prairies; other arid areas.

Range
S. Alberta, Saskatchewan, and Manitoba south through E. Montana and Wyoming, NE. Colorado, the Dakotas, Nebraska, W. Kansas and Oklahoma, E. New Mexico, and N. Texas.

Comments
This mostly nocturnal, solitary fox excavates its own den or enlarges a Badger or marmot den in open country. Its calls include a shrill yap, several whines, purrs, and growls. For short distances, it can run as fast as 25 mph (hence its common name).

Red Fox
Vulpes vulpes
41, 42, 44, 45

35⅜–40⅜″ (90–103 cm) long. Small, doglike. Rusty reddish above; white underparts, chin, and throat. Long, bushy tail with white tip. Prominent pointed ears. Back of ear, lower legs, feet black. Elliptical pupils. Color variations include a black phase (almost completely black), a silver phase (black with silver-tipped hairs), a cross phase (reddish brown with a dark cross across shoulders), and intermediate phases, all with white-tipped tail.

Sign
Den: Maternity den usually in sparse ground cover; commonly enlarged den of marmot or Badger on slight rise, providing view of all approaches, but also in stream bank, slope, or rock pile; less often in hollow tree or log. Typical earthen mound has main entrance up to 1′ wide, slightly higher, with littered

fan or mound of packed earth and 1–3 less conspicuous smaller escape holes. Den well marked with excavated earth, cache mounds where food is buried, holes where food has been dug up, and scraps of bones and feathers. Dens established shortly after mating (usually late January or February), abandoned by late August when families disperse.
Tracks: Similar to those of Gray Fox, but usually slightly larger, with smaller toeprints. Foreprint about 2¼″ long, hindprint slightly smaller, narrower, more pointed. Often blurred, especially in winter, with lobes and toes less distinctly outlined than those of Gray Fox, as Red Fox's feet are heavily haired. In heavy snow, tail may brush out tracks.

Breeding
Mates January–early March. After 51–53 days gestation, 1–10 kits, average 4–8, born March–May in maternity den.

Habitat
Varied: mixed cultivated and wooded areas, brushlands.

Range
Most of Canada and United States except for much of West Coast: Southwest (S. California, N. Nevada, Arizona); S. Alberta and SW. Saskatchewan to SW. Oklahoma; NW. Texas and Southeast (coastal North Carolina to peninsular Florida).

Comments
Even when fairly common, the Red Fox may be difficult to observe, as it is shy, nervous, and primarily nocturnal (though it may be abroad near dawn or dusk or on dark days). Omnivorous, it eats whatever is available.

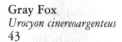

Gray Fox
Urocyon cinereoargenteus
43

31½–44¼″ (80–113 cm) long. Grizzled gray above, reddish below and on back of head; throat white. Tail with black "mane" on top and black tip; feet rusty-colored. Prominent ears.

Sign
Tree and scent posts: Marked with urine, noticeable on snow by spattered urine stains and melting.
Caches: Heaped or loosened dirt, moss, or turf, frequently paler than surrounding ground; dug-up cache holes are shallow and wide, since foxes seldom bury very small prey except near a den in whelping season.
Den: Entrance size varies considerably, as most dens are in natural cavities, with entrance occasionally marked by snagged hair or a few telltale bone scraps; several auxiliary or escape dens nearby. Dens are in rare instances conspicuously marked with mounds like those of the Red Fox.
Tracks: When in straight line, similar to those of a very large domestic cat, except that nonretractile claws may show. Similar to Red Fox's, but often smaller with larger toes and more sharply defined because of less hair around pads. Foreprint about 1½″ long; hindprint as long, slightly

narrower; 4 toes with claws. On fairly hard ground, hind heel pad leaves only a round dot if side portions fail to print. A fox digs in when running, leaving claw marks even in hard ground, where pads do not print.

Breeding
Mates February–March; 2–7 young, average 3–4, born in March or April; weaned at 3 months, when they weigh about 7 lb. Male helps tend young, but does not den with them.

Habitat
Varied, but associated much more with wooded and brushy habitats than are Red Foxes.

Range

Eastern United States west to E. North and South Dakota, Nebraska, Kansas, Oklahoma, most of Texas, New Mexico, Arizona, and California, north through Colorado, S. Utah, S. Nevada, and W. Oregon.

Comments
Although primarily nocturnal, the Gray Fox is sometimes seen foraging by day in brush, thick foliage, or timber. The only American canid with true climbing ability, it occasionally forages in trees and frequently takes refuge in them, especially in leaning or thickly branched ones. Favored den sites include woodlands among boulders on the slopes of rocky ridges.

Black-tailed Jack Rabbit
Lepus californicus
6

18¼–24¾" (46.5–63 cm) long. Buffy gray or sandy above, peppered with black; white below. Tail has black stripe above, extending onto rump, with white border. Very long ears, brownish with black tips. Very large hind foot.

Sign
Trails worn between feeding and resting sites; scarred or freshly nipped prickly-pear cactus or light tufts of fur on thorns; nesting forms: shallow scrapes often beneath sagebrush or rabbit brush.

Breeding
Mating is year-round but more frequent in milder seasons; 1–4 litters per year of 1–8 young (usually only 2–4) are born in a relatively deep form lined with hair from the mother's chest.

Habitat
Barren areas and prairies, meadows, and cultivated fields.

Range

Western United States: Texas and California north to south-central Washington; also in northern Mexico. Introduced in New Jersey and Kentucky.

Comments
This most abundant and widespread jack was originally called a jackass rabbit, after its very large ears; like other jacks, it is not really a rabbit but a hare, as its young are born well furred and with eyes open. By day, it generally rests in dense

vegetation or in a form, becoming active in late afternoon. Somewhat social, it often feeds in loose groups.

White-tailed Jack Rabbit
Lepus townsendii
47

22¼–25¾" (56.5–65.5 cm) long. Buffy gray above; white or pale gray below. Tail white above and below, or sometimes with dusky stripe on top but not extending onto rump. Long ears; on outsides buff or gray on front, whitish with black stripe to tip on back. In winter, white or very pale gray in most of range (except most southern parts).

Breeding
1–6 young (averaging 4) are born late May–early June in a form or on the ground.

Habitat
Barren, grazed, or cultivated land; grasslands.

Range
E. Washington and N. California east through Minnesota, Iowa, and Kansas.

Comments
Traveling in 12–20' leaps, this jack rabbit can maintain a speed of 36 mph, with spurts up to 45 mph. Bucks fight furiously during the mating season in April and May, kicking out with their hind feet and biting when they can.

Eastern Cottontail
Sylvilagus floridanus
48

14¾–18¼" (37.5–46.3 cm) long. Grayish brown above, interspersed with some black; forehead often has white spot. Distinct rust-colored nape. Short tail cottony white below. Whitish feet. Long ears.

Sign
Small, woody sprigs cut off cleanly and at an angle (sprigs browsed by deer, which lack upper incisors, are raggedly torn). Young trees stripped of bark to height of 3–4' when snow is deep.
Tracks: In clusters of 4; foreprints almost round, about 1" wide, slightly longer hindprints oblong, about 3–4" long, depending on size and speed of rabbit. When sitting or standing: 2 foreprints side by side just ahead of 2 more widely spaced hindprints. When moving: one foreprint slightly ahead of the other; hindprints ahead of foreprints, as forefeet are fulcrums for hops. Hindprints relatively short when moving fast, as less of the leg touches down. Straddle 4–5"; stride variable with speed.

Breeding
Mates February–September and usually produces 3–4 litters per year of 1–9 young (usually 4–5), which are nursed at dawn and dusk. Within hours after giving birth the female mates again. If no young were lost, a single pair, together with their offspring, could produce 350,000 rabbits in 5 years. However, this rabbit's death rate vies with its birth rate, and few rabbits live more than one year.

Habitat
Brushy areas, old fields, woods, cultivated areas; especially thickets and brush piles.

Range
Eastern United States south of New England, west to North Dakota, Kansas, Texas, N. New Mexico, and into Arizona.

Comments
The Eastern Cottontail is the most common rabbit in our range. Cottontails usually hop, but they can leap 10–15′; sometimes they stand on hind feet to view their surroundings. When pursued, they usually circle their territory and often jump sideways to break their scent trail.

triped Skunk
1ephitis mephitis
9

20½–31½″ (52.2–80 cm) long. Black with 2 broad white stripes on back meeting in cap on head and shoulders; thin white stripe down center of face. Bushy black tail, often with white tip or fringe. Coloration varies from mostly black to mostly white. Males larger than females.

Sign
Strong odor if skunk has recently sprayed. Den entrance sometimes marked with nesting material, snagged hairs. Small pits in ground or patches of clawed-up earth from foraging may be skunk signs if confirmed by tracks or hair.
Tracks: Show 5 toes when clear, sometimes claws. Hindprints 1¼–2″ long, less wide, broadest at front, flat-footed; foreprints 1–1¾″ long, slightly wider; stride 4–6″ (because skunk shuffles and waddles, tracks are closer than in other mustelids, and foreprint and hindprint usually do not overlap); when running, stride longer and hind feet print ahead of forefeet. Trail undulates due to waddling walk.

Breeding
Mates in late winter; in mid-May, 4–7 young born blind, with very fine hair clearly marked with black-and-white pattern.

Habitat
Grassy plains, woodlands, deserts, suburbs.

Range
Most of United States and southern tier of Canadian provinces; also northern Mexico.

Comments
The Striped Skunk is boldly colored, advertising to potential enemies that it is not to be bothered. Its anal glands hold a fetid, oily, yellowish musk, enough for 5 or 6 jets of spray—though 1 is usually enough. When threatened, it raises its tail straight up and sprays scent 10–15′; the mist may reach 3 times as far, and the smell may carry a mile. Fluid in the eyes causes intense pain and fleeting loss of vision. Ammonia or tomato juice can be used to remove the odor; carbolic soap and water are best for washing skin.

Eastern Spotted Skunk
Spilogale putorius
50

13½–22¼″ (34.3–56.3 cm) long. Small. Black with horizontal white stripes on neck and shoulders, irregular vertical stripes and elongated spots on sides. Tail with white tip; white spots on top of head, between eyes.

Sign
Tracks: Like Striped Skunk's but smaller. Hindprint 1¼″ long; heel pad shows more definite lobing. Unlike other skunks, stride very irregular.

Breeding
Mates in late winter; 4–5 young born in spring, blind, furred, and achieve adult coloration in early summer.

Habitat
Mixed woodlands and open areas, scrub, and farmlands.

Range
In the Midwest and Southeast, Minnesota and South Dakota south to Texas and Louisiana; in the East, S. Illinois and south-central Pennsylvania south to Mississippi, W. South Carolina, and Florida; also in extreme northern Mexico.

Comments
Faster and more agile than the larger skunks, the Spotted Skunk is also a good climber, ascending trees to flee predators and occasionally to forage. More social than other skunks, several may share a den in winter. The Spotted Skunk's spraying behavior is unique: if a predator refuses to retreat when it raises its tail, the skunk turns its back, stands on its forefeet, raises its tail again, spreads its hind feet, and sprays, often for a distance of 12′.

Badger
Taxidea taxus
51

20½–34¼″ (52.1–87 cm) long. Flattish body, wider than high, with short bowed legs. Shaggy coat grizzled gray to brown. White stripe from shoulder to pointed, slightly upturned snout. Short, bushy, yellowish tail; cheeks white with black patch; ears small; dark feet with large foreclaws. Males larger than females.

Sign
Den: "Badger hole" or burrow with 8–12″ elliptical entrance to accommodate Badger's flattish shape, surrounded by large mound of earth scattered with bone, fur, rattlesnake rattles, and droppings. Vicinity of burrow marked by other elliptical holes dug when foraging. Burrows of prairie dogs with openings enlarged to capture occupants.
Tracks: Turn in sharply. Foreprint 2″ wide (as long as wide even though little heel pad shows), longer when claw tips show; hindprint narrower than foreprint, 2″ long. Gait variable, with hind foot printing before or behind forefoot. Stride 6–12″; straddle 5–7″, wider in snow.

Breeding
Mates in late summer; delayed implantation; 2–5 young born well furred, blind, March–April; weaned June.

Habitat
Open plains, farmland, sometimes edge of woods.

Range
Western United States east to E. Texas, Oklahoma, N. Missouri, N. Illinois, N. Indiana, N. Ohio, north to SE. British Columbia, Alberta, Manitoba, and S. Saskatchewan.

Comments
This powerful burrower has become nocturnal in areas where it encounters man, but otherwise it is often active by day, usually waddling about but occasionally moving at a clumsy trot. It feeds mainly on small mammals—especially ground squirrels, pocket gophers, rats, and mice—which it usually captures by digging out their burrows. Occasionally a Badger will dig itself into a deserted burrow and await the occupant's return.

Ermine
Mustela erminea
52

7½–13½″ (19–34.4 cm) long. Elongated body, dark brown above, white below. Tail brown with black tip; feet white. In winter, throughout northern range, white with black tail tip, nose, and eyes. Males almost twice as large as females.

Sign
Tracks: Similar to Long-tailed Weasel's but usually smaller.

Breeding
Mates in July; 4–9 young born blind, with fine hair, in spring in some protected area, such as under a log, a rockpile, or tree stump; eyes open at 35 days.

Habitat
Varied: open woodlands, brushy areas, grasslands, wetlands, farmlands.

Range
Most of Canada south to N. Iowa, Michigan, Pennsylvania, and Maryland in East; to N. California, W. Colorado, and N. New Mexico in West.

Comments
Though the Ermine hunts mainly on the ground, often running on fallen logs, it can climb trees and occasionally even pursues prey into water. After a rapid dash, it pounces on its victim with all 4 feet, biting through the neck near the base of the skull.

Long-tailed Weasel
Mustela frenata
53

11–21¾″ (28–55 cm) long. Brown above, white below. Tail brown with black tip; feet brownish. In Southwest, white on face. During winter in northern latitudes, entirely white except for black nose, eyes, and tail tip. Males almost twice as large as females.

Sign
Cache of several dead mice under log or in burrow. Drag marks in deep snow; holes where weasel plunged under snow.

Tracks: Hindprints ¾" wide, 1" long or more, usually with only 4 of the 5 toes printing; foreprints slightly wider, but approximately half as long. Hind feet usually placed in or near foreprints, but prints are sometimes side by side, more often with 1 slightly ahead; straddle 3". Stride varies as weasels run and bound, often alternating long and short leaps: when carrying prey or stalking, 12"; when running, 20".

Breeding
Mates in midsummer; 4–9 young born blind, nearly naked, in early May in abandoned dens of other small mammals; disperse at 7–8 weeks, when males are already larger than mother. Females mate in first year, males not until second season.

Habitat
Varied: forested, brushy, and open areas, including farmlands, preferably near water.

Range
S. British Columbia, Alberta, Manitoba, and Saskatchewan south through most of United States except SE. California and much of Arizona.

Comments
Weasels are wholly carnivorous, preying mainly on mice but also taking rabbits, chipmunks, shrews, rats, and birds, including poultry. They attack prey several times their size, climb 15–20' up a tree after a squirrel, and occasionally go on killing sprees. Their killing instinct is triggered by the smell of blood; even an injured sibling will be killed and eaten.

Least Weasel
Mustela nivalis
54

6¾–8⅛" (17.2–20.6 cm) long. Tiny. Brown above, white below. Tail very short, brown; feet white. All white in winter except in southern part of range.

Sign
Tracks: Similar to those of larger weasels but much smaller; straddle 1¼–1¾"; leaps occasionally 2'.

Breeding
Mates year round; up to 3 litters per year; 3–6 young born in any month, usually in the abandoned burrow of another animal; weaned at 4–7 weeks.

Habitat
Grassy and brushy fields; marsh areas.

Range
Most of Canada south in Midwest to E. Montana, Nebraska, Iowa, N. Illinois, N. Indiana, Ohio, Pennsylvania, West Virginia, through the southern Appalachian Mountains.

Comments
The Least Weasel is the smallest carnivore in North America and one of the most ferocious. Previously known as *Mustela rixosa,* it is now considered to be the same species as the European Least Weasel. Although primarily nocturnal, it is

abroad by day over its home range of less than 2 acres. It feeds almost entirely on meadow mice, chasing them over their runways, pouncing upon them, and killing them with a swift bite at the base of the skull; it also takes an occasional shrew or mole.

Southern Bog Lemming
Synaptomys cooperi
55

4⅝–6⅛" (11.8–15.4 cm) long. Brown above; silvery below. Very short tail brownish above, lighter below. Ears and eyes inconspicuous. Upper incisors shallowly grooved.

Sign
Grass cuttings about 3" long.

Habitat
Grassy meadows; sometimes burrows in northeastern forests; rarely bogs.

Range
SE. Manitoba east to Newfoundland, south to Kansas, NE. Arkansas, W. North Carolina, and NE. Virginia.

Comments
This lemming lives in a system of subsurface runways and burrows about 6" below the ground; it also commonly uses the runways of other small mammals. Its globular grass nest, up to 7" in diameter with 2–4 entrances, may be an underground chamber or above ground among vegetation.

Meadow Vole
Microtus pennsylvanicus
56

5½–7¾" (14–19.5 cm) long. Color variable: from yellowish brown or reddish brown peppered with black, to blackish brown above; usually gray with silver-tipped hair below. Tail long, dark above, lighter below. Feet dark.

Sign
Grass cuttings, 1–1½" long, in piles in runways 1" wide found in dense vegetation.
Tracks: In light snow, hindprint ⅝" long, with 5 toes printing; foreprint ½" long, with 4 toes printing; hindprints ahead of foreprints, with distance between individual walking prints ½–⅞"; straddle, approximately 1½". Print patterns vary greatly, from an overlapping 2-2 pattern to a 4-print pattern. Jumping distances between tracks range from 1¾–4¼".

Habitat
Lush grassy fields; also marshes, swamps, woodland glades, and mountaintops.

Range
Canada and Alaska (except for northern portions) south and east to N. Washington, Idaho, Utah, New Mexico, Wyoming, Nebraska, N. Missouri, N. Illinois, Kentucky, NE. Georgia, and South Carolina.

Comments
This vole lives in a system of surface runways and underground

burrows, often nesting in the burrows during the summer; it may also nest in a depression on the surface under matted vegetation. In winter, the Meadow Vole usually places its spherical grass nest on the surface as long as there is snow cover for protection and insulation.

California Vole
Microtus californicus
57

6¼–8⅜″ (15.7–21.4 cm) long. Grizzled brownish with scattered black hairs above; gray below with hairs often white-tipped. Long tail bicolored. Feet pale.

Habitat
Grassy meadows from sea level to mountains.

Range
California and SW. Oregon; also N. Baja California.

Comments
This vole feeds on grasses and other green vegetation when available; in winter it eats mostly roots and other underground parts of plants. Hawks, owls, weasels, and snakes are its main predators.

Sagebrush Vole
Lagurus curtatus
58

4¼–5⅝″ (10.8–14.2 cm) long. Pale gray above; whitish to silvery or buff below and on feet. Bicolored, well-furred tail usually short. Ears and nose buff.

Sign
Burrow entrances, often under sagebrush clumps, containing greenish scat; grass cuttings; paths between burrows.

Habitat
Sagebrush and grass-sage communities.

Range
E. Washington, S. Alberta, and SW. Manitoba south through E. Oregon to Nevada, Utah, and NE. Colorado.

Comments
These voles are usually found in colonies, which vary greatly in size and density from year to year. There are several entrances to their relatively short burrows, which are often under 2′ long and usually less than 12″ deep with a nest chamber 7–10″ in diameter. The nest is constructed of shredded sagebrush bark lined with grass.

Prairie Vole
Microtus ochrogaster
59

5⅛–6¾″ (13–17.2 cm) long. Grizzled yellowish brown above; buff below. Relatively short tail bicolored. Incisors not grooved.

Habitat
Dry grass prairie or mixed grassy-weed situations.

Range
SE. Alberta, S. Saskatchewan, and S. Manitoba south to E. Colorado, N. Oklahoma, NW. Tennessee, and NW.

Kentucky. Isolated populations in SE. Texas and SW. Louisiana.

Comments
Like many microtines, Prairie Voles are subject to cyclical population fluctuations, with populations peaking, then declining, every 3–4 years. Their diet consists mainly of green vegetation and tubers, which they often cache in underground chambers or tree stumps. These voles often damage orchards and other crops.

Hispid Cotton Rat
Sigmodon hispidus
60

8¼–14⅜″ (20.7–36.5 cm) long. Dark brown or blackish coarse grizzled fur above; grayish below. Tail less than half total length, scaly, scantily haired, slightly lighter below.

Sign
Tracks: In mud, foreprint and hindprint overlap; combined prints about ½″ wide and long; straddle to 1½″; walking stride 1¼″. Those of other cotton rats (*Sigmodon*) similar.

Habitat
Grassy and weedy fields.

Range
SE. Virginia south through Florida, west to SE. Colorado, SE. New Mexico, and SE. Arizona; also northern Mexico.

Comments
Hispid Cotton Rats are among the most prolific of mammals. They begin breeding at 6 weeks and produce several litters per year; however, their enormous reproductive potential is kept in check by their many predators, including birds, reptiles, and other mammals. Omnivorous, Cotton Rats consume vegetation, insects, and small animals.

House Mouse
Mus musculus
61

5⅛–7¾″ (13–19.8 cm) long. Grayish brown above; nearly as dark below. Long tail dusky above and below, nearly naked. Incisors not grooved.

Sign
In buildings: damaged materials and shredded nesting material; in fields: small dark droppings, small holes in ground.

Habitat
Buildings; areas with good ground cover, including cultivated fields. Uncommon in undisturbed or natural habitats.

Range
Throughout United States and southwestern Canada north to central British Columbia, and along the Pacific Coast north to Alaska; also northern Mexico.

Comments
The House Mouse originated in Asia and spread through Europe many centuries ago. In the early 16th century, it

arrived in Florida and Latin America on ships of the Spanish conquistadores and about a century later came to the northern shores of this continent along with English and French traders, and colonists. It makes its own nest but lives in groups, sharing escape holes and areas for eating and defecating.

Deer Mouse
Peromyscus maniculatus
62

4¾–8¾″ (11.9–22.2 cm) long. Grayish to reddish brown above; white below; tail distinctly bicolored and short-haired. Prairie forms usually smaller, with tail shorter and feet smaller than woodland form.

Sign
Tracks: Similar to those of the White-footed Mouse.

Habitat
Prairies; brushy areas; woodlands.

Range
Mexico to S. Yukon and Northwest Territories, east through Canada to Hudson Bay, and south to Pennsylvania, the southern Appalachians, central Arkansas, and central Texas.

Comments
Highly variable, this species comprises numerous subspecies, which differ both in structure and habitat. There are, however, 2 primary forms: the prairie and the woodland. The smaller prairie form (*P. m. bairdii*) occurs through much of the Midwest, whereas the many woodland forms occur to the north, presumably forming a series of interconnecting populations with the prairie form.

Western Harvest Mouse
Reithrodontomys megalotis
63

4½–6¾″ (11.4–17 cm) long. Brownish above, buff along sides; white below.

Habitat
Early-stage dry weedy or grassy areas.

Range
Much of western United States and extreme southwestern Canada east to SW. Wisconsin, NW. Indiana, NE. Arkansas, and W. Texas; also northern Mexico.

Comments
The Western frequently makes use of the ground runways of other rodents and is a nimble climber. Although primarily a seed-eater, in spring it also eats new growth and in summer consumes many insects, especially grasshoppers. It stores surplus food, such as seeds, in underground caches.

Fulvous Harvest Mouse
Reithrodontomys fulvescens
64

5¼–7⅞″ (13.4–20 cm) long. Reddish brown interspersed with black above, shading to yellowish on sides; white below. Tail more than half total length. Feet reddish above.

Habitat
Grassy or weedy areas; arid inland valleys.

Range
SE. Arizona, SW. and E. Texas, E. Oklahoma, SE. Kansas,
SW. Missouri, W. Arkansas, Louisiana, and W. Mississippi.

Comments
In arid areas, these mice live in burrows; elsewhere they
inhabit nests constructed up to 4' above ground. Nests have
only one opening. This species eats mostly seeds and the soft
parts of green plants.

Eastern Harvest Mouse
Reithrodontomys humulis
65

4¼–5⅞" (10.7–15 cm) long. Brownish above, with dark
middorsal stripe; dusky below. Tail about half total length
and not sharply bicolored. Grooved upper incisors.

Habitat
Old fields; brushy areas; briar patches; broom sedges; low
areas.

Range
Southeastern United States: E. Texas, NW. Arkansas,
Mississippi, Tennessee, Kentucky, S. Ohio, West Virginia,
Virginia, Pennsylvania, and Delaware.

Comments
These mice feed on seeds and young sprouts. They store
surplus seeds in their nests and, occasionally, in an extra cache.

Western Jumping Mouse
Zapus princeps
66

8½–10¼" (21.5–26 cm) long. Yellow sides; dark band down
middle of back; belly white, sometimes tinged yellow. Long
tail darker above, whitish below. Enlarged hind feet.

Breeding
Mating occurs soon after emergence from hibernation. The
young are usually born in June or July, sometimes much later.

Habitat
Variable: primarily moist fields, thickets, or woodlands,
especially where grasses, sedges, or other green plant cover is
dense; grassy edges of streams, ponds, or lakes.

Range
Western North America from S. Yukon, all of British
Columbia, southern half of Alberta and Saskatchewan, extreme
SW. Manitoba, south through NE. South Dakota, NE. and
W. Montana, to central New Mexico and east-central Arizona,
Utah, N. Nevada, W. California, and W. Oregon.

Comments
Although it often runs on all four feet, the Western Jumping
Mouse may make a series of jumps 3–5' long when startled
from its hiding place, then "disappear" by remaining
motionless in a new one. It can swim and climb. Although
primarily nocturnal like other jumping mice, by day it has
been observed 1' or more off the ground while foraging in
salal thickets. The seeds of grasses, dock, and many other
green plants, strawberries, blueberries, blackberries, and

subterranean fungi are chief foods. It lives in burrows it digs itself or in those of other animals.

Meadow Jumping Mouse
Zapus hudsonius
67

7¼–10″ (18.7–25.5 cm) long. Yellowish sides; brownish back; white belly. Long tail with tip usually not white.

Breeding
In late April or early May, males emerge from hibernation first; 1–2 weeks later females emerge and the first mating takes place. Gestation is 19 days. There are often two litters of 2–9 young (usually 5–6) per year, with most produced in June and August.

Habitat
Mainly moist fields; but also brush, brushy field, marsh, stands of touch-me-not, woods with thick vegetation.

Range
S. Alaska and most of southern tier of Canadian provinces; northeastern United States west to E. Wyoming, and south to NE. Oklahoma and NE. Georgia.

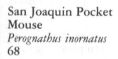

Comments
When startled from a hiding place, this mouse may take a few long jumps of 3–4′, then shorter ones, but generally soon stops and remains motionless, which is its best means of eluding predators. In spring, animal foods are particularly important, with caterpillars, beetles, and other insects constituting about half of its diet. It feeds on the seeds of grasses and many other green plants, either cutting off grasses at the base and pulling the stem down to reach the head, or climbing a stalk and cutting off the head.

San Joaquin Pocket Mouse
Perognathus inornatus
68

5–6⅜″ (12.8–16 cm) long. Soft-furred. Orange-buff above; whitish below. Tail nearly uniform light brown above and below and has a small tuft. Ears may have light spots at base.

Habitat
Weedy or grassy areas on fine soil.

Range
West-central California.

Comments
Under adverse conditions of great heat or cold the San Joaquin Pocket Mouse may become torpid and retire to its burrow. The Latin species name *inornatus* alludes to its uniform coloration, which lacks dramatic "ornamental" markings.

Great Basin Pocket Mouse
Perognathus parvus
69

5¾–7¾″ (14.8–19.8 cm) long. Medium-sized. Soft-furred. Pinkish buff or yellowish above, interspersed with blackish hairs, white or buff below; indistinct olive-greenish line on sides. Long tail, darker above, whitish below, slightly crested toward tip.

Sign
Burrow systems with several openings and packed piles of soil near entrance.

Habitat
Arid, sparsely vegetated plains and brushy areas.

Range
South-central British Columbia south through E. Washington, E. Oregon, and S. Idaho, to NE. and central California, Nevada, extreme NW. Arizona, Utah, and extreme SE. Wyoming.

Comments
It is active from April through September, eating many kinds of insects and collecting seeds to be stored in its burrow, including those of Russian thistle, pigweed, wild mustard, and bitterbrush. Water is metabolized from food. Summer nesting and storage burrows are shallow, but a deep tunnel is dug to a hibernation nest of dry vegetation in a chamber 3–6' deep, where it spends the winter. It mates in April, after emerging from hibernation, and may produce 2 litters per year of 2–8 young born May and August.

Northern Grasshopper Mouse
Onychomys leucogaster
70

5⅛–7½" (13–19 cm) long. Heavy-bodied. 2 color phases above: grayish, or cinnamon-buff; white below. Short, thick, bicolored tail with white tip usually less than one-third total length. Juvenile pelage dark gray.

Sign
Tracks: In mud or dust, foreprint and hindprint overlap partially or completely, each about ⅝" long, ½" wide, with hindprint sometimes slightly longer; straddle 1¼".

Habitat
Low valleys; deserts; prairies.

Range
Much of western North America from SE. Washington, S. Alberta and SW. Manitoba south to NE. California, E. Arizona, and W. Texas; also northern Mexico.

Comments
These mice are most active on moonless nights or under heavy cloud cover. As their name suggests, they feed heavily on grasshoppers, but they also eat other insects, scorpions, mice, and a small amount of plant material. Grasshopper Mice either dig burrows or take over those abandoned by other animals. Their complex burrow systems include a nest burrow, retreat burrows, cache burrows, and signpost burrows.

Oldfield Mouse
Peromyscus polionotus
71

4¾–6" (12.2–15.3 cm) long. Whitish to fawn above; white below. Tail short, bicolored.

Habitat
Waste fields; beaches.

Range
Southeastern United States from E. Alabama, Georgia, and
SW. South Carolina south through N. and E. coastal Florida.

Comments
This burrowing species plugs up the entrance to its tunnels
with sand while inside. At the far end of the burrow, above
the nest, a branch of the tunnel extends upward, ending just
below the ground surface. A predator digging into the burrow
will often cause the mouse to "explode" through this escape
hatch, thereby eluding the startled predator. Seeds and insects
form the bulk of the Oldfield's diet, although blackberries and
wild pea (*Galactia*) are also eaten.

Ord's Kangaroo Rat
Dipodomys ordii
72

8⅛–11⅛″ (20.8–28.2 cm) long. Buff above; white below.
Long tail, usually not white-tipped. Usually conspicuous
white spots at base of ears and above eyes. 5-toed. White tail
stripes narrower than dark stripes. Lower incisors rounded in
front.

Sign
3″ burrow openings often in banks or sand dunes, with small
mounds outside; small, shallow, scooped-out dusting spots, as
well as burrows, reveal a colony area; a tap at a burrow
entrance may get a response of "drumming," the occupant's
foot thumping as an alarm signal.
Tracks: When moving slowly, all 4 feet touch the ground and
heel of hind foot leaves a complete print about 1½″ long,
somewhat triangular, much wider at front than rear; foreprints
much smaller, round, and between hindprints; when resting
on ground, tail leaves a long drag mark. When hopping, heel
of hind foot is off ground, so hindprints are shorter, little or
no tail mark shows, and forefeet may or may not print. Width
of straddle over 2″. Trails radiate and crisscross.

Habitat
Sandy waste areas; sand dunes; sometimes hard-packed soil.

Range
SE. Alberta, SW. Saskatchewan, S. Idaho, south-central
Washington, and E. Oregon south to extreme NE. California,
Arizona, New Mexico, W. Texas, and W. Oklahoma; also
northern Mexico.

Comments
This kangaroo rat is active all winter in Texas, but farther
north it is seldom seen above ground in very cold weather. It
spends its days in deep burrows in the sand, which it plugs to
maintain stable temperature and humidity. Extra holes are
dug throughout the home range as escape hatches. It eats the
seeds of mesquite, tumbleweed, Russian thistle, sunflowers,
and sandbur. Interesting behavior includes skirmishes between
individuals, with each jumping into the air and striking out at
the other with its feet; and kicking sand into the face of an
enemy, such as a rattlesnake.

Heermann's Kangaroo Rat
Dipodomys heermanni
73

9¾–13⅜″ (25–34 cm) long. Brownish above; white below. Tail uniformly dusky, with little or no crest. 5-toed. Ears dusky or nearly black. Juveniles gray.

Sign
Tracks: When resting on hind legs, base of tail forms drag marks between complete hindprints, 1½–2″ long; when moving slowly, smaller round foreprints made between or just in front of hindprints; when making long jumps, only fronts of hind feet touch ground, leaving round prints 1″ across.

Habitat
Open sloping terrain; grassland and woodland in foothills; live oak and pines in low valleys.

Range
Central and S. California.

Comments
Burrow systems may be 6–10′ long, with 2–3 passages, usually with a nest in one, and with 2–3 blind "escape" passages, ending an inch below the surface. It eats seeds of many plants and the green parts of *Lotus, Dudleya, Lupinus,* and *Bromus.* This fast-moving species has been clocked at 12 mph.

Northern Pygmy Mouse
Baiomys taylori
74

3⅜–4⅞″ (8.7–12.3 cm) long. Smallest tree mouse in North America. Body and tail grayish brown above; slightly lighter below. Tail nearly one-half total length.

Habitat
Grassy or weedy areas.

Range
Eastern and S. Texas, extreme SE. Arizona, extreme SW. New Mexico.

Comments
Pygmy Mice utilize small home ranges, usually less than 100′ in diameter. For reasons not yet known, populations occur in isolated pockets, frequently separated by areas seemingly suitable for habitation. They construct nests either underground or in low tangled vegetation; a typical nest consists of a ball of grass, usually with 2 entrances. These mice also maintain networks of tiny runways beneath the matted grass.

Plains Pocket Mouse
Perognathus flavescens
75

4⅜–5⅛″ (11.3–13 cm) long. Soft-furred. Yellowish buff sprinkled with black hairs above; white below. No yellow patches behind ears.

Sign
Tiny burrows leading in all directions from under plants in sandy areas.

Habitat
Sandy plains with sparse vegetation.

Range
SE. North Dakota, W. and S. Minnesota, and N. Iowa
southwest to E. Colorado and Texas Panhandle; also SW.
Colorado, most of W. New Mexico, NE. Arizona, and SE.
Utah.

Comments
During the day it closes the main burrow entrance but usually
leaves open other less conspicuous ones. A subspecies of the
Plains Pocket Mouse is the larger Apache Pocket Mouse
(*Perognathus flavescens apache*), which is distinguished from the
former by its distinct buff side stripe. It is found in
southeastern Utah, southwestern Colorado, northeast Arizona,
and western New Mexico.

Least Shrew
Cryptotis parva
76

2¾–3½″ (6.9–8.9 cm) long. Grayish brown or brownish
above; paler below. Short tail. Only 3 unicuspids visible (the
fourth is behind the third).

Habitat
Grassy or weedy fields, sometimes in marshy areas or wet
woods.

Range
Throughout southeastern United States north to southeast-
central New York and S. Minnesota, west to South Dakota,
NE. Oklahoma, and E. Texas.

Comments
Most active at night but sometimes moving about by day, the
Least Shrew has a metabolism that demands voracious, almost
constant feeding; it eats moth and beetle larvae, earthworms,
spiders, and internal organs of large grasshoppers and crickets.
It probes loose soil and leaf litter for prey, which it detects
chiefly with the stiff hairs around its mouth.

Eastern Mole
Scalopus aquaticus
77

3¼–8¾″ (8.2–22.3 cm) long. Short, velvety fur; gray in
northern parts of range, brownish or tan in southern and
western parts. Forefeet broader than long, with palms turned
out; toes slightly webbed. Tail very short and nearly naked.
Snout long, flexible, and naked. No visible eyes.

Habitat
Open fields, waste areas, lawns, gardens, and sometimes
woods, in well-drained loose soil.

Range
Most of eastern United States from Gulf Coast north to
extreme SE. Wyoming, S. Minnesota, lower peninsula of
Michigan, most of Ohio, E. West Virginia, central
Pennsylvania, and Massachusetts.

Comments
This mole spends nearly all of its time underground,
becoming most active at dawn or dusk. In winter it prefers

deeper burrows. It feeds mainly on earthworms but also eats
larvae and adults of many kinds of insects and other
invertebrates.

ains Pocket Gopher
eomys bursarius
3

7⅜–14⅛″ (18.7–35.7 cm) long. Larger in north, smaller in
south. Light brown to black (in Illinois), varying with color of
soil; slightly lighter below. Long, sparsely haired tail. White
feet. Upper incisors with 2 distinct grooves.

Sign
Mounds of dirt up to 1′ high, more than 2′ wide, often in a
line, with fresh mounds indicating direction of excavation.

Habitat
Prairie areas with sandy loam or loam soils; pastures; lawns;
sometimes plowed ground.

Range
E. North Dakota, Minnesota, and W. Wisconsin south
through central Illinois, NW. Indiana, much of Missouri and
Arkansas to W. Louisiana; west and south through S. South
Dakota, SE. Wyoming, E. Colorado, E. New Mexico, and
northeastern two-thirds of Texas.

Comments
In early spring, the male leaves his burrow to seek a female,
and after having mated returns to his solitary ways. Its
burrows are shallow in summer, usually within 1′ of the
surface, and deeper in winter, when dirt is pushed up into the
snow, leaving earthen cores when the snow melts.

Voodchuck
Marmota monax
9

16½–32¼″ (41.8–82 cm) long. Large. Grizzled brown (or
reddish to blackish); uniformly colored. Prominent bushy tail.
Small ears. Short legs. Feet dark brown or black.

Sign
Large burrow openings 8–12″ across, with mounds just
outside main entrance; often additional escape entrances with
no mound. When hay is high, Woodchucks tramp down trails
radiating from burrows.

Breeding
A litter of 4–5 blind and naked young is born in April or
early May; the young open their eyes and crawl at about 1
month and disperse at 2 months.

Habitat
Pastures, meadows, old fields, and woods.

Range
East-central Alaska, British Columbia, most of southern
Canada, N. Idaho, E. Kansas, NE. North Dakota; in the East,
south to Virginia and N. Alabama.

Comments
The sun-loving Woodchuck is active by day, especially in

early morning and late afternoon. A good swimmer and climber, it will go up a tree to escape an enemy or obtain a vantage point but never travels far from its den. Green vegetation such as grasses, clover, alfalfa, and plantain forms its diet; at times it will feed heavily on corn and can cause extensive damage in a garden. Its burrow, up to 5' deep and 30' long, has one or more tunnels terminating in a chamber containing a large grass nest and is used by other mammals—including cottontail rabbits, Opossums, Raccoons, skunks, and foxes—which enlarge it for use as a nursery den.

Fox Squirrel
Sciurus niger
80

17⅞–27½" (45.5–69.8 cm) long. Largest tree squirrel. 3 color phases: in northeastern part of range, gray above, yellowish below; in western part, bright rust; in South, black often with white blaze on face and white tail tip. Large bushy tail with yellow-tipped hairs. In South Carolina, typically black with white ears and nose.

Sign
Large leaf nests in trees, fairly well hidden in summer but obvious in winter; remains of nuts, tulip tree fruits.

Habitat
Woods, particularly oak-hickory, and prairie edges; in the South, live oak and mixed forests, cypress and mangrove swamps, and piney areas.

Range
Eastern United States except for New England, most of New Jersey, extreme W. New York, N. and E. Pennsylvania; west to the Dakotas, NE. Colorado, and E. Texas.

Comments
The Fox Squirrel is most active in morning and late afternoon burying nuts, which in winter it will locate by its keen sense of smell, even under snow. It eats mainly hickory nuts and acorns but also other nuts and seeds, including the fruit of tulip poplar, the winged seeds of maple trees, ripening corn along wooded areas, open buds, various berries in season, and some fungi. It spends much time in trees feeding or cutting (chewing on) nuts or sunbathing on a limb or in a crotch. In summer it makes a leaf nest in a tree crotch; in winter it lives in a nest in a tree hole, often with a family group.

Columbian Ground Squirrel
Spermophilus columbianus
81

12⅞–16⅛" (32.7–41 cm) long. Grayish mixed with black above, with indistinct buff spotting. Front of face, front legs, and belly reddish brown. Front feet buff. Bushy tail mostly reddish, but edged with white and with some black hairs above, especially at base and tip.

Breeding
1 litter per year of 2–7 young (averaging 3–4).

Habitat
Variable: alpine meadows, arid grasslands, and brushy areas.

Range
SE. British Columbia and SW. Alberta south to NE. Oregon, N. Idaho, and NW. Montana.

Comments
This colonial estivator and hibernator sleeps 7–8 months of the year, starting estivation as early as July in a chamber it seals off from its main tunnels by a plug 2' long.

Uinta Ground Squirrel
Spermophilus armatus
2

11–11⅞" (28–30.3 cm) long. Brownish to buff above, with paler sides; belly buff. Tail buff mixed with black above and below, with pinkish-buff edge. Head, front of face, and ears cinnamon, with grayish dappling on top of head. Sides of face and neck gray. Forelegs and forefeet buff; hind legs cinnamon, hind feet buff.

Breeding
Average of 4–5 young born in May, first year, 6–7 thereafter.

Habitat
Dry sage, sage-grass; also on lawns.

Range
SW. Montana, W. Wyoming, E. Idaho, and north-central Utah.

Comments
Adults begin estivation in July, juveniles later; by September all individuals have·disappeared. From estivation they directly enter the long hibernation. In Utah, adult males emerge first, in late March to mid-April, and remain active only about 3½ months before reentering their sleep cycles. Seeds, other types of vegetation, invertebrates, and some vertebrates are eaten.

Richardson's Ground Squirrel
Spermophilus richardsonii
3

9¾–14" (24.8–35.5 cm) long. Gray or yellowish gray above, tinged with brown or buff and indistinctly mottled; whitish or pale buff below. Tail bordered with white or buff; light brownish or buff below.

Breeding
6–11 young (usually 7–8) born May; forage with mother in June.

Habitat
Open prairies.

Range
S. Alberta, Saskatchewan, and Manitoba south to NE. Idaho, Wyoming, NW. Colorado, NE. South Dakota, extreme W. Minnesota.

Comments
This rather solitary squirrel sometimes appears colonial in favorable habitats, being especially abundant where vegetation is short. Because it often stands erect on its hind legs to survey surroundings, it has acquired the nickname Picket Pin. It is

also called Flickertail, after the way it accompanies its shrill
whistle with a flick of its tail.

**Franklin's Ground
Squirrel**
Spermophilus franklinii
84

15–15⅝" (38.1–39.7 cm) long. Brownish gray peppered with
black above; almost as dark below. Tail blackish mixed with
buff above and below, bordered with white.

Sign
Burrows concealed in tall grass, with some mounds.

Breeding
1 litter of 5–8 young born in May.

Habitat
Dense grassy areas; hedges; brush borders.

Range
East-central Alberta, S. Saskatchewan, and S. Manitoba south
to N. Kansas, N. Illinois, and NW. Indiana.

Comments
The largest and darkest ground squirrel in its range, it
sometimes gathers in small colonies but usually is solitary. It
is active on sunny days but usually retires when the sky is
overcast. In summer it puts on a layer of fat, and it hibernates
from about October to April, depending upon latitude.
Although a good climber, it is believed to spend more than 90
percent of its life underground.

**Belding's Ground
Squirrel**
Spermophilus beldingi
85

10–11¾" (25.3–30 cm) long. Gray washed with reddish or
pinkish above, with broad brown streak down middle of back,
top of head pinkish; pale gray below washed with pinkish
especially toward front. Tail pinkish gray above, reddish to
hazel below, edged with pinkish buff, tipped with black.

Breeding
3–8 young born late June–early July, depending on locale and
spring weather, conditions that determine time of mating.

Habitat
Old fields, roadsides, and other grassy areas, where vegetation
is very short; hay and alfalfa fields in Utah.

Range
E. Oregon, SW. Idaho, NE. California, extreme NW. Utah,
and N. Nevada.

Comments
This semicolonial hibernator feeds on weed and grain seeds,
leaves and stems of green plants, and grasshoppers, crickets,
caterpillars, and other insects. It often stands up on its hind
legs to view its surroundings. Large colonies of these ground
squirrels may damage pastures and grain fields. Their 8-month
hibernation is one of the longest of any North American
mammal.

White-tailed Prairie Dog
Cynomys leucurus
5

13⅜–14⅝″ (34–37 cm) long. Stocky. Pinkish buff mixed with black above; slightly lighter below. Short, white-tipped tail. Dark patches above and below eyes; yellowish nose. Small ears.

Sign
Burrow openings with mounds up to 3′ high, 8–10′ wide. Burrow mounds of White-tailed Prairie Dogs less conspicuous than those of Black-tailed Prairie Dogs, as well as looser and not tamped down as thoroughly. An occasional burrow may have no discernible mound at all, probably because the loose earth has washed away.
Tracks: Similar to those of other prairie dogs.

Breeding
Mates chiefly in March at higher elevations. Gestation requires only a month, but the young (an average of 5 in an annual litter) do not appear at burrow entrances until May or June.

Habitat
Sagebrush plains at high elevations.

Range
SE. Utah, SW. Colorado, NE. Arizona, and NW. New Mexico.

Comments
Although the habits of the White-tail are similar to those of the Black-tailed Prairie Dog, the White-tail is less colonial, with only a few of its burrows interlinked with those of other individuals; it also engages in fewer social contacts such as "kissing," mutual grooming, and cooperative burrow-building. It lives at high, cool elevations (mountain meadows and high pastures rather than level plains) and hibernates throughout the resulting longer winters, entering the burrows by late October and reemerging in March. It is believed to awaken occasionally, at which times it does not emerge but probably feeds underground on roots and seeds. Preferred foods are grasses and forbs. In some areas, White-tailed Prairie Dogs are forced to rely heavily on saltbush.

Black-tailed Prairie Dog
Cynomys ludovicianus
7

14–16¼″ (35.5–41.5 cm) long. Large. Pinkish brown above; whitish or buffy white below. Slim, sparsely haired tail unique among prairie dogs for black tip. Short rounded ears; large black eyes.

Sign
Conical entrance mound to burrow of hard-packed earth at least 1′ high, about 2′ wide, and often wider, resembling miniature volcano.
Tracks: Hindprint 1¼″ long, with 5 toes printing; foreprint slightly smaller, with 4 toes printing. White-tailed and other prairie dogs with similar tracks.

Breeding
Breed February–March and about a month later have their one

annual litter, usually of 4–5 young born deaf, blind, and hairless. The young emerge from the burrow at about 6 weeks

Habitat
Shortgrass prairies.

Range
E. Montana and SW. North Dakota south to NW. Texas, New Mexico, and extreme SE. Arizona; also northern Mexico.

Comments
During the hot summers in most of its range the usually diurnal Black-tailed Prairie Dog often sleeps in its burrow to escape midday heat and is most active above ground mornings and evenings. In cool overcast weather it may be active all day, but it retreats to its burrow to wait out storms. Among the most gregarious of mammals, it lives in "towns" of several thousand individuals covering 100 acres or more. The town is divided into territorial neighborhoods, or "wards," which, in turn, are composed of several "coteries," or family groups of 1 male, 1–4 females, and their young up to two years of age.

Spotted Ground Squirrel
Spermophilus spilosoma
88

7¼–10″ (18.5–25.3 cm) long. Grayish or brownish above, with small, squarish indistinct light spots scattered on back; whitish below. Rather scantily haired tail similar to back, with black tip; buff below. Ears small.

Sign
Burrows about 2″ wide, usually opening under bushes or overhanging rocks.

Breeding
2 litters of 5–7 young abroad by late April.

Habitat
Dry sandy areas especially; also grassy areas and pine woods.

Range
SW. South Dakota south to W. Texas, New Mexico, and Arizona; also northern Mexico.

Comments
Active in the morning and late afternoon, in the heat of the day it often retires to its burrow. In southern parts of its range it is active all year but may hibernate in northern ones. Green vegetation and seeds are its primary foods.

Thirteen-lined Ground Squirrel
Spermophilus tridecemlineatus
89

6¾–11¾″ (17–29.7 cm) long. Brownish, with 13 alternating brown and whitish longitudinal lines (sometimes partially broken into spots) on back and sides. Rows of whitish spots within dark lines.

Sign
Burrow openings with radiating runways; however, openings are often hidden under a clump and no mound marks them, for excess dirt is spread evenly over the ground.

Breeding
Mates in April; 1 litter of 8–10 young born in May.

Habitat
Originally shortgrass prairies; now along roadsides, in yards, cemeteries, golf courses, and wherever grass is kept mowed.

Range
Much of central North America, from SE. Alberta and S. Manitoba south to N. New Mexico, N. and SE. Texas, and east through Minnesota and Missouri to Michigan and Ohio.

Comments
This handsome little spotted animal, also called the Striped Gopher, was known as the leopard-spermophile in Audubon's day. Strictly diurnal, it is especially active on warm days and is easily seen, often scurrying along the side of the road.

Eastern Chipmunk
Tamias striatus
90

8½–11¾″ (21.5–29.9 cm) long. Reddish brown above; belly white. 1 white stripe on sides (bordered by 2 black stripes); stripes end at rump. Dark center stripe down back; light facial stripes above and below eyes. Tail brown on tip, edged with black. Prominent ears. Large internal cheek pouches.

Sign
Burrow entrances 2″ wide without piles of dirt, often on a woody slope or bank; occasional sprinklings of nutshells, opened on one side; bits of chaff on logs, stumps, and rocks. Tracks: In mud, hindprint 1⅛″ long, foreprint considerably smaller; straddle 1¾–3½″; stride 7–15″, with hindprints closer together and printing ahead of foreprints.

Breeding
Mates in early spring; 3–5 young born in May; litters in late July–August probably by first-year females not breeding in early spring.

Habitat
Open woodland; forest edges; brushy areas; bushes and stone walls in cemeteries and around houses.

Range
Southeastern Canada and northeastern United States west to North Dakota and E. Oklahoma, and south to Mississippi, NW. South Carolina, and Virginia.

Comments
The Eastern Chipmunk is a forest dweller, but can often be seen darting into cracks in stone walls along abandoned fields. Although it is essentially a ground species, this pert chipmunk does not hesitate to climb large oak trees when acorns are ripe. Like the Gray and Fox squirrels, it often feeds on acorns and hickory nuts; the cutting sounds it makes as it eats can be heard for some distance. It is single-minded in its food gathering, making trips from tree to storage burrow almost continuously.

GRASSES

The prairies, plains, fields, and meadows of North America support a wide variety of grasses—plants that give these areas their distinctive look and make them habitable for many different kinds of animals. Some grasses are taller than a person, while others often grow no higher than 12 inches. Some species grow in open clusters, while others form strange-looking clumps that sprawl out across the landscape. This section describes some of the most often seen and easily recognized species of the North American grasslands.

Kentucky Bluegrass
Poa pratensis
91

A densely tufted grass with smooth, erect stems topped by pyramidal clusters of ovoid, green spikelets borne on threadlike, spreading, or ascending branches.
Flowers: tiny, lacking petals; stamens 6; styles 2. Flowers enclosed in scales; scales grouped into spikelets about ¼" (6 mm) long; spikelets at the ends of branches, together forming a cluster to 6" (15 cm) long; May–August.
Leaves: to 8" (20 cm) long and ¼" (6 mm) wide, basal and on lower part of stem.
Fruit: lustrous red, linear-elliptic grain.
Height: 1–3' (30–90 cm).

Habitat
Moist or dry soil, meadows, fields.

Range
Throughout North America.

Comments
This grass is often cultivated as a lawn or pasture grass. It gives Kentucky the name Bluegrass State, even though it is not originally from Kentucky. The Bluegrass region near Lexington is noted for its famous racehorses that graze on the limestone-rich grasses.

Velvet Grass
Holcus lanatus
92

Distinctive for its velvety texture and gray-green color, this grass has small flowers in a loose pyramidal cluster.
Flowers: tiny, lacking petals; stamens 3, styles 2. Flowers enclosed by fuzzy scales; entire flower cluster up to 6" (15 cm) long; May–July.
Leaves: to 6" (15 cm) long, velvety.
Fruit: a tiny grain.
Height: 12–25" (30–100 cm).

Habitat
Fields, meadows, roadsides, moist places.

Range
Throughout the United States except for Great Plains and Rocky Mountains.

Comments
A field of Velvet Grass is recognizable from a distance by its soft gray-green color. The plant flowers in the moist spring months, then the flowering stalks disintegrate, leaving little trace through the winter or late summer. Velvet Grass was introduced from Europe and has spread on its own, though it is occasionally planted in meadows.

Redtop
Agrostis alba
93

A delicate grass with many small, 1-flowered spikelets on branches toward the top of the stem, together forming a reddish-brown, pyramidal, open cluster.
Flowers: tiny, lacking petals; stamens 3; styles 2. Flower enclosed by scales, the scales grouped in a spikelet ¹⁄₁₂" (2 mm) long on branches up to 3" (7.5 cm) long; entire cluster

up to 9″ (22.5 cm) long; June–September.
Leaves: blades 2–8″ (5–20 cm) long, ½″ (6 mm) wide,
tapering to a point, hairy on upper surface, smooth on lower
surface; sheathe stem at base.
Fruit: reddish grain.
Height: 8–30″ (20–75 cm).

Habitat
Fields, roadsides, and low places.

Range
Throughout North America.

Comments
The fine, pinkish-tinged, cone-shaped flowering panicles are
especially beautiful in open fields. In flower the tiny stamens,
with conspicuous yellow anthers, hang out of the scales. This
perennial is widely cultivated as a pasture and lawn grass. It
spreads by underground rhizomes or stems, forming colonies.
Grasses used for golf courses belong to this genus.

Indian Grass
Sorghastrum nutans
94

A tall, loosely tufted grass with spikelets forming shiny,
golden-brown, plumelike masses on tall stems.
Flowers: tiny, lacking petals; stamens 3, with prominent,
yellow anthers protruding; styles 2. Flowers enclosed in hairy
scales, with a long, slender twisted bristle projecting. Scales
grouped into spikelets up to ⅓″ (8 mm) long; spikelets in a
narrow cluster to 10″ (25 cm) long; August–September.
Leaves: blades to 2′ (60 cm) long, ½″ (1.3 cm) wide;
projecting from the stem at a 45° angle.
Height: 3–8′ (90–240 cm).

Habitat
Prairies; dry fields.

Range
S. Ontario and Quebec; south through New England to
Florida; west to Texas; north to North Dakota, Wyoming,
and Manitoba.

Comments
This is a beautiful grass with a somewhat metallic golden
sheen to its flowering parts. It is an important associate in the
tallgrass prairies and is relished by livestock. It appears to be
favored by occasional flooding and repeated burning and
sometimes forms nearly pure stands in the lowlands.

Switch Grass
Panicum virgatum
95

Grows in large clumps, with many persistent, curly leaves.
Flowers: tiny, lacking petals; stamens 3, rarely visible; styles
2, small, purple, feathery. Each flower enclosed in several
scales, forming an ovate spikelet ½₂″–¼″ (2.8–6 mm) long.
Flower cluster large, 2–18″ (5–50 cm) long, loose and open,
branches delicate, small flowers widely spaced; July–
September.
Leaves: 4–25″ (10–60 cm) long, numerous, curly.

Fruit: a small, hard grain.
Height: 3–6' (1–2 m).

Habitat
Moist prairies, open ground, roadsides, upper edge of salt marshes.

Range
Throughout the United States except for Pacific Coast states.

Comments
Switch Grass is one of the dominant species of the tallgrass prairie, but also grows as a weed along roadsides. The rich, yellow-colored clumps last throughout the winter.

Sweet Vernal Grass
Anthoxanthum odoratum
96

Tufted, slender stems bear compact, spikelike clusters of narrow, greenish-brown spikelets with projecting bristles.
Flowers: tiny, lacking petals; stamens 3; styles 2. Flowers enclosed in scales, the scales grouped in spikelets ⅓" (8 mm) long; spikelets in a cluster to 3" (7.5 cm) long; April–August.
Leaves: blades to 6" (15 cm) long, up to ¼" (6 mm) wide, flat, rough above; sheathe stem at base; long ligule (projection at base of blade) present.
Fruit: yellowish grain.
Height: 12–28" (30–70 cm).

Habitat
Fields, roadsides, and waste places.

Range
Newfoundland south to Georgia; west to Louisiana and Mississippi; north to Ontario; on the Pacific Coast from British Columbia to California.

Comments
When in flower, the exerted anthers on their long filaments are most conspicuous. This grass is very fragrant when dried and has a sweet, cloverlike flavor when chewed. The genus name is from the Greek *anthos* ("flower") and *xanthos* ("yellow") and refers to the yellowish flowers of some species.

Little Bluestem
Andropogon scoparius
97

An erect, yellowish-tan, tufted grass (reddish tan in fall) with spikelets in narrow terminal clusters on slender stems that intermingle with the leaves.
Flowers: tiny, lacking petals; stamens usually 3; styles 2. Flowers enclosed by scales tipped with long, slender bristles. Scales grouped in small spikelets to ⅓" (8 mm) long; the spikelets in cluster to 2½" (6.3 cm) long; August–October.
Leaves: blades to 10" (25 cm) long, 1½" (3.8 cm) wide; slightly folded, sheathe stem at base.
Fruit: purplish or yellowish grain.
Height: 1½–4½' (45–135 cm).

Habitat
Old fields, prairies, open woods and roadsides.

Range
Throughout the United States, except California,
Washington, Oregon, and Nevada.

Comments
The dominant species of the mixed-green prairie, Little
Bluestem gets its name from the bluish color of the stem bases
in the spring, but most striking is the plant's reddish-tan
color in fall, persisting through winter snows. The seeds
become fuzzy white when they mature; during the winter they
are of particular value to several species of small birds that
spend the cold months in grasslands.

Broomsedge
Andropogon virginicus
98

Short, gold-tan leaves run the full length of the stem, partly
enclosing the short, fuzzy, flowering branches.
Flowers: tiny, lacking petals; stamens 3, styles 2, both barely
visible. Each flower subtended by tufts of white hairs, flowers
arranged in a line along short branches that run the length of
stem, partly hidden in leaf sheaths; August–October.
Leaves: basal leaves sometimes slightly hairy.
Fruit: tiny grain.
Height: 20–40" (50–100 cm).

Habitat
Fields, roadsides, dry soils, open woods.

Range
Central New England, New York west to Iowa, Nebraska,
Oklahoma, Texas, east to Florida; also California.

Comments
The tawny leafstalks last through the winter. Broomsedge is
similar in appearance and habitat to Little Bluestem (*A.
scoparius*), except that it is not a prairie dominant. In
appearance, Broomsedge is leafier, the hairs under the flowers
are whiter, and the flowering branches are more hidden in the
leaf sheaths. A variety of Broomsedge, with large tufts of
leaves at the top of the stem, is extremely common in the
Southeast, filling roadside ditches for endless miles; it is also
found in coastal plain bogs.

Needlegrass
Stipa spartea
99

A shiny, nodding grass, with long bristles.
Flowers: slightly fuzzy, topped with a long bristle twisted in
the middle, and subtended by a fuzzy, sharp-pointed callus.
Each flower enclosed in 2 papery scales that persist after the
grain is dispersed. Entire flower cluster 6–8" (15–20 cm)
long; May–June.
Leaves: narrow, edges often rolled over, 6–12" (20–30 cm)
long.
Fruit: a narrow, sharp-pointed grain, like the flower.
Height: 1¾–7' (0.5–1.2 m).

Habitat
Prairies, sandy soil.

Range
Pennsylvania and Ohio to Oklahoma, New Mexico, Colorado, Wyoming, and Montana.

Comments
Needlegrass is one of the cool-season species that gives the spring prairie its greenness. It is easily recognized by its long bristles and papery scales.

Idaho Fescue
Festuca idahoensis
100

Grows in large tufts with flowers in narrow clusters on stiff stalks, flower stalks twice the height of the leaves.
Flowers: tiny, lacking petals, stamens 3, styles 2, not easily visible; with short bristles; arranged in narrow clusters, 4–8" (10–20 cm) long; May–August.
Leaves: long, threadlike, very rough.
Fruit: a small grain.
Height: 11–40" (30–100 cm).

Habitat
Rocky slopes, open woods, sagebrush plains, mountain meadows.

Range
Washington to California, Nevada, Utah, Colorado, north to Montana.

Comments
In spite of its rough leaves, Idaho Fescue is still an important native forage grass.

Big Bluestem
Andropogon gerardi
101

A tall, gangly grass, rich in a variety of colors: bronze, tan, crimson, green, and lead-gray.
Flowers: each with a short bristle, lined on short stalks that radiate in bunches of 2–6 from a single point, like fingers; August–October.
Leaves: long, often curly, the lower ones sometimes hairy.
Fruit: small grain.
Height: 3½–7' (1–2 m), sometimes taller.

Habitat
Prairies, fields, roadsides, dry woods, rocky shorelines.

Range
Maine to Florida, west to Montana, south to Arizona.

Comments
Big Bluestem is the chief grass of the tallgrass prairie and once covered solid acres. The basal leaves are very nutritious for cattle, and it is now being rediscovered as a commercial hay and forage plant. Another name for it is Turkey Claw.

Reed Canary Grass
Phalaris arundinacea
102

Grows in large patches, the flowering stalks jutting in a uniform layer over the leaves, which also grow to a uniform height. The flower stalks do not persist long after flowering.

Flowers: tiny, lacking petals; stamens 3, styles 2; flowers enclosed in small, papery scales, entire flower cluster erect, 2–8″ (5–20 cm) long, narrow, tapering to a point at the top; June–August.
Leaves: flat, relatively wide; to ½″ (2 cm).
Fruit: a small, shiny grain.
Height: 2–7′ (0.6–2 m).

Habitat
Low, wet places, riverbanks, marshes.

Range
Maine to Virginia, west to Washington and California.

Comments
This introduced grass is much planted for hay but is also naturally established. Like many marsh plants, Reed Canary Grass spreads by rhizomes and soon forms large patches. The inflorescences can be mistaken for those of Orchard Grass (*Dactylis glomerata*), but they are more fragile and smooth-textured, and the growth habit is different: Orchard Grass grows in distinct clumps on drier soil. A variety of Reed Canary Grass, *Phalaris arundinacea* (var. *picta*), with white stripes on the leaves, is known as Ribbon Grass and is often planted in gardens.

Buffalo Grass
Buchloe dactyloides
103

A low, gray-green grass, spreading to form dense mats.
Flowers: male and female flowers separate, unusual among grasses. Male flowers tiny, arranged in 2 rows along 2 or 3 branches ¼–½″ (6–12 mm) long; female flowers in round, hard, somewhat spiny clusters tucked in sheaths of the leaves; May–August.
Leaves: short and curly, slightly hairy.
Fruit: a small, hard grain.
Height: male flower stalks 4–12″ (10–30 cm).

Habitat
Dry plains.

Range
North Dakota, Montana, south to Texas, New Mexico, Arizona, and Nevada.

Comments
The range of this grass is almost synonymous with that of the shortgrass prairie, of which Buffalo Grass is one of the dominant species. The plant is called Buffalo Grass because it apparently sustained the buffalo, which in turn trampled the ground and created conditions favorable for its growth.

Orchard Grass
Dactylis glomerata
104

A coarse grass; flowering branches few, short and stiff.
Flowers: tiny, lacking petals, stamens 3, styles 2. Flowers enclosed in small, rough, gray-green scales, which are then arranged in small, irregularly shaped clusters at the end of the short, stiff branches; May–September.

Leaves: rough, blue-green, shaggy.
Fruit: a tiny grain.
Height: 16–60″ (40–150 cm).

Habitat
Meadows, roadsides, waste places.

Range
Throughout North America.

Comments
Orchard Grass was imported early in colonial times and
planted for hay. It has now spread successfully and in some
places is an extremely common spring grass.

Prairie Cordgrass
Spartina pectinata
105

A tall grass, with stiff, widely spaced flowering branches, the
entire flower cluster reaching well above the leaves.
Flowers: tiny, lacking petals, stamens 3, styles 2, not easily
visible; enclosed in rough, papery scales, each one with a short
bristle at tip. Arranged in tight rows along 1 side of the
flowering branches, like the teeth of a comb. Flowering
branches ½–4½″ (2–11 cm) long; widely spaced along top
part of main stalk; July–September.
Leaves: 11–50″ (30–120 cm) long, very rough along edges.
Fruit: a small grain.
Height: 1½–7′ (0.5–2.5 m).

Habitat
Wet prairies, shores, roadsides, salt marsh edges.

Range
Maine to Washington, south to Virginia, Tennessee,
Missouri, Texas, New Mexico, Utah, and Oregon.

Comments
This is one of our tallest grasses and is probably the species
that gave rise to Midwestern settlers' accounts of grass higher
than a horse's back. Prairie Cordgrass is one of the dominants
of the tallgrass prairie, growing mainly in low, wet areas. The
species name derives from the Greek word *pecten* ("comb"),
referring to the appearance of the plant's flowering branches.
Also known as Sloughgrass.

Timothy
Phleum pratense
106

Recognizable by the narrow, compact, cylindrical flower
cluster.
Flowers: tiny, lacking sepals and petals; stamens 3, styles 2,
plumose. Flowers enclosed by flattened bristle-tipped scales
about 1/12″ (2 mm) long. Scales grouped into spikelets, the
spikelets in a cluster up to 7″ (17.5 cm) long; June–August.
Leaves: 4–10″ (10–25 cm) long, ¼″ (6 mm) wide; tapering to
a point.
Height: 1½–3′ (45–90 cm).

Habitat
Fields, roadsides, clearings.

Range
Throughout North America, but particularly in cooler areas.

Comments
This common old field or pasture grass is easily recognized by the somewhat bristly spike, especially fuzzy when in flower with the stamens projecting. It is an excellent hay plant; songbirds enjoy the seeds and the cover provided by the plants growing along roadsides and fencerows.

Foxtail Barley
Hordeum jubatum
107

Small and shiny. When in flower, the nodding clusters are purple to pale green, with many long, straight bristles; after flowering, the bristles frizz up, and the flower heads dry to a bleached tan and disintegrate easily.
Flowers: tiny, lacking petals, stamens 3, styles 2, not easily visible; enclosed in narrow scales, with bristles 1¼–2½" (3–6 cm) long. Flower cluster soft, 2–4" (5–10 cm) long; June–August.
Leaves: short and rough, not numerous.
Fruit: a small grain.
Height: 12–24" (30–60 cm).

Habitat
Waste places, roadsides, meadows, bare soil.

Range
Throughout the United States, except for the Southeast.

Comments
In parts of the West, this grass is exceedingly common, carpeting roadsides and waste areas. In the presettlement prairies, it was probably one of the colonizers of temporarily bare soil. Beautiful as it is, this grass is unpopular with ranchers because the bristles pierce the mouths of the livestock that graze it.

Blue Grama
Bouteloua gracilis
108

A fine-textured, clump-forming grass, easily recognized by its leafy base and delicate, arching flower stalks with flowers along one side.
Flowers: 1–3, stalkless, purplish, borne on 1 side of stem, with up to 80 spikelets; somewhat resembling a toothbrush or tiny comb; to 2" (5cm) long; May–August.
Leaves: 3–5" (7.5–12.5 cm) long; flat, smooth, somewhat curly at base.
Fruit: a small grain.
Height: 6–20" (15–50 cm).

Habitat
Arid shortgrass prairie and plains, often in shallow, rocky, or sandy soils.

Range
Alberta and Manitoba to Wisconsin, south to S. California, Texas, and Arkansas; also in Mexico.

Comments
Together with Buffalo Grass (*Buchloe dactyloides*), Blue
Grama, which is also known as Mosquito Grass and
Mesquite Grass, dominates the shortgrass prairie of North
America's Great Plains region.

Tobosa Grass
Hilaria mutica
109

A rough grass with stiff leaves, often growing in patches.
Flowers: flower clusters arranged in groups of 3, the middle
clusters with many short bristles and producing seed, the
outer 2 clusters male and producing no seed; all flowers hairy-
tufted at base; June–October.
Leaves: very stiff, hairy-tufted at the nodes.
Fruit: a small grain.
Height: 12–24" (30–60 cm).

Habitat
Plains, low hills, valleys.

Range
California to Texas and Colorado; Wyoming.

Comments
Many areas formerly occupied by Tobosa Grass have now been
taken over by mesquite and other shrubs.

Needle-and-Thread
Stipa comata
110

An upright grass, with long bristles.
Flowers: fuzzy, topped by a bristle 4–9" (10–24 cm) long,
twisted at the base, loosely twisted above, and curved at tip;
each flower subtended by a sharp-pointed, hairy callus. Entire
flower cluster loose, 1–4" (4–16 cm) long; June–July.
Leaves: narrow; basal leaves threadlike, 4–12" (10–30 cm)
long.
Fruit: a long, sharp-pointed grain, like the flower.
Height: 12–24" (30–60 cm).

Habitat
Prairies, plains, and dry hills.

Range
Michigan, Indiana, Wisconsin, Minnesota to Washington,
south to California and Texas.

Comments
This species is similar to *S. spartea* but occurs further west and
is usually found on drier sites. *S. comata* does not nod like *S.
spartea,* and the bristles are curved at the tip and twisted at the
base.

Purple Needlegrass
Stipa pulchra
111

When in flower, this grass has a purplish cast; it is also
recognizable by its many long bristles.
Flowers: each flower only slightly hairy, topped by a twice-
twisted bristle 2½–3½" (7–9 cm) long and subtended by a
sharp-pointed, hairy callus. Entire flower cluster loose,
nodding, 6–8" (15–20 cm) long.

Leaves: long, narrow.
Fruit: a narrow, pointed grain, like the flower.
Height: 2–3½' (60–100 cm).

Habitat
Native grasslands, serpentine barrens, open places.

Range
Only in California.

Comments
As far as anyone can tell, Purple Needlegrass was once the dominant plant of the Central Valley prairies. Because most of these prairies are now lost to agricultural or urban development, Purple Needlegrass is much less frequent.

Bluebunch Wheatgrass
Agropyron spicatum
112

Grows in large bunches, with stiff, straight flowering stalks; often blue-green.
Flowers: tiny, lacking petals, stamens 3, styles 2, not easily visible; flower clusters flat, arranged in narrow spikes 3½–6" (8–15 cm) long; June–August.
Leaves: long, hairy on upper surface, green or blue-green.
Fruit: a small grain.
Height: 20–40" (60–100 cm).

Habitat
Dry slopes, plains, open woods.

Range
Washington to California, east to Montana, New Mexico, also North and South Dakota.

Comments
A former dominant of the intermountain grasslands, this species is now much diminished in distribution due to competition from Downy Brome and Sagebrush.

Common Sagebrush
Artemisia tridentata
113

A shrub of variable size, with strong-smelling, fuzzy, gray-green foliage.
Flowers: small, dull-colored, arranged in small, round clusters on short branches at top of stem; August–November.
Leaves: gray-green, fuzzy, with a pungent smell; wedge-shaped, 3–5 lobed at tip; to 1" (3 cm) long; upper leaves sometimes without lobes.
Fruit: small, hard, grainlike.
Height: usually 2–7' (0.6–2 m); can grow to be a small tree.

Habitat
High plains, dry mountain slopes, dry woods.

Range
Montana to Washington, south to Nebraska, New Mexico, and California.

Comments
Some have labeled Common Sagebrush the most abundant

shrub in North America. In some parts of the West, it grows for seemingly interminable distances, regularly spaced like orchard trees to the apparent exclusion of anything else. Its abundance has increased due to settlement and the overexploitation of grasslands. Although Common Sagebrush might not make very palatable cattle food, it is attractive to mule deer and pronghorn, and it provides cover and nesting sites for many species of birds. There are many species of shrubby *Artemisia* in the West, but none of the others has wedge-shaped, 3-lobed leaves.

Creosote Bush
Larrea tridentata
14

A medium-sized shrub, with dark green, strong-smelling, leathery leaves.
Flowers: sepals 5; petals 5, twisted, yellow, ¼–½" (5–8 mm) long; stamens 10; April–June.
Leaves: compound, each consisting of 2 oblong to obovate leaflets ¼–½" (5–10 cm) long; evergreen, resinous, strong-smelling.
Fruit: a densely white, hairy capsule, about ¼" (5 mm) in diameter.
Height: to 7' (2 m).

Habitat
Low plains, sandy flats, dry slopes.

Range
Texas to S. Utah, New Mexico, Arizona, and California.

Comments
It has been said that Creosote Bush is to the low, hot deserts as Common Sagebrush is to the high, cold deserts: a relentless, ubiquitous dominant. Like Common Sagebrush, Creosote Bush often grows in endless pure stands, so regularly spaced that it appears to have been planted. It is instantly recognizable by the smell of the leaves, which is especially strong after a rain.

WILDFLOWERS

From early spring to late fall, the grasslands put on a brilliant display of color as thousands of wildflowers burst into bloom. Some of these, such as the daisies and sunflowers, are easily recognized; others, like the Rain Lily and Prairie Gentian, are less well known and offer the visitor a special kind of delight. In this section, you will find descriptions of some of the most typical and beautiful wildflowers of the grasslands.

Flatpod
Idahoa scapigera
15

Tiny, with a basal rosette of leaves and several slender, leafless stems tipped with 1 minute white flower or a round flat pod.
Flowers: petals 4, about ⅛″ (3 mm) long.
Leaves: blades ¼–⅝″ (6–15 mm) long, ovate, on petioles up to 3 times as long.
Fruit: pod ¼–½″ (6–13 mm) wide; green, often mottled with reddish brown.
Height: 1–5″ (2.5–12.5 cm).

Flowering
February–April.

Habitat
Open places in grassland or among sagebrush, commonly where moist early in season.

Range
N. California to E. Washington, S. Idaho, and N. Nevada.

Comments
When the 2 sides of the pod fall away, the silvery partition remains attached to the tip of the flower stalk.

Rattlesnake Master
Eryngium yuccifolium
16

Smooth, rigid stem bearing thistlelike flower heads made up of small greenish-white florets mingled with pointed bracts.
Flowers: head ¾″ (2 cm) wide, slightly ovoid, surrounded by larger pointed bracts.
Leaves: to 3′ (90 cm) long, linear, sharp-pointed, parallel-veined, bristly, clasping stem.
Height: 2–6′ (60–180 cm).

Flowering
July–August.

Habitat
Prairies, open woods, and thickets.

Range
S. Connecticut south to Florida; west to Texas and Kansas; north to Minnesota, Wisconsin, and Michigan.

Comments
Their spiny leaves make walking through clumps of these plants difficult, and also make them unpalatable to grazing livestock. They were once credited with curative powers.

Marijuana
Cannabis sativa
17

Coarse, branching plant with erect stems and clusters of small greenish flowers in the leaf axils.
Flowers: to ⅛″ (3 mm) wide; male and female on separate plants.
Leaves: palmately divided, hairy, with 5–7 long, narrow, coarsely toothed, tapering leaflets 2–6″ (5–15 cm) long.
Height: 3–10′ (90–300 cm).

Flowering
June–October.

Habitat
Waste places and roadsides.

Range
Widespread as a weed in the Eastern United States; also occurs in most western states.

Comments
This annual was introduced from Asia and grown for making rope. It has been displaced on a commercial basis by synthetics and other natural fibers and its cultivation prohibited because the narcotic marijuana is obtained from its female flowers.

Devil's Claw
Proboscidea altheaefolia
118, 197

A coarse plant with stems lying on the ground and a few yellowish-green bilaterally symmetrical flowers in racemes.
Flowers: corolla 1–1½" (2.5–3.8 cm) long, commonly flecked with maroon or rust-brown, the 5 lobes spreading from a broad opening.
Leaves: blades ¾–3" (2–7.5 cm) long, fleshy, roundish, edges plain, scalloped, or deeply lobed.
Fruit: pod about 2½" (6.3 cm) long, with curved horn nearly 5" (12.5 cm) long.
Height: creeper, with flower stalks to about 1' (30 cm) high, and stems spreading to nearly 3' (90 cm) wide.

Flowering
June–September.

Habitat
Sandy soil in arid grassland and deserts.

Range
S. California to W. Texas.

Comments
As the plump fruit matures, it divides into halves, the single "horn" forming two curved "devil's claws."

Green Pitaya
Echinocereus viridiflorus
119

A small cactus with 1 cylindrical stem or several in a clump; flowers yellowish green or magenta with many petals.
Flowers: near top of stem, ¾–1" (2–2.5 cm) wide.
Stems: 4" (10 cm) wide; 6–14 ribs.
Spines: ½–1" (1.3–2.5 cm) long, red, brownish, white, gray, or greenish yellow, making bands of color on stem.
Fruit: green, with spines that eventually drop.
Height: 1–10" (2.5–25 cm).

Flowering
May–July.

Habitat
Dry plains and hills.

Range
SE. Wyoming and W. South Dakota; south to E. New Mexico and W. Texas.

Comments
Pitaya (pronounced *pee-tah'-yah*) is the phonetic spelling of the
original Spanish *pitahaya,* a name broadly applied to a number
of cacti that produce sweet, edible fruit.

agged Fringed Orchid
abenaria lacera
20

Whitish-green or creamy-yellow flowers with highly lacerated,
3-parted lip petals are in spikelike clusters.
Flowers: ½″ (1.3 cm) long; sepals and petals colored alike;
upper sepal and 2 narrow petals erect; lateral sepals ovate,
spreading; lip petal deeply 3-parted, the lateral divisions
deeply cut, the middle division coarsely fringed; spur curved,
slender, ½″ (1.3 cm) long.
Leaves: lower ones to 8″ (20 cm) long, lanceolate, sheathing
the stem; upper ones smaller.
Height: 1–2′ (30–60 cm).

Flowering
June–September.

Habitat
Bogs, wet woods, and dry to wet meadows and fields.

Range
Nova Scotia and New England; south to Florida; west to
Texas; north to Tennessee, Minnesota, and Ontario.

Comments
This Orchid is one of the more common and widespread
members of the genus.

indweed
onvolvulus arvensis
21

Long trailing and twining stems with rather triangular leaves
have, on short stalks, white or pinkish, funnel-shaped flowers.
Flowers: about 1″ (2.5 cm) wide; corolla with 5 veins leading
to low lobes on edge; 2 narrow bracts about ¼″ (6 mm) long
on stalk well below calyx.
Leaves: ¾–1½″ (2–3.8 cm) long, generally triangular, but
sometimes arrow-shaped or ovate; short stalk.
Height: 1–3′ (30–90 cm).

Flowering
May–October.

Habitat
Fields, lots, gardens, and roadsides.

Range
Throughout North America.

Comments
Bindweed's very deep roots make it a troublesome weed,
difficult to eradicate.

ego Lily
alochortus nuttallii
22

Erect, unbranched stems with a few leaves are topped by 1–4
showy, white, bell-shaped flowers in an umbel-like cluster.
Flowers: 1–2″ (2.5–5 cm) wide; sepals 3, lanceolate, slightly

shorter than petals; petals 3, broad, fan-shaped; yellow around
the gland at base, marked with reddish brown or purple above
the gland; gland circular, surrounded by a fringed membrane.
Leaves: 2–4″ (5–10 cm) long, narrow; edges rolled upward.
Height: 6–18″ (15–45 cm).

Flowering
May–July.

Habitat
Dry soil on plains, among sagebrush, and in open pine forests.

Range
E. Montana and W. North Dakota; south to E. Idaho and
NW. Nebraska; across Utah and W. Colorado to N. Arizona
and NW. New Mexico.

Comments
This is Utah's state flower; the Utes called it "sago" and
taught Mormon settlers to eat the bulbs in times of scarcity.

Horse Nettle
Solanum carolinense
123

Starlike, white or pale lavender flowers with yellow centers are
in lateral clusters on a prickly, erect stem.
Flowers: ¾–1¼″ (2–3.1 cm) wide; petals 5; stamens 5 with
yellow, elongated anthers forming central cone.
Leaves: 3–5″ (8–12.5 cm) long, rough, elliptic-oblong,
coarsely lobed, and covered with prickles.
Fruit: yellow, tomatolike berries, ¾″ (2 cm) across.
Height: 1–3′ (30–90 cm).

Flowering
May–October.

Habitat
Fields, waste places, and gardens.

Range
S. Ontario to New England and New York; south to Florida;
west to Texas; north to Nebraska; sparingly established as a
weed in several western states.

Comments
This plant is not related to the true Nettles. A coarse, native,
deep-rooted perennial, it is considered a weed by some, yet the
flowers are attractive.

Elegant Camas
Zigadenus elegans
124

Long, basal, grasslike leaves and cream or greenish-white,
bowl-shaped flowers in a raceme or branched flower cluster.
Flowers: about ¾″ (2 cm) wide; 6 broad, petal-like segments,
each with a greenish, heart-shaped gland at base; flower parts
attached around sides of ovary rather than at base.
Leaves: 6–12″ (15–30 cm) long.
Height: 6–28″ (15–70 cm).

Flowering
June–August.

Habitat
Mountain meadows, rocky slopes, and forests.

Range
Western Canada; south to W. Washington, E. Oregon, Arizona, New Mexico, and Texas.

Comments
Also known as Alkali Grass. Camases are among the most infamous western plants, poisoning many livestock, especially sheep. Indians and early settlers were also poisoned whenever they mistook the bulbs for those of edible species, such as the Camas Lily (*Camassia*). The highly poisonous *Z. venenosus* grows throughout most of the western United States. It has petal-like segments about ¼" (6 mm) long, the inner 3 slightly longer and with a short stalk at the base, and stamens about as long as the segments.

Velvety Nerisyrenia
Nerisyrenia camporum
125

This grayish, hairy plant has clumps of leafy, branched stems and at the ends of branches bears racemes of white or lavender flowers.
Flowers: about ¾" (2 cm) wide; petals 4.
Leaves: ½–2½" (1.3–6.3 cm) long, lanceolate, toothed, with short stalks.
Fruit: pods ½–1½" (1.3–3.8 cm) long, narrow, 4-sided, and slightly flattened, held erect, the partition in center of pod perpendicular to broad sides.
Height: 8–24" (20–60 cm).

Flowering
February–October.

Habitat
Gravelly or rocky soils derived from limestone, or on limestone in deserts and arid grassland.

Range
W. Texas, SW. New Mexico, and northern Mexico.

Comments
This is the most common species of Mustard in its region that has large white flowers.

Common Strawberry
Fragaria virginiana
126

This low perennial forms runners and produces several small, white flowers and long-stalked, 3-parted basal leaves.
Flowers: ¾" (2 cm) wide; sepals 5; petals 5, roundish; stamens many, numerous; pistils many, on a domelike structure.
Leaves: leaflets 1–1½" (2.5–3.8 cm) long, toothed, and with hairy stalks.
Fruit: dry, seedlike, sunken within enlarged, fleshy cone—the "strawberry."
Height: creeper, with flower stalk 3–6" (7.5–15 cm) high.

Flowering
April–June.

Habitat
Open fields; edges of woods.

Range
Throughout North America except in the Southwest.

Comments
Found in patches in fields and dry openings, this plant produces the finest, sweetest, wild strawberry. The edible portion of the strawberry is actually the central portion of the flower (receptacle), which enlarges greatly with maturity and is covered with the embedded, dried, seedlike fruit.

Multiflora Rose
Rosa multiflora
127

On prickly, arching stems are clusters of many small, fragrant, white flowers.
Flowers: ¾–1½″ (2–3.8 cm) wide; sepals 5, lanceolate, sharp-tipped; petals 5; stamens and pistils numerous.
Leaves: pinnately divided into 7–9 ovate, toothed leaflets, about 1″ (2.5 cm) long; highly fringed, winged leaf appendages present at base of leaf stalks. Thorns curved, flattened.
Fruit: small, fleshy, many-seeded hip.
Height: 6–16″ (1.8–4.5 m).

Flowering
May–June.

Habitat
Borders of fields and woods; roadsides.

Range
Southern New England to Kansas, Texas, and Florida.

Comments
This small-flowered Rose is sold as a living hedge by nurseries. It forms dense impenetrable masses and provides excellent wildlife cover; however, it has become a pest in many areas.

Douglas' Meadow Foam
Limnanthes douglasii
128, 187

The broadly bell-shaped flowers of this delicate, branched plant usually have a yellow center with a white rim, or are all yellow, and bloom on slender stalks in upper leaf axils.
Flowers: about ¾″ (2 cm) wide; petals 5, broad, notched at tip; stamens 10, each about ¼″ (6 mm) long.
Leaves: 2–5″ (5–12.5 cm) long, divided into segments.
Fruit: divides into 5 smooth or slightly warty, seedlike sections.
Height: 4–16″ (10–40 cm).

Flowering
March–May.

Habitat
Low, moist places in grassland and open woodland.

Range
S. Oregon to S. California.

Comments
A form with all-yellow petals grows on Point Reyes in northern California; in the Coast Ranges, the flower may have white petals often with dark purple veins. Near the Central Valley, petals may be white with rose veins, becoming pink.

Yarrow
Achillea millefolium
29

Flat-topped clusters of small, whitish flowers grow at the top of a gray-green, leafy, usually hairy stem.
Flowers: heads about ¼" (6 mm) across, composed of 4–6 ray flowers surrounding tiny central disk flowers.
Leaves: 6" (15 cm) long, very finely dissected, gray-green, fernlike, aromatic; lanceolate in outline, stalkless. Basal leaves longer.
Height: 1–3' (30–90 cm).

Flowering
June–September.

Habitat
Old fields, roadsides.

Range
Throughout temperate North America.

Comments
Yarrow was formerly used for medicinal purposes: to break a fever by increasing perspiration, to treat hemorrhaging, and as a poultice for rashes. A tea used by the Indians to cure stomach disorders was made by steeping the leaves.

Blackfoot Daisy
Melampodium leucanthum
30

A low, round, bushy plant with flower heads of 8–10 broad white rays surrounding a small yellow disk.
Flowers: heads about 1" (2.5 cm) wide, with 5 broad outer bracts joined to one another for half or two-thirds their length.
Leaves: ¾–2" (2–5 cm) long, opposite, narrow.
Fruit: seedlike, with several narrow scales at tip.
Height: 6–20" (15–50 cm).

Flowering
March–November.

Habitat
Rocky soil on dry plains and in deserts.

Range
Arizona to Kansas; south to Mexico.

Comments
At first glance Blackfoot Daisy appears the twin of White Zinnia (*Zinnia acerosa*), but heads of that species have 4–6 white rays and a narrow base of several overlapping scales.

English Daisy
Bellis perennis
31

Short, slender, leafless stalks, each bearing 1 flower head with many narrow white or pinkish rays and yellow disk flowers, grow from a basal rosette of leaves.

Flowers: heads about 1" (2.5 cm) wide, with bracts the same length.
Leaves: to 1½" (3.8 cm) long, the blade elliptic or round and with small teeth on edges, tapered at base to a broad petiole as long or longer.
Fruit: seedlike, no hairs or scales at tip.
Height: 2–8" (5–20 cm).

Flowering
March–September.

Habitat
Lawns, fields, and roadsides.

Range
Introduced from Europe and found scattered throughout the United States.

Comments
The word "daisy" comes from Anglo-Saxon *daeges ege* and means "day's eye." English Daisy folds up its rays at night and opens them again at dawn–the "eye of the day."

Oxeye Daisy
Chrysanthemum leucanthemum
132

The common white-and-yellow daisy of the fields, with solitary flower heads on slender, erect stems.
Flowers: heads 1–2" (2.5–5 cm) wide; ray flowers white, all female; disk flowers yellow, both male and female; disk depressed at center.
Leaves: dark green, coarsely toothed or pinnately lobed, basal ones to 6" (15 cm) long, upper ones to 3" (7.5 cm).
Height: 1–3' (30–90 cm).

Flowering
June–August.

Habitat
Waste places, meadows, pastures, and roadsides.

Range
Throughout much of North America, but less abundant southward.

Comments
This species–the "day's eye"—is disliked by farmers because it can produce an unwanted flavor in milk if eaten by cattle.

Spreading Fleabane
Erigeron divergens
133

A well-branched plant covered with short, grayish hairs, those on stems standing straight out; at the tip of each of the many branches blooms a flower head with many narrow white, pink, or lavender rays surrounding a yellow disk.
Flowers: heads about 1" (2.5 cm) wide, with very narrow bracts, mostly lined up side by side, and not overlapping like shingles; rays each ¼–½" (6–10 mm) long.
Leaves: largest in tufts at base, ½–1" (1.3–2.5 cm) long, the lanceolate blade evenly tapered to the stalklike base; those on stem numerous, but slightly smaller.

Fruit: seedlike, with numerous fragile, fine bristles at top.
Height: 4–28″ (10–70 cm).

Flowering
April–September.

Habitat
Open sandy areas in deserts, plains, valleys, and foothills.

Range
S. British Columbia to California; east to W. Texas, Colorado, and Montana; also Mexico.

Comments
This is one of a large number of similar species. Most usually can be recognized as *Erigeron* by their low form, many white, pink, or lavender rays, and bracts around the head.

anicled Aster
ster simplex
34

Tall stem bears a loose cluster of white, occasionally violet-tinged flower heads.
Flowers: heads ¾–1″ (2–2.5 cm) wide; ray flowers numerous, bracts surrounding the flower heads very narrow, green-tipped.
Leaves: lanceolate, sharp-pointed; lower leaves 3–6″ (7.5–15 cm) long, upper ones smaller.
Height: 2–5′ (60–150 cm).

Flowering
August–October.

Habitat
Damp thickets, meadows, and shores.

Range
Eastern Canada to North Dakota, Kansas, and Virginia.

Comments
This plant spreads by underground rootstocks to form colonies. It has many varieties, differing in color, size of the ray flowers, leaf form, and serration.

Calico Aster
Aster lateriflorus
35

Several small flower heads of white or pale purple ray flowers surrounding yellow or purple disk flowers are on one side of straggly, divergent branches.
Flowers: less than ½″ (1.3 cm) wide with 9–15 ray flowers surrounding the central disk, bracts under flower heads with greenish midrib.
Leaves: 2–6″ (5–15 cm) long, lanceolate to elliptic, coarsely toothed.
Height: 1–5′ (30–150 cm).

Flowering
August–October.

Habitat
Fields; thickets.

Range
Ontario to Nova Scotia south to Georgia, east to Texas, and north to Minnesota.

Comments
The heads are at first yellow and later turn purplish red, so that flowers on a single head may include both colors at once.

Chickweed
Stellaria media
136

A weak-stemmed, much-branched, low plant having small white flowers with deeply cleft petals, in terminal clusters or solitary in leaf axils. Stems with a line of hairs down the side.
Flowers: ¼" (6 mm) wide; petals 5, so deeply divided as to appear to be 10; sepals 5, green, longer than the petals.
Leaves: ½–1" (1.3–2.5 cm) long; relatively smooth, opposite ovate, lower with petioles, upper without.
Height: 3–8" (7.5–20 cm), with stem to 16" (40 cm) long.

Flowering
February–December.

Habitat
Lawns and disturbed areas.

Range
Introduced from Eurasia; throughout North America.

Comments
This highly variable annual is a cosmopolitan weed. It can be eaten in a salad and is a favorite of chickens and wild birds.

Prairie Star
Lithophragma parviflorum
137

Flowers in open, slender racemes have white or pale pink petals cleft into 3 or 5 fingerlike lobes; the leaves of plant mostly at base and lower part of stem.
Flowers: ½–1" (1.3–2.5 cm) wide; sepals 5, short, triangular, attached near rim of bell-shaped base; petals 5; stamens 5.
Leaves: ½–1¼" (1.3–3.1 cm) wide, roundish, deeply cleft into 3 or 5 sections, these less deeply divided into narrow lobes.
Height: to 20" (50 cm).

Flowering
March–June.

Habitat
Prairies, among sagebrush, and in open forest at lower elevations.

Range
British Columbia to N. California; east to W. Nebraska, W. South Dakota, Montana, and Alberta.

Comments
The white or pinkish petals on starlike flowers in racemes are characteristic of the genus. Those species that grow in woods are called Woodland Star.

Mouse-ear Chickweed
Cerastium vulgatum
138

Low, horizontally spreading plant with hairy sticky stems, fuzzy leaves, and small white flowers in clusters at the top of slender stalks.
Flowers: ¼" (6 mm) wide; 5 deeply notched petals.
Leaves: to ½" (1.3 cm) long, paired, oblong, stalkless.
Fruit: small cylindrical capsule.
Height: 6–12" (15–30 cm).

Flowering
May–September.

Habitat
Waste places, fields, and roadsides.

Range
Throughout North America.

Comments
This naturalized European plant takes its common name from the fuzzy leaves. Although a troublesome weed in the garden, its leaves can be boiled and eaten as greens.

Carolina Anemone
Anemone caroliniana
139

A tuberous underground stem gives rise to a set of 1–3 deeply cut basal leaves and a slender stalk bearing a single white or pale blue flower subtended by a set of paired or whorled, stalkless leaves.
Flowers: about 1½" (3.8 cm) wide; sepals 5–20, petal-like; petals absent; stamens numerous.
Leaves: basal ones deeply palmately 3-parted, with segments ½–1¼" (1.3–3.1 cm) long, lobed; stem leaves 3-cleft.
Fruit: seedlike, woolly, cylindrical head.
Height: 4–10" (10–25 cm).

Flowering
April–May.

Habitat
Prairies; open places; on limestone soils.

Range
North Dakota, Minnesota, and Wisconsin south to Texas, Louisiana, and Georgia.

Comments
This Anemone is distinguished by having more sepals than others. The similar Canada Anemone (*A. canadensis*), abundant in the prairies, extends east into New England. It has more stem leaves, and its flowers have 5 broad sepals.

Bladder Campion
Silene cucubalus
140

White flowers with deeply notched petals and globular calyx, in loose clusters.
Flowers: 1" (2.5 cm) wide, with 5 petals, each cut into 2 lobes; calyx inflated, prominently veined; styles 3.
Leaves: 1½–4" (3.8–10 cm) long, opposite, lanceolate to oblong, often clasping the stem.
Height: 8–30" (20–75 cm).

Flowering
April–August.

Habitat
Fields and roadsides.

Range
Across southern Canada, south to Virginia, Tennessee, west to Missouri, Kansas, Colorado, and California.

Comments
Its common name refers to the distinctive, balloonlike calyx.

Evening Lychnis
Lychnis alba
141

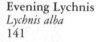

Downy, much-branched plant having white (occasionally pinkish), sweet-scented flowers with an inflated calyx.
Flowers: 1″ (2.5 cm) wide, with 5 deeply notched petals; female flower has 5 curved styles protruding from center, inflated, sticky calyx with 20 veins and 5 sharp teeth; male flower has a slender, 10-veined calyx and 10 stamens.
Leaves: 1½–4″ (3.8–10 cm) long, opposite, hairy, ovate or lanceolate.
Fruit: vase-shaped capsule.
Height: 1–3′ (30–90 cm).

Flowering
July–October.

Habitat
Fields, roadsides, and waste places.

Range
Southern Canada south to California, Colorado, Kansas, Missouri, Alabama, and South Carolina.

Comments
This European introduction blooms at night and attracts moths that pollinate the flowers.

White Prairie Clover
Petalostemum candidum
142

A plant with several branched stems; smooth, bright green leaves, and dense spikes of white bilateral flowers.
Flowers: less than ¼″ (6 mm) long, in clusters to 2½″ (6.3 cm) long; petals 5, the upper one broader than the 4 lower; stamens 5; calyx with glands just beneath the 5 teeth.
Leaves: pinnately compound, with 5–9 oblong leaflets, each ½–1¼″ (1.3–3.8 cm) long, minutely dotted with glands on the lower side.
Fruit: pod ⅛″ (3 mm) long, with glands on walls.
Height: 1–2′ (30–60 cm).

Flowering
May–September.

Habitat
Plains, arroyos, along roads, and among pinyon and juniper.

Range
Central Canada; south, mostly along the eastern slope of the

Rocky Mountains, to Colorado; west to Utah and Arizona; east across the plains to Illinois and Alabama; south into Mexico.

Comments

The genus is closely related to Dalea and by one expert recently included within it. White Dalea (*D. albiflora*), from Arizona, SW. New Mexico, and Mexico, resembles White Prairie Clover, but has 10 stamens.

English Plantain
Plantago lanceolata
43

From a basal rosette of long, narrow, strongly ribbed leaves rises a floral stalk with a dense, globose to cylindrical head of tiny, spirally arranged, greenish-white flowers.
Flowers: about ⅛" (3 mm) long; corolla 4-lobed; stamens 4, white, protruding; bracts present under flowers.
Leaves: 4–16" (10–40 cm) long, about one sixth as wide; narrowly elliptic or lanceolate.
Fruit: small, 2-seeded capsule, opening around the middle.
Height: 6–20" (15–50 cm).

Flowering
May–October.

Habitat
Waste places.

Range
Introduced; now widespread.

Comments
This weed is troublesome in lawns and gardens. The seeds are often eaten by songbirds and are used for feeding caged birds. The leaves are a favorite food of rabbits.

Death Camas
Zigadenus nuttallii
144

From an onionlike bulb arise grasslike basal leaves and a leafless stem with a branching cluster of numerous greenish-white, starlike flowers.
Flowers: about ½" wide; 6 similar parts (sepals 3 and petals 3) each with 1 gland at base.
Leaves: 8–24" (20–60 cm).
Height: 1–2½' (30–75 cm).

Flowering
April–May.

Habitat
Prairies; open woodlands.

Range
Tennessee west to Texas and Kansas.

Comments
Grazing livestock can be poisoned by this plant, or by hay containing any part of it. The toxic substance, also present in the bulb, is an alkaloid that causes vomiting, breathing difficulties, and coma in humans. There are other species of *Zigadenus* in the West, not all of them poisonous.

Queen Anne's Lace
Daucus carota
145

Plant having lacy, flat-topped clusters of tiny cream-white flowers, with one dark reddish-brown floret usually at center of umbel.
Flowers: in clusters (compound umbels) 3–5" (7.5–12.5 cm) wide, with stiff 3-forked, leaflike bracts below.
Leaves: 2–8" (5–20 cm) long, very finely cut, fernlike.
Fruit: bristly, not barbed; umbels curled inward, forming "bird's nest."
Height: 1–3' (30–90 cm).

Flowering
May–October.

Habitat
Dry fields, waste places.

Range
Throughout most of North America.

Comments
Also known as Wild Carrot. An attractive, hairy biennial, Queen Anne's Lace is considered a troublesome weed. It was the ancestor of the garden carrot, and its long, first-year taproot can be cooked and eaten.

Flowering Spurge
Euphorbia corollata
146

Flowers are in an umbellate cluster, with each flower having 5 round, white, petal-like structures (bracts) surrounding a group of minute true flowers; stem juice is milky.
Flowers: bracted groups ⅜" (9 mm) wide.
Leaves: about 1½" (3.8 cm) long, linear to oblong, mostly alternate but whorled just below flower cluster.
Height: 10–36" (25–90 cm).

Flowering
June–October.

Habitat
Dry open woods, fields, and roadsides.

Range
Ontario; New York south to Florida; west to Texas; north to Michigan, Wisconsin, and Minnesota.

Comments
The petal-like bracts, which are often colored, are typical of the spurges, as is the milky juice.

Hoary Cress
Cardaria draba
147

Patches of leafy stems, branched near the top and bearing numerous tiny white flowers in racemes, grow from an extensive underground system of runners. Leaves and stems grayish with dense hairs.
Flowers: petals 4, about ⅛" (3 mm) long; 4 sepals drop upon opening.
Leaves: 1½–4" (3.8–10 cm) long, oblong, pointed at tip, edges with small teeth, base of blade attached to stem in notch between 2 backward-projecting pointed lobes.

Fruit: pod about ¼" (6 mm) wide, roundish, slightly flat, smooth, 2-lobed, 1 seed in each lobe.
Height: 8–20" (20–50 cm).

Flowering
April–August.

Habitat
Roadsides, fields, and old lots.

Range
Nearly throughout North America.

Comments
Also called White Top. A second but less common species, Globepodded Hoary Cress (*C. pubescens*), is distinguished by its downy pod.

White Snakeroot
Eupatorium rugosum
148

Solitary or clustered firm stems bear flat-topped clusters of small fuzzy white flower heads composed entirely of disk flowers.
Flowers: heads about ⅓" (5 mm) long and ¹/₁₆" (4 mm) wide.
Leaves: 2½–7" (6–18 cm) long, opposite, ovate, stalked, coarsely or sometimes sharply toothed.
Fruit: tiny, seedlike, bearing white bristles.
Height: 1–3' (30–90 cm).

Flowering
July–October.

Habitat
Woods and thickets.

Range
S. Ontario to New Brunswick; south through New England to Virginia and upland Georgia; west to Louisiana and NE. Texas; north to Wisconsin.

Comments
Cattle sometimes graze on White Snakeroot. When cows eat this plant, the toxins it contains result in milk that can be fatal to humans.

Meadowsweet
Spiraea latifolia
149

A woody shrub with a dense, pyramidal terminal cluster of small, white or pale pinkish flowers.
Flowers: about ¼" (6 mm) wide; sepals 5; petals 5; stamens numerous; pistils usually 5.
Leaves: 1½–2¾" (3.8–7 cm) long, narrowly ovate to broadly lanceolate, smooth, coarsely toothed, pale on underside.
Fruit: dry, splitting open along 1 side and persisting.
Height: 2–5' (60–150 cm).

Flowering
June–September.

Habitat
Low, moist ground, meadows, and old fields.

Range
Newfoundland to Nova Scotia; south from New England to
the mountains of North Carolina; west to Michigan.

Comments
The brown fruits, which persist after flowering, are a
distinctive feature. Although less spectacular than the showy
introduced garden Spiraeas, this native species is most suitable
for naturalistic landscaping.

Boneset
Eupatorium perfoliatum
150

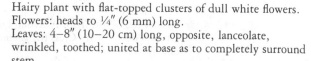

Hairy plant with flat-topped clusters of dull white flowers.
Flowers: heads to ¼" (6 mm) long.
Leaves: 4–8" (10–20 cm) long, opposite, lanceolate,
wrinkled, toothed; united at base as to completely surround
stem.
Height: 2–4' (60–120 cm).

Flowering
July–October.

Habitat
Low woods and wet meadows.

Range
Throughout North America.

Comments
As suggested by the Latin species name, the stem appears to
be growing through the leaf. To early herb doctors, this
indicated the plant would be useful in setting bones, so its
leaves were wrapped with bandages around splints.

White Sweet Clover
Melilotus alba
151

Small flowers, fragrant when crushed, are in long, slender,
cylindrical, spikelike clusters rising in the leaf axils on a bushy
plant.
Flowers: ¼" (6 mm) long, in clusters up to 8" (20 cm) long.
Leaves: pinnately divided into 3 lanceolate, toothed leaflets,
each ½–1" (1.3–2.5 cm) long.
Fruit: small, ovoid pod.
Height: 3–8' (90–240 cm).

Flowering
May–October.

Habitat
Roadsides and fields.

Range
Throughout North America.

Comments
This tall, introduced legume has the fragrance of new-mown
hay when crushed. Both this plant and yellow Sweet Clover
(*M. officinalis*) are widely used as pasture crops for nitrogen
enrichment of the soil.

Wild Madder
Galium mollugo
152

A mostly smooth plant with an erect stem arising from a sprawling base; numerous, small, white flowers form a loose, branched, terminal cluster; leaves in whorls of 6–8.
Flowers: about ⅙" (4 mm) wide; no sepals; corolla 4-lobed.
Leaves: ½–1¼" (1.3–3.1 cm) long, linear-oblong to lanceolate, margins rough.
Fruit: dry, dark brown, smooth.
Height: 1–3' (30–90 cm).

Flowering
June–August.

Habitat
Roadsides; fields.

Range
Ontario to Newfoundland and Nova Scotia; south through New England to Virginia; west to Indiana; occasionally established in the Pacific states.

Comments
Introduced from Europe, this weed has now become common over its range. The generic name is from the Greek *gala* ("milk") and refers to an old use of the plant to curdle milk in making cheese.

Illinois Tick Trefoil
Desmodium illinoense
153

Tall, spindly, hairy stem topped with a slender elongated cluster of many white, purple, or pinkish-lavender flowers.
Flowers: up to ½" (1.3 cm) long; 1 broad upper petal and 2 lateral petals nearly enclosing 2 lower petals that are joined and shaped like prow of a boat; on stalks to ¾" (2 cm) long.
Leaves: divided into 3 segments, with terminal one 2–3½" (5–8.8 cm) long, strongly veined beneath; ovate stipules at base of leafstalks.
Fruit: flattened, jointed pod with 3–7 segments.
Height: 2–5' (60–150 cm).

Flowering
July–August.

Habitat
Dry prairies.

Range
Ontario; south from Ohio and Missouri to Texas and Oklahoma; north to Nebraska and Iowa.

Comments
A showy plant when in flower, Illinois Tick Trefoil develops long fruits with segments that separate and attach themselves to clothing, thereby promoting seed dispersal.

Prairie False Indigo
Baptisia leucantha
154

Bushy perennial with smooth leaves and white or cream-colored flowers held in stiffly erect clusters. Stem covered with whitish bloom.
Flowers: to 1" (2.5 cm) long; 1 broad upper petal and 2 lateral

petals nearly enclosing 2 lower petals that are joined and shaped like prow of a boat; in clusters to 12″ (30 cm) long.
Leaves: palmately divided into 3 oblong segments, each 1–2½″ (2.5–6.3 cm) long.
Fruit: black, drooping, oblong, beaked pod, about 1″ (2.5 cm) long.
Height: 2–5′ (60–150 cm).

Flowering
May–July.

Habitat
Prairies, waste places, and open woods.

Range
Ontario; Ohio south to Mississippi, west to Texas; north to Nebraska and Minnesota.

Comments
Also called White Wild Indigo. This showy legume, with its stiff clusters of white flowers, often stands out above surrounding prairie grasses.

Prairie Larkspur
Delphinium virescens
155, 156

The white to pale blue spurred flowers are borne in a narrow cluster on a finely downy stalk.
Flowers: about 1″ (2.5 cm) long; sepals 5, petal-like, the upper prolonged into a spur ½″ (1.3 cm) or more long; petals 4, inconspicuous, the upper pair extending into the spur, the lower pair with short claws.
Leaves: palmately divided, with narrow leaf segments, each about ¼″ (6 mm) wide.
Fruit: 3 or more seedpods that split open along one side.
Height: 1–3′ (30–90 cm).

Flowering
May–July.

Habitat
Prairies and dry, open woods.

Range
Manitoba and NW. Wisconsin and Minnesota, south to Missouri, Kansas, Oklahoma, and Texas; NE. Colorado to SE. Arizona.

Comments
The flowers of this midwestern species can cover acres of prairie before the grasses take over. Prairie Larkspur's showy sepals range from white to pale blue to greenish, which accounts for the species name (Latin for "to become green").

White Clover
Trifolium repens
157

White or pale pinkish, rounded headlike flower clusters and 3-part leaves rise on separate stalks from a short creeping stem.
Flowers: ¼–½″ (6–13 mm) long; 1 broad upper petal and 2

lateral petals nearly enclosing 2 lower petals that are joined and shaped like prow of a boat; in long-stalked clusters about ¾" (2 cm) wide; turning brown with age.
Leaves: on long stalks, leaflets ¾–1" (2–2.5 cm) long, ovate.
Height: creeper, with stem 4–10" (10–25 cm) long.

Flowering
May–October.

Habitat
Lawns, roadsides, and fields.

Range
Throughout North America.

Comments
This introduced perennial is common in lawns, where one may sometimes find a "4-leaf" clover.

rairie Mimosa
esmanthus illinoensis
58

Erect plant with ball-like clusters of small whitish or greenish flowers, on tall stalks arising in the axils of compound leaves.
Flowers: cluster about ½" (1.3 cm) wide; 5 petals, each less than ¹⁄₁₂" (2 mm) long, and 5 projecting stamens.
Leaves: 2–4" (5–10 cm) long, doubly pinnately divided into numerous small leaflets.
Fruit: 20–30 curved or twisted pods, each up to 1" (2.5 cm) long, forming dense spherical structure.
Height: 2–4' (60–120 cm).

Flowering
June–August.

Habitat
Plains, prairies, and riverbanks.

Range
South Carolina to Florida; west to Texas and beyond; north to North Dakota and Minnesota; also Illinois and Ohio.

Comments
Also called Prairie Desmanthus. Distinguished from Prairie Acacia (*Acacia angustissima*) by its fruit, this nutritious plant is considered by some to be our most important range legume.

rairie Acacia
cacia angustissima
59

A shrub with round masses of creamy white or salmon-colored flowers resembling shaving brushes, rising on slender stalks from the axils of the compound leaves.
Flowers: florets minute, in clusters up to ¾" (2 cm) wide; stamens numerous, protruding beyond sepals.
Leaves: about 2½" (6.3 cm) long; twice-compound, with 10–50 pairs of narrow leaflets.
Fruit: oblong to linear seedpod.
Height: 1–5' (30–150 cm).

Flowering
June–October.

Habitat
Dry bluffs, prairies, and rocky woodlands.

Range
Missouri and Louisiana west to Arizona.

Comments
This attractive native legume has seeds that are rich in protein; the plant is readily eaten by livestock and decreases in abundance with heavy grazing. The species name, meaning "most narrow" in Latin, refers to the nature of the leaflets.

Fiddleneck
Amsinckia retrorsa
160

Coils of small yellow-orange flowers grow at ends of branches; the leafy stems have both long, spreading, bristly hairs and very short, dense, downward-projecting ones.
Flowers: calyx with 5 narrow lobes; corolla about ⅛" (3 mm) wide, all petals joined, forming a funnel with a narrow tube and an abruptly flared end.
Leaves: ¾–6" (2–15 cm) long, narrowly or broadly lanceolate
Fruit: divided into 4 grayish nutlets about ⅛" (3 mm) long, somewhat wrinkled on the back and with a rough surface.
Height: 1–3' (30–90 cm).

Flowering
April–May.

Habitat
Along roadsides, fields, and other dry, open places.

Range
Baja California to Arizona; north to Idaho and Washington.

Comments
The name Fiddleneck refers to the coiled inflorescence. As blooming proceeds the coil opens; maturing fruits are farther down the stem.

Many-spined Opuntia
Opuntia polyacantha
161

Fleshy, sprawling perennial with pale yellow flowers and flat pads having groups of 5–12 whitish spines, 1" (2.5 cm) long, with tufts of bristles above the spines; may form clumps 8–12' (2.4–3.6 m) in width.
Flowers: 2–3" (5–8 cm) wide, stalkless with numerous sepals, petals, and stamens; stamens much shorter than petals.
Leaves: tiny; soon deciduous.
Fruit: 1" (2.5 cm) long; prickly berry reddish, edible.
Height: 2–24" (5–60 cm).

Flowering
May–June.

Habitat
Plains and dry soil.

Range
S. British Columbia to E. Oregon and N. Arizona; east to W. Texas, Missouri, and central Canada.

Comments
This plant spreads as a result of drought and overgrazing; its seeds are also carried by rodents. It is one of several "Prickly Pears" with yellow or orange flowers found on plains and prairies in the West and Southwest.

Yellow Thistle
Cirsium horridulum
62

A tall branching stem with large yellow flower heads and very spiny, clasping leaves.
Flowers: heads 2½" (6.3 cm) wide, made up of tiny, 5-parted, tubular disk flowers enclosed in weakly spined bracts. Heads surrounded by erect, narrow, spiny bractlike leaves.
Leaves: 6–10" (15–25 cm) long, lanceolate in outline, pinnately lobed, stalkless and clasping the stem, with spiny margins and tips.
Height: 1–5' (30–150 cm).

Flowering
May–August.

Habitat
Shores, marshes, sandy or peaty fields.

Range
Coastal Plain from S. Maine to Florida; west to Texas.

Comments
Often found along the edges of salt marshes, it is also a pasture weed in the South, where it is frequently red-purple instead of yellow. Prairie Thistle (*C. plattense*), also yellow, has leaves white and velvety beneath and grayish above with leaf bases extending, winglike, down the stem.

Pale Agoseris
Agoseris glauca
163

Several leafless stalks, each with a yellow flower head at the top, grow from a basal cluster of leaves. Sap milky.
Flowers: head ½–1¼" (1.3–3.1 cm) wide; flowers all of ray type, those in middle very short.
Leaves: 2–14" (5–35 cm) long, very narrow to broadly lanceolate, broader above middle, without teeth, with a few teeth, or sometimes deeply pinnately divided.
Fruit: seedlike, with fine ridges at tip and fine white hairs on tip of the stalk.
Height: 4–28" (10–70 cm).

Flowering
May–September.

Habitat
Open areas in coniferous forests and in sagebrush.

Range
Western Canada; south through the California mountains; east across the West to New Mexico, South Dakota, and Minnesota.

Comments
Several other yellow-flowered species of *Agoseris,* all called

False Dandelion or Mountain Dandelion, are distinguished from this one by technical features of the fruit.

Yellow Hawkweed
Hieracium pratense
164

Hairy, mostly leafless stalk bears several heads of bright yellow ray flowers.
Flowers: heads ½" (1.3 cm) wide, each surrounded by bracts covered with gland-tipped black hairs.
Leaves: basal leaves 2–10" (5–25 cm) long, oblong, untoothed, covered with stiff hairs.
Height: 1–3' (30–90 cm).

Flowering
May–August.

Habitat
Pastures and roadsides.

Range
S. Ontario and Quebec to Nova Scotia; New England south to upland Georgia; west to Tennessee.

Comments
Also called King Devil. This perennial is similar to the Orange Hawkweed (*H. aurantiacum*), differing primarily in flower color. Both introduced from Europe, they are considered weeds by farmers, since they spread quickly by leafy runners. New England meadows covered with a mixture of both flowers, however, are a beautiful sight.

Yellow Goatsbeard
Tragopogon dubius
165

Smooth stems bear grasslike leaf blades and single yellow flower heads that open in the morning and usually close by noon; stems swollen just below flower heads.
Flowers: heads 1–2½" (2.5–6.3 cm) wide, with all ray flowers, surrounded at base by long-pointed green bracts.
Leaves: to 1' (30 cm) long, broad at base where they clasp the stem, then narrow to long sharp tip.
Fruit: heads large and plumose, with seedlike fruits bearing parachute of bristles.
Height: 1–3' (30–90 cm).

Flowering
May–August.

Habitat
Fields and waste places.

Range
Massachusetts south to Virginia; west to the Pacific Coast.

Comments
The basal leaves of this plant can be eaten raw in salads or as cooked greens. The delicate fruiting heads can be preserved by spraying them with hair spray or artist's fixative.

Elecampane
Inula helenium
66

Yellow sunflowerlike heads with long, narrow, straggly ray flowers surrounding a darker central disk atop a tall, hairy stem.
Flowers: 2–4″ (5–10 cm) wide.
Leaves: large, rough, toothed leaves, white-woolly beneath; stem leaves stalkless, clasp stem; basal leaves up to 20″ (50 cm) long, with long leafstalks.
Height: 2–6′ (60–180 cm).

Flowering
July–September.

Habitat
Fields and roadsides.

Range
S. Ontario to Nova Scotia; south to North Carolina; west to Missouri; north to Minnesota.

Comments
Perhaps of Asian origin, Elecampane was introduced to Europe, then brought to America by early colonists. In the 19th century a tincture of its roots was thought useful in reducing fevers and as a diuretic, but it may have caused more illness than it cured.

Threadleaf Groundsel
Senecio douglasii
67

A bluish-green, bushy, leafy plant covered with close white wool, bearing yellow flower heads in branched clusters.
Flowers: heads about 1¼″ (3.1 cm) wide, with rays about ½″ (1.3 cm) long surrounding a narrow disk; most bracts about same length, lined up side by side and not overlapping.
Leaves: 1–5″ (2.5–12.5 cm) long, divided into few very narrow lobes; upper leaves often simply very narrow.
Fruit: seedlike, with a tuft of slender white hairs at top.
Height: 1–3′ (30–90 cm).

Flowering
April–September.

Habitat
Dry rocky plains, deserts, and pinyon-juniper rangeland.

Range
S. Colorado and Utah to Arizona, Texas, and Mexico.

Comments
One of the most toxic range plants to livestock, especially the tender new growth; because it is generally avoided, it tends to increase on overstocked ranges.

Camphorweed
Heterotheca subaxillaris
68

Yellow daisylike flower heads on tall, hairy stems; plant often has 1-sided, unbalanced look.
Flowers: heads ½–¾″ (1.3–2 cm) wide.
Leaves: alternate, oblong; basal ones 2–3″ (5–7.5 cm) long, stalked; upper ones smaller, wavy-edged, clasping stem.
Height: 1–3′ (30–90 cm).

Flowering
July–November.

Habitat
Sandy soils of prairies, waste places, and roadsides.

Range
New Jersey and Delaware south to Florida; west to Texas; north to Kansas and Illinois.

Comments
This native annual or biennial has been extending its range northward. It is unpalatable to grazing livestock on open rangeland.

Mule's Ears
Wyethia amplexicaulis
169

Plant seems varnished with resin, the stout leafy stems growing from clumps of lanceolate leaves, ending in several large deep yellow flower heads on long stalks, the central head largest.
Flowers: central head 3–5″ (7.5–12.5 cm) wide, with lanceolate bracts that often extend past top of disk; about 13–21 rays and scales enfold bases of disk flowers.
Leaves: those at base 8–24″ (20–60 cm) long, with lanceolate blades on short stalks; those on stem smaller, their bases wrapped partly around the stem.
Fruit: seedlike, narrow, 4-sided, with a low crown of scales at top.
Height: 12–32″ (30–80 cm).

Flowering
May–July.

Habitat
Open hillsides and meadows, open woods, from foothills to moderate elevations in mountains.

Range
Central Washington to W. Montana; south to NW. Colorado, N. Utah, and Nevada.

Comments
All species have leaves on the stem, distinguishing them from *Balsamorhiza,* which has all leaves at the base.

Hairy Golden Aster
Chrysopsis camporum
170

The stiff, rough, hairy and leafy stem bears few flower heads with golden-yellow ray flowers and slightly darker disk flowers that turn brown with age.
Flowers: heads 1″ (2.5 cm) or more wide.
Leaves: 1–3″ (2.5–7.5 cm) long, oblong to lanceolate, covered with short hairs; upper leaves stalkless, lower leaves narrowed into short leafstalks.
Fruit: seedlike, ovate, tipped with soft hairs.
Height: 1–2′ (30–60 cm).

Flowering
July–September.

Habitat
Dry plains and prairies.

Range
Manitoba south to Wisconsin, W. Indiana, and E. Missouri.

Comments
Also known as Prairie Golden Aster. The heights of these
plants vary greatly with environmental conditions.

Compass Plant
Silphium laciniatum
371

Tall plant with heads made up of yellow ray and disk flowers
enclosed by large, hairy-edged, green bracts; stem exudes
resinous juice.
Flowers: heads to 3″ (7.5 cm) wide.
Leaves: 12–18″ (30–45 cm) long, alternate, rough, large,
deeply divided, vertical, edges mostly oriented in north-south
direction, unstalked or short-stalked.
Height: 3–12′ (90–360 cm).

Flowering
July–September.

Habitat
Prairies.

Range
Michigan and Indiana south to Alabama; west to Texas; north
to North Dakota.

Comments
Compass Plant is one of a group of tall, mostly prairie
Sunflowers, some with very large leaves. The common name
refers to the north-south orientation of the leaves.

Jerusalem Artichoke
Helianthus tuberosus
372

Stout, rough branching stems bear large golden flower heads.
Flowers: heads to 3″ (7.5 cm) wide, with 10–20 ray flowers;
bracts beneath heads narrow, spreading.
Leaves: to 4–10″ (10–25 cm) long, ovate to lanceolate, thick
and rough, toothed, opposite below and alternate above, with
winged stalks, 3 main veins.
Height: 5–10′ (150–300 cm).

Flowering
August–October.

Habitat
Moist soil.

Range
Great Plains to the Atlantic Coast; sparingly introduced into
the western states.

Comments
This large, coarse Sunflower was cultivated by the Indians and
has spread eastward. The edible tuber is highly nutritious and,
unlike potatoes, contains no starch, but rather carbohydrate in
a form that is metabolized into natural sugar.

Giant Sunflower
Helianthus giganteus
173

Tall, rough, reddish stem bears several to many light yellow flower heads.
Flower heads 1½–3″ (3.8–7.5 cm) wide, with 10–20 ray flowers and numerous yellow disk flowers; bracts beneath heads narrow, thin, green.
Leaves: 3–7″ (7.5–17.5 cm) long, mostly alternate; rough, lanceolate, pointed, finely toothed, occasionally opposite.
Height: 3–12′ (90–360 cm).

Flowering
July–October.

Habitat
Swamps, wet thickets, and meadows.

Range
Minnesota to N. Georgia, east to the Atlantic Coast.

Comments
Considering its name, the flowers of this plant are comparatively small; the "Giant" in its common name actually refers to the plant's overall height.

Arrowleaf Balsam Root
Balsamorhiza sagittata
174

An almost leafless stalk with 1 large bright yellow flower head at tip grows from a basal cluster of large silvery-gray leaves covered with feltlike hairs.
Flowers: heads 4–5″ (10–12.5 cm) wide, with densely woolly bracts, 8–25 rays, each 1–1½″ (2.5–3.8 cm) long, and many disk flowers, each enfolded by a parchmentlike scale.
Leaves: blades to 1′ (30 cm) long, on petioles about the same length.
Fruit: seedlike, no hairs or scales at tip.
Height: 8–32″ (20–80 cm).

Flowering
May–July.

Habitat
Open hillsides and flats in grasslands, sagebrush, or open pine forest.

Range
British Columbia south through the Sierra Nevada of California; east to W. Montana, W. South Dakota, and Colorado.

Comments
Indians prepared medicine from the roots of this plant.

Common Sunflower
Helianthus annuus
175

Rough erect stem bears from one to several terminal flower heads, with sterile, overlapping, yellow ray flowers and brownish disk flowers that produce the fruit.
Flowers: heads 3–6″ (7.5–15 cm) wide; bracts enclosing heads edged with bristles.
Leaves: 3–12″ (7.5–30 cm) long, ovate to nearly triangular, pointed, with rough stiff hairs, mostly alternate.

Fruit: dry, seedlike, with a white seed inside.
Height: 3–10' (90–300 cm).

Flowering
July–November.

Habitat
Prairies and rich soils, but spread to waste places and
roadsides.

Range
Throughout most of the United States, much of North
America.

Comments
This native annual is appreciably smaller than the familiar
cultivated variety. The Common Sunflower was much used by
the Indians for bread flour made from its ground seeds.

Black-eyed Susan
Rudbeckia hirta
176

Coarse, rough-stemmed plant with daisylike flower heads
made up of showy golden-yellow ray flowers, with disk flowers
forming a brown central cone.
Flowers: head 2–3" (5–7.5 cm) wide.
Leaves: 2–7" (5–17.5 cm) long, lanceolate to ovate, rough,
hairy; lower ones untoothed or scantily toothed, with 3
prominent veins and winged leafstalks.
Fruit: tiny, dry, seedlike, lacking the typical bristles.
Height: 1–3' (30–90 cm).

Flowering
June–October.

Habitat
Fields, prairies, and open woods.

Range
Native to the central United States, but introduced nearly
throughout.

Comments
This native prairie biennial forms a rosette of leaves the first
year, followed by flowers the second year. It is covered with
hairs that give it a slightly rough texture.

Maximilian's Sunflower
Helianthus maximiliani
177

Heads of yellow ray and disk flowers rise from upper half of
stalk on 1 or more rough stems.
Flowers: heads 2–3" (5–7.5 cm) wide.
Leaves: 4–6" (10–15 cm) long, stiff, narrow, tapering at both
ends, rough on both sides, often folded lengthwise and curved
downward at tips, mostly alternate.
Height: 3–10' (90–300 cm).

Flowering
July–October.

Habitat
Prairies.

Range
SE. British Columbia to Idaho, Montana, and Minnesota; south to Missouri, Oklahoma, and Texas; escaped from cultivation eastward to Atlantic states; occurs occasionally as a weed in the Pacific states.

Comments
A native perennial, associated with the tallgrass prairie, it is a desirable range plant, eaten by many livestock. A heavy crop of seeds is produced; thus it is a valuable plant for wildlife. It was named for the naturalist Prince Maximilian of Wied Neuweid, who led an expedition into the West in the 1830s.

Goldfields
Lasthenia chrysostoma
178

A small, slender annual with reddish stems, very narrow opposite leaves, and a small golden-yellow flower head at the end of each branch.
Flowers: heads ¾–1″ (2–2.5 cm) wide, with about 10 oblong rays surrounding a conical disk.
Leaves: ½–2½″ (1.3–6.3 cm) long, stiffly hairy at base.
Fruit: seedlike, slender, with several narrow, brownish, pointed scales at top, or sometimes without scales.
Height: 4–10″ (10–25 cm).

Flowering
March–May.

Habitat
Open fields and slopes at low elevations.

Range
SW. Oregon to Baja California and central Arizona.

Comments
On open areas with poor soils, where grass is sparse, this plant will form carpets of gold if moisture is ample.

Cowpen Daisy
Verbesina encelioides
179

A well-branched grayish-green plant with mostly opposite, toothed, nearly triangular leaves and yellow flower heads.
Flowers: heads 1½–2″ (3.8–5 cm) wide, with rays about ½″ (1.3 cm) long around the disk.
Leaves: 1–4″ (2.5–10 cm) long, with coarse teeth on edges, the base narrowed to a broad stalk.
Fruit: seedlike; those of disk flowers with 2 slender, rigid bristles at tip; none on fruit of ray flowers.
Height: 4–60″ (10–150 cm).

Flowering
June–September.

Habitat
Along roads, fields, in pastures, washes, and on rangeland.

Range
Central California to Arizona, New Mexico, and Texas; north through E. Utah and Colorado to Montana; east to Kansas and southeastern United States; south into tropical America.

Comments
This plant, common on disturbed ground and sometimes coloring acres or miles of roadside solid yellow, was used by Indians and early settlers to treat skin ailments.

nakehead
Ialacothrix coulteri
80

Pale, smooth, branched stems with most leaves near the base, and at the tips pale yellow flower heads. Sap milky.
Flowers: heads 1–1½" (2.5–3.8 cm) wide, with only flowers of ray type, those in center smaller.
Leaves: those near base 2–4" (5–10 cm) long, lanceolate, the edges coarsely toothed; those on stem ovate, the bases "clasping" the stem.
Fruit: seedlike, narrow, pale greenish brown, with 4 or 5 sharp angles and 2 fine lines between the angles, and topped with slender bristles, most of which break off easily.
Height: 4–20" (10–50 cm).

Flowering
March–May.

Habitat
Open flats and hills in grassland or desert.

Range
Central California to Baja California east to SW. Utah and S. Arizona.

Comments
The flower head's broad, round bracts have parchmentlike edges and a purplish or greenish central band that resembles a serpent's scales, and the bud resembles a fanciful snake head, thus the common name.

Common Madia
Madia elegans
81

Slender, erect leafy stems have mostly yellow flower heads at the ends of branches in the upper part.
Flowers: heads 1¼–2" (3.1–5 cm) wide, with about 13 yellow rays ½–¾" (1.3–2 cm) long, each with 3 teeth at broad end and often a maroon patch near base, and bracts that completely enfold the adjacent fruit. Among the disk flowers are erect hairs.
Leaves: to 8" (20 cm) long, narrow.
Fruit: seedlike, flat, dark, produced only by ray flowers.
Height: 1–4' (30–120 cm).

Flowering
July–September.

Habitat
Dry, open, usually grassy places, often along roadsides.

Range
SW. Washington to Baja California.

Comments
Species of *Madia* are covered with sticky, glandular hairs and are often called Tarweed.

Gumweed
Grindelia squarrosa
182

Stout erect stem bears several branches with yellow daisylike flower heads.
Flowers: heads about 1″ (2.5 cm) wide, with ray flowers encircling darker central disk flowers; entire head surrounded by pointed, outward-curling, green bracts that produce sticky material.
Leaves: 1–2½″ (2.5–6.3 cm) long, oblong, stalkless, toothed, covered with translucent dots.
Height: 6–36″ (15–90 cm).

Flowering
July–September.

Habitat
Prairies and waste places.

Range
British Columbia to Minnesota, south to California and Texas; eastward to Mid-Atlantic states and north to Ontario and Quebec.

Comments
This tough but short-lived perennial, a common invader of overgrazed rangeland in the West, has now spread to dry waste places in the East. Because of its bitter taste it is not eaten by cattle.

Common Tansy
Tanacetum vulgare
183

Erect perennial with flat-topped clusters of bright orange-yellow, buttonlike flower heads.
Flowers: heads ½″ (1.3 cm) wide, composed entirely of disk flowers with occasional raylike extensions developing from marginal flowers.
Leaves: 4–8″ (10–20 cm) long, pinnately divided into linear, toothed segments, strongly aromatic.
Height: 2–3′ (60–90 cm).

Flowering
July–September.

Habitat
Roadsides and edges of fields.

Range
Throughout North America, except for the Southwest.

Comments
For centuries this plant was used medicinally to cause abortions, with sometimes fatal results. The bitter-tasting leaves and stem contain tanacetum, a toxic oil.

Rosin Weed
Calycadenia truncata
184

A slender, odorous plant with yellow flower heads in a narrow cluster, and very narrow leaves, the upper ones tipped with a broad dish-shaped gland.
Flowers: heads about 1″ (2.5 cm) wide, with 3–8 broad rays, each about ¼–½″ (6–13 mm) long, with 3 teeth at end, the central tooth narrowest.

Leaves: ¾–3½" (2–8.8 cm) long.
Fruit: seedlike; those from disk flowers are slender, sparsely hairy, and topped by several short scales; those from ray flowers are short, squat, wrinkled, and without hairs or scales.
Height: 1–4" (30–120 cm).

Flowering
June–October.

Habitat
Dry, sunny, sparsely grassy slopes.

Range
S. Oregon to central California.

Comments
The genus name comes from the Greek *kalyx* ("cup") and *adenos* ("gland"), referring to the peculiar glands that distinguish all but one species of this primarily California genus. Rays on some species are white, changing to rose as they age.

ittle Golden Zinnia
innia grandiflora
85

Several short, leafy, slightly woody stems in a low, round clump have numerous small flower heads with 3–6 nearly round yellow-orange rays.
Flowers: heads 1–1½" (2.5–3.8 cm) wide; disk flowers reddish or greenish; bracts overlap, with translucent tips.
Leaves: 1" (2.5 cm) long, very narrow, opposite, with 3 veins at base.
Fruit: seedlike, usually with 1 or 2 spines at tip.
Height: 3–9" (7.5–22.5 cm).

Flowering
June–October.

Habitat
Dry areas on plains and in desert.

Range
E. Arizona to SE. Colorado and SW. Kansas; south to Mexico.

Comments
The genus is named for Johann Zinn, an 18th-century German professor, who collected seeds of *Z. elegans* (from which the garden *Zinnia* descends) in Mexico. There he was accosted by bandits who, after searching his bag, left him alone, believing him crazy and therefore unlucky.

ough-fruited Cinquefoil
otentilla recta
86

Erect, hairy plant with flat-topped, sparse clusters of pale yellow flowers with notched petals.
Flowers: ¾" (2 cm) wide; sepals and petals usually 5, the petals large compared to the sepals; stamens and pistils numerous.
Leaves: compound, divided into 5–7 blunt-tipped, toothed leaflets, each 1–3" (2.5–7.5 cm) long.
Height: 1–2' (30–60 cm).

Flowering
May–August.

Habitat
Roadsides; dry fields.

Range
Ontario to Nova Scotia; south from New England to Virginia; west to Tennessee, Arkansas, Kansas; north to Minnesota; sporadic in the West.

Comments
With low forage value this seldom-grazed introduced species is now considered to be a rapidly increasing weed.

Twinleaf
Cassia bauhinioides
188

A low plant with few stems and 1–3 slightly bilateral yellow flowers on short stalks in axils of grayish leaves with only 2 leaflets.
Flowers: ½″ (1.3 cm) wide; sepals 5, narrow; petals 5, round, with upper petal forward of others; stamens 10, brown, the 3 upper ones very small.
Leaves: leaflets ¾–2″ (2–5 cm) long.
Fruit: pod ¾–1½″ (2–3.8 cm) long, hairy.
Height: 4–16″ (10–40 cm).

Flowering
April–August.

Habitat
Hills and flats in arid grassland and deserts.

Range
Central Arizona to W. Texas; south to northern Mexico.

Comments
This large genus, many species of which are trees or shrubs, is found primarily throughout the world's tropics.

Cream Cup
Platystemon californicus
189

A softly haired plant with several stems, each with 1 small, bowl-shaped flower at top that resembles a pale yellow or cream buttercup.
Flowers: ½–1″ (1.3–2.5 cm) wide; petals 6; sepals 3, drop as flower blooms; stamens many, with flat stalks; stigmas 6–25 on an ovary that separates into sections when fruit forms.
Leaves: ¾–3″ (2–7.5 cm) long, opposite, narrowly lanceolate, mostly on lower half of plant.
Height: 4–12″ (10–30 cm).

Flowering
March–May.

Habitat
Open grassy areas.

Range
Most of California; east to SW. Utah, central Arizona, and N. Baja California.

Comments
Only one species, some races with nearly white petals, some with yellow petals, others with cream petals yellow at base.

Hooker's Evening Primrose
Oenothera hookeri
190

A tall, erect, usually unbranched stem with large yellow flowers in a raceme.
Flowers: 2–3″ (5–7.5 cm) wide; sepals 4, reddish; petals 4, broad; becoming rather orange as they age the following day; stamens 8.
Leaves: 6–12″ (15–30 cm) long, lanceolate, numerous, progressively smaller from base to top of stem.
Fruit: slender, rigid pod 1–2″ (2.5–5 cm) long.
Height: 2–3′ (60–90 cm).

Flowering
June–September.

Habitat
Open slopes, road banks, and grassy areas from the plains well into the mountains.

Range
E. Washington to Baja California; east to W. Texas and S. Colorado.

Comments
This plant is closely related to the garden primrose (*O. erythrosepala*), scattered in the wild from western Washington to California, which is a taller plant, with redder sepals and paler petals about 1½″ (3.8 cm) long.

Shrubby Cinquefoil
Potentilla fruticosa
191

A small shrub with reddish-brown, shredding bark on the young twigs, and yellow flowers, 1 in each upper leaf axil, or a few in clusters at ends of branches.
Flowers: about 1″ (2.5 cm) wide; petals 5, broad; stamens 25–30.
Leaves: pinnately divided, generally with 5 crowded leaflets, each ½–¾″ (1.3–2 cm) long, hairy and grayish, especially on lower side.
Height: 6–36″ (15–90 cm).

Flowering
June–August.

Habitat
Ridges, open forests, and plains from low to high elevations.

Range
Alaska south to California, Arizona, New Mexico, South Dakota, Illinois, and New Jersey.

Comments
This handsome shrub, common in the West, adapts well to cultivation and among the many horticultural variants are dwarf, low-growing, and unusually large-flowered forms, some with white flowers, others with yellowish-orange ones.

Moth Mullein
Verbascum blattaria
192

Yellow or white flowers with rounded petals, marked with brownish purple on the back, are in a slender, open, spikelike cluster on an erect stem.
Flowers: 1″ (2.5 cm) wide; petals 5; stamens 5, with orange anthers and violet hairs on the filaments; pistil 1.
Leaves: 1–5″ (2.5–12.5 cm) long; triangular to oblong or lanceolate, coarsely toothed, clasping the stem.
Height: 2–4′ (60–120 cm).

Flowering
June–September.

Habitat
Old fields, roadsides.

Range
Throughout North America.

Comments
This plant's fuzzy stamens resemble the antennae of a moth; hence the common name.

Common Buttercup
Ranunculus acris
193

A tall, erect, hairy, branching plant with yellow flowers.
Flowers: 1″ (2.5 cm) wide; petals 5, longer than sepals; sepals 5, spreading, greenish; stamens and pistils numerous.
Leaves: basal ones, 1–4″ (2.5–10 cm) wide, long-petioled, blades deeply and palmately cut into unstalked segments; upper leaves smaller, scattered.
Fruit: dry, seedlike, in a globose cluster.
Height: 2–3′ (60–90 cm).

Flowering
May–September.

Habitat
Old fields, meadows, and disturbed areas, especially moist sites.

Range
Throughout North America, especially in the West and East.

Comments
This European introduction is one of our tallest and most common Buttercups. The acrid juice from stems and leaves discourages browsing animals.

Yellow Mariposa Tulip
Calochortus luteus
194

The slender stems of this plant bear a few narrow leaves and at the top 1–4 large, deep yellow, bell-shaped flowers in an umbel-like cluster.
Flowers: 1–1½″ (2.5–3.8 cm) wide; sepals 3, lanceolate; petals 3, broad, fan-shaped, long, usually with fine red-brown lines on lower portion and also often with a central red-brown blotch; gland near base of petals broadly crescent-shaped, covered with short, matted hairs.
Leaves: 4–8″ (10–20 cm) long.
Height: 8–24″ (20–60 cm).

Flowering
April–June.

Habitat
Heavy soil in grassland and open forests at low elevations.

Range
California Coast Ranges and western foothills of the Sierra
Nevada.

Comments
This species and some others frequently reproduce asexually by
means of small "bulblets" in the leaf axils, which drop to the
ground and grow into new plants.

ain Lily
ephyranthes longifolia
95

Resembling a Daffodil, but much smaller and more delicate,
the single yellow, funnel-shaped flower is held erect on a
slender stem.
Flowers: ¾–1" (2–2.5 cm) long, the 6 petal-like parts, yellow
inside, copper-tinged outside, join above ovary.
Leaves: to 9" (22.5 cm) long, few, basal, very narrow, often
not present at flowering.
Fruit: nearly spherical 3-chambered capsule about ¼" (2 cm)
wide, filled with flat, black, D-shaped seeds.
Height: to 9" (22.5 cm).

Flowering
April–July.

Habitat
Sandy grasslands and deserts.

Range
S. Arizona to W. Texas and northern Mexico.

Comments
Zephyranthes means "flower of the west wind." Flowers of this
species appear very soon after substantial rains; hence its
common name.

uffalo Gourd
ucurbita foetidissima
96

A malodorous plant with large, gray-green, triangular leaves
growing along long, prostrate stems. Mostly hidden under
leaves are funnel-shaped orange to yellow flowers.
Flowers: 2–3" (5–7.5 cm) wide; some with stamens, others
only with an ovary; corolla with 5 lobes.
Leaves: to 1' (30 cm) long, rough.
Fruit: 3" (7.5 cm) in diameter, spherical, hard, striped, pale
and dark green when immature, lemon-yellow when ripe.
Height: creeper, with leaves reaching about 1' (30 cm) high,
on trailing stems to 20' (6 m).

Flowering
April–July.

Habitat
Open areas on plains and deserts.

Range
S. California to E. Colorado; east to Missouri; south into Mexico.

Comments
The fruits are easily dried and often brightly painted for decorative use. They are foul-tasting, inedible, and when mature somewhat poisonous. Massive roots of large specimens may weigh several hundred pounds.

Yellow Bell
Fritillaria pudica
198

This dainty little plant has 1 yellow, narrowly bell-shaped flower hanging at the top of the flower stalk.
Flowers: ½–1″ (1.3–2.5 cm) long; 6 petal-like segments.
Leaves: 2–8″ (5–20 cm) long, 2 or several borne near middle of stem.
Height: 4–12″ (10–30 cm).

Flowering
March–June.

Habitat
Grasslands, among sagebrush, and in open coniferous woods.

Range
British Columbia; south on the eastern side of the Cascade Mountains to N. California; east to Utah, W. North Dakota, Wyoming, W. Montana, and Alberta.

Comments
A charming modest Lily that can be mistaken for no other; th narrow yellow bell becomes rusty red or purplish as the flower ages.

Birdsfoot Trefoil
Lotus corniculatus
199

Low plant, often with a reclining stem, with cloverlike leaves and yellow flowers in flat-topped terminal clusters.
Flowers: ½″ (1.3 cm) long; 1 broad upper petal and 2 lateral petals nearly enclosing 2 lower petals that are joined and shaped like prow of a boat.
Leaves: compound, with 3 ovate leaflets about ½″ (1.3 cm) long, and 2 leafletlike stipules at base of stalk.
Fruit: slender pod about 1″ (2.5 cm) long.
Height: 6–24″ (15–60 cm).

Flowering
June–September.

Habitat
Fields and roadsides.

Range
Throughout North America; more common in the East.

Comments
This showy plant was introduced from Europe. The pod arrangement suggests a bird's foot; hence the common name.

Yellow Rattlebox
Rhinanthus crista-galli
200

Erect stem, simple or branched, bears stalkless yellow flowers in a leafy, 1-sided spike. Calyx becomes inflated in fruit.
Flowers: ½" (1.3 cm) long; calyx 4-toothed, flattened vertically at first, later becoming nearly globose. Corolla 2-lipped; upper lip arched, with a low tooth on each side; lower lip 3-lobed. Bracts with bristle-tipped teeth present beneath flowers.
Leaves: ¾–2½" (2–6.3 cm) long, opposite, stalkless, triangular-lanceolate to oblong, toothed.
Fruit: flattened, circular capsule.
Height: 4–32" (10–80 cm).

Flowering
May–September.

Habitat
Fields; thickets.

Range
Alaska to Labrador, south to New York, Michigan, Colorado, and Oregon.

Comments
As the name implies, the seeds rattle in the capsule at maturity. The plant is parasitic on the roots of other plants.

Butter-and-eggs
Linaria vulgaris
201

Yellow, 2-lipped, spurred flowers bloom in a terminal cluster on a leafy stem.
Flowers: about 1" (2.5 cm) long; sepals 5; petals 5, united, the upper lip 2-lobed, the lower lip 3-lobed with orange ridges, and a prominent spur at base; stamens 4; pistil 1, with green style.
Leaves: 1–2½" (2.5–6.3 cm) long, gray-green; the upper alternate, linear, grasslike, the lower ones opposite or whorled.
Height: 1–3' (30–90 cm).

Flowering
May–October.

Habitat
Dry fields, waste places, and roadsides.

Range
Throughout North America.

Comments
This European introduction grows well in dry sites and forms sizable masses. An orange path on the lower lip leads to nectar in the long spur and serves as a "honey guide" for insects when they alight.

Common St. Johnswort
Hypericum perforatum
202

An herb with bright yellow flowers in broad, branched, terminal clusters.
Flowers: ¾–1" (2–2.5 cm) wide; petals 5, with black dots on margins; stamens numerous, in 3 sets; styles 3.

Leaves: 1–2″ (2.5–5 cm) long; opposite, elliptic, numerous, and small, with translucent dots.
Fruit: ovoid, brown capsule.
Height: 1–2½′ (30–75 cm).

Flowering
June–September.

Habitat
Fields, roadsides, waste places.

Range
Throughout eastern United States and in Pacific states; sporadic elsewhere.

Comments
The common name derives from the fact that the flowers are said to bloom on St. John's Eve, June 24.

Broom Snakeweed
Gutierrezia sarothrae
203, 211

Oblong yellow flower heads of this sticky bushy plant occur in clusters at ends of the smooth branches.
Flowers: heads ¼″ (6 mm) wide, in clusters of 2–5.
Leaves: about 1½″ (3.8 cm) long, alternate, narrow, untoothed.
Height: 6–20″ (15–50 cm).

Flowering
July–September.

Habitat
Dry plains, prairies, and deserts, and among pinyon and juniper.

Range
E. Washington to south-central Canada and Minnesota, and south to Mexico.

Comments
Also called Turpentine Weed. The fine, brittle stems of this shrubby perennial, which are somewhat broomlike, account for its common name; they die back nearly to the ground each year. It is poor grazing fodder, and the new spring growth may be toxic to animals. Since it tends to increase with overgrazing, its abundance often indicates overused rangeland.

Yellow Bee Plant
Cleome lutea
204

A branched plant with palmately compound leaves and racemes of small yellow flowers at the tops.
Flowers: petals 4, about ¼″ (6 mm) long; stamens 6, long.
Leaves: palmately compounded, 3–7 leaflets, each ¾–2½″ (6–6.3 cm) long, lanceolate.
Fruit: pod ½–1½″ (1.3–3.8 cm) long, slender, on long arched stalks, jointed at middle.
Height: 1½–5′ (45–150 cm).

Flowering
May–September.

Habitat
Desert plains and lower valleys in mountains, commonly near water or areas formerly filled with water.

Range
E. Washington to E. California; east to S. Arizona, N. New Mexico, W. Nebraska, and Montana.

Comments
The genus name was used by the Greek philosopher Theophrastus for a plant resembling Mustard, and while the flowers resemble those of Mustards, the ovary on a jointed stalk and palmately compound leaves are typical of Capers.

Evening Primrose
Oenothera biennis
205

At the top of a leafy stalk bloom lemon-scented, large yellow flowers. Stem hairy, often purple-tinged.
Flowers: 1–2″ (2.5–5 cm) wide; petals 4; sepals 4, reflexed, arising from top of long, floral tube; stamens 8, prominent; stigma cross-shaped.
Leaves: 4–8″ (10–20 cm), slightly toothed, lanceolate.
Fruit: oblong capsule, about 1″ (2.5 cm) long, often persisting.
Height: 2–5′ (60–150 cm).

Flowering
June–September.

Habitat
Fields, roadsides.

Range
Wisconsin south to Louisiana, east to the Atlantic.

Comments
The flowers of this night-flowering biennial open in the evening and close by noon. The plant takes 2 years to complete its life cycle, with basal leaves becoming established the first year, and flowering occurring the second. The roots are edible, and the seeds are important as bird feed.

Common Winter Cress
Barbarea vulgaris
206

Tufted plant with elongated clusters of small bright yellow flowers atop erect leafy stems.
Flowers: ⅓″ (8 mm) wide, with 4 petals forming a cross; 6 stamens.
Leaves: lower ones 2–5″ (5–12.5 cm) long, with stalks, pinnately divided into 5 segments, terminal one large and rounded; upper leaves lobed, clasping the stem.
Fruit: erect seedpod, ¾–1½″ (2–3.8 cm) long, with a short beak.
Height: 1–2′ (30–60 cm).

Flowering
April–August.

Habitat
Moist fields, meadows, and brooksides.

Range
Ontario to Nova Scotia; south to Virginia; west to Missouri and Kansas; north to Canada; occasionally in Pacific states.

Comments
This introduced early-blooming mustard frequently forms showy yellow patches in open fields. The young leaves can be used in salads or cooked as greens.

Sweet Fennel
Foeniculum vulgare
207

A tall plant with feathery leaves, and on the upper branches tiny yellow flowers in compound umbels.
Flowers: umbels 2–7″ (5–17.5 cm) wide; each flower with 5 petals, no sepals.
Leaves: to 12–16″ (30–40 cm) long, triangular, pinnately divided several times into hairlike segments.
Fruit: ³⁄₁₆″ (4.5 mm) long, cylindrical, bluntly tapered at ends, ribbed.
Height: 3–7′ (90–210 cm).

Flowering
May–September.

Habitat
Roadsides, old lots, and fields.

Range
Sporadic throughout, most frequent in Pacific states and in warmer regions to the south.

Comments
All parts are edible and have a mild anise or licorice flavor but wild plants should not be eaten unless you are absolutely sure of their identification. The plant could be mistaken for the deadly water hemlock (*Circuta maculata*).

Stiff Goldenrod
Solidago rigida
208

Tall, coarse, hairy stem bears a dense, rounded or flat-topped, terminal group of large, dark yellow, bell-shaped flower heads.
Flowers: heads about ⅓″ (8 mm) long, each with 7–10 ray flowers, 20–30 disk flowers.
Leaves: basal rough, elliptic, long-stalked, the blade up to 10″ (25 cm) in length; upper leaves oval, clasping, rigid, rough.
Height: 1–5′ (30–150 cm).

Flowering
August–October.

Habitat
Prairies, thickets, and open woods.

Range
Massachusetts south to Georgia; west to Texas and Colorado; north to Saskatchewan.

Comments
This deep-rooted species is usually found in clumps. It is common in prairies; in the East it is found in dry, rocky areas.

ommon Barberry
erberis vulgaris
09

Spiny, gray-twigged shrub bears pendulous clusters of small yellow flowers and clustered leaves; 3-pronged thorns.
Flowers: about ¼" (6 mm) wide; 6 sepals, 6 petals with 2 glandular spots inside, 6 stamens, and a circular and depressed stigma.
Leaves: 1–3" (2.5–7.5 cm) long, bristle-toothed.
Fruit: elliptical berries, scarlet when mature.
Height: 3–10' (90–300 cm).

Flowering
May–June.

Habitat
Pastures and thickets.

Range
S. Ontario to Nova Scotia; south to Delaware and Pennsylvania; west to Missouri; north to Minnesota.

Comments
Barberry is very susceptible to the black stem rust of wheat, a fungus that spends part of its life cycle on these shrubs and the remainder on the grain.

lains Wallflower
rysimum asperum
10

Erect, leafy stems, branched in upper part, have dense racemes of bright yellow flowers at top.
Flowers: ½–1" (1.3–2.5 cm) wide; petals 4, each with a long slender base and a broad tip spreading at right angles.
Leaves: 1–5" (2.5–12.5 cm) long, crowded, sometimes with teeth.
Fruit: very slender 4-sided pod 3–5" (7.5–12.5 cm) long, projecting upward at an angle from the stem.
Height: 6–14" (15–35 cm).

Flowering
April–July.

Habitat
On open hills and plains.

Range
Central Canada to Texas, most frequent east of the Rocky Mountains, but found sporadically to the Cascades and Sierra Nevada.

Comments
This species is very closely related to Western Wallflower (*E. capitatum*), which is taller and has erect pods, and many botanists consider the two as one species, *E. asperum*.

Rabbit Brush
Chrysothamnus nauseosus
12

A shrub with erect, slender, flexible branches covered with dense, feltlike, matted hairs (often overlooked until one scrapes the surface lightly), very narrow leaves, and small yellow flower heads in dense clusters at ends of stems.
Flowers: heads ¼–½" (6–13 mm) high, slender, without rays, bracts oriented in 5 vertical rows, outer bracts short.

Leaves: ¾–3″ (2–7.5 cm) long.
Fruit: seedlike, with fine hairs at tip.
Height: up to 7′ (210 cm).

Flowering
August–October.

Habitat
Dry open places with sagebrush; grassland or open woodland.

Range
S. British Columbia to Saskatchewan south to California, Texas, and northern Mexico.

Comments
Rabbit Brush is a common and variable species in a genus found only in western North America.

Lance-leaved Goldenrod
Solidago graminifolia
213

Smooth or finely downy stem branches above the middle, with each branch bearing a flat-topped cluster of small yellow flower heads.
Flowers: heads about ⅕″ (5 mm) long, with 10–20 ray flowers and 8–12 disk flowers.
Leaves: 3–5″ (7–12.5 cm) long, narrow, elongated, pointed, with 3–5 veins.
Height: 2–4′ (60–120 cm).

Flowering
July–October.

Habitat
Roadsides, fields, and thickets.

Range
Across southern Canada south to North Carolina, Minnesota, South Dakota, and New Mexico.

Comments
The flat-topped floral arrangements and narrow leaves of this Goldenrod are distinctive.

Tall Goldenrod
Solidago altissima
214

Small yellow flower heads on outward-arching branches form a pyramidal cluster atop a grayish, downy stem.
Flowers: heads about ⅛″ (3 mm) long.
Leaves: lanceolate, rough above, hairy below, sometimes toothed; lower ones up to 6″ (15 cm) long, upper ones smaller.
Height: 2–7′ (60–210 cm).

Flowering
August–November.

Habitat
Thickets, roadsides, and clearings.

Range
S. Ontario and Quebec and New York south to Florida; west to North Dakota, Nebraska, Oklahoma, and Texas.

Comments
Another similar species with arching flowerstalks is Late
Goldenrod (*S. gigantea*), smooth-stemmed, often with a
whitish bloom, and flower heads up to ¼″ (6 mm) high.

**Rough-stemmed
Goldenrod**
Solidago rugosa
215

Tall, rough, hairy stem bears divergent or arching branches
with small, light yellow flower heads concentrated on the
upper side.
Flowers: heads about ⅛″ (4 mm) long, each with 6–11 ray
flowers and 4–7 disk flowers.
Leaves: 1½–5″ (3.8–12.5 cm) long, rough, sharply toothed,
very hairy, and wrinkled.
Height: 1–6′ (30–180 cm).

Flowering
July–October.

Habitat
Fields, roadsides, and borders of woods.

Range
Ontario to Nova Scotia and Newfoundland; New England
south to Florida; west to Texas; north to Michigan.

Comments
This highly variable Goldenrod can form large masses in fields
that were once cultivated. Physicians in ancient times believed
that Goldenrod had healing powers; in recent times these
plants have been popularly blamed for causing hay fever, but
its irritating symptoms are actually caused by Ragweed, whose
pollen is abundant when Goldenrod is in flower.

Sweet Goldenrod
Solidago odora
216

Smooth, tall, anise-scented plant bears crowded, cylindrical,
yellow flower clusters, with flower heads arranged along one
side of slightly arching branches.
Flowers: heads about ⅙″ (4 mm) long.
Leaves: 1–4″ (2.5–10 cm) long, smooth, narrow, stalkless,
with small translucent dots.
Height: 2–3′ (60–90 cm).

Flowering
July–September.

Habitat
Dry fields and open woods.

Range
New England south to Florida; west to Texas and north to
Ohio, Missouri, and Oklahoma.

Comments
The crushed leaves of Sweet Goldenrod give off a licorice scent
that readily identifies this widespread species. A tea can be
brewed from its leaves.

Desert Plume
Stanleya pinnata
217

Slender wands of yellow flowers top tall, stout, smooth, bluish-green, leafy stems.
Flowers: petals 4, yellow, ⅜–⅝″ (9–15 mm) long, densely hairy on inner side of brownish base; sepals 4, yellow.
Leaves: at base 2–6″ (5–15 cm) long, pinnately divided, broadly lanceolate; those on stem smaller, often also pinnately divided.
Fruit: pod 1¼–2½″ (3.1–6.3 cm) long, very slender, each on slender stalk ½–¾″ (1.3–2 cm) long joined to slightly thicker stalk.
Height: 1½–5′ (45–150 cm).

Flowering
May–July.

Habitat
Plains and deserts to lower mountains, often with sagebrush.

Range
SE. Oregon to SE. California; east to W. Texas; north to W. North Dakota.

Comments
This is a conspicuous wildflower in the arid West, its flowers generally standing above any nearby shrubs.

Yellow Sweet Clover
Melilotus officinalis
218

A smooth, loosely branched plant with small yellow flowers in slender, cylindrical, spikelike clusters rising in the axils of 3-parted leaves.
Flowers: ¼″ (6 mm) long; 1 broad upper petal and 2 lateral petals nearly enclosing 2 lower petals that are joined and shaped like prow of a boat; in clusters to 6″ (15 cm) long.
Leaves: each leaflet ½–1″ (1.3–2.5 cm) long; lanceolate to ovate, toothed.
Fruit: small, ovoid, wrinkled pod.
Height: 2–5′ (60–150 cm).

Flowering
May–October.

Habitat
Waste places, fields.

Range
Throughout North America.

Comments
The leaves of this plant have a vanillalike fragrance when crushed and can be used as a flavoring. The seeds are eaten by upland game birds such as grouse.

Common Mullein
Verbascum thapsus
219

An erect, woolly stem has a tightly packed, spikelike cluster of yellow flowers and white, woolly stem leaves, and rises from a rosette of thick, velvety basal leaves.
Flowers: ¾–1″ (2–2.5 cm) wide; petals 5, nearly regular; stamens 5; pistil 1.

Leaves: basal ones to 12″ (30 cm) oblong, stalked; upper leaves smaller, stalkless.
Height: 2–6′ (60–180 cm).

Flowering
June–September.

Habitat
Fields, roadsides, and waste places.

Range
Throughout North America.

Comments
An introduced biennial with velvety leaves, it has long been used for many purposes. Roman soldiers are said to have dipped the stalks in grease for use as torches. Indians lined their moccasins with the leaves to keep out the cold, and colonists used them in their stockings for the same purpose.

⹄rly Dock
⹄mex crispus
⹄0

A stout plant with small, reddish or greenish flowers in a long, slender, branching cluster at the top of a stem bearing leaves with very wavy margins.
Flowers: about ⅙″ (4 mm) long; sepals in 2 cycles of 3; petals absent.
Leaves: 6–10″ (15–25 cm) long, oblong to lanceolate, margins crisped.
Fruit: seedlike, brown, enclosed by calyx of 3 "wings" with smooth margins.
Height: 2–4′ (60–120 cm).

Flowering
June–September.

Habitat
Old fields; waste places.

Range
Throughout North America.

Comments
A somewhat similar plant, Bitter Dock (*R. obtusifolius*), has heart-shaped leaves with reddish veins and calyx lobes with toothed margins. These introduced species are common pasture, meadow, garden, or roadside weeds.

⹄eep Sorrel
⹄mex acetosella
⹄1

A sour-tasting weed with distinctive arrowhead-shaped leaves and long, spikelike clusters of tiny, reddish or greenish flowers; male and female flowers are on separate plants.
Flowers: about 1/12″ (2 mm) long, in clusters up to half the length of the stem. Calyx 6-parted; petals absent. Male flowers nodding on short, jointed stalks; female flowers with fruit protruding from deciduous sepals.
Leaves: ¾–2″ (2–5 cm) long.
Fruit: seedlike, shiny golden brown.
Height: 6–12″ (15–30 cm).

Flowering
June–October.

Habitat
Open sites, especially sour soils.

Range
Throughout North America.

Comments
This vigorous, perennial weed, with running rootstalks, is especially favored by acid soils low in nutrients. In pure stand the flowers are sufficiently showy to be attractive, and bees an small butterflies serve as pollinators. The seeds are eaten by songbirds and the leaves by rabbits and deer.

Winged Dock
Rumex venosus
222

Stout, erect, leafy, reddish stems, with conspicuous white sheaths where leaves join, have reddish-orange flowers in thic clusters.
Flowers: at first inconspicuous, with 6 sepal-like segments, tl inner 3 greatly enlarging to broadly heart-shaped bracts, each ½–1½″ (1.3–3.8 cm) long, which surround a tiny fruit.
Leaves: up to 6″ (15 cm) long, numerous, ovate or lanceolate.
Height: 6–20″ (15–50 cm).

Flowering
April–June.

Habitat
Open banks, ravines, grassland or sagebrush desert, often where sandy.

Range
S. British Columbia to NE. California; east to central Canada and throughout the Great Plains.

Comments
The reddish-orange flower clusters are conspicuous in the late spring; later the broad sepals catch the wind and tumble the seed to new places.

California Poppy
Eschscholtzia californica
223

A smooth, bluish-green plant with several stems, fernlike leaves, and usually orange flowers borne singly on a long stalk
Flowers: 1–2″ (2.5–5 cm) wide; petals 4, fan-shaped, deep orange or yellow-orange, sometimes yellow at tips and orange at base, rarely cream; sepals joined into a cone, which is pushed off as flower opens; stamens many; beneath ovary a flat conspicuous, pinkish rim.
Leaves: ¾–2½″ (2–6.3 cm) long, divided into narrow segments, on long stalks.
Fruit: capsule 1¼–4″ (3.1–10 cm) long, slender, slightly curved.
Height: 8–24″ (20–60 cm).

Flowering
February–September.

Habitat
Open areas, common on grassy slopes.

Range
S. California to S. Washington and east to W. Texas; often cultivated.

Comments
On sunny days in spring, California Poppies, the state flower, often turn hillsides orange. Responsive to sunlight, the flowers close at night and on cloudy days. The spicy fragrance attracts mainly beetles, which serve as pollinators. Flowers produced early in the season tend to be larger than those later on.

Canada Lily
Lilium canadense
24

From 1 to several nodding flowers, each on a long stalk and ranging in color from yellow to orange-red with dark spots, are at the top of a stem that also bears whorled leaves.
Flowers: 2–3″ (5–7.5 cm) wide; 3 petals and 3 petal-like sepals arch outward but not backward; stamens 6, with brown anthers.
Leaves: to 6″ (15 cm) long; lanceolate, in whorls of 4–10, with veins beneath bearing minute prickles.
Fruit: erect capsule 1–2″ (2.5–5 cm) long.
Height: 2–5′ (60–150 cm).

Flowering
June–August.

Habitat
Wet meadows, woodlands, and borders.

Range
Ontario, Quebec, and Nova Scotia; south to New England, E. Maryland, Pennsylvania, and, in the mountains, to South Carolina; Florida west to Alabama; north to S. Indiana.

Comments
As many as 16–20 of these beautiful, stalked, nodding flowers may be borne on one plant, either rising from the axils of leafy bracts or in a group at the end of the flowering stalk.

Indian Paintbrush
Castilleja coccinea
25

The actual flowers are hidden in the axils of scarlet-tipped, fan-shaped bracts and arranged in a dense spike.
Flowers: about 1″ (2.5 cm) long, greenish yellow, tubular, with a long, 2-lobed upper lip arching over shorter 3-lobed lower lip; styles protrude beyond bracts.
Leaves: basal ones 1–3″ (2.5–7.5 cm) long; in rosettes, elliptic, untoothed; stem leaves stalkless, divided into narrow segments.
Height: 1–2′ (30–60 cm).

Flowering
May–July.

Habitat
Meadows; prairies; damp sandy soil.

Range
S. Manitoba to S. New Hampshire; south to N. Florida; west to Louisiana and Oklahoma.

Comments
The conspicuous, red-tipped, brushlike bracts appear to have been dipped in paint, as is suggested by the common name.

Indian Blanket
Gaillardia pulchella
226

Branching hairy stems bear solitary flower heads with reddish ray flowers, tipped with yellow, surrounding central disk flowers.
Flowers: heads 1–3″ (2.5–7.5 cm) wide; ray flowers occasionally all yellow; disk flowers same color as rays.
Leaves: 1–3″ (2.5–7.5 cm) long, bristle-haired or downy, mostly stalkless; lower bluntly lobed, upper lanceolate.
Height: 8–16″ (20–40 cm).

Flowering
June–July.

Habitat
Prairies, sandy fields, and roadsides.

Range
E. Colorado to Arkansas, Texas, SE. Arizona, and Mexico.

Comments
This lovely annual may produce many color variants and combinations in the red-pink-yellow range.

Orange Hawkweed
Hieracium aurantiacum
227

A slender, hairy, usually leafless floral stalk bears dandelionlike orange flower heads.
Flowers: heads ¾″ (2 cm) wide, with all ray flowers, each having 5 teeth (tips of fused petals); disk flowers absent; green bracts around flower head covered with black, gland-tipped hairs.
Leaves: 2–5″ (5–12.5 cm) long, in basal rosette, elliptic, coarsely hairy.
Height: 1–2′ (30–60 cm).

Flowering
June–August.

Habitat
Fields, clearings, and roadsides.

Range
Newfoundland and Nova Scotia; south through New England to North Carolina; west to Iowa; north to Minnesota; also on Pacific Coast.

Comments
This showy, introduced Hawkweed is found across the northern part of the East, particularly New England. The name Hawkweed derives from a folk belief that hawks ate the flowers to aid their vision.

Butterfly Weed
Asclepias tuberosa
228

Small, bright orange, clustered flowers crown the leafy stem.
Flowers: ⅜" (9 mm) wide, with 5 curved-back petals and a
central crown in clusters about 2" (5 cm) wide.
Leaves: alternate, oblong, narrow, 2–6" (5–15 cm) long, with
juice that is watery, not milky.
Fruit: spindle-shaped, narrow, hairy, erect pods.
Height: 1–2½' (30–75 cm).

Flowering
June–September.

Habitat
Dry open soil, roadsides, and fields.

Range
Ontario to Newfoundland; New England south to Florida;
west to Texas; north to Colorado, South Dakota, and
Minnesota.

Comments
Because its tough root was chewed by the Indians as a cure for
pleurisy and other pulmonary ailments, Butterfly Weed was
given another common name, Pleurisy Root.

Red Clover
Trifolium pratense
229

Dense, rounded, headlike masses of magenta flowers on an
erect, hairy stem, with leaves divided into 3 oval leaflets.
Flowers: ½" (1.3 cm) long; in heads about 1" (2.5 cm) long
and ½–1" (1.3–2.5 cm) wide; upper petal (standard) folded
over 2 fused lower petals (keel) and lateral petals (wings).
Leaves: leaflets ½–2" (1.3–5 cm) long, each with a lighter V-
shaped pattern near the middle.
Height: 6–24" (15–60 cm).

Flowering
May–September.

Habitat
Old fields, lawns, and roadsides.

Range
Throughout North America.

Comments
Introduced from Europe and extensively planted here as a hay
and pasture crop, this is one of our most common perennial
covers. It stores nitrogen in its root nodules and is used in
crop rotation to improve soil fertility.

Field Milkvetch
Astragalus agrestis
230

This soft, green plant tends to grow in patches, the weak
stems often leaning on other vegetation; lavender or purple
flowers are crowded in short heads.
Flowers: about ¾" (2 cm) wide; 1 broad upper petal and 2
lateral petals nearly enclose 2 lower petals that are joined and
shaped like the prow of a boat; calyx with short, black hairs.
Leaves: pinnately compound, narrow, with 13–21 broadly
lanceolate or oval leaflets ¼–¾" (6–20 mm) long.

Fruit: pod about ½" (1.3 cm) long, erect, 3 sides, the lowest with a groove.
Height: 2–12" (5–30 cm).

Flowering
May–August.

Habitat
Commonly in moist meadows and prairies or on cool brushy slopes.

Range
Across much of Canada; south to NE. California, S. Utah, central New Mexico, Kansas, and Iowa.

Comments
Representative of many of the low *Astragalus* with lilac or purple flowers, of which the hundreds in the West are difficult to identify. The poisonous species are known as Locoweeds; apparently this species is not toxic.

Feather Peabush
Dalea formosa
231

A low, scraggly shrub with tiny pinnately compound leaves, and flowers in short, headlike racemes, the petals yellow and vivid reddish lavender.
Flowers: about ½" (1.3 cm) wide; 1 broad upper petal and 2 lateral petals nearly enclosing 2 bottom petals that are joined and shaped like prow of a boat; upper petal yellow, the remaining 4 bright purple; long, slender teeth of calyx have silky hairs and resemble little feathers.
Leaves: less than ½" (1.3 cm) long, divided into 7 or 9 plump, folded little leaflets.
Height: 1–3' (30–90 cm).

Flowering
March–May, often again in September.

Habitat
Scrubby vegetation on high plains and in deserts.

Range
W. Oklahoma to central Arizona; south to northern Mexico.

Comments
One of many shrubby species of *Dalea,* its dark bark, contorted branches, and small leaves make it an excellent candidate for bonsai. This and other shrubby *Dalea* species are hosts of a very strange flowering parasite, Thurber's Pilostyles (*Pilostyles thurberi*), which remains under the bark most of the year, then produces tiny, inconspicuous, yellowish-brown flowers that burst through and bloom early in the summer.

Vase Flower
Clematis hirsutissima
232, 233

A hairy plant generally with several stems in a dense clump, and at the end of each stem a purplish-brown, dull reddish-lavender, or dull violet flower hanging like a small, inverted urn.
Flowers: about 1" (2.5 cm) long; sepals 4, leathery, lanceolate,

petal-like, hairy on outside, joined at base, their tips flared outward; petals absent; stamens many inside "urn."
Leaves: up to 5″ (12.5 cm) long, opposite, finely divided, carrotlike.
Fruit: styles form plumes 1–2 ″ (2.5–5 cm) long above the seedlike base, all together forming a shaggy, silvery cluster.
Height: 8–24″ (20–60 cm).

Flowering
April–July.

Habitat
Grassland, among sagebrush, and in open pine forests.

Range
British Columbia to E. Washington; east to Montana and Wyoming; south to N. Arizona and New Mexico.

Comments
Unlike most other *Clematis* species, this plant is not a vine. Another common name for it, Lion's Beard, refers to the shaggy fruit head.

Spreading Dogbane
Apocynum androsaemifolium
234

Bushy plant with numerous small pink, nodding, bell-like flowers, fragrant and striped inside with deeper pink. Milky juice exudes from broken stems and leaves.
Flowers: ⅓″ (8 mm) wide; clustered at top or rising from leaf axils.
Leaves: opposite, ovate, blue-green, 2–4″ (5–10 cm) long.
Fruit: 2 long, slender seedpods, 3–8″ (7.5–20 cm) opening along one side, with seeds ending in a tuft of hair.
Height: 1–4′ (30–120 cm).

Flowering
June–August.

Habitat
Borders of dry woods, thickets, and fields; roadsides.

Range
Southern Canada south to Georgia, Texas, Arizona, and S. California.

Comments
These plants are relatives of the milkweeds. Indian Hemp (*A. cannabinum*), a slightly smaller species with erect clusters of greenish-white flowers, is also found in fields and is poisonous.

Showy Evening Primrose
Oenothera speciosa
235

Nodding buds, opening into pink or white flowers, are in the upper leaf axils on slender, downy stems.
Flowers: 3″ (7.5 cm) wide; petals 4, broad, sometimes white with pink lines.
Leaves: 2–3″ (5–7.5 cm) long, wavy-margined or pinnately cleft, linear to lanceolate.
Fruit: club-shaped, 8-ribbed capsule up to 2″ (5 cm) long.
Height: 8–24″ (20–60 cm).

Flowering
May–July.

Habitat
Prairies, plains, and roadsides.

Range
Virginia south to Florida, west to Louisiana, north to Illinois.

Comments
There are many species of *Oenothera* throughout the West and Midwest, most of them with yellow flowers but some with pink or white.

Threadleaf Phacelia
Phacelia linearis
236

Slender, commonly branched, erect stems are topped with reddish-lavender flowers in loose coils.
Flowers: corolla ⅜–¾" (9–20 mm) wide, broadly bell-shaped, with 5 round lobes; stamens 5, barely protruding.
Leaves: ½"–4" (1.3–10 cm) long, narrowly lanceolate, hairy, sometimes with 1–4 pairs of small lobes in lower half.
Fruit: small capsule; 6–15 seeds with pitted surfaces.
Height: 4–20" (10–50 cm).

Flowering
April–June.

Habitat
Brushy and open grassy areas in foothills and on plains.

Range
S. British Columbia to N. California; east across much of Utah and Idaho to W. Wyoming.

Comments
A common, showy species, distinguished from other Phacelias by its comparatively large, broad corolla and narrow leaves.

Corn Cockle
Agrostemma githago
237

Tall, densely hairy plant with showy pink flowers at tips of long stalks.
Flowers: 2" (5 cm) wide; calyx with 10 prominent ribs and 5 narrow sepals longer than the 5 wide petals.
Leaves: to 4" (10 cm) long, opposite, narrow, pale green.
Height: 1–3' (30–90 cm).

Flowering
June–September.

Habitat
Grain fields, roadsides, and waste places.

Range
Throughout North America; most abundant in the North.

Comments
This European introduction is especially bothersome in grain fields, because its seeds contain poisonous enzymes like those of Bouncing Bet.

:rairie Rose
:sa suffulta
38

Small clusters of flowers, white or tinged deep pink, are on densely prickly stems of new growth or the short lateral branches from older stems.
Flowers: about 2″ (5 cm) wide; sepals and petals 5; stamens and pistils numerous.
Leaves: pinnately divided into 9–11 toothed, ovate to oblong leaflets to 2″ (5 cm) long, covered with soft hairs underneath; size variable according to moisture conditions.
Fruit: a bright red, fleshy hip.
Height: 2′ (60 cm).

Flowering
June.

Habitat
Prairies, roadsides, and ditches.

Range
Manitoba south to Indiana and southwest to Texas.

Comments
The flower buds are a deeper pink than the open flowers, which can range from white to pink. The colorful fruits remain on the plants into the fall and winter.

:alse Baby Stars
inanthus androsaceus
39

A knoblike cluster of prickly leaves and deep pink, lilac, white, or yellow, trumpet-shaped flowers top this small, spindly plant.
Flowers: corolla ½–¾″ (1.3–2 cm) wide, tube slender, with 5 lobes; calyx with 5 needle-pointed lobes, membrane between them short and inconspicuous.
Leaves: ½–1¼″ (1.3–3.1 cm) long, most in the cluster at top, but several in pairs widely spaced apart on the slender stem; each leaf divided into 5–9 narrow, pointed lobes, the pair of leaves seeming to form a ring of needles.
Height: 2–12″ (5–30 cm).

Flowering
April–June.

Habitat
Grassy slopes and open places.

Range
Through most of California west of the Sierra Nevada to the edge of the southern desert.

Comments
The many *Linanthus* species are mostly slender, perky little annuals, commonly forked, with prickly leaves often clustered near the top, and colorful flowers that seem almost too big for the plant. Almost 40 species occur in California, few elsewhere.

:arewell to Spring
larkia amoena
40

An open plant with showy, pink, cup-shaped flowers in a loose inflorescence.
Flowers: sepals 4, reddish, remain attached by tips, twisted to

one side; petals 4, fan-shaped, ¾–1½" (2–3.8 cm) wide, eac‹
often with a red-purple blotch in center; stamens 8.
Leaves: ¾–3" (2–7.5 cm) long, lanceolate.
Height: 6–36" (15–90 cm).

Flowering
June–August.

Habitat
Dry grassy slopes and openings in brush and woods.

Range
S. British Columbia to central California.

Comments
As the lush grass watered by spring rains begins to turn gold
in the dry heat of summer, Farewell to Spring begins to
flower. The flowers close at night, and reopen in the morning.

Common Milkweed
Asclepias syriaca
241

A tall, downy plant with slightly drooping purplish to pink
flower clusters.
Flower: ½" (1.3 cm) wide, with 5 downward-pointing petals
and a conspicuous 5-part central crown; in clusters 2" (5 cm)
wide.
Leaves: 4–10" (10–25 cm) long, opposite, broad-oblong,
light green with gray down beneath, exude a milky juice
when bruised.
Fruit: rough-textured pod that splits open on one side, filled
with many overlapping seeds, each covered with tuft of silky
hairs.
Height: 2–6' (60–180 cm).

Flowering
June–August.

Habitat
Old fields, roadsides, and waste places.

Range
Saskatchewan to New Brunswick; south to Georgia; west
through Tennessee to Kansas and Iowa.

Comments
This plant contains cardiac glycosides, allied to digitalins use‹
in treating some heart disease. These glycosides, when
absorbed by monarch butterfly larvae, whose sole source of
food is milkweed foliage, make the larvae and adult butterflie‹
toxic to birds and other predators.

Centaury
Centaurium calycosum
242

An erect, sparsely leaved plant with pink, trumpet-shaped
flowers in small clusters at ends or in forks of the many
branches.
Flowers: ⅜–½" (9–13 mm) wide; calyx with 5 very slender
lobes pressed against the tube of corolla; corolla with 5
abruptly flared ovate lobes as long as its tube; stamens 5, with
spirally twisted anthers.

Leaves: ½–2½" (1.3–6.3 cm) long, opposite.
Height: 5–24" (12.5–60 cm).

Flowering
April–June.

Habitat
Moist, open areas along streams, prairies, and meadows, and
on hillsides.

Range
SE. California to S. Utah and central Texas; south to northern
Mexico.

Comments
Also called Rosita. The brilliant pink corolla resembles that of
Phlox, which has 3 branches on the style, whereas the
Centaurium style always ends with a small knob or 2 short
branches.

Western Pink Vervain
Verbena ambrosifolia
43

Gently rounded clusters of bilaterally symmetrical pink,
lavender, or purple flowers bloom atop stems with highly
divided leaves.
Flowers: corolla ¼–½" (6–13 mm) wide, the tubular base 1–
1½ times the length of the calyx; calyx glandular-hairy, the
teeth at the tip of the 5 narrow lobes about ⅛" (3 mm) long.
Leaves: ¾–2½" (2–6.3 cm) long, pinnately divided, the main
divisions again pinnately divided, the final divisions
lanceolate.
Height: 8–16" (20–40 cm).

Flowering
February–October.

Habitat
Open fields and weedy areas.

Range
South Dakota to Arizona and Louisiana south into Mexico.

Comments
Also called Moradilla. This plant often forms brilliant displays
covering acres of ground. The Spanish name comes from
"morado," meaning purple, and in this species means "little
purple flower."

Deptford Pink
Dianthus armeria
44

Deep pink flowers in flat-topped clusters at the top of stiff,
erect stems.
Flowers: ½" (1.3 cm) wide; 5 petals, with jagged edges and
tiny white spots; leaflike bracts below flowers are lanceolate or
awl-shaped.
Leaves: 1–4" (2.5–10 cm) long, narrow, erect, light green.
Height: 6–24" (15–60 cm).

Flowering
May–September.

Habitat
Dry fields and roadsides.

Range
S. Ontario to Nova Scotia; south to Georgia; northwest to Missouri; also in Idaho, Montana, Washington, and Oregon.

Comments
This European introduction somewhat resembles Sweet William. The common name refers to Deptford, England (now part of London), where the flower was once abundant.

Ragged Robin
Lychnis flos-cuculi
245

Deep pink (sometimes white) flowers with deeply cut petals are in clusters at the ends of thin branching stalks; stem slightly sticky toward the top, downy below.
Flowers: ½" (1.3 cm) wide, 5 petals, each cut into four thin lobes, appearing ragged.
Leaves: opposite, lanceolate, decreasing in size as they go up the stem, the lower ones 2–3" (5–7.5 cm) long.
Height: 1–3' (30–90 cm).

Flowering
May–July.

Habitat
Moist fields, meadows, and waste places.

Range
Quebec; south through New England to New York and Pennsylvania.

Comments
This plant, introduced from Europe, has become naturalized in the northeastern United States. The genus name *Lychnis,* derived from *lychnos* ("flame"), was originally used by the ancient Greeks for some flame-colored species.

New England Aster
Aster novae-angliae
246

Large, stout, hairy, leafy plant with bright lavender to purplish-blue flower heads clustered at ends of branches.
Flowers: heads 1–2" (2.5–5 cm) wide; ray flowers 35–45; disk flowers yellowish; bracts beneath flower heads narrow, hairy, sticky; flower stalk with sticky hairs (glandular).
Leaves: 1½–5" (3.8–12.5 cm) long, lanceolate, toothless, clasping large stem.
Height: 3–7' (90–210 cm).

Flowering
August–October.

Habitat
Wet thickets, meadows, and swamps.

Range
Across southern Canada; south from New England to Maryland and Alabama, west to North Dakota, Wyoming, and New Mexico.

Comments
The flower color is variable, ranging from lavender to blue to white. A pink variety is sometimes grown commercially.

New York Ironweed
Vernonia noveboracensis
247

Tall erect stem branches toward the summit, with each branch bearing a cluster of deep lavender to violet flower heads; together, clusters form a loose spray.
Flowers: clusters 3–4″ (7.5–10 cm) wide, each head about ⅓″ (8 mm) wide, with 30–50 5-lobed disk flowers; ray flowers absent; bracts surrounding flower heads with hairlike tips.
Leaves: 4–8″ (10–20 cm) long, alternate, finely toothed, lanceolate, pointed.
Fruit: seedlike, with double set of purplish bristles.
Height: 3–6′ (90–180 cm).

Flowering
August–October.

Habitat
Moist low ground and stream margins.

Range
Massachusetts and New York south to Georgia; west to Mississippi; north to West Virginia and Ohio.

Comments
This often roughish plant is common in wet open bottomland fields.

Spotted Joe-Pye Weed
Eupatorium maculatum
248

Atop a sturdy purple or purple-spotted stem, hairy above, is a large pinkish-purplish, flat-topped cluster of fuzzy flower heads.
Flowers: heads ⅓″ (8 mm) wide, in clusters 4–5½″ (10–14 cm) wide, of all disk flowers.
Leaves: 2½–8″ (6.3–20 cm) long, in whorls of 3–5, thick, lanceolate, coarsely toothed.
Height: 2–6′ (60–180 cm).

Flowering
July–September.

Habitat
Damp meadows, thickets, and shores.

Range
Across southern Canada south to Utah, New Mexico, Oklahoma, Iowa, Illinois, and North Carolina.

Comments
Folklore tells that an Indian, Joe Pye, used this plant to cure fevers and that colonists used it to treat an outbreak of typhus.

Prairie Smoke
Geum triflorum
249

A softly hairy plant with reddish-brown or pinkish flowers, often in groups of 3, at the summit of a stalk that rises from a set of fernlike basal leaves.

Flowers: up to ¾″ (2 cm) long; calyx lobes 5; petals 5; narrow bracts alternate with sepals.
Leaves: 4–9″ (10–22.5 cm) long, pinnately divided into wedge-shaped to oblong, toothed or lobed leaflets; stem leaves few, small.
Fruit: seedlike, with long, plumy, gray "tails" 2″ (5 cm) long.
Height: 6–16″ (15–40 cm).

Flowering
Late April–July.

Habitat
Woods and prairies.

Range
Southern Canada to California, Nevada, Utah, New Mexico, Nebraska, Illinois, and New York.

Comments
One of the earliest flowers to appear on the prairies, it attracts attention when in fruit with its "feather duster" look, especially when it forms colonies. Indians once made a tea from the roots.

Coyote Thistle
Eryngium leavenworthii
250

A stiff, prickly, purplish plant with narrow, leafy, forked stems topped by spiny, egg-shaped, lavender or reddish flower heads.
Flowers: heads to 1½″ (3.8 cm) long; flowers tiny, with 5 purplish petals.
Leaves: to 2½″ (6 cm) long with prickly edges.
Height: 20–40″ (60–100 cm).

Flowering
July–September.

Habitat
Plains and prairies.

Range
Much of Texas; north to Kansas.

Comments
The prickly nature of this plant is unusual for the Carrot Family, but the individual flowers are typical. This "thistle" represents several species of *Eryngium* that grow in the West, all with flowers in prickly heads. One Mexican meaning of the word "coyote" is a "shyster," a foxy or tricky person.

Showy Thistle
Cirsium pastoris
251

A white, woolly, prickly plant with crimson flower heads at the ends of the few upper branches terminating the main stem.
Flowers: heads 1½–2½″ (3.8–6.3 cm) long, with bracts the same length, tipped with spines; bright red disk flowers extend about 1″ (2.5 cm) beyond the bracts.
Leaves: 4–12″ (10–30 cm) long, narrow, pinnately lobed, edged prickly and continuing down the stem as narrow wings.

Fruit: seedlike, with long white hairs at tip, each hair with many smaller hairs along its length.
Height: 2–4' (60–120 cm).

Flowering
June–September.

Habitat
Dry open slopes in brushy or grassy areas, or in open woods.

Range
N. California, S. Oregon, and W. Nevada.

Comments
With its blaze of red flowers and white foliage, this is perhaps the handsomest Thistle, a group considered obnoxious weeds.

Teasel
Dipsacus sylvestris
252

Small lavender flowers are clustered in an egg-shaped, thistlelike spike on a prickly stem.
Flowers: less than ½" (1.3 cm) long, tubular; calyx 5-lobed; corolla 4-lobed, cluster 1½–4" (3.8–10 cm) long and 1–2" (2.5–5 cm) wide. Spiny bracts project between flowers and longer, horizontal or upward-curving spiny bracts surround base of flowering spike.
Leaves: 4–16" (10–40 cm) long; lanceolate, toothed, opposite, the upper ones fused at their bases around the stem.
Height: 2–6' (60–180 cm).

Flowering
July–October.

Habitat
Old fields and roadsides, in basic or neutral soils.

Range
Throughout much of North America; more frequent in the northern half.

Comments
Originally brought from Europe, this biennial was cultivated by wool manufacturers. The dried flower heads were placed on spindles and used to raise the nap, or tease the cloths; hence the common name. The progression of flowers opening on the spike in all species of *Dipsacus* is unique. They start in a belt around the center of the spike, and new ones open daily in both directions, in time forming 2 bands of flowers.

Purple Prairie Clover
Petalostemum purpureum
253

Tiny rose-purple flowers in cylindrical, headlike masses at the ends of upright wiry stems.
Flowers: about ⅛" (4 mm) long, in clusters up to 2" (5 cm) long; corolla with 1 main heart-shaped petal (the standard) and 4 narrow petal-like structures (modified stamens); calyx 5-part, hairy; 5 true stamens.
Leaves: pinnately divided into 3–7 (usually 5) narrow segments, each ½–¾" (1.3–2 cm) long.
Height: 1–3' (30–90 cm).

Flowering
June–September.

Habitat
Prairies and dry hills.

Range
Alberta south to N. Arizona, New Mexico, and W. Texas;
east to Manitoba, Wisconsin, Illinois, Tennessee, and
Alabama.

Comments
This is one of the most widespread of the perennial Prairie
Clovers, identifiable by their conelike flower heads. An
excellent range species, with high protein content, Purple
Prairie Clover decreases in abundance with overgrazing.

Bull Thistle
Cirsium vulgare
254

This very prickly plant has a spiny-winged stem and large
rose-purple flower heads, composed entirely of disk flowers and
surrounded by spiny, yellow-tipped bracts.
Flowers: heads 1½–2″ (3.8–5 cm) wide.
Leaves: 3–6″ (7.5–15 cm) long, coarsely pinnately lobed,
spiny.
Height: 2–6′ (60–180 cm).

Flowering
June–September.

Habitat
Roadsides, pastures, and waste places.

Range
Throughout North America.

Comments
This, our spiniest thistle, should be handled only with gloves.
A biennial, it produces a rosette of leaves the first year, and an
upright flowering stalk the second year. The bristles on the
fruits serve as parachutes to carry the light seeds.

Nodding Thistle
Carduus nutans
255

A nodding, rose-purple, thistlelike flower head is borne alone
on a long floral stalk at the end of the main stem and its
branches. A cobweblike covering may be present on the stem.
Flowers: heads 1½–2½″ (3.8–6.3 cm) wide, surrounded by
broad, pointed, purple bracts, the outer ones curving outward.
Leaves: to 10″ (25 cm) long, lanceolate, deeply lobed, very
spiny, with bases extending up and down the stem as prickly
wings.
Fruit: seedlike, with long, white, minutely barbed bristles.
Height: 2–9′ (60–270 cm).

Flowering
June–October.

Habitat
Waste places; fields.

Range
Throughout much of the United States, especially the Rocky Mountain region.

Comments
This European introduction spread rapidly into the rangeland of the Midwest.

Canada Thistle
Cirsium arvense
256

Numerous fragrant pale magenta or lavender flower heads top this highly-branched, smooth-stemmed plant.
Flowers: heads 1" (2.5 cm) wide, all disk type, heads surrounded by spine-tipped bracts.
Leaves: 5–8" (12.5–20 cm) long, gray-green with matted hairs, spiny, lanceolate, deeply cut, wavy-edged, mostly stalkless.
Height: 1–5' (30–150 cm).

Flowering
June–October.

Habitat
Pastures, roadsides, waste places.

Range
Throughout North America; more frequent in the northern half.

Comments
This is a European introduction that reached us by way of Canada, hence the common name.

Wild Bergamot
Monarda fistulosa
257

A dense, rounded cluster of lavender tubular flowers is at the top of a square stem.
Flowers: 1" (2.5 cm) long; corolla with hairy 2-lobed upper lip, broader 3-lobed lower lip, stamens 2, projecting; bracts under flower cluster often pink-tinged.
Leaves: about 2½" (6.3 cm) long; gray-green, opposite, lanceolate, coarsely toothed.
Height: 2–4' (60–120 cm).

Flowering
June–September.

Habitat
Dry fields, thickets, borders; usually common in calcareous regions.

Range
Southern Canada south to Arizona, New Mexico, Texas, Louisiana, and Georgia; more frequent east of the Rockies.

Comments
A showy perennial, frequently in cultivation, its aromatic leaves can be used to make mint tea. Long ago, oil from the leaves was used to treat respiratory ailments.

Queen-of-the-Prairie
Filipendula rubra
258

This plant bears large, feathery clusters of small, fragrant, pink flowers.
Flowers: ⅓–½" (8–13 mm) wide; sepals and petals 5; stamens numerous, protruding; pistils 5–7.
Leaves: pinnately compound, divided into lobed and toothed leaflets, the terminal leaflet to 8" (20 cm) wide and long.
Fruit: dry, 1-seeded.
Height: 3–6' (90–180 cm).

Flowering
June–August.

Habitat
Prairies, meadows, and thickets.

Range
Pennsylvania south to Georgia; west to Kentucky, Illinois, Iowa, and Michigan; escaped from cultivation in New England and New York.

Comments
A showy species, this coarse-leaved perennial can be grown readily in wildflower gardens.

Rough Blazing Star
Liatris aspera
259

Rounded lavender flowers in a loose spikelike cluster on stiff, erect stem covered with grayish hairs.
Flowers: heads about ¾" (2 cm) wide, all disk flowers, both stalkless and stalked; bracts beneath heads broadly rounded, flaring, with pinkish translucent margins.
Leaves: rough, lanceolate to linear; lower leaves 4–12" (10–30 cm) long, upper ones progressively smaller.
Height: 16–48" (40–120 cm).

Flowering
August–October.

Habitat
Open plains and thin woods, in sandy soil.

Range
S. Manitoba and Ontario; North Carolina south to Florida; west to Texas; north through Oklahoma and Missouri to North Dakota.

Comments
This species is distinguished from others of its genus by its roughness and rounded floral bracts.

Rocky Mountain Bee Plant
Cleome serrulata
260

Branched stems have palmately compound leaves and, in racemes at ends of branches, pink or reddish-purple flowers.
Flowers: ½" (1.3 cm) long; petals 4; stamens 6, long; ovary on a long, protruding stalk.
Leaves: 3 lanceolate leaflets, each ½–3" (1.3–7.5 cm) long.
Fruit: pod 1½–2½" (3.8–6.3 cm) long, slender, on long, arched stalks jointed at middle.
Height: ½–5' (15–150 cm).

Flowering
June–September.

Habitat
Plains and rangeland, foothills of lower mountains.

Range
E. Washington to N. California; east on most of the Great
Plains; south to central Arizona, central New Mexico, and N.
Texas; naturalized to northern New England.

Comments
Flowers produce copious nectar and attract bees, hence the
common name. Indians boiled the strong leaves for food and as
a stomachache remedy. Rocky Mountain Bee Plant sometimes
has white flowers.

Prairie Blazing Star
Liatris pycnostachya
261

Rose-purple, cylindric, stalkless flower heads made up of all
disk flowers, densely crowded on a coarse, hairy, leafy stem.
Flowers: heads about ½″ (1.3 cm) wide, in spikelike clusters;
bracts beneath heads with long-pointed purplish tips,
spreading or bent backward.
Leaves: lower 4–12″ (10–30 cm) long, upper much smaller,
punctate, linear.
Height: 2–5′ (60–150 cm).

Flowering
July–October.

Habitat
Damp prairies.

Range
Wisconsin south to Kentucky and Louisiana; west to Texas
and Oklahoma; north to South Dakota and Minnesota.

Comments
One of the most popular of the Blazing Stars, this is
sometimes grown as an ornamental. The species name, from
the Greek for "crowded," describes both the leaves and the
flower heads.

Dense Blazing Star
Liatris spicata
262

Rose-purple flower heads closely set on a spike 1′ (30 cm) or
more in length.
Flowers: heads ¼″ (6 mm) wide, stalkless, all disk flowers;
long styles protrude beyond corolla lobes; thin scalelike bracts
beneath flower heads, blunt, with purple edges.
Leaves: numerous, linear, crowded, 1′ (30 cm) or more in
length at base of plant, decreasing in size upward.
Height: 1–6′ (30–180 cm).

Flowering
July–September.

Habitat
Moist, low ground.

Range
Long Island south to Florida; west to Louisiana; north to Michigan and Wisconsin; escaped from cultivation in southern New England and New York.

Comments
The protruding styles give the flowers of Dense Blazing Star an overall feathery appearance; hence its occasional alternate name, Gay Feather.

Steeplebush
Spiraea tomentosa
263

An erect shrub, with dense, steeple-shaped, branched clusters of pink flowers.
Flowers: less than ¼″ (6 mm) wide; sepals 5; petals 5; stamens numerous; pistils 5–8.
Leaves: 1–2″ (2.5–5 cm) long, oblong, toothed, very woolly on underside.
Fruit: small, dry, woody follicle in persisting clusters.
Height: 2–4′ (60–120 cm).

Flowering
July–September.

Habitat
Old fields, meadows, sterile low grounds.

Range
Ontario to Nova Scotia; south through New England to Georgia; west to Arkansas; north to Minnesota.

Comments
A similar species, the pink-flowered Japanese Spiraea (*S. japonica*), from Asia, differs from Steeplebush in having flat-topped clusters of flowers and smooth leaves. It occurs from New England to Georgia, and west to Tennessee and Indiana.

Common Owl's Clover
Orthocarpus purpuracens
264

The flower cluster of this erect little plant is rose and yellow, or rose and white, for the floral bracts are velvety and rose-purple on their divided tips.
Flowers: bilaterally symmetrical corollas 1–1¼″ (1.3–3.1 cm) long, each exposing a white or yellow 3-lobed pouch as they "peer" from bracts, strongly angled upward; at end of pouch are 3 tiny teeth; above pouch's upper lip is a short, hooked, velvety, rose-purple beak.
Leaves: ½–2″ (1.3–5 cm) long, divided into a few very narrow segments.
Fruit: capsule about ½″ (1.3 cm) long.
Height: 4–16″ (10–40 cm).

Flowering
March–May.

Habitat
Fields and open wooded areas.

Range
S. California to W. Arizona and northern Mexico.

Comments
Following a wet spring, acre upon acre is carpeted with this beautiful wildflower, whose Spanish name means "little broom," descriptive of the distinctive, broomlike flower cluster.

.ocoweed
xytropis splendens
65

Tufted plant with silvery, silky-hairy, leafless stems, topped by dense spikes of rich lavender flowers, rising from among pinnately compound basal leaves.
Flowers: about ¾" (2 cm) long; in clusters 1½–7" (3.8–17.5 cm) long; 1 broad upper petal and 2 lateral petals nearly enclosing 2 lower petals that are joined and shaped like prow of a boat.
Leaves: to 9½" (23.8 cm) long, pinnately divided into numerous lanceolate leaflets, often in groups of 3–4.
Fruit: ovoid, hairy, beaked capsule, up to ⅔" (1.6 cm) long.
Height: 4–12" (10–30 cm).

Flowering
June–July.

Habitat
Prairies and plains.

Range
Alaska south to N. New Mexico and east to Minnesota.

Comments
This is one of the poisonous Locoweeds, similar to the members of the genus *Astragalus* (whose flowers have a blunt keel) also known as Locoweeds or Poison Vetches. There are nonpoisonous members of both genera as well.

:ow Vetch
'icia cracca
66

Climbing plant with gray-green leaves and long, 1-sided, crowded spikes of tubular, lavender to blue flowers, directed downward on a long stalk.
Flowers: ½" (1.3 cm) long; 1 broad upper petal and 2 lateral petals nearly enclosing 2 lower petals that are joined and shaped like prow of a boat.
Leaves: pinnately compound, with 8–12 pairs of narrow bristle-tipped leaflets, each 1" (2.5 cm) long; pair of tendrils at end of each leafstalk.
Fruit: narrow, lanceolate pod.
Height: vine, to 4' (1.2 m) long.

Flowering
May–August.

Habitat
Roadsides and fields.

Range
Across southern Canada to Newfoundland and Nova Scotia; south from New England to North Carolina; west to Illinois; occasional in the Rocky Mountains and westward.

Comments
This is one of 17 vetches in the East. They are mostly
climbing plants with compound leaves ending in tendrils.
Used as cover crops, they frequently escape from cultivation.

Crazyweed
Oxytropis lambertii
267

Hairy, deep-rooted plant sending its compound leaves directly
up through the soil from the plant crown, with clusters of
sweet-scented, pink to lavender flowers on leafless stalks that
rise above the leaves.
Flowers: about ¾" (2 cm) long; 1 broad upper petal and 2
lateral petals nearly enclosing 2 lower petals joined and shaped
like prow of a boat.
Leaves: pinnately divided into 9–19 linear to oblong, hairy
leaflets, each up to 1" (2.5 cm) long.
Fruit: erect, hairy, beaked pod.
Height: 8–12" (20–30 cm).

Flowering
May–July.

Habitat
Dry prairies and limestone sites.

Range
South-central Canada to Montana and Minnesota, and south to
Arizona, New Mexico, and Texas.

Comments
Also called Stemless Loco. This is one of the most dangerous
of the poisonous locoweeds that are widely distributed
throughout the West and Midwest. Its huge taproot can
penetrate to a depth of 8' (2.4 m). Fortunately, livestock do
not like it and avoid it unless other forage is scarce.

Woolly Locoweed
Astragalus mollissimus
268

Low-growing, hairy, bushy plant with compound woolly
leaves and dense spikes of violet flowers.
Flowers: 1" (2.5 cm) long; 1 broad upper petal and 2 lateral
petals nearly enclosing 2 united lower petals of flower that
form a blunt keel.
Leaves: about 6" (15 cm) long; pinnately compound, with
8–12 pairs of narrow leaflets.
Fruit: roundish pod with shallow depressions on each side.
Height: 8–18" (20–45 cm).

Flowering
June.

Habitat
Prairies and sandy soil.

Range
South Dakota and E. Wyoming to E. Nevada, Arizona, New
Mexico, and W. Texas.

Comments
It is similar to Locoweeds in the genus *Oxytropis,* whose flowers

have a pointed, rather than blunt, keel and leaves arising directly from the ground. Some members of both genera are called "locoweeds" and are poisonous. They contain a toxin that affects an animal's muscular control and may impair its vision (so a horse may behave oddly, jumping high over small depressions or knocking into objects)—hence the name.

Wild Lupine
Lupinus perennis
269

Blue flowers are in an upright, elongated, terminal cluster on an erect stem with palmately compound leaves.
Flowers: up to ⅔" (1.6 cm) long; 1 broad upper petal and 2 lateral petals nearly enclosing 2 lower petals that are joined and shaped like prow of a boat.
Leaves: the 7–11 lanceolate leaflets, up to 2" (5 cm) long, radiate from a central point.
Fruit: hairy pod, up to 2" (5 cm) long.
Height: 8–24" (20–60 cm).

Flowering
April–July.

Habitat
Dry open woods and fields.

Range
Maine south to Florida; west to Louisiana and Minnesota.

Comments
The plant was once thought to deplete or "wolf" the mineral content of the soil; hence the genus name derived from the Latin *lupus* ("wolf"). Actually, the plant and all the family enhance soil fertility by fixing atmospheric nitrogen.

Texas Bluebonnet
Lupinus subcarnosus
270

Small, deep blue flowers in a tall, dense, terminal cluster above palmately compound leaves.
Flowers: ½" (1.3 cm) long; banner (upper petal) of flower bears central white or yellowish spot that turns red with age.
Leaves: 4–7 blunt segments, each about 1" (2.5 cm) long, radiating from a central point.
Height: 12–15" (30–37.5 cm).

Flowering
April–May.

Habitat
Grasslands.

Range
S. Texas.

Comments
Although there are four species of Lupines in Texas, this one has been designated the official state flower. It is restricted to the eastern and southern part of the state. A most showy and important prairie species, *L. texensis,* grows up to 2' (60 cm) tall and has a reddish or yellow blotch at the center of its purple or lavender flowers.

Blue Salvia
Salvia azurea
271

A tall, delicate plant with large, 2-lipped, blue flowers whorled around the square stem and forming a terminal spikelike cluster.
Flowers: ⅔–1″ (1.6–2.5 cm) long; corolla glandular and hairy on the outside, lower lip much larger than upper lip; stamens 2.
Leaves: up to 4″ (10 cm) long; linear to lanceolate, opposite; basal leaves absent.
Height: 2–5′ (60–150 cm).

Flowering
July–October.

Habitat
Dry prairies and pastures, open or shaded; open pinelands.

Range
North Carolina south to Florida; west to Texas; north to Nebraska and Minnesota.

Comments
A widespread perennial of the grasslands, it also extends east to the Carolinas. It begins to flower early and may continue until fall, or into early winter in Florida.

Silverleaf Scurf Pea
Psoralea argophylla
272

Small, very dark blue flowers in groups of 2–4 at tops of branches with silvery foliage.
Flowers: ⅓″ (8 mm) long; 1 broad upper petal and 2 lateral petals nearly enclosing 2 lower petals that are joined and shaped like prow of a boat; stalkless.
Leaves: compound, palmately divided into 3–5 elliptic leaflets, each ¾–2″ (2–5 cm) long, covered with soft whitish hairs.
Fruit: ovate, 1-seeded, silky pod.
Height: 1–2′ (30–60 cm).

Flowering
Late June–August.

Habitat
Prairies and moist, level land.

Range
Wisconsin south to Missouri; west to the eastern slope of the Rocky Mountains from Canada to New Mexico.

Comments
This legume is often associated with Little Bluestem (*Andropogon scoparius*) in midwestern grasslands. It is reported to be poisonous to cattle.

Miniature Lupine
Lupinus bicolor
273

A usually small, grayish, hairy, branched plant with palmately compound leaves and blue-violet and white flowers arranged in whorls in short, thick, conelike racemes.
Flowers: about ⅜″ (9 mm) long; 1 broad upper petal, its central part white and dotted with black, and 2 lateral petals

nearly enclosing 2 lower petals that are joined and shaped like the prow of a boat (keel); upper edge with a few hairs near the tip; stalks of individual flowers only about ⅛" (3 mm) long.
Leaves: 5–7 leaflets, each ½–1¼" (1.3–3.1 cm) long, arranged like wheel spokes.
Fruit: pods about ¾" (2 cm) long, less than ¼" (6 mm) wide, hairy.
Height: 4–16" (10–40 cm).

Flowering
March–May.

Habitat
Mostly in open, often grassy, places from sea level to moderate elevations.

Range
S. British Columbia to S. California.

Comments
The Miniature Lupine and the California Poppy (*Eschscholtzia californica*) are common companions, the blue cast given to fields by the Lupine complementing perfectly the fiery orange of the Poppy. There are many other annual Lupines. The oldest known viable seeds, discovered in 1967 frozen in a lemming burrow, are from an arctic Lupine, estimated at 10,000 years old; when planted they germinated in just 48 hours.

Blue Vervain
Verbena hastata
74

Stiff, pencil-like spikes of numerous small, tubular, blue-violet flowers are at the top of a square, grooved stem and its branches.
Flowers: ⅛" (3 mm) wide; flaring petals 5; stamens in 2 pairs of different lengths; pistil 1, with 4-lobed ovary.
Leaves: 4–6" (10–15 cm) long, opposite, lanceolate, doubly toothed, rough-textured.
Height: 2–6' (60–180 cm).

Flowering
July–September.

Habitat
Damp thickets, shores, and roadsides.

Range
Nearly throughout North America.

Comments
An attractive perennial, it has flowers on showy candelabra-like spikes. Bumblebees are among the important pollinators.

Leadplant
Amorpha canescens
275

A gray-colored shrub with white-hairy stems, pinnately compound leaves, and many small, blue flowers in spikelike clusters.
Flowers: about ⅙" (4 mm) long; only 1 petal (the standard); stamens 10, bright orange.

Leaves: 2–4" (5–10 cm) long; covered with dense short hairs giving a grayish appearance, divided into 15–45 leaflets, each about ½" (1.3 cm) long.
Height: 1–3' (30–90 cm).

Flowering
May–August.

Habitat
Dry prairies; hills.

Range
Indiana to Arkansas, Texas, and New Mexico; north to Saskatchewan and Michigan.

Comments
This is one of the most conspicuous and characteristic shrubs of the upland prairies. It is also called Prairie Shoestring, probably because of the laced-shoestring look of the leaves and roots. It has very deep roots, 4' (1.2 m) or more, and thus avoids competition from the associated grasses.

Great Lobelia
Lobelia siphilitica
276

Showy, bright blue flowers are in the axils of leafy bracts and form an elongated cluster on a leafy stem.
Flowers: about 1" (2.5 cm) long, 2-lipped, the lower lip striped with white; calyx hairy, with 5 pointed lobes; stamens 5, forming a united tube around style.
Leaves: 2–6" (5–15 cm) long, oval to lanceolate, untoothed or irregularly toothed.
Height: 1–4' (30–120 cm).

Flowering
August–September.

Habitat
Rich lowland woods and meadows; swamps.

Range
Western New England south to E. Virginia and uplands of North Carolina and Alabama, west to E. Kansas and Minnesota.

Comments
This blue counterpart of the Cardinal Flower is a most desirable plant for wildflower gardens. The unfortunate species name is based on the fact that it was a supposed cure for syphilis. The root contains alkaloids that cause vomiting.

Vinegar Weed
Trichostema lanceolatum
277

Tall, leafy, unpleasant-smelling plant with pale blue bilaterally symmetrical flowers in long clusters in leaf axils.
Flowers: about ½" (1.3 cm) long; corolla with a narrow tube strongly bent upward near the base of the 5 narrow lobes; stamens 4, long, with the style projecting from between 2 upper corolla lobes, bent toward back of flower, then arching up and forward.
Leaves: ¾–3" (2–7.5 cm) long, narrowly lanceolate, opposite.

usually much longer than section of stem between pairs of leaves.
Height: 2–5′ (60–150 cm).

Flowering
July–October.

Habitat
Dry slopes and fields.

Range
NW. Oregon to Baja California.

Comments
The genus name comes from Greek words *trichos* ("hair") and *stemon* ("stamen"), referring to the long, slender stamens, characteristic of the genus.

Tough-leaved Iris
Iris tenax
78

Large, delicate, lavender to deep purple (sometimes white, rarely yellow) flowers, commonly with dark violet veins, grow at top of short stalks in dense clumps of narrow, tough leaves about the same height.
Flowers: 3–4″ (7.5–10 cm) wide; sepals 3, resembling petals, curved downward; petals 3, erect, slightly shorter than sepals; sepals and petals join to form a tube at base ¼–½″ (6–13 mm) long; bracts beneath flower joined to stem at distinctly different levels.
Leaves: to 16″ (40 cm) long.
Height: to 16″ (40 cm).

Flowering
April–June.

Habitat
Pastures, fields, and open areas in forests.

Range
SW. Washington to NW. California.

Comments
In the Willamette Valley of Oregon these handsome flowers provide brilliant color displays along highways throughout late spring and early summer.

Douglas' Iris
Iris douglasiana
79

Large, reddish-purple, pinkish, white or cream flowers (with lilac veins) bloom on stout, branched stalks rising from clumps of sword-shaped leaves.
Flowers: 3–4″ (7.5–10 cm) wide; sepals 3, long, resembling petals, curved downward; petals 3, erect, about same length as sepals and slightly narrower; sepals and petals join to form a tube at base ½–1″ (1.3–2.5 cm) long. Pair of bracts beneath flower grow nearly opposite one another, bases not separated by space on stem.
Leaves: to 3′ (90 cm) long, usually shorter, ¾″ (2 cm) wide, flexible, tough.
Height: 6–32″ (15–80 cm).

Flowering
March–May.

Habitat
Grassy slopes and open brush.

Range
Coast Ranges from S. Oregon to central California.

Comments
A common Iris in the redwood region. *Iris,* Greek for "rainbow," refers to the variegated colors of the beautiful flowers.

Elegant Brodiaea
Brodiaea elegans
280

An umbel of several violet or blue-violet, funnel-shaped flowers at top of a leafless stalk with a few long, very narrow basal leaves that are usually withered by flowering time.
Flowers: 1–1½" (2.5–3.8 cm) long; 6 narrow petal-like segments; inside, alternating with 3 stamens, are flat, white scales separated from, and shorter than, stamens.
Leaves: 4–16" (10–40 cm) long.
Height: 4–16" (10–40 cm).

Flowering
April–July.

Habitat
Dry plains and grassy hillsides.

Range
N. Oregon to S. California.

Comments
This plant begins to flower as fields dry out in the early summer. Several species of *Brodiaea* are similar.

Pasqueflower
Anemone patens
281

From a cluster of deeply cut basal leaves rises a silky-hairy stalk with a solitary, blue to purple or white flower above a circle of 3 unstalked leaves with linear segments.
Flowers: about 2½" (6.3 cm) wide; sepals 5–7, petal-like, about 1" (2.5 cm) long; petals absent; stamens numerous; pistils numerous, with long styles.
Leaves: basal to 3" (7.5 cm) long, hairy, palmately divided into segments cut again into narrow divisions; leaves beneath flowers hairy, divided into linear lobes.
Fruit: seedlike, in heads with long, feathery styles.
Height: 6–16" (15–40 cm).

Flowering
April–June.

Habitat
Grasslands.

Range
Northwestern Canada east to N. Wisconsin and Michigan; south to Utah, New Mexico, Texas, Missouri, and Illinois.

Comments
The feathery, silky fruiting head is the distinctive feature of this western grasslands species. The common name refers to the Eastertime flowering throughout much of its range.

Prairie Gentian
Eustoma grandiflorum
282

Erect stems, with evenly spaced opposite leaves, grow in small clumps; at their tops bloom small clusters of large, erect, bell-shaped, usually bluish flowers.
Flowers: 1¼–1½″ (3.1–3.8 cm) long; calyx to 1¼″ (3.1 cm) long, with 5 needlelike lobes; bluish-purple, pinkish, white, white and purplish- or yellowish-tinged corolla with a short broad tube and 5 broad lobes 1¼–1½″ (3.1–3.8 cm) long.
Leaves: to 3″ (7.5 cm) long, ovate, with 3 conspicuous veins.
Height: 10–28″ (25–70 cm).

Flowering
June–September.

Habitat
Moist places in prairies and fields.

Range
E. Colorado to Nebraska; south to E. New Mexico and Texas.

Comments
One of the most handsome prairie wildflowers. *Eustoma*, from the Greek *eu* ("good") and *stoma* ("mouth"), refers to the large opening into the flower's "throat" where the corolla lobes join.

Ivy-leaved Morning Glory
Ipomoea hederacea
283

This leafy, hairy vine has 3-lobed leaves, and blue, funnel-shaped flowers (white on the inside) that turn rose-purple late in the day.
Flowers: about 1½″ (3.8 cm) wide; corolla of 5 fused petals; sepals 5, with long tips and narrow hairy base.
Leaves: 2–5″ (5–12.5 cm) long or wide; deeply indented into 3 lobes, tapering to points.
Height: vine, 3–6′ (90–180 cm) long.

Flowering
July–October.

Habitat
Fields and disturbed areas.

Range
New England and New York south to Florida; west to Texas; north to North Dakota.

Comments
Introduced from tropical America, this twining plant is often a troublesome weed, especially in Alabama.

Baby Blue Eyes
Nemophila menziesii
284

A low plant with pale or clear blue, bowl-shaped flowers that bloom singly on slender stalks growing near the ends of slender, leaning, branched stems.

Flowers: ½–1½″ (1.3–3.8 cm) wide; corolla with 5 broad, pale or bright blue petals, often paler near base, generally with small black spots; stamens 5; style with 2 branches at tip.
Leaves: ¾–2″ (2–5 cm) long, opposite, oblong, pinnately divided into segments with teeth along edges.
Height: 4–12″ (10–30 cm).

Flowering
March–June.

Habitat
Grassy hillsides and among brush.

Range
Central Oregon to S. California.

Comments
One of the most charming and best-known spring wildflowers in California, it is often included in commercial wildflower seed mixtures and has been cultivated in England for more than a century.

Purple Groundcherry
Physalis lobata
285

Blue-violet or violet, nearly round, saucer-shaped flowers bloom on slender stalks in leaf axils of short, erect stems that grow from a rosette of leaves, or on longer, leafy stems that lie on ground, their ends turning upward.
Flowers: corolla about ¾″ (2 cm) wide; hairy pads alternate with bases of 5 slender stamens near center of flower, the anthers like small yellow knobs; calyx enlarges as fruit matures and forms a 5-sided bladder ¾″ (2 cm) long.
Leaves: to 4″ (10 cm) long, lanceolate, pinnately lobed or divided.
Fruit: berry about ¼″ (6 mm) in diameter enclosed in the calyx.
Height: creeper, with some branches to about 6″ (15 cm).

Flowering
March–September.

Habitat
Open areas in desert plains, frequent in agricultural areas.

Range
Arizona to Kansas, south to Mexico.

Comments
The berry is edible, but caution is advised, for the flower resembles some of those of *Solanum,* a genus with both edible and deadly berries, and unripe berries of some species of *Physalis* are also poisonous.

Bird-foot Violet
Viola pedata
286

This smooth plant has deep blue-violet flowers and deeply cut leaves on separate stalks.
Flowers: often 1½″ (3.8 cm) wide, larger than most violets; petals 5, beardless, the lower one whitish, veined with violet,

grooved and spurred; stamens 5, with orange anthers
conspicuous in throat of flower.
Leaves: 1–2″ (2.5–5 cm) long, fan-shaped, with linear,
toothed segments.
Height: 4–10″ (10–25 cm).

Flowering
March–June.

Habitat
Dry, sandy fields; wood openings.

Range
Maine to Minnesota, south to Florida and Texas.

Comments
This plant is one of the earliest spring flowers of the tallgrass
prairie. Its showy, light violet-blue flowers and distinctive
"bird's-foot"-shaped leaves make it easy to identify.

Wild Blue Flax
Linum perenne
287

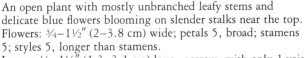

An open plant with mostly unbranched leafy stems and
delicate blue flowers blooming on slender stalks near the top.
Flowers: ¾–1½″ (2–3.8 cm) wide; petals 5, broad; stamens
5; styles 5, longer than stamens.
Leaves: ½–1¼″ (1.3–3.1 cm) long, narrow, with only 1 vein.
Height: 6–32″ (15–80 cm).

Flowering
March–September.

Habitat
Well-drained soil in prairies, meadows, and open mountain
slopes and ledges.

Range
Alaska to S. California; east to W. Texas, central Kansas,
Wisconsin, and Saskatchewan; also northern Mexico; reported
in West Virginia.

Comments
Several Indian tribes used Wild Blue Flax for making cordage.
Common Flax (*L. usitatissimum*), from which linen is made and
linseed oil is obtained, often escapes from cultivation. It has
blue petals about ½″ (1.3 cm) long and leaves with 3 veins.

Bluets
Houstonia caerulea
288

A low plant with erect, slender stems bearing pale blue flowers
with golden-yellow centers.
Flowers: about ½″ (1.3 cm) wide; corolla tubular, with 4
flattish lobes. Flowers pistillate (female), with sterile stamens,
or staminate (male), with sterile pistils.
Leaves: basal ones to ½″ (1.3 cm) long, oblong, in tufts; stem
leaves tiny, opposite.
Height: 3–6″ (7.5–15 cm).

Flowering
April–June.

Habitat
Grassy slopes and fields, thickets, and lawns on acid soils.

Range
Ontario to Nova Scotia; south to Georgia; west to Alabama; north to Wisconsin.

Comments
This lovely, delicate, flowering plant is often found in striking patches of light blue.

Pointed Blue-eyed Grass
Sisyrinchium angustifolium
289

Small blue or violet-blue flowers with yellow centers are at the top of a long, flat, twisted stalk that is usually branched.
Flowers: ½″ (1.3 cm) wide; petals 3; sepals 3, petal-like, each tipped with a thornlike point.
Leaves: 4–20″ (10–50 cm) long, less than ¼″ (6 mm) wide; basal, linear and grasslike, may be shorter or longer than the floral stalk.
Height: 4–20″ (10–50 cm).

Flowering
May–July.

Habitat
Meadows, low woods, shores.

Range
Eastern Canada south to Texas and Florida.

Comments
Although the plant is small and has grasslike leaves, the flowers have all the features of the Iris family. The various species are all much alike and separation is based on such characteristics as branching pattern and leaf length. Common Blue-eyed Grass (*S. montanum*) is also a widespread species.

Wild Blue Phlox
Phlox divaricata
290

A loose cluster of slightly fragrant, light blue flowers tops a somewhat sticky stem that produces leafy, creeping shoots at the base.
Flowers: ¾–1½″ (2–3.8 cm) wide; petals 5, united, form a trumpet-shaped corolla; stamens 5, short, arise from inside of corolla tube; pistil 1, with stigmas 3.
Leaves: 1–2″ (2.5–5 cm) long, opposite, ovate to lanceolate, unstalked.
Height: 10–20″ (25–30 cm).

Flowering
April–June.

Habitat
Rich woods; fields.

Range
Quebec and Vermont south to South Carolina; west to N. Alabama and E. Texas; north to Illinois, Minnesota, Wisconsin, and Michigan.

Comments
This beautiful species is most common in midwestern woods and fields. It is sometimes known as Wild Sweet William.

Chicory
Cichorium intybus
291

A stiff stem bears several stalkless, showy blue flower heads, with square-tipped, fringed ray flowers.
Flowers: heads to 1½" (3.8 cm) wide, disk flowers absent; 2-part style is surrounded by dark blue, fused anthers.
Leaves: basal leaves 3–6" (7.5–15 cm) long, dandelionlike. Stem leaves much smaller, oblong to lanceolate, clasping.
Height: 1–4' (30–120 cm).

Flowering
June–October.

Habitat
Fields, roadsides, and waste places.

Range
Throughout most of the United States.

Comments
Only a few flower heads open at a time, and each lasts only a day. While this Old World weed has in some places proliferated to become a plant pest, it is also sought for its food uses and is cultivated as well. The roots can be roasted and ground as a coffee substitute or additive.

Tahoka Daisy
Machaeranthera tanacetifolia
292

Branched stems with fernlike leaves end in heads with many bright purple, very narrow rays surrounding a yellow disk.
Flowers: heads 1¼–2½" (3.1–6.3 cm) wide.
Leaves: 2–5" (5–12.5 cm) long, pinnately divided, the main segments also pinnately divided.
Fruit: seedlike, covered with short hairs lying flat on the surface, the top with many slender bristles.
Height: 4–16" (10–40 cm).

Flowering
May–September.

Habitat
Sandy open ground on plains or deserts.

Range
Alberta to Texas, Arizona, and Mexico.

Comments
The fernlike leaves of this beautiful species make it one of the easiest to identify in a complex group.

Smooth Aster
Aster laevis
293

A smooth-leaved perennial with many rich lavender-blue ray and yellow disk flowers and a light grayish-white bloom on its stem.
Flowers: to 1" (2.5 cm) wide, green-tipped bracts around flower head.

Leaves: 1–4″ (2.5–10 cm) long, thick, slightly toothed, elliptic or lanceolate, lower ones stalked, upper unstalked and clasping the stem.
Fruit: dry, 1-seeded, often with reddish bristles.
Height: 2–4′ (60–120 cm).

Flowering
August–October.

Habitat
Fields, open woods and roadsides.

Range
S. Ontario to New Brunswick; Maine south to Georgia; west to Louisiana; north to Kansas.

Comments
One of the most attractive blue Asters, it has bright green foliage that is very smooth to the touch. At least 11 other related species are found within its range.

Tall Ironweed
Vernonia altissima
294

Tall erect stem bears deep purple-blue flower heads in loose terminal clusters.
Flowers: heads about ¼″ (6 mm) wide, with 13–30 5-lobed disk flowers; ray flowers absent; bracts beneath flower heads blunt-tipped, usually purple.
Leaves: 6–10″ (15–25 cm) long, thin, lanceolate, pointed, lower surfaces downy.
Fruit: seedlike, with a double set of purplish bristles.
Height: 3–7′ (90–210 cm).

Flowering
August–October.

Habitat
Damp, rich soil.

Range
New York south to Georgia; west to Louisiana; north to Missouri, Illinois, and Michigan.

Comments
The common name refers to the toughness of the stem. The genus name honors the English botanist William Vernon, who did fieldwork in North America. At least 6 additional species are found in the East; some were once used for treating stomach ailments.

BUTTERFLIES AND MOTHS

Grasslands vegetation provides ample shelter, moisture, and nectar for a large variety of butterflies and moths. These delicate creatures are often especially abundant after a rainfall, and in wet years the numbers of some species are large indeed. Some moths and butterflies will colonize almost any open space, where various kinds of legumes or grasses are abundant. A few species are migratory, turning up at various times during the year. This section describes many of the most common butterflies and moths of the grasslands.

Orange Sulphur
Colias eurytheme
295

Wingspan: 1⅝–2⅜″ (41–60 mm). Male and female above bright gold-orange with pink blush and black borders (broken by yellow spots of female); black spot in fore-wing cell, red-orange spot in hind-wing cell. Below, orange, yellow, or greenish yellow with single or double red-rimmed silvery spot in hind-wing cell and row of brown spots just inside margin. Both wings have pink fringe.

Life Cycle
Egg whitish, long and pitcher-shaped; laid singly on top or bottom of leaves. Caterpillar dark grass-green with pink stripes low on sides, white stripes higher, and covered with tiny white hair. Chrysalis green, dashed with yellow and black; overwinters.

Flight
Overlapping broods; March–December.

Habitat
Nearly any open space, particularly alfalfa fields.

Range
Most of North America.

Comments
Like the Common Sulphur, this species breeds with enormous success on native and naturalized legumes. These food preferences, along with strong and probing flight habits, allow the Orange and Common sulphurs to colonize disturbed and cultivated areas as well as natural habitats. When these 2 sulphur species are superabundant in an alfalfa field, they often hybridize and produce many part-orange, part-yellow butterflies that are difficult to classify. However, the species have not merged; they breed true where density is lower.

Common Sulphur
Colias philodice
296

Wingspan: 1⅜–2″ (35–51 mm). Above, male light yellow with sharp black borders; female yellow or white with yellow-spotted black border. Below, both sexes greenish yellow in spring and fall broods, clear yellow in midsummer; double red-rimmed silvery spot near end of cell and row of brown spots slightly inward from edges of both wings. Albino female has pink fringes.

Life Cycle
Chartreuse egg laid singly. Caterpillar bright green with darker back stripe and light side stripes. Green chrysalis overwinters.

Flight
Several broods; March–December, weather permitting.

Habitat
Almost any open country; especially numerous in clover meadows, and pastures; absent from forests and deserts.

Range
Throughout United States except for most of Florida.

Comments
Because it feeds on clover, alfalfa, vetches, and many other pervasive legumes, the Common Sulphur has spread dramatically. It was probably originally a northern and eastern species, while the Orange Sulphur occupied the West and the South. Now, due to the spread of agriculture, their territories have largely merged.

Prairie Ringlet
Coenonympha inornata
297

Wingspan: 1–1⅞" (25–48 mm). Pale orange-brown to rich ocher above, sometimes dusky, without markings. Below, fore wing mostly ocher, paler at tip, sometimes with 1 small black, yellow-rimmed eyespot; hind wing below pale dusky olive with fragmentary, curved white band across disk and whitish veins; hind wing often darker at base and sometimes has a partial row of minute eyespots around margin.

Life Cycle
Egg yellowish. Caterpillar tan or olive with 2 tails. Chrysalis rounded, greenish brown.

Flight
2 broods; June–September.

Habitat
Prairies, meadows, pastures, and grassy woodland glades and embankments.

Range
W. Ontario east to Labrador, south to E. British Columbia, Dakotas, Iowa, Wisconsin, New England, and upper New York.

Comments
The relatively recent colonization of northern New York by the Prairie Ringlet has raised some concern that it might swamp another related species of the Northeast, the local Nipisquit Ringlet (*C. nipisquit*).

Sleepy Orange
Eurema nicippe
298

Wingspan: 1⅜–1⅞" (35–48 mm). Male bright golden orange above with broad, uneven black border and a black fore-wing cell spot; yellow beneath with small brown blotches. Female orange or yellow; black border breaks down halfway along hind wing; below, hind wing cocoa-brown with darker blotches; fore wing orange. In autumn individuals hind wing below is darker.

Life Cycle
Egg long, narrow. Caterpillar, to 1" (25 mm), slender, green, downy, and side-striped with white, yellow, and black. Chrysalis ash-green to brown-black.

Flight
March–November in South with 2–3 overlapping broods; shorter flight period northerly. Adults may be seen in all months in Deep South.

Habitat
Old fields, wood edges, desert scrub, open pine woods, mountain canyons, watersides, and wet meadows.

Range
Throughout South and Southwest, northward east of Rockies, rarely well into Northeast.

Comments
This sulphur cannot withstand cold winters yet annually penetrates the northerly latitudes. The common name, Sleepy Orange, may have come from the butterfly's habit of hibernating through the cooler days of the southern winter. In summer it seems anything but sleepy with its rapid flight.

European Skipper
Thymelicus lineola
299

Wingspan: ¾–1" (19–25 mm). Small. Above, brassy-orange with narrow dark border, male has tiny stigma; veins darkened above, especially on female. Below, fore wing clear orange, hind wing olive-ocher, greenish gray, or copper-colored.

Life Cycle
Egg whitish; laid in strips of 30 or 40; overwinters. Caterpillar green with brown head and dark midstripe. Chrysalis yellow-green with down-curved horn.

Flight
1 brood; June–August.

Habitat
Meadows, pastures, and grassy waste ground.

Range
Minnesota, New Brunswick, and west-central British Columbia south to Maryland and Illinois.

Comments
The European Skipper was introduced to North America in London, Ontario, in 1910, and has since spread dramatically. The population of the butterfly fluctuates markedly.

Indian Skipper
Hesperia sassacus
300

Wingspan: 1–1⅜" (25–35 mm). Long, triangular wings. Above, male has slender bar of scent scales and broad, jagged dark border; female dark brown or black, with orange confined to sharply bordered patches. Both sexes below, fore wing orange and tawny, black at base; hind wing light tan with pale band of large, connected spots.

Life Cycle
Mature caterpillar reddish brown mottled with green highlights and light speckling.

Flight
1 brood; May–July. Perhaps 2 broods in South.

Habitat
Dry, old fields and pastures, acid soil scrub, and damp meadows and roadsides.

Range
S. Ontario east to Maine, south to Virginia and Tennessee, and west to Wisconsin and Iowa.

Comments
The Indian Skipper is more often seen in May, but flies until mid-July. It is one of the few springtime skippers, and the time of its appearance will separate it from most others with which it might be confused.

Woolly Bear Caterpillar Moth
sia isabella
01

Wingspan: 1⅝–2″ (40–50 mm). Fore wings yellow-brown with a series or row of small black dots. Hind wings slightly paler, slightly pinkish with several indistinct gray dots. Abdomen has 3 black spots above on rear edge of each segment. Caterpillar, to 2⅛″ (55 mm), is black, covered with stiff bristles, and has a broad band of red-brown bristles around the middle.

Flight
June–August in the North, February–November in the South.

Habitat
Meadows, pastures, uncultivated fields, and road edges.

Range
Throughout North America, except northern Canada.

Comments
Familiar since Colonial times as the "Woolly Bear," the caterpillar is often seen crossing roads and paths on warm days in late fall. According to superstition, the amount of black in the caterpillar's bristle coating forecasts the severity of the coming winter. Actually, the coloration indicates how near the caterpillar is to full growth.

Ornate Tiger Moth
pantesis ornata
02

Wingspan: 1⅛–1⅝″ (30–40 mm). Fore wings black, crosshatched with ivory-white. Hind wings pink to red, spotted with black. Body black, thorax streaked with ivory; dull brownish yellow often along sides of abdomen. Caterpillar is mostly black with yellow midline stripe and often has pale spots above each side of stripe.

Flight
Spring–summer.

Habitat
Fields and roadsides.

Range
Great Basin to Pacific Coast.

Comments
Male moths are attracted to artificial lights at night, but females generally remain close to breeding areas and food plants.

Acraea Moth
Estigmene acraea
303

Wingspan: 1⅞–2" (48–50 mm). Thorax and fore wings above white with 4–6 black dots on front margin, with further speckling elsewhere. Hind wings brownish yellow (male) or white (female). In both sexes, hind wings have 3 black spots near outer margin, middle spot largest. Caterpillar, to 2½" (65 mm), is black covered with dense, long rusty-red hair.

Flight
June–July.

Habitat
Fields, pastures, and marshes.

Range
Throughout North America, except northern Canada.

Comments
Because these caterpillars often feed on grasses in salt marshes, they are sometimes called Salt Marsh Caterpillars.

Yellow Woolly Bear Moth
Diacrisia virginica
304

Wingspan: 1½–2" (38–50 mm). Wings snow-white with small gray dots; 1 on each fore wing, 3–4 on each hind wing. Abdomen yellowish with black dots on midline and along each side. Front femora and leg bases are orange or yellowish brown. Caterpillar has short and long hair on pale yellow to white body, and yellow legs.

Flight
May–summer.

Habitat
Meadows, roadsides, and crop fields.

Range
Throughout most of North America.

Comments
This moth's caterpillars are sometimes pests on crops and garden flowers. There are 2 generations a year.

Sod Webworm Moths
Crambus spp.
305

Wingspan: ½–1½" (12–39 mm). Wings grayish white to brown, often with silvery streaks. At rest, wings curl around the body, giving insect an almost cylindrical form; pattern of darker and paler areas on fore wings inconspicuous until wings are spread. Caterpillar is dirty white to pale brown with pairs of dark spots on back and side and a few coarse hairs.

Flight
Throughout the summer. There are 2–3 generations a year.

Habitat
Grasslands, open fields, and pastures.

Range
Throughout North America.

Comments
Adults rest on grass blades, head down or up, and fly away if

approached closely. A single caterpillar may produce an irregular brown spot in a new lawn; many may cause severe damage by destroying grass roots.

Milkweed Tiger Moth
Euchaetias egle
406

Wingspan: 1–1¾″ (25–45 mm). Wings silvery to grayish brown. Abdomen yellow with 3 lengthwise rows of black spots. Wings disproportionately long for body, but of characteristic tiger moth shape—fore wings slant backward to form a nearly smooth contour with shorter hind wings. Caterpillar, to 1⅝″ (40 mm), is densely hairy with long tufts of black and white hair at each end, shorter tufts along sides, and orange hair down midline, which has short black hair on each side.

Flight
June–early August.

Habitat
Meadows and roadsides, where milkweed is common.

Range
Ontario and northeastern United States, to North Carolina mountains, west to Great Plains.

Comments
The colorful black, white, and orange caterpillar is often called the Harlequin Caterpillar.

Cabbage White
Artogeia rapae
307

Wingspan: 1¼–1⅞″ (32–48 mm). Milk-white above with charcoal fore-wing tips, black patches of scent scales just inside margin of fore wing (1 on male, 2 on female) and on leading edge of hind wing. Below, fore-wing tip and hind wing pale to bright mustard-yellow, specked with grayish spots and black fore-wing spots.

Life Cycle
Egg yellowish, vase-shaped. Caterpillar, to ¾″ (19 mm), bright green with yellowish back stripes and side stripes; covered with short pile. Chrysalis, to ¾″ (19 mm), speckled, green or tan.

Flight
3 or more broods; from last to first hard frost.

Habitat
Gardens, agricultural and abandoned fields, cities, plains, foothills; wandering virtually everywhere except where the most extreme climatic conditions exist.

Range
All of North America south of Canadian Taiga, including Hawaii.

Comments
Exceedingly well known to most gardeners, the Cabbage White has spread throughout North America after its

unintentional introduction to Quebec in 1860. It is native to Eurasia. No other butterfly is so successful over such a great expanse of landscape. Farmers and gardeners consider it a pest, so great is its appetite for cabbages and radishes.

Becker's White
Pontia beckerii
308

Wingspan: 1⅜–1⅞" (35–48 mm). White above with open, squarish black spot in fore-wing cell and bold black spotting around fore-wing tip and margin. Female may also have black spots on hind wing above. Below, gray-green or moss-green scaling broadly outlines veins of hind wing, broken by clear white band across wing; fore-wing tips below have some green scaling and black spot in fore-wing cell. Brightness of green scaling variable.

Life Cycle
Egg spindle-shaped, ridged. Caterpillar pale green, black-dotted, yellow cross-banded. Chrysalis smooth gray with white wing case; resembles bird dropping.

Flight
2 distinct broods; May–June, August–September. More broods in some southerly locales.

Habitat
Arid lands such as sage flats, dry coulees, foothill canyons, and lower mountains.

Range
Drier, intermontane western North America from interior British Columbia through Montana to Black Hills of South Dakota, SE. Colorado, and across Great Basin to Baja California.

Comments
A hardy butterfly of harsh environments, Becker's White is at home on a hot wind in a dusty canyon. Its association with sagebrush arises from a common adaptation to the desert. Look for this bright green-marked butterfly on rabbit brush, where it takes nectar, or find it roosting among sparse vegetation at dawn or dusk.

Checkered White
Pontia protodice
309

Wingspan: 1¼–1¾" (32–44 mm). Generally white above with charcoal or brown markings; hind-wing veins below lined with brown- or olive-green. Female more heavily marked than male; spring brood more marked than summer—heavily checkered with charcoal above and lined with olive below. Summer male nearly immaculate white except for black cell spot above and tan tracery below. All gradations in between can occur.

Life Cycle
Yellow, spindle-shaped eggs. Caterpillar becomes blue-green, black-speckled, and downy with 4 lengthwise yellow stripes. Blue-gray chrysalis has black speckles; overwinters in California.

Flight
Early spring–late fall in several broods; year-round in parts of California.

Habitat
Mostly lowland open spaces, especially disturbed areas, fields, vacant lots, railroad yards, and other weedy plots.

Range
Lower margins of Canada southward to northern Mexico; absent from most of Pacific Northwest. Scarcer in East.

Comments
The distributions of native white butterflies have probably changed considerably since pre-colonial times, possibly due in part to competition from the introduced Cabbage White. However, these changes may be caused to a greater extent by the expansion and contraction of various habitats by people.

Alfalfa Looper
Autographa californica
310

Wingspan: 1⅛–1⅝″ (30–40 mm). Fore wings gray with a silvery mark near middle. Hind wings and body dull gray to brown, paler toward base, darker along outer margin. Caterpillar, to 1″ (25 mm), is olive-green with paler head.

Flight
Midsummer.

Habitat
Crop fields, wastelands, and open areas.

Range
Western half of the United States, extreme S. Saskatchewan, and British Columbia.

Comments
These moths are members of a large, widespread genus in North America. Most adults have a silvery mark, or "autograph," on the fore wings. Their caterpillars move in a looping gait and sometimes seriously damage crops.

Common Checkered Skipper
Pyrgus communis
311

Wingspan: ¾–1¼″ (19–32 mm). Extremely variable. Above can be quite blackish with little white checkering (especially in female) or very pale with broad bands of white spots (particularly males); usually some black at base and often considerable bluish hairy scaling. Below, fore wing similar to upper side but paler; hind wing pale eggshell-white to yellowish, crossed by 2 major and 2 minor rows of olive-tan to olive-green spots normally linked into solid bands, outlined finely with black or brown scales. Fringes checkered with gray and white.

Life Cycle
Egg changes from green to cream-color before hatching. Caterpillar tan with darker median line, brown and white side lines, and black head. Chrysalis greener toward head and browner toward tip; has dark speckles and dashes in bands.

Flight
Successive broods; year-round in far South, April–October in Midwest.

Habitat
Foothills, weedy plains, fields, roadsides, riverbanks, valley bottoms, gardens, vacant lots, and parks.

Range
Southern Canada to Argentina, but absent from northwest states and north of Massachusetts.

Comments
This is considered by many to be the most common skipper in North America. Highly aggressive males patrol tightly circumscribed territories, darting out at passing objects.

Yucca Giant Skipper
Megathymus yuccae
312

Wingspan: 2–2⅞" (51–73 mm). Black above with yellow rays outward from bases and cloudy-yellow hind-wing borders; fore wing has bright yellow cell spot, narrow or pointed in western populations and rounded in others, and band of squarish yellow spots just inside margin above; sometimes hind wing has yellow spotting above. Below, dark hind wing frosty-violet with some black dusting and white spotting. Big, rounded body, generally black to dark brown, brownish gray, or gray.

Life Cycle
Caterpillars make silk shelter of 2 or more yucca leaves strapped together. Caterpillar overwinters, pupates in spring before feeding.

Flight
Late January–June, only about 4 weeks in any one locale except central Florida.

Habitat
Forest edges, granite outcroppings, old fields, and bottomlands with yucca.

Range
Utah and Great Basin east through Arkansas and Carolinas, south to Florida and Gulf, west to Nevada, S. California, Baja California, and Mexico.

Comments
By far the most widely distributed giant skipper, the Yucca Giant Skipper may be seen as readily in Georgia's pine woods as in Utah's deserts, and from the bottom of Black Canyon of the Gunnison to high elevations in North Park, Colorado.

Small Checkered Skipper
Pyrgus scriptura
313

Wingspan: ⅝–1" (16–25 mm). Tiny. Shiny dark gray to dark brown above, with small and separate white checks. Long white fringes with little dark checkering. Below, fore wing gray-olive; hind wing crossed by alternating rows of clean white and olive-tan, without black outlines.

Flight
Successive broods; most of year in California and Southwest,
April–August further north.

Habitat
Open grasslands, prairies, high plains, abandoned fields, and
canal sides; marshes in California.

Range
SE. Alberta and North Dakota south to Mexico and west to
Arizona, S. Nevada, California, and Baja California.

Comments
This species is one of the few butterflies to emerge just after
the snow melts in foothill canyons. It also flies in parched
weedy patches in late summer.

Dakota Skipper
Hesperia dacotae
314

Wingspan: 1–1⅜″ (25–35 mm). Compact, with short,
rounded wings. Male above bright tawny-orange with short
but prominent stigma, little border; clear yellow-orange
below, usually with only vague suggestion of pale spot band.
Female above olive-brown, with tawny-orange mostly
restricted to upper marginal area of fore wing, and square
glassy spot below end of cell; often traces of light yellow spot
band on hind wing above and whitish band on golden-gray
hind wing below.

Life Cycle
Female lays single egg quite near ground on grass blade.
Caterpillar constructs shelter partly or wholly beneath soil.

Flight
1 brood; June–early July.

Habitat
Well-drained, unplowed, ungrazed or lightly grazed prairie.

Range
S. Manitoba and Dakotas to Minnesota, Iowa, and Illinois.

Comments
There are 2 other prairie *Hesperias*. Like them, the Dakota
Skipper is severely limited by its need for intact grasslands.
The only hope for the survival of this species lies in the
preservation of its native prairie habitat.

Artichoke Plume Moth
Platyptilia carduidactyla
315

Wingspan: ¾–1⅛″ (20–28 mm). Fore wings narrow,
shallowly notched at outer margin; mostly pale brown with
1 pale spot just beyond 1 dark spot at the front margin toward
the tip. Hind wings somewhat broader, twice notched on
outer margin; mostly grayish. Body and appendages tan to
gray. Caterpillar is yellowish with shiny black head, black
cervical shield, and black plate on last abdominal segment.

Flight
Midsummer.

Habitat
Meadows and cultivated fields.

Range
Coast to coast.

Comments
This graceful little plume moth rests easily on long slender legs, ready to flutter away from any disturbance. The caterpillars spin webs on plants while feeding.

Funereal Duskywing
Erynnis funeralis
316

Wingspan: 1⅛–1¾" (28–44 mm). Fore wing very long and narrow; hind wing rather square. Fore wing patterned, hind wing plain. Above, dark brown with blacker, mottled markings across fore wing; hind wing almost uniform blackish brown. Female lighter than male with some buff spots on hind wing above. Small glassy white spots from leading edge to middle of fore wing. Below, lighter overall.

Life Cycle
Caterpillar greenish with distinctive yellow-spotted yellow lines along sides. Chrysalis green.

Flight
Successive broods in S. Texas; year-round. 3 broods in S. California; February–October.

Habitat
Prairie and desert edges; mountains with pine, juniper, oak; moist valleys.

Range
California, S. Nevada, S. Utah, Colorado and W. Kansas south to Argentina and Chile.

Comments
Named for its sober coloring, the Funereal Duskywing wanders far afield to colonize such pioneer legumes as vetch, lotus, and alfalfa. It is therefore common over a large range.

Beard-grass Skipper
Atrytone arogos
317

Wingspan: ⅞–1¼" (22–32 mm). Male tawny-orange above with fairly broad brown margins; female has broader dark margins, with tawny-orange restricted to upper border on fore wing above and small patch on hind wing above. Below, clear tawny to bright yellow.

Life Cycle
Egg cream-colored. Caterpillar pale chartreuse with rust-colored spots and stripes; pupates in loose cocoon spun between 2 grass blades about a yard above ground. Chrysalis yellowish with paler thorax, abdomen, wing pads, and tongue case.

Flight
1 brood in North; June–July. 2 broods in South; March–May and August–September.

Habitat
Beard-grass fields and barrens.

Range
Minnesota east to New York, south to Florida, west to Texas, and north to Nebraska, Colorado, and Wyoming.

Comments
Beard-grass Skippers live in local colonies, never in large numbers. Their virgin prairie habitats have been largely eliminated; however, they can live near civilization, as demonstrated by the colony on one of the last serpentine barrens of Staten Island, New York.

Great Gray Copper
Gaeides xanthoides
318

Wingspan: 1¼–1¾" (32–44 mm). Large. Male above uniform gray-brown, with orange scaling and small black dots along hind-wing margin. Female above has few black spots and often light orange scaling, especially on fore wing; orange margins on hind wing more extensive than male. Both sexes below very light gray with small black spots and either prominent orange hind-wing margins (East) or thin orange hind-wing marginal band (West).

Life Cycle
Egg white. Mature caterpillar green, yellow-green, or magenta with dark orange stripes. Chrysalis pink-buff; found in loosely constructed cocoon of silk and soil in debris.

Flight
1 brood; late May–early August.

Habitat
In West, dry slopes, sandy flats, and dry riverbeds. In East, prairie swamps, marshes, and meadows.

Range
Oregon south to Baja California, east through Rockies and across to Great Plains from Manitoba to Oklahoma.

Comments
The Great Gray Copper is the largest American copper and one of the largest gossamer wings. Its rapid and jerky flight makes this butterfly difficult to watch, except when it stops to take nectar from milkweed. In prairie gullies, the Great Gray Copper may fly side by side with Viceroys, and sometimes the 2 species clash in flight.

Gray Hairstreak
Strymon melinus
319

Wingspan: 1–1¼" (25–32 mm). Above, deep slate-gray with orange spot on hind wing; female browner. Below, dove-gray; straight, thin red and black midband on fore wing and hind wing lined with white; bold orange and blue patches above tail, black spot at outer angle of hind wing. Abdomen has orange sides.

Life Cycle
Egg pale green. Caterpillar variable, usually grass-green to

translucent green, with white to mauve diagonal side stripes. Chrysalis brown with copious black mottling.

Flight
Variable, number of broods increasing southward: 2 in North, 3 or more in South; April–October.

Habitat
Open deciduous woods, coastlines, roadsides, chaparral, old fields, parks, vacant lots, and other open spaces.

Range
British Columbia to Maritimes, and south to Baja California and Florida.

Comments
Absent only from the far North, the Gray Hairstreak is one of the most generally distributed butterflies.

Pipevine Swallowtail
Battus philenor
320

Wingspan: 2¾–3⅜″ (70–86 mm). Coal-black to dark gray above with brilliant, metallic blue, especially toward hind-wing margin (male brighter than female); hind wing above ha row of cream to yellow spots around rim. Fore wing dull gray below; hind wing has row of big, bright orange spots curving through blue patch along margin and white marginal spots.

Life Cycle
Clustered, rust-colored eggs. Mature caterpillar, 1⅞–2⅛″ (48–54 mm), rust-black with black or red projections, longest on head. Chrysalis, to 1⅛″ (28 mm), lavender to greenish yellow or pale brown; has sculptured curves, angles, and horns.

Flight
2 broods in North, 3 in South; January–October depending on latitude, late April–early autumn in New England.

Habitat
Open woodlands, canyons, meadows, fields, gardens, streamsides, orchards, and roadsides.

Range
S. Ontario and New England south throughout East to Florida, west through Nebraska and Texas to Arizona and California, north to Oregon; also south into Mexico.

Comments
Horticulture has caused the spread of pipevines, and thereby extended the range of this butterfly. The adult favors honeysuckle, swamp milkweed, orchids, buddleia, azalea, lilac, and thistle. But the distasteful host plants of its caterpillars give this swallowtail an unpleasant flavor, causing birds to avoid it.

Red-spotted Purple
Basilarchia astyanax
321, 330

Wingspan: 3–3⅜″ (76–86 mm). Large. Fore wing long, hind wing very squared, sometimes quite scalloped. Above, coal-black with brilliant blue to blue-green iridescence, especially over hind wing. Below, brick-red spots line borders and cluster around wing bases. Eastern populations have some red in fore-wing tips above.

Life Cycle
Caterpillar humped, dark-saddled and mottled; basically cream-colored with 2 large brushlike bristles behind head.

Flight
Up to 3 broods in South; mid-spring through summer.

Habitat
Open woodlands, forest edges, nearby meadows, watercourses, shorelines, and roads and paths; arroyos and canyons in Southwest.

Range
Eastern Dakotas and NE. Colorado east to southern New England, south to central Florida, and west to Arizona and Mexico.

Comments
Along the northern edge of its range, the Red-spotted Purple hybridizes with the White Admiral to produce partially banded offspring. The Red-spotted Purple mimics the toxic, bright blue Pipevine Swallowtail, thus gaining protection from birds.

Acmon Blue
caricia acmon
322, 323

Wingspan: ¾–1″ (19–25 mm). Above, male bright lilac-blue with narrow black margins; hind wing has pinkish-orange band just inside margin surrounding small marginal black dots. Female dark brownish; blue, if present, limited to wing bases (mostly fore wing); red-orange band just inside margin more prominent. Below, both sexes white to gray with many small black dots; prominent orange band just inside margin of hind wing; outermost row of hind-wing black dots have metallic green caps. Fringes are white; fore wing below has black dot in middle of cell.

Life Cycle
Egg pale green. Young caterpillar overwinters; mature caterpillar dirty yellow, covered with fine white hair, green back stripe, and various side markings. Chrysalis brown with green abdomen.

Flight
Multiple broods; February–October, according to locale.

Habitat
Virtually any habitat in West except driest deserts, dense forests, and urban areas, sea level to 10,000′ (3050 m); rarer at higher elevations.

Range
Canada to Mexico; Pacific Coast east to Saskatchewan and Dakotas, western edge of Great Plains, and W. Texas. Isolated populations in Minnesota, Nebraska, and Kansas.

Comments

Nearly the most ubiquitous western blue, this species flies close to the ground between flower visits. Spring brood females may be quite blue. Almost any crowd of blues at a mountain mud puddle will include some Acmon Blues. As they drink they twitch their hind wings, and in so doing, flash their emerald scales in the sunshine. This immediately distinguishes them from the similar, smaller buckwheat blues in the genus *Euphilotes*.

Orange-bordered Blue
Lycaeides melissa
324

Wingspan: ⅞–1¼″ (22–32 mm). Above, male vivid silver-blue or dark blue with very narrow black margins. Female slate-colored gray-brown above, sometimes shot with blue; has orange margins. Below dusky, whitish to tan; solid, bold black line along extreme margins; black markings crisp, solid extensive orange flanks iridescent blue-green hind-wing spots.

Life Cycle

Egg pale green with frosty white ridges. Caterpillar green covered by delicate brown pile, darker green above, with faint oblique side stripes. Overwinters in East as egg and very young caterpillar. Chrysalis is green with many translucent yellowish spots.

Flight

2 broods; May to mid-June and July–August. Apparently 3 broods in lowland West, especially in alfalfa fields.

Habitat

Open sunny areas, such as lupine stands and dry mountain meadows in West, and sand barrens and dry woods in East.

Range

Mid-Canada south through the Sierra Nevada and Rockies to Mexico, east to western Great Plains States and Manitoba; Minnesota and Michigan east to New Hampshire in spotty colonies.

Comments

Along with sulphurs and whites, lowland western Orange-bordered Blues swarm over alfalfa fields, where their caterpillars eat flowers and young leaves. The northeastern subspecies, known as the Karner Blue, was named by novelist Vladimir Nabokov. It is a protected insect in New York State

---

Western Tailed Blue
Everes amyntula
325

Wingspan: ⅞–1⅛″ (22–28 mm). Above, bright lavender-blue with very narrow dark margin; female more brown and black than blue. Below, chalk-white, with grayish markings hazy and reduced, sometimes absent; orange spot above threadlike hind-wing tail inconspicuous, sometimes absent.

Life Cycle

Egg pale green. Caterpillar varies from straw-color to jade-green; has transverse mauve and maroon side slashes, and short fine white hair. Mature caterpillar overwinters.

Flight
2 staggered broods at lower elevations and latitudes; January–September, peaking in May and June in California. 1 brood at higher elevations and farther north; June–August.

Habitat
Moist meadows, canyons, and along roadsides, sandy clearings, and forest margins.

Range
Alaska south to Baja California and Mexico, east across Canada to north-central states, and south in Rockies to Arizona and New Mexico.

Comments
This butterfly largely replaces the Eastern Tailed Blue in the West and in mountains. Offshore, it often abounds on the California Islands in far greater numbers than are normally seen on the mainland.

Silvery Blue
Glaucopsyche lygdamus
26

Wingspan: 1–1¼″ (25–32 mm). Above, male silver-blue with narrow black margins; female dark with diffuse, wide dark margins, sometimes blue restricted to base, or wings totally brown. Both sexes pale gray to dark brownish gray below, usually with 1 bold, crooked row of black rounded dots, each ringed with white (missing in northern populations); sometimes a bluish cast to wing bases.

Life Cycle
Mature caterpillars variable: green to tan with darker (often reddish) back stripe and lighter, oblique dashes on sides. Pale brown chrysalis marked with small black dots; chrysalis overwinters.

Flight
1 brood; about 1 month, precise time varying with altitude and latitude; March–July, depending on location.

Habitat
Widespread from sea level to above timberline: mountain meadows, open woodlands, brush, disturbed or burned areas, canyons, seeps, and streamsides.

Range
E. Alaska and Nova Scotia south to Baja California, central Arizona, New Mexico, Oklahoma, Alabama, and Georgia.

Comments
The slow-flying Silvery Blue is among the first species to appear in spring. It is easily recognized by the small number of dots on the underside. Over 10 geographic races are identified; the shade of blue, depth of iridescence, and size of spots vary dramatically from area to area.

Greenish Blue
Plebejus saepiolus
327

Wingspan: 7/8–1¼" (22–32 mm). Above, male silver-blue (sometimes faintly greenish) with dark margins, sometimes with marginal dot row on hind wing. Female 2 forms: brown form with or without orange just inside margin of hind wing or hind wing and fore wing; also blue form (not as blue as male). Both sexes usually have dark spots at ends of cells on fore wing and hind wing above. Below, male silver-white to gray, often with blue tinge at base; female browner; both sexes have black dots on fore wing and hind wing of nearly equal size, those on hind-wing base have more black than surrounding white; any orange inconspicuous, limited to outer dot rows, usually only 1 faint rust-colored spot near outer angle of hind wing.

Life Cycle
Formally undescribed. Caterpillar greenish or reddish; overwinters half grown.

Flight
1 brood in some areas, 2 in others; late spring and early summer, mostly June and July.

Habitat
Sea level to high mountains and high latitudes in wet areas: bogs, meadows, grassy slopes, roadside ditches.

Range
Alaska south to mountains of S. California; east through southern Canada to Great Lakes, Gaspé, and Maine; also to W. South Dakota and Nebraska, Colorado west of plains, and N. New Mexico.

Comments
In almost any moist, clovery meadow within its range, the Greenish Blue abounds in summertime. Its taste for clovers no doubt has enabled it to extend its range, for the Greenish Blue may now be found along roadsides and in other disturbed sites, where European white clover has been used as a ground cover. Adults take nectar at bistort, asters, and other flowers.

Eastern Tailed Blue
Everes comyntas
328

Wingspan: ¾–1" (19–25 mm). Above, male bright silver-blue with thin dark margin and orange and black hind-wing spots near threadlike tail; female slate-gray and black shot with blue. Grayish white below with distinct curved rows of gray-black spots becoming hazier toward borders; conspicuous orange black-edged spots above hind-wing tail. Both sexes have white fringe.

Life Cycle
Eggs laid in flower buds and stems. Caterpillar variable, often dark green and downy with obscured brown and lighter side stripes. Caterpillar overwinters. Chrysalis buff-colored.

Flight
3 broods in North, probably more in South, often overlapping; first flight begins in early spring.

Habitat
Disturbed sites; fields, gardens, powerline cuts, railroad lines, and crop fields.

Range
Southern Canada to Central America, covering entire area east of Rockies; more spottily west to Pacific at low elevations.

Comments
One of the East's most abundant butterflies, the low-flying Eastern Tailed Blue readily adapts to human activities; roadsides and rights-of-way create new suitable habitats for its leguminous host plants. Color patterns vary seasonally, spring females bearing much more blue than those of later summer. Populations west of the Rockies may have been introduced after people altered the natural landscape.

Common Blue
Icaricia icarioides
329

Wingspan: 1–1⅜″ (25–35 mm). Above, male silver-blue to violet-blue, with dark margins, usually without fore-wing cell mark. Female completely brown or with blue restricted to wing bases, with or without fore-wing cell mark. Below, both sexes pale or silver-gray to cream-tan or brownish with black spots on fore wing, black or white spots on hind wing; sometimes marginal crescent row (often very faint) and orange absent or limited to a few rust-colored hind-wing spots usually smaller than fore-wing spots, prominently encircled with or replaced by white. Bar near hind-wing cell below more white than black.

Life Cycle
Egg delicate green. Caterpillar, to ⅜″ (10 mm), green and covered with short white hair, many diagonal marks along sides; overwinters half grown. Chrysalis, to ⁵⁄₁₆″ (8 mm), green with red-brown on abdomen; adult emerges in a few weeks.

Flight
1 brood; 1 month or more from April in S. California to August in mountains of California and in Rockies.

Habitat
Sea level to over 10,000′ (3050 m), including coastal sand dunes, mountains, valleys, meadows, streams, sagelands, and roadsides. Always close to lupines.

Range
British Columbia to S. California, and east to W. Saskatchewan, the Dakotas, Nebraska, western edge of Colorado plains, and south to E. New Mexico.

Comments
This highly variable species has over a dozen named subspecies, yet many populations have individuals resembling several varieties. One of these, the Mission Blue, is restricted to the San Bruno Mountains of San Francisco; it has been listed as an endangered species.

**Eastern Black
Swallowtail**
Papilio polyxenes
331

Wingspan: 2⅝–3½" (67–89 mm). Black to blue-black above
with blue cloud on outer hind wing (more blue on female).
Small cream-yellow spots and chevrons rim wings above and
below (larger on male). Bright orange eyespot with round,
black-centered pupil at corner of hind wing toward body.
Sometimes band of yellow spots across outer third of wings
inside row of blue patches, more commonly present or
enlarged on male.

Life Cycle
Egg yellow. Mature caterpillar, to 2" (51 mm), white to leaf-
green with black bands on each segment broken by yellow or
red-orange spots. Chrysalis brown or green; overwinters.

Flight
2 or 3 broods; February–November, depending on latitude.
Late spring, midsummer, and early autumn flights in midcontinent.

Habitat
Open spaces including gardens, farmland, meadows, and
banks of watercourses; seldom in woodlands.

Range
Southern Canada along eastern Rockies into Arizona and
Mexico, and east to Atlantic.

Comments
Eastern Black Swallowtails may be attracted to gardens by
parsley or carrot plants, and nectar sources such as phlox and
milkweed.

Tiger Swallowtail
Pterourus glaucus
332

Wingspan: 3⅛–5½" (79–140 mm). Males and some females
above and below are yellow with black tiger-stripes across
wings and black borders spotted with yellow. Long, black tail
on each hind wing. Hind wing above and below usually has
row of blue patches inside margin, with orange spot above and
sometimes much orange below, running through yellow.
Dark-form females are black above, with border-spotting of
yellow, blue, and orange (blue sometimes becomes cloud on
hind wing), below brown-black with shadowy "tiger" pattern.
Yellow spots along outer edge of fore wing below are separate
in all but northernmost populations. Most have orange
uppermost spot on outer margin of hind wing above and
below and orange spot on trailing edge.

Life Cycle
Very large yellow-green, globular egg. Young caterpillar
brown and white, resembling bird droppings; mature
caterpillar, to 2" (51 mm), is green, swollen in front, with big
orange and black eyespots and band between third and fourth
segments. Mottled green or brown sticklike chrysalis, to 1¼"
(32 mm), overwinters.

Flight
1–3 broods; spring–autumn, actual dates vary with latitude.

Habitat
Broadleaf woodland glades, gardens, parks, orchards, and along roads and rivers.

Range
Central Alaska and Canada to Atlantic; southeast of Rockies to Gulf. Rarer at northern and southern edges of range.

Comments
This species is the most widely distributed tiger swallowtail, and one of the most common and conspicuous butterflies of the East. Feeding in groups, adults take nectar from a wide range of flowers. The black female form has evolved to mimic the distasteful Pipevine Swallowtail; its presence in the population reflects the abundance of the species it mimics.

ark Zebra Swallowtail
urytides philolaus
33

Wingspan: 2½–3½" (64–89 mm). Long triangular wings with long tails. Milk-white with submarginal, parallel, broad black bands; crimson spots at hind-wing inner angle. Alternate female form all black with small white crescents around hind-wing margin ending with crimson spots. Similar below, with long scarlet streak. Antennae black.

Life Cycle
Unreported.

Flight
Early spring and midsummer broods in Mexico; more common at beginning of rainy season.

Habitat
Lowland dry forests, roads, clearings, pastures, and forest openings.

Range
Reported once from Texas (Padre Island, Cameron County); Mexico south through Central America.

Comments
The Dark Zebra should be watched for in Texas. In Yucatan, it gathers by the hundreds around damp spots. The Maya knew this butterfly and named it "X-Chail."

iceroy
asilarchia archippus
34

Wingspan: 2⅝–3" (67–76 mm). Above and below, rich, russet-orange with black veins, a black line usually curving across hind wing, white-spotted black borders, and white spots surrounded by black in diagonal band across fore-wing tip. Color ranges from pale tawny in Great Basin to deep, mahogany-brown in Florida.

Life Cycle
Egg compressed oval. Caterpillar, 1–1¼" (25–32 mm), mottled brown or olive with saddle-shaped patch on back; fore parts humped; 2 bristles behind head. Chrysalis, to ⅞" (22 mm), also brown and cream-colored with brown, rounded disk projecting from back.

Flight
2, 3, or more broods depending upon latitude; April–September in middle latitudes, later in South. Sometimes a distinct gap between broods, with no adults for some weeks i mid- to late summer.

Habitat
Canals, riversides, marshes, meadows, wood edges, roadsides, lakeshores, and deltas.

Range
North America south of Hudson Bay, from Great Basin eastward, and west to eastern parts of Pacific States.

Comments
In each life stage, the Viceroy seeks protection through a different ruse. The egg blends with the numerous galls that afflict the willow leaves upon which it is laid. Hibernating caterpillars hide themselves in bits of leaves they have attache to a twig. The mature caterpillar looks mildly fearsome with its hunched and horned foreparts. Even most birds pass over the chrysalis, thinking it is a bird dropping. The adult, famed as a paramount mimic, resembles the distasteful Monarch. Since birds learn to eschew Monarchs, they also avoid the look-alike Viceroy. Southern populations of Viceroys mimic the much deeper chestnut-colored Queen instead. In flight, the Viceroy flaps frenetically in between brief glides.

Monarch
Danaus plexippus
335

Wingspan: 3½–4″ (89–102 mm). Very large, with fore wing long and drawn out. Above, bright, burnt-orange with black veins and black margins sprinkled with white dots; fore-wing tip broadly black interrupted by larger white and orange spots. Below, paler, duskier orange. 1 black spot appears between hind-wing cell and margin on male above and below. Female darker with black veins smudged.

Life Cycle
Egg pale green, ribbed, and pitted, is shaped like lemon with flat base. Caterpillar, to 2″ (51 mm), is off-white with black and yellow stripes; 1 pair of fine black filaments extends from front and rear. Chrysalis, to ⅞″ (28 mm), pale jade-green, studded with glistening gold; plump, rounded, appears lidded, with lid opening along abdominal suture.

Flight
Successive broods; April–June migrating northward, July–August resident in North, September–October migrating southward, rest of year in overwintering locales. Year-round resident in S. California and Hawaii.

Habitat
On migration, anywhere from alpine summits to cities; when breeding, habitats with milkweeds, especially meadows, weedy fields and watercourses. Overwinters in coastal Monterey pine, Monterey cypress, eucalyptus groves in California, and fir forests in Mexican mountains.

Range
Nearly all of North America from south of Hudson Bay through South America; absent from Alaska and Pacific Northwest Coast. Established in the Hawaiian Islands.

Comments
One of the best known butterflies, the Monarch is the only butterfly that annually migrates both north and south as birds do, on a regular basis. But no single individual makes the entire round-trip journey. In the fall, Monarchs in the North begin to congregate and to move southward. Midwestern and eastern Monarchs continue south all the way to the Sierra Madre of middle Mexico, where they spend the winter among fir forests at high altitudes. Far western and Sierra Nevada Monarchs fly to the central and southern coast of California, where they cluster in groves of pine, cypress, and eucalyptus in Pacific Grove and elsewhere. Winter butterflies are sluggish and do not reproduce; they venture out to take nectar on warm days. In spring they head north, breed along the way, and their offspring return to the starting point.

Regal Fritillary
Speyeria idalia
436

Wingspan: 2⅝–3⅝" (66–92 mm). Very large. Above, both sexes have red-orange fore wing with blue-black spots and white-dotted black margin; hind wing black with 2 rows of light spots (cream-white on female, outer row rust-orange on male) and orange at base. Below, fore wing similar to upper side; hind wing deep olive-brown with many silver spots. Female larger, darker than male.

Life Cycle
Eggs tan; laid in late summer. Caterpillar yellowish brown with black blotches and lines, yellowish bands, and many spines (some silver on back and orange on side); overwinters. Chrysalis light brown with black spots.

Flight
1 brood; June–early September.

Habitat
Moist tallgrass prairies, especially virgin grasslands and wet meadows in woodland areas.

Range
Manitoba and E. Montana east to S. Ontario and Maine, south to E. Colorado, N. Arkansas, and W. North Carolina.

Comments
The Regal Fritillary may one day be very rare and restricted because its natural grassland habitat is rapidly disappearing as land is plowed or developed.

American Painted Lady
Vanessa virginiensis
337

Wingspan: 1¾–2⅛" (44–54 mm). Fore-wing tip extended, rounded. Above, pinkish orange with black marks across fore wing; margins black-spotted and fore-wing tip has white spots; row of black-rimmed blue spots crosses outer hind wing.

Underside has complex pattern of olive, black, and white, dominated by large bright pink area on fore wing and 2 large blue eyespots in olive field on hind wing.

Life Cycle
Egg yellowish green, barrel-shaped; laid singly. Caterpillar, to 1⅜" (35 mm), black with yellow crossbands and white to rust-colored spots; makes solitary nest of silk and leaves. Gold spotted brown chrysalis, to ⅞" (22 mm), is often formed in nest. Reported to overwinter as adult or chrysalis.

Flight
2 or 3 broods; summer–fall.

Habitat
Sunny, flowery open spots, sandy wastes, gardens, streambeds riversides, and canyons.

Range
Subarctic North America south to Mexico; quite common in East, rarer in West; naturalized in Hawaii.

Comments
Of the painted ladies and their close relative the Red Admiral, this species seems to be the most tolerant of cold, and is quite likely the only one able to overwinter in the North.

Painted Lady
Vanessa cardui
338

Wingspan: 2–2¼" (51–57 mm). Fore-wing tip extended slightly, rounded. Above, salmon-orange with black blotches, black-patterned margins, and broadly black fore-wing tips with clear white spots; outer hind wing crossed by small black-rimmed blue spots. Below, fore wing dominantly rose-pink with olive, black, and white pattern; hind wing has small blue spots on olive background with white webwork. Fore wing above and below has white bar running from leading edge across black patch near tip.

Life Cycle
Egg pale green, barrel-shaped; laid singly. Caterpillar, to 1¼" (32 mm), varies from chartreuse with black marbling to purplish with yellow back stripe; has short spines. Chrysalis, to ⅞" (22 mm), lavender-brown, bumpy, bluntly beaked; hangs upside down.

Flight
2 or more broods; all year in southern deserts, April–June until hard frosts in North.

Habitat
Anywhere, especially flowery meadows, parks, and mountaintops.

Range
All of North America well into sub-Arctic, and south to Panama; naturalized in Hawaii.

Comments
This species deserves its alternate name, Cosmopolite.

Despite its inability to overwinter in any stage above a certain undetermined latitude, the Painted Lady is perhaps the most widespread butterfly in the world, found throughout Africa, Europe, Asia and many islands, as well as in North America.

West Coast Lady
Vanessa annabella
339

Wingspan: 1¾–2″ (44–51 mm). Fore-wing tip extended, clipped. Orange to salmon-orange above with black patterning; small white spots near fore-wing tip and blue to purplish spots along outer hind wing. Beneath, complex blurred marbling of olive, tan, and white webbing on hind wing, with small, indistinct, unrimmed blue spots outwardly; fore wing pink with blue, black, and buff spotting below. Orange to pale yellow bar outside fore-wing cell both above and below, runs from leading edge across black area near tip.

Life Cycle
Egg greenish, barrel-shaped; laid singly. Caterpillar, 1–1¼″ (25–32 mm), variable, from light brown to black, with yellow or orange blotches, lines, and spines, Chrysalis olive-straw, rounded, bluntly beaked, with whitish tubercles.

Flight
Year-round in warmer parts of California; elsewhere spottily from early spring–late fall; autumn in eastern part of range.

Habitat
Vacant lots, flowerbeds, canals, fields, mountain canyons, and slopes.

Range
Pacific Slope from British Columbia to Baja California, east as a transient to western edge of Great Plains.

Comments
The West Coast Lady's numbers vary dramatically from year to year, but it does not undergo the massive emigrations of the Painted Lady. Its cold tolerance may be in between that of the other ladies; it can withstand moderate but not frigid winters.

Pearly Crescentspot
Phyciodes tharos
340

Wingspan: 1–1½″ (25–38 mm). Male has broad, open orange areas above with wide black margin; female has heavier black markings. Below, orange fore wing has black patches, especially along margin, and several cream-colored spots; hind wing yellowish to cream-colored with fine brown lines and purplish-brown patch containing light crescent on margin. Spring broods have hind wing mottled with brown below.

Life Cycle
Eggs laid in clusters. Caterpillar brown with yellow bands and many branching spines; last brood overwinters when half grown. Chrysalis mottled gray, yellowish, or brown.

Flight
Usually several broods; April–November. 1 brood in Rockies and northern Canada; June–August.

Habitat
Open spaces, moist meadows, fields, roadsides, and streamsides.

Range
Yukon and Newfoundland to southern Mexico, and from E. Washington and SE. California to Atlantic.

Comments
One of our most common meadow butterflies, the Pearly Crescentspot flies low over the grasses with alternating flaps and glides. Often described as highly pugnacious, the males dart out from perches, or break their flight pattern to investigate any passing form—butterfly, bird, or human.

Mylitta Crescentspot
Phyciodes mylitta
341

Wingspan: 1⅛–1⅜" (28–35 mm). Fore wing slightly indented along outer margin. Above, orange with open pattern of fine black lines. Beneath, fore wing orange with dark lines and spots and small black spot on trailing margin; hind wing has yellowish-brown areas, white bands, and white marginal crescent in brown patch.

Life Cycle
Egg cream-colored; laid in clusters. Caterpillar overwinters half grown; mature caterpillar, to ⅞" (22 mm), black with yellowish stripes and spots; many branching spines. Chrysalis, to ⅜" (10 mm), mottled brown to gray with golden sheen and tubercles.

Flight
Several overlapping broods; March–October.

Habitat
Agricultural fields, dry canyons, mountains, open woods, shorelines, marshes, vacant lots, meadows, and roadsides.

Range
British Columbia and Montana south to Baja California, New Mexico, and southern Mexico.

Comments
In the 1800's weedy thistles spread all over the West and were followed by the Mylitta Crescentspot. Now this species seems ubiquitous and is found in many disturbed as well as natural habitats. Flying from early spring to autumn, it is most abundant in August.

Variegated Fritillary
Euptoieta claudia
342

Wingspan: 1¾–2¼" (44–57 mm). Fore wing somewhat elongated. Tawny-brown above with zigzag black band in middle of both wings, followed by blackish shadowy line, black dots, and finally 2 bands of black along margin; fore wing has several black circles and crescents. Below, whitish brown with fore wing orange on basal half and pattern of upper side faintly repeated; hind wing somewhat mottled or variegated, with whitish veins.

Life Cycle
Egg cream-colored, ribbed. Caterpillar, to 1¼" (32 mm), white with red bands, black spines; red head has 2 very long black spines. Chrysalis, to ¾" (19 mm), pale shiny blue-green with black, yellow, and orange marks and gold bumps. Adult overwinters in extreme South, but not in North.

Flight
Continuous broods; spring–fall.

Habitat
Open areas such as grasslands, subtropical fields, and mountain summits and meadows; everywhere but deep forests.

Range
Resident from Arizona to Florida and southern plains, emigrating periodically to S. California and northward to SE. British Columbia, Northwest Territories, and Quebec.

Comments
The caterpillars of this species eat more different types of plants than those of almost any other butterfly.

Little Metalmark
Calephelis virginiensis
43

Wingspan: ⅝–¾" (16–19 mm). Small. Above, uniform bright rust to orange, with marginal and inner bands of conspicuous, glistening silver-green spots. Below, dull orange, flecked with black or lead-gray, not much paler than above.

Flight
3 broods in mid-Atlantic states; May, July, September. Broods less defined farther south; every month in Florida.

Habitat
Open grassy fields, pine savannah, salt marsh meadows, and wood margins.

Range
Virginia to Florida, west to Texas and Arkansas.

Comments
Distributed sporadically in all of the Gulf States, the Little Metalmark becomes progressively more local to the north. It is fond of pine flats, woodland edges, and damp habitats.

Meadow Fritillary
Clossiana bellona
44

Wingspan: 1¼–1⅞" (32–48 mm). Tan to brownish orange above with black dashes and dots; fore-wing tip angled outward as if clipped; no heavy black margin. Beneath, orange fore wing has black spots and purplish tip; brownish hind wing has orange-brown patch band and whitish, keel-shaped patch near base along leading edge; outer half of wing soft grayish to violet with row of bluish spots.

Life Cycle
Egg greenish yellow. Purplish-black caterpillar has yellow and black mottling and brown branching spines; overwinters half grown. Chrysalis yellowish brown.

Flight
Up to 3 broods; May–September. 1 brood in Rockies and colder parts of Canada; June–July.

Habitat
Moist meadows in wooded areas, hayfields, pastures, and streamsides.

Range
British Columbia and Quebec, south to Washington, Colorado, Missouri, and North Carolina.

Comments
Along with the Silver-bordered Fritillary, the Meadow Fritillary is one of the most abundant bog fritillaries, particularly in the East. Rocky Mountain and northwestern populations are fewer and sparser.

Buckeye
Junonia coenia
345

Wingspan: 2–2½" (51–63 mm). Wings scalloped and rounded except at drawn-out fore-wing tip. Highly variable. Above, tawny-brown to dark brown; 2 orange bars in fore-wing cell, orange band just inside margin of hind wing, white band diagonally crossing fore wing. 2 bright eyespots on each wing above: on fore wing, 1 very small eyespot near tip and 1 large eyespot in white fore wing bar; on hind wing, 1 large eyespot near upper margin and 1 small eyespot below it. Eyespots black, yellow-rimmed, with iridescent blue and lilac irises. Beneath, fore wing resembles above in lighter shades; hind-wing eyespots tiny or absent, rose-brown to tan, with vague crescent-shaped markings.

Life Cycle
Egg dark green, stubby, ribbed, flat-topped. Caterpillar, to 1¼" (32 mm), dark or greenish to blackish gray with orange and yellowish markings. Chrysalis, to 1" (25 mm), mottled pale brown.

Flight
2–4 broods; year-round in Deep South, elsewhere March–October.

Habitat
Shorelines, roadsides, railroad embankments, fields and meadows, swamp edges, and other open places.

Range
Resident throughout South, in North to east and west of Rockies to Oregon, Ontario, and New England.

Comments
Although the Buckeye flies in summer throughout much of North America south of the Canadian taiga, it is not able to overwinter very far north. In the autumn along the East Coast, there are impressive southward emigrations. In places such as Cape May, New Jersey, the October hordes of Buckeyes drifting southward rival those of Monarchs in number and spectacle.

Eyed Brown
Satyrodes eurydice
346

Wingspan: 1⅝–2″ (41–51 mm). Wings rounded. Above, warm tan to olive-brown, often but not always with light patch on outer third of fore wing. Variable dark eyespots near margins of both wings above and below; eyespots have small white pupils below. Below, light brown crossed by darker, deeply zigzagged lines near yellow-rimmed eyespots.

Life Cycle
Caterpillar slender, light green, with lengthwise yellow and dark green stripes and red-tipped horns extending from head and tail. Chrysalis green, with small, blunt hook on head.

Flight
1 staggered brood; June–September.

Habitat
Open, damp meadows, sedge marshes, and wetter parts of prairies.

Range
South-central Northwest Territories, south through Dakotas to NE. Colorado, east across Canada and northeastern United States south to N. Illinois and Delaware.

Comments
This locally abundant species occupies a very broad range and is familiar throughout much of the Northeast; its colonies are small, separate, and local.

Riding's Satyr
Neominois ridingsii
347

Wingspan: 1½–1⅞″ (38–48 mm). Above, graduated shades of gray (lead, putty, or sandy brown-gray dominate in different populations); bands of oblong orbs of cream-white or milk-white cross all wings. 1, 2, or 3 black eyespots with white pupils lie in fore-wing bands, more rarely 1 small eyespot appears on hind wing. Below, grayish tan, heavily speckled and striated, with upper-side pattern repeated less distinctly.

Life Cycle
Egg chalk-white, keg-shaped. Caterpillar light reddish, banded with green on sides and back, covered with minute bumps and hair. After feeding in clumps of grass, caterpillar pupates in soil. Chrysalis color similar to that of caterpillar.

Flight
1 brood; June–August, emerging and remaining later at higher altitudes. Occasionally second brood.

Habitat
Dry, sunny prairies and other grasslands; sage flats and subalpine sagebrush summits.

Range
S. Alberta and Saskatchewan south through Rockies, along western edge of Great Plains to Nebraska, Great Basin, central Arizona, and New Mexico, and E. California and south-central Oregon.

Comments
No other American butterfly looks at all like the Riding's Satyr, with its pattern of spotted gray. This species is the only New World representative of a Eurasian group of satyrs that includes many Himalayan butterflies. North American populations vary in appearance from dark gray with clean white spots in Colorado and California, to pale and sandy-colored with cream-colored spots in the Great Basin, to very pale in Arizona. Wherever it lives, this satyr's colors and patterns elegantly blend with sandy, stony backgrounds. When disturbed, it flies short distances close to the ground.

Large Wood Nymph
Cercyonis pegala
348

Wingspan: 2–2⅞" (52–73 mm). Large. Highly variable. Above, light cocoa-brown to deep chocolate-brown (very pale in N. Great Basin). Below, paler and heavily striated with darker scales. Normally fore wing above and below has 1 or 2 small to very large black eyespots, often yellow-rimmed, with small white or large blue pupil; eyespots may lie in a vague or discrete broad band of bright or dark yellow. Hind wing above may have small eyespots; hind wing below may have 1 or 2 small eyespots or a full row of 6 eyespots. Hind wing below usually divided into darker inner and lighter outer portion by single zigzagged, dark line. Female normally larger, paler, with bigger eyespots.

Life Cycle
Egg lemon-yellow, keg-shaped, and ribbed. Caterpillar grass-green, with 4 lengthwise yellow lines, fine, fuzzy pile, and 2 reddish tails; overwinters shortly after hatching. Chrysalis green, rather plump.

Flight
1 brood; generally June–August or September, varying with locality.

Habitat
Open oak, pine, and other woodlands; meadows, fields, and along slow watercourses with long, overhanging grasses; marshes, prairie groves, thickets, and roadsides.

Range
Central Canada to central California, Texas, and central Florida. Absent from Pacific Northwest Coast and much of Gulf region.

Comments
The Large Wood Nymph occupies much of North America; it is the largest wood nymph and the only one east of the Mississippi. Extremely variable, this butterfly has been given dozens of names. Today, all are considered a single species. As they perch on tree trunks or boughs to bask or drink sap, Large Wood Nymphs blend beautifully with the bark. When disturbed or seeking mates, they fly erratically through tall grasses, with little speed but great skill and endurance.

INSECTS AND SPIDERS

Among the most numerous animals on earth, insects and spiders are also fascinating. Some have carved out a niche for themselves as tiny predators in an immense landscape; others have developed complex social systems of communal life. A few—the grasshoppers and crickets—sometimes swarm by the thousands. Included in this section are descriptions of some of the most common and typical insects, spiders, and related creatures of the grasslands.

Locust Treehopper
Thelia bimaculata
349

⅜–½" (9–13 mm). Male gray mottled with yellow, lemon-yellow stripe along each side of front portion of thorax; female larger, mottled gray-black and brownish. Upper part of thorax projects in large thornlike crest.

Habitat
Woods, meadows, and gardens.

Range
New Hampshire to Florida, northwest to Ohio.

Life Cycle
Eggs are laid at roots of host tree, just below leaf litter. Nymphs remain close to adults. 1 or 2 generations a year.

Comments
Nymphs produce a sweet secretion that attracts ants; this probably protects them from predators.

Field Cricket
Gryllus pennsylvanicus
350

⅝–1" (15–25 mm). Black to dark reddish brown. Black antennae longer than body; projections from tail hairy, longer than head and front portion of thorax combined. Wings do not extend beyond tail projections.

Habitat
Undergrowth where there is moderate humidity and protection from night winds and cold.

Range
Throughout North America to Alaska.

Sound
Common song is a series of triple chirps. Courtship song is a continuous trill at a pitch near the upper limits of audibility.

Life Cycle
Female inserts eggs singly deep into the soil. Eggs overwinter in the North, where all unmatured nymphs and adults die of the frost. In the South nymphs and adults may overwinter.

Comments
This cricket enters houses in autumn, attracted by the warmth. In courtship the male dances about and "sings" to excite the female.

Mormon Cricket
Anabrus simplex
351

1–2⅜" (25–60 mm). Dark brown to bluish black, sometimes with pale markings. Large upper part of thorax extends backward, concealing female's vestigial wings and almost covering male's reduced wings. Female's egg-laying organ upcurved, as long as body. Antennae as long as body.

Habitat
Open fields.

Range
Missouri River to N. Arizona, west to SE. California, north to Alberta.

Sound
A hoarse chirp, repeated at intervals.

Life Cycle
Dark brown eggs are deposited below soil surface in midsummer. They turn gray, overwinter, and hatch in spring. Up to 100 nymphs emerge, maturing in about 60 days.

Comments
This common cricket got its common name after thousands suddenly attacked the Mormon pioneers' first crops in Utah in 1848. Fortunately, many California gulls arrived in time to devour the crickets and save the crops.

Spur-throated Grasshopper
Melanoplus ponderosus
352

1–1⅜″ (25–34 mm). Mostly yellowish to pale brown. Hind tibiae often orange or reddish with yellowish and brown rings near base. Blunt projection below front portion of thorax.

Habitat
Open fields and grasslands.

Range
Tennessee and Mississippi to New Mexico, north to Iowa.

Life Cycle
Egg masses, each containing about 20 eggs, overwinter in soft soil. Nymphs appear in spring and become adults by June in the South, where they feed until December.

Comments
The Migratory Grasshopper (*M. sanguinipes,* formerly *M. bilituratus*), 1–1⅜″ (25–34 mm), also has a spur-throat. It is pale brown and yellow with red hind tibiae. This species ranges from the Atlantic Coast to Georgia, southwest to Mexico, north to Alaska.

Green Valley Grasshopper
Schistocerca shoshone
353

1½–2¾″ (38–70 mm). Green with yellow midline stripe on head and upper part of thorax. Hind tibiae red-pink.

Habitat
Tall grasses and open, sandy woods.

Range
Colorado to Texas and Mexico, northwest to California.

Life Cycle
Egg masses are thrust into soft soil, hatching in a week or less except when soil is very dry. Often nymphs do not hatch until rains soften soil.

Comments
One of the largest grasshoppers, the Green Valley Grasshopper sometimes appears in devastating hordes and severely damages range grasses.

**Two-striped
Grasshopper**
Mermiria bivittata
354

1⅛–2⅛″ (29–55 mm). Pale green to brown with 2 dark
brown stripes extending backward from compound eyes over
head and thorax, becoming vague on fore wings. Hind tibiae
have 15 or more spines in outer row; tibiae reddish.

Habitat
Grasslands.

Range
South Carolina to Florida, west to Texas, north to Nebraska.

Life Cycle
Female works abdominal tip into soft moist soil, deposits eggs
in compact mass as deep as possible. Nymphs work way to
surface, where they begin feeding. Adults active in summer.

Comments
This grasshopper flies as well as leaps to avoid disturbance.
The Three-striped Grasshopper (*M. maculipennis*) has an
additional dark stripe along its midline and ranges from
Mexico to Alberta and Saskatchewan.

Nebraska Cone-head
Neoconocephalus nebrascensis
355

Male 1⅛–1¼″ (28–31 mm); female 1⅛–1⅜″ (28–36 mm),
egg-laying organ 1⅛–1½″ (29–39 mm). Body and wings
leaf-green or tan, with narrow yellowish edging. Black
beneath conical projection of head. Hind edge of upper part of
thorax rounded. Egg-laying organ curved, swordlike.

Habitat
Marshes, thickets, and cornfields.

Range
Maine to Tennessee, west to Nebraska, north to Minnesota.

Sound
Tsip-tsip, almost continuous by day, sometimes at night. At
close range a loud monotonous buzz.

Life Cycle
Eggs are thrust into soft plant tissues, where they overwinter.
1 generation a year in the North, 2 in the South.

Comments
The Robust Cone-head (*N. robustus*), to 2⅜″ (60 mm), has a
narrow yellow line on each side of the flat-topped prothorax. It
ranges from the Appalachians to the Great Lakes and Atlantic
Coast, and is also in California.

Praying Mantis
Mantis religiosa
356

2–2½″ (50–65 mm), including wings, which extend beyond
abdominal tip. Green to tan. Compound eyes tan to chocolate-
brown. Bases of forelegs bear black-ringed spot beneath.

Habitat
Meadows, on foliage and flowers.

Range
Eastern United States into Ontario.

Life Cycle

Eggs overwinter in flat mass attached to exposed twigs above snow. They hatch almost simultaneously in late spring. Nymphs are dispersed by wind or eat one another. Survivors are solitary. 1 generation matures in late summer or in fall.

Comments

This mantid was accidentally introduced in 1899 on nursery stock from southern Europe. At a time when Gypsy Moth caterpillars were burgeoning in the eastern states, it was recognized almost immediately as a beneficial predator. However, mantids are so cannibalistic that they rarely have much effect in depleting caterpillar populations.

Chinese Mantid
Tenodera aridifolia
357

2½–3⅜″ (65–85 mm), including wings. Tan to pale green. Fore wings tan with green along front margin. Compound eyes chocolate-brown at sunset, pale tan soon after sunrise and during the day.

Habitat

Meadows and gardens, on herbs, flower clusters, and shrubs.

Range

Massachusetts to New Jersey, west to Ohio.

Life Cycle

Overwinters in egg masses along tree stem exposed above snow. Nymphs hatch in late spring, disperse in wind, and thereafter are solitary. Mating pairs are seen mostly in September.

Comments

The largest mantid, this insect was introduced from China around 1896 as a beneficial insect.

Green Lacewings
Chrysopa spp.
358

⅜–⅝″ (10–15 mm). Body pale yellow to pale green. Compound eyes brilliant golden or coppery, hemispherical. Threadlike antennae two-thirds body length. Wings are clear with green veins and are at least one-fourth longer than body.

Habitat

Meadows, gardens, and forest edges.

Range

Throughout North America.

Life Cycle

Eggs on slender white silk stalks hang from the underside of leaves. All species pupate in silken cocoons. Some fly in May and June, others in late summer.

Comments

California Green Lacewings (*C. californica*), found west of the Rocky Mountains, are raised indoors by the thousands for release in greenhouses and vineyards, where they prey on destructive mealy bugs.

Green Midges
Tanytarsus spp.
359

¼–⅜″ (5–10 mm). Cylindrical; abdomen tapering to a point. Head small, projecting beyond cylindrical front portion of thorax. Pale green; front portion of thorax faintly marked with brown above. Antennae feathery with long hair on segments. Legs long, pale brown; front outermost leg segments long. Wings milky, transparent.

Habitat
Meadows and woods, near wetlands.

Range
Most of North America.

Life Cycle
Males perform aerial dances in large swarms, often above a shrub or treetop, usually in the evening. Females enter swarm and are seized by males. Pairs drop below swarm to mate. Mated females thrust eggs through water surface film. Larvae wriggle through bottom silt to reach decomposing plant matter. At end of pupal stage, pupae float to surface and explode suddenly to release adults.

Comments
Midges do not bite but are often mistaken for mosquitoes, particularly when swarming. On cooler days they usually swarm in the late afternoon when they are warmed by the sun.

Malaria-carrying Mosquitoes
Anopheles spp.
360

⅛″ (4 mm). Dark brown. Head bears patch of pale hair. Antennae narrowly feathery. Proboscis, palps, and thorax have dark scales. Abdomen may be hairy. Legs slender. Each wing has several dark patches of scales. Upon landing, it does headstand with hind legs up in the air and head pointing downward.

Habitat
Deciduous and mixed forests, and around human habitations.

Range
Throughout North America; individual species more local.

Life Cycle
Eggs are laid singly on water surface film, hatching in 2–3 days. Larvae float parallel to surface, swimming to greater depths if disturbed. They pupate in about 2 weeks. Adults emerge after 2–3 days. Many survive winter weather.

Comments
These mosquitoes transmit infectious malaria, obtained from taking blood of infected people. The disease afflicted many in the early days of prairie settlement. The Eastern Malaria Mosquito (*A. quadrimaculatus*), same size, has 4 dark patches of scales on each fore wing and ranges east of the Rocky Mountains from Quebec and Nova Scotia to Florida, west to Mexico, and north to North Dakota. The Western Malaria Mosquito (*A. freeborni*), same size, has a bronze patch at the tip of each black-spotted wing. It is common from Montana to Texas, south to northern Mexico, north to British Columbia.

obber Flies
olmerus spp.
51

⅝–¾″ (15–20 mm). Abdomen slender, tapering to tip. Gray with black markings on thorax and abdomen. Legs mostly black, with black bristles. Wings clear.

Habitat
Pastures, open fields, and gardens.

Range
East of the Rocky Mountains in the United States and Canada.

Life Cycle
Female presses abdomen into holes in the soil and deposits eggs. Larvae tunnel downward in search of prey and pupate in the soil close to surface. Adults fly July–September.

Comments
Adults in mated pairs often rest on leaves or flowers, flying off quickly if disturbed. The more vigorous takes the other by the tail and tows the mate, which makes no attempt to fly away.

ouse Mosquito
ulex pipiens
62

⅛–¼″ (4–5 mm). Thorax light brown to brownish gray. Abdomen banded white and brown above. Proboscis brown. Wings brown. Male's antennae more feathery than female's. Abdomen kept parallel to support.

Habitat
Near swamps, ponds, and other bodies of stagnant water.

Range
Throughout North America.

Life Cycle
Eggs are deposited in raftlike masses of 100–300 on water surface film. They hatch in 1–5 days. Larvae feed head down in water. They pupate after 1–2 weeks. Adults emerge after a few days. Many generations possible; the last overwinter.

Comments
The Northern House Mosquito (*C. p. pipiens*), found in the northern United States and Canada, is the most common night-flying mosquito. The Southern House Mosquito (*C. p. quinquefasciatus*) is common in the Southeast, ranging west to California.

ellow-faced Bees
ylaeus spp.
63

¼″ (5–6 mm). Slender; abdomen wasplike with almost no hair. Black with yellow markings on face, upper part of thorax, and tibiae. Wings clear to smoky, veins often reddish.

Habitat
Meadows and abandoned crop fields.

Range
Throughout North America.

Life Cycle
Most species prepare brood cells in pith of stems, such as sumac. Some construct cells in soil using old tunnels or

burrows. Cells are lined with silky secretions and provisioned with nectar and small amounts of pollen.

Comments
These bees do not have external pollen-collecting apparatuses but carry pollen and nectar in the stomach. The different species in this genus can be identified only by an expert.

Yellow Jackets
Vespula spp.
364

½–⅝" (12–16 mm). Body stout, slightly wider than head. Abdomen narrow where attached to thorax with short "waist." First antennal segment yellow, others black. Head, thorax, and abdomen black and yellow or white. Wings smoky.

Habitat
Meadows and edges of forested land, usually nesting in ground or at ground level in stumps and fallen logs.

Range
Throughout North America; various species more localized.

Life Cycle
In spring mated female constructs small nest and daily brings food to larvae until first brood matures and females serve as workers, extending nest and tending young. In late summer males develop from unfertilized eggs and mate. When cold weather begins, all die except mated females, which overwinter among litter and in soil.

Comments
Yellow jackets can be pests at picnics, and they will carry off bits of food. Females sting repeatedly at the least provocation. If the nest can be found and its opening covered at night with a transparent bowl set firmly into the ground, adults will be confused by their inability to escape and seek food in daylight; they will not dig a new escape hole and will soon starve.

American Hover Fly
Metasyrphus americanus
365

⅜" (9–10 mm). Stout. Black to metallic green. Abdomen has 3 broad yellow crossbands not reaching margins of abdomen. Face yellow with black stripe and black cheeks. Wings clear.

Habitat
Meadows and fields on flowers and foliage.

Range
Throughout North America.

Life Cycle
Elongated white eggs are laid singly on plants infested by aphids. Pale grayish, sluglike larvae feed, then drop to soil to pupate under debris. Adults are active June–August.

Comments
This fly gets its name from the way it hovers in the air above flowers. It is considered to be highly beneficial because its larvae help eliminate insects that attack plants and crops.

xomerus Hover Flies
xomerus spp.
6

¼–½" (7–13 mm). Mostly black. Face yellow. Thorax has yellow stripe on sides. Abdomen has 3–4 sets of broken yellow bands. Legs brownish yellow. Wings clear.

Habitat
Meadows on foliage and flowers.

Range
Throughout North America.

Life Cycle
Chalky white eggs are laid singly on plants, usually near aphids. Larvae feed and, when fully grown, pupate in soil cavities. Adults emerge in summer.

Comments
This fly cannot bite or sting. Its larvae are probably as important as ladybug beetles in controlling aphid populations.

ant Hornet
spa crabro germana
7

¾–1⅛" (18–30 mm). Short "waist" between thorax and abdomen. Head, antennae, thorax, legs, and first abdominal segment reddish brown. Back of head and sides of thorax sometimes have yellow stripe. Rest of abdomen bright yellow with dark crossbands and small spots. Wings amber.

Habitat
Forests and towns.

Range
S. Massachusetts to Georgia, west to Indiana.

Life Cycle
A covered, tan-colored paper nest is built in a hollow tree, under porch floor, or in an outbuilding. First generation is all female workers, which feed later generations. In late summer unfertilized eggs produce males that mate and then die.

Comments
This hornet is common locally around the western limits of its range. It defends its nest from intruders but otherwise avoids confrontations when possible.

per Wasps
listes spp.
8

½–1" (13–25 mm). Slender, hornetlike. Short 1-segmented "waist" between thorax and abdomen. Upper portion of head pointed. Head and body mostly reddish brown to black with yellow rings and reddish areas on abdomen. Male's face pale, with antennal tips hooked; female has brown face. Wings amber to reddish brown.

Habitat
Meadows, fields, and gardens on flowers, and near buildings.

Range
Throughout North America.

Life Cycle
In spring several females work together to construct

uncovered, paperlike hanging nest of wood pulp and saliva. One female becomes dominant queen. First few generations in summer are all females, cared for as larvae by unmated female workers. Unfertilized eggs produce fertile males. Only mated young queens overwinter under leaf litter and in stone walls.

Comments
Paper wasps are much more tolerant of people and minor disturbances than are hornets and yellow jackets.

Digger Wasp
Scolia dubia
369

½–¾" (13–18 mm). Wingspan: 1" (26 mm). Hairy. Black with yellow or reddish-orange markings on abdomen. Wings blackish with many longitudinal wrinkles near outer margin.

Habitat
Gardens and meadows with flowers.

Range
Massachusetts to Florida, west to Arizona and California.

Life Cycle
Female digs into ground in search of beetle larvae, sometimes tunneling a few feet deep. Female stings beetle larva, subduing it, then digs cell around body and lays 1 egg on its back. Larva feeds on host. Wasp larva spins cocoon and overwinters as pupa.

Comments
Adults are usually found on flower clusters or scampering over the ground in early morning searching for beetle larvae. Mating males and females perform a mating dance, flying low in an "S" or figure-8.

Large Bee Flies
Bombylius spp.
370, 371

¼–½" (7–12 mm). Mostly black. Mouthparts slender, beaklike, almost as long as body. Thorax and abdomen densely covered with pile of long yellow, brown, gray, and black hairs, making fly appear fuzzy like a bee. Wings clear with black patterns from base along front margin.

Habitat
Meadows, open fields, and gardens on flowers frequented by solitary bees.

Range
Most of North America.

Life Cycle
Female fly follows solitary bee female from flower to nest, waits until bee departs, then lays eggs in entrance tunnel. Fly larvae feed on bee larvae, pupate in nest, and emerge as adults in early summer.

Comments
Bee flies are capable of hovering motionless while waiting for a female bee but can dart quickly in pursuit. They often settle on foliage or bare ground, but are difficult to capture.

rly Tachinid Fly
alpus signifer
2

¼–⅜" (6–10 mm). Head pale grayish tan, hairy. Eyes brownish red. Antennal bristle about as long as rest of antenna. Thorax grayish with dark tan stripes above. Abdomen black except for striking large yellow abdominal spot; abdomen has long black bristles, especially prominent at rear. Wings amber.

Habitat
Fields and meadows near flowers.

Range
Nova Scotia to Georgia, west to California, north to British Columbia.

Life Cycle
Female places 1 or 2 eggs on undersurface of caterpillar host, beyond reach of its jaws. Fly larvae burrow into host and feed. Fully grown larvae drop from host to pupate in soil. Adults fly late spring–early summer.

Comments
This fly is rather inactive but it is very alert and will fly away swiftly if approached.

igger Bees
nthophora spp.
3

⅝" (15–17 mm). Tongue very long. Black, densely covered with short yellow hair on head, thorax, and first abdominal segment. Legs black, covered by short black hair; outermost leg segments brownish or yellowish. Wings clear, smoky at tip; very small spot in fore wings. Pollen-collecting brush on hind tibia.

Habitat
Meadows and gardens.

Range
Most of North America.

Life Cycle
Nest is constructed in clay or sand bank. Entrance is concealed by a downslanted chimney made of mud. The chimney and brood cells at ends of inner branching tunnels are thinly lined with mud. Each cell contains mixture of honey and pollen plus 1 egg. Larvae feed, overwinter, and pupate in cell. Adults emerge in late spring.

Comments
Digger bees often nest together in large numbers. They are sometimes called flower-loving bees, because they visit such a wide variety of flowers.

olden Northern
umble Bee
mbus fervidus
74

Male drone ⅜–⅝" (10–15 mm); workers ½–¾" (13–18 mm); spring queen ¾–⅞" (18–23 mm). Robust, hairy. Face and head mostly blackish. Black band between wings. Female is yellow on most of thorax and abdominal segments 1–4, black on 5–6; male is yellow on segments 1–5, black on 6–7. Wings smoky. Pollen-collecting apparatus on hind tibia.

Habitat
Clearings in forests, roadsides, and open areas.

Range
Quebec and New Brunswick south to Georgia, west to California, and north to British Columbia.

Life Cycle
Queen overwinters until early spring, enters opening in soil t build honeypots and brood cells. Small workers develop first. With warmer weather, new honeypots and brood cells are constructed, producing larger adults. Only young mated females (new queens) overwinter. Adults fly May–September

Comments
The similar Golden-orange Bumble Bee (*B. borealis*), same size, is orangish yellow and has more black near the legs. It occurs from the Yukon to Nova Scotia, south to Georgia. Th larger American Bumble Bee (*B. pennsylvanicus*) is black behind the wings with yellow on abdominal segments 1–3. I is found in the United States and southern Canada.

Honey Bee
Apis mellifera
375

Male drone ⅝" (15–17 mm); queen ¾" (18–20 mm); sterile female worker ⅜–⅝" (10–15 mm). Drone more robust with largest compound eyes; queen elongate with smallest compound eyes and larger abdomen; worker smallest. All mostly reddish brown and black with paler, usually orange-yellow rings on abdomen. Head, antennae, legs almost black with short, pale erect hair. Wings translucent. Pollen-collecting apparatus on hind tibia.

Habitat
Bee hives. Workers visit flowers of many kinds in meadows, open woods, and gardens.

Range
Worldwide.

Life Cycle
Complex social behavior centers on maintaining queen for ful life-span, usually 2 or 3 years, sometimes up to 5. Queen lays eggs at intervals, producing a colony of 60,000–80,000 workers, which collect, produce, and distribute honey and maintain hive. Workers feed royal jelly to queen continuousl and to all larvae for first 3 days; then only queen larvae continue eating royal jelly while other larvae are fed bee breac a mixture of honey and pollen. By passing food mixed with saliva to one another, members of hive have chemical bond. New queens are produced in late spring and early summer; old queen then departs with a swarm of workers to found new colony. About a day later the first new queen emerges, kills other new queens, and sets out for a few days of orientation flights. In 3–16 days queen again leaves hive to mate, sometimes mating with several drones before returning to hive. Drone dies after mating; unmated drones are denied food and die.

Comments

Settlers brought the Honey Bee to North America in the 17th century. Today these bees are used to pollinate crops and produce honey. They are frequently seen swarming around tree limbs.

Rough Harvester Ant
Pogonomyrmex rugosus
476

¼–½" (6–13 mm), depending on caste. Reddish brown. 2-segmented "waist" between thorax and abdomen. Winged female and wingless queen larger and darker than workers; winged male smaller.

Habitat

Lowlands, especially cultivated fields and relatively bare areas, and sandy areas near roads.

Range

Southwestern states.

Life Cycle

Mated female, with help from mate, digs small chamber to conceal clusters of milk-white capsule-shaped eggs and, later, larvae and pupae. First workers to emerge enlarge nest; nest opening may be level with ground or protected by conical crater of small pebbles. Separate chambers are dug to shelter eggs, larvae, and pupae. Ants swarm April–October.

Comments

Workers, active only by day, can bite and sting painfully. They can severely damage crops by cutting down plants and creating large barren areas.

European Earwig
Forficula auricularia
577

⅜–⅝" (9–15 mm), including abdominal pincers. Body reddish brown to almost black. Antennae, legs, and elytra yellow. Underside yellowish brown. Pincers reddish brown; male's curved, female's almost straight and parallel. Short wings do not cover abdomen. Antennae have 15 or fewer segments; second outermost segment of leg lobed beneath.

Habitat

Dark damp crevices and ground litter; grasses, herbs, shrubs, trees, and even buildings.

Range

Eastern Canada; southern New England; Pacific Northwest.

Life Cycle

Female digs cup-shaped nest in upper soil, deposits mass of up to 30 oval grayish-white eggs, and stays with them until a few days after they hatch. Nymphs mature in about 10 weeks. Eggs and adults overwinter in soil or under boards and stones. 1 or 2 generations a year.

Comments

Gardeners often lure these tiny insects by spreading poisoned bran sweetened with molasses. In California a tachinid fly has been introduced from Europe to control this minor pest.

Eastern Wood Ticks
Dermacentor spp.
378

⅛″ (3–4 mm). Male's body pale gray with reddish-brown spots and legs. Female's body reddish brown with small shield of gray near head. Legs brown; head often orange above.

Habitat
Woodlands and shrubbery beside trails.

Range
Eastern North America.

Life Cycle
Tick clings to plants while extending forelegs to seize passing host. Tick climbs on prey for a meal, dropping off after fully engorged. If not yet mature, tick molts and repeats process. Mature female, if mated before last major meal, drops many eggs, producing 6-legged larvae.

Comments
This tick can transfer disease organisms from one host to the next. After a walk through a field, it is wise to inspect clothing and hair for ticks. Then the ticks should be removed and burned or drowned in alcohol.

Tumblebugs
Canthon spp.
379

⅜–¾″ (10–20 mm). Dull black, sometimes with bluish, greenish, or coppery tinge. Minute sculpturing on surface.

Habitat
Pastures and areas where dung of large mammals is available.

Range
Most of the United States.

Life Cycle
Male helps female form a ball of dung and roll it some distance, perhaps to compact it, before they dig a vertical tunnel and tumble the ball inside. A single egg is deposited on the dung ball, which is then covered with earth. Larvae feed alone and pupate in the soil close to dung. Adults are active August–September.

Comments
This beetle helps turn dry dung into fertilizer for plants and is considered beneficial. In ancient Egypt, the related Sacred Scarab (*Scarabaeus sacer*) was associated with rebirth. Scarabs—both real and clay images—were placed on mummies in tombs.

Nine-spotted Ladybug Beetle
Coccinella novemnotata
380

¼″ (5–7 mm). Almost hemispherical. Head and thorax black with yellowish or white markings on margin; legs and underside black. Elytra are yellowish red or orange with 9 black spots.

Habitat
Meadows, crop fields, gardens, and marshes.

Range
North America, except the Southwest.

Life Cycle
Lemon-yellow egg clusters are attached to leaves near aphids. Larvae feed, then pupate without cocoons, attached to leaves. Adults overwinter and emerge May–September.

Comments
The pattern of black spots on this ladybug varies geographically. The Seven-spotted Ladybug Beetle (*C. septapunctata*), same size, has 7 black spots. Recently introduced into New Jersey, it occurs throughout most of the Northeast. The Three-banded Ladybug Beetle (*C. trifasciata*), ⅛–¼" (4–6 mm), has 3 black bands across its orange or yellow elytra and is found in the North.

Red-blue Checkered Beetle
Trichodes nuttalli
381

⅜" (8–11 mm). Elongate, almost cylindrical, with many upright fine stiff bristles. Mostly dark blue-black, sometimes purplish or greenish; with 3 orange to reddish crossbands. Antennae pale to dark brown with 3-segmented club.

Habitat
Meadows, fields, and gardens; adult on flowers and foliage; larva in nests of wasps and bees.

Range
East of the Rocky Mountains; also straying into Idaho and British Columbia.

Life Cycle
Eggs are laid on flowers. Larvae attach themselves to bees and wasps, ride to nests, and prey on or parasitize their larvae. Larvae or pupae overwinter. Adults emerge in midsummer.

Comments
This handsome little insect is easily noticed on daisy heads and other open flowers, where it often rests or feeds voraciously.

Tarnished Plant Bug
Lygus lineolaris
382

¼" (6–7 mm). Dark brown to pale green with reddish-brown, black, and yellow markings. Head yellow with 3 narrow dark stripes. Upper part of thorax has yellowish margins and lengthwise stripes. Legs pale.

Habitat
Meadows, gardens, and crop fields.

Range
Eastern North America.

Life Cycle
Tiny, pale green, seedlike eggs are inserted into leafstalks and soft stems. Nymphs grow rapidly. In the North only adults overwinter. Often 5 generations a year in the South, where nymphs as well as adults overwinter.

Comments
This genus probably includes the most common leaf bugs in the United States and Canada, with about 40 species.

Pennsylvania Firefly
Photuris pennsylvanicus
383

⅜–⅝" (9–15 mm). Elongate, flattened. Head visible from above, eyes large, widely separated. Antennae threadlike. Head and upper part of thorax are dull yellowish, latter with a black spot surrounded by reddish ring. Elytra are brown or gray and have yellow bands along sides near midline and a narrow pale stripe down middle. Both sexes have flashing green light. Larva is spindle-shaped with light organ below abdomen at rear.

Habitat
Meadows and open woods.

Range
Atlantic Coast to Texas, north to Manitoba.

Life Cycle
Eggs are concealed singly among rotting wood and humid debris on ground. Larvae hatch in spring. Fully grown larvae overwinter in pupal chambers just below soil surface and pupate the following spring. Adults emerge early summer–late August.

Comments
Eggs, larvae, and pupae are all luminous. This firefly flashes its light every 2 or 3 seconds while in flight.

Pyralis Firefly
Photinus pyralis
384

⅜–½" (10–14 mm). Head concealed from above by rounded front of upper part of thorax. Upper part of thorax is rosy pink with dull yellow edges and black spot in center. Elytra are mostly blackish brown. Both sexes have flashing yellow light, smaller in female, which does not fly.

Habitat
Meadows.

Range
East of the Rocky Mountains.

Life Cycle
Eggs are left on damp soil. Larvae overwinter at end of first and second year, then pupate in chambers in moist soil.

Comments
The smaller Scintillating Firefly (*P. scintillans*), ¼–⅜" (5–10 mm), is yellow and pink and has a large black spot on its pronotum. It is found from New England to Texas.

Striped Blister Beetle
Epicauta vittata
385

½–⅝" (13–17 mm). Dull yellow above, black below with yellow hair. Thorax and each elytron with 2 black stripes. Bulbous head loosely linked to nearly cylindrical thorax.

Habitat
Fields, including pastures, and croplands.

Range
Nova Scotia to North Carolina, west to Louisiana, north to Saskatchewan.

Life Cycle
Egg clusters of 100 are deposited in holes made in soil and hatch in 10–21 days. Larvae burrow in search of grasshopper eggs, pupate in 2 weeks, and overwinter in soil. Adults emerge in early summer. Usually 1 generation a year.

Comments
The population of these beetles increases or decreases according to the availability of grasshopper egg masses. Larvae are beneficial—one larva can destroy 30 or more eggs, which is a full pod for some grasshoppers. But adult beetles are detrimental when they attack field crops.

Japanese Beetle
Popilla japonica
386

⅜–½″ (8–12 mm). Oval, sturdy. Body bright metallic green; elytra mostly brownish or reddish orange. Grayish hair on underside and 5 patches of white hair along each side of abdomen with 2 white tufts at tip. Male has pointed tibial spurs; female's are rounded.

Habitat
Open woods and meadows.

Range
Maine to South Carolina.

Life Cycle
Elongate, yellowish-white eggs are deposited on soil, 1–4 at a time. Fully grown larvae overwinter in soil and pupate in the spring. 1 generation of adults emerges in summer when blackberries ripen. In the North, cycle takes 2 years.

Comments
The Japanese Beetle was introduced accidentally in 1916 on iris roots imported from Japan and has been a major pest for years. Its numbers have been reduced by the controlled use of tachinid flies and tiphiid wasps that prey on beetle larvae.

Green June Beetle
Cotinus nitida
387

¾–⅞″ (20–23 mm). Robust, elongate, somewhat flattened. Head dark, with a horn. Upper part of thorax and elytra are metallic green, with brownish yellow on the sides; the underside is glittery green and brownish yellow. Tibiae green; femora are brownish yellow.

Habitat
Gardens, orchards, open woods, and crop fields, particularly above sandy soil.

Range
New York to Florida and Gulf states, north to Missouri.

Life Cycle
Grayish, spherical eggs are laid in soil with high organic content. Larvae emerge after a rain and overwinter deep in soil. Larvae develop in earthen cells near soil surface and pupate in the late spring of the second year after hatching. Adults emerge June–July. 1 generation a year.

Comments
This beetle is often an agricultural pest because its larvae destroy the roots of valuable plants, especially tobacco.

Three-lined Potato Beetle
Lema trilineata
388

¼" (6–7 mm). Reddish yellow. Black eyes. Upper part of thorax has 2 black dots (sometimes absent). Elytra have 3 black stripes. Thorax is constricted in front of elytra.

Habitat
Meadows and potato fields.

Range
Throughout North America.

Life Cycle
Yellow eggs are laid singly or clustered on leaves. Larvae pupate in silk-lined cells in the soil. Adults overwinter. 2 generations a year.

Comments
Voracious larvae gather in clusters on potato leaves, nibbling lacy holes and eventually consuming all but the midvein. Unlike the larvae of other potato-feeders, they are blanketed in a wet froth of their own secretions. Adults usually can be distinguished from the Striped Cucumber Beetle by the constriction behind the thorax.

Meadow Spittlebug
Philaenus spumarius
389

⅜" (9–10 mm). Near bubbly froth. Elongated, pear-shaped. Rounded head, very short antennae. Gray to green, yellow, or chocolate-brown with pale spots. Wings short.

Habitat
Meadows and croplands where forage plants are raised.

Range
New England south to Florida; West Coast to north-central states and adjacent Canada.

Life Cycle
Frost-resistant eggs are deposited in angle between leaf and stem, hatching in spring. Nymphs soon cover themselves with froth consisting of self-made bubbles, which provides protection from dry air, predators, and potential parasites. Nymphs maintain their cover until they mature. Winged adults crawl or fly into open. 1 generation a year.

Comments
Adults are often inconspicuously colored, and nymphs are overlooked because of their bubbly covering. This pest destroys alfalfa and clover crops.

Rose, Pea, and Potato Aphids
Macrosiphum spp.
390

⅛" (3–4 mm). Pear-shaped. Light to medium green or pink, with darker midline stripe, or mottled green and pink. Antennae longer than body; legs long. Abdomen tapers to narrow projection between tubes on rear of abdomen.

Habitat
Crop fields, gardens, and meadows.

Range
Throughout North America.

Life Cycle
In autumn, eggs are laid on woody stems of a shrub or tree, where they overwinter and produce wingless females in spring. These feed, then reproduce asexually for a month or so, creating several generations of wingless females. A winged generation appears and moves to another host plant, primarily annual herbs and grasses, where asexual reproduction continues. In autumn another winged generation returns to the woody host shrub or tree, then a wingless sexual generation develops, mates, and repeats the cycle.

Comments
The best-known species in this genus is the Potato Aphid (*M. euphorbiae*), known also as the Pink-and-green Tomato Aphid. It places overwintering eggs primarily on roses. Summer hosts include rose, apple, potato, tomato, eggplant, corn, gladiolus, iris, and various weeds.

Brown Daddy-long-legs
Phalangium opilio
391

⅛–¼″ (4–6 mm). Long thin legs. Body reddish brown. Legs dark with bases of legs paler and prominent. Eyes on black turret; 1 eye to right, 1 to left.

Habitat
Fields on tree trunks and open ground.

Range
Throughout North America.

Life Cycle
Female thrusts egg-laying organ into soil to deposit eggs. When warm weather arrives, young creep out and grow slowly. Normally they mature in summer, then mate without courtship. 1 generation a year.

Comments
On cool afternoons adults often climb trees or sides of buildings, seemingly to benefit from residual heat of the sun. A warm knothole may attract dozens of daddy-long-legs.

Goldenrod Spider
Misumena vatia
392, 396

Male ⅛″ (3–4 mm), female ¼–⅜″ (5–10 mm). Female yellowish to white with crimson streaks on each side of abdomen and a reddish-brown stain between eyes. Female's legs pale. Male's cephalothorax dark reddish brown with white spot in center and in front of eyes; abdomen white with 2 red bands. Male has 2 pairs of reddish-brown forelegs, 2 pairs of yellow hind legs.

Habitat
Meadows, fields, and gardens on daisies, goldenrod, and other white or yellow flowers.

Range
Throughout North America and southern Canada.

Life Cycle
Eggs are protected in a silken sac. Female usually dies before spiderlings hatch and disperse.

Comments
This spider's coloring often changes to yellow, camouflaging it on yellow daisies and goldenrod.

Metaphid Jumping Spiders
Metaphidippus spp.
393

Male ⅛–¼″ (3–5 mm), female ⅛–¼″ (3–6 mm). Brown to yellow. Body and legs somewhat grayish due to covering of dense hair. Male usually has white band on sides of abdomen. Both sexes have spots, bands, and chevrons.

Habitat
Meadows and woods, on foliage, tree bark, fence posts, and tall grasses.

Range
Throughout North America; individual species more restricted.

Life Cycle
After mating, female constructs cocoon for eggs, attaches it to twigs, and stays close by. Spiderlings disperse rapidly.

Comments
These spiders run freely, producing an anchor line when they leap on potential prey or walk about on the ground.

Jumping Lynx Spiders
Oxyopes spp.
394

Male ⅛–¼″ (3–5 mm), female ⅛–⅜″ (4–8 mm). Cephalothorax yellow with 4 lengthwise vague, pale stripes; 2 black lines from below eyes to tip of fangs. Male's abdomen gray or black with iridescent scales; female's pale, darker below and on sides. Narrow black line below each yellow femur; legs spiny.

Habitat
Fields in tall grasses and among herbaceous vegetation.

Range
Throughout the United States; most common in the East, the Rocky Mountains, and Canadian Great Basin.

Life Cycle
Female attaches spherical egg sac to plant, tying several leaves together with silk. Female guards egg sac until spiderlings disperse, each soon hunting on its own. In the North, egg sac, embryos, or spiderlings overwinter. Adults are usually seen June–September. Usually 1 generation a year.

Comments
This hunting spider does not build a web or nest. Active by day, it hunts among herbaceous vegetation, including tall grasses and low plants.

Orb Weavers
Araneus spp.
95

Male ¼″ (6 mm), female ⅜–¾″ (10–20 mm). Abdomen bulbous. Brown to orange, with distinctive pattern for each species. Legs long, yellowish, sometimes ringed with black.

Habitat
Among tall grasses and shrubbery.

Range
Throughout North America; individual species more restricted.

Life Cycle
Spider usually hangs head downward near center of web, or remains at a nearby resting site connected to the web by a signal line. Egg sac is attached to plant near this retreat or on foliage nearby. Spiderlings disperse after hatching.

Comments
Each night the old web is replaced with a new one, spun in complete darkness by touch alone.

TREES

A variety of distinctive trees grow in the grasslands. Many common and widespread conifers and hardwoods are found here, along with trees adapted to arid grasslands—such as yuccas and mesquite. The fruit of many species is consumed in large quantities by a wide range of animals. Included in this group are descriptions of some of the most common and typical trees of the grasslands.

Alligator Juniper
Juniperus deppeana
97, 477

Evergreen tree with short, stout trunk and rounded, spreading crown, becoming irregular and with branches partly dead.
Height: 20–50′ (6–15 m). Diameter: 2–4′ (0.6–1.2 m).
Leaves: opposite; in 4 rows, forming slender, 4-angled twigs; 1/16–1/8″ (1.5–3 mm) long. Scalelike, sharp-pointed; blue-green, with gland-dot and often whitish resin drop.
Bark: blackish or gray; thick and rough, deeply furrowed into checkered plates, suggesting an alligator's back.
Cones: 1/2″ (12 mm) in diameter; berrylike, brownish with whitish bloom, hard and dry, mealy; 3–5 seeds; maturing second year.

Habitat
Rocky hillsides and mountains; with pinyons, other junipers, oaks, and Ponderosa Pine.

Range
Trans-Pecos Texas northwest to N. Arizona; also Mexico; at 4500–8000′ (1372–2438 m).

Comments
Alligator Juniper is easily recognized by its distinctive bark. New sprouts often appear at the base of cut stumps. The large "berries" are consumed by birds and mammals. Large trees often have a partially dead crown of grotesque appearance with some branches that die and turn light gray instead of falling; other branches die only in a vertical strip and continue to grow on the other side.

Utah Juniper
Juniperus osteosperma
98, 476

Tree with short upright trunk, low spreading branches, and rounded or conical open crown.
Height: 15–40′ (4.6–12 m). Diameter: 1–3′ (0.3–0.9 m).
Leaves: generally opposite in 4 rows, forming stout, stiff twigs; 1/16″ (1.5 mm) long. Scalelike, short-pointed; yellow-green, usually without gland-dot.
Bark: gray, fibrous, furrowed, shreddy.
Cones: 1/4–5/8″ (6–15 mm) in diameter; berrylike, bluish with a bloom, becoming brown, hard and dry; mealy and sweetish; 1–2 seeds.

Habitat
Dry plains, plateaus, hills, and mountains, mostly on rocky soils; often in pure stands or with pinyons.

Range
Nevada east to Wyoming, south to W. New Mexico, and west to S. California; local in S. Montana; at 3000–8000′ (914–2438 m).

Comments
The most common juniper in Arizona, it is conspicuous at the south rim of the Grand Canyon and on higher canyon walls. Utah Juniper grows slowly, becoming craggier and more contorted with age. Scattered tufts of yellowish twigs with whitish berries found on the trees are a parasitic mistletoe, which is characteristic of this tree.

Oneseed Juniper
Juniperus monosperma
399

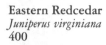

Evergreen shrub or small tree with several branches curving up
from ground, sometimes with short trunk, and much-
branched, spreading, and often scraggly crown.
Height: 10–25′ (3–7.6 m). Diameter: 1′ (0.3 m).
Leaves: opposite: in 4 rows on short, stout, crowded twigs;
⅟₁₆″ (1.5 mm) long. Scalelike: yellow-green, usually with
gland-dot.
Bark: gray, fibrous, shreddy.
Cones: ¼″ (6 mm) in diameter; berrylike, dark blue with a
bloom, soft, juicy, sweetish and resinous, 1-seeded. Male or
pollen cones on separate trees.

Habitat
Dry plains, plateaus, hills, and mountains, mostly on rocky
soils; often in pure, orchardlike stands.

Range
Central Colorado south to NW. and Trans-Pecos Texas and
west to central Arizona; also northern Mexico; at 3000–7000
(914–2134 m).

Comments
This abundant juniper is one of the most common small trees
in New Mexico. The wood is important for fence posts and
fuel, and Indians used to make mats and cloth from the bark.

Eastern Redcedar
Juniperus virginiana
400

Evergreen, aromatic tree with trunk often angled and
buttressed at base and narrow, compact, columnar crown;
sometimes becoming broad and irregular.
Height: 40–60′ (12–18 m). Diameter: 1–2′ (0.3–0.6 m).
Leaves: evergreen; opposite in 4 rows forming slender 4-angle
twigs; ⅟₁₆″ (1.5 mm) long, to ⅜″ (10 mm) long on leaders.
Scalelike, not toothed; dark green, with gland-dot.
Bark: reddish brown; thin, fibrous and shreddy.
Cones: ¼–⅜″ (6–10 mm) in diameter; berrylike; dark blue
with a bloom; soft, juicy, sweetish, and resinous;
1–2 seeds. Pollen cones on separate trees.

Habitat
From dry uplands, especially limestone, to floodplains and
swamps; also abandoned fields and fencerows; often in
scattered pure stands.

Range
S. Ontario and widespread in eastern half of United States
from Maine south to N. Florida, west to Texas, and north to
North Dakota.

Comments
The most widely distributed eastern conifer, native in 37
states, Eastern Redcedar is resistant to extremes of drought,
heat, and cold. The aromatic wood is used for fence posts,
cedar chests, cabinetwork, and carvings. First observed at
Roanoke Island, Virginia, in 1564, it was prized by the
colonists for building furniture, rail fences, and log cabins.

Common Juniper
Juniperus communis
01, 475

Usually a spreading low shrub, sometimes forming broad or prostrate clumps; rarely a small tree with an open crown.
Height: 1–4' (0.3–1.2 m), rarely 15–25' (4.6–7.6 m).
Diameter: 8" (20 cm).
Leaves: evergreen; ⅜–½" (10–12 mm) long. Awl-shaped; stiff, very sharp-pointed, jointed at base; in 3's spreading at right angles. Whitish and grooved above, shiny yellow-green beneath.
Bark: reddish brown to gray; thin, rough, scaly, and shreddy.
Twigs: light yellow; slender, 3-angled, hairless.
Cones: ¼–⅜" (6–10 mm) in diameter; berrylike; whitish blue with a bloom; hard; mealy; sweetish and resinous; aromatic; maturing in 2–3 years and remaining attached; 1–3 brown, pointed seeds. Pollen cones mostly on same plant.

Habitat
Rocky slopes in coniferous forests of mountains and plains.

Range
Widespread from Alaska east to Labrador and S. Greenland, south to New York, and west to Minnesota and Wyoming; also south in mountains to NW. South Carolina and central Arizona; to 8000–11,500' (2438–3505 m) in South.

Comments
Although usually a tree in Eurasia, Common Juniper is only rarely a small tree in northeastern states. Juniper "berries" are consumed by wildlife; they are also used to make gin, producing that liquor's distinctive aroma and tang. Also called Dwarf Juniper.

Virginia Pine
Pinus virginiana
02

Short-needled tree with open, broad, irregular crown of long spreading branches; often a shrub.
Height: 30–60' (9–18 m). Diameter: 1–1½' (0.3–0.5 m).
Needles: evergreen; 1½–3" (4–7.5 cm) long; 2 in bundle; stout, slightly flattened and twisted; dull green.
Bark: brownish gray, thin, with narrow scaly ridges, becoming shaggy; on small trunks, smoothish, peeling off.
Cones: 1½–2¾" (4–7 cm) long; narrowly egg-shaped, shiny reddish brown; almost stalkless; opening at maturity but remaining attached; cone-scales slightly raised and keeled, with long slender prickle.

Habitat
Clay, loam, and sandy loam on well-drained sites. Forms pure stands, especially on old fields or abandoned farmland, even in poor or severely eroded soil. Also in mixed forest types.

Range
SE. New York (Long Island) south to NE. Mississippi, and north to S. Indiana; at 100–2500' (30–762 m).

Comments
Common in old fields as a pioneer after grasses on hills of the Piedmont, growing rapidly and forming thickets. Later this pine is replaced by taller, more valuable hardwoods.

Shortleaf Pine
Pinus echinata
403, 479

The most widely distributed of the southern yellow pines, a large tree with broad, open crown.
Height: 70–100' (21–30 m). Diameter: 1½–3' (0.5–0.9 m).
Needles: evergreen; 2¾–4½" (7–11 cm) long. 2 or sometimes 3 in bundle; slender, flexible; dark blue-green.
Bark: reddish brown, with large irregular flat scaly plates.
Cones: 1½–2½" (4–6 cm) long; conical or narrowly egg-shaped, dull brown; short-stalked; opening at maturity but remaining attached; cone-scales thin, keeled, with prickle.

Habitat
From dry rocky mountain ridges to sandy loams and silt loams of floodplains, and in old fields; often in pure stands or with other pines and oaks.

Range
Extreme SE. New York and New Jersey south to N. Florida, west to E. Texas, and north to S. Missouri; to 3300' (1006 m).

Comments
Shortleaf Pine is native in 21 southeastern states. Seedlings and small trees will sprout after fire damage or injury.

Loblolly Pine
Pinus taeda
404

The principal commercial southern pine, a large, resinous, and fragrant tree with rounded crown of spreading branches.
Height: 80–100' (24–30 m). Diameter: 2–3' (0.6–0.9 m).
Needles: evergreen; 5–9" (13–23 cm) long. 3 in bundle; stout, stiff, often twisted; green.
Bark: blackish gray; thick, deeply furrowed into scaly ridges exposing brown inner layers.
Cones: 3–5" (7.5–13 cm) long; conical; dull brown; almost stalkless; opening at maturity but remaining attached; cone-scales raised, keeled, with short stout spine.

Habitat
From deep, poorly drained floodplains to well-drained slopes of rolling, hilly uplands. Forms pure stands.

Range
S. New Jersey south to central Florida, west to E. Texas, north to extreme SE. Oklahoma; to 1500–2000' (457–610 m).

Comments
Loblolly Pine is native in 15 southeastern states. Among the fastest-growing southern pines, it is extensively cultivated in forest plantations for pulpwood and lumber.

Eastern White Pine
Pinus strobus
405, 478

The largest northeastern conifer, a magnificent evergreen tree with straight trunk and crown of horizontal branches. 1 row added a year, becoming broad and irregular.
Height: 100' (33 m), formerly 150' (46 m) or more.
Diameter: 3–4' (0.9–1.2 m) or more.
Needles: evergreen; 2½–5" (6–13 cm) long, 5 in bundle; slender, blue-green.

Bark: gray; smooth becoming rough; thick and deeply
furrowed into narrow scaly ridges.
Cones: 4–8″ (10–20 cm) long; narrowly cylindrical; yellow-
brown; long-stalked; cone-scales thin, rounded, flat.

Habitat
Well-drained sandy soils; sometimes in pure stands.

Range
SE. Manitoba east to Newfoundland, south to N. Georgia,
and west to NE. Iowa; a variety in Mexico. From near sea level
to 2000′ (610 m); in the southern Appalachians to 5000′
(1524 m).

Comments
The largest conifer and formerly the most valuable tree of the
Northeast. Younger trees and plantations have replaced the
once seemingly inexhaustible lumber supply of virgin forests.
The tall straight trunks were prized for ship masts in the
colonial period.

Longleaf Pine
Pinus palustris
406

Large tree with the longest needles and largest cones of any
eastern pine and an open, irregular crown of a few spreading
branches, 1 row added each year.
Height: 80–100′ (24–30 m). Diameter: 2–2½′ (0.6–0.8 m).
Needles: evergreen; mostly 10–15″ (25–38 cm) long, on
small plants to 18″ (46 cm). Densely crowded, 3 in bundle;
slightly stout, flexible; spreading to drooping; dark green.
Bark: orange-brown, furrowed into scaly plates; on small
trunks, gray and rough.
Twigs: dark brown; very stout, ending in large white bud.
Cones: 6–10″ (15–25 cm) long; narrowly conical or
cylindrical; dull brown; almost stalkless; opening and
shedding at maturity; cone-scales raised, keeled, with small
prickle.

Habitat
Well-drained sandy soils of flatlands and sandhills; often in
pure stands.

Range
Coastal Plain from SE. Virginia to E. Florida, and west to E.
Texas. Usually below 600′ (183 m); to 2000′ (610 m) in
foothills of Piedmont.

Comments
Frequent fires caused by man or by lightning have perpetuated
subclimax, pure stands of this species. The seedlings pass
through a "grass" stage for a few years, in which the stem
grows in thickness rather than height and the taproot develops
rapidly. Later, the unbranched stem produces long needles.

Slash Pine
Pinus elliottii
407

Large tree with narrow, regular, pointed crown of horizontal
branches and long needles.
Height: 60–100′ (18–30 m). Diameter: 2–2½′ (0.6–0.8 m).

Needles: evergreen; 7–10″ (18–25 cm) long; 2 and 3 in bundle; stout, stiff; slightly shiny green.
Bark: purplish brown, with large, flattened, scaly plates; on small trunks, blackish gray, rough and furrowed.
Cones: 2½–6″ (6–15 cm) long; narrowly egg-shaped; shiny .dark brown; short-stalked; opening and shedding at maturity, leaving a few cone-scales on twig; cone-scales flat, slightly keeled, with short stout prickle.

Habitat
Low areas such as pond margins, flatwoods, swamps or "slashes," including poorly drained sandy soils; also uplands and old fields. In pure stands as a subclimax after fires and in mixed forests.

Range

Coastal Plain from S. South Carolina to S. Florida, and west to SE. Louisiana; mostly near sea level, locally to 500′ (152 m).

Comments
An important species both for lumber and naval stores and one of the fastest-growing southern pines, Slash Pine is extensively grown in forest plantations both in its natural range and farther north.

Soaptree Yucca
Yucca elata
408

Evergreen, palmlike shrub or small tree with single trunk or several clustered trunks; unbranched or with few upright branches; and very long, narrow leaves.
Height: 10–17′ (3–5 m), rarely to 25′ (7.6 m). Diameter: 6–10″ (15–25 cm).
Leaves: evergreen; numerous, spreading, grasslike; 1–2½′ (0.3–0.8 m) long, ⅛–⅜″ (3–10 mm) wide. Linear, flat, leathery, and flexible; ending in sharp spine. Yellow-green, with fine whitish threads along edges.
Trunk: gray and slightly furrowed in lower part, covered by dead leaves above.
Flowers: 1½–2″ (4–5 cm) long; bell-shaped, with 6 white, broad, pointed sepals; crowded on upright branches, in clusters 3–10′ (0.9–3 m) or more in height including long stalk; in spring.
Fruit: 1½–3″ (4–7.5 cm) long; a cylindrical capsule, light brown, dry, 3-celled; maturing in early summer, splitting open in 3 parts and remaining attached; many small, flat, thin, rough, dull black seeds.

Habitat
Dry, sandy plains, mesas, and washes; in desert grassland and desert, often in pure stands with grasses.

Range

Trans-Pecos Texas west to central New Mexico and central Arizona and local in SW. Utah; also northern Mexico; at 1500–6000′ (457–1829 m).

Comments
Cattle relish the young flower stalks, and chopped trunks and

leaves serve as emergency food during droughts. Indians ate
the flower buds, flowers, and young flower stalks of this and
other yuccas, either raw or boiled.

Glossy Buckthorn
hamnus frangula
09, 474

Introduced, ornamental shrub or small tree with glossy foliage
and red-to-black berries.
Height: 20′ (6 m). Diameter: 4″ (10 cm).
Leaves: 1½–2¾″ (4–7 cm) long, ¾–2″ (2–5 cm) wide.
Elliptical; usually widest above middle; not toothed; with
several almost straight parallel side veins; nearly hairless.
Shiny dark green above, paler beneath; turning yellow in fall.
Bark: grayish, thin, slightly fissured and warty.
Twigs: slender; covered with fine hairs; thornless, ending in
naked bud of tiny hairy leaves.
Flowers: ⅛″ (3 mm) wide; bell-shaped; with 5 pointed
greenish-yellow sepals; in short clusters at leaf bases; in late
spring and early summer.
Fruit: ⁵⁄₁₆″ (8 mm) in diameter; berrylike; turning from red to
black; clustered; 2–3 seeds; in late summer and autumn.

Habitat
Hardy in various soils, escaping especially in wet areas along
fences and in bogs.

Range
Native to Europe, western Asia, and northern Africa.
Naturalized from S. Manitoba east to Nova Scotia, south to
New Jersey and west to Illinois.

Comments
Glossy Buckthorn is a handsome ornamental with shiny,
alderlike leaves, turning yellow in autumn. It has long been
planted, both as a tree and as a tall hedge, especially in
Europe; however, it spreads rapidly and may become a pest.

Southern Catalpa
Catalpa bignonioides
10

Short-trunked tree with broad, rounded crown of spreading
branches, large, heart-shaped leaves, large clusters of showy
white flowers, and long, beanlike fruit.
Height: 50′ (15 m). Diameter: 2′ (0.6 m).
Leaves: 3 at a node (whorled) and opposite; 5–10″ (13–25 cm)
long, 4–7″ (10–18 cm) wide. Ovate, abruptly long-pointed at
tip, notched at base; without teeth. Dull green above, paler
and covered with soft hairs beneath; turning blackish in
autumn. With unpleasant odor when crushed. Slender
leafstalk 3½–6″ (9–15 cm) long.
Bark: brownish gray; scaly.
Twigs: green, turning brown; stout, hairless or nearly so.
Flowers: 1½″ (4 cm) long and wide; with bell-shaped corolla
of 5 unequal rounded fringed lobes, white with 2 orange
stripes and many purple spots and stripes inside; slightly
fragrant; in upright branched clusters to 10″ (25 cm) long and
wide; in late spring.
Fruit: 6–12″ (15–30 cm) long, ⁵⁄₁₆–⅜″ (8–10 mm) in

diameter; narrow, cylindrical, dark brown capsule; cigarlike, thin-walled, splitting into 2 parts; many flat light brown seed with 2 papery wings; maturing in autumn, remaining attached in winter.

Habitat
Moist soils in open areas such as roadsides and clearings.

Range
Probably native in SW. Georgia, NW. Florida, Alabama, and Mississippi; widely naturalized from southern New England south to Florida, west to Texas, and north to Michigan; at 100–500' (30–152 m).

Comments
Catalpa is the American Indian name, while the scientific name refers to a related vine with flowers of similar shape.

Osage-orange
Maclura pomifera
411, 459, 469

Medium-sized, spiny tree with short, often crooked trunk, broad rounded or irregular crown of spreading branches, singl straight stout spines at base of some leaves, and milky sap.
Height: 50' (15 m). Diameter: 2' (0.6 m).
Leaves: 2½–5" (6–13 cm) long, 1½–3" (4–7.5 cm) wide. Narrowly ovate, long-pointed; not toothed; hairless. Shiny dark green above, paler beneath; turning yellow in autumn.
Bark: gray or brown; thick, deeply furrowed into narrow forking ridges; inner bark of roots orange, separating into thir papery scales.
Twigs: brown, stout, with single spine ¼–1" (0.6–2.5 cm) long at some nodes and short twigs or spurs.
Flowers: tiny; greenish; crowded in rounded clusters less than 1" (2.5 cm) in diameter; male and female on separate trees in early spring.
Fruit: 3½–5" (9–13 cm) in diameter; a heavy yellow-green ball, hard and fleshy, containing many light brown nutlets; maturing in autumn and soon falling.

Habitat
Moist soils of river valleys.

Range
The native range uncertain. SW. Arkansas to E. Oklahoma and Texas; widely planted and naturalized in eastern and northwestern states.

Comments
Rows of these spiny plants served as fences in the grassland plains before the introduction of barbed wire. The fruit is eaten by livestock, which has given rise to yet another common name, Horseapple.

Common Persimmon
Diospyros virginiana
412, 468, 470

Tree with a dense cylindrical or rounded crown, or sometimes a shrub, best known by its sweet, orange fruit in autumn.
Height: 20–70' (6–21 m). Diameter: 1–2' (0.3–0.6 m).
Leaves: alternate; 2½–6" (6–15 cm) long, 1½–3" (4–7.5 cm)

wide. Ovate to elliptical; long-pointed; without teeth; slightly
thickened. Shiny dark green above, whitish green and hairless
to densely hairy beneath; turning yellow in autumn.
Bark: brown or blackish; thick, deeply furrowed into small
square scaly plates.
Twigs: brown to gray, slightly zigzag, often hairy.
Flowers: with bell-shaped, 4-lobed white corolla; fragrant;
scattered and almost stalkless at leaf bases. Male and female on
separate trees in spring. Male, 2–3 together, 3″ (10 mm)
long. Female, solitary, ⅝″ (15 mm) long.
Fruit: ¾–1½″ (2–4 cm) in diameter; a rounded or slightly
flat, orange to purplish-brown berry; 4–8 large flat seeds;
maturing in autumn before frost and often remaining attached
into winter; orange pulp becoming soft and juicy at maturity.

Habitat
Moist alluvial soils of valleys and in dry uplands; also at
roadsides and in old fields, clearings, and mixed forests.

Range
S. Connecticut south to S. Florida, west to central Texas, and
north to extreme SE. Iowa; to 3500′ (1067 m).

Comments
Persimmons are consumed fresh and are used to make
puddings, cakes, and beverages. American Indians made
persimmon bread and stored the dried fruit like prunes. Many
mammals and birds also feed upon the fruit.

Pussy Willow
Salix discolor
413, 460

Many-stemmed shrub or small tree with open, rounded crown;
silky, furry catkins appear in late winter and early spring.
Height: 20′ (6 m). Diameter: 8″ (0.2 m).
Leaves: 1½–4″ (4–10 cm) long, ⅜–1¼″ (1–3 cm) wide.
Lance-shaped or elliptical, wavy-toothed, stiff; hairy when
young; slender-stalked. Green above, whitish beneath.
Bark: gray, fissured, scaly.
Twigs: brown, stout, hairy when young.
Flowers: catkins 1–2½″ (2.5–6 cm) long; cylindrical, thick
with blackish scales, covered with silky, whitish hairs: in late
winter and early spring long before leaves.
Fruit: ⁵⁄₁₆–½″ (8–12 mm) long; narrow, light brown, finely
hairy capsules; in early spring before leaves.

Habitat
Wet meadow soils and borders of streams and lakes; usually in
coniferous forests.

Range
N. British Columbia to Labrador, south to Delaware, west to
NE. Missouri, and north to N. Wyoming and North Dakota;
to 4000′ (1219 m).

Comments
The large flower buds burst and expose their soft, silky hairs,
or "pussy fur," early in the year. In winter, cut Pussy Willow
twigs can be put in warm water and the flowers forced.

Curlleaf Cercocarpus
Cercocarpus ledifolius
414, 486

Slightly resinous and aromatic evergreen shrub or small tree with compact, rounded crown of widely spreading, curved, and twisted branches and many stiff twigs.
Height: 15–30′ (4.6–9 m). Diameter: ½–1½′ (0.15–0.5 m).
Leaves: evergreen; alternate; usually clustered; ½–1¼″ (1.2–3 cm) long, less than ⅜″ (10 mm) wide. Narrowly lance-shaped or elliptical, thick and leathery, with edges rolled under, slightly resinous and aromatic, almost stalkless. Shiny dark green with grooved midvein and obscure side veins above, pale and with fine hairs beneath.
Bark: reddish brown, thick, deeply furrowed into scaly ridges.
Twigs: reddish brown, hairy when young.
Flowers: ⅜″ (10 mm) long; funnel-shaped, slightly 5-lobed, yellowish, hairy, without petals, stalkless; 1–3 at leaf bases; in early spring.
Fruit: ¼″ (6 mm) long; narrowly cylindrical, hairy, with twisted tail 1½–3″ (4–7.5 cm) long, covered with whitish hairs; maturing in summer.

Habitat
Dry, rocky mountain slopes; in grassland, with sagebrush, pinyons, and oaks, and in coniferous forests.

Range
Extreme SE. Washington east to S. Montana, south to N. Arizona, and west to S. California; at 4000–10,500′ (1219–3200 m).

Comments
This species is a small tree characteristic of lower mountain slopes throughout the Great Basin. Deer browse the evergreen foliage year-round.

Southern Crab Apple
Malus angustifolia
415

Small tree with short trunk, spreading branches, and broad, open crown.
Height: 30′ (9 m). Diameter: 1′ (0.3 m).
Leaves: alternate; 1–2¾″ (2.5–7 cm) long, ½–¾″ (12–19 mm) wide. Elliptical or oblong, usually blunt at tip; wavy saw-toothed; hairy when young. Dull green above, paler beneath; turning brown in autumn. Leafstalks slender, ½–¾″ (12–19 mm) long, hairy when young.
Bark: gray or brown; furrowed into narrow scaly ridges.
Twigs: brown; densely covered with hairs when young.
Flowers: 1–1½″ (2.5–4 cm) wide; with 5 rounded pink petals; in clusters, on long stalks; fragrant; in spring.
Fruit: ¾–1″ (2–2.5 cm) in diameter; like small apples; yellow-green, sour, long-stalked; maturing in late summer.

Habitat
Moist soils of valleys and lower slopes, borders of forests, fence rows, and old fields.

Range
S. Virginia south to N. Florida, west to Louisiana, and north

to Arkansas; local from S. New Jersey to S. Ohio, and in SE. Texas; to 2000' (610 m).

Comments
This is the crab apple that grows at low altitudes in the Southeast, often forming thickets. Quantities of the fruit are consumed by bobwhites, rabbits, and other wildlife.

Siberian Elm
Ulmus pumila
416

Small to medium-sized, introduced tree with open, rounded crown of slender, spreading branches.
Height: 60' (18 m). Diameter: 1½' (0.5 m), usually smaller.
Leaves: alternate in 2 rows; ¾–2" (2–5 cm) long, ½–1" (1.2–2.5 cm) wide. Narrowly elliptical, blunt-based; saw-toothed; with many straight side veins; slightly thickened. Dark green above, paler and nearly hairless beneath; yellow in autumn.
Bark: gray or brown; rough, furrowed.
Flowers: ⅛" (3 mm) wide; greenish; in clusters; in spring.
Fruit: ⅜–⅝" (10–15 mm) long; several clustered rounded flat 1-seeded keys (samaras), bordered with broad notched wing; in early spring.

Habitat
Dry regions, tolerant of poor soils and city smoke; also scattered in moist soils along streams.

Range
Native from Turkestan to eastern Siberia and northern China. Naturalized from Minnesota south to Kansas and west to Utah; at 1000–5000' (305–1524 m).

Comments
A fast-growing, often-planted tree in dry regions such as the Great Plains, Siberian Elm is less suited to moist regions. Hardy and resistant to the Dutch Elm disease.

Pin Cherry
Prunus pensylvanica
417, 456, 473

Small tree or shrub with horizontal branches; narrow, rounded, open crown; shiny red twigs; bitter, aromatic bark and foliage; and tiny red cherries.
Height: 30' (9 m). Diameter: 1' (0.3 m).
Leaves: alternate; 2½–4½" (6–11 cm) long, ¾–1¼" (2–3 cm) wide. Broadly lance-shaped, long-pointed; finely and sharply saw-toothed; becoming hairless. Shiny green above, paler beneath; turning bright yellow in autumn. Slender leafstalks often with 2 gland-dots near tip.
Bark: reddish gray, smooth, thin; becoming gray and fissured into scaly plates.
Flowers: ½" (12 mm) wide; with 5 rounded white petals; 3–5 flowers on long equal stalks; in spring with leaves.
Fruit: a cherry ¼" (6 mm) in diameter; red skin; thin sour pulp; large stone; in summer.

Habitat
Moist soil, often in pure stands on burned areas and clearings.

Range
British Columbia and S. Mackenzie east across Canada to Newfoundland, south to N. Georgia, west to Colorado; to 6000′ (1829 m) in southern Appalachians.

Comments
This species is often called Fire Cherry because its seedlings come up rapidly after forest fires. It is also a "nurse" tree, providing cover and shade for the establishment of seedlings of the next generation of larger hardwoods.

American Plum
Prunus americana
418, 455

A thicket-forming shrub or small tree with short trunk, many spreading branches, broad crown, showy large white flowers, and red plums.
Height: 30′ (9 m). Diameter: 1′ (0.3 m).
Leaves: alternate; 2½–4″ (6–10 cm) long, 1¼–1¾″ (3–4.5 cm) wide. Elliptical, long-pointed at tip; sharply and often doubly saw-toothed; slightly thickened. Dull green with slightly sunken veins above, paler and often slightly hairy on veins beneath.
Bark: dark brown; scaly.
Twigs: light brown, slender, hairless.
Flowers: ¾–1″ (2–2.5 cm) wide; with 5 rounded white petals; in clusters of 2–5 on slender equal stalks; slightly unpleasant odor; in early spring before leaves.
Fruit: a plum ¾–1″ (2–2.5 cm) in diameter; thick red skin; juicy sour edible pulp; large stone; maturing in summer.

Habitat
Moist soils of valleys and low upland slopes.

Range
SE. Saskatchewan east to New Hampshire, south to Florida, west to Oklahoma, and north to Montana; to 3000′ (914 m) in the South and to 6000′ (1829 m) in the Southwest.

Comments
The plums are eaten fresh and used in jellies and preserves, and are also consumed by many kinds of birds. Numerous cultivated varieties with improved fruit have been developed.

Black Cherry
Prunus serotina
419, 458

Aromatic tree with tall trunk, oblong crown, abundant small white flowers, and small black cherries; crushed foliage and bark have distinctive cherrylike odor and bitter taste.
Height: 80′ (24 m). Diameter: 2′ (0.6 m).
Leaves: alternate; 2–5″ (5–13 cm) long, 1¼–2″ (3–5 cm) wide. Elliptical; 1–2 dark red glands at base; finely saw-toothed with carved or blunt teeth; slightly thickened. Shiny dark green above, light green and often hairy along midvein beneath; turning yellow or reddish in autumn.
Bark: dark gray; smooth, with horizontal lines; becoming irregularly fissured and scaly, exposing reddish-brown inner bark; bitter and aromatic.
Twigs: red-brown, slender, hairless.

Flowers: ⅜″ (10 mm) wide; 5 rounded, white petals; many
flowers along spreading or drooping axis of 4–6″ (10–15 cm)
at end of leafy twig; in late spring.
Fruit: a cherry ⅜″ (10 mm) in diameter; skin dark red turning
blackish; slightly bitter, juicy, edible pulp; elliptical stone;
maturing in late summer.

Habitat
On many sites except very wet or very dry soils.

Range
S. Quebec to Nova Scotia, south to central Florida, west to E.
Texas, and north to Minnesota; varieties from central Texas
west to Arizona and south to Mexico; to 5000′ (1524 m) in
southern Appalachians and at 4500–7500′ (1372–2286 m) in
the Southwest.

Comments
This widespread species is the largest and most important
native cherry. Black Cherry is quick to appear in an old field,
its seeds spread by birds.

Canyon Live Oak
Quercus chrysolepis
420, 482

Evergreen tree with short trunk, large, spreading, horizontal
branches, and broad, rounded crown; sometimes shrubby.
Height: 20–100′ (6–30 m). Diameter: 1–3′ (0.3–0.9 m).
Leaves: evergreen; alternate; 1–3″ (2.5–7.5 cm) long, ½–
1½″ (1.2–4 cm) wide. Elliptical to oblong; short-pointed at
tip, rounded or blunt at base; with edges turned under and
often with spiny teeth (especially on young twigs); thick and
leathery. Shiny green above; with yellow hairs or becoming
gray and nearly hairless beneath.
Bark: light gray, nearly smooth or scaly.
Acorns: ¾–2″ (2–5 cm) long; variable in size and shape, egg-
shaped, turbanlike with shallow, thick cup of scales densely
covered with yellowish hairs; stalkless or short-stalked;
maturing second year.

Habitat
In canyons and on sandy, gravelly, and rocky slopes; in pure
stands and mixed forests.

Range
SW. Oregon south through Coast Ranges and Sierra Nevada
to S. California; local in W. Nevada and in W. and central
Arizona; at 1000–6500′ (305–1981 m); in Arizona at 5500–
7500′ (1676–2286 m).

Comments
Many consider this to be the most beautiful of the California
oaks. The species name, meaning "golden-scale," refers to the
yellowish acorn cups.

Common Chokecherry
Prunus virginiana
421, 457, 472

Shrub or small tree, often forming dense thickets, with dark
red or blackish chokecherries.
Height: 20′ (6 m). Diameter: 6″ (15 cm).

Leaves: alternate; 1½–3¼" (4–8 cm) long, ⅝–1½" (1.5–4 cm) wide. Elliptical; finely and sharply saw-toothed; slightly thickened. Shiny dark green above, light green and sometimes slightly hairy beneath; turning yellow in autumn. Leafstalks slender, usually with 2 gland-dots.
Bark: brown or gray; smooth or becoming scaly.
Twigs: brown, slender, with disagreeable odor, bitter taste.
Flowers: ½" (12 mm) wide; with 5 rounded white petals; in unbranched clusters to 4" (10 cm) long; in late spring.
Fruit: a chokecherry ¼–⅜" (6–10 mm) in diameter; shiny dark red or blackish skin; juicy, astringent or bitter pulp; large stone; maturing in summer.

Habitat

Moist soils, especially along streams in mountains, forest borders, clearings and roadsides.

Range

N. British Columbia east to Newfoundland, south to W. North Carolina, and west to S. California; to 8000' (2438 m) in the Southwest.

Comments

As the common name suggests, chokecherries are astringent or puckery, especially when immature or raw; but they can be made into preserves and jelly. However, the fruit stones are poisonous; also wilted foliage occasionally contains hydrocyanic acid that can poison livestock.

Apple
Malus sylvestris
422, 452

This familiar fruit tree naturalized locally has a short trunk, spreading rounded crown, showy pink-tinged blossoms, and delicious red fruit.
Height: 30–40' (9–12 m). Diameter: 1–2' (0.3–0.6 m).
Leaves: alternate; 2–3½" (5–9 cm) long, 1¼–2¼" (3–6 cm) wide. Ovate or elliptical; wavy saw-toothed; hairy leafstalk. Green above, densely covered with gray hairs beneath.
Bark: gray; fissured and scaly.
Twigs: greenish, turning brown; densely covered with white hairs when young.
Flowers: 1¼" (3 cm) wide; with 5 rounded petals, white tinged with pink; in early spring.
Fruit: the familiar edible apple; 2–3½" (5–9 cm) in diameter; shiny red or yellow; sunken at ends; thick sweet pulp; star-shaped core contains up to 10 seeds; matures in late summer.

Habitat

Moist soils near houses, fences, roadsides, and clearings.

Range

Native of Europe and western Asia. Naturalized locally across southern Canada, in eastern continental United States, and in Pacific states.

Comments

Although well known, the Apple is sometimes not recognized when growing wild. For nearly fifty years Jonathan Chapman

(1774–1845), better known as Johnny Appleseed, traveling mostly on foot, distributed apple seeds to everybody he met. With seeds from cider presses, he helped to establish orchards from Pennsylvania to Illinois. Wildlife consume quantities of fallen fruit after harvest.

Mexican Plum
Prunus mexicana
423

Small tree with single trunk and open crown.
Height: 20' (6 m). Diameter: 6" (15 cm).
Leaves: alternate; 2–4½" (5–11 cm) long, 1¼–2" (3–5 cm) wide. Elliptical; abruptly long-pointed at tip; base often with glands; finely doubly saw-toothed. Yellow-green and usually hairless above; paler, with soft hairs, and prominently veined beneath. Leafstalks mostly with 1–3 gland-dots near tip.
Bark: gray; scaly, becoming rough and deeply furrowed.
Twigs: light brown, shiny, slender, hairless.
Flowers: ¾" (19 mm) wide; with 5 rounded white petals; 2–4 flowers clustered on equal stalks; in spring before leaves.
Fruit: a plum ½–1" (1.2–2.5 cm) in diameter; skin purplish red with whitish bloom; thick sweetish pulp; large stone; maturing in late summer.

Habitat
Moist soils of valleys and dry uplands, prairies, open areas, and oak forests; not forming thickets.

Range
S. Ohio south to Alabama, west to S. Texas, north to SE. South Dakota; also northeastern Mexico; to 1500' (457 m).

Comments
The common wild plum of the forest-prairie border from Missouri and eastern Kansas to Texas. The fruit is eaten fresh and made into preserves and is also consumed by wildlife.

Prairie Crab Apple
Malus ioensis
424, 451

A sometimes spiny shrub or small tree, with spreading branches and broad, open crown.
Height: 10–30' (3–9 m). Diameter: 1' (0.3 m).
Leaves: alternate; 2½–4" (6–10 cm) long, 1–1½" (2.5–4 cm) wide. Elliptical; wavy saw-toothed, often slightly lobed; with prominent veins; slightly thickened; hairy when young; leafstalks slender and hairy. Shiny dark green above, paler and hairy beneath; turning yellow in autumn.
Bark: reddish brown; scaly.
Twigs: reddish brown; hairy when young.
Flowers: 1½–2" (4–5 cm) wide; 5 rounded pink or white petals; in clusters, on long stalks; in spring.
Fruit: 1–1¼" (2.5–3 cm) in diameter; like a small apple; yellow-green, long-stalked; maturing in late summer.

Habitat
Moist soils along streams in prairie and forest borders.

Range
N. Indiana south to Arkansas and Oklahoma, and north to

extreme SE. South Dakota; local in central Texas and
Louisiana; at 500–1500' (152–457 m).

Comments
This is the crab apple of the eastern prairie region in the upper
Mississippi Valley. Numerous species of birds, including
bobwhites and pheasants, and squirrels, rabbits, and other
mammals consume the fruit.

Coast Live Oak
Quercus agrifolia
425

Evergreen tree with short, stout trunk; many large, crooked,
spreading branches; and broad, rounded crown.
Height: 30–80' (9–24 m). Diameter: 1–3' (0.3–0.9 m).
Leaves: evergreen; alternate; ¾–2½" (2–6 cm) long, ½–1½"
(1.2–4 cm) wide. Oblong or elliptical, short-pointed or
rounded at both ends; with edges turned under and bearing
spiny teeth; thick and leathery. Shiny dark green above,
yellow-green and often hairy beneath.
Bark: dark brown, thick, deeply furrowed.
Acorns: 1–1½" (2.5–4 cm) long; narrowly egg-shaped, one-
third enclosed by deep, thin cup with many brownish, finely
hairy scales outside and silky hairs inside; 1 or few together;
stalkless; maturing first year.

Habitat
In valleys and on slopes, usually in open groves; often with
Canyon Live Oak and California Black Oak.

Range
Coast Ranges mostly, central to S. California, including Santa
Cruz and Santa Rosa islands; also N. Baja California; to about
3000' (914 m).

Comments
This is the common oak of the California coast and foothills.
The acorns were among those preferred by Indians; after
removing the shells, they ground the seeds into meal, which
was washed to remove the bitter taste, and boiled into mush
or baked in ashes as bread.

European Buckthorn
Rhamnus cathartica
426

Introduced, ornamental, spiny shrub or sometimes small tree.
Height: 20' (6 m). Diameter: 4" (10 cm).
Leaves: mostly opposite or clustered on short spurs; ¾–2½"
(2–6 cm) long, ¾–2" (2–5 cm) wide. Broadly elliptical;
finely wavy-toothed; with few long curved side veins; hairless
or nearly so; slender-stalked. Green above, paler beneath;
falling in late autumn.
Bark: brown; smooth, peeling off in thin curly strips to reveal
reddish inner bark.
Twigs: gray; often paired and with short spurs; slender,
hairless or nearly so; ending in narrow pointed scaly buds or
sharp spines; sometimes thornless.
Flowers: ³⁄₁₆" (5 mm) wide; bell-shaped with 4 spreading
pointed greenish-yellow sepals; clustered on stalks at leaf bases;
male and female generally on separate plants; in late spring.

Fruit: ⁵⁄₁₆″ (8 mm) in diameter; berrylike; black; with bitter pulp; usually 4 seeds; maturing in late summer and autumn.

Habitat
Dry soils in open woods, clearings, and along fences and roadsides; spread by birds.

Range
Native of Europe and Asia. Naturalized locally from S. Ontario east to Nova Scotia, south to North Carolina, west to NE. Kansas, and north to North Dakota.

Comments
The hardy, thorny shrubs can be sheared into good hedges. Widely planted in Europe for centuries. The fruit has been used medicinally as a cathartic, hence the Latin species name.

Oneflower Hawthorn
Crataegus uniflora
27

A low spreading shrub or sometimes a small bushy tree, with short, stout trunks and dense, rounded crown of stout, crooked branches.
Height: 2–5′ (0.6–1.5 m), sometimes to 16′ (5 m).
Diameter: 6″ (15 cm).
Leaves: alternate; ¾–1½″ (2–4 cm) long, ½–1¼″ (1.2–3.2 cm) wide. Spoon-shaped, broadest beyond middle and tapering to almost stalkless base; coarsely and wavy saw-toothed, sometimes lobed; slightly thick; with sunken veins. Shiny dark green, rough, and becoming hairless above, paler and hairy beneath.
Bark: gray-brown; smooth, becoming fissured into scaly plates near base.
Twigs: stiff, hairy, with many slender spines.
Flowers: nearly ⅝″ (15 mm) wide; with 5 white petals, about 20 pale yellow or white stamens, and 3–5 styles; usually solitary (sometimes 2–3); in late spring after leaves.
Fruit: to ½″ (12 mm) in diameter; rounded; yellow to dull red to brown; large gland-toothed calyx at tip; hard dry mealy pulp; 3–5 nutlets; maturing in late summer or autumn.

Habitat
Dry sandy and rocky uplands in open woods, forest borders, and old fields.

Range
New York (Long Island) and New Jersey south to N. Florida, west to E. Texas, and northeast to S. Missouri; to 2000′ (610 m) or above.

Comments
This species occurs in tree form only in northern Florida. Sometimes planted as a curiosity in botanical gardens because of its dwarf size.

Gray Birch
Betula populifolia
428

Small, bushy tree with open, conical crown of short slender branches reaching nearly to the ground; more often a clump of several slightly leaning trunks from an old stump.

Height: 30' (9 m). Diameter: 1' (0.3 m).
Leaves: alternate; 2–3" (5–7.5 cm) long, 1½–2½" (4–6 cm)
wide. Triangular, tapering from near base to long-pointed tip
sharply and double saw-toothed; usually with 4–8 veins on
each side; leafstalks slender, with black gland-dots. Shiny dark
green above, paler with tufts of hairs along midvein beneath;
turning pale yellow in autumn.
Bark: chalky or grayish white; smooth, thin, not papery;
becoming darker and fissured at base.
Twigs: reddish brown, slender, with warty gland-dots.
Flowers: tiny; in early spring. Male yellowish, with 2 stamens
many in long drooping catkins near tip of twigs. Female
greenish, in short upright catkins back of tip of same twig.
Cones: ¾–1¼" (2–3 cm) long; cylindrical, brownish,
spreading, short-stalked; with many hairy scales and hairy
2-winged nutlets; maturing in autumn.

Habitat
Dry barren uplands, also on moist soils, in mixed woodlands.

Range

S. Ontario east to Cape Breton Island, south to Pennsylvania
and New Jersey; local to W. North Carolina and NW.
Indiana; to 2000' (610 m).

Comments
A pioneer tree on clearings, abandoned farms, and burned
areas, Gray Birch grows rapidly but is short-lived. A nurse
tree, it shades and protects seedlings of the larger, long-lived
forest trees.

Paper Birch
Betula papyrifera
429

One of the most beautiful native trees, with narrow, open
crown of slightly drooping to nearly horizontal branches;
sometimes a shrub.
Height: 50–70' (15–21 m). Diameter: 1–2' (0.3–0.6 m).
Leaves: alternate; 2–4" (5–10 cm) long, 1½–2" (4–5 cm)
wide. Ovate, long-pointed; coarsely and doubly saw-toothed;
usually with 5–9 veins on each side. Dull dark green above,
light yellow-green and nearly hairless beneath; turning light
yellow in autumn.
Bark: chalky to creamy white; smooth, thin, with long
horizontal lines; separating into papery strips to reveal orange
inner bark; becoming brown, furrowed, and scaly at base;
bronze to purplish in varieties.
Twigs: reddish brown, slender, mostly hairless.
Flowers: tiny; in early spring. Male yellowish, with 2 stamens
many in long drooping catkins near tip of twigs. Female
greenish, in short upright catkins back of tip of same twig.
Cones: 1½–2" (4–5 cm); narrowly cylindrical, brownish,
hanging on slender stalk; with many 2-winged nutlets;
maturing in autumn.

Habitat
Moist upland soils and cutover lands; often in nearly pure
stands.

Range
Transcontinental across North America near northern limit of trees from NW. Alaska east to Labrador, south to New York, and west to Oregon; local south to N. Colorado and W. North Carolina; to 4000' (1219 m), higher in southern mountains.

Comments
Indians made their lightweight birchbark canoes by stretching the stripped bark over frames of Northern White-cedar, sewing it with thread from Tamarack roots, and caulking the seams with pine or Balsam Fir resin.

Quaking Aspen
Populus tremuloides
0

The most widely distributed tree in North America; with a narrow, rounded crown of thin foliage.
Height: 40–70' (12–21 m). Diameter: 1–1½' (0.3–0.5 m).
Leaves: alternate; 1¼–3" (3–7.5 cm) long. Nearly round; abruptly short-pointed; rounded at base; finely saw-toothed; thin. Shiny green above, dull green beneath; turning golden yellow in autumn before shedding. Leafstalks slender, flattened.
Bark: whitish, smooth, thin; on very large trunks becoming dark gray, furrowed, and thick.
Twigs: shiny brown; slender, hairless.
Flowers: catkins 1–2½" (2.5–6 cm) long; brownish; male and female on separate trees; in early spring before leaves.
Fruit: ¼" (6 mm) long; narrowly conical light green capsules in drooping catkins to 4" (10 cm) long; maturing in late spring and splitting in 2 parts. Many tiny cottony seeds; rarely produced in the West, where propagation is by root sprouts.

Habitat
Many soil types, especially sandy and gravelly slopes; often in pure stands.

Range
Across northern North America from Alaska to Newfoundland, south to Virginia, and in Rocky Mountains south to S. Arizona and northern Mexico; from near sea level northward to 6500–10,000' (1981–3048 m) southward.

Comments
The names refer to the leaves, which in the slightest breeze tremble on their flattened leafstalks. A pioneer tree after fires and logging and on abandoned fields, it is short-lived and replaced by conifers. The twigs and foliage are browsed by deer, elk, and moose, also by sheep and goats. Beavers, rabbits, and other mammals eat the bark, foliage, and buds, and grouse and quail feed on the winter buds.

Balsam Poplar
Populus balsamifera
1

Large tree with narrow, open crown of upright branches and fragrant, resinous buds with strong balsam odor.
Height: 60–80' (18–24 m). Diameter: 1–3' (0.3–0.9 m).
Leaves: 3–5" (7.5–13 cm) long, 1½–3" (4–7.5 cm) wide. Ovate, pointed at tip, rounded or slightly notched at base;

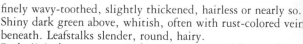

finely wavy-toothed, slightly thickened, hairless or nearly so.
Shiny dark green above, whitish, often with rust-colored veir
beneath. Leafstalks slender, round, hairy.
Bark: light brown, smooth; becoming gray and furrowed into
flat, scaly ridges.
Twigs: brownish, stout, with large, gummy or sticky buds
producing fragrant, yellowish resin.
Flowers: catkins 2–3½" (5–9 cm) long; brownish; male and
female on separate trees; in early spring.
Fruit: ⁵⁄₁₆" (8 mm) long; egg-shaped capsules, pointed, light
brown, hairless; maturing in spring and splitting into 2 parts
many tiny, cottony seeds.

Habitat
Moist soils of valleys, mainly stream banks, sandbars, and
floodplains, also lower slopes; often in pure stands.

Range

Across North America along northern limit of trees from NW
Alaska, south to SE. British Columbia, and east to
Newfoundland, south to Pennsylvania and west to Iowa; local
south to Colorado and in eastern mountains to West Virginia
to 5500' (1676 m) in Rocky Mountains.

Comments
The northernmost New World hardwood, Balsam Poplar
extends in scattered groves to Alaska's Arctic Slope. Balm-of-
Gilead Poplar, an ornamental with broad, open crown and
larger, heart-shaped leaves, is a clone or hybrid.

Eastern Cottonwood
Populus deltoides
432

Large tree with a massive trunk often forked into stout
branches, and broad, open crown of spreading and slightly
drooping branches.
Height: 100' (30 m). Diameter: 3–4' (0.9–1.2 m).
Leaves: alternate; 3–7" (7.5–18 cm) long, 3–5" (7.5–13 cm)
wide. Triangular; long-pointed; usually straight at base;
curved, coarse teeth; slightly thickened; shiny green, turning
yellow in autumn. Leafstalks long, slender, flattened.
Bark: yellowish green and smooth; becoming light gray,
thick, rough, and deeply furrowed.
Twigs: brownish; stout, with large resinous or sticky buds.
Flowers: catkins 2–3½" (5–9 cm) long; brownish; male and
female on separate trees; in early spring.
Fruit: ⅜" (10 mm) long; elliptical capsules, light brown;
maturing in spring and splitting into 3–4 parts; many on
stalks in catkin to 8" (20 cm) long; many tiny cottony seeds.

Habitat
Bordering streams and in wet soils in valleys; in pure stands o
often with willows. Pioneers on new sandbars and bare
floodplains.

Range

Widespread. S. Alberta east to extreme S. Quebec and New
Hampshire, south to NW. Florida, west to W. Texas, and

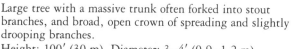

north to central Montana; to 1000′ (305 m) in East, to 5000′ (1524 m) in West.

Comments
Scarcely a riverbank in the West is not lined with Eastern Cottonwoods, which are also planted for shade and shelterbelts. Although short-lived, it is one of the fastest-growing native trees; on favorable sites in the Mississippi Valley, trees average 5′ (1.5 m) in height growth annually with as much as 13′ (4 m) the first year.

gtooth Aspen
pulus grandidentata
3

Medium-sized tree with narrow, rounded crown.
Height: 30–60′ (9–18 m). Diameter: 1–1½′ (0.3–0.5 m).
Leaves: alternate; 2½–4″ (6–10 cm) long, 1¾–3½″ (4.5–9 cm) wide. Broadly ovate; short-pointed tip; rounded at base; coarse, curved teeth; with white hairs when young. Dull green above, paler beneath, turning pale yellow in autumn. Leafstalks long, slender, flattened.
Bark: greenish, smooth, thin; becoming dark brown and furrowed into flat, scaly ridges.
Twigs: brown, slender, hairy when young.
Flowers: catkins 1½–2½″ (4–6 cm) long; brownish; male and female on separate trees; in early spring.
Fruit: ¼″ (6 mm) long; narrowly conical capsules; light green; slightly curved; finely hairy; maturing in spring and splitting into 2 parts; many tiny cottony seeds.

Habitat
Sandy upland soils, also floodplains of streams, often with Quaking Aspen.

Range
SE. Manitoba east to Cape Breton Island, south to Virginia, and west to NE. Missouri; local south to W. North Carolina; to 2000′ (610 m), or to 3000′ (914 m) in south.

Comments
Bigtooth Aspen is a pioneer tree after fires and logging and on abandoned fields, short-lived and replaced by other species. The foliage, twig buds, and bark are consumed by wildlife.

iltmore Hawthorn
rataegus intricata
34, 454

Much-branched, thicket-forming shrub or small tree with irregular, open crown.
Height: 20′ (6 m). Diameter: 6′ (15 cm).
Leaves: alternate; 1–2½″ (2.5–6 cm) long, 1–2″ (2.5–5 cm) wide. Elliptical or broadly ovate; mostly blunt at ends; sharply or doubly saw-toothed, with gland-tipped teeth; often shallowly lobed; hairless or nearly so. Green above, paler beneath. Stout leafstalks often with gland-dots.
Bark: brown or gray; scaly.
Twigs: hairless, with long spines.
Flowers: ⅝″ (15 mm) wide; with 5 white petals, 10 pale yellow or pink stamens, and 3–5 styles; short-stalked; usually 4–8 flowers in compact, slightly hairy clusters; in late spring.

Fruit: nearly ½″ (12 mm) in diameter; rounded to elliptical, greenish or reddish brown; large gland-toothed calyx often shedding early; thick hard dry pulp; 3–5 nutlets; maturing and usually falling in autumn.

Habitat
Dry uplands and moist valleys, open areas, borders of woods, and stream banks.

Range
S. Ontario east to New Hampshire, south to Georgia, west to SE. Oklahoma, and north to S. Michigan; to 3000′ (914 m) southern Appalachians.

Comments
The common name honors the Biltmore Estate in North Carolina, where early studies of hawthorns were made.

Fanleaf Hawthorn
Crataegus flabellata
435

Much-branched shrub or small tree with irregular crown.
Height: 20′ (6 m). Diameter: 6″ (15 cm).
Leaves: alternate; 1½–3″ (4–7.5 cm) long, 1¼–2½″ (3–6 cm) wide. Broadly ovate or fan-shaped; short- or long-pointed at tip, blunt or rounded at base; sharply and doubly saw-toothed with 4–6 shallow lobes. Green, becoming nearly hairless above, paler beneath; yellow and brown in autumn.
Bark: dark gray or brown; scaly.
Twigs: stout, hairless, with many long slender curved spines.
Flowers: ⅝″ (15 mm) or more wide; with 5 white petals, 5–20 dark red stamens, and 3–5 styles; 5–15 flowers on slender stalks in compact hairless clusters; in spring.
Fruit: ½″ (12 mm) in diameter; rounded; red; soft sweet pulp 3–5 nutlets; few in drooping clusters; maturing in autumn.

Habitat
Rocky upland soils in thickets, borders of forests, pastures, and old fields.

Range
Newfoundland and Nova Scotia south to Georgia, west to Louisiana, and north to Minnesota; to 3000′ (914 m), locally in southern Appalachians to 6000′ (1829 m).

Comments
One of the common hawthorns, known also by the scientific name *Crataegus macrosperma*. There are innumerable species of hawthorn. Quite difficult to distinguish, many of them grow as invaders in old fields.

Sweetgum
Liquidambar styraciflua
436, 481

Large, aromatic tree with straight trunk and conical crown that becomes round and spreading.
Height: 60–100′ (18–30 m). Diameter: 1½–3′ (0.5–0.9 m)
Leaves: alternate; 3–6″ (7.5–15 cm) long and wide. Star-shaped or maplelike, with 5, sometimes 7, long-pointed, finely saw-toothed lobes and 5 main veins from notched base; with resinous odor when crushed; leafstalks slender, nearly as

long as blades. Shiny dark green above; reddish in autumn.
Bark: gray; deeply furrowed into narrow scaly ridges.
Twigs: green to brown, stout, often forming corky wings.
Flowers: tiny; in greenish ball-like clusters in spring; male in
several clusters along a stalk; female in drooping cluster on
same tree.
Fruit: 1–1¼" (2.5–3 cm) in diameter; a long-stalked
drooping brown ball composed of many individual fruits, each
ending in 2 long curved prickly points and each with 1–2
long-winged seeds; maturing in autumn and persisting.

Habitat
Moist soils of valleys and lower slopes; in mixed woodlands.
Often a pioneer after logging, clearing, and in old fields.

Range
Extreme SW. Connecticut south to central Florida, west to
E. Texas, and north to S. Illinois; also a variety in eastern
Mexico; to 3000' (914 m) in southern Appalachians.

Comments
A frequent old-field invader in the Southern and Middle
Atlantic states, Sweetgum is also an important timber tree,
second in production only to oaks among hardwoods. In
pioneer days, a gum was obtained from the trunks by peeling
the bark and scraping off the resinlike solid.

Blackjack Oak
Quercus marilandica
37

Tree with irregular crown of crooked, spreading branches.
Height: 20–50' (6–15 m). Diameter: 6–12" (15–30 cm).
Leaves: alternate; 2½–5" (6–13 cm) long, 2–4" (5–10 cm)
wide. Slightly triangular or broadly obovate, broadest near tip
with 3 shallow broad bristle-tipped lobes; gradually narrowed
to rounded base; slightly thickened. Shiny yellow-green above,
light yellow-green with brownish hairs (especially along veins)
beneath; turning brown or yellow in fall.
Bark: blackish; rough, thick, deeply furrowed into broad,
nearly square plates.
Acorns: ⅝–¾" (15–19 mm) long; elliptical, ending in stout
point; one-third to two-thirds enclosed by deep, thick, top-
shaped cup of rusty brown, hairy, loosely overlapping scales;
short-stalked; maturing second year.

Habitat
Dry sandy and clay soils in upland ridges and slopes with
other oaks and with pines.

Range
Long Island and New Jersey south to NW. Florida, west to
central and SE. Texas, and north to SE. Iowa; local in S.
Michigan; to 3000' (914 m).

Comments
This species and Post Oak form the Cross Timbers in Texas
and Oklahoma, the forest border of small trees and transition
zone to prairie grassland.

California Black Oak
Quercus kelloggii
438

Tree with large branches and irregular, broad, rounded crown of stout, spreading branches.
Height: 30–80′ (9–24 m). Diameter: 1–3′ (0.3–0.9 m).
Leaves: alternate; 3–8″ (7.5–20 cm) long, 2–5″ (5–13 cm) wide. Elliptical, usually 7-lobed about halfway to midvein, each lobe with few bristle-pointed teeth; slightly thick. Shiny dark green above, light yellow-green and often hairy beneath; turning yellow or brown in autumn.
Bark: dark brown, thick, becoming furrowed into irregular plates and ridges; on small trunks, smooth, light brown.
Acorns: 1–1½″ (2.5–4 cm) long; elliptical, one-third to two-thirds enclosed by deep, thin, scaly cup; 1 or few on short stalk; maturing second year.

Habitat
Sandy, gravelly, and rocky soils of foothills and mountains; often in nearly pure stands and in mixed coniferous forests.

Range
SW. Oregon south in Coast Ranges and Sierra Nevada to S. California; at 1000–8000′ (305–2438 m).

Comments
This is the common oak in valleys of southwestern Oregon and in the Sierra Nevada. The large, deeply lobed leaves with bristle-tipped teeth differ from all other western oaks.

Bur Oak
Quercus macrocarpa
439

Tree with very large acorns, stout trunk, and broad, rounded, open crown of stout, often crooked, spreading branches; sometimes a shrub.
Height: 50–80′ (15–24 m). Diameter: 2–4′ (0.6–1.2 m).
Leaves: alternate; 4–10 ″ (10–25 cm) long, 2–5″ (5–13 cm) wide. Obovate, broadest beyond middle, lower half deeply divided into 2–3 lobes on each side; upper half usually with 5–7 shallow rounded lobes on each side to broad rounded tip. Dark green and slightly shiny above, gray-green and with fine hairs beneath; turning yellow or brown in fall.
Bark: light gray; thick, rough, furrowed into scaly ridges.
Acorns: large; ¾–2″ (2–5 cm) long and wide; broadly elliptical, large deep cup with hairy gray scales (the upper scales very long-pointed), forming fringelike border; maturing first year.

Habitat
From dry uplands on limestone and gravelly ridges, sandy plains, and loamy slopes to moist floodplains of streams; often in nearly pure stands.

Range
Extreme SE. Saskatchewan east to S. New Brunswick, south to Tennessee, west to SE. Texas and north to North Dakota; local in Louisiana and Alabama. Usually at 300–2000′ (91–610 m) to 3000′ (914 m) or above in Northwest.

Comments
Bur Oak is the most characteristic tree of the prairies,

bordering and invading the grassland, individual trees often surviving in isolated splendor.

Valley Oak
Quercus lobata
440, 483

Large, handsome tree with stout, short trunk and large, widely spreading branches drooping at ends, forming broad, open crown.
Height: 40–100′ (12–30 m). Diameter: 3–4′ (0.9–1.2 m), sometimes much greater.
Leaves: alternate; 2–4″ (5–10 cm) long and 1¼–2½″ (3–6 cm) wide. Elliptical, rounded or blunt at both ends; deeply 7- to 11-lobed more than halfway to midvein, larger lobes broadest and notched at end. Dark green and nearly hairless above, paler and finely hairy beneath.
Bark: light gray or brown; thick, deeply furrowed and broken horizontally into thick plates.
Acorns: 1¼–2¼″ (3–6 cm) long; oblong, pointed, one-third enclosed by deep, half-round cup with light brown scales, the lowest ones thick and warty or knobby; sweetish and edible; maturing first year.

Habitat
Valleys and slopes on rich loam soils; forming groves in foothill woodland.

Range
N. to S. California, also Santa Cruz and Santa Catalina islands; to 5000′ (1524 m).

Comments
Valley Oak is the largest of the western deciduous oaks and a handsome, graceful shade tree. It is common through California's interior valleys.

Post Oak
Quercus stellata
441

Tree with dense, rounded crown and distinctive leaves suggesting a Maltese cross; sometimes a shrub.
Height: 30–70′ (9–21 m). Diameter: 1–2′ (0.3–0.6 m).
Leaves: alternate; 3¼–6″ (8–15 cm) long, 2–4″ (5–10 cm) wide. Obovate; with 5–7 deep broad rounded lobes, 2 middle lobes largest; with short-pointed base and rounded tip; slightly thickened. Shiny dark green and slightly rough with scattered hairs above, gray-green with tiny star-shaped hairs beneath; turning brown in fall.
Bark: light gray; fissured into scaly ridges.
Acorns: ½–1″ (1.2–2.5 cm) long; elliptical, a third to a half enclosed by deep cup; green becoming brown; usually stalkless or short-stalked; maturing first year.

Habitat
Sandy, gravelly, and rocky ridges, also moist loamy soils of floodplains along streams; sometimes in pure stands.

Range
SE. Massachusetts south to central Florida, west to NW. Texas, and north to SE. Iowa; to 3000′ (914 m).

Comments
Of large size in the lower Mississippi Valley, where it is
known as Delta Post Oak. Post Oak and Blackjack Oak form
the Cross Timbers in Texas and Oklahoma, the forest border
of small trees and transition zone to prairie grassland.

Sassafras
Sassafras albidum
442, 466

Aromatic tree or thicket-forming shrub with variously shaped
leaves and narrow, spreading crown of short, stout branches.
Height: 30–60′ (9–18 m). Diameter: 1½′ (0.5 m),
sometimes larger.
Leaves: 3–5″ (7.5–13 cm) long, 1½–4″ (4–10 cm) wide.
Elliptical, often with 2 mitten-shaped lobes or 3 broad and
blunt lobes; not toothed; base short-pointed; long slender
leafstalks. Shiny green above, paler and often hairy beneath;
turning yellow, orange, or red in autumn.
Bark: gray-brown; becoming thick and deeply furrowed.
Twigs: greenish, slender, sometimes hairy.
Flowers: ⅜″ (10 mm) long; yellow-green; several clustered at
end of leafless twigs in early spring; male and female usually
on separate trees.
Fruit: ⅜″ (10 mm) long; elliptical shiny bluish-black berries;
each in red cup on long red stalk, containing 1 shiny brown
seed; maturing in autumn.

Habitat
Moist, particularly sandy, soils of uplands and valleys, often in
old fields, clearings, and forest openings.

Range
Extreme S. Ontario east to SW. Maine, south to central
Florida, west to E. Texas, and north to central Michigan; to
5000′ (1524 m) in southern Appalachians.

Comments
A frequent invader in old fields, Sassafras spreads rapidly by
underground stems. The roots and root bark supply oil of
sassafras (used to perfume soap) and sassafras tea, and have
been used to flavor root beer.

Gregg Catclaw
Acacia greggii
443, 462

Spiny, much-branched, thicket-forming shrub; occasionally a
small tree with a broad crown.
Height: 20′ (6 m). Diameter: 6″ (15 cm).
Leaves: clustered; bipinnately compound; 1–3″ (2.5–7.5 cm)
long; the slender axis usually with 2–3 pairs of side axes. 3–7
pairs of leaflets ⅛–¼″ (3–6 mm) long; oblong; rounded at
ends; thick; usually hairy; almost stalkless; dull green.
Bark: gray; thin, becoming deeply furrowed.
Twigs: brown, slender, angled, covered with fine hairs; with
many scattered stout spines ¼″ (6 mm) long, hooked or
curved backward.
Flowers: ¼″ (6 mm) long; light yellow; fragrant; stalkless;
including many tiny stamens in long narrow clusters 1–2″
(2.5–5 cm) long; in early spring and irregularly in summer.

Fruit: 2½–5″ (6–13 cm) long, ½–¾″ (12–19 mm) wide;
thin, flat, ribbonlike, oblong pod; brown, curved, much
twisted, often narrowed between seeds; maturing in summer
and shedding in winter, remaining closed; several beanlike,
nearly round, flat, brown seeds.

Habitat
Washes, slopes, and rocky canyons, especially limestone soils,
desert, and desert grassland; forming impenetrable thickets.

Range
Central, S., and Trans-Pecos Texas west to S. Nevada and SE.
California, south to northern Mexico; to 5000′ (1524 m).

Comments
One of the most despised southwestern shrubs. As indicated
by the common names (including the Spanish, *uña de gato*),
the sharp, stout, hooked spines, like a cat's claws, tear
clothing and flesh.

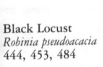

Black Locust
Robinia pseudoacacia
444, 453, 484

Medium-sized, spiny tree with a forking, often crooked and
angled trunk and irregular, open crown of upright branches.
Height: 40–80′ (12–24 m). Diameter: 1–2′ (0.3–0.6 m).
Leaves: alternate; pinnately compound; 6–12″ (15–30 cm)
long. 7–19 leaflets 1–1¾″ (2.5–4.5 cm) long, ½–¾″
(12–19 mm) wide; paired (except at end); elliptical; with tiny
bristle tip; without teeth; hairy when young; drooping and
folding at night. Dark blue-green above, pale and usually
hairless beneath.
Bark: light gray; thick, deeply furrowed into long rough
forking ridges.
Twigs: dark brown, with stout paired spines ¼–½″
(6–12 mm) long at nodes.
Flowers: ¾″ (19 mm) long; petals unequal; 1 broad upper
petal and 2 lateral petals nearly enclosing 2 lower petals that
are joined and shaped like prow of a boat; white, with the
largest yellow near base; very fragrant; in showy drooping
clusters 4–8″ (10–20 cm) long at base of leaves; in late
spring.
Fruit: 2–4″ (5–10 cm) long; narrowly oblong flat pod; dark
brown; maturing in autumn, remaining attached into winter
months, splitting open; 3–14 dark brown, flattened, beanlike
seeds.

Habitat
Moist to dry sandy and rocky soils, especially in old fields and
other open areas, and in woodlands.

Range
Central Pennsylvania and S. Ohio south to NE. Alabama, and
from S. Missouri to E. Oklahoma; naturalized from Maine to
California and in southern Canada; from 500′ (152 m) to
above 5000′ (1524) in southern Appalachians.

Comments
Black Locust is widely planted for ornament and shelterbelts,

and for erosion control particularly on lands strip-mined for coal. Although it grows rapidly and spreads by sprouts like a weed, it is short-lived.

Honey Mesquite
Prosopis glandulosa
445, 461, 485

Spiny, large, thicket-forming shrub or small tree with short trunk, open spreading crown of crooked branches, and narrow beanlike pods.
Height: 20' (6 m). Diameter: 1' (0.3 m).
Leaves: alternate; bipinnately compound; 3–8" (7.5–20 cm) long; the short axis bearing 1 pair of side axes or forks, each fork with 7–17 pairs of stalkless leaflets ⅜–1¼" (1–3.2 cm) long; narrowly oblong; hairless or nearly so; yellow-green.
Bark: dark brown; rough, thick, becoming shreddy.
Twigs: slightly zigzag; with stout, yellowish, mostly paired spines ¼–1" (0.6–2.5 cm) long at enlarged nodes, which afterwards bear short spurs.
Flowers: ¼" (6 mm) long; nearly stalkless, light yellow; fragrant; crowded in narrow clusters 2–3" (5–7.5 cm) long; in spring and summer.
Fruit: 3½–8" (9–20 cm) long, less than ⅜" (10 mm) wide; narrow pod ending in long narrow point, slightly flattened, wavy-margined between seeds; sweetish pulp; maturing in summer, remaining closed; several beanlike seeds within 4-sided case.

Habitat
Sandy plains and sandhills and along valleys and washes; in shortgrass, desert grasslands, and deserts.

Range
E. Texas and SW. Oklahoma west to extreme SW. Utah and S. California; also northern Mexico; naturalized north to Kansas and SE. Colorado; to 450' (1372 m).

Comments
Cattlemen regard mesquites as range weeds and eradicate them. In sandy soils, dunes often form around shrubby mesquites, burying them except for a rounded mass of branching tips.

Huisache
Acacia farnesiana
446, 463

Spiny much-branched shrub or small tree with a widely spreading, flattened crown and yellow balls of tiny flowers.
Height: 16' (5 m). Diameter: 4" (10 cm).
Leaves: alternate or clustered; bipinnately compound; 2–4" (5–10 cm) long; usually with 3–5 pairs of side axes. 10–20 pairs of leaflets ⅛–¼" (3–6 mm) long; oblong; mostly hairless; stalkless; gray-green.
Bark: grayish brown; thin; smooth or scaly.
Twigs: slightly zigzag, slender, covered with fine hairs when young; with straight, slender, paired white spines at nodes.
Flowers: 3/16" (5 mm) long; yellow or orange; very fragrant; including many tiny stamens clustered in stalked balls ½" (12 mm) in diameter; mainly in late winter and early spring.

Fruit: 1½–3″ (4–7.5 cm) long, ⅜–½″ (10–12 mm) in diameter; a cylindrical pod; short-pointed at ends, dark brown or black, hard; maturing in summer, remaining attached, often opening late; many elliptical flattened brown seeds.

Habitat
Sandy and clay soils, especially in open areas, borders of woodlands, and roadsides.

Range
S. Texas and local in S. Arizona; cultivated and naturalized from Florida west to Texas and S. California; also in Mexico; to 5000′ (1524 m).

Comments
In southern Europe this species is extensively planted for the "cassie" flowers, which are a perfume ingredient. After drying in the shade, the flowers can be used in sachets to keep clothes smelling fragrant. The tender foliage and pods are browsed by livestock; it is also a honey plant.

Staghorn Sumac
Rhus typhina
447, 471

Tall shrub or small tree with irregular, open, flat crown of a few stout, spreading branches; whitish sticky sap turns black on exposure.
Height: 30′ (9 m). Diameter: 8″ (20 cm), sometimes larger.
Leaves: alternate; pinnately compound; 12–24″ (30–61 cm) long; with stout, soft, hairy, reddish-tinged axis. 11–31 leaflets 2–4″ (5–10 cm) long; lance-shaped; often slightly curved; saw-toothed; nearly stalkless. Dark green above, whitish (with reddish hairs when young) beneath; turning bright red with purple and orange in autumn.
Bark: dark brown; thin; smooth or becoming scaly.
Twigs: few, very stout, brittle, dense velvety covering of long, brown hairs.
Flowers: ⅛–³⁄₁₆″ (3–5 mm) wide; with greenish petals; crowded in upright clusters to 8″ (20 cm) long; branches densely covered with hairs; male and female usually on separate plants; in early summer.
Fruit: ³⁄₁₆″ (5 mm) in diameter; rounded, 1-seeded, dark red, covered with long dark red hairs; numerous, crowded in upright clusters; maturing in late summer and autumn, remaining attached in winter.

Habitat
Open uplands, edges of forests, roadsides, and old fields.

Range
S. Ontario east to Nova Scotia, south to NW. South Carolina, west to Tennessee, and north to Minnesota; to 5000′ (1524 m) in the Southeast.

Comments
Staghorn Sumac reaches tree size more often than related species and commonly forms thickets. In winter, the bare, widely forking, stout, hairy twigs resemble deer antlers "in velvet," hence the alternate common name, Velvet Sumac.

Smooth Sumac
Rhus glabra
448, 465

The most common sumac; a large shrub or sometimes a small tree with open, flattened crown of a few stout, spreading branches and with whitish sap.
Height: 20' (6 m). Diameter: 4" (10 cm).
Leaves: alternate; pinnately compound; 12" (30 cm) long; with slender axis. 11–31 leaflets 2–4" (5–10 cm) long; lance-shaped; saw-toothed; hairless; almost stalkless. Shiny green above, whitish beneath; turning reddish in autumn.
Bark: brown; smooth or becoming scaly.
Twigs: gray, with whitish bloom; few, very stout, hairless.
Flowers: less than ⅛" (3 mm) wide; with 5 whitish petals; crowded in large upright clusters to 8" (20 cm) long, with hairless branches; male and female usually on separate plants; in early summer.
Fruit: more than ⅛" (3 mm) in diameter; rounded, 1-seeded, numerous, crowded in upright clusters; dark red, covered with short sticky red hairs; maturing in late summer, remaining attached in winter.

Habitat
Open uplands including edges of forests, grasslands, clearings, roadsides, and waste places, especially in sandy soils.

Range
E. Saskatchewan east to S. Ontario and Maine, south to NW. Florida, and west to central Texas; also in mountains from S. British Columbia south to SE. Arizona and in northern Mexico; to 4500' (1372 m) in the East; to 7000' (2134 m) in the West.

Comments
The only shrub or tree species native to all 48 contiguous states. Deer browse the twigs and fruit throughout the year. It is also consumed by birds of many kinds and small mammals, mainly in winter.

Shining Sumac
Rhus copallina
449, 464

Shrub or small tree with a short trunk and open crown of stout, spreading branches.
Height: 25' (7.6 m). Diameter: 6" (15 cm).
Leaves: alternate; pinnately compound; to 12" (30 cm) long; with flat broad-winged axis. 7–17 leaflets (27 in southeastern variety) 1–3¼" (2.5–8 cm) long; lance-shaped; usually without teeth; slightly thickened. Shiny dark green and nearly hairless above, paler and covered with fine hairs beneath; turning dark reddish purple in autumn; stalkless.
Bark: light brown or gray; scaly.
Twigs: brown, stout, slightly zigzag, covered with fine hairs; with watery sap.
Flowers: ⅛" (3 mm) wide; with 5 greenish-white petals; crowded in spreading clusters to 3" (13 cm) wide, with hairy branches; male and female usually on separate plants; in late summer.
Fruit: more than ⅛" (3 mm) in diameter; 1-seeded; crowded in clusters; rounded and slightly flattened, dark red, covered

with short sticky red hairs; maturing in autumn, remaining attached in winter.

Habitat
Open uplands, valleys, edges of forests, grasslands, clearings, roadsides, and waste places.

Range
S. Ontario east to SW. Maine, south to Florida, west to central Texas, and north to Wisconsin; to 4500' (1372 m) in the Southeast.

Comments
The sour fruit can be nibbled or made into a drink like lemonade. Wildlife eat the fruit, and deer also browse the twigs. It is easily distinguishable from other sumacs by the winged leaf axis and watery sap.

Common Prickly-ash
Zanthoxylum americanum
450

Much-branched shrub, often forming thickets, and rarely a round-crowned tree; aromatic, spiny, and with tiny gland-dots on foliage, flowers, and fruit.
Height: 20' (6 m) or more. Diameter: 6" (15 cm).
Leaves: pinnately compound; 5–10" (13–25 cm) long; 5–11 paired leaflets, 1–2" (2.5–5 cm) long; elliptical or ovate; blunt-pointed at ends; edges straight or slightly wavy; hairy when young; stalkless. Dull green with sunken veins above, paler and hairy on veins beneath.
Bark: gray to brown; smooth.
Twigs: brown or gray; hairy when young; often with paired short stout spines less than ⅜" (10 mm) long.
Flowers: less than 3/16" (5 mm) wide; with 5 spreading fringed yellow-green petals; in short-stalked clusters; male and female on separate plants; in spring before leaves.
Fruit: 3/16" (5 mm) long; podlike, elliptical, brown, slightly fleshy; maturing in late summer and splitting open.

Habitat
Moist soils in valleys and rocky uplands.

Range
S. Ontario east to S. Quebec, south to Pennsylvania, west to central Oklahoma, and north to E. North Dakota; local to Georgia; to 2000' (610 m).

Comments
This shrub is the northernmost representative of a tropical genus named from Greek words meaning "yellow" and "wood." A drug formerly was obtained from the dried, bitter, aromatic bark.

Russian-olive
Elaeagnus angustifolia
467

Introduced shrub or small tree often with crooked or leaning trunk, dense crown of low branches, silvery foliage, and sometimes spiny twigs.
Height: 20' (6 m). Diameter: 4" (10 cm).
Leaves: 1½–3¼" (4–8 cm) long, ⅜–¾" (10–19 mm) wide.

Lance-shaped or oblong; without teeth; short-stalked. Dull gray-green with obscure veins above, silvery, scaly, and brown-dotted beneath.
Bark: gray-brown; thin, fissured and shedding in long strips.
Twigs: silvery, scaly when young, becoming reddish brown; long and slender; often ending in short spine.
Flowers: ⅜" (10 mm) long; bell-shaped; with 4 calyx lobes, yellow inside, silvery outside (petals absent); fragrant; short-stalked; scattered along twigs at leaf bases; in late spring or early summer.
Fruit: ⅜–½" (10–12 mm) long; berrylike, elliptical, yellow to brown with silvery scales, becoming shiny; thin, yellow, mealy, sweet edible pulp; large brown stone; scattered along twig; maturing in late summer and autumn.

Habitat
Moist soils, from salty to alkaline; spreading in valleys.

Range
Native of southern Europe and Asia; planted and naturalized from British Columbia east to Ontario and from New England west to California; to 5000' (1524 m) or above.

Comments
The fruit is consumed by songbirds, such as cedar waxwings, robins, and grosbeaks, and by pheasants and quail. The plants sprout and spread from roots, sometimes becoming pests.

Singleleaf Pinyon
Pinus monophylla
480

Slow-growing, small pine with spreading, rounded, gray-green crown and low, horizontal branches; often shrubby.
Height: 16–30' (5–9 m). Diameter: 1–1½' (0.3–0.5 m).
Needles: evergreen; 1 in bundle (rarely 2), sheath shedding after first year; 1–2¼" (2.5–6 cm) long. Stout, stiff, sharp-pointed; straight or slightly curved; dull gray-green, with many whitish lines; resinous.
Bark: dark brown or gray, smoothish, becoming furrowed into scaly plates and ridges.
Cones: 2–3" (5–7.5 cm) long; egg-shaped or rounded, dull yellow-brown, almost stalkless, resinous; opening and shedding, with thick, 4-angled cone-scales, often with tiny prickle; seeds large, wingless, thin-walled, mealy, edible.

Habitat
Dry, gravelly slopes of mesas, foothills, and mountains; in open, orchardlike pure stands and with junipers.

Range
SE. Idaho and N. Utah south to NW. Arizona and west to S. California; also N. Baja California; at 3500–7000' (1067–2134 m).

Comments
This species is easily recognized by the needles borne singly, instead of in bundles of 2–5, as in other native pines. The large edible seeds are sold locally as pinyon or pine nuts.

BIRDS

A tremendous number of birds—large and small, silent and noisy—find a congenial home in North American grasslands. Birds of prey find perfect hunting in the open country, while other species look for insects amid grasses or lead a secretive existence among the shrubs. Bright yellow American Goldfinches travel in flocks, looking for seeds, while the inconspicuous Common Nighthawk perches lengthwise on branches. This section describes these and many of the other typical birds of the grasslands.

Cattle Egret
Bubulcus ibis
487

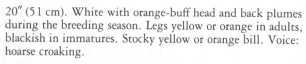

20" (51 cm). White with orange-buff head and back plumes during the breeding season. Legs yellow or orange in adults, blackish in immatures. Stocky yellow or orange bill. Voice: hoarse croaking.

Habitat
Dry land in open fields where it feeds alongside livestock, but breeds near water with other herons.

Range
Chiefly southern and eastern states. Also tropics of Mexico, Central and South America, West Indies, and the Old World.

Comments
Originating in the Old World, the Cattle Egret crossed the Atlantic, probably flying from Africa to South America, where this species was first reported early in the present century. These birds follow livestock, feeding on insects flushed up from the grass.

Turkey Vulture
Cathartes aura
488

26–32" (66–81 cm). Wingspan: 72" (1.8 m). One of North America's largest birds of prey. Brown-black overall; with unfeathered red head (dark in young); yellow feet. In flight, conspicuously short-necked; broad wings appear 2-toned with dark gray flight feathers looking lighter than black wing linings. Wings in flight are held at a slight V angle, or dihedral, often with outermost flight feathers separated. Rarely gives a soft hiss or groan, but generally silent.

Habitat
Dry open country or along roadsides.

Range
Common from southern Canada throughout the United States and Mexico. Also widespread through Central and South America. In the West, winters in California and S. Arizona.

Comments
Vultures are often called buzzards, a Western misnomer originally applied to *Buteo* hawks in the Old World. Although many people find the vulture's eating habits repulsive, it fills a useful role by consuming the flesh of dead animals.

Northern Harrier
Circus cyaneus
489

16–24" (40–61 cm). Wingspan: 42" (1.1 m). Long-winged, long-tailed hawk with a white rump, usually seen soaring unsteadily over marshes with its wings held in a shallow V. Female and young are brown above, streaked below, young birds with a rusty tone. Male, seen less than young birds and females, has gray back, head, and breast. Usually silent. At the nest it utters a *kee-kee-kee-kee* or a sharp whistle.

Habitat
Marshes and open grasslands.

Range
Eastern Aleutians, Alaska, Mackenzie, and Newfoundland to

Virginia and northern Mexico. Winters north to British
Columbia, Wisconsin, and New Brunswick.

Comments
This is the only North American member of a group of hawks
known as harriers. All hunt by flying close to the ground,
taking small animals by surprise.

wainson's Hawk
uteo swainsoni
90

18–22″ (45–56 cm). Wingspan: 49″ (1.2 m). A large hawk
with longer, more pointed wings than the Red-tail. Uniform
brown above, white below with brown breast; tail dark brown
and indistinctly banded. Young birds similar to immature
Red-tails but tend to have darker markings on the breast
whereas young Red-tails are more heavily marked on flanks
and belly. A rare all-dark form also occurs. Call a long,
plaintive, whistled *kreee.*

Habitat
Open plains, grasslands, and prairies.

Range
Alaska and Mackenzie south to northern Mexico and Texas.
Winters chiefly in South America and often migrates eastward
to Florida, where small numbers winter.

Comments
This species is a highly gregarious *Buteo,* often migrating in
great soaring flocks containing thousands of birds. On its
breeding grounds in the western plains, this hawk preys
mainly on rodents and grasshoppers. It is named after the
English naturalist William Swainson (1789–1855).

.ed-tailed Hawk
.uteo jamaicensis
91, 492

19–25″ (48–64 cm). Wingspan: 48–54″ (1.2–1.4 m). Large
hawk. Dark brown above, most typically light below with a
dark belly band. Rufous tail has a narrow dark band and light
tip. Finely streaked grayish tail of immature is often light at
base. Plumage variation widespread, including an overall dark
brown phase and a pale white-tailed phase. Call a loud, harsh
downslurred scream or a prolonged *kee-ahrrr.*

Habitat
A variety of habitats from tundra to semidesert, wherever
there are open hunting areas with woodland seclusion for
nesting. Its most characteristic habitat is natural savanna or its
man-made counterpart, farmlands with woods.

Range
North and Central America.

Comments
Commonly sighted at roadsides, perching atop telephone
poles, haystacks, or fence posts, this hawk may sit for hours,
then suddenly glide off to surprise a ground squirrel, lizard, or
other ground-dwelling prey.

Ferruginous Hawk
Buteo regalis
493

22½–25" (57–64 cm). Wingspan: 56" (1.4 m). Largest
member of hawk family. Light phase: rufous above, whitish
below, with rufous wrist patch and leg feathers. Black flight
feather tips. Dark phase (rare): deep rufous above and below.
Whitish tail. Legs feathered down to talons. Immatures
resemble light-phase adults but lack rufous markings. Call a
loud descending *kre-ah;* gull-like *krag* notes.

Habitat
Prairies, brushy open country, badlands.

Range
Nests from the Canadian prairie provinces south to Oregon,
Nevada, Arizona, and Oklahoma. Winters in southern half of
breeding range and southwestern states from S. California to
SW. Texas.

Comments
The clutch is large for a *Buteo* hawk and may well reflect a
fluctuating food supply. These hawks lay more eggs when prey
abounds, fewer in years when rodent populations decrease.
They feed mainly on prairie dogs and ground squirrels.

Golden Eagle
Aquila chrysaetos
494

30–41" (76–104 cm). Wingspan: 76–92" (2–2.4 m). Shaped
like a hawk but when soaring its wingspan is much greater;
bill also larger, and the "eagle look" of the eye seems more
pronounced because of the deep socket. Adult dark brown
overall with "golden" nape (visible only at close range). Legs
feathered down to talons. Immatures in flight show large
white wing patch at base of outermost flight feathers and
white tail with dark band at tip. Rarely heard: soft mewing or
yelping notes; sometimes a high squeal.

Habitat
Remote rangeland, alpine tundra, mountainous badlands, and
canyons.

Range
Mountains and rangeland of western North America, from
Alaska to Mexico; also in northeastern states and provinces,
where rare. Northern populations migratory.

Comments
These majestic birds are common in many places in the West.
They feed mainly on rabbits and large rodents, and sometimes
scavenge dead lambs.

Crested Caracara
Polyborus plancus
495

20–22" (51–56 cm). Wingspan: 48" (1.2 m). Dark brown,
with black cap and bare red face; white throat, neck, base of
tail, and wing tips; black band at tip of tail. Call a high,
harsh crackle.

Habitat
Prairies, savannas, and semiarid areas with open groves of
palms, mesquites, and cacti.

Range
Central and S. Florida, where it is becoming scarce; local in the southern portions of Texas and Arizona. South to southern South America.

Comments
This scavenger has probably the most varied diet of any bird of prey. It often accompanies and dominates vultures at fresh kills or carrion and also eats small animals.

American Kestrel
Falco sparverius
96

9–12″ (23–30 cm). Wingspan: 21″ (0.5 m). Jay-sized. Wings long and pointed, tail long. May be recognized in any plumage by its rusty tail and back. The adult male has pale blue-gray wings, rusty in the female. Often seen hovering. Call a shrill *killy-killy-killy*.

Habitat
Towns and cities, parks, farmlands, and open country.

Range
Alaska, the Northwest Territories, and Newfoundland south to Tierra del Fuego. Winters from British Columbia, Illinois, and New England southward.

Comments
Unlike the larger falcons it has adapted to man and nests even in our largest cities, where it preys chiefly on House Sparrows. In the countryside it takes insects, small birds, and rodents, capturing its prey on the ground rather than in the air. This species was formerly called "Sparrow Hawk."

Gray Partridge
Perdix perdix
97

12–14″ (30–35 cm). A small, stocky, chickenlike bird, largely gray with a black U-shaped mark on the underparts and a rust-colored tail. Call a hoarse *kee-ah*. When flushed, a rapid cackle.

Habitat
Grain fields, agricultural grasslands.

Range
Introduced and locally established in Nova Scotia, New Brunswick, N. New York, Ontario, Ohio, Indiana, S. Michigan, Iowa, Minnesota, and across the northern part of the United States to British Columbia.

Comments
This species is well adapted to areas of intensive agriculture, where no native game bird can exist. It forms coveys outside the breeding season, like the Bobwhite, but does not defend a territory. In the spring the flocks break up into pairs.

Ring-necked Pheasant
Phasianus colchicus
98

30–36″ (76–91 cm). Larger than a chicken, with a long, pointed tail. Male has a red eye-patch, brilliant green head, and white neck-ring; body patterned in soft brown and

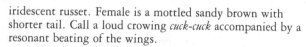

iridescent russet. Female is a mottled sandy brown with
shorter tail. Call a loud crowing *cuck-cuck* accompanied by a
resonant beating of the wings.

Habitat
Farmlands, pastures, and grassy woodland edges.

Range
Introduced from British Columbia, Alberta, Minnesota,
Ontario and the Maritime Provinces south to New Jersey,
Maryland, Oklahoma, and central California.

Comments
These birds are very tolerant of man, often nesting on the
outskirts of large cities. Although successful in most grassland
habitats, its North American headquarters is the central plains.

Sage Grouse
Centrocercus urophasianus
499

Male, 26–30" (66–76 cm); female, 22–23" (56–58 cm). Both
sexes streaked gray above with a black belly. Male has a long
pointed tail; black throat, white collar, and white breast
flanked by elongated neck plumes. Female's head, back, and
breast uniformly barred. In courtship display male's tail is
fanned and tilted forward; white neck and breast are inflated
by pair of naked yellowish-green air sacs. When flushed, it
may give a chickenlike *cluck cluck cluck*.

Habitat
Open country, plains, foothills, sagebrush semideserts.

Range
From S. British Columbia, Alberta, and Saskatchewan south
to W. Colorado, Utah, Nevada, and E. California.

Comments
As its name suggests, this grouse feeds on sagebrush buds and
leaves, where it also nests and hides. The males gather each
spring on a traditional display ground, or lek, for its elaborate
courtship ritual.

Greater Prairie-Chicken
Tympanuchus cupido
500

16–18" (40–46 cm). A chickenlike bird with a short black
tail, heavily barred above and below with grayish brown. Male
has orange air sacs inflated during courtship display and long
black feathers on sides of neck, erected into "horns" during
courtship; horns of female shorter. Gives a hollow "booming"
call during display; also cackles and clucks.

Habitat
Undisturbed tallgrass prairie.

Range
Locally in Wisconsin, Illinois, and Michigan, and from
Manitoba south through the Great Plains to Oklahoma; also
on the coastal prairies of Texas.

Comments
Once found from the Atlantic Coast west to Wyoming, the

Greater Prairie-Chicken has been exterminated from much of this vast range through the destruction of the undisturbed prairies on which it breeds. Where they still survive, Greater Prairie-Chickens perform striking courtship dances on communal display grounds.

esser Prairie-Chicken
ympanuchus pallidicinctus
01

16″ (40 cm). A smaller and paler edition of the Greater Prairie-Chicken. In the male, the air sacs on the neck are reddish, rather than yellowish. Call consists of various cackling and clucking notes; the male "booms" during courtship.

Habitat
Sandy prairies and plains, especially with shrubby oak.

Range
Resident in S. Colorado and Kansas, south locally in W. Oklahoma, Texas, and E. New Mexico.

Comments
As in the Greater Prairie-Chicken, males of this species gather and engage in communal courtship displays. These birds replace the Greater Prairie-Chicken in more arid grasslands; some authorities consider the two to be a single species.

harp-tailed Grouse
ympanuchus phasianellus
02

16–18″ (40–46 cm). Similar to the Greater Prairie-Chicken, but speckled rather than barred and with a pointed tail edged with white. Call a dovelike *coo,* guttural clucks and cackles. A booming sound during courtship dance.

Habitat
Prairie grassland and grassy edges of woodland.

Range
Alaska, N. Manitoba, and Quebec south to Michigan, Colorado, and Washington.

Comments
The habitat requirements of this grouse are not as specialized as those of the Greater Prairie-Chicken, and so this species has managed to survive in much larger numbers. The cutting of large areas of northern coniferous forest, creating vast tracts of brushland, has actually helped the Sharp-tail.

Northern Bobwhite
Colinus virginianus
03

8–11″ (20–28 cm). A small, chunky, brown bird; underparts pale and streaked; throat and eyebrow white in males and buff in females. Usually seen in groups called coveys. Call a clear whistled *bob-WHITE* or *poor-bob-WHITE.* The assembly call for a covey is a *ho-ha,* with each note higher than the last.

Habitat
Pastures, grassy roadsides, and farmlands.

Range
Wyoming, Minnesota, Ontario, and Massachusetts south to

Florida, the Gulf Coast, and Mexico. Introduced locally elsewhere.

Comments

One of our most popular game birds, the Bobwhite is undoubtedly more numerous than it was when unbroken forest covered most of the eastern United States, but in recent years the species has declined somewhat due to the cutting of roadside brush, trimming of farmland borders, and gradual replacement of former pastures with stands of young trees.

Scaled Quail
Callipepla squamata
504

10–12" (25–30 cm). White, cottony crest; pale unstreaked gray head; bluish-gray feathers of breast and back and upper surface of wing have black semicircular edge, creating scaled effect; belly also has brown "scales"; white lines on flanks. Sexes look alike. The call is often interpreted as a nasal *pay-cos pay-cos*.

Habitat

Semideserts such as yucca flats, juniper hillocks, canyon bottoms.

Range

Its distribution centers on the Chihuahuan Desert of Mexico; it extends north to SE. Arizona, New Mexico, Utah, S. Colorado, and parts of Texas.

Comments

Though birds of arid habitat, Scaled Quails must visit water holes regularly. They nest in the rainy season, when moisture produces some vegetation, and do not breed during extremely dry summers.

Sandhill Crane
Grus canadensis
505

34–48" (86–122 cm). Over 36" (90 cm) tall. Large bird with long legs and neck but relatively short bill; color of ash or wet sand, with red cap on forehead. Like all cranes, flies with neck and legs outstretched. In flight formation some utter a *krooo-ooo* or *garooo-a* call incessantly, audible at great distances; when disturbed, the whole flock calls.

Habitat

Breeds in marshes; in the North on tundra, prairies, and swampy bogs.

Range

Breeds from NE. Siberia across coastal Alaska to the central Canadian Arctic, south to NE. California, Nevada, Colorado, South Dakota, and Michigan. Also from S. Mississippi through Florida to Cuba. Winters from California to W. Texas and south to central Mexico.

Comments

The Sandhill is still common at some places in the North, but the nesting population in British Columbia and the United States is decreasing due to loss of its habitat. In winter the

Sandhill chooses not only marshes but also extensive prairies and fields, where it thrives on spilled grain.

Killdeer
Charadrius vociferus
506

9–11″ (23–28 cm). Robin-sized. Brown above and white below, with 2 black bands on the breast and a blackish bill. In flight, tail appears bright rufous. Often bobs its head. Call a clear *kill-DEEE,* repeated endlessly.

Habitat
Open country generally—plowed fields, golf courses, and shortgrass prairies.

Range
Breeds from British Columbia, Mackenzie, and Newfoundland south to the West Indies, Mexico, and Peru. Winters regularly from New Jersey and Ohio southward.

Comments
This is probably our most familiar shorebird. Not only is it abundant and conspicuous, but its loud call compels attention. When the nest is approached, the adult feigns injury, hobbling along with wings dragging as if badly wounded. This behavior often succeeds in luring a predator away from the eggs or young; the bird then "recovers" and flies off calling loudly.

Upland Sandpiper
Bartramia longicauda
507

12″ (30 cm). Pigeon-sized. Long neck and tail, short bill, small head; overall warm brown with a dark rump and outermost flight feathers. Well known for its beautiful song, whistled trills, and mournful windlike sounds.

Habitat
Open grassland, prairies, and hay fields in breeding season; also, while on migration, open country generally.

Range
Alaska and central Canada to central United States. Winters in southern South America.

Comments
This attractive bird of open grasslands was formerly shot in great numbers for food and sport, until it became very scarce. Now given complete protection, it has increased once again.

Long-billed Curlew
Numenius americanus
508

20–26″ (51–66 cm). Very large shorebird with extraordinarily long downcurved bill. Cinnamon-brown with dark mottling above, clear buff below, with light side streaking on neck and belly, cinnamon underwing linings, long neck. Call a far-reaching, loud *cur-lee?,* often answered by *kli-li-lili-lili.*

Habitat
Salt marshes, mud flats, beaches; nests on upland prairies.

Range
Southern Canada throughout the Great Basin, east to Texas

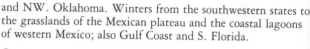

and NW. Oklahoma. Winters from the southwestern states to the grasslands of the Mexican plateau and the coastal lagoons of western Mexico; also Gulf Coast and S. Florida.

Comments
Although territorial when nesting, curlews are social birds that feed, roost, and migrate in flocks. They avoid cover, feeling safe only in the open.

Mourning Dove
Zenaida macroura
509

11–13″ (28–33 cm). Light brownish gray above, pale buffy below; wings darker, with black spots along inside edge; light blue eye-ring, large black spot at lower base of ear feathers; iridescent light violet neck shield. Very long central tail feathers (shorter in female), with sharply tapered white-tipped outer tail feathers. The common name comes from the male's melancholy cooing, the last 3 notes lower than the first: *coo-ooh, coo, coo-coo*. It is uttered from a prominent perch and followed by a courtship flight, which begins with an upward arc and audible wing clapping and ends in a glide with flamboyant tail display.

Habitat
Dry uplands, grain fields, suburban areas; deserts.

Range
Throughout temperate North America, including Mexico but not in mountain and northern forests. Migratory in the North.

Comments
The breeding season starts early—in March in California—and continues to mid-September. Bird may nest 2–4 times each year. Thus it is easily able to maintain its numbers even though it is hunted extensively.

Common Ground-Dove
Columbina passerina
510

6½″ (16 cm). Sparrow-sized. A short-tailed, brown dove with much rufous in the wings and a heavily scaled breast. Call a soft cooing with rising inflection.

Habitat
Open areas such as fields, gardens, farmland, and roadsides.

Range
S. United States to northern South America. Not migratory.

Comments
This bird, as its name implies, spends much of its time on the ground, and is most commonly seen when flushed from a roadside or path in a brushy pasture. It is a rather retiring bird, and is somewhat locally distributed.

Greater Roadrunner
Geococcyx californianus
511

24″ (61 cm). Crow-sized. A long-legged, gray-brown long-tailed ground bird with a bushy crest. Bright yellow eyes at close range. Utters clucks, crows, dovelike coos, doglike whines, and hoarse guttural notes.

Habitat
Open arid country with plenty of thickets to serve as cover.

Range
Breeds in central California, Nevada, Utah, Colorado, Kansas, Oklahoma, Arkansas, and Louisiana south to central Mexico.

Comments
The comical-looking Roadrunner, or "Chaparral Cock" as it is called by cowboys, would rather run than fly. With its twisting and turning in and out of cactus thickets, it can easily outdistance a man.

Common Barn-Owl
Tyto alba
512

18″ (46 cm). Wingspan: 44″ (1.1 m). Crow-sized. Buff-brown above and white below, with heart-shaped face and numerous small dark dots on white underparts; dark eyes, long legs. Its weird calls include rapid gracklelike clicks, hissing notes, screams, guttural grunts, and bill snapping.

Habitat
Open country, forest edge, clearings, cultivated areas, cities.

Range
Nearly worldwide; in America from southernmost Canada to Tierra del Fuego.

Comments
This nocturnal ghost of a bird frequents such places as belfries, deserted buildings, and hollow trees. It hunts its food— almost entirely rodents—in garbage dumps, neglected cemeteries, rundown farms, and similar waste lots of cities.

Burrowing Owl
Athene cunicularia
513

9″ (23 cm). Pigeon-sized. Short-tailed and long-legged; yellow eyes; no ear tufts; face framed in white with a blackish collar. Call a liquid cackling; also a mellow *coo-coooo,* repeated twice.

Habitat
Plains, deserts, fields, and airports.

Range
Southwestern Canada, Florida, and the West Indies to Tierra del Fuego.

Comments
This comical little bird is one of the most diurnal of all owls. It often perches near its hole, and when approached too closely will bob up and down and finally dive into its burrow rather than take flight. The burrows have usually been abandoned by prairie dogs or pocket gophers, but the owls are quite capable of digging their own.

Short-eared Owl
Asio flammeus
514

16″ (40 cm). Crow-sized. A long-winged, tawny-brown owl of open country, rather heavily streaked, and with a blackish patch around each eye. The very short ear tufts are rarely visible. Usually silent; on the nesting ground gives a variety of barks, hisses, and squeals.

Habitat
Freshwater and salt marshes; open grassland, prairies, dunes; open country generally during migration.

Range
Breeds locally from Alaska and northern Canada south to New Jersey and California; winters in the southern part of the breeding range and south to Guatemala. Also in South America.

Comments
This owl is most commonly seen late in the afternoon, as it begins to move about in preparation for a night of hunting. It can often be identified at a great distance by its habit of hovering; its flight is erratic and bounding.

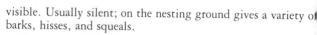

Common Nighthawk
Chordeiles minor
515

10″ (25 cm). Wingspan: 23″ (0.6 m). Blue Jay-sized, usually seen in flight. Dark with long, pointed wings and white patches on the outer wing. Perches motionless and lengthwise on branches. Call a loud, nasal, buzzy *peent* or *pee-yah*.

Habitat
Aerial, but open country generally; also cities and towns.

Range
Canada to Panama and the West Indies; winters in South America.

Comments
Its name is somewhat inappropriate, since it is not strictly nocturnal, often flying in sunlight, and it is not a hawk, although it does "hawk," or catch flying insects on the wing.

Cassin's Kingbird
Tyrannus vociferans
516

8–9″ (20–23 cm). Similar to Western Kingbird but darker; back more olive-gray, black tail lightly white-tipped but lacks white margins. Darker gray breast makes white throat patch appear smaller and more clearly defined than Western Kingbird's. A noisy kingbird, its common utterances are a loud, *chi-beer!* and a rapid *chi-beer, ch-beer-beer-beer-r-r*.

Habitat
Highland counterpart of the Western Kingbird in savanna, rangeland, pinyon-juniper woodland.

Range
From S. Montana and Wyoming to Mexico; also coastal savanna areas of S. California where some winter as well. Winters in Mexico and Guatemala.

Comments
It is often found high on a tree, where it sits quietly as compared with the nervous Western Kingbird.

Western Kingbird
Tyrannus verticalis
517

9" (23 cm). Robin-sized. Pale gray above, yellow below with white throat; black tail edged with white. Call a noisy chattering and twittering; also a sharp *whit*.

Habitat
Open country; ranches, roadsides, streams, and ponds with trees.

Range
British Columbia, Manitoba, and Minnesota, south to Kansas, Oklahoma, and northern Mexico. Winters in Central America.

Comments
Like the Horned Lark and others, the Western Kingbird has benefited from the cutting of forests; the species has moved eastward in recent decades. During fall migration a few are always seen along the Atlantic Coast.

Eastern Kingbird
Tyrannus tyrannus
518

8½" (21 cm). Dark gray above, blackish on head, white below; black tail with white tip; red crown patch. Call consists of harsh and strident notes, often ascending, like *killy-killy-killy,* and others that sound like very squeaky chattering.

Habitat
Open country; farms, roadsides, and lake and river shores.

Range
Central Canada to southern United States. Winters from Peru to Bolivia.

Comments
These noisy, conspicuous birds are named for their aggressive behavior, often driving away birds much larger than themselves, especially if their territory is invaded. In late summer and early fall they often flock, and large numbers pursue flying insects; they also feed on wild berries, which they deftly pluck while on the wing.

Scissor-tailed Flycatcher
Tyrannus forficatus
519

14" (35 cm), of which more than half is a very long and deeply forked black-and-white tail; adult has bright salmon-pink sides and belly; head, upper back, and breast pale grayish white. Call a harsh *kee-kee-kee-kee*. Also a chattering and twittering like that of the Kingbird.

Habitat
Open country along roadsides and on ranches with scattered trees and bushes; also fence wires and posts.

Range
South-central United States north to Missouri and Nebraska. Winters from Mexico to Panama and on the Florida Keys.

Comments
Scissor-tails are noisy and aggressive and will chase birds much larger than themselves. In spring they put on a wonderful

aerial courtship display. With their long scissorlike tail they can maneuver and "sky-dance" gracefully.

Horned Lark
Eremophila alpestris
520

7–8" (17–20 cm). Larger than a sparrow. Brown, with black stripe below eye, black crescent on breast, and black "horns" (not always seen). Walks rather than hops. In flight, tail seen as black with white edges. Similar-looking pipits have brown tails and lack the face pattern. Call: *Ti-ti.* Song delivered in flight is a high-pitched series of tinkling notes.

Habitat
Plains, fields, airports, and beaches.

Range
Arctic south to North Carolina, Missouri, coastal Texas, and northern South America.

Comments
This species favors the most barren habitats; as soon as thick grass begins to grow in an area, the birds abandon it. In the fall they roam over the open countryside in large flocks, often in company with pipits, longspurs, and Snow Buntings.

Cliff Swallow
Hirundo pyrrhonota
521

5–6" (13–15 cm). Sparrow-sized. A stocky, square-tailed swallow with pale buff rump. Upperparts dull steel-blue, underparts buff-white; throat dark chestnut, forehead white. Call consists of constant squeaky chattering and twittering.

Habitat
Open country near buildings or cliffs; lake shores and marshes in migration.

Range
Alaska, Ontario, and Nova Scotia south to Virginia, Missouri, and Central America. Winters in South America.

Comments
As its name implies, this swallow originally nested on cliffs. The introduction of House Sparrows was a disaster for these birds, since the sparrows usurp their nests and often cause the swallows to abandon a colony.

Barn Swallow
Hirundo rustica
522

5¾–7¾" (15–20 cm). Sparrow-sized. Our most familiar swallow, and the only one with a deeply forked tail. Upperparts dark steel-blue, underparts creamy buff, throat and forehead rusty. Call: constant liquid twittering and chattering.

Habitat
Agricultural land, suburban areas, marshes, lake shores.

Range
Aleutians west to Unalaska Island, Alaska, and the Maritime Provinces to the Carolinas, Arkansas, and Mexico; winters in South America.

Comments
The great majority of these birds now nest on or in buildings, but originally they used rocky ledges over streams and perhaps attached their nests to tree trunks in the shelter of branches (as do related species in Africa).

Black-billed Magpie
Pica pica
23

17½–22" (44–56 cm). Large black and white bird with long tail and dark bill. Bill, head, breast, and underparts black, with green iridescence on wings and tail. White belly, shoulders, and outermost flight feathers, which are conspicuous as white wing patches in flight. Call a rapid, nasal *mag? mag? mag?* or *yak yak yak.*

Habitat
Open savanna, brush-covered country, streamside growth.

Range
Northern part of the Northern Hemisphere. In North America from Alaska south to E. California, and east to Oklahoma.

Comments
Magpies generally nest individually but can sometimes be found in loose colonies; they are social when feeding or after the breeding season.

Eastern Bluebird
Sialia sialis
24

7" (17 cm). Sexes similar; the male bright blue above with a reddish-brown breast and white belly; the female is duller. Its call, when flying overhead, is an unmistakable liquid and musical *turee* or *queedle.* Song is a soft melodious warble.

Habitat
Open farmlands with scattered trees.

Range
East of the Rockies from southern Canada to the Gulf of Mexico and as far as the mountains of central Mexico.

Comments
This beautiful bird is a favorite of many people and is eagerly awaited in the spring after a long, cold winter. In the past 25 years bluebirds have become uncommon in the East for reasons not altogether clear. Competition for nest sites may be a critical factor.

Mountain Bluebird
Sialia currucoides
25

7" (18 cm). Male pure sky-blue above, paler blue below, with a white abdomen; female similar but duller and grayer. Utters soft warbling notes.

Habitat
Breeds in high mountain meadows with scattered trees and bushes; in winter descends to lower elevations, where it occurs on plains and grasslands.

Range
S. Alaska, Mackenzie, and Manitoba south to W. Nebraska,

New Mexico, Arizona, and S. California; winters from British
Columbia and Montana south through the western United
States to central Mexico.

Comments

This species has longer wings and a more graceful, swallow-
like flight than the Eastern Bluebird. In eastern North
America, it is mainly a winter visitor to the western
plains.

Water Pipit
Anthus spinoletta
526

6–7" (15–17 cm). Sparrow-sized. A slender brown bird of
open country. Often wags its tail and usually walks rather
than hops. Crown and upperparts uniform brown, underparts
buff with streaks; outer tail feathers white; legs usually black.
In contrast, sparrows have conical bills and hop. Call a paired,
high-pitched *pip-pip*. Flight song weak and tinkling trills.

Habitat

Arctic and alpine tundra; in migration and winter it is found
on beaches, barren fields, agricultural land, and golf courses.

Range

Aleutians, N. Alaska, Mackenzie, the Arctic islands, and
western Greenland south to Newfoundland, Hudson Bay, and
Oregon, and in the mountains to N. Maine and New Mexico.
Winters south to Florida, the Gulf Coast, and Guatemala.

Comments

Although mainly breeding on the tundra in both hemispheres,
some populations in western Europe have colonies on rocky
coasts and are known as Rock Pipits. The lack of a breeding
species of pipits in the open country of the eastern United
States is due to the fact that until recently forests covered this
area. In winter large flocks gather in open fields.

Northern Shrike
Lanius excubitor
527

9–10½" (23–26 cm). Robin-sized. Pale gray above, white
below, with faint barring on underparts and a bold black mask
ending at bill. Black tail with white edges. Stout, hooked
bill. Usually seen perched in the top of a tree in the open. Call
a mixture of warbles and harsh tones with a Robinlike quality.

Habitat

Open woodlands and brushy swamps in summer; open
grasslands with fence posts and scattered trees in winter.

Range

Alaska and the Labrador Peninsula to Quebec, Saskatchewan,
and N. British Columbia. Winters south to Virginia, Texas,
and N. California.

Comments

Unusual among songbirds, shrikes prey on small birds and
rodents, catching them with the bill and sometimes impaling
them on thorns or barbed wire for storage. Like other northern
birds that depend on rodent populations, the Northern

Shrike's movements are cyclical, becoming more abundant in the South when northern rodent populations are low.

oggerhead Shrike
anius ludovicianus
28

8–10" (20–25 cm). Robin-sized. Slightly smaller than a Northern Shrike, pale gray above, white below, with black face mask extending over the bill; dark crown. Utters a variety of harsh and musical notes and trills, often with long pauses in between.

Habitat
Grasslands, orchards, and open areas, with scattered trees; open grassy woodlands; deserts in the West.

Range
Breeds from S. British Columbia, central Alberta, central Saskatchewan, S. Manitoba, S. Ontario, S. Quebec, and Maritime Provinces to S. Florida, the Gulf Coast, and Mexico. Winters north to Virginia and N. California.

Comments
Since this shrike has no talons, it impales its prey—usually a small bird, mouse, or insect—on a thorn or barbed wire fence to facilitate tearing it apart then or at a later time; hence its other name, "Butcher Bird."

)ickcissel
biza americana
29

6" (15 cm). Male with yellow breast with black V, somewhat like miniature Meadowlark; has a heavy bill and a chestnut wing patch. Female patterned like the male, but lacks V on breast; has narrow streaks along the sides and yellowish throat and breast. Song sounds like *dick-dick-cissel,* the first 2 notes being sharp sounds followed by a buzzy, almost hissed *cissel,* repeated over and over again from a perch on a fence, bush, or weed.

Habitat
Open country in grain or hay fields and in weed patches.

Range
Chiefly in the north-central states south to the Gulf states. Winters from Mexico to northern South America.

Comments
Formerly common in farming regions of the eastern states, it disappeared from that region by the middle of the last century and is now most numerous in the Midwest. It appears in small numbers on the East Coast during the fall migration and rarely but regularly in winter at feeders.

American Tree Sparrow
pizella arborea
30

5½–6½" (14–16 cm). Gray head with rufous crown and ear-stripe; streaked brown above; plain gray below with dark spot in center of breast. Similar to Field Sparrow but larger and without white eye-ring or pink bill. Gives 1 or 2 clear notes followed by a sweet, rapid warble. Winter feeding call a silvery *tsee-ler.*

Habitat
Arctic willow and birch thickets, fields, weedy woodland edges, and roadside thickets in winter.

Range
Alaska, N. Saskatchewan, N. Manitoba, and N. Quebec sout to Newfoundland, central Quebec, and British Columbia. Winters south to the Carolinas, Arkansas, and California.

Comments
This northern species is a winter visitor. Unlike northern finches such as siskins and crossbills, its numbers seem to depend on weather, not on the food supply—the birds are les numerous in mild winters.

Clay-colored Sparrow
Spizella pallida
531

5–5½" (13–14 cm). A small sparrow with streaked crown an upperparts and clear gray breast; bright, buff-brownish rump gray sides of neck, and buff cheek patch bordered above and below with black. Call consists of a series of 4 or 5 toneless, insectlike buzzes.

Habitat
Brushy grasslands and prairies.

Range
North-central Canada and Illinois south to Nebraska and Montana; occasionally east to W. New York. Winters regularly north to S. Texas and New Mexico.

Comments
This western relative of the Chipping Sparrow has been gradually extending its range eastward and now breeds in the eastern Great Lakes region. Each spring and fall a few individuals, most of them immatures, appear in the East.

Field Sparrow
Spizella pusilla
532

5¼" (13 cm). The combination of the bright pink bill, rufous cap, white eye-ring and unstreaked buff breast distinguishes it from other sparrows. Call a series of soft, plaintive notes, all on the same pitch, accelerating to a trill at the end.

Habitat
Abandoned fields and pastures grown up to weeds, scattered bushes, and small saplings.

Range
Breeds from N. North Dakota, central Minnesota, N. Wisconsin, and central New England south to Georgia, Mississippi, Louisiana, and central Texas. Winters south to the Gulf of Mexico and northeastern Mexico.

Comments
When farms and pastures become overgrown with weeds and bushes, Field Sparrows move in and nest. Although shyer thar its close relative the Chipping Sparrow—and thus more difficult to observe—it may be studied at leisure when it sings its plaintive song from a perch atop a bush or fence post.

esper Sparrow
oecetes gramineus
33

5–6½" (13–16 cm). A grayish, streaked sparrow with white outer tail feathers, narrow white eye-ring, and a small patch of chestnut on the bend of the wing. Call a slow series of 4 clear musical notes, the last 2 higher, ending in a descending series of trills—sometimes rendered as *come-come-where-where-all-together-down-the-hill.*

Habitat
Fields, pastures, and roadsides in farming country.

Range
British Columbia, Ontario, and Nova Scotia south to the Carolinas, Texas, Colorado, and California. Winters from New England to the Gulf Coast and Mexico.

Comments
The rich, musical song of this sparrow is a most distinctive sound on rolling farmlands. Long known as the "Bay-winged Bunting," the bird was given the pleasing if somewhat inappropriate name Vesper Sparrow by the naturalist John Burroughs, who thought the song sounded more melodious in the evening.

ark Sparrow
hondestes grammacus
34

5½–6½" (14–16 cm). Head boldly patterned with black, chestnut, and white; streaked above; white below with a black spot in the center of the breast; tail black with white edges. Call consists of alternating buzzes and melodious trills.

Habitat
Grassland with scattered bushes and trees; open country generally in winter.

Range
British Columbia, Saskatchewan, N. Minnesota, and S. Ontario to Alabama, Louisiana, and northern Mexico. Winters from the Gulf Coast and California south to El Salvador. It has long been recorded along the eastern seaboard in fall.

Comments
The easiest way to find Lark Sparrows is to drive through grasslands and watch for the birds to fly up into trees along the road.

ark Bunting
alamospiza melanocorys
35

6–7½" (15–19 cm). Sparrow-sized. Male black with conspicuous white wing patches, most evident in flight. Female duller and streaked with brown, but also shows much white in wings. Usually seen in flocks. Call a long, varied series of trills. Call a soft *hoo-ee.*

Habitat
Open plains and fields.

Range
Breeds from British Columbia, Manitoba, and Minnesota south to Texas and New Mexico. Winters from S. Texas and Arizona to central Mexico.

Comments
Usually seen in large flocks feeding along roadsides. On the breeding grounds they are quite gregarious, several pairs crowding into a few acres of suitable habitat. Since there are few elevated song perches in their grassland breeding area, males advertise their presence with a conspicuous song flight. Often one can see several singing males in the air at one time

Savannah Sparrow
Passerculus sandwichensis
536

4½–6" (11–15 cm). Pale and streaked, with a bright yellow eyebrow and flesh-colored legs. Tail notched; other grassland sparrows have shorter, more pointed tails. Call a high-pitched buzzy *tsip-tsip-tsip-se-e-e-srr.*

Habitat
Fields, prairies, salt marshes, and grassy dunes.

Range
Aleutians, Alaska, Mackenzie, and Labrador south to New Jersey, Missouri, and northern Mexico. Winters regularly north to Massachusetts and SE. Alaska.

Comments
This most abundant and familiar of the grass sparrows shows great deal of color variation over its wide range. These birds are able runners; once discovered, they drop into the grass and dart away. In the fall they migrate southward in huge numbers.

Grasshopper Sparrow
Ammodramus savannarum
537

4½–5" (11–13 cm). A small, chunky grassland sparrow with a clear buff breast and dark rufous, scaly upperparts; has pale central stripe on crown; tail short and pointed. Call a high-pitched, insectlike *kip-kip-kip, zeeee,* usually uttered from the top of a weed stalk.

Habitat
Open grassy and weedy meadows, pastures, and plains.

Range
British Columbia, Manitoba, and New Hampshire south to Florida, the West Indies, and Mexico. Winters north to North Carolina, Texas, and California.

Comments
This elusive sparrow—named for its buzzy song—is sensitive to subtle changes in its habitat. As soon as a weedy field grows up or trees have filled in abandoned pastures, it no longer uses them as breeding sites.

Henslow's Sparrow
Ammodramus henslowii
538

5" (13 cm). Dull olive-green head, red-brown back and necklace of streaks on the breast. Call an explosive 2-note sneeze, *tsi-lick.*

Habitat
Local in grassland with scattered weeds and small shrubs.

Range
Northeastern United States south to east-central, wintering in the Gulf and south Atlantic states.

Comments
Sometimes found in loose colonies of several pairs, this sparrow is secretive and mouselike, skulking low in the grass. It relies on running rather than flying, and is seldom observed unless perched atop some weed stalk uttering its insect-like "song." It was named for John Henslow, prominent early 19th-century English botanist.

McCown's Longspur
Calcarius mccownii
39

5¾–6" (14–16 cm). Sparrow-sized. Breeding male streaked above with black crown, whitish face, and black mustache; gray below with a bold black band across breast. Female and winter male duller and more streaked; best identified by tail pattern, which is largely white with central pair of tail feathers black and with narrow black band at tip. Call a dry rattle; also a clear sweet warble given during a fluttering flight with wings raised high over back.

Habitat
Arid plains.

Range
Alberta, W. Manitoba, and SW. Manitoba south to the Dakotas, Wyoming, and Colorado. Winters from Nebraska and Colorado south to northern Mexico.

Comments
This longspur nests in higher and more arid shortgrass plains than does the Chestnut-collared Longspur, and so has been less affected by plowing of the prairie. They so dislike moisture that in wet seasons they may abandon areas where they normally are abundant.

Lapland Longspur
Calcarius lapponicus
40

6–7" (15–17 cm). Sparrow-sized. The only longspur in most of the East. Breeding male has black face, crown, and upper breast; chestnut nape; streaked above and white below with streaked flanks. Female and winter male dull and without bold pattern; best identified by largely black tail with white outermost tail feathers. Smith's Longspur has a similar tail but is always buff above and below and usually shows a small white wing patch. Rattling call. Flight song is sweet and bubbling.

Habitat
Arctic tundra; winters in open windswept fields and on grassy coastal dunes. Often found on parking lots along the coast in winter.

Range
Aleutians, N. Alaska, the Arctic islands, and Greenland to N. Quebec and S. Alaska. Winters regularly to New York and California.

Comments
This species is the only one of four longspurs that is found in both hemispheres. Like other longspurs, it is almost invisible on the ground; often a whole flock will dart into the air at an observer's feet, only to disappear again when they land.

Smith's Longspur
Calcarius pictus
541

5¾–6½" (15–16 cm). Sparrow-sized. Breeding male streaked dark brown and buff above, clear warm buff below; bold black-and-white head pattern. Small white wing patch most evident in flight; tail black, with white outer feathers. Females and winter males duller and without head pattern, but with more buff color than other longspurs. Call a dry rattle, like running a finger along the teeth of a comb.

Habitat
Arctic tundra and forest edge; winters on open grassy plains.

Range
N. Alaska across northern Canada to Hudson Bay. Winters from Nebraska south to Texas.

Comments
Longspur identification is difficult in the Midwest, where all four species winter, but this species, clad in warm buff the year around, can be told at a glance.

Chestnut-collared Longspur
Calcarius ornatus
542

5½–6½" (14–16 cm). Sparrow-sized. Similar to the Lapland Longspur, but breeding male has wholly black underparts and some white on its face. Tail of female and winter male similar to that of Lapland Longspur but with more white at sides. Call is soft, sweet, and tumbling.

Habitat
Dry elevated prairies and shortgrass plains.

Range
Alberta and Manitoba south to Minnesota and Wyoming. Winters from Colorado and Kansas south to Texas and northern Mexico.

Comments
The upland prairies favored for nesting have been extensively planted in wheat, so these longspurs are much less numerous than formerly. They need only a small area, however, and often several pairs will crowd into a patch of land or even the narrow strips of unplowed grassland along highways.

Snow Bunting
Plectrophenax nivalis
543

6–7¼" (15–18 cm). Sparrow-sized. Breeding male has black back with much white on head, underparts, wings, and tail. Female similar but duller. Winter birds have brown on crown and upperparts, duller underparts, but still show much white in wings. Call a clear whistle or low soft purring. Song is a sweet warble.

Habitat
Arctic tundra. Winters on windswept grasslands and beaches.

Range
Aleutians, N. Alaska and Greenland south to N. Quebec and central Alaska. Winters regularly to Pennsylvania and Oregon.

Comments
This circumpolar bird, often called "Snowflake," breeds farther north than almost any other land bird. In severe winters large flocks descend to our northern states, where they favor the most barren places.

Bobolink
Dolichonyx oryzivorus
544

6–8" (15–20 cm). Larger than a House Sparrow. Breeding male largely black with white rump and back, dull yellow nape. Female and winter male rich buff-yellow, streaked on back and crown. Short, conical bill. Flight song is a series of joyous, bubbling, tumbling, gurgling phrases with each note on a different pitch. Call a soft *pink*, often heard during migration.

Habitat
Prairies and meadows; marshes during migration.

Range
Breeds from British Columbia, Manitoba, and Newfoundland south to Pennsylvania, Colorado, and N. California. Winters in southern South America.

Comments
The Bobolink was probably confined to the central grasslands originally, but with the settling of the Northeast it quickly spread into New England. Now, with farms abandoned and the land returning to forest, the species is declining.

Red-winged Blackbird
Agelaius phoeniceus
545, 546

7–9½" (18–24 cm). Male black with red and buffy yellow epaulets. Female is streaked brown. Immature males resemble female but are darker, with faint epaulets. Freshly molted fall males have tan feather edges Shoulder patches of adult males in the Central Valley of California are pure red. Utters a loud, liquid, ringing *ok-a-lee!* Call is a low *chuck* and a thin *teeyee*.

Habitat
Marshes, preferring a narrow edge of cattails, tall weeds, and even blackberry tangles, surrounded by meadows or fields.

Range
Widespread from subarctic Canada to the tropical swamplands of Central America and Cuba. Migratory in the northern United States and Canada.

Comments
Red-wings form the nucleus of the huge flocks of mixed blackbird species that feed in fields, pastures, and marshes from early fall to spring.

Eastern Meadowlark
Sturnella magna
547

9–11″ (23–28 cm). Robin-sized. A stocky, brown-streaked bird with white-edged tail; throat and breast bright yellow, breast crossed by a black V. Western Meadowlark is very similar, but paler above and the yellow of its throat extends onto cheeks. Best distinguished by voice. Call a clear, mellow whistle, *see-you, see-yeeeer;* a loud rattling alarm note.

Habitat
Meadows, pastures, and prairies; in migration, in open country generally.

Range
Breeds from SE. Ontario, Nova Scotia, Minnesota, SW. South Dakota, New Mexico, and Arizona through Central America to northern South America. Winters as far north as New England and Nebraska.

Comments
Its cheerful song, usually delivered from a conspicuous perch, is familiar in most rural areas. Meadowlarks are often polygamous; more than one female may be found nesting in the territory of a single male. Because they often breed in hay fields, the nests may be destroyed by mowing; unless the season is well advanced, they will normally nest again.

Western Meadowlark
Sturnella neglecta
548

8½–11″ (21–28 cm). Robin-sized. Streaked brown above, bright yellow below, with a bold black V on the breast. Very similar to Eastern Meadowlark, but upperparts paler, and yellow of throat extending onto cheeks. Best told by voice: rich, flutelike jumble of gurgling notes, usually descending the scale; very different from the Eastern Meadowlark's series of simple, plaintive whistles.

Habitat
Meadows, plains, and prairies.

Range
British Columbia, Manitoba, N. Michigan, and NW. Ohio south to Louisiana, central Texas, and northern Mexico. Has spread eastward. Winters north to Nebraska and Utah.

Comments
The clearing of eastern North American forests has caused this species to extend its range eastward beyond the Great Lakes, where it has occasionally interbred with the Eastern Meadowlark. They are so similar that it was not until 1844 that Audubon noticed the difference and named the western bird *neglecta* because it had been overlooked for so long.

Brewer's Blackbird
Euphagus cyanocephalus
549, 550

8–10″ (20–25 cm). Robin-sized. Male is solid black with purplish-blue iridescent head and yellow eyes. Female is gray with dark eyes. Utters gurgles, squawks, and whistles.

Habitat
Prairies, fields, and farm yards.

Range
British Columbia and Manitoba east to the Great Lakes and south to Indiana, Texas, and northern Mexico. Winters north to Tennessee and S. British Columbia.

Comments
This blackbird, named for 19th-century ornithologist Dr. Thomas M. Brewer of Boston, is best known as a winter visitor to stockyards and farms, where it feeds on spilled grain. It also takes insects that are stirred up by livestock and plows. It nests in hay fields, but its young are usually fledged before the hay is harvested.

Bronzed Cowbird
Molothrus aeneus
551

6½–8¾″ (17–22 cm). Male is all black, with bronze, iridescent sheen; red or orange eyes; thick, rather conical bill. Smaller female is blackish, and has red eyes, but lacks sheen. Utters bubbling, mechanical, squeaking notes, similar to song of Brown-headed Cowbird, but higher-pitched and more prolonged. Call is a rattling sound.

Habitat
Fields, pastures, savannas, and feedlots.

Range
From the southwestern United States, along the Mexican border, in S. Arizona and Texas, south to Panama.

Comments
A strongly social bird, it associates with blackbirds as well as its own species and roosts in huge flocks, often in city parks.

American Goldfinch
Carduelis tristis
552

4½–5″ (11–14 cm). Smaller than a sparrow. Breeding male bright yellow with a white rump, black forehead, white edges on black wings and tail, and yellow at bend of wing. Female and winter male duller and grayer with black wings, tail, and white wing bars. Travels in flocks; undulating flight. Call a bright *per-chick-o-ree,* also rendered as *potato-chips,* delivered in flight and coinciding with each undulation.

Habitat
Brushy thickets, weedy grasslands, and nearby trees.

Range
SE. British Columbia and Newfoundland and south to Georgia, Arkansas, central Oklahoma, S. Colorado, central Utah, and Baja California; widespread in the Northeast. Winters south to the Gulf Coast and southern Mexico.

Comments
This familiar common species is often called the "Wild Canary." Since their main food is seeds, nesting does not begin until midsummer or late summer, when weed seeds are available. Thus goldfinches remain in flocks until well past the time when other species have formed pairs and are nesting.

MUSHROOMS

Several species of mushrooms can be found on prairies and plains after a rain. Some of these grow on the ground, while others spring to life on fallen tree trunks and branches. Some species are quite inconspicuous; others lend a touch of unexpected color—bright reds and oranges—to somber areas. This section provides descriptions of some of the most familiar and conspicuous mushrooms that grow in North America's grasslands.

Japanese Umbrella Inky
Coprinus plicatilis
553

Cap ⅜–1″ (1–2.5 cm) wide; stalk 2–3″ (5–7.5 cm) tall. Young cap brownish, becoming gray; conical first but flat or depressed at center at maturity; distinctly radially grooved, thin and fragile. Gills black at maturity, free from stalk but attached to small collar. Stalk white; dry and fragile.

Season and Habitat
May–September in grassy areas.

Range
Widely distributed throughout North America.

Comments
The gills of mushrooms in the genus *Coprinus* typically transform into an inky ooze at maturity, giving them the common name "inky caps." However, that does not happen in this species.

Fairy Ring Mushroom
Marasmius oreades
554

Cap ⅜–1⅝″ (1–4 cm) wide; stalk ⅜–3″ (1–7.5 cm) tall. Cap usually yellowish brown or paler, sometimes reddish brown, with a broad knob; dry, smooth, suggesting felt. Gills free or attached to stalk; close to somewhat distant; yellowish white. Stalk varying in color from white to yellowish or reddish brown. Stalk finely hairy and usually twisted.

Season and Habitat
May–September, all year in California; in grassy areas.

Range
Widespread in North America.

Comments
While it is a good edible, this species is not recommended here because it resembles poisonous ones. Fairy Ring Mushrooms shrivel in dry seasons and revive with rain; they frequently grow in a circular pattern, giving rise to the common name.

Common Psathyrella
Psathyrella candolleana
555

Cap 1–4″ (2.5–10 cm) wide; stalk 2–4″ (5–10 cm) tall. Cap brownish buff to almost white (sometimes tinged purplish); nearly flat and low-knobbed at maturity, usually with white veil remnants at margin. Gills attached to stalk, crowded, becoming purple-brown. Stalk shiny white, usually without a ring from the delicate veil.

Season and Habitat
May–September in grassy areas, and on or near hardwood stumps.

Range
Widespread throughout North America.

Comments
This is an excellent edible, but has not much substance.

Hemispheric Agrocybe
Agrocybe pediades
556

Cap ⅜–1″ (1–2.5 cm) wide; stalk ¾–2″ (2–5 cm) tall. Cap creamy to light yellow; more or less hemispherical; sticky in humid weather. Gills attached to stalk, close, rust-brown at maturity. Stalk buff to brownish. No veil.

Season and Habitat
Spring, summer, and early fall in grassy areas and wood mulch.

Range
Widespread in North America.

Comments
Although this species is edible, it is not recommended because it resembles poisonous mushrooms of the genus *Hebeloma*.

White Waxy Cap
Hygrophorus eburneus
557

Cap 1–4″ (2.5–10 cm) wide; stalk 2–6 ″ (5–15 cm) tall. Cap white or lightly tinted yellow-pink; slimy to sticky; often low-knobbed, varying to flat overall or sunken in center. Gills white, separated, running down stalk. Stalk white, slimy.

Season and Habitat
August–January in grassy areas; also coniferous, beech, or mixed forests.

Range
Across northern North America south to North Carolina, and in Colorado and California.

Comments
The White Waxy Cap is a good edible. Without doubt its range is wider than is today known.

Smooth Lepiota
Lepiota naucina
558

Cap 2–4″ (5–10 cm) wide; stalk 2–6″ (5–15 cm) tall. Cap white, with a low knob, dry and smooth but occasionally with tiny gray scales. Gills free, close to crowded; white when young, becoming pink-tinged. Stalk white, smooth or finely hairy; usually enlarged at base.

Season and Habitat
September–October; November–January in California; in grassy areas.

Range
Widely distributed throughout North America.

Comments
This species closely resembles a few of the virulently poisonous *Amanita* mushrooms. Furthermore, the Smooth Lepiota has made some people ill.

Fried-chicken Mushroom
Lyophyllum decastes
559

Cap 1–5″ (2.5–12.5 cm) wide; stalk 2–4″ (5–10 cm) tall. Cap grayish yellow or yellow-brown, almost flat; moist in humid weather; smooth. Gills close and off-white, attached to stalk or running down it. Stalk stout, off-white, smooth.

Season and Habitat
June–October; winter in California; in grassy areas.

Range
Widespread in North America.

Comments
Growing in dense clusters, this edible mushroom provides an ample meal for experienced collectors. Those lacking experience are cautioned that the Fried-chicken Mushroom resembles other, possibly dangerous species.

Meadow Mushroom
Agaricus campestris
560

Cap 1–4″ (2.5–10 cm) wide; stalk 1–2″ (2.5–5 cm) tall. Cap white when young, gray-brown in age; smooth or a bit hairy (sometimes with flat scales); dry. Gills free and crowded, pink at first and deep chocolate-brown or darker at maturity. Stalk white, sometimes narrowing at base; smooth above and hairy below a thin ring.

Season and Habitat
August–September; sometimes in spring. In fall and winter in California. In grassy areas.

Range
Widely distributed throughout North America.

Comments
The Meadow Mushroom is a highly prized edible, but even the most experienced collectors must be certain to check gill color to avoid picking dangerous white-gilled *Amanita* mushrooms by mistake. Inexperienced mushroomers should avoid it.

Purple-gilled Laccaria
Laccaria ochropurpurea
561

Cap 2–8″ (5–20 cm) wide; stalk 2–8″ (5–20 cm) tall. Cap brownish purple fading to grayish white; flat with usually wavy margin; smooth to almost hairless; dry. Gills attached to stalk, distant, light to deep purple. Stalk stout, dry, fibrous; gray-white, perhaps tinged purple or brown.

Season and Habitat
July–November in open oak woods and grassy areas.

Range
Eastern North America.

Comments
This species is edible and substantial but is usually considered best when eaten in combination with other vegetables.

Shaggy Mane
Coprinus comatus
562

Cap 1¼–2″ (3–5 cm) wide, 1⅝–6″ (4–15 cm) high; stalk 2⅜–8″ (6–20 cm) tall. Cap primarily white with reddish-brown scales; more or less egg-shaped at first, slowly opening and transforming to black oozy mass from margin of cap inward as spores mature. Gills just about free, crowded; white when young but black, oozy mass at maturity, slowly dripping from cap. Stalk white; has ring from partial veil.

Season and Habitat
Late spring and in the fall. November–January in the Southeast. In grassy areas, wood chips, and hardpacked soil.

Range
Widespread throughout North America.

Comments
A distinctive and choice edible when eaten in the young stage, the Shaggy Mane must be consumed soon after picking. The transformation of the cap to a black ooze does not represent rotting but is this mushroom's manner of dispersing spores. The spores develop in sequence from the margin inward, and the mushroom "clears away" all used tissue to give mature spores clear sailing.

Tumbling Puffball
Bovista pila
563

Mushroom 1¼–3¼″ (3–8 cm) wide; no stalk. Mushroom white at first. This layer flakes off, revealing shiny bronze-colored spore sac, with opening through which brown spores escape. Mushroom initially attached to ground by cordlike strands; later rolls free.

Season and Habitat
June–October in pastures and open woods.

Range
Widespread across North America.

Comments
This puffball is the mushroom equivalent of tumbleweed. The bronze spore sacs roll about as weather and ground surface dictate, frequently lasting more than one season.

Giant Puffball
Calvatia gigantea
564

Mushroom 8–20″ (20–50 cm) wide, sometimes larger; no stalk. Entire mushroom almost spherical; white and smooth, suggesting fine felt; darkening with age to yellowish brown, opening irregularly to reveal yellowish-green to brownish spore mass. Interior of immature mushroom white. Rootlike attachment present.

Season and Habitat
Late spring–midsummer, and in the fall in pastures and open woods.

Range
Eastern United States.

Comments
This is an excellent edible mushroom when in the immature white stage. Several Giant Puffballs sometimes form a fairy ring (mushrooms growing in a circle). It is reported that large specimens of this species have been mistaken for sheep in the distance.

AMPHIBIANS AND REPTILES

Warm, sunny mornings in the grasslands are ideal for basking—one of the favorite pastimes of many reptiles and amphibians. Early in the morning, slow-moving turtles and stealthy snakes may venture out in search of a meal, retreating to a rock to bask or to a shady burrow as the day grows hotter. Many reptiles and amphibians avoid the heat of the day entirely, never stirring from their homes until nightfall. In this section are included descriptions of many of the most common reptiles and amphibians found in the grasslands, from venomous rattlesnakes to inconspicuous toads and noisy frogs.

**Great Plains
Narrowmouth Frog**
Gastrophryne olivacea
565

⅞–1⅛″ (2.2–4.1 cm). Small, plump, smooth-skinned, with egg-shaped body, pointed snout, and fold of skin across back of head. Gray to olive, with scattered black flecks. Single spade on each hind foot. Male has dark throat. Voice a high-pitched buzzing bleat.

Habitat
Desert from sea level to 4000′ (1200 m), montane woodlands, and grasslands. Moist or damp areas.

Range
In a band from E. Nebraska and W. Missouri through Oklahoma and Texas into Mexico, west through northern Mexico into south-central Arizona.

Comments
Nocturnal. This frog often shares the burrow of a tarantula, a lizard, or a mole. It feeds primarily on ants.

Western Spadefoot
Scaphiopus hammondi
566

1½–2½″ (3.8–6.4 cm). Stout-bodied toad with wedge-shaped spade on each hind foot. External eardrum apparent. Dusky-olive to brown or gray, with irregular light stripes and random darker blotches. Skin relatively smooth with scattered small tubercles, red- or orange-tipped in some specimens. Belly white. Voice a rolling trill like the purr of a cat. Males call while floating on surface of water.

Habitat
Tolerates wide range of conditions from semiarid to arid. Prefers shortgrass plains and sandy, gravelly areas.

Range
Arizona, New Mexico, parts of S. Colorado, and W. Oklahoma south into Mexico. Separate population in California south of San Francisco through the central valley and foothills into N. Baja California.

Comments
Nocturnal. When handled, the Western Spadefoot produces a secretion that smells like peanuts and can inflame the skin or cause hay-fever symptoms of runny nose and watery eyes. The Western and Plains Spadefoots hybridize in areas where their ranges coincide.

Plains Spadefoot
Scaphiopus bombifrons
567

1½–2½″ (3.8–6.3 cm). A stout-bodied toad with round- to wedge-shaped spade on hind feet and prominent bony hump between eyes. External eardrum apparent. Skin relatively smooth with scattered small tubercles; gray to brown, often with overtones of green; tubercles orange. Usually light stripes on back are vaguely discernible. Belly white. Male throat bluish gray on sides. Voice a dissonant grating note given at 1-second intervals; sometimes a hoarse trill lasting 1 second.

Habitat
Shortgrass prairie where soil is loose and dry, rainfall low.

Range
The Great Plains from S. Alberta and Saskatchewan southeast through Montana to Missouri and central Oklahoma, south through W. Texas and E. Arizona and into Mexico. Separate population in extreme S. Texas.

Comments
Nocturnal. A single sharp-edged spade on the inside of each hind foot pushes aside soil as the Spadefoot backs into the ground. Burrows may be a few inches to several feet long. They remain open but are difficult to locate in sandy soil.

ed-spotted Toad
ufo punctatus
68

1½–3″ (3.8–7.6 cm). Small flat toad with round parotoids. Olive to grayish brown, usually with reddish warts. Bony ridges on head weak or absent. Voice a high-pitched musical trill. Males call while sitting near water's edge.

Habitat
Desert and rocky regions and prairie grasslands, usually near source of permanent water or dampness, natural or man-made, from sea level to 6000′ (1800 m).

Range
From central Texas west into SE. California and south into Mexico.

Comments
Active at twilight. Red-spotted Toads are most often collected at breeding choruses, but animals have been encountered over a mile from water and even in prairie dog burrows.

Voodhouse's Toad
ufo woodhousei
69

2½–5″ (6–12.7 cm). Large toad with light stripe down middle of back. Prominent bony ridges on head touch elongate partoids. Yellow to green to brown. Voice like the bleat of a sheep with a cold. Males call while sitting in quiet water.

Habitat
Sandy areas near marshes, irrigation ditches, backyards, and temporary rain pools.

Range
Widespread throughout most of the United States.

Comments
Primarily nocturnal; it is the toad commonly seen at night catching insects beneath lights. Occasionally it is active during the day, but more frequently remains hidden.

Great Plains Toad
ufo cognatus
70

2–4½″ (5.1–11.4 cm). Large, with prominent bony ridges on head that converge to form bony hump on snout. Behind eyes, bony ridges on head meet elongate parotoid glands. Gray to olive to brown, with large, symmetrical, light-bordered dark blotches. Sharp-edged tubercle on each hind foot. Flap of skin conceals the deflated male vocal sac. Voice a high-pitched, almost metallic trill.

Habitat
Grasslands of the prairie and drier bushy areas.

Range
From SE. Alberta to W. Wisconsin in the north, south through the Great Plains to NW. Texas and into Mexico, west to S. New Mexico, Arizona, and SE. California, and north to parts of SE. Nevada and central Utah.

Comments
Primarily nocturnal, but sometimes found foraging on cloudy, rainy days. This frog prefers loose soil where burrowing is easy. When in danger, it inflates, closes its eyes, and lowers its head to the ground.

Striped Chorus Frog
Pseudacris triseriata
571

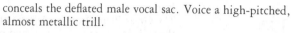

¾–1½" (1.9–3.8 cm). Skin smooth, greenish gray to brown. 3 dark stripes down back; may be broken, reduced, or absent. Dark stripe through eye and white stripe along upper lip. Small round toe tips. Voice a rasping, rising trill lasting 1–2 seconds, like the sound of a fingernail running over the teeth of a comb. Males call while sitting upright on floating vegetation.

Habitat
Grassy areas from dry to swampy to agricultural.

Range
Widespread. Alberta to N. New York (except New England, the northern Appalachians, and the southern coast) south to Georgia, west to Arizona.

Comments
Nocturnal. Chorus frogs may be heard calling on warm nights in early spring even before all the ice has disappeared from the water. At the slightest threat they go beneath the surface.

Plains Leopard Frog
Rana blairi
572

2–4⅜" (5.1–11.1 cm). Stout green to brown frog. Large dark spots between yellow dorsolateral ridges—ridges broken near hind legs. Prominent light-colored jaw stripe. Usually has light spot on eardrum. Groin and underside of thigh yellow. Voice 2 or 3 guttural notes a second; almost a chuckle.

Habitat
Prairies and other grassy, moist areas, along margins of ponds, streams, marshes.

Range
From central Nebraska to Illinois and extreme W. Indiana, south through Kansas to central Texas, north to E. Colorado.

Comments
Primarily nocturnal. It can be found foraging along the water's edge on cloudy days.

een Toad
fo debilis
3

1¼–2⅛″ (3.2–5.4 cm). Small, flat, bright green toad with many small warts and black spots. Large parotoids extend onto sides. Male has dark throat. Voice a piercing cricketlike trill. Males call while floating head-up in the water.

Habitat
The shelter of rocks in semiarid regions; also prairies.

Range
From SW. Kansas south through Texas to the Gulf Coast and into Mexico, north to SE. areas of Arizona, New Mexico, and Colorado.

Comments
Active at twilight, but forages by day after heavy rains. When threatened, it often flattens itself against the ground.

estern Box Turtle
rapene ornata
4

4–5¾″ (10.2–14.6 cm). Carapace high-domed, keelless, with distinctive pattern of radiating yellowish lines on a brown or black background. Plastron has distinct movable hinge; is often as long as carapace; plates continuously patterned, with radiating yellow lines. Male has red eyes, and hind portion of plastron is slightly concave; female's eyes are yellowish brown.

Habitat
Primarily open prairies; also grazed pasturelands, open woodlands, and waterways in arid, sandy-soiled terrain.

Range
S. South Dakota, Iowa, and E. Illinois south to Louisiana and Texas, west to SW. Arizona. Separate population in NW. Indiana and adjacent Illinois.

Comments
In the morning the Western Box Turtle basks briefly, then searches for food. By midday it seeks shady shelter. Where cattle share its habitat, it searches dung piles for beetles.

inted Turtle
rysemys picta
5

4–9⅞″ (10.2–25.1 cm). Carapace olive or black; oval, smooth, flattened, and unkeeled; plate seams bordered with olive, yellow, or red. Red bars or crescents on marginal plates. Plastron yellow, unpatterned or intricately marked. Yellow and red stripes on neck, legs, and tail. Notched upper jaw.

Habitat
Slow-moving shallow streams, rivers, and lakes.

Range
British Columbia to Nova Scotia, south to Georgia, west to Louisiana, north to Oklahoma, and northwest to Oregon. Isolated populations in the Southwest.

Comments
The most widespread turtle in North America. It is fond of basking and often dozens can be observed on a single log. Young turtles are carnivorous, but become herbivorous.

Snapping Turtle
Chelydra serpentina
576

8–18½" (20–47 cm). The familiar "snapper," with massive head and powerful jaws. Carapace tan to dark brown, often masked with algae or mud, bearing 3 rows of weak to prominent keels, and serrated toward the back. Plastron yellow to tan, unpatterned, relatively small, and cross-shaped in outline. Tail as long as carapace; with saw-toothed keels. Tubercles on neck.

Habitat
Fresh water. Likes soft mud bottoms and abundant vegetation Also enters brackish waters.

Range
S. Alberta to Nova Scotia, south to the Gulf.

Comments
Highly aquatic, it likes to rest in warm shallows, often buried in mud, with only its eyes and nostrils exposed. It emerges in April from a winter retreat beneath an overhanging mudbank under vegetative debris, or inside a muskrat lodge. Snappers eat invertebrates, carrion, aquatic plants, fish, birds, and small mammals. They strike viciously when lifted from water or teased and can inflict a serious bite.

Many-lined Skink
Eumeces multivirgatus
577

5–7⅝" (12.7–19.4 cm). Long-bodied, with many alternating light and dark stripes, including light stripe at juncture of back and sides along third scale row counting from middle of back. Back striping faded or absent in some populations. Tail tapers so gradually it appears swollen. Young have bright blue tail.

Habitat
Areas of rocks and small brush in open grassy plains, sand hills, and deserts; also occurs in mountainous wooded areas to 8200' (2500 m).

Range
SW. South Dakota through SE. Wyoming, south to Arizona and New Mexico; scattered populations are found in W. Texas and in Mexico.

Comments
Diurnal. This skink typically burrows under rocks, logs, trash, even dry cow chips. It feeds on insects.

Western Skink
Eumeces skiltonianus
578

6½–9⁵⁄₁₆" (16.5–23.7 cm). 4 light stripes extending well onto tail. Broad brown band on back between light stripes; broad dark band on side between light stripes. Tail usually gray or brown; bright blue in juveniles. Breeding male has orange on sides of head, tip of tail.

Habitat
Forest, open woodland, and grassy areas, especially where rocks are abundant. Often under leaf litter, logs, twigs, or rocks.

Range
N. Arizona and S. Nevada to S. British Columbia; south along the coast through California into Baja peninsula.

Comments
Diurnal. The Western Skink feeds on a variety of insects, their larvae, spiders, and earthworms.

airie Skink
meces septentrionalis
'9

5–8⅛" (13–20.6 cm). Brown, with 4 dark-edged light stripes extending onto tail. Light stripes on side separated by dark band. Pale stripe may run down middle of back. Breeding male may have orange on head. Young have bright blue tail.

Habitat
Moist terrain with vegetation and loose soil; gravelly washes.

Range
S. Manitoba south through E. North Dakota, Minnesota, and W. Wisconsin; south to coastal Texas.

Comments
Active at dawn and dusk; terrestrial. When disturbed, it retreats into a burrow or disappears into the vegetation.

acerunner
emidophorus sexlineatus
0

6–10½" (15.2–26.7 cm). Slender, with 6 or 7 light stripes separated by dark greenish-brown to black bands without spots. Sometimes a narrow light stripe down middle of back. Back scales small and granular. Throat green or blue in males, white in females. Belly white or blue-white; 8 lengthwise rows of large, smooth, rectangular belly scales. Tail brown, prominently striped on sides; light blue in juveniles.

Habitat
Dry sunny areas; grasslands, open woodlands.

Range
Delaware south through Florida, west to Texas, New Mexico, Colorado, SE. Wyoming, South Dakota.

Comments
Diurnal. The Racerunner is most active in the morning, when it can be seen basking or hunting for insects. It avoids cool seasonal and night temperatures by burrowing into the soil.

ender Glass Lizard
hisaurus attenuatus
1

22–42" (56–106.7 cm). Stiff legless lizard with eyelids and external ear openings. White markings in center of back scales. Groove along sides, dark stripes or speckling below groove. Prominent dark stripe down middle of back.

Habitat
Dry grassland and dry open woodland.

Range
Virginia to Florida, west to Texas, Oklahoma, and Nebraska, north to S. Wisconsin, and Illinois.

Comments
Diurnal. If the tail is grabbed or takes a blow, it may shatter into several pieces—hence the name glass lizard.

Great Plains Skink
Eumeces obsoletus
582

6½–13¾" (16.5–34.9 cm). The largest skink. Scale rows on sides oblique to rows on back. Dark edges of brown scales may align to form indistinct lengthwise stripes. Sides yellow. Juveniles black with white spots on lips, bright blue tail.

Habitat
Open rocky grasslands of the Great Plains; near permanent or semipermanent water in otherwise drier areas.

Range
SE. Wyoming, S. Nebraska, and extreme SW. Iowa through the Great Plains to central Arizona, Mexico, and Texas.

Comments
Diurnal. This husky skink feeds on insects, spiders, and small lizards. It will bite if handled.

Tiger Salamander
Ambystoma tigrinum
583

6–13⅜" (15.2–40 cm). World's largest land-dwelling salamander. Stoutly built, with broad head and small eyes. Color and pattern extremely variable—large light spots, bars, or blotches on dark background or network of spots on lighter background. Tubercles on soles of feet. 11–14 (usually 12–13) grooves on sides.

Habitat
Varied: arid sagebrush plains, pine barrens, mountain forests, and damp meadows where ground is easily burrowed; also in mammal and invertebrate burrows.

Range
Widespread from central Alberta and Saskatchewan, south to Florida and Mexico, but absent from New England, Appalachian Mountains, Far West.

Comments
Often seen at night after heavy rains, especially during breeding season; they live beneath debris near water or in crayfish or mammal burrows. They are voracious consumers of earthworms, large insects, small mice, and amphibians.

Bluntnose Leopard Lizard
Gambelia silus
584

8–9¼" (20.3–23.5 cm). Head short, nose blunt. Tail round, not flattened. Narrow white to yellow crossbars separated by wide gray or brown crossbars containing numerous dark-edged brown spots. Throat blotched with gray.

Habitat
Sandy areas, alkali flats, canyon floors, foothills, with sparse, open vegetation.

Range
San Joaquin Valley and surrounding foothills, California.

Comments
Diurnal. This lizard usually "freezes" when danger threatens, only to dash for cover if closely approached. Because much of its habitat has been converted to farms and communities, this lizard is threatened with extinction.

:sser Earless Lizard
olbrookia maculata
35

4–5⅛" (10–13 cm). Small; with smooth granular back scales, 2 folds across throat, no external ears. Gray to brownish, depending on earth color. Usually has lengthwise rows of dark blotches separated by pale stripe down center of back and light stripes where back meets sides. Male has 2 blue and black marks on belly. Female has orange throat in breeding season.

Habitat
Sandy soil areas in grassy prairie, cultivated fields, dry streambeds, desert grasslands.

Range
S. South Dakota through the Great Plains to central Texas, west through most of New Mexico and Arizona into Mexico.

Comments
Diurnal. Loss of the external ear may be an adaptation of this lizard's habit of burrowing headfirst into sand.

exas Horned Lizard
hrynosoma cornutum
86

2½–7⅛" (6.3–18.1 cm). Flat-bodied lizard with large crown of spines on head; 2 center spines longest. 2 rows of pointed scales fringe each side. Belly scales keeled. Red to yellow to gray; dark spots have light rear margins. Dark lines radiate from eye.

Habitat
From sea level to 6000' (1800 m) in dry areas, mostly open country with loose soil supporting grass, mesquite, cactus.

Range
Kansas to Texas and west to SE. Arizona. Isolated population in Louisiana; introduced in N. Florida.

Comments
Diurnal. Since this lizard, the common "horned toad" of the pet trade, feeds mainly on live large ants unavailable to pet owners, most in captivity slowly starve to death.

pot-tailed Earless Lizard
olbrookia lacerata
87

4½–6" (11–15.2 cm). Smooth granular back scales, 2 folds across throat, no external ears. Gray with paired dark blotches extending from head to tail. Up to 6 dark spots or streaks on side of belly. Round dark spots under tail. Egg-bearing female has yellow-green neck and body.

Habitat
Arid areas with sparse vegetation; dry prairie brushland.

Range
Central and S. Texas and adjacent Mexico.

Comments
Diurnal. This wary lizard scrambles for cover at the first sign of a human. However, in open areas where cover is scarce, it tires after a 50–100 yard chase and can be caught by hand. Some elude capture by "swimming" into loose sand.

Western Whiptail
Cnemidophorus tigris
588

8–12″ (20.3–30.5 cm). Slender; 4–8 light stripes, often with many dark spots and lines on light gray or tan. Stripes and spotting sometimes faded or absent. Throat and belly usually white or yellow (rarely all black), with black spotting on chest. 8 longitudinal rows of large smooth rectangular belly scales. Tail gray or gray-green, usually with black speckling.

Habitat
Arid and semiarid desert to open woodlands; where vegetation is sparse enough to make running easy.

Range
Baja California and California to E. Oregon and S. Idaho, south to W. Texas and Mexico.

Comments
Diurnal. This species digs burrows both for safe retreats and to find underground prey. Like most whiptails, it stalks any small moving object, even fluttering leaves.

Eastern Fence Lizard
Sceloporus undulatus
589

3½–7½″ (9.0–19.0 cm). Dark band along rear of thigh. Color varies geographically: gray to brown or rusty, dark or light stripes down back, sometimes vague crossbars or spots. Back and belly scales about same size. Males usually marked by black-bordered blue patches on belly and blue throat patch.

Habitat
Generally sunny locations: favors rotting logs, open woodlands, open grassy dunes, prairies.

Range
Delaware to Florida and west to New Mexico and Arizona.

Comments
Diurnal. In the east this lizard is primarily a tree-dweller, seldom far from a tree or wall up which it will flee to avoid capture. In the prairie states it is more terrestrial, sheltering under brush or in burrows.

Side-blotched Lizard
Uta stansburiana
590

4–6⅜″ (10.0–16.2 cm). A small lizard with small back scales, some larger scales on head; a fold with granular scales across throat. Brown; back pattern may consist of blotches, spots, speckles, stripes. Single dark blue to black spot on side behind foreleg. External ear openings.

Habitat
Arid and semiarid regions with coarse, gravelly soil and low-growing vegetation.

Range
Central Washington southeast to W. Texas and Mexico; west to Pacific Coast and Baja California, north through central and E. California to central Oregon.

Comments
Diurnal. These lizards live on or near the ground and are voracious consumers of insects. In the northern parts of their range they become inactive in the winter.

ollared Lizard
rotaphytus collaris
91

8–14″ (20–35.6 cm). Large head; conspicuous black-and-white collar across back of neck. Inside of mouth dark. Tail not flattened side to side. Yellow-brown to green with bluish highlights and usually light spots and dark bands. Mature male has blue-green or orange throat without black center seen in Desert Collared Lizard. Pregnant female has orange spots and bars on sides. Young show dark and light crossbanding.

Habitat
Hardwood forests to arid areas with large rocks for basking. More frequent in hilly regions, especially among limestone ledges that provide crevices for good cover.

Range
E. Utah and Colorado to extreme SW. Illinois, south through central Texas into Mexico, and west into central Arizona.

Comments
Diurnal. A wary, feisty lizard that will bite readily and hard, given the chance. When fleeing would-be captors, it lifts body and tail and dashes along on its hind legs, giving it the appearance of a fierce little dinosaur.

ommon Garter Snake
hamnophis sirtalis
92

18–51⅝″ (45.7–131.1 cm). Most widely distributed snake in North America. Coloration highly variable, but back and side stripes usually well defined. Red blotches or a double row of alternating black spots often present between stripes. Scales keeled. Scale in front of anus undivided.

Habitat
Near water—wet meadows, marshes, prairie swales, irrigation and drainage ditches, damp woodland, farms, parks.

Range
Atlantic to Pacific coasts; except desert regions of Southwest.

Comments
The most commonly encountered snake in many parts of its range. Active during the day and most frequently seen amid moist vegetation. This species is able to tolerate cold weather and may be active all year in the southerly part of its range. It hibernates in great numbers in community dens in northerly range. Ill-tempered when first captured, it will bite or expel musk, but it tames quickly and soon becomes docile.

Plains Garter Snake
Thamnophis radix
593

20–40″ (51–102 cm). Distinct bright yellow or orange back stripe. Cream to yellow side stripes occupy third and fourth scale rows above belly. Double row of squarish black spots between side and back stripes, and a row of black spots below side stripe. Black vertical bars on lips. Scales keeled. Scale in front of anus undivided.

Habitat
Wet meadows, open boggy areas, vacant lots, parks, and open prairies along margins of lakes, streams, and marshes.

Range
NW. Indiana northwest and southwest through the Great Plains to the Rockies from S. Alberta to NE. New Mexico. Isolated populations in north-central Ohio, NW. Arkansas, SW. Illinois and SE. Missouri.

Comments
A common species through much of its range, including urban areas. Spends warm days basking or searching for frogs, salamanders, and small rodents.

Checkered Garter Snake
Thamnophis marcianus
594

18–42½″ (45.7–108 cm). Brown, olive, or tan, with bold checkered pattern of large squarish black blotches on sides. Uppermost blotches intrude into yellow back stripe. Light side stripe on neck and farther back on body. Large paired black blotches at back of head separated from corners of mouth by light crescent; 8 upper lip scales. Scales keeled. Scale in front of anus undivided.

Habitat
Arid and semiarid grassland near streams, springs, ponds, and irrigation sites; sea level to ca. 5000′ (1500 m).

Range
Extreme SE. California, S. Arizona, E. and SW. New Mexico to E. Texas, north to SW. Kansas, south to Costa Rica.

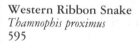

Comments
Active during the day in the more northerly portions of its range. On warm summer nights it can be found foraging for frogs, fishes, and crayfish.

Western Ribbon Snake
Thamnophis proximus
595

19–48½″ (48.3–123.2 cm). Slim-bodied, 3 well-defined light stripes contrast sharply with dark back and sides. Side stripe involves third and fourth scale rows. Dark stripe bordering belly scales is narrow or absent. Lip scales and belly unmarked; 2 fused spots on crown of head. Tail long. Scales strongly keeled, in 19 rows. Anal plate single.

Habitat
Weedy margins of lakes, ponds, cattle tanks, marshes, ditches, streams, rivers; sea level to 8000′ (2400 m).

Range
S. Wisconsin, Indiana, and Mississippi Valley, west to

E. Nebraska, SE. Colorado, E. New Mexico, and south through Texas to Costa Rica.

Comments
Forages amid vegetation along water's edge for frogs, tadpoles, and small fish. Young ribbon snakes, in turn, often fall prey to bullfrogs, fish, and birds.

Lined Snake
Tropidoclonion lineatum
596

7½–21" (19.1–53.3 cm). Resembles garter snakes. Dark or light olive-gray with 3 distinct stripes; back stripe whitish, pale gray, yellow or orange; side stripe on second and third scale rows. Belly white or yellow with 2 rows of dark spots down midline. 5–6 upper lip scales. Scales keeled. Scale in front of anus undivided.

Habitat
Open prairie hillsides, edges of woodland, and vacant suburban lots; sea level to ca. 5300' (1600 m).

Range
SE. South Dakota, south to south-central Texas; west through Oklahoma panhandle to central Colorado and NE. New Mexico. Isolated populations in Illinois, Iowa, Missouri, and New Mexico.

Comments
Crepuscular and nocturnal; during the day it hides under rocks or debris. May be found around trash dumps. Like its relatives, the garter and water snakes, the Lined Snake often voids excrement and anal secretions when first handled.

Western Terrestrial Garter Snake
Thamnophis elegans
597

18–42" (45.7–106.7 cm). Variable color and markings. Side stripe narrow, but back stripe is usually well defined. Space between stripes marked with dark spots or with scattered light specks. Scales keeled. Scale in front of anus undivided.

Habitat
Moist situations near water; margins of streams, ponds, lakes, damp meadows; open grassland to forest.

Range
SW. Manitoba and S. British Columbia southward into Mexico, extreme SW. South Dakota and extreme W. Oklahoma west to Pacific Coast.

Comments
Diurnal. Occasionally seen basking during morning hours in the open. When disturbed, it often takes to water.

Pine-Gopher Snake
Pituophis melanoleucus
598

48–100" (122–254 cm). Large and powerfully built; small head. Light-colored with black, brown, or reddish-brown blotches on back and sides. Snout somewhat pointed, with enlarged scale extending upward between nostrils. Scales keeled. Scale in front of anus undivided.

Habitat
Dry, sandy pine–oak woodlands and pine flatwoods, cultivated fields, prairies, open brushland, rocky desert, chaparral.

Range
S. New Jersey, western Virginia, S. Kentucky, Wisconsin, SW. Saskatchewan, S. Alberta, and south-central British Columbia south to S. Florida, east-central and west-central Mexico, and tip of Baja.

Comments
Generally diurnal, but may be active at night during hot weather. When confronted, the Pine-Gopher Snake hisses loudly, sometimes flattening its head and vibrating its tail, and then lunges at the intruder.

Western Diamondback Rattlesnake ⊗
Crotalus atrox
599

34–83⅞″ (86.4–213 cm). Largest western rattlesnake. Heavy-bodied with large head sharply distinct from neck. Back patterned with light-bordered dark diamonds or hexagonal blotches; blotches often obscured by randomly distributed small dark spots, which give back a mottled or dusky look. 2 light diagonal lines on side of face; stripe behind eye meets upper lip well in front of angle of jaw. Tail encircled by broad black and white rings. Scales keeled.

Habitat
Arid and semiarid areas from plains to mountains; brushy desert, rocky canyons, bluffs along rivers, sparsely vegetated rocky foothills; sea level to 7000′ (2100 m).

Range
SE. California eastward to central Arkansas south into northern Mexico.

Comments
The "coon-tail rattler" is capable of delivering a fatal bite! When disturbed it usually stands its ground, lifts its head well above its coils, and sounds a buzzing warning. Take heed! Active late in the day and at night in summer months.

Massasauga ⊗
Sistrurus catenatus
600

18–39½″ (45.8–100.3 cm). Unlike other rattlers, has 9 enlarged scales on top of head. Tail stocky with moderately developed rattle. Rounded dark blotches on back and sides; interspaces narrow. Light-bordered dark bar extends from eye to rear of jaw. Dark bars (often lyre-shaped) on top of head and neck. Scales keeled. Scale in front of anus undivided.

Habitat
Rocky hillsides, grassy wetland, sagebrush prairie, into desert grassland in the West; sphagnum bogs, swamps, marshland, and floodplains to dry woodland in the East.

Range
S. Ontario and NW. Pennyslvania south to NE. Mexico and extreme SE. Arizona. Isolated populations in New York.

Comments
Massasauga means "great river mouth" in the Chippewa language and probably alludes to the snake's habitat in Chippewa country—swampland surrounding mouths of rivers.

Glossy Snake
Arizona elegans
601

26–70″ (66–178 cm). Resembles Gopher snake but has smooth glossy scales rather than keeled scales. Snout somewhat pointed; lower jaw inset. Variable number of black-edged tan, brown, or gray blotches mark cream, pinkish, or light brown upper surfaces. Dark line runs from angle of jaw to eye. Belly unmarked. Scale in front of anus undivided.

Habitat
Dry, open sandy areas, coastal chaparral, creosote—mesquite desert, sagebrush flats, and oak—hickory woodland.

Range
SE. Texas and extreme SW. Nebraska west to central California, south into Mexico.

Comments
Occasionally called the Faded Snake because of its bleached appearance. It is a capable burrower and is usually seen on the surface in the early evening hours during the warmer months.

Northern Water Snake
Nerodia sipedon
602

22–53″ (55.9–134.6 cm). Reddish, brown, or gray to brownish black, with dark crossbands on neck region, and alternating dark blotches on back and sides at midbody. Pattern darkens with age, becoming black. Belly white, yellow, or gray, with reddish-brown or black crescent-shaped spots. No dark line from eye to corner of mouth. Juveniles more vivid. Scales keeled. Scale in front of anus divided.

Habitat
Found in most aquatic situations from sea level to about 4800′ (1450 m); lakes, ponds, swamps, marshes, canals, ditches, bogs, rivers, even salt marshes of Carolina Outer Banks.

Range
Maine to coast of North Carolina, NW. South Carolina and Georgia to S. Alabama and E. Louisiana, west to E. Colorado and northeast through Minnesota to S. Ontario and Quebec.

Comments
Active day and night. Will flee if given the chance, but flattens body and strikes repeatedly if cornered. Wounds caused by bite bleed profusely because of the anticoagulant quality of the snake's saliva, but there is no poison. Northern Water Snakes are often mistaken for venomous "water moccasins" and killed on sight.

Corn Snake
Elaphe guttata
603

24–72″ (61–182.9 cm). Long and slender; orange or brownish yellow to light gray, with large black-edged red, brown, olive-brown, or dark gray blotches down middle of back. 2

alternating rows of smaller blotches on each side, extending
onto edges of belly scales. Large squarish black marks on
belly, becoming stripes under tail. Dark spear-point mark on
top of head, and dark stripe extending from eye onto neck.
Belly scales flat in middle, with ends angled up sharply. Scales
smooth or weakly keeled. Scale in front of anus divided.

Habitat
Wooded groves, rocky hillsides, meadowland; along
watercourses, around springs, woodlots, barnyards, and
abandoned houses. Sea level to ca. 6000' (1850 m).

Range
S. New Jersey south through Florida and S. Tennessee to
Texas, Mexico, and E. New Mexico, SE. Colorado,
SE. Nebraska to SW. Illinois. Separate population in E. Utah
and W. Colorado.

Comments
Primarily nocturnal, but often active in early evening. It
readily climbs trees and enters abandoned houses and barns in
search of prey: mice, rats, birds, and bats. The common name
probably originated from the similarity of the belly markings
to the checkered patterns of kernels on Indian corn.

Western Hognose Snake
Heterodon nasicus
604

16–35¼" (40.6–89.5 cm). Sharply upturned and pointed
snout. Stout body with broad neck. Tan, brown, gray or
yellowish gray above with distinct or somewhat faded series of
dark blotches down back and 2 or 3 rows of side spots. Belly
and underside of tail distinctly patterned with large black
blotches. Scales keeled. Scale in front of anus divided.

Habitat
Sand and gravelly-soiled prairie, scrubland, river floodplains.

Range
SE. Alberta and NW. Manitoba, south to SE. Arizona, Texas,
and into northern Mexico. Isolated populations in Minnesota,
Iowa, Illinois, Missouri, and Arkansas.

Comments
Primarily active during morning and late afternoon hours;
burrows into loose soil to escape hot or cold conditions. Sense
of smell enables it to find buried toads, lizards, snakes, and
reptile eggs; also eats birds and small rodents.

Western Rattlesnake ⊗
Crotalus viridis
605

16–64" (40.6–162.6 cm). Size and color vary greatly.
Brownish blotches down midline of back, generally edged
with dark brown or black and often surrounded by light
border; begin as oval, squarish, diamondlike, or hexagonal
markings and tend to narrow into inconspicuous crossbands
near tail. Scales keeled.

Habitat
Great Plains grassland to brush-covered sand dunes on Pacific

Coast, and to timberline in the Rockies and the coniferous forests of the Northwest; rocky outcrops, talus slopes, stony canyons, and prairie dog towns; sea level to 11,000′ (3350 m).

Range
Extreme W. Iowa, south into Mexico and west to S. Alberta, SW. Saskatchewan, south-central British Columbia, Washington, Oregon, coastal California, and into Mexico.

Comments
Western counterpart of the Timber Rattlesnake but much more excitable and aggressive. Active April to October over much of range, and becomes crepuscular and nocturnal during hot summer months. Adults prey chiefly on small mammals; young like lizards and mice.

astern Hognose Snake
eterodon platyrhinos
)6

20–45½″ (50.8–115.6 cm). A stout-bodied snake with pointed, slightly upturned snout and wide neck. Color extremely variable: yellow, tan, brown, gray, or reddish with squarish dark blotches on back interspaced with round dark blotches at juncture of back and sides. All-black individuals common in some areas. Belly mottled; underside of tail conspicuously lighter than belly color. Scales keeled. Scale in front of anus divided.

Habitat
Prefers open sandy-soiled areas; thinly wooded upland hillsides, cultivated fields, woodland meadows; sea level to 2500′ (750 m).

Range
East-central Minnesota to extreme S. New Hampshire south to S. Florida, west to E. Texas and W. Kansas.

Comments
Active in the daytime. Burrows deep into loose earth during cold winter months. When disturbed, it "hoods" its neck, inflates its body, hisses loudly, and strikes. If this fails to discourage a would-be predator, it rolls over and plays dead with mouth agape and tongue hanging out. It becomes limp and will remain "dead" when picked up; however, it will roll over again if placed right-side up. It rarely bites people.

rairie Kingsnake
ampropeltis calligaster
07

30–52⅛″ (76.2–132.4 cm). A slender, variably patterned kingsnake. Tan, grayish brown, or yellowish brown above with black-edged, dark brown to reddish-brown or greenish blotches down back and 2 alternating rows of smaller, less conspicuous spots on sides. V-shaped arrowheadlike marking on crown of head. Pattern of older specimens may be lost or obscured by dark pigment; some develop 4 longitudinal dusky stripes. Scales smooth. Scale in front of anus undivided.

Habitat
Open fields, cultivated farmland, barnyards, pastures, prairies, rocky hillsides, open woodland.

Range
Central Maryland to N. Florida west to SE. Nebraska and
E. Texas.

Comments
Secretive; spends much of the day in animal burrows or under
rocks or several inches of loose soil. Most frequently seen
crossing roads after a rainstorm or on warm spring or summer
nights.

Fox Snake
Elaphe vulpina
608

34–70½" (86.4–179 cm). Yellowish or light brown, marked
with bold chocolate-brown to black blotches down midline of
back and tail; 2 alternating rows of smaller blotches on sides.
Belly yellow with dark squarish blotches. Dark band runs
from eye to angle of mouth, a second band extends vertically
from eye to mouth. Scales usually keeled. Scale in front of
anus divided.

Habitat
Rolling prairies, farmland, wooded stream valleys, Lake
Michigan dune country, marshland bordering lakes Erie and
Huron.

Range
Great Lakes region west to SE. South Dakota, E. Nebraska,
and N. Missouri.

Comments
Although an excellent climber, it is usually seen on the
ground in fields near streams or marshes. Unfortunately, it is
often mistaken for a Copperhead and killed. When excited, it
may rapidly vibrate its tail in surface litter—the sound
somewhat suggestive of an aroused rattler.

Longnosed Snake
Rhinocheilus lecontei
609

22–41" (55.9–104.1 cm). A tricolored snake with a tapered,
pointed snout protruding beyond lower jaw. Most scales under
tail in a single row. Light-bordered, cream-flecked black
saddle-shaped blotches extend down sides to edge of belly
scales. Spaces between blotches pink or reddish with black
spotting on sides. Scales smooth. Scale in front of anus
undivided.

Habitat
Dry open prairie, desert brushland, coastal chaparral to
tropical habitat in Mexico; sea level to 5400′ (1600 m).

Range
SW. Kansas, SE. Colorado, and New Mexico, south into
Mexico, and northwest to Arizona, W. Utah, Nevada, and
central California.

Comments
A good burrower. Active at night; hides amid rocks or in
underground burrows during day. When first captured it
exhibits an unusual defense reaction: it tries to hide its head,

then coils its body, vibrates its tail, and discharges a bloody
fluid and anal gland secretions.

round Snake
onora semiannulata
10

8–19" (20.3–48.3 cm). Tiny glossy snake; grayish, brownish,
or reddish with great variation in back pattern. Some
essentially patternless; others with a wide red, orange, or beige
back stripe; others with crossbanding ranging from a single
neck band to evenly spaced, saddle-shaped blotches to bands
with red interspaces encircling body. Small dark blotch on
back scales. Scales smooth and shiny. Scale in front of anus
divided.

Habitat
Dry open areas with loose sandy soil; rocky wooded or prairie
hillsides, mesquite thickets along river beds, sand hummocks,
vacant lots, brushy desert; sea level to 6000' (1800 m).

Range
SW. Idaho, SE. Oregon south through Nevada, SE.
California, and Arizona into Baja California and northern
Mexico, east to E. Texas, and north through Oklahoma, SE.
Colorado, S. Kansas, and SW. Missouri.

Comments
Until recently this secretive burrower was considered to be 2
species: *Sonora episcopa* with 2 subspecies and *S. semiannulata*
with 5 subspecies. Plain-colored, striped, and crossbanded
individuals may be found in the same area.

Milk Snake
ampropeltis triangulum
11

14–78¼" (35.6–199 cm). Gray or tan marked with a light
Y-shaped or V-shaped patch on neck and chocolate-brown to
reddish-brown, black-bordered blotches down back and sides.
Or colorfully ringed and blotched with red (or orange), black,
and yellow (or white). Light neck collar followed by black-
bordered red bands separated by light rings. Light rings widen
near belly. Scales smooth. Scale in front of anus undivided.

Habitat
Diverse situations: semiarid to damp coastal bottomland to
Rocky Mountains and tropical hardwood forests; pine forests,
open deciduous woodland, meadows, rocky hillsides, prairies,
high plains, sand dunes, farmland, and suburban areas; sea
level to ca. 8000' (2450 m).

Range
SE. Maine, SW. Quebec, SE. and south-central Ontario,
S. Wisconsin, and central and SE. Minnesota south through
most of United States east of the Rocky Mountains; Mexico
south to Colombia and Venezuela.

Comments
Usually discovered under rotting logs or stumps or damp
trash. Secretive and usually not seen in the open except at
night. It eats small rodents, birds, lizards, and snakes—
including venomous species. In the north, it is often mistaken

for the Copperhead, in the south for the Eastern Coral Snake. Its common name is based on the absurd belief that it milks cows, taking prodigious amounts in the process.

Ringneck Snake
Diadophis punctatus
612

10–30″ (25.4–76.2 cm). A small slender snake with a yellow, cream, or orange neck ring and bright yellow, orange, or red belly. Back gray, olive, brownish, or black; belly frequently marked with black spots. Neck ring may be interrupted, obscure, or occasionally absent. Scale present between eye and snout. Scales smooth. Scale in front of anus divided.

Habitat
Moist situations in varied habitat; forest, grassland, rocky wooded hillsides, chaparral, into upland desert along streams; sea level to ca. 7000′ (2150 m).

Range
Nova Scotia to Florida Keys, west to the Pacific Coast, south to central Mexico.

Comments
Secretive. Most often seen under flat rocks, logs, or loose bark of dead trees. When threatened, red-bellied forms tightly coil the tail and elevate it to display brightly colored underside. Rarely attempts to bite when picked up, but will void musk and foul-smelling contents. Partially constricts prey.

Rat Snake
Elaphe obsoleta
613

34–101″ (86.4–256.5 cm). Long, powerful constrictor with different adult color patterns predominating: plain, striped, and blotched. Plain is black, often with white showing between scales. Striped is red, orange, yellow, brown, or gray with 4 dark stripes. Blotched is light gray, yellow, or brown with dark brown, gray, or black blotches down back. Belly uniformly white, yellow, orange, or gray, often with dark mottling or checks. Belly scales flat in middle, ends angled up sharply. Underside of tail not striped. If present, dark stripe through eye does not reach neck. All young vividly blotched. Scales weakly keeled. Scale in front of anus divided.

Habitat
Hardwood forest, wooded canyons, swamps, rocky timbered upland, farmland, old fields, barnyards; from wet to arid situations; sea level to 4400′ (1350 m).

Range
E. Ontario and S. Vermont to Florida Keys, W. Texas, and adjacent Mexico, north to SW. Minnesota, and S. Michigan.

Comments
Active during the day in spring and fall but becomes nocturnal in summer. A skillful climber, it ascends trees or rafters of abandoned buildings in search of birds, eggs, and mice. Also eats other small mammals and lizards. Hawks may home in on a nest-raiding Rat Snake when it is being heckled by other birds.

...achwhip
...asticophis flagellum
...4

36–102" (91.4–259 cm). Large, lithe, long-tailed and fast-moving. Western races generally yellow, tan, brown, gray, or pinkish; essentially patternless or with dark crossbars on neck. Eastern form: head and neck region dark brown to almost black, gradually fading to light brown toward rear. Occasionally all black. No pale side stripes. Scales smooth. Scale in front of anus divided.

Habitat
Dry, relatively open situations; pine and palmetto flatwoods, rocky hillsides, grassland prairies, desert scrub, thorn forest, and chaparral; sea level to ca. 7000' (2150 m).

Range
SE. North Carolina, SW. Tennessee, extreme SW. Illinois, extreme SW. Nebraska, E. Colorado, north-central New Mexico, SW. Utah, west-central and S. Nevada, and central California, through Florida, Texas, California, and Mexico.

Comments
Perhaps our fastest snake. When pursued, it may climb a tree or enter a mammal burrow. If cornered, it coils, vibrates its tail, and strikes repeatedly. Contrary to legend, it does not chase down an adversary and whip it to death.

...lains Blackhead Snake
...ntilla nigriceps
...5

7–14¾" (17.8–37.5 cm). Uniform tan to brownish gray. Belly white, with pink or orange midline. Distinct black headcap extends downward but does not reach corner of mouth, ends abruptly with convex border on neck, 3–5 scales behind head shields. Scales smooth. Scale in front of anus divided.

Habitat
Rocky and grassy prairie; hillsides where soil is moist.

Range
S. Nebraska south through W. Kansas and E. Colorado to S. Texas, New Mexico, SE. Arizona and into Mexico.

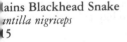

Comments
Nocturnal. Found under surface litter, in small burrows, occasionally wandering in basements. Specimens have been uncovered 8' (2.4 m) beneath the surface in January.

...athead Snake
...ntilla gracilis
...16

7–9⅝" (17.8–24.5 cm). Slender light brown or reddish-brown snake with a slightly darker head. Sometimes has dark gray headcap ending abruptly with concave border on neck, 1–2 scales behind head shields. Belly pink, color extending onto side of head. Scales smooth; scale in front of anus divided.

Habitat
Rocky prairie and wooded hillsides; sea level to 2,000' (600 m).

Range
Extreme SW. Illinois to E. Nebraska south through Oklahoma and Arkansas to E. Texas and adjacent Coahuila.

Comments
Nocturnal. A secretive species, found in rotting stumps and logs and under slabs of rocks, where it feeds on insect larvae, centipedes, slugs, and sowbugs.

Texas Blind Snake
Leptotyphlops dulcis
617

5–10¾" (12.7–27.3 cm). Smooth, shiny cylindrical snake; reddish brown, pink, or silvery tan, with blunt head and tail. Small spine on tip of tail. Eyes mere black spots beneath scales; more than 1 scale on top of head between large scale covering each eye.

Habitat
Semiarid deserts, prairies, hillsides, mountain slopes with sandy or loamy soil suitable for burrowing; sea level to 5000' (1500 m).

Range
South-central Kansas through Oklahoma and Texas to Mexico, west to S. New Mexico and SE. Arizona.

Comments
Nocturnal. This burrowing snake is seldom seen on the surface except in the evening following heavy summer rains. It is most frequently found in damp soil under slabs of rock, logs, or other surface debris. In farming areas it is sometimes uncovered and eaten by chickens scratching through barnyard soil for worms. It defends itself by coiling and writhing about, smearing cloacal fluid over its body.

Racer
Coluber constrictor
618

34–77" (86.4–195.5 cm). Large, slender, agile, and fast moving. Adults uniformly black, blue, brown, or greenish above; white, yellow, or dark gray below. Young typically gray and conspicuously marked with dark spots on sides and dark gray, brown, or reddish-brown blotches down midline of back. Scales smooth. Scale in front of anus divided.

Habitat
Abandoned fields, grassland, sparse brushy areas along prairie land, open woodland, mountain meadows, rocky wooded hillsides, grassy-bordered streams, and pine flatwoods; sea level to ca. 7000' (2150 m).

Range
S. British Columbia and extreme S. Ontario; every state in continental United States, except Alaska; scattered populations through eastern Mexico to northern Guatemala.

Comments
Diurnal. May be encountered in most any terrestrial situation except atop high mountains and in hottest deserts. When annoyed it may make a buzzing sound like a rattler by vibrating the tail tip in dead vegetation. If grabbed, it will bite repeatedly and thrash about violently. Despite the scientific name, it is not a constrictor.

GLOSSARY

Abdomen In insects, the hindmost of the 3 subdivisions of the body; in spiders, the hindmost of the 2 subdivisions of the body.

Achene A small, dry, hard fruit that does not open and contains one seed.

Agricultural grassland An area deliberately kept in grass, such as a meadow or pasture. A meadow is periodically cut for hay; a pasture is grazed.

Alternate Arising singly along the stem, not in pairs or whorls.

Annual Having a life cycle completed in one year or season.

Anther The saclike part of a stamen, containing pollen.

Axil The angle formed by the upper side of a leaf and the stem from which it grows.

Biennial Plant that lives two years, usually flowering the second year.

Biomass The total weight of all living organisms in a particular area.

Bipinnate With leaflets arranged on side branches off a main axis; twice-pinnate; bipinnately compound.

Bloom A whitish, powdery coating found on certain fruits and leaves.

Bract A modified and often scalelike leaf, usually located at the base of a flower, a fruit, or a cluster of flowers or fruits.

Brood A generation of butterflies hatched from the eggs laid by females of a single generation.

Calyx Collective term for the sepals of a flower, usually green.

Cambium In woody plants, the sheath of embryonic cells, between wood and bark, that divides to form new tissue.

Capsule A dry, thin-walled fruit containing 2 or more seeds and splitting along natural grooved lines at maturity.

Carapace Upper part of a turtle's shell.

Caste In social insects, a specialized form of adult with a distinct role in the colony.

Catkin A compact and often drooping cluster of reduced, stalkless, and usually unisexual flowers.

Cell The area of a butterfly's wing that is entirely enclosed by veins; also called discal cell.

Cephalothorax The first subdivision of a spider's body, combining the head and the thorax.

Chaparral Low, thick, scrubby growth consisting of evergreen shrubs or low trees; common in semiarid climates, especially in California.

Climax The plants and animals in a given community that will persist in that community so long as conditions remain stable.

Composite Any of a large family of shrubs, herbs, and trees. Includes such daisylike flowers as asters, sunflowers, coneflowers, etc.

Compound eye One of the paired visual organs consisting of several or many light sensitive units, or ommatidia, usually clustered in a radiating array with exposed lenses fitting together.

Corolla Collective term for the petals of a flower.

Creeper Technically, a trailing shoot that takes root at the nodes; used here to denote any trailing, prostrate plant.

Crepuscular Active at twilight.

Cutin An impermeable covering on the epidermis of plants.

Dewclaw A functionless digit or "toe," usually on the upper part of a mammal's foot.

Disk The central portion of a butterfly's wing.

Dispersal The spread of organisms from one place to another by migration of passive transfer.

Diurnal Active during the daytime hours.

Drone One of a caste of social bees, consisting only of reproductive males.

Drupe A stone fruit; a fleshy fruit with the single seed enveloped by a hard covering (stone).

Ecosystem A system of ecologically linked animals and plants that have evolved together in a certain environment. The elements of an ecosystem are mutually dependent.

Ecotone The transition area between 2 communities; ecotones contain species from each area as well as organisms unique to it.

Elytron The thickened forewing of beetles, serving as protective covers for the hind wings (*pl.* elytra).

Entire Smooth-edged, not lobed or toothed.

Epiphyte A plant growing on another plant but deriving little or no nutrition from it; also called an air plant.

Evapotranspiration Total water loss from the soil both by transpiration from plant surfaces and direct evaporation.

Exotic Not native to a given area; also, an introduced plant.

Eyespots Spots resembling eyes on winged insects, such as butterflies and moths.

Femur The third segment of an insect's leg, between trochanter and tibia.

Floodplain An area formed by and subject to a river's process of periodic flooding and deposition.

Follicle A dry, 1-celled fruit, splitting at maturity along a single grooved line.

Fungus A plant that lacks chlorophyll and reproduces by means of spores.

Habitat The place or community where a plant or animal naturally grows and lives.

Head A crowded cluster of flowers on very short stalks, or without stalks as in the sunflower family.

Herb A plant with soft, not woody, stems that dies to the ground in winter.

Host plant The food plant of a caterpillar.

Hybrids The offspring of two different varieties, races, species, or genera.

Hygroscopic Taking up moisture from the air.

Inflorescence A flower cluster on a plant; especially the arrangement of flowers on a plant.

Intergrades Animals of related and adjoining subspecies that may resemble either form or exhibit a combination of their characteristics.

Introduced Intentionally or accidentally established in an area by man, and not native; exotic or foreign.

Invader Plant—usually annual—or animal that tends to establish itself on a disturbed area.

Involucre A whorl or circle of bracts beneath a flower or flower cluster.

Key A dry, 1-seeded fruit with a wing; a samara.

Lanceolate Shaped like a lance, several times longer than wide, pointed at the tip and broadest near the base.

Larva A post-hatching immature stage that differs in appearance from the adult and must metamorphose before assuming adult characters (e.g., a tadpole).

Loam A rich soil of clay, silt, sand, and humus.

Lobed Indented on the margins, with the indentations not reaching to the center or base.

Loess Fine-grained, yellow-brown loam, very fertile. Chiefly deposited by wind.

Margin The edge of the wing.

Molt The periodic loss and replacement of feathers; most species have regular patterns and schedules of molt.

Moraine A formation of boulders, gravel, sand, clay, etc., deposited directly by a glacier.

Nitrogen fixation Conversion by plants of atmospheric nitrogen into a usable form (nitrates) by certain soil bacteria in their nodules.

Nocturnal Active at night.

Node The place on the stem where leaves or branches are attached.

Oblanceolate Reverse lanceolate; shaped like a lance, several times longer than wide, broadest near the tip and pointed at the base.

Obovate Reverse ovate; oval, with the broader end at the tip.

Old field Formerly cultivated or grazed land. An old field, if undisturbed, will undergo a succession that ends in a forest.

Opposite leaves Occurring in pairs at a node, with one leaf on either side of the stem.

Ovary The swollen base of a pistil, within which seeds develop.

Ovate leaf Egg-shaped, pointed at the top, technically broader near the base.

Overwinter To go through a period of dormancy during the cold season.

Palmate Having 3 or more divisions or lobes, looking like the outspread fingers of a hand.

Palp A sensory structure associated with an insect's mouthparts.

Panicle Loosely branched flower cluster in a pyramidal form.

Parasite A plant or animal living in or on another plant or animal, and deriving its nutrition from the host organism to the detriment of the host.

Parotoid gland A large glandular structure on each side of the neck or behind the eyes of toads and some salamanders.

Parthenogenesis Reproduction by the development of an unfertilized egg; some animals produce only one sex and reproduce by means of unfertilized eggs.

Pedicel The stalk of an individual flower.

Pedipalp One of the second pair of appendages of the cephalothorax of a spider, usually leglike in a female but enlarged at the tip in a male as a special organ for transferring sperm; used by both sexes for guiding prey to the mouth.

Peduncle The main flowerstalk or stem holding an inflorescence.

Perennial Living more than two years; also, any plant that uses the same root system to produce new growth.

Petal Of a flower, the basic unit of the corolla; flat, usually broad, and brightly colored.

Petiole The stalklike part of a leaf, attaching it to the stem.

Pheromones Sex-attractant scent molecules produced by the scent scales, or androconia, of some insects and other animals.

Phloem The vascular tissue in a plant that conducts food material.

Photosynthesis The process by which plant cells use the sun's energy to produce carbohydrates from carbon dioxide and water; the reaction is catalyzed by the green pigment chlorophyll, and uses free oxygen as a byproduct.

Pinnate leaf A compound leaf with leaflets along the sides of a common central stalk, much like a feather.

Pioneer species A plant or animal that begins a new cycle of life in a barren area; pioneers prepare the way for, and eventually are replaced by, different species.

Pistil The female organ of a flower, consisting of an ovary, style, and stigma.

Plastron The lower part of a turtle's shell.

Pod A dry, one-celled fruit, splitting along natural grooved lines, with thicker walls than a capsule.

Pollen Spores formed in the anthers of a flower that produce the male cells.

Pome A fruit with fleshy outer tissue and a papery-walled inner chamber containing the seeds.

Pothole A circular body of water created by melting glacial ice, often frequented by waterfowl; kettle.

Prehensile Adapted for grasping or wrapping around; said of the toes, claws, and tails of certain animals.

Primaries The outermost and longest flight feathers on a bird's wing.

Proboscis A prolonged set of mouthparts adapted for reaching into or piercing a food source.

Pupa The inactive stage of insects during which the larva transforms into the adult form, completing its metamorphosis

Raceme A long flower cluster on which individual flowers each bloom on a small stalk all along a common, larger, central stalk.

Rain shadow Area of little rainfall on the lee side of high mountains.

Ray flower The bilaterally symmetrical flowers around the edge of the head in many members of the sunflower family; each ray flower resembles a single petal.

Regular flower With petals and/or sepals arranged around the center, like the spokes of a wheel; always radially symmetrical.

Relict community Prairie outlier whose origin, survival, and dynamics are a mystery.

Reproductive In social insects, a member of the caste capable of reproduction; reproductives usually gain wings for brief mating flights, as occurs in termites and ants.

Rhizome A horizontal underground stem, distinguished from roots by the presence of nodes, often enlarged by food storage.

Rosette A crowded cluster of leaves; usually basal, circular, and appearing to grow directly out of the ground.

Saprophyte A plant lacking chlorophyll and living on dead organic matter.

Scale One of millions of shinglelike plates covering the wings of butterflies.

Scent scales Specialized scales that produce and disperse sex attractants; also called androconia or pheromones.

Sepal A basic unit of the calyx, usually green, but sometimes colored and resembling a petal.

Sessile leaf A leaf that lacks a petiole, the blade being attached directly to the stem.

Sheath A more or less tubular structure surrounding a part, as the lower portion of a leaf surrounding the stem.

Simple eye A light-sensitive organ consisting of a convex lens bulging from the surface of the head, concentrating and guiding light rays to a cup-shaped cluster of photoreceptor cells.

Simple leaf A leaf with a single blade, not compound or composed of leaflets.

Soil A mixture of disintegrated rock and organic materials; characteristically broken down as clay, silt, and sand. The organic component is humus.

Spadix A dense spike of tiny flowers, usually enclosed in a spathe, as in members of the arum family.

Spathe A bract or pair of bracts, often large, enclosing the flowers.

Spike An elongated flower cluster, each flower of which is without a stalk.

Stamen One of the male structures of a flower, consisting of a threadlike filament and a pollen-bearing anther.

Steppe A dry, shortgrass prairie, sometimes also with shrubs such as sagebrush.

Stigma The tip of a pistil, usually enlarged, that receives the pollen.

Stipules Small appendages, often leaflike, on either side of some petioles at the base.

Stolon A stem growing along or under the ground; a runner.

Style The narrow part of the pistil, connecting ovary and stigma.

Subspecies A more or less distinct geographic population of a species that is able to interbreed with other members of the species.

Symbiosis An intimate biological relationship between two species. Symbiosis may take the form of parasitism, where one organism lives at the expense of the other; commensalism, where the presence of one neither helps nor damages the other; and mutualism, where both gain from the relationship.

Taproot The main root of a tree or plant, growing vertically downward, from which smaller, lateral roots extend.

Tarsus In butterflies, the foot section of the leg; it has hooks at the end for clinging; in birds, the lower, usually featherless, part of the leg.

Thorax The subdivision of the body between head and abdomen, consisting of three segments (the prothorax, mesothorax, and metathorax) and bearing whatever legs and wings are present.

Transpiration Loss of water by evaporation from leaves and other parts of plants.

Trenching Process in which soil compaction (from overgrazing) causes increased runoff and the formation of deep gullies (trenches).

Trophic Related to, or functioning in, nutrition.

Tubercle A raised, wartlike knob.

Type Tree species growing together in an association; forest types are defined by the trees actually growing on a site.

Umbel A flower cluster in which the individual flower stalks grow from the same point, like the ribs of an umbrella.

Venation The pattern of veins on a wing.

Vernal pool Low, wet depression, sometimes extensive, water-filled in spring, dry in summer.

Virgin forest Woodland that exists in its primeval state.

Whorl A circle of three or more leaves, branches, or pedicels at a node.

Wing bar A conspicuous, crosswise wing mark.

Wing stripe A conspicuous mark running along the opened wing.

Worker One of a caste of social insects, usually incapable of reproduction, that procures and distributes food or provides defense for the colony.

Xeric Low in the amount of moisture available to plants.

BIBLIOGRAPHY

Grassland enthusiasts might enjoy reading some of the following related materials:

Allen, Durward L.
The Life of Prairies and Plains.
New York: McGraw-Hill Book Company, 1967.
A highly readable, generously illustrated overview of the ecology and history of the nation's grasslands.

Brown, Lauren.
Grasses.
Boston: Houghton Mifflin Company, 1979.
A fully illustrated, simplified identification guide to common grasses and grasslike plants. Covers eastern grasslands, tallgrass, and mixed prairie species.

Costello, David F.
The Prairie World.
New York: Thomas Y. Crowell Company, 1969.
An excellent description of the ecology of the midcontinent prairies, enlivened with personal anecdotes and observations.

Crampton, Beecher.
Grasses in California.
Berkeley: University of California Press, 1974.
Paperback; describes and illustrates the common California grasses.

Hitchcock, A. S.
Manual of the Grasses of the United States. Washington, D.C.: U.S. Government Printing Office, 1950.
Describes and illustrates every grass growing in the United States at the time of publication. A standard reference and a handsome publication.

Madson, John.
Where the Sky Began. Land of the Tallgrass Prairie.
Boston: Houghton Mifflin Company, 1982.
A vivid description of the history and ecology of the tallgrass prairie.

McPhee, John.
Basin and Range.
New York: Farrar, Straus, Giroux, 1981.
Even the desolate Nevada basins become interesting in this book, which is about geology, but conveys the general feeling of the Intermountain area.

Phillips Petroleum Company.
Pasture and Range Plants.
Bartlesville, Oklahoma: Phillips Petroleum Company, 1963.
A handsomely illustrated guide to selected grasses and forbs, with notes on the growth and uses of each.

CREDITS

Photo Credits

The numbers in parentheses are plate numbers. Some photographers have pictures under agency names as well as their own.

David H. Ahrenholz (297, 309 left, 316, 324 left and right, 327, 331, 346)
Durward L. Allen (99, 102 left, 110 left, 203 left)
Ruth Allen (214)

Amwest
Charles G. Summers, Jr. (37)

Dennis Anderson (285)

Animals Animals
Tom Brakefield (570) George K. Bryce (395 left and right)
Zig Leszczynski (578, 599, 609) C. W. Perkins (356) Lynn M. Stone (571)

William Aplin (463)

Ardea London
C. R. Knight (497)

Charles Arneson (19, 111)
Ray E. Ashton, Jr. (590)
Ron Austing (506, 524)
Stephen F. Bailey (508, 516)
Gregory Ballmer (308, 325)
Roger W. Barbour (55, 59, 64–66, 70, 71, 74, 77, 78, 84, 575, 580)
Erwin A. Bauer (41)
Mabel Boulet (227)
Tom Brakefield (53)
Jim Brandenburg (6)
Harold E. Broadbooks (75)
Lauren Brown (92 left, 102 right, 104 left)
Richard W. Brown (429 left)
Fred Bruemmer (44)
Sonja Bullaty (4th frontispiece)
Sonja Bullaty and Angelo Lomeo (22, 400 left and right, 402 right, 403 left and right, 404 left and right, 405 left and right, 406 left and right, 409 left and right, 410 left and right, 411 left and right, 412 left and right, 413 left and right, 415 left and right, 416 left and right, 417 left and right, 418 left and right, 419 left and right, 421 left and right, 422 left and right, 424 left and right, 426 left and right, 428 left, 429 right, 432 left and right, 433 left, 434 left and right, 435 left and right, 436 left and right, 437 left and right, 439 left and right, 441 left and right, 442 left, 444 left and right, 447 left and right, 448 left and right, 449 left and right, 450 left and right, 451, 452, 454, 468, 469, 481)
Karen Bussolini (23)
S. R. Cannings (522)
David Cavagnaro (398 left, 401 right, 420 left, 425 left and right, 430 left, 438 left and right, 440 left and right, 443 left

and right, 445 left, 446 left, 480, 486)
Glenn Chambers (40)
Norden H. Cheatham (482)
Scooter Cheatham (423 left and right, 445 right, 446 right)
Herbert Clark (509)
Anna-Jean Cole (194, 207)
C. J. Cole (588)

Bruce Coleman, Inc.
Bill Brooks (191 right) Bob and Clara Calhoun (39)
R. Schonbeck (165) James Simon (161) Peter Ward (245)
Dale and Marian Zimmerman (379)

Stephen Collins (96, 106, 138, 148, 192, 209, 216)

Cornell Laboratory of Ornithology
Mary Tremaine (537)

Steve Crouch (461, 483, 485)
James A. Cunningham (146, 151, 202, 274)
Robert Dana (314 left and right, 317 left and right)
Thase Daniel (88, 154, 171, 232, 492, 535)
Kent and Donna Dannen (163, 210, 471)
Harry N. Darrow (309 right, 326 left, 333, 337 left, 342
left, 344 left and right, 367, 371, 378, 386, 392, 489, 495,
543)
Thomas W. Davies (311 left, 326 right, 339 left, 353, 354,
372)
Edward R. Degginger (49, 126, 134, 224, 247, 301, 358,
364, 380, 383, 389, 391, 408 left)
David M. Dennis (25, 569, 586, 600)
Jack Dermid (26, 27, 98)
Larry Ditto (498, 518)

DRK Photo
Stephen J. Krasemann (21, 83, 264, 546) Wayne
Lankinen (552)

Georges Dremeaux (542)
Wilbur H. Duncan (92 right)
John Earl (228)
Frances Eikum (218)
John F. Eisenberg/Smithsonian Institution Photographic
Services (68)
Harry Ellis (150, 349, 373, 592)
Harry Engels (47, 174)
Jon Farrar (Cover, 10, 238)
William Fehrenbach (401 left)
P. R. Ferguson (170, 217)
William E. Ferguson (302, 305, 315, 366, 384, 388, 394)
Davis Finch (507)
Kenneth W. Fink (48, 85, 86, 493, 501, 502, 525, 549,
550)
Richard B. Fischer (166, 213)
R. Wills Flowers (359)
Jeff Foott (1st frontispiece, 52, 499, 505)
Richard S. Funk (336 right, 572)

John Gerlach (513)
Susan Gibler (101 right, 103 left and right, 109)
François Gohier (2nd frontispiece, 3rd frontispiece, 31)
Lois Theodora Grady (93, 94, 407 right, 474)
William D. Griffin (58)
Joseph A. Grzybowski (533)
Raymond P. Guries (430 right)
Pamela J. Harper (453, 458)

Grant Heilman Photography (460)

Douglass Henderson (17, 100 left and right, 110 right, 112, 114)
Elizabeth Henze (177, 292)
David Hillis (587)
Walter H. Hodge (455, 457, 470)
Michael Hopiak (544)
Joseph R. Jehl (541)
Charles C. Johnson (117, 123, 130, 131, 139, 142, 155, 159, 173, 175, 181, 187, 190, 196, 204, 235, 239–242, 248, 250, 253, 259–262, 272, 277, 290, 407 left)
Emily Johnson (555)
J. Eric Juterbock (568, 591)
Peter Katsaros (563)
G. C. Kelley (35, 504, 511)
Dwight R. Kuhn (390)
Carl Kurtz (249)
Frank A. Lang (115)
Wayne Lankinen (51, 491, 523, 530)
Calvin Larsen (488)
Marion Latch (340 left)
Donald J. Leopold (402 left)
Jack Levy (318, 323 right)
Ken Lewis (152 left and right, 162, 219, 258)
William B. Love (574, 596–598)
John A. Lynch (456)
John R. MacGregor (50, 56, 60, 135, 237, 289, 294, 573, 601, 604, 608, 614)
Thomas W. Martin (529, 532, 545, 547)
Peter May (307 left)
Joe McDonald (512)
Sturgis McKeever (320)
Ron Mellott (95 right, 101 left, 105 left)
Anthony Mercieca (73, 496, 521, 534)
Robert W. Mitchell (13, 303, 352, 375, 376, 382, 387)
C. Allan Morgan (351, 370, 490, 503)
David Muench (2, 3, 7–9, 15)

National Audubon Society Collection/Photo Researchers, Inc.
A. W. Ambler (140, 465) N. E. Beck, Jr. (306) Bob Behme (178) Charles R. Belinky (472, 576) John Bova (536) Gary Braasch (160) Ken Brate (186, 266, 304, 381) Louise K. Broman (275) Richard L. Carlton (293) Joseph T. Collins (579, 581, 585, 589, 593, 595, 606, 610–612, 615–617) Stephen Collins (54) Alford W. Cooper (267, 270) Helen

Cruickshank (89) R. Dimond (223) M. dos Passos (141) Phil
Dotson (45) Michael P. Gadomski (340 right) W. Grace (200)
Patrick W. Graco (132) Farrell Grehan (265) W. Harlow
(478) Verna R. Johnston (57) G. C. Kelley (82) Russ Kinne
(108) Stephen Krasemann (156) Ruth Laming (144) Karl H.
Maslowski (67) C. G. Maxwell (189) Tom McHugh (38, 46,
565) Sturgis McKeever (76) Irvin L. Oakes (246, 288) Charles
Ott (191 left) Hiram L. Parent (212 left) Richard Parker (116,
143, 153, 158, 182, 185 right, 203 right, 226, 268, 271,
276, 385) Lawrence Pringle (164 left) Noble Proctor (206)
Louis Quitt (341 left) Leonard Lee Rue III (613) John Serrao
(335 left) Jeff Simon (577) Alvin E. Staffan (602) Mary M.
Thacher (475) Virginia P. Weinland (296, 433 right) Jerome
Wexler (91) Jeanne White (220, 221, 462)

John and Vikki Neyhart (323 left)
Peter Nice (329 left)
Theodore F. Niehaus (273, 282)
William A. Niering (97, 215, 225)
Philip Nordin (313, 329 right)
Irvin L. Oakes (127)
Dorothy Orians (118)
Margaret C. Orr (20)
Robert T. Orr (11, 553)
Robert and Margaret Orr (284)
Dennis R. Paulson (510)
Ray Pawley (603)
Charles E. Peck (63)
C. W. Perkins (201, 234, 244, 255)
O. S. Pettingill, Jr. (539)
Mary Plant (558)
Robert Potts (128)
Betty Randall (287, 431 left and right)
Betty Randall and Robert Potts (397 left and right, 414 left
and right, 420 right, 476, 477)
William Ratcliffe (124)
Susan Rayfield (172, 183, 193, 205, 229, 252, 256, 263,
464)
Dorothy M. Richards (120, 283)
Manuel Rodriguez (368)
Edward S. Ross (121, 279, 295, 310, 322 right, 334 right,
339 right, 341 right, 360, 363, 365, 369, 377)
Thomas Ruckstuhl (299 left)
Leonard Lee Rue III (33, 81, 87, 164 right)

Leonard Rue Enterprises
Len Rue Jr. (32)

Kit Scates (554, 557, 560–562)
Clark Schaack (399 left, 408 right)
Werner W. Schulz (233)
John Shaw (5th frontispiece, 299 right, 321, 330, 332, 335
right, 337 right, 338 left and right, 357, 362, 374, 396,
399 right)
Ervio Sian (514)

Robert S. Simmons (583, 607)
James R. Simon (137 right)
Richard Singer (336 left)
Arnold Small (1, 16, 487, 517, 528, 531, 540)
Arlo I. Smith (479)
John J. Smith (428 right, 442 right)
Paul Spade (322 left)
Richard Spellenberg (125, 184, 185 left, 188, 197, 231, 251 left and right, 398 right, 459, 467)
Bob and Ira Spring (198)
Joy Spurr (107, 122, 137 left, 169, 212 right, 222, 236, 278)

Tom Stack and Associates
Harry Ellis (556) J. Madeley (269) Rick McIntyre (69) Rod Planck (34) Al Nelson (257) P. Urbanski (281)

Alvin E. Staffan (42, 43, 61, 80, 90, 145, 199, 208, 254, 286, 291, 350, 466, 473, 484)
Lynn M. Stone (5, 12, 30, 105 right)
Edo Streekman (129, 136, 157, 176)
Gayle T. Strickland (311 right, 312, 343, 526)
Phil and Judy Sublett (28)
Rick Sullivan and Diana Rogers (427 left and right)
K. H. Switak (584, 618)
Arthur Swoger (149, 168)
George Taylor (334 left)
Scott B. Terrill (515)
Bill Thomas (4, 29)
T. K. Todsen (133, 167, 195, 211, 243)
Bob Tucher (519)
Edmund Tylutki (559)
University of Colorado Museum (147, 179, 180, 230)
William Vandivert (62, 79)
Charles S. Weber (280)
Wardene Weisser (548, 551)
Larry West (24, 298, 300, 342 right, 345, 347, 348, 355, 393, 564)
Jack Wilburn (18, 113, 527, 538)
D. Dee Wilder (361)
John Wilkie (307 right, 319)
Michael A. Williamson (605)
Marilyn Wolff (95 left, 104 right)
David Wright (328)
Gary Zahm (500, 520)
Dale and Marian Zimmerman (14, 36, 72, 119, 494)
Richard G. Zweifel (566, 567, 582, 594)

Illustrations

The drawings of plants were executed principally by Robin Jess. The following artists also contributed drawings of plants and tree silhouettes to this guide: Daniel Allen, Bobbi Angell Margaret Kurzius, Steven Phillips, Dolores R. Santoliquido, and Wendy B. Zomlefer. Dot Barlowe contributed the drawings of mammal tracks.

INDEX

umbers in boldface type refer
plate numbers. Numbers in
alic refer to page numbers.

A

Acacia, Prairie, 159, *385*
Acacia
angustissima, 159, *385*
farnesiana, 446, 463, *524*
greggii, 443, 462, *522*
Achillea millefolium, 129,
373
Agaricus campestris, 560,
557
Agelaius phoeniceus, 545,
546, *551*
Agoseris, Pale, 163, *387*
Agoseris glauca, 163, *387*
Agrocybe, Hemispheric,
556, *556*
Agrocybe pediades, 556, *556*
Agropyron spicatum, 112,
364
Agrostemma githago, 237,
418
Agrostis alba, 93, *355*
Ambystoma tigrinum, 583,
566
Ammodramus
henslowii, 538, *548*
savannarum, 537, *548*
Amorpha canescens, 275, *435*
Amsinckia retrorsa, 160, *386*
Anabrus simplex, 351, *476*
Andropogon
gerardi, 101, *359*
scoparius, 97, *357*
virginicus, 98, *358*
Anemone, Carolina, 139,
377
Anemone
caroliniana, 139, *377*
patens, 281, *438*
Anopheles spp., 360, *480*
Ant, Rough Harvester,
376, *487*
Anthophora spp., 373, *485*
Anthoxanthum odoratum, 96,
357
Anthus spinoletta, 526, *544*
Antilocapra americana, 34,
325
Apantesis ornata, 302, *449*
Aphids, Rose, Pea, and
Potato, 390, *492*
Apis mellifera, 375, *486*
Apocynum androsaemifolium,
234, *417*

Apple, 422, 452, *510*
Prairie Crab, 424, 451, *511*
Southern Crab, 415, *506*
Aquila chrysaetos, 494, *532*
Araneus spp., 395, *495*
Arizona elegans, 601, *573*
Artemisia tridentata, 113,
364
Artichoke, Jerusalem,
172, *391*
Artogeia rapae, 307, *451*
Asclepias
syriaca, 241, *420*
tuberosa, 228, *415*
Ash, Common Prickly-,
450, *527*
Asio flammeus, 514, *539*
Aspen
Bigtooth, 433, *517*
Quaking, 430, *515*
Aster
Calico, 135, *375*
Hairy Golden, 170, *390*
New England, 246, *422*
Panicled, 134, *375*
Smooth, 293, *443*
Aster
laevis, 293, *443*
lateriflorus, 135, *375*
novae-angliae, 246, *422*
simplex, 134, *375*
Astragalus
agrestis, 230, *415*
mollissimus, 268, *432*
Athene cunicularia, 513, *539*
Atrytone arogos, 317, *456*
Autographa californica, 310,
453

B

Baby Blue Eyes, 284, *439*
Baby Stars, False, 239,
419
Badger, 51, *334*
Baiomys taylori, 74, *345*
Balsam Root, Arrowleaf,
174, *392*
Balsamorhiza sagittata, 174,
392
Baptisia leucantha, 154, *383*
Barbarea vulgaris, 206, *405*
Barberry, Common, 209,
407
Barley, Foxtail, 107, *362*

Bartramia longicauda, 507,
537
Basilarchia
archippus, 334, 465
astyanax, 321, 330, 458
Battus philenor, 320, 458
Bee
Digger, 373, 485
Golden Northern Bumble,
374, 485
Honey, 375, 486
Yellow-faced, 363, 481
Bee Plant
Rocky Mountain, 260, 428
Yellow, 204, 404
Beetle
Green June, 387, 491
Japanese, 386, 491
Nine-spotted Ladybug,
380, 488
Red-blue Checkered, 381,
489
Striped Blister, 385, 490
Three-lined Potato, 388,
492
Bell, Yellow, 198, 402
Bellis perennis, 131, 373
Berberis vulgaris, 209, 407
Bergamot, Wild, 257, 427
Betula
papyrifera, 429, 514
populifolia, 428, 513
Bindweed, 121, 369
Birch
Gray, 428, 513
Paper, 429, 514
Bison, 31, 323
Bison bison, 31, 323
Blackbird
Brewer's, 549, 550, 552
Red-winged, 545, 546, 551
Black-eyed Susan, 176,
393
Blanket, Indian, 226, 414
Blazing Star
Dense, 262, 429
Prairie, 261, 429
Rough, 259, 428
Blue
Acmon, 322, 323, 459
Common, 329, 463
Eastern Tailed, 328, 462
Greenish, 327, 462
Orange-bordered, 324, 460

Silvery, 326, 461
Western Tailed, 325, 460
Bluebird
Eastern, 524, 543
Mountain, 525, 543
Bluebonnet, Texas, 270,
433
Bluegrass, Kentucky, 91,
355
Bluestem
Big, 101, 359
Little, 97, 357
Bluets, 288, 441
Bobolink, 544, 551
Bobwhite, 503, 535
Bombus fervidus, 374, 485
Bombylius, 370, 371, 484
Boneset, 150, 382
Bouteloua gracilis, 108, 362
Bovista pila, 563, 558
Brodiaea, Elegant, 280,
438
Brodiaea elegans, 280, 438
Broomsedge, 98, 358
Brown, Eyed, 347, 473
Bubulcus ibis, 487, 530
Buchloe dactyloides, 103, 360
Buckeye, 345, 472
Buckthorn
European, 426, 512
Glossy, 409, 474, 503
Buffalo Gourd, 196, 401
Bufo
cognatus, 570, 561
debilis, 573, 563
punctatus, 568, 561
woodhousei, 569, 561
Bug, Tarnished Plant,
382, 489
Bunting
Lark, 535, 547
Snow, 543, 550
Buteo
jamaicensis, 491, 492, 531
regalis, 493, 532
swainsoni, 490, 531
Butter-and-eggs, 201, 403
Buttercup, Common,
193, 400
Butterfly Weed, 228, 415

C
Calamospiza melanocorys,
535, 547

alcarius
pponicus, **540,** *549*
ccownii, **539,** *549*
natus, **542,** *550*
ictus, **541,** *550*
alephelis virginiensis, **343,**
71
allipepla squamata, **504,**
36
alochortus
teus, **194,** *400*
uttallii, **122,** *369*
alvatia gigantea, **564,** *558*
alycadenia truncata, **184,**
96
amas
Death, **144,** *379*
legant, **124,** *370*
amphorweed, **168,** *389*
ampion, Bladder, **140,**
77
anis latrans, **37, 38,** *327*
annabis sativa, **117,** *367*
anthon spp., *379,* **488**
aracara, **495,** *532*
ardaria draba, **147,** *380*
arduelis tristis, **552,** *553*
arduus nutans, **255,** *426*
assia bauhinioides, **188,**
98
astilleja coccinea **225,** *413*
atalpa, Southern, **410,**
03
atalpa bignonioides, **410,**
03
atclaw, Gregg, **443,**
62, **522**
athartes aura, **488,** *530*
entaurium calycosum, **242,**
20
entaury, **242,** *420*
entrocercus urophasianus,
99, **534**
erastium vulgatum, **138,**
77
ercocarpus, Curlleaf,
14, *486,* **506**
ercocarpus ledifolius, **414,**
86, **506**
ervus elaphus, **32,** *323*
eryonis pegala, **348,** *474*
haradrius vociferus, **506,**
37
helydra serpentina, **576,** *564*

Cherry
Black, **419, 458,** *508*
Pin, **417, 456, 473,** *507*
Chicken
Greater Prairie, **500,** *534*
Lesser Prairie, **501,** *535*
Chickweed, **136,** *376*
Mouse-ear, **138,** *377*
Chicory, **291,** *443*
Chipmunk, Eastern, **90,**
353
Chokecherry, Common,
421, 457, 472, *509*
Chondestes grammacus, **534,**
547
Chordeiles minor, **515,** *540*
Chrysanthemum
leucanthemum, **132,** *374*
Chrysemys picta, **575,** *563*
Chrysopa spp., **358,** *479*
Chrysopsis camporum, **170,**
390
Chrysothamnus nauseosus,
212, *407*
Cichorium intybus, **291,** *443*
Cinquefoil
Rough-fruited, **186,** *397*
Shrubby, **191,** *399*
Circus cyaneus, **489,** *530*
Cirsium
arvense, **256,** *427*
horridulum, **162,** *387*
pastoris, **251,** *424*
vulgare, **254,** *426*
Clarkia amoena, **240,** *419*
Clematis hirsutissima, **232,**
233, *416*
Cleome
lutea, **204,** *404*
serrulata, **260,** *428*
Clossiana bellona, **344,** *471*
Clover
Purple Prairie, **253,** *425*
Red, **229,** *415*
White, **157,** *384*
White Prairie, **142,** *378*
White Sweet, **151,** *382*
Yellow Sweet, **218,** *410*
Cnemidophorus
sexlineatus, **580,** *565*
tigris, **588,** *568*
Coachwhip, **614,** *579*
Coccinella movemnotata, **380,**
488

Coenonympha inornata, **297,**
447
Colias
eurytheme, **295,** *446*
philodice, **296,** *446*
Colinus virginianus, **503,**
535
Coluber constrictor, **618,** *580*
Columbina passerina, **510,**
538
Compass Plant, **171,** *391*
Cone-head, Nebraska,
355, *478*
Convolvulus arvensis, **121,**
369
Copper, Great Gray, **318,**
457
Coprinus
comatus, **562,** *557*
plicatilis, **553,** *555*
Cordgrass, Prairie, **105,**
361
Corn Cockle, **237,** *418*
Cotinus nitida, **387,** *491*
Cottontail, Eastern, **48,**
332
Cottonwood, Eastern,
432, *516*
Cowbird, Bronzed, **551,**
553
Coyote, **37, 38,** *327*
Crambus spp., **305,** *450*
Crane, Sandhill, **505,** *536*
Crataegus
flabellata, **435,** *518*
intricata, **434, 454,** *517*
uniflora, **427,** *513*
Crazyweed, **267,** *432*
Cream Cup, **189,** *398*
Creosote Bush, **114,** *365*
Crescentspot
Mylitta, **341,** *470*
Pearly, **340,** *469*
Cress, Hoary, **147,** *380*
Cricket
Field, **350,** *476*
Mormon, **351,** *476*
Crotalus
atrox, **599,** *572*
vividis, **605,** *574*
Crotaphytus collaris, **591,** *569*
Cryptotis parva, **76,** *346*
Cucurbita foetidissima, **196,**
401

Culex pipiens, 362, *481*
Curlew, Long-billed, 508, *537*
Cynomys
leucurus, 86, *351*
ludovicianus, 87, *351*

D
Dactylis glomerata, 104, *360*
Daddy-long-legs, Brown, 391, *493*
Daisy
Blackfoot, 130, *373*
Cowpen, 179, *394*
English, 131, *373*
Oxeye, 132, *374*
Tahoka, 292, *443*
Dalea formosa, 231, *416*
Danaus plexippus, 355, *466*
Daucus carota, 145, *380*
Deer
Mule, 35, *326*
White-tailed, 33, *324*
Delphinium virescens, 155, 156, *384*
Dermacentor spp., 378, *488*
Desmanthus illinoensis, 158, *385*
Desmodium illinoense, 153, *383*
Devil's Claw, 118, 197, *368*
Diacrisia virginica, 304, *450*
Diadophis punctatus, 612, *577*
Dianthus armeria, 244, *421*
Dickcissel, 529, *545*
Dicotyles tajacu, 36, *327*
Diospyros virginiana, 412, 468, 470, *504*
Dipodomys
heermanni, 73, *345*
ordii, 72, *344*
Dipsacus sylvestris, 252, *425*
Dock
Curly, 220, *411*
Winged, 222, *412*
Dogbane, Spreading, 234, *417*
Dolichonyx oryzivorus, 544, *551*
Dove
Common Ground, 510, *538*

Mourning, 509, *538*
Duskywing, Funereal, 316, *456*

E
Eagle, Golden, 494, *532*
Earwig, European, 377, *487*
Echinocereus viridiflorus, 119, *368*
Egret, Cattle, 487, *530*
Elaeagnus angustifolia, 467, *527*
Elaphe
guttata, 603, *573*
obsoleta, 613, *578*
vulpina, 608, *576*
Elecampane, 166, *389*
Elk, 32, *323*
Elm, Siberian, 416, *507*
Epalpus signifer, 372, *485*
Epicauta vittata, 385, *490*
Eremophila alpestris, 520, *542*
Erigeron divergens, 133, *374*
Ermine, 52, *335*
Eryngium
leavenworthii, 250, *424*
yuccifolium, 116, *367*
Erynnis funeralis, 316, *456*
Erysimum asperum, 210, *407*
Eschscholtzia californica, 223, *412*
Estigmene acraea, 303, *450*
Euchaetias egle, 306, *451*
Eumeces
obsoletus, 582, *566*
septentrionalis, 579, *565*
skiltonianus, 578, *564*
Eupatorium
maculatum, 248, *423*
perfoliatum, 150, *382*
ragosum, 148, *381*
Euphagus cyanocephalus, 549, 550, *552*
Euphorbia corollata, 146, *380*
Euptoieta claudia, 342, *470*
Eurema nicippe, 298, *447*
Eurytides philolaus, 333, *465*
Eustoma grandiflorum, 282, *439*
Everes
amyntula, 325, *460*
comyntas, 328, *462*

'alco sparverius, 496, *533*
'arewell to Spring, 240,
19
'ennel, Sweet, 207, *406*
'escue, Idaho, 100, *359*
'estuca idahoensis, 100, *359*
'iddleneck, 160, *386*
'ilipendula rubra, 258, *428*
'irefly
'ennsylvania, 383, *490*
'yralis, 384, *490*
'latpod, 115, *367*
'lax, Wild Blue, 287, *441*
'leabane, Spreading, 133,
74
'ly
American Hover, 365, *482*
.arly Tachinid, 372, *485*
.arge Bee, 370, 371, *484*
.obber, 361, *481*
'oxomerus Hover, 366,
83
'lycatcher, Scissor-tailed,
19, *541*
'oeniculum vulgare, 207, *406*
'orficula auricularia, 377,
87
'ox
'ray, 43, *330*
Kit, 39, *328*
.ed, 41, 42, 44, 45, *329*
.wift, 40, *329*
'ragaria virginiana, 126,
71
'ritillaria pudica, 198, *402*
'ritillary
Meadow, 344, *471*
.egal, 336, *467*
Variegated, 342, *470*
'rog
'reat Plains Narrowmouth,
-65, *560*
'lains Leopard, 572, *562*
.triped Chorus, 571, *562*

'
'aeides xanthoides, 318, *457*
'aillardia pulchella, 226,
14
'alium mollugo, 152, *383*
'ambelia silus, 584, *566*
'arter Snake
Checkered, 594, *570*

Common, 592, *569*
Plains, 593, *570*
Western Terrestrial, 597,
571
Gastrophryne olivacea, 565,
560
Gentian, Prairie, 282, *439*
Geococcyx californianus, 511,
538
Geomys bursarius, 78, *347*
Geum triflorum, 249, *423*
Glaucopsyche lygdamus, 326,
461
Goatsbeard, Yellow, 165,
388
Goldenrod
Lance-leaved, 213, *408*
Rough-stemmed, 215, *409*
Stiff, 208, *406*
Sweet, 216, *409*
Tall, 214, *408*
Goldfields, 178, *394*
Goldfinch, American,
552, *553*
Gopher, Plains Pocket,
78, *347*
Grass
Blue Grama, 108, *362*
Buffalo, 103, *360*
Indian, 94, *356*
Orchard, 104, *360*
Pointed Blue-eyed, 289,
442
Red Canary, 102, *360*
Sweet Vernal, 96, *357*
Switch, 95, *356*
Tobosa, 109, *363*
Velvet, 92, *355*
Grasshopper
Green Valley, 353, *477*
Spur-throated, 352, *477*
Two-striped, 354, *478*
Grindelia squarrosa, 182,
396
Groundcherry, Purple,
285, *440*

Groundsel, Threadleaf,
167, *389*
Grouse
Sage, 499, *534*
Sharp-tailed, 502, *535*
Grus canadensis, 505, *536*
Gryllus pennsylvanicus, 350,
476
Gumweed, 182, *396*
Gutierrezia sarothrae, 203,
211, *404*

H
Habenaria lacera, 120,
369
Hairstreak, Gray, 319,
457
Harrier, Northern, 489,
530
Harvest Mouse
Eastern, 65, *341*
Fulvous, 64, *340*
Western, 63, *340*
Hawk
Ferruginous, 493, *532*
Red-tailed, 491, 492, *531*
Swainson's, 490, *531*
Hawkweed
Orange, 227, *414*
Yellow, 164, *388*
Hawthorn
Biltmore, 434, 454, *517*
Fanleaf, 435, *518*
Oneflower, 427, *513*
Helianthus
annuus, 175, *392*
giganteus, 173, *392*
maximiliani, 177, *393*
tuberosus, 172, *391*
Hesperia
dacotae, 314, *455*
sassacus, 300, *448*
Heterodon
nasicus, 604, *574*
platyrhinos, 606, *575*
Heterotheca subaxillaris, 168,
389
Hieracium
aurantiacum, 227, *414*
pratense, 164, *388*
Hilaria mutica, 109, *363*
Hirundo
pyrrhonota, 521, *542*
rustica, 522, *542*

Holbrookia
lacerata, 587, *567*
maculata, 585, *567*
Holcus lanatus, 92, *355*
Hordeum jubatum, 107, *362*
Hornet, Giant, 367, *483*
Houstonia caerulea, 288, *441*
Huisache, 446, 463, *524*
Hygrophorus eburneus, 557,
556
Hylaeus spp., 363, *481*
Hypericum perforatum, 202,
403

I
Icaricia
acmon, 322, 323, *459*
icarioides, 329, *463*
Idahoa scapigera, 115, *367*
Indigo, Prairie False,
154, *383*
Inky, Japanese Umbrella,
553, *555*
Inula helenium, 166, *389*
Ipomoea hederacea, 283, *439*
Iris
Douglas', 279, *437*
Tough-leaved, 278, *437*
Iris
douglasiana, 279, *437*
tenax, 278, *437*
Ironweed
New York, 247, *423*
Tall, 294, *444*
Isia isabella, 301, *449*

J
Jack Rabbit
Black-tailed, 46, *331*
White-tailed, 47, *332*
Joe-Pye Weed, Spotted,
248, *423*
Juniper
Alligator, 397, 477, *497*
Common, 401, 475, *499*
Oneseed, 399, *498*
Utah, 398, 476, *497*
Juniperus
communis, 401, 475, *499*
deppeana, 397, 477, *497*
monosperma, 399, *498*
osteosperma, 398, 476, *497*
virginiana, 400, *498*
Junonia coenia, 345, *472*

K
Kestrel, American, 496,
533
Killdeer, 506, *537*
Kingbird
Cassin's, 516, *540*
Eastern, 518, *541*
Western, 517, *541*
Kingsnake, Prairie, 607,
575

L
Laccaria, Purple-gilled,
561, *557*
Laccaria ochropurpurea, 561,
557
Lacewings, Green, 358,
479
Lady
American Painted, 337,
467
Painted, 338, *468*
West Coast, 339, *469*
Lagurus curtatus, 58, *338*
Lampropeltis
calligaster, 607, *575*
triangulum, 611, *577*
Lanius
excubitor, 527, *544*
ludovicianus, 528, *545*
Lark, Horned, 520, *542*
Larkspur, Prairie, 155,
156, *384*
Larrea tridentata, 114, *365*
Lasthenia chrysostoma, 178,
394
Leadplant, 275, *435*
Lema trilineata, 388, *492*
Lemming, Southern Bog,
55, *337*
Lepiota, Smooth, 558, *556*
Lepiota naucina, 558, *556*
Leptotyphlops dulcis, 617,
580
Lepus
californicus, 46, *331*
townsendii, 47, *332*
Liatris
aspera, 259, *428*
pycnostachya, 261, *429*
spicata, 262, *429*
Lilium canadense, 224, *413*
Lily
Canada, 224, *413*

Rain, 195, *401*
Sego, 122, *369*
Limnanthes douglasii, 128, 187, *372*
Linanthus androsaceus, 239, *419*
Linaria vulgaris, 201, *403*
Linum perenne, 287, *441*
Liquidambar styraciflua, 436, 481, *518*
Lithophragma parviflorum, 137, *376*
Lizard
Bluntnose Leopard, **584**, *566*
Collared, **591**, *569*
Eastern Fence, **589**, *568*
Lesser Earless, **585**, *567*
Side-blotched, **590**, *568*
Slender Glass, **581**, *565*
Spot-tailed Earless, **587**, *567*
Texas Horned, **586**, *567*
Lobelia, Great, 276, *436*
Lobelia siphilitica, 276, *436*
Locoweed, 265, *431*
Wooly, **268**, *432*
Locust, Black, 444, 453, 484, *523*
Longspur
Chestnut-collared, **542**, *550*
Lapland, **540**, *549*
McCown's, **539**, *549*
Smith's, **541**, *550*
Looper, Alfalfa, 310, *453*
Lotus corniculatus, 199, *402*
Lupine
Miniature, **273**, *434*
Wild, **269**, *433*
Lupinus
bicolor, 273, *434*
perennis, 269, *433*
subcarnosus, 270, *433*
Lycaeides melissa, 324, *460*
Lychnis, Evening, 141, *378*
Lychnis
alba, 141, *378*
flos-cuculi, 245, *422*
Lygus lineolaris, 382, *489*
Lyophyllum decastes, 559, *556*

M
Machaeranthera tanacetifolia, 292, *443*
Maclura pomifera, 411, 459, 469, *504*
Macrosiphum spp., 390, *492*
Madder, Wild, 152, *383*
Madia, Common, 181, *395*
Madia elegans, 181, *395*
Magpie, Black-billed, 523, *543*
Malacothrix coulteri, 180, *395*
Malus
angustifolia, 415, *506*
ioensis, 424, 451, *511*
sylvestris, 422, 452, *510*
Mantid, Chinese, 357, *479*
Mantis, Praying, 356, *478*
Mantis religiosa, 356, *478*
Marasmius oreades, 554, *555*
Marijuana, 117, *367*
Marmota monax, 79, *347*
Massasauga, 600, *572*
Masticophis flagellum, 614, *579*
Meadow Foam, Douglas', 128, 187, *372*
Meadowlark
Eastern, **547**, *552*
Western, **548**, *552*
Meadowsweet, 149, *381*
Megathymus yuccae, 312, *454*
Melampodium leucanthum, 130, *373*
Melanoplus ponderosus, 352, *477*
Melilotus
alba 151, *382*
officinalis, 218, *410*
Mephitis mephitis, 49, *333*
Mesquite, Honey, 445, 461, 485, *524*
Metalmark, Little, 343, *471*
Metaphidippus spp., 393, *494*
Metasyrphus americanus, 365, *482*
Microtus
californicus, 57, *338*

ochrogaster, 59, *338*
pennsylvanicus, 56, *337*
Midges, Green, 359, *480*
Milkvetch, Field, 230, *415*
Milkweed, Common, 241, *420*
Mimosa, Prairie, 158, *385*
Misumena vatia, 392, 396, *493*
Mole, Eastern, 77, *346*
Molothrus aeneus, 551, *553*
Monarch, 335, *466*
Monarda fistulosa, 257, *427*
Morning Glory, Ivy-leaved, 283, *439*
Mosquito
House, **362**, *481*
Malaria-carrying, **360**, *480*
Moth
Acraea, **303**, *450*
Artichoke Plume, **315**, *455*
Milkweed Tiger, **306**, *451*
Ornate Tiger, **302**, *449*
Sod Webworm, **305**, *450*
Woolly Bear Caterpillar, **301**, *449*
Yellow Woolly Bear, **304**, *450*
Mouse
Deer, **62**, *340*
Eastern Harvest, **65**, *341*
Fulvous Harvest, **64**, *340*
Great Basin Pocket, **69**, *342*
House, **61**, *339*
Meadow Jumping, **67**, *342*
Northern Grasshopper, **70**, *343*
Northern Pygmy, **74**, *345*
Oldfield, **71**, *343*
Plains Pocket, **75**, *345*
San Joaquin Pocket, **68**, *342*
Western Harvest, **63**, *340*
Western Jumping, **66**, *341*
Mule's Ears, 169, *390*
Mullein
Common, **219**, *410*
Moth, **192**, *400*
Mus musculus, 61, *339*
Mushroom
Fairy Ring, **554**, *555*
Fried-chicken, **559**, *556*
Meadow, **560**, *557*

Mustela
erminea, 52, _335_
frenata, 53, _335_
nivalis, 54, _336_

N
Needle-and-Thread, 110, _363_
Needlegrass, 99, _358_
Purple, 111, _363_
Nemophia menziesii, 284, _439_
Neoconocephalus nebrascensis, 355, _478_
Neominois ridingsii, 347, _473_
Nerisyrenia, Velvety, 125, _371_
Nerisyrenia camporum, 125, _371_
Nerodia sipedon, 602, _573_
Nettle, Horse, 123, _370_
Nighthawk, Common, 515, _540_
Numenius americanus, 508, _537_

O
Oak
Blackjack, 437, _519_
Bur, 439, _520_
California Black, 438, _520_
Canyon Live, 420, 482, _509_
Coast Live, 425, _512_
Post, 441, _521_
Valley, 440, 483, _521_
Odocoileus
hemionus, 35, _326_
virginianus, 33, _324_
Oenothera
biennis, 205, _405_
hookeri, 190, _399_
speciosa, 235, _417_
Onychomys leucogaster, 70, _343_
Ophisaurus attenuatus, 581, _565_
Opuntia, Many-spined, 161, _386_
Opuntia polyacantha, 161, _386_
Orange, Sleepy, 298, _447_
Orb Weavers, 395, _495_

Orchid, Ragged Fringed, 120, _369_
Orthocarpus purpuracens, 264, _430_
Osage-orange, 411, 459, 469, _504_
Owl
Common Barn, 512, _539_
Burrowing, 513, _539_
Short-eared, 514, _539_
Owl's Clover, Common, 264, _430_
Oxyopes spp., 394, _494_
Oxytropis
lambertii, 267, _432_
splendens, 265, _431_

P
Paintbrush, Indian, 225, _413_
Panicum virgatum, 95, _356_
Papilio polyxenes, 331, _464_
Partridge, Gray, 497, _533_
Pasqueflower, 281, _438_
Passerculus sandwichensis, 536, _548_
Peabush, Feather, 231, _416_
Peccary, Collared, 36, _327_
Perdix perdix, 497, _533_
Perognathus
flavescens, 75, _345_
inornatus, 68, _342_
parvus, 69, _342_
Peromyscus
maniculatus, 62, _340_
polionotus, 71, _343_
Persimmon, Common, 412, 468, 470, _504_
Petalostemum
candidum, 142, _378_
purpureum, 253, _425_
Phacelia, Threadleaf, 236, _418_
Phacelia linearis, 236, _418_
Phalangium opilio, 391, _493_
Phalaris arundinacea, 102, _360_
Phasianus colchicus, 498, _533_
Pheasant, Ring-necked, 498, _533_
Philaenus spumarius, 389, _492_

Phleum pratense, 106, *361*

Phlox, Wild Blue, 290, *442*

Phlox divaricata, 290, *442*

Photinus pyralis, 384, *490*

Photuris pennsylvanicus, 383, *490*

Phrynosoma cornutum, 586, *567*

Phyciodes

tylitta, 341, *470*

tharos, 340, *469*

Physalis lobata, 285, *440*

Pica pica, 523, *543*

Pine

Eastern White, 405, 478, *500*

Loblolly, 404, *500*

Longleaf, 406, *501*

Shortleaf, 403, 479, *500*

Slash, 407, *501*

Virginia, 402, *499*

Pink, Deptford, 244, *421*

Pinus

chinata, 403, 479, *500*

elliottii, 407, *501*

monophylla, 480, *528*

palustris, 406, *501*

strobus, 405, 478, *500*

taeda, 404, *500*

virginiana, 402, *499*

Pinyon, Singleleaf, 480, *528*

Pipit, Water, 526, *544*

Pitaya, Green, 119, *368*

Pituophis melanoleucus, 598, *571*

Plantago lanceolata, 143, *379*

Plantain, English, 143, *379*

Platyptilia carduidactyla, 315, *455*

Platystemon californicus, 189, *398*

Plebejus saepiolus, 327, *462*

Plectrophenax nivalis, 543, *550*

Plum

American, 418, 455, *508*

Mexican, 423, *511*

Plume, Desert, 217, *410*

Poa pratensis, 91, *355*

Pocket Gopher, Plains, *78, 347*

Pocket Mouse

Great Basin, 69, *342*

Plains, 75, *345*

San Joaquin, 68, *342*

Pogonomyrmex rugosus, 376, *487*

Polistes spp., 368, *483*

Polyborus plancus, 495, *532*

Pontia

beckerii, 308, *452*

protodice, 309, *452*

Pooecetes gramineus, 533, *547*

Popilla japonica, 386, *491*

Poplar, Balsam, 431, *515*

Poppy, California, 223, *412*

Populus

balsamifera, 431, *515*

deltoides, 432, *516*

grandidentata, 433, *517*

tremuloides, 430, *515*

Potentilla

fruticosa, 191, *399*

recta, 186, *397*

Prairie Dog

Black-tailed, 87, *351*

White-tailed, 86, *351*

Prairie Smoke, 249, *423*

Prickly-ash, Common, 450, *527*

Primrose

Evening, 205, *405*

Hooker's Evening, 190, *399*

Showy Evening, 235, *417*

Proboscidea altheaefolia, 118, 197, *368*

Pronghorn, 34, *325*

Prosopis glandulosa, 445, 461, 485, *524*

Prunus

americana, 418, 455, *508*

mexicana, 423, *511*

pensylvanica, 417, 456, 473, *507*

serotina, 419, 458, *508*

virginiana, 421, 457, 472, *509*

Psathyrella, Common, 555, *555*

Psathyrella candolleana, 555, *555*

Pseudacris triseriata, 571, *562*

Psoralea argophylla, 272, *434*

Pterourus glaucus, 332, *464*

Puffball

Giant, 564, *558*

Tumbling, 563, *558*

Purple, Red-spotted, 321, 330, *458*

Pussy Willow, 413, 460, *505*

Pyrgus

communis, 311, *453*

scriptura, 313, *454*

Q

Quail, Scaled, 504, *536*

Queen Anne's Lace, 145, *380*

Queen-of-the-Prairie, 258, *428*

Quercus

agrifolia, 425, *512*

chrysolepis, 420, 482, *509*

kelloggii, 438, *520*

lobata, 440, 483, *521*

macrocarpa, 439, *520*

marilandica, 437, *519*

stellata, 441, *521*

R

Rabbit

Black-tailed Jack, 46, *331*

White-tailed Jack, 47, *332*

Rabbit Brush, 212, *407*

Racer, 618, *580*

Racerunner, 580, *565*

Ragged Robin, 245, *422*

Rana blairi, 572, *562*

Ranunculus acris, 193, *400*

Rat

Heermann's Kangaroo, 73, *345*

Hispid Cotton, 60, *339*

Ord's Kangaroo, 72, *344*

Rattlebox, Yellow, 200, *403*

Rattlesnake

Western, 605, *574*

Western Diamondback, 599, *572*

Rattlesnake Master, 116, *367*

Redcedar, Eastern, 400, *498*

Redtop, 93, *355*
Reithrodontomys
fulvescens, **64,** *340*
humulis, **65,** *341*
megalotis, **63,** *340*
Rhamnus
cathartica, **426,** *512*
frangula, **409, 474,** *503*
Rhinanthus crista-galli, **200,**
403
Rhinocheilus lecontei, **609,**
576
Rhus
copallina, **449, 464,** *526*
glabra, **448, 465,** *526*
typhina, **447, 471,** *525*
Ringlet, Prairie, 297, *447*
Roadrunner, Greater,
511, *538*
Robinia pseudoacacia, **444,**
453, 484, *523*
Rosa
multiflora, **127,** *372*
suffulta, **238,** *419*
Rose
Multiflora, **127,** *372*
Prairie, **238,** *419*
Rosin Weed, 184, *396*
Rudbeckia hirta, **176,** *393*
Rumex
acetosella, **221,** *411*
crispus, **220,** *411*
venosus, **222,** *412*
Russian-olive, 467, *527*

S
Sagebrush, Common,
113, *364*
St. Johnswort, Common,
202, *403*
Salamander, Tiger, 583,
566
Salix discolor, **413, 460,**
505
Salvia, Blue, 271, *434*
Salvia azurea, **271,** *434*
Sandpiper, Upland, 507,
537
Sassafras, 442, 466, *522*
Sassafras albidum, **442, 446,**
522
Satyr, Riding's, 347, *473*
Satyrodes eurydice, **346,** *473*
Scalopus aquaticus, **77,** *346*

Scaphiopus
bombifrons, **567,** *560*
hammondi, **566,** *560*
Sceloporus undulatus, **589,**
568
Schistocerca shoshone, **353,**
477
Sciurus niger, **80,** *348*
Scolia dubia, **369,** *484*
Scurf Pea, Silverleaf, 272,
434
Senecio douglasii, **167,** *389*
Shaggy Mane, 562, *557*
Shrew, Least, 76, *346*
Shrike
Loggerhead, **528,** *545*
Northern, **527,** *544*
Sialia
currucoides, **525,** *543*
sialis, **524,** *543*
Sigmodon hispidus, **60,** *339*
Silene cucubalus, **140,** *377*
Silphium laciniatum, **171,**
391
Sistrurus catenatus, **600,** *572*
Sisyrinchium angustifolium,
289, *442*
Skink
Great Plains, **582,** *566*
Prairie, **579,** *565*
Western, **578,** *564*
Skipper
Beard-grass, **317,** *456*
Common Checkered, **311,**
453
Dakota, **314,** *455*
European, **299,** *448*
Indian, **300,** *448*
Small Checkered, **313,** *454*
Yucca Giant, **312,** *454*
Skunk
Eastern Spotted, **50,** *334*
Striped, **49,** *333*
Snake
Checkered Garter, **594,** *570*
Common Garter, **592,** *569*
Corn, **603,** *573*
Eastern Hognose, **606,** *575*
Flathead, **616,** *579*
Fox, **608,** *576*
Glossy, **601,** *573*
Ground, **610,** *577*
Lined, **596,** *571*
Longnosed, **609,** *576*

Milk, 611, *577*
Northern Water, 602, *573*
Pine Gopher, 598, *571*
Plains Blackhead, 615, *579*
Plains Garter, 593, *570*
Rat, 613, *578*
Ringneck, 612, *577*
Texas Blind, 617, *580*
Western Hognose, 604, *574*
Western Ribbon, 595, *570*
Western Terrestrial Garter, 597, *571*
Snakehead, 180, *395*
Snakeroot, White, 148, *381*
Snakeweed, Broom, 203, 211, *404*
Solanum carolinense, 123, *370*
Solidago
altissima, 214, *408*
graminifolia, 213, *408*
odora, 216, *409*
rigida, 208, *406*
rugosa, 215, *409*
Sonora semiannulata, 610, *577*
Sorghastrum nutans, 94, *356*
Sorrel, Sheep, 221, *411*
Spadefoot
Plains, 567, *560*
Western, 566, *560*
Sparrow
American Tree, 530, *545*
Clay-colored, 531, *546*
Field, 532, *546*
Grasshopper, 537, *548*
Henslow's, 538, *548*
Lark, 534, *547*
Savannah, 536, *548*
Vesper, 533, *547*
Spartina pectinata, 105, *361*
Spermophilus
armatus, 22, *349*
beldingi, 85, *350*
columbianus, 81, *348*
franklinii, 84, *350*
richardsonii, 83, *349*
spilosoma, 88, *352*
tridecemlineatus, 89, *352*
Speyeria idalia, 336, *467*
Spider
Goldenrod, 392, 396, *493*

Jumping Lynx, 394, *494*
Metaphid Jumping, 393, *494*
Spilogale putorius, 50, *334*
Spiraea
latifolia, 149, *381*
tomentosa, 263, *430*
Spittlebug, Meadow, 389, *492*
Spiza americana, 529, *545*
Spizella
arborea, 530, *545*
pallida, 531, *546*
pusilla, 532, *546*
Spurge, Flowering, 146, *380*
Squirrel
Belding's Ground, 85, *350*
Columbian Ground, 81, *348*
Fox, 80, *348*
Franklin's Ground, 84, *350*
Richardson's Ground, 83, *349*
Spotted Ground, 88, *352*
Thirteen-lined, 89, *352*
Uinta Ground, 82, *349*
Stanleya pinnata, 217, *410*
Star, Prairie, 137, *376*
Steeplebush, 263, *430*
Stellaria media, 136, *376*
Stipa
comata, 110, *363*
pulchra, 111, *363*
spartea, 99, *358*
Strawberry, Common, 126, *371*
Strymon melinus, 319, *457*
Sturnella
magna, 547, *552*
neglecta, 548, *552*
Sulphur
Common, 296, *446*
Orange, 295, *446*
Sumac
Shining, 449, 464, *526*
Smooth, 448, 465, *526*
Staghorn, 447, 471, *525*
Sunflower
Common, 175, *392*
Giant, 173, *392*
Maximilian's, 177, *393*
Swallow
Barn, 522, *542*

Cliff, 521, *542*
Swallowtail
Dark Zebra, 333, *465*
Eastern Black, 331, *464*
Pipevine, 320, *458*
Tiger, 332, *464*
Sweetgum, 436, 481, *518*
Sylvilagus floridanus, 48, *332*
Synaptomys cooperi, 55, *337*

T
Tamias striatus, 90, *353*
Tanacetum vulgare, 183, *396*
Tansy, Common, 183, *396*
Tantilla
gracilis, 616, *579*
nigriceps, 615, *579*
Tanytarsus spp., 359, *480*
Taxidea taxus, 51, *334*
Teasel, 252, *425*
Tenadera aridifolia, 357, *479*
Terrapene ornata, 574, *563*
Thamnophis
elegans, 597, *571*
marcianus, 594, *570*
proximus, 595, *570*
radix, 593, *570*
sirtalis, 592, *569*
Thelia bimaculata, 349, *476*
Thistle
Bull, 254, *426*
Canada, 256, *427*
Coyote, 250, *424*
Nodding, 255, *426*
Showy, 251, *424*
Yellow, 162, *387*
Thymelicus lineola, 299, *448*
Tick, Eastern Wood, 378, *488*
Timothy, 106, *361*
Toad
Great Plains, 570, *561*
Green, 573, *563*
Red-spotted, 568, *561*
Woodhouse's, 569, *561*
Tolmerus spp., 361, *481*
Toxomerus spp., 366, *483*
Tragopogon dubius, 165, *388*
Treehopper, Locust, 349, *476*

Trefoil
Birdsfood, **199,** *402*
Illinois Tick, **153,** *383*
Trichodes nutalli, **381,** *489*
Trichostema lanceolatum, **277,**
436
Trifolium
pratense, **229,** *415*
repens, **157,** *384*
Tropidoclonion lineatum, **596,**
571
Tulip, Yellow Mariposa,
194, *400*
Tumblebugs, 379, *488*
Turtle
Painted, **575,** *563*
Snapping, **576,** *564*
Western Box, **574,** *563*
Twinleaf, 188, *398*
Tympanuchus
cupido, **500,** *534*
pallidicinctus, **501,** *535*
phasianellus, **502,** *535*
Tyrannus
forficatus, **519,** *541*
tyrannus, **518,** *541*
verticalis, **517,** *541*
vociferans, **516,** *540*
Tyto alba, **512,** *539*

U
Ulmus pumila, **416,** *507*
Urocyon cinereoargenteus, **43,**
330
Uta stansburiana, **590,** *568*

V
Vanessa
annabella, **339,** *469*
cardui, **338,** *468*
virginiensis, **337,** *467*
Vase, Flower, 232, 233,
416
Verbascum
blataria, **192,** *400*
thapsus, **219,** *410*
Verbena
ambrosifolia, **243,** *421*
hastata, **274,** *435*
Verbesina encelioides, **179,**
394
Vernonia
altissima, **294,** *444*

noveboracensis, **247,** *423*
Vervain
Blue, **274,** *435*
Western Pink, **243,** *421*
Vespa crabro germana, **367,**
483
Vespula spp., **364,** *482*
Vetch, Cow, 266, *431*
Viceroy, 334, *465*
Vicia cracca, **266,** *431*
Vinegar Weed, 277, *436*
Viola pedata, **286,** *440*
Violet, Bird-foot, 286,
440
Vole
California, **57,** *338*
Meadow, **56,** *337*
Prairie, **59,** *338*
Sagebrush, **58,** *338*
Vulpes
macrotis, **39,** *328*
velox, **40,** *329*
vulpes, **41, 42, 44, 45,** *329*
Vulture, Turkey, 488,
530

W
Wallflower, Plains, 210,
407
Wasp
Digger, **369,** *484*
Paper, **368,** *483*
Waxy Cap, White, 557,
556
Weasel
Least, **54,** *336*
Long-tailed, **53,** *335*
Wheatgrass, Bluebunch,
112, *364*
Whiptail, Western, 588,
568
White
Becker's **308,** *452*
Cabbage, **307,** *451*
Checkered, **309,** *452*
Willow, Pussy, 413, 460,
505
Winter Cress, Common,
206, *405*
Wood Nymph, Large,
348, *474*
Woodchuck, 79, *347*
Wyethia amplexicaulis, **169,**
390

Y
Yarrow, 129, *373*
Yellow Jackets, 364, *482*
Yucca, Soaptree, 408,
502
Yucca elata, **408,** *502*

Z
Zanthoxylum americanum,
450, *527*
Zapus
hudsonius, **67,** *342*
princeps, **66,** *341*
Zenaida macroura, **509,** *538*
Zephyranthes longifolia, **195,**
401
Zigadenus
elegans, **124,** *370*
nuttalii, **144,** *379*
Zinnia, Little Golden,
185, *397*
Zinnia grandiflora, **185,** *397*

THE AUDUBON SOCIETY

The National Audubon Society is among the oldest and largest private conservation organizations in the world. With over 560,000 members and more than 500 local chapters across the country, the Society works in behalf of our natural heritage through environmental education and conservation action. It protects wildlife in more than eighty sanctuaries from coast to coast. It also operates outdoor education centers and ecology workshops and publishes the prizewinning AUDUBON magazine, AMERICAN BIRDS magazine, newsletters, films, and other educational materials. For further information regarding membership in the Society, write to the National Audubon Society, 950 Third Avenue, New York, New York 10022.

CHANTICLEER STAFF

Publisher: Paul Steiner
Editor-in-Chief: Gudrun Buettner
Managing Editor: Susan Costello
Series Editor: Mary Beth Brewer
Text Editor: Ann Whitman
Associate Editor: Marian Appellof
Assistant Editors: David Allen, Constance Mersel
Editorial Assistant: Karel Birnbaum
Production: Helga Lose, Amy Roche, Frank Grazioli
Art Director: Carol Nehring
Art Associate: Ayn Svoboda
Art Assistant: Ellen Pugatch
Picture Library: Edward Douglas, Dana Pomfret
Maps and Symbols: Paul Singer
Senior Editor: Jane Opper
Natural History Consultant: John Farrand, Jr.
Design: Massimo Vignelli